DATE DUE

A HANDBOOK OF
TIBETAN
CULTURE

May any goodness generated
by the creation of this book
be dedicated to the long-life and well-being
of all those who work for global peace
and nurture the welfare of our world.

A HANDBOOK OF
TIBETAN
CULTURE

A GUIDE TO TIBETAN CENTRES AND
RESOURCES THROUGHOUT THE WORLD

Compiled by The Orient Foundation

Edited by Graham Coleman

SHAMBHALA
Boston
1994

Shambhala Publications, Inc.
Horticultural Hall
300 Massachusetts Avenue
Boston, Massachusetts 02115

© 1993 by The Orient Foundation.
First published in the United Kingdom by Rider, an
imprint of Random House Ltd, 20 Vauxhall Bridge Road,
London SW1V 2SA

9 8 7 6 5 4 3 2 1
First Shambhala Edition

Printed in the United States of America on acid-free paper ⊗

Distributed in the United States by Random House, Inc., and
in Canada by Random House of Canada Ltd

Library of Congress Cataloging-in-Publication Data

A Handbook of Tibetan culture: a guide to Tibetan centres
and resources throughout the world/compiled by The Orient
Foundation and edited by Graham Coleman.—
1st Shambhala ed.
p.   cm.
Originally published: London: Rider, 1993.
Includes bibliographical references and index.
ISBN 1-57062-002-4 (acid-free)
1. Tibet (China)—Civilization—Handbooks, manuals, etc. 2.
Tibet (China)—Civilization—Societies, etc.—Directories. I.
Coleman, Graham. II. Orient Foundation.
DS786.H327   1994   93-33363
951'.5—dc20   CIP

CONTENTS

PREFACE BY THE DALAI LAMA

More than thirty years after the communist Chinese completed the occupation of our land and many of us came into exile, many people are unaware that Tibet ever was independent or that it had its own government, distinct language, culture and way of life.

While the indigenous Bon tradition is probably as old as the Tibetan nation itself, Tibetans have also been custodians of the full range of the Buddha's teachings for more than a thousand years. These have been analysed, refined and, most important of all, put into practice, becoming the mainstay of Tibetan culture. Over recent decades in Tibet, the institutions, literature, artifacts and even individual proponents of our culture have come under attack. Therefore, those of us in exile have had a responsibility to preserve what we could, not only for the benefit of our brothers and sisters who remain in Tibet, but also for the world at large.

There is a great deal in Tibet's culture, in its medical knowledge, peaceful outlook and respectful attitude to the environment that can be of widespread benefit to others. For example, living experience of meditation has given Tibetan practitioners a profound knowledge of the workings and nature of the mind, an inner science to complement conventional scientists' understanding of the physical world.

In this century, in particular, it has become clear that no amount of technological development on its own leads to lasting happiness. What is also required is a corresponding inner development. Many people have remarked that Tibetans seem to have just such a sense of inner peace and hope, even in the face of adversity. I think the source of this lies mostly in the Buddhist teachings of love, kindness, tolerance and especially the theory that all things are relative.

So, recognising the importance and value of our own language, literature and traditions, we have made every effort to preserve and promote our cultural heritage in all its aspects. The four major Buddhist traditions and the Bon tradition have re-established their monastic institutions, and educational and training facilities have been provided for the young. Schools have also been created to ensure the survival of Tibet's performing arts, its medical sciences, its arts, crafts and literary skills.

Besides this, a huge expansion of interest in Tibetan culture throughout the world has resulted in a proliferation of academic and cultural organisations, libraries, museums, teaching and retreat centres and publications concerned with Tibetan civilisation.

The Orient Foundation's *A Handbook of Tibetan Culture* fills a growing need for a sourcebook that brings together in a convenient form much of the information needed by anyone interested in Tibetans and their way of life. It will also play a valuable role in facilitating the development of further exchanges between Tibetan and global culture, as well as serving to increase awareness of the distinct Tibetan identity and the justice of the Tibetan people's will to be free.

February 25th, 1993.

INTRODUCTION BY THE EDITOR

The Chinese occupation of Tibet in the nineteen fifties, the flight into exile of approximately one hundred thousand Tibetans, China's cultural revolution in Tibet, during the sixties and seventies, and the continued cultural repression in Tibet, have combined to make the last forty years one of the darkest periods in Tibet's long history. It is estimated that more than 1.2 million Tibetans died in the first ten years of Chinese rule. Many of these individuals were highly esteemed cultural figures: scholars, poets, doctors, writers and artists.

Paradoxically, an ever-growing appreciation of Tibet's rich and sophisticated cultural inheritance has arisen within the global community, simultaneous with the dislocation in Tibet, largely as a result of contact with the exiled Tibetan communities. This access to an ancient aspect of our shared cultural inheritance has occurred at a time when intense global pressures are generating a crucial shift of perspective in the dominant world view. Development models which have cultivated an established fascination with a short-term, non-empathetic, individualist, view of the world have inspired what could be called a 'global depression', a pervasive sense of estrangement and lack of personal fulfilment. Present and future generations are faced with awesome environmental problems, the breakdown of communities and the growth of societies that are no longer self-sustaining. To ensure that our developing global cultural perspectives and policy shifts are successful, we must reflect on the cultural perspectives and societal structures which have been successful in the past.

The people of Tibet have carried into the modern world, intact, a two-and-a-half-thousand-year-old cultural inheritance. This living inheritance is the result of a continuous dedication to the exploration of the nature of mind and phenomena; a pervasive, natural sense of the value of artistic expression; and a sustained integration of thoughtful perspectives on the place of human beings in nature and society. Tibet's inherited cultural skills and insights cover a deep and panoramic range of disciplines. These include understandings which relate to evolving shifts of appreciation in the fields of physics, cosmology, bio-chemistry, biology, art, philosophy, the science of consciousness, psychology, the relationship between the mind and the body, attitudes toward death and dying, ecology, and the place of the individual in society. The Tibetan legacy provides a powerful interface with the value systems of other cultures and their methods in the multi-disciplinary pursuit of social cohesion and well-being.

Since 1982, The Orient Foundation, has collaborated with an ever-growing network of co-participants, to assist the exiled Tibetan communities in their efforts to maintain the continuity and vitality of their cultural inheritance and to provide a cross-cultural interface between Tibetan and other cultures. The focus of this work has been the creation of the *Tibetan Cultural Resources Database* and the development of a multi-site Tibetan National Archive.

The Tibetan literary tradition is largely set down on the assumption that the insights and meaning expressed in a particular text will be explicated and continued through the oral tradition. Up until 1959, these oral traditions had remained unbroken, having been continuously cultivated and passed on from one generation of accomplished scholars and practitioners to the next, for more than two

ACKNOWLEDGMENTS

Our heartfelt thanks go out to all the lamas, scholars, curators, librarians, translators, students and staff of all the organisations throughout the world who have contributed to the compilation of this *Handbook*. Their care and timeliness has been a source of inspiration throughout the project.

The initial financial support for the compilation of the *Tibetan Cultural Resources Database*, from which the *Handbook* is extracted, came from the distribution of our films: *Tibet: A Buddhist Trilogy* (Arts Council of Great Britain/Thread Cross Films, 1979), which I wrote and directed. First and foremost, therefore, I would like to thank David Lascelles, a founding trustee of the Orient Foundation and producer of the *Trilogy*, for personally co-funding the films and also for allowing the resources generated from the distribution of the *Trilogy*, in the cinemas of North America, Europe and Australasia, to be applied in support of this work. Fond appreciation is also especially offered to Elinore and Jacques Detiger of the Tiger Trust, who have consistently supported the Foundation's work from 1985 up to the present. We will always be indebted to their warmth, vision and kindness. Others who made substantial and invaluable contributions to the development of this work are: The Elmgrant Trust, Geoff Jukes, The Howe Green Trust, Richard Gere, The Tibet Society (UK), Mr & Mrs Herb Lundberg and Sir Cyril Pickard. In each case, their generous contributions between 1985 and 1988 secured the continuity of the project's development. Since 1988, the compilation of the *Tibetan Cultural Resources Database* has been funded by the Ford Foundation. Our especial thanks, therefore, go to the staff, officers and trustees of the Ford Foundation, whose kind support has brought these extracts from the *Tibetan Cultural Resources Database* to publication.

Since 1983 the project has been co-managed by myself and Judith Lundberg, a founding trustee and the distributor of the Foundation's films in North America. Data entry has been primarily the responsibility of our project staff: David Noyce (1987–89), Matthew Poulton (1989–91), and Ruth Winocour (1988–93) and I thank them sincerely for their perseverance, patience and rigour. Our appreciation goes also to the project's computer programmer Peter Le Blond for his skill and dedication throughout the last six years and to Microrim, who donated and continuously up-graded our database software *Rbase*.

Throughout the development of this work, the Orient Foundation has been managed and advised by its founding trustees: Judith Lundberg, who co-initiated this project and whose consistent close participation has been an inspiration and strong guiding hand, David Lascelles, whose friendship and personal support I honour, James Heywood, who edited our films *Tibet: A Buddhist Trilogy* and whose sincerity, clarity and good-nature I deeply value, Barrie Gavin, whose firmness and oversight has played a critical role, and Prof Dr Jan Andersson and Dr Lawrence Epstein, who have both been kind and loyal supporters and advisors.

As the reader will discover, the *Handbook* owes much to Geshe Thupten Jinpa and Dr Gyurme Dorje, who co-wrote the glossary entries and provided much advice throughout the development of the project. Working with both of these gifted scholars has been a privilege and consistent joy.

thousand years. This process has, in the last forty years, been severely disrupted. The primary focus of our work has therefore been to assist in the preservation and continuity of the oral traditions. Over the last ten years (1983 – 1993), The Orient Foundation, working with the leaders of Tibetan community organisations in India and Nepal, many of the principal scholars of the five main Tibetan cultural traditions, the Dalai Lama's administration and more than 600 Tibetan related organisations throughout the world, has traced and catalogued more than 30,000 hours of audio and video recordings of oral commentarial discourse by Tibet's leading cultural figures. Also catalogued, in the *Tibetan Cultural Resources Database*, are the writings of Tibetans published in Western languages since 1959. Over the last two years, in collaboration with leading lineage holders and facilitated by *The Tibetan Cultural Resources Database*, it has been possible to analyse which oral commentarial traditions have been recorded and which have not. Based on this analysis an extensive oral recording program is now underway in the Tibetan communities of India and Nepal to record as much as possible of the endangered oral traditions, while the elder scholars and practitioners who hold these lineages, and who were trained and brought up in pre-occupation Tibet, are still teaching. The culmination of this work will be the creation of an interactive multi-media, multi-site Tibetan National Archive which is truly representative of the full range of oral lineages and oral history subjects which has survived from ancient times to the present.

The publication of *The Handbook of Tibetan Culture*, which is extracted from *The Tibetan Cultural Resources Database*, serves three purposes. First, the handbook provides the only comprehensive sourcebook to Tibetan related organisations around the world. Secondly, it includes a biographical dictionary to many of Tibet's more widely known contemporary cultural figures. Thirdly, it offers an authoritative glossary to key Tibetan, Buddhist and Sanskrit terms, which a reader in the Tibetan cultural field may encounter. This is the first edition of a work which is continuously expanding. We hope that it will be helpful in establishing cross-cultural exchange between Tibetan and other cultures and in the sharing of information upon which the future of our societies depend.

March 10th, 1993
The Orient Foundation
Bath, Avon, England.

Additional scholastic consultants who have generously contributed to specific aspects of this project are: Dr Paul Williams, who advised on Gelug and classical Indian references, Dr David Jackson who advised on the Sakya biographies, Dr Gyurme Dorje, who advised on the Kagyu and Nyingma biographies, Peter Roberts, who provided additional information for the Kagyu biographies and Dr Alex Berzin who advised on the Gelug biographies and also provided much of the initial information in the Resource Directory for Eastern Europe, the former Soviet Union, China, South America and Africa.

I would like to thank the Tibet Institut, Switzerland, and particularly Peter Kessler for allowing us to reproduce, in revised form, his painstakingly researched map of the distribution of monasteries in ethnic Tibet and my friend Robert Beer, an extraordinarily gifted artist, for illuminating the text with images which wonderfully make vivid the presence of the lineage holders of the past.

Our especial thanks go out also to: H.H. Menri Trizin, for providing the history of the Bon tradition, to the late H.H. Dilgo Khyentse Rinpoche for writing the history of the Nyingma, to H.E. Shamar Rinpoche for writing the history of the Kagyu, to H.H. Sakya Trizin for writing the history of the Sakya tradition and to H.H. the Ganden Tri Rinpoche for the history of the Gelug. Finally, I offer my deepest thanks and appreciation to H.H. the Dalai Lama, for providing the preface and for his advice, support and participation in our work, since 1975.

Graham Coleman
President, The Orient Foundation.

INTRODUCTION TO THE HISTORIES OF THE
FIVE MAJOR CULTURAL TRADITIONS OF TIBET

During Tibet's long history, a rich and inter-related array of cultural lineages have developed and been sustained. Today, however, it is commonly said that there are five principal traditions, which represent the coalescence of these lineages into five formal traditional structures. These five traditions are the: Bon, Nyingma, Kagyu, Sakya and Gelug. The Bon tradition represents the earliest pre-classical Indian Buddhist culture of Tibet. The Nyingma represents the first wave of transmission of classical Indian Buddhist lineages into Tibet, beginning in the seventh to eighth centuries. The Kagyu and Sakya represent the second wave of transmission of classical Buddhist lineages from India, beginning in the eleventh century. The Gelug represents a distinct tradition which formed towards the end of the fourteenth century.

These five traditions share the same goal, namely to develop an enlightened insight into the nature of mind and phenomena, based on the compassionate motivation to benefit all beings.

Despite their commonality of purpose, each tradition has a distinct and vital inheritance of oral, literary and artistic lineages, each of which have been passed from generation to generation and remained unbroken since the time of their first expression. Within the myriad lineages of each of these traditions, there exists a broad array of highly sophisticated and tested systems of inner development, a rich store of highly articulate and polished philosophical insights and a highly developed and richly expressive range of artistic, ritual, and performing arts skills.

By way of introduction to *The Handbook of Tibetan Culture*, leading lineage holders of each of the five main cultural traditions have kindly contributed a short history of their tradition. These are presented in order of their chronology.

A BRIEF HISTORY OF THE BON TRADITION

By the Bon Monastic Centre, Dolanji

The Origin of Bon

According to the Bon tradition, Bon originated in the land of Olmo Lungring, a part of a larger country called Tazig. Ol, symbolizes the unborn; Mo, the undiminishing; Lung, the prophetic words of Tonpa Shenrab the founder of Bon; and Ring, his everlasting compassion. Olmo Lungring is said to constitute one third of the existing world and is situated to the west of Tibet. It is described as an eight-petalled lotus under a sky which appears like an eight-spoked wheel. In the centre rises Mount Yungdrung Gutseg, 'Pyramid of Nine Svastikas'. The svastika is the symbol of permanence and indestructability. The nine svastikas piled up represent the Nine ways of Bon. At the base of Mount Yungdrung spring four rivers, flowing towards the four cardinal directions. The mountain is surrounded by temples, cities and parks. To the south is the palace Barpo Sogye where Tonpa Shenrab was born. To the west and north are the palaces in which lived the wives and children of Tonpa Shenrab. A temple named Shampo Lhatse is to the east. The complex of palaces, rivers and parks with Mount Yungdrung in the centre constitutes the inner region of Olmo Lungring. The intermediate region consists of twelve cities, four of which are towards the cardinal directions. The third region includes the outer land. These three regions are encircled by an ocean and again by a range of snowy mountains. The access to Olmo Lungring is gained by the so-called 'arrow way'. Before his visit to Tibet, Tonpa Shenrab shot an arrow, thus creating a passage through the mountain range.

This sophisticated description of Olmo Lungring has been tentatively related by some scholars to different geographical locations. Some see it as a description of Mount Kailash and the four great rivers that spring from its base; China being the land to the east, India to the south, Orgyen to the west and Khotan to the north. To other scholars, the description seems to resemble the geography of the Middle East and Persia in the time of Cyrus the Great. To a Bonpo, the question of the geographic identification of Olmo Lungring is less important than its symbology which is clearly made use of to indicate the supramandane origin of the tradition. Symbolic descriptions which combine history, geography and mythology are well known phenomena in ancient texts. The Buddhist description of the universe with Mount Meru supporting the sky, the four Chief Continents to the four cardinal points and this earth as the southern continent is another similar example.

The Founder and His Teachings.

The founder of the Bon tradition is the Lord Shenrab Mibo. In past ages there were three brothers, Dagpa, Salba, and Shepa, who studied the Bon doctrines in the heaven named Sridpa Yesang, under the Bon sage Bumtri Logi Chechan. When their studies were completed, they visited the Deity of Compassion, Shenlha Okar and asked him how they could help living beings submerged in the misery and sorrow of suffering. He advised them to act as guides to mankind in three successive ages of the world. To follow his advice, the eldest brother Dagpa completed his work in the past world age. The second brother Salba took the name Shenrab and became the teacher and guide of the present world-age. The youngest brother Shepa will come to teach in the next world-age.

The Lord Shenrab was born in the Barpo Sogye Palace to the south of Mount Yungdrung. He was born a prince, married while young and had children. At the age of thirty-one, he renounced the world and lived in austerity, teaching the doctrine. During his whole life, his efforts to propagate the Bon teachings were obstructed by the demon Khyabpa Lagring. This demon fought to destroy or impede the work of Tonpa Shenrab until he was eventually subdued and became a disciple. Once, pursuing the demon to regain his stolen horses, Tonpa Shenrab arrived in Tibet; it was his only visit to Tibet. There he imparted instructions concerning the performance of rituals but, on the whole, found the land unprepared to receive fuller teachings. Before leaving Tibet, he prophesied that all his teachings would flourish in Tibet when the time was ripe. Tonpa Shenrab departed this life at the age of eighty-two. .

The Propagation of Bon in Zhang-Zhung and Tibet.

The first Bon sacred texts were brought to Zhang-zhung by six disciples of Mucho Demdrug, the successor of Tonpa Shenrab. They were first translated into the Zhang-zhung language, and then later into Tibetan. The works included in the Bonpo canon, as we know it now, are written in the Tibetan language, but a number of them, especially the older ones, retain the titles and at times whole passages in Zhang-zhung.

Until the seventh century, Zhang-zhung existed as a separate state which comprised the land to the west of the Central Tibetan Provinces of U and Tsang and generally known as Western Tibet. The historical evidence is incomplete but there are some reliable indications that it may have extended over the vast area from Gilgit in the west to the lake of Namtsho in the east, and from Khotan in the north to Mustang in the south. The capital of Zhang-zhung was a place called Khyunglung Ngulkhar – 'The Silver Palace of the Garuda Valley' – the ruins of which are to be found in the upper Sutlej Valley to the south-west of Mount Kailash. The people of Zhang-zhung spoke a language which is classified among the Tibeto-Burmese group of Sino-Tibetan languages.

The country seems to have been ruled by a dynasty of kings which ended in the eighth century when the last king Ligmirya was assassinated and Zhang-zhung became an integral part of Tibet. Since the annexation, Zhang-zhung became gradually Tibetanised and its language and culture were integrated into the general frame of Tibetan culture. Through Zhang-zhung, which was geographically situated near the great cultural centres of Central Asia such as Gilgit and Khotan, many spiritual and philosophical concepts infiltrated Tibet.

With the increasing interest in the Buddhist tradition, the founding of Samye monastery in 779 AD, and the establishment of Buddhism as the principal cultural tradition, the Bon tradition was generally discouraged and serious attempts were made to eradicate it. However, the adherents of Bon among the nobility and especially among the common people, who for generations had followed the Bon traditions, retained their cultural convictions and Bon survived. During the seventh and eighth centuries, which were particularly difficult times, many Bonpo scholars and lamas fled Central Tibet, having first concealed their texts for fear of their destruction, and to preserve them for future generations. Drenpa Namkha, one of the greatest Bonpo masters of that time, embraced Buddhism out of fear of being killed and for the sake of preserving the Bonpo teachings in secret .

From the eighth to the eleventh centuries, we know practically nothing of the developments among the Bonpos. The revival of Bon began with the discovery of a number of important texts by Shenchen Luga in the year 1017 A.D. With him, the Bon tradition emerged as a fully systematized system. Shenchen Luga was born in the clan of Shen, which descended from Kongtsha Wangden, one of the sons of Tonpa Shenrab. The descendants of this important Bonpo family still live in Tibet.

Shenchen Luga had a large following. To three of his disciples, he entrusted the task of continuing three different traditions. To the first one, Druchen Namkha Yungdrung, born in the clan of Dru which migrated to Tibet from Druzha (the Tibetan name for Gilgit), he entrusted the studies of cosmology and metaphysics. Namkha Yungdrung's disciple founded the monastery of Yeru Bensakha in 1072. This monastery remained a great centre of learning until 1386, when it was badly damaged by floods and, later, it was abandoned. With the decline of Yeru Bensakha the Dru family continued to sponsor the Bon tradition but this lineage came to an end in the 19th century when, for the second time, a reincarnation of the Panchen Lama was found in this family. (The first reincarnation was the second Panchen Lama (b.1663) and the second, the fifth Panchen Lama (b.1854).

The second disciple, Zhuye Legpo, was assigned to maintain the Dzogchen teachings and practices. He founded the monastery of Kyikhar Rizhing. The descendants of the Zhu family now live in India.

The third disciple, Paton Palchog, took responsibility for upholding the tantric teachings. The members of the Pa family moved from Tsang to Kham where they still live.

Meukhepa Palchen (b.1052) who came from the Meu clan founded the Zangri monastery, which also became a centre for philosophical studies. Thus, during the period from the eleventh to the fourteenth centuries, the Bonpos had four important centres of studies, all of which were in Tsang Province.

At the beginning of the fifteenth century, Bon studies were substantially strengthened by the founding of Menri monastery in 1405 by the great Bonpo teacher, Nyamed Sherab Gyaltshan (1356–1415). Menri monastery and the two mentioned below, remained the most important centres of study until the Chinese takeover of Tibet in 1959. The monastery of Yungdrung Ling was founded in 1834 and, soon afterwards, the monastery of Kharna, both in the vicinity of Menri. With these monasteries as centres of study and spiritual inspiration, many monasteries were established throughout the whole of Tibet (except the Central Province of U), especially in Khyungpo, Kham, Amdo, Gyarong and Hor. By the beginning of the twentieth century, there were three hundred and thirty Bonpo monasteries in Tibet.

The Present Situation.

Menri, the mother monastery in Tibet, and most of the other monastic establishments, lie wasted and ruined. This situation is a great sadness and of concern to us. We pray and take heart that Tibet will once again become a free and spiritual land.

The Bon Monastic Centre
Dolanyi, India

A BRIEF HISTORY OF THE NYINGMA TRADITION OF TIBETAN BUDDHISM

by H.H. Dilgo Khyentse Rinpoche

Although the dawn of Buddhism in Tibet might be said to have occurred in the seventh century during the reign of King Songtsen Gampo (617–650), it was just 100 years later that the teachings of the Buddha began to flourish in the Land of Snow. This was due to three remarkable figures: King Trisong Detsen, the abbot Shantarakshita, and, above all, Guru Padmasambhava, the Lotus Born Guru, also known as the 'Second Buddha'.

The king Trisong Detsen had invited Shantarakshita, the abbot of Nalanda Monastery in India, to build a large monastery at Samye. However, the work done by men in the day-time was destroyed by malevolent spirits during the night. The abbot then predicted that the only solution was to invite the powerful siddha Guru Padmasambhava, who alone would be capable of building this, the first monastery in Tibet. Guru Padmasambhava came, subjugating along the way all the malevolent forces adverse to the Dharma, and built Samye with the help of both human and non-human beings.

Then, Guru Padmasambhava inspired the translation of most of the Buddhist canon, by outstanding Indian pandits and Tibetan translators. He also taught the whole corpus of Buddhist teachings, especially those of the esoteric tradition of the Vajrayana, the Adamantine Vehicle, and bestowed empowerments and pith instructions on countless followers, especially those renowned as his 'twenty-five disciples'. For the sake of future generations, he and the wisdom Dakini Yeshe Tsogyal, concealed countless teachings in the form of spiritual treasures, or termas, travelling miraculously throughout Tibet and blessing all its mountains, caves and lakes. Finally, he left Tibet, riding his horse through the sky, and flew to the land of Camara in the south-west. There he is said to remain in the 'immortal rainbow-body of great transference'.

It is through the generosity of King Trisong Detsen, the monastic ordinations given by the abbot Shantarakshita, and the spiritual transmissions given by Guru Padmasambhava, that the Buddhist tradition was able to spread and flourish in Tibet from early times up to the present. The tradition they thus established is called the 'Nga-gyur Nyingma', the Ancient Tradition of the Early Translation. It is the oldest Buddhist school in Tibet.

The Nyingma tradition has three main streams of transmission: the distant canonical lineage, kama (bka'-ma); the close lineage of spiritual treasures, terma (gter-ma); and the profound pure visions, dagnang (dag-snang).

The first one is the 'distant' lineage of the canonical scriptures, which has been transmitted without interruption from master to disciple, from the primordial Buddha, Samantabhadra, through Guru Padmasambhava and other great masters. The second is the 'close', or direct lineage of the revealed treasures, concealed by Guru Padmasambhava for the sake of future generations, which represents the quintessence of the kama lineage. After bestowing the ripening empowerments and the liberating instructions on his disciples, Guru Padmasambhava entrusted particular teachings to each of them and miraculously concealed these as spiritual treasures in various places: temples, images, the sky, rocks and lakes. He prophesied that, in the future, these disciples would reincarnate, take these teachings from their place of concealment, and propagate them far and wide for the sake of beings. Such reincarnate lamas are called 'treasure masters' or Tertons. In due time, a terton has visions or signs indicating how and where to discover the treasure. In the case of 'mind treasures', the teachings are not physically unearthed but arise in the Terton's mind. Many such masters have appeared, throughout the centuries, down to the present day. In the third case, that of Pure Vision, Guru Padmasambhava appears to the Terton and actually speaks to him in person.

Many great luminaries have appeared in the Nyingma lineage, among them Gyalwa Longchen Rabjampa (1308–1363), who was the first to write down and systematically compile the teachings of the Great Perfection or Dzogchen, the ultimate teachings of the Tantras on the nature of mind and phenomena. Minling Terchen Gyurme Dorje (1646–1714) also played a major role in preserving and collecting the whole Nyingma Canon or Kama lineage. Rigdzin Jigme Lingpa (1729–1798), Patrul Rinpoche (1808–1887), Lama Mipham (1846–1912), Jamyang Khyentse Wangpo (1820–1892) and Jamgon Kongtrul (1813–1899) appeared in the world at crucial moments to ensure that this precious lineage would endure through the troubles of our present age.

H.H. Dilgo Khyentse Rinpoche
Kathmandu, Nepal

A BRIEF HISTORY OF THE KAGYU TRADITION OF TIBETAN BUDDHISM

by H.E. Shamar Rinpoche

The Kagyu (bka'-brgyud) lineage was founded by the great siddha Tilopa (988–1069), also known as Prajnabhadra. Tilopa was a holder of the entire teachings of the various classes of Tantra which can be divided into two types of lineages: a direct sambhogakaya lineage and an extensive nirmanakaya lineage. The first of these involves either one or a few previous lineage holders, in that the related teachings were revealed by the 'Enjoyment Body' (sambhogakaya) directly to a master. Hence, it is known as a direct sambhogakaya lineage. The second of these involves many lineage holders in that the related teachings were passed on from master to disciple in a long unbroken line. Hence, it is known as an extensive nirmanakaya lineage. As to a direct sambhogakaya lineage, Tilopa received the entire teachings from Vajradhara and Vajrayogini. As to an extensive nirmanakaya lineage, Tilopa received the four special transmissions (bka'-babs-bzhi) from his four main teachers. He received the oral instructions on the yoga of luminosity ('od-gsal) (prabhasvara) and the yoga of illusory form (sgyu-lus)(mayadeha) from Matangi, whose lineage originated with Nagarjuna. Nagarjuna had passed on these teachings to Aryadeva who gave them to Candrakirti who transmitted them to Matangi. These masters are associated with the south of India.

Tilopa received the oral instructions on the yoga of dream (rmi-lam) (svapna) from Indrabhuti, whose lineage originated with Dombi Heruka, followed by Vinapa and Lavapa, to Indrabhuti. These masters are associated with the western part of India. Tilopa received the oral instruction on the yoga of tummo (gtum-mo)(candali) from Tsaryapa, whose lineage originated with Mahasukhasiddhi, followed by Tanglopa, Shinglopa and Karnaripa, to Krishnacarya. These masters are associated with the eastern part of India. Tilopa received the oral instruction on the yoga of transference of consciousness ('pho-ba)(samkranti) and the yoga of the intermediate state (bar-do)(antarabhava) from Sukhasiddhi, whose lineage originated with Luipa, followed by Dengipa and Darikapa, to Sukhasiddhi. These masters are associated with the north of India.

Thus, Tilopa received the four special transmissions. Having mastered these teachings, he passed them on to his main disciple Naropa (1016–1100), also known as Jnanasiddhi. Naropa mastered the same teachings and passed them on to Marpa (Mar-pa) (1012–1097) the translator. Marpa, having mastered the same instructions, spread them in Tibet. He transmitted them to his main disciple Milarepa (Mi-la-ras-pa) (1052–1135). Milarepa passed them on to Gampopa (sGam-po-pa) (1079–1153), his principal disciple, who was a great scholar as well as an accomplished meditator. Gampopa himself had numerous accomplished disciples, and through him many lineages arose.

Baram Darma Wangchuk ('bab-ram dar-ma dbang-phyug) was one prominent disciple. He founded the Baram Kagyu ('bab-ram bka'-brgyud). Pagtru Dorje Gyalpo (phag-gru rdo-rje rgyal-po), another outstanding disciple, founded the Pagtru Kagyu (phag-gru bka'-brgyud). Karmapa Dusum Khyenpa (ka-rma-pa dus-gsum mkhyen-pa) (1110–1193), an extraordinary disciple, founded the Karma Kamtsang Kagyu (ka-rma kam-tshang bka'-brgyud). Shang Tsalpa Tsondru Trag (zhang tsal-pa brtson-grus grags), also a prominent disciple, founded the Tsalpa Kagyu (tshal-pa bka'-brgyud). These are the four major Kagyu lineages.

What is known as the eight minor Kagyu lineages originated with Pagtru's eight main disciples. These eight lineages are: Taglung Kagyu (rtag-lung bka'-brgyud), Trophu Kagyu (khro-phu bka'-brgyud), Drukpa Kagyu ('brug-pa bka'-brgyud), Martsang Kagyu (smar-tshang bka'-brgyud), Yerpa Kagyu (yer-pa bka'-brgyud), Yazang Kagyu (g-ya'-bzang bka'-brgyud), Shugseb Kagyu (shugs-gseb bka'-brgyud) and Drikung Kagyu ('bri-gung bka'-brgyud). These lineages are not referred to as major and minor in terms of the instructions they contain; they are equal in that respect. The four major lineages are known as major in that they originate with Gampopa himself, whereas the eight minor lineages originate with a later generation of disciples.

Gampopa was a follower of the Kadampa (bka'-gdams-pa) tradition at the outset of his spiritual training. He perfected these teachings through detailed study of them, by contemplating their profound meaning, and subsequently integrating the ensuing understanding into the practice of meditation. Gampopa, having met with Milarepa, received all the instructions of the Kagyu lineage, which he mastered by progressively proceeding through the four stages of mahamudra: one-pointedness (rtse-gcig), free from conceptual elaboration (spros-bral), one taste (ro-gcig) and non-meditation (sgom-med), this process culminating in perfect realisation of mahamudra.

Thus, the particular feature of the Kagyu lineage is that the teacher, having mastered the instructions, clears away defects – relating to intellectual understanding, meditation experience and the various levels of realisation. Upon completion of this process, the teacher is able to point out and introduce mahamudra to the disciple. The Kagyu teachings have been transmitted and preserved in this way, in an unbroken line, until the present time.

H.E. Shamar Rinpoche
New Delhi, India

A BRIEF HISTORY OF THE SAKYA TRADITION OF TIBETAN BUDDHISM

by H.H. Sakya Trizin

The Sakya Tradition originated in the eleventh century, and has been closely connected with one of the 'holy families' of Tibet, the Khon Family, since early times. One of the family members, Khon Lui Wangpo Sungwa, became a disciple of the great Indian saint Padmasambhava in the eighth century, being amongst the first seven monks to be ordained in Tibet. Through the next thirteen generations, the Khon family was an acknowledged pillar of the 'early propagation' in Tibet. However, it was Khon Konchok Gyalpo who, in 1073, built Sakya monastery and thereby established the foundations of the Sakya Tradition in Tibet. He studied under Drokmi the Translator (992–1072) and soon became a master of many deep teachings. The next two centuries saw the rise of the Sakya Tradition to great heights, not only as a pre-eminent spiritual centre but also as a political power in Tibet.

The five great masters known as 'Gongma Nga' (the Five Exalted Ones) hold a special place in the annals of the Sakya Tradition. Sachen Kunga Nyingpo (1092–1158), the first Gongma, was the son of Khon Konchok Gyalpo. Through his efforts, hundreds of sutras and tantras, as well as oral instructions, were gathered and they became the basis for the Sakya canon. Thus the new school was firmly established as a distinct tradition with a philosophical system of its own. Lobpon Sonam Tsemo (1142–1182) and Jetsun Dakpa Gyaltsen (1147–1216) succeeded him as the fourth and fifth patriarchs of the Sakya school, and greatly enhanced the school through their meditation, their writings, and their demonstration of Dharma. The Fourth Gongma and sixth patriarch of the Sakya order, popularly known as Sakya Pandita (1182–1251), was the most famous of all. The fame of his knowledge and scholasticism spread as far as Mongolia and China, from where he received invitations from the imperial court. His nephew, Chogyal Phakpa (1235–1280), succeeded him as the Fifth Gongma and seventh patriarch of the Sakya school. During his time, the Sakya Tradition reached its political zenith, with the introduction of Mahayana Buddhism into China and Mongolia. The Mongol ruler Kublai Khan, in devotion, offered the thirteen myriarchies of Tibet to Chogyal Phakpa, and thus Tibet was united under a joint spiritual and political authority. These five masters – known to the Tibetans as 'Jetsun Gongma Nga' – are regarded as the real founders of the Sakya Tradition.

Hundreds of Indian sutras and tantric teachings were assimilated into the spiritual life of Tibet through the efforts of the founders of the Sakya Tradition. The most famous of these are: the *Hevajra Tantras*, whose transmission originated with the Mahasiddha Virupa, the *Vajrakila Tantras* of Padmasambhava, the *Vajrayogini precepts* of Naropa, the *Guhyasamaja Tantra* teachings of Nagarjuna, and the *Mahakala precepts* of Vararuci. The distinct philosophical system taught by the Sakya school is known as the *Lamdre*, '*the Path and its Fruit*', and is based on the *Hevajra Tantra*. These instructions originated with the Mahasiddha Virupa and had been brought to Tibet by the yogin Gayadhara, the teacher of Drokmi the Translator. The special philosophical view of the Sakya school is called the 'Non-differentiation of Samsara and Nirvana' and posits a 'Non-dual luminosity-emptiness' beyond all extremes. In terms of spiritual training, the Sakya masters have always stressed study and meditation in like measure; this ideal, so often embodied in the lives of its eminent teachers, has won respect for the Sakya Tradition as one not only of learned scholars but of enlightened sages. The Sakya Tradition has the distinction of having a close connection with the other three major schools of Tibetan Buddhism. The Vajrakila lineage, which the Sakyapas follow, originates from Guru Padmasambhava, the founding master of the Nyingma school. The Kagyu and the Sakya schools originated almost at the same time, and both received important lineages from Naropa: the Sakyas follow the Vajrayogini of Naropa. Lama Tsongkhapa, the founder of the Gelug school, studied under many Sakya lamas, including Rendawa Shonnu Lodo, who was one of his most influential teachers.

For the past 900 years, the adherents of the Sakya Tradition have preserved, studied, expounded and disseminated their unique tradition. In addition to this, over the centuries, the followers of the other schools of Tibetan Buddhism have also diligently studied Sakya philosophical and ethical teachings.

H.H. Sakya Trizin
Rajpur, India

A BRIEF HISTORY OF THE GELUG TRADITION OF TIBETAN BUDDHISM

by H.H. Tri Rinpoche Yeshe Dhondup
(the Ninety-ninth Throne-Holder of Tsongkhapa)·

The Gelug tradition evolved into a fully independent school of Tibetan Buddhism towards the end of the fourteenth century, A.D. The founder of the tradition, the great philosopher saint of Tibet, Tsongkhapa (1357–1419), popularly known as Je Rinpoche, was a great admirer of the Kadam tradition of the celebrated eleventh century Indian master Atisha and his chief Tibetan disciple, Dromtonpa. Tsongkhapa was particularly attracted by the Kadam's emphasis on the Mahayana principles of universal compassion and altruism, valuing these qualities not only as a spiritual orientation, but more importantly, as a way of life. In this regard, Tsongkhapa saw the study and practice of such Indian classics as the *Bodhisattvacaryavatara* of Shantideva and the *Ratnavali* (Precious Garland) of Nagarjuna as highly supportive to an individual's path to Buddhahood. However, in Tsongkhapa's tradition, the Kadam approach is combined with a strong emphasis on the cultivation of an in-depth insight into the doctrine of emptiness as propounded by Nagarjuna and Candrakirti. Tsongkhapa enshrined into a system of learning and contemplation the need to base the above two elements of the path on a whole-hearted wish for liberation, impelled by a genuine sense of renunciation. He called these three elements: renunciation, bodhicitta and the correct view of emptiness, 'the Three Principal Aspects of the Path'. In Tsongkhapa's view, a sound foundation based on these three principles is essential for a successful practice of Vajrayana Buddhism. It is as a result of this emphasis that the Gelug tradition is said to represent a genuine union of sutra and tantra.

Tsongkhapa's written inheritance is enshrined in his collected works, which run into eighteen volumes. These cover an enormously wide spectrum of learning and meditative practices, ranging from explications of the most profound aspects of Highest Yoga Tantra, and the Madhyamaka philosophy of emptiness, to the minute enumeration and analysis of the rules and precepts of a fully ordained monk.

In terms of meditative traditions, Tsongkhapa became the master holder of the three main classical Indian lineages of the Mahayana Buddhist path. He inherited the lineage of *Rgya chen spyod brgyud* (The Vast Practice), stemming from the Buddha Shakyamuni through to Maitreya; the lineage of *Zab mo lta brgyud* (The Profound View), which came from the Buddha Shakyamuni through to Manjushri and onto Nagarjuna; and was also the master of the lineage of *Nyams len byin rlabs brgyud* (The Inspirational Lineage of Realisation), which came from Vajradhara through the various lineages of Tantric practices. Through Lama Tsongkhapa these three lineages merged into a single major lineage. Additionally, in Gelug there are also several important transmissions known as *Dag snang*, (The close lineage of pure vision). Teachings belonging to this category are based on profound mystical experiences of highly realised meditation masters.

After a long, devoted and inspired spiritual training, studying with many of the great masters of his time, Tsongkhapa established Ganden monastery to the east of Lhasa, in 1409. Ganden very quickly became a foremost centre of Buddhist philosophical studies attracting students and scholars from all parts of Tibet. The followers of Tsongkhapa who gathered at Ganden, (also known as Geden), later became known as Gelugpa, those from the Geden school.

Among Tsongkhapa's foremost disciples were Gyaltsab Je (1364–1431); Khedrup Gelek Pelsang (1385–1438); and the First Dalai Lama, Gedun Drup (1391–1474). Following the establishment of Ganden monastery, many other monastic institutions were founded by his principal disciples. Jamyang Choje Tashi Palden (1379–1449) founded Drepung Monastery, reputed to be the largest monastery in the world before 1959. Jamchen Choje Shakya Yeshe (1354–1435) established Sera monastery. The first Dalai Lama founded Tashilhunpo monastery, in Tsang province.

Subsequent generations also saw great luminaries who contributed to the flourishing of Lama Tsongkhapa's tradition. These include such masters as the successive Dalai Lamas and Panchen Lamas, Kachen Yeshe Gyaltsen (1713–1793), Gungthang Tenpai Donme (1762–1823), Ngulchu Dharma Bhadra (1772–1851), and more recently the great Phabongkha Dechen Nyingpo (1878–1941). It is through the establishment of the major monastic universities, and also through the noble contribution of these great masters, that the Gelug tradition eventually became the most pervasively established Buddhist school of Tibet.

H.H. Tri Rinpoche Yeshe Dhondup
Mundgod, India

MAPS OF ETHNIC TIBET

Showing the distribution of Monasteries
of the five major cultural traditions
from 1280–1965

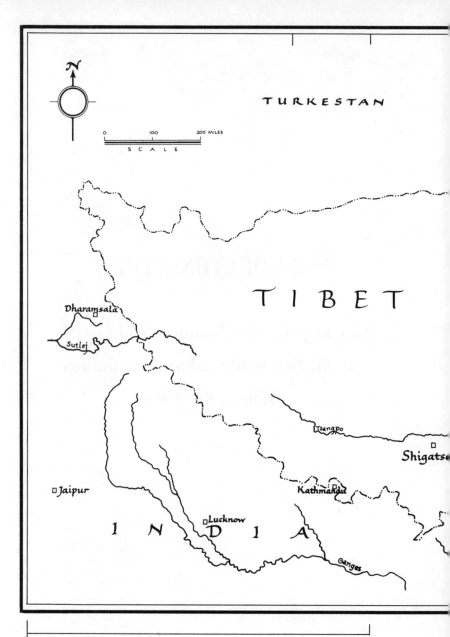

Area covered in detail by Map 1

Area covered in
detail by Map 2

ETHNIC

Showing the distribution of Monasteries of th

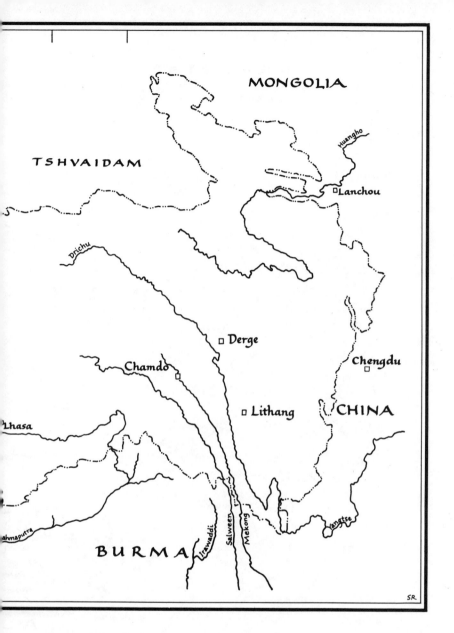

Area covered in detail by Map 3

TIBET
five major cultural traditions from 1280-1965

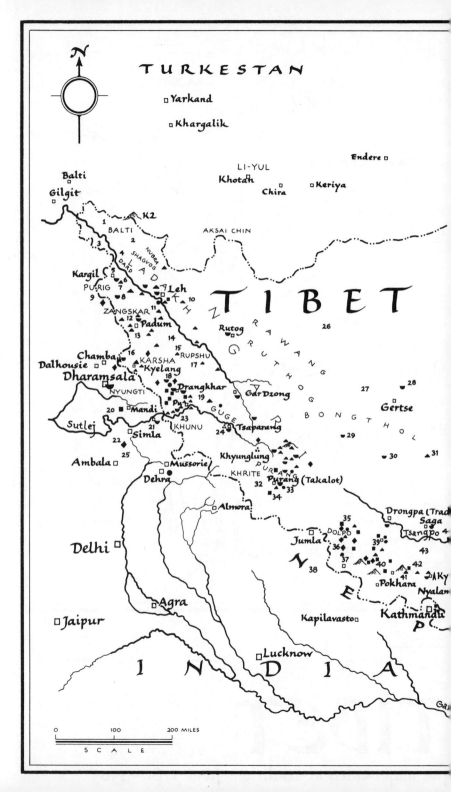

Map 1

1 Drak Chung
2 Dongkhor
3 Skardu
4 Hanu
5 Kargil
6 Lamayuru
7 Shargol
8 Rangdum
9 Suru
10 Drangtse
11 Hemis
12 Zangla
13 Bardan
14 Phug-g'a
15 Kordzog
16 Repag
17 Wamle
18 Kyi
19 Samur
20 Rewalsar
21 Rampur
22 Dolanji
23 Kanam
24 Toling
25 Thopgyal-Sarpa
26 Rungmar
27 Kundo
28 Nagrong
29 Selephug
30 Lungkar
31 Mendong (Tso Chen)
32 Shingpheling
33 Khorlhag
34 Tingkar
35 Tchiyor
36 Shugtsal
37 Dorpatan
38 Salyan
39 Lowo Matang
40 Muktinath
41 Nagtsa
42 Mu
43 Dzongka
44 Chatu
45 Zangden
46 Shindarding
47 Jonang
48 Tanag
49 Phuntsoling
50 Narthang
51 Ngor
52 Rongphug
53 Namche
54 Jumbesi

K · E · Y

◆ Bon
■ Nyingma
▲ Kagyu
● Sakya
⏷ Gelug
∴ Historical Sites
⋀ Pagodas
▫ Cities, Towns
⛰ Mountains
◌ Ethnic Minorities
⌇ Ethnic Border of Tibet
〰 Great Wall of China

Map 2

28 Nagrong
30 Lungkar
31 Mendong (Tso Chen)
39 Lowo Matang
40 Muktinath
41 Nagtsa
42 Mu
43 Dzongka
44 Chatu
45 Zangden
46 Shindarding
47 Jonang
48 Tanag
49 Phuntsoling
50 Narthang
51 Ngor
52 Rongphug
53 Namche
54 Jumbesi
55 Jiwang
56 Walung
57 Gangtok
58 Rumtek
59 Darjeeling (Dorjeling)
60 Kalimpong
61 Paro
62 Phari
63 Punakha
64 Khangmar
65 Gyangtse
66 Zhalu
67 Kyilphug
68 Tashilhunpo
69 Shigatse
70 Menri
71, 72 Yungdrung Ling
73 Rinpung
74 Nakartse Dzong
75 Ralung
76 Lhalung
77 Tongsa
78 Lhuntse Dzong
79 Tawang
80 Samding
81 Dorje Drak
82 Mindroling
83 Yarlung
84 Lhagyari
85 Tsethang
86 Tropu
87 Drepung
88 Tsurphu
89 Samye
90 Densatil
91 Ganden
92 Sera
93 Phenpo Nalandra
94 Yerpa
95 *see* 93
96 Taglung
97 Reting
98 Drikung
99 Gyatsa
100 Dvagla Gampo
101 Gyamda
102 Tselha
103 Driru
104 Sok Dzong
105 Shakcuka
106 Tashiling
107 Garsha
108 Tashi
109 'Adza Sumdo
189 Balgatai
190 Kar-ri

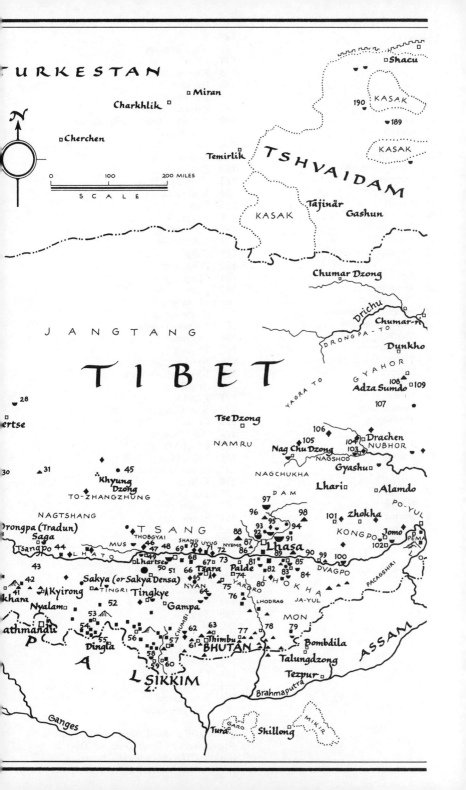

Map 3

102 Tselha
103 Driru
104 Sok Dzong
105 Shakcuka
106 Tashiling
107 Garsha
108 Tashi
109 'Adza Sumdo
110 Zahor Dzogchen
111 Surmang
112 Khampagar
113 Karma
114 Riwoche
115 Chamdo
116 Tsawa Pasho
117 Shobamdo (Pelwar)
118 Showa (Tangme)
119 Senge Dzong
120 Shing-gi
121 Shugden
122 Sangngak Chodzong
123 Shikathang
124 Menkong
125 Dechenling
126 Yartri
127 Balung
128 Dongakrong
129 Satam
130 Dokardzong
131 Tharlam
132 Mili
133 Yanyuan
134 Barong
135 Do
136 Sampel Ling
137 Tsakhalo
138 Gartok
139 Batang
140 Samar
141 Drayab
142 Konjo
143 Rinagjangsum
144 Palyul
145 Kathog
146 Palpung
147 Dzongchen
148 Drolma Lhakang
149 Tengchen (*might be* Rongpasta *or* Manigango)
150 Beri
151 Trewo
152 Drango
153 Nyarong Dzong
154 Nyakcu Dzong
155 Dartsedo
156 Rongdrak
157 Barkham
158 Tsawakhalo
159 Kargu
160 Zungphen
161 Murge
162 Ngawa
163 Metsang
164 Dome Gongma
165 Tarhang Gonpa
166 Sogtsang
167 Doyung
168 Bagchen (Gade)
169 Khar Rishodbarma
170 Arig Rabgya
171 Lhamo
172 Khar Chagtse
173 Cone
174 Balsa Gonpa
175 Rongpo Gon
176 Trikhakhar (Ku'e Te)
177 Enchung Nam Dzong
178 Ja Kyung
179 Dentig
180 Kumbum
181 Shara Koto
182 Tongkhor
183 Ziling
184 Martsang Lhamo
185 Bar Koto *(hist. site)*
186 Azha Khar *(hist. site)*
187 Dulan
188 Kurlyk
189 Balgatai
190 Kar-ri
191 Lungwang
192 Suchou
193 Jayang
194 Chenkor
195 Mathise
196 Bawo Gon
197 Talung Gonpa

The map of ethnic Tibet is based on an original work by Peter Kessler © Tibet Institut, CH 8486, Rikon (Schweiz).

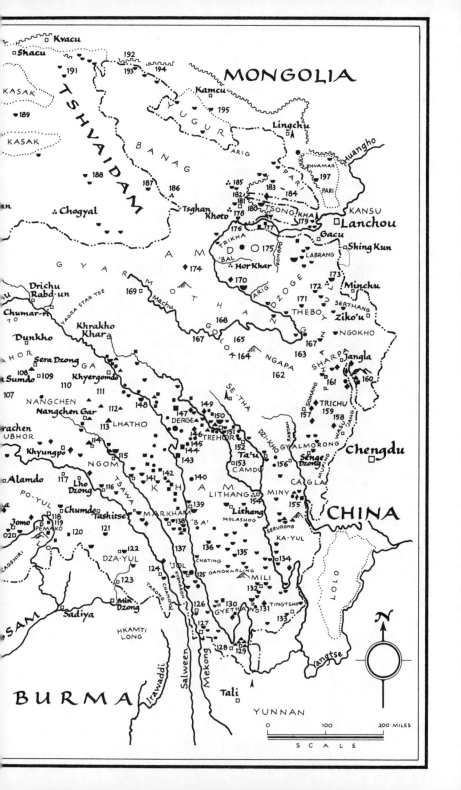

Avalokiteshvara

INTERNATIONAL
RESOURCES DIRECTORY

NOTES TO THE RESOURCES DIRECTORY

The Resources Directory has been in the process of compilation, and its entries have been continuously updated, since 1983. Friends, colleagues and participating institutions around the world have kindly provided a growing list of initial contact addresses. The Foundation has consequently contacted each organisation individually and invited them to describe their activities and resources. These descriptions, and their updates, have been edited, entered into the *Tibetan Cultural Resources Database,* and returned to each organisation for proofing. The entries are therefore written and updated by each organisation. Only in a very few cases have entries been compiled from secondary sources.

The entries are organised according to country, in alphabetical order. Within each country the entries are divided into sections, where applicable, and these are: Academic Organisations; Cultural Organisations and Tibetan Refugee Aid Societies; Ecumenical Centres; Government Offices; Libraries; Medical Institutions; Monasteries and Nunneries; Museums; Publishing Companies and Journals; and Teaching Centres. Descriptions of each organisation include the following: Address; Telephone/fax; Distribution Details; Year Established; Founder; Lama/ Scholar (current staff); General Description; Teaching Programme; Facilities and Services; Project Descriptions.

This directory focuses on culturally related organisations. For a list of Tibet Support Groups, comprehensive Tibetan Government-in-Exile listings and Human Rights Organisations, the reader should consult the Resource Directory of The International Campaign for Tibet, Washington D.C.

Every care has been taken in the compilation of the following entries. However, since each organisation composed their own entries, this leads to inconsistencies, in the phoneticisation of Tibetan in particular. Spelling of Tibetan and Sanskrit terms has been standardised as much as possible, and where applicable, the Tibetan transliteration in a Wylie derived standard, and Sanskrit transliteration with diacritics, can be found in the glossary.

We apologise sincerely for any errors or omissions. We invite all participating organisations to inform us as they wish to update their entries and invite all those not currently included to contact us, so that they may be represented in the *Tibetan Cultural Resources Database* and future editions of the *Handbook.*

ARGENTINA

Cultural Organisations and Tibetan Refugee Aid Societies

FRIENDS OF TIBETAN CULTURE FOUNDATION
Address Paseo Colon 1131–2–11 CAP, Buenos Aires, Argentina, 1063. **Tel** 01 361 2746. **Lama/Scholar** Kamala Di Tella (President), Alejandro Chaoul.

Ecumenical Centres

INSTITUTO DE ESTUDIOS BUDISTOS
Address Arribenos 2350 Casa 1, Buenos Aires, Argentina, 1428. **Tel** 01 782 6939. **Lama/Scholar** Dr. Carmen Dragonetti (President). **General Description** The Institute translates and prepares scholarly articles, particularly for the Latin American magazine of Buddhist studies published in Mexico City, Mexico.

Teaching Centres

KAGYU OSEL LING
Address Antolin Torres 3435, Barrio San Daniel, Cordoba, Argentina, 5000. **Founder** Lama Sherab.

TANGYULING
Address Soldado de la Independencia 1086, Buenos Aires, Argentina, 1426. **Tel** 01 771 0896. **Founder** Dorzang Rinpoche and Chogyal Rinpoche. **Lama/Scholar** Gerardo Abboud. **General Description** This centre invites Lamas from the Drukpa Kagyu lineage, primarily from Tashi Jong, India, for occasional visits to Argentina.

TASHI GAR
Address c/o Raquel Ramponi, Av Federico, La Crozel, 395–9Mo Pisodto 60, Buenos Aires, Argentina, 1426. **Founder** Namkhai Norbu Rinpoche.

AUSTRALIA

Academic Organisations

AUSTRALIAN NATIONAL UNIVERSITY, SOUTH AND WEST ASIA CENTRE
Address Faculty of Asian Studies, A.N.U., Canberra, A.C.T., Australia, 2601. **Tel** 062 49 3163. **Telex/Fax** 062 49 0745. **Distribution Details** No materials are distributed. **Year Established** 1965. **Lama/Scholar** Dr T. Rajapatirana. **General Description** The centre specialises in the languages and literatures of South and West Asia, from the earliest times until the present. There is a three-year pass and a four-year honours degree

course in Sanskrit, Hindi, and Arabic. Also offered is a two-year course in Classical Tibetan for those students wanting to study Tibetan, particularly with reference to Sanskrit texts. There is no course in Spoken Tibetan. The centre participates in lecturing and tutoring for the Religions of India course, offered in the Asian History Centre, and also the Religious Studies course offered in the Dept. of Philosophy. **Teaching Programme** The three-year course in Sanskrit is devoted to the study of grammar, and in the first year the reading is of selections from the Epics and easy prose texts. The works studied in the second and third years represent a diversity of styles and subject matter. The four-year honours course includes the study of Pali, Prakrit, Vedic and more difficult philosophical and Buddhist Hybrid Sanskrit texts. The Sanskrit course consists of four hours of lectures a week; the Classical Tibetan course, which usually has Sanskrit I as a prerequisite, is taught for two hours per week. **Facilities and Services** The Australian National University library system has an excellent collection of Tibetan material, mostly from the PL–480 collection. The National Library, also in Canberra, has the Japanese reprint of the Peking *Kangyur* (*bKa' 'gyur*) and *Tengyur* (*bsTan 'gyur*), and also the new Nyingma Institute reprint.

UNIVERSITY OF NEWCASTLE, DEPARTMENT OF SOCIOLOGY AND ANTHROPOLOGY

Address Rankin Drive, Shortland, Newcastle, New South Wales, Australia, 2308. **Tel** (049) 685307. **Distribution Details** No materials are distributed. **Lama/Scholar** Dr Geoffrey Samuel. **General Description** The Department possesses only one Tibetanist, Dr. Geoffrey Samuel, who is a social anthropologist specialising in religion and politics in Tibetan society. There is consequently only limited Tibetan input into the range of courses offered. **Teaching Programme** Dr Samuel teaches a third year one-semester course on 'Society and Culture – Thailand and Tibet' incorporating material on Tibetan religion, politics and society. **Facilities and Services** The University Library houses a reasonably good collection of Western language material on Tibet, together with a few works in Tibetan. In particular, the *Lam 'bras* series has been recently acquired from the Sakya Centre in India. Dr Geoffrey Samuel has a personal collection of Tibetan books. He also possesses a quantity of Tibetan secular music (mainly *nang ma* and *stod gzhas*, and the Gesar epic) on tape, along with a few other items.

Cultural Organisations and Tibetan Refugee Aid Societies

AUSTRALIAN TIBETAN SOCIETY

Address P.O. Box 39, Gordon, New South Wales, Australia, 2072. **Tel** (2) 371 4239. **Telex/Fax** (2) 628 3292. **Distribution Details** Newsletter published three times a year and subscription to *Tibetan Review* available.

BODHI AUSTRALIA

Address P.O. Box 668, Devonport, Tasmania, Australia, 7310. **Tel** (004) 24 6276. **General Description** The Benevolent Organisation for Development, Health and Insight (BODHI), Australia, is involved in two major projects among Tibetan refugees in India: health education for monks and wild dog sterilization. It is hoped that the success of these projects will contribute indirectly to TB eradication. The organisation is also developing proposals for an environment project to reduce the problem of deforestation. A periodical newsletter, the *Bodhi Times* is published.

DROGMI TIBETAN TRANSLATION SERVICES

Address 2 Sage Close, Chisholm, A.C.T., Australia, 2905. **Tel** (06) 292 8150. **Founder** Lama Choedak. **Lama/**

Scholar Lama Choedak. **General Description** Established by Lama Choedak, Drogmi Tibetan Translation Services has begun the translation of selected Lamdre works. Translation or Tibetan word processing services are available.

TIBET INFORMATION SERVICE
Address P.O. Box 87, Ivanhoe, Victoria, Australia, 3079. **Tel** (3) 499 7347. **Telex/Fax** (3) 663 4484. **Distribution Details** Monthly newsletter published called *News Digest*.

Ecumenical Centres

SIDDHARTHA'S INTENT SOUTHERN DOOR
Address PO Box 330, Round Corner, New South Wales, Australia, 2158. **Tel** 02–653 1762. **Telex/Fax** 02–653 1762. **Founder** H.H. Dilgo Khyentse Rinpoche. **Lama/Scholar** Dzongsar Jamyang Khyentse Rinpoche. **General Description** Siddhartha's Intent Southern Door is the Australian branch of an international voluntary world peace organisation. Guided and directed by Dzongsar Jamyang Khyentse, the centre organises, facilitates and arranges teachings, seminars, workshops and public talks in Australia for Buddhist teachers of all schools in association with Vajradhara Gonpa in northern New South Wales.

Educational and Healing Centres

HOSPICE OF MOTHER TARA
Address 13 Picton Cresent, Bunbury, Western Australia, Australia, 6230. **Tel** 097 219 497. **General Description** The Hospice of Mother Tara is a member of the Foundation for the Preservation of the Mahayana Tradition (FPMT). Apart from the work with dying people the centre offers courses based on learning and using techniques from Tibetan Buddhism, healing courses using meditation, yoga, relaxation massage and other alternative healing methods. Support is offered (when requested) to the dying, offering meditation or whatever is appropriate for the individual concerned.

KARUNA CENTRE
Address 38 Lamont Road, Wilston, Queensland, Australia, 4051. **Tel** 356–7100. **Year Established** 1985. **Founder** Lama Thubten Zopa Rinpoche. **General Description** The Karuna Centre was founded in 1985 by Lama Thubten Zopa Rinpoche. It is a therapy centre providing relaxation classes and support groups as well as individual counselling, physiotherapy, massage, acupuncture and podiatry. In March 1989 the centre established the 'Karuna Hospice Fund', a recognised tax-deductible Public Benevolent Institution, providing a service to the dying. **Teaching Programme** The centre holds classes and support groups on a regular basis, as well as individual consultations and treatments. **Facilities and Services** There is a small lending library.

SHAKYAMUNI BUDDHA HOSPICE
Address P.O. Box A453, Sydney South, New South Wales, Australia, 2000. **Tel** 02 967 2020. **Telex/Fax** 02 904 1247.

Museums

ART GALLERY OF NEW SOUTH WALES

Address Art Gallery Road, Domain, Sydney, New South Wales, Australia, 2000. **Tel** 02 225 1700. **Telex/Fax** 02 221 6226. **Year Established** 1880. **Lama/Scholar** Ms Jacqueline Menzies (Curator of Asian Art), Mr Edmund Capon (Director). **General Description** The Asian Department of the Art Gallery of New South Wales has a small collection of Tibetan art which includes eight late eighteenth century thangkas and one gilt bronze figure of Avalokiteshvara.

Publishing Companies and Journals

WISDOM PUBLICATIONS AUSTRALIA
Address PO Box 1326, Chatswood, New South Wales, Australia, 2067. **Tel** 02 417 1897. **Telex/Fax** 02 417 1857.

Teaching Centres

ATISHA CENTRE

Address RMB 1530 Eaglehawk, Bendigo, Victoria, Australia, 3556. **Tel** (054) 412 705. **Telex/Fax** (054) 425 301. **Distribution Details** Books and cassettes are available at the centre. **Founder** Lama Yeshe. **General Description** Atisha Centre is located some twenty minutes from the centre of Bendigo, two hours from Melbourne. It is a local centre for the people of Bendigo and also serves as a retreat centre for a wider area including Melbourne. **Teaching Programme** The regular weekly programme comprises evening meditation classes, and discourses on Sunday mornings. When visiting teachers are present weekend courses take place;

usually two weekends per year Geshe Doga of Tara House teaches. **Facilities and Services** The centre has a meditation/lecture room, kitchen/dining facilities, a library, and accommodation for a visiting teacher. Visiting students are accommodated in railway carriages with room for up to fifty-five beds. The facilities are available to individual retreaters and those attending courses. **Project Description** It is aimed to develop further the centre's facilities, especially for group and individual retreats.

BUDDHA HOUSE

Address 3, Nelson Street, Fullarton, Adelaide, South Australia, Australia, 5063. **Tel** (08) 379 9153. **Telex/Fax** (08) 373 1051. **Year Established** 1981. **Founder** Lama Thubten Yeshe. **Lama/Scholar** Khenzur Lobsang Thubten Rinpoche. **General Description** Buddha House is a city centre, set up to cater for the needs of the local population through providing: meditation instruction, Buddhist philosophy courses, and related information. It is also intended to include retreat facilities, and to be continually open for people to practice meditation. Since September 1988, Khenzur Lobsang Thubten Rinpoche has been the resident teacher. **Teaching Programme** The teaching programme comprises a combination of different level courses, consonant with the varying needs of individual students. Every Monday there is an Introduction to Meditation class, and bi-monthly 'Basic Buddhism' weekend courses are held. For students who have some understanding of Buddhism, more advanced courses examining classic texts or particular Tantric practices, are offered. There is also a Tibetan language class held at the centre. Pujas are held on the appropriate days of the Tibetan calendar. In coordination with the other FPMT centres in Australia, tours of visiting lamas and other teachers from abroad are arranged. Also, the nine Australian FPMT centres exchange resident teachers throughout the year. Jampa Gendun, the translator, teaches twice weekly on the themes 'Introduction to Buddhism' and 'A Look at Buddhism', and helps new students. A yoga class and day-time meditation classes are also held weekly. **Facilities and Services** The meditation room is open from 8 am to 10 pm daily. There is opportunity to receive advice from the resident teacher, whenever it is needed. There is a comprehensive library and bookshop. Accommodation is provided for the resident teacher, and there are rooms for three other residents. **Project Description** There is an ongoing commitment to provide a service to the community in which the centre is situated. Healing workshops are run each term and community based talks and workshops are given to businesses by appointment.

CHENREZIG CITY CENTRE
Address 51 Enoggera Road, Newmarket, Brisbane, Queensland, Australia, 4051. **Tel** 07 356 9523.

CHENREZIG INSTITUTE FOR WISDOM CULTURE
Address Highlands Road, P.O. Box 41, Eudlo, Queensland, Australia, 4554. **Tel** (074) 450077. **Telex/Fax** (074) 450088. **Distribution Details** Contact centre for further information. **Year Established** 1974. **Founder** Lama Thubten Yeshe. **Lama/Scholar** Geshe Thubten Lodan (formerly), Geshe Puntsok Thinley (formerly), Geshe Tashi Tsering (present). **General Description** Chenrezig Institute was one of the earliest Australian Buddhist centres to be established. It is located in the countryside behind Queensland's Sunshine Coast, about one hour north of Brisbane. A Tibetan lama is normally resident and teaching at the centre. Courses and ongoing teachings are given regularly for the growing number of residents. Facilities include a meditation hall, a library, a motel block, retreat huts, a kitchen and dining hall, together with an office, shop, and community and school buildings. The centre functions as a community and group meditations are held daily. Monks and nuns are usually present to guide and give advice. There are regular discussion groups, pujas, retreats, study groups, and collective work periods. **Teaching Programme** Regular courses on all aspects of Tibetan Buddhism, philosophy, and meditational techniques are given by both resident and visiting teachers. The Centre follows Gelugpa traditions and methods in meditation, philosophy, approaches to retreat practices, tantric yoga, and sangha training. **Facilities and Services** The meditation hall holds 200 for teaching and meditation, and there is a meeting room for up to fifty. Accommodation is available for up to seventy in rooms, dormitories and huts. A well stocked library is open daily. The kitchen and dining area is of a commercial standard, and there is a community room with cooking facilities and an eating and relaxing area for many residents. There is a kindergarten hall with cooking facilities, which functions three mornings per week. An amenities block includes showers and a laundry. There are two teaching staff houses, which are fully self-contained.

KAGYU EVAM BUDDHIST INSTITUTE
Address P.O. Box 444, Hawthorn, Melbourne, Victoria, Australia, 3122. **Tel** (03) 387 0442. **Telex/Fax** (03) 380 8296. **Distribution Details** The Institute will distribute publications and cassettes world-wide to any enquiry on receipt of payment for materials ordered (most publications not restricted). **Year Established** 1980. **Founder** Traleg Kyabgon Rinpoche. **Lama/Scholar** Traleg Kyabgon Rinpoche. **General Description** The Kagyu Evam Buddhist Institute was established by Ven. Traleg Kyabgon Rinpoche and has, over the last eight years, attracted an impressive list of Buddhist scholars and meditation teachers. The institute has as its policy a two-pronged approach to the preservation and propagation of the teachings of the Buddha: 1) To bring different Buddhist traditions together ie, Theravada, Mahayana & Vajrayana on the one hand (which has been done through the very successful annual Buddhist Summer School), and to promote Tibetan Buddhism with particular emphasis on Kagyu and Nyingma teachings. 2) To encourage and foster greater understanding amongst world religions, specifically between Buddhism and Christianity through 'dialogue' and other means, so that each can have greater appreciation of the other. The institute also sees the importance of engaging in dialogue with secular Western thought and, starting in 1993, will conduct an annual Buddhism and Psychotherapy Conference. **Teaching Programme** Throughout the year KEBI offers courses and retreats led by various Buddhist masters from all traditions. Besides these special occasions with visiting teachers, the institute has an ongoing teaching programme that includes regular introductory meditation classes held on Sundays and Wednesdays; and a special class every Monday conducted by the Institute's resident teacher Traleg Kyabgon Rinpoche for the growing number of Ngondro students (original Tibetan texts on Mahayana teachings are used). Every year Rinpoche offers two retreats, one during Easter and the other in November. Students of the institute are encouraged to practise meditation (Shamatha and Vipassana) and to be involved in serious study of Mahayana texts, leading to the practise of Ngondro (preliminary practise). This culminates in the study and practise of Tantra (Mahamudra and Maha Ati).

SAKYA CENTRE
Address 50A Swains Avenue, Rose Park, South Australia, Australia, 5067.

SAKYA LOSAL CHOE DZONG, THE TIBETAN BUDDHIST SOCIETY OF ACT
Address P.O. Box 3430, Manuka, A.C.T., Australia, 2603. **Year Established** 1989. **Founder** Lama Choedak. **Lama/Scholar** Lama Choedak. **General Description** The centre has about sixty members who meet twice a week to attend Chenrezig meditation on Wednesday evenings and guided Shamatha meditation and Dharma study classes on Sunday mornings. Lama Choedak teaches at these classes on classic texts and gives occasional workshops, seminars and retreats on diverse topics. On the first Sunday of each month senior students meet for a White Tara practice. The centre also hosts visits of prominent Tibetan teachers, and co-ordinates joint retreats and seminars with other Buddhist organisations. The centre facilitates sponsorship to assist Tibetan refugee children in Nepal and India. **Facilities and Services** There is a quarterly newsletter *"The Clear Mind Newsletter"*.

SAKYA THARPA LING
Address 26 Louisa Road, Birchgrove, New South Wales, Australia, 2041.

SHAKYAMUNI CENTRE FOR BUDDHIST STUDIES
Address P.O. Box 166, Bondi Road, Bondi, New South Wales, Australia, 2026. **Tel** 02–3650010.

TARA INSTITUTE

Address 3 Mavis Avenue, East Brighton, Melbourne, Victoria, Australia, 3187. **Tel** (03) 596 8900. **Telex/Fax** (03) 596 4856. **Distribution Details** Please contact the Centre for further information. **Year Established** 1973. **Founder** Lama Thubten Yeshe. **Lama/Scholar** Geshe Lobsang Doga, Samdup Tsering (Translator), Ven. Thubten Donyo (Translator). **General Description** In 1987 the Tara Institute moved to an imposing Edwardian house set in a beautiful suburb of Melbourne. It is located opposite an attractive park and is surrounded by an acre of grounds. The main building contains a converted Catholic church, that now serves as the main prayer hall, seating 400. Other features of the building include extensive residential quarters, an indoor theatre, and a commercial kitchen and large restaurant/dining area. The institute is a member of the Foundation for the Preservation of the Mahayana Tradition, and links with the other Australian FPMT centres to coordinate tours of visiting lamas. **Teaching Programme** The weekly programme of the Tara Institute consists of classes on introductory Buddhism, general teachings, and seminars on more advanced philosophy. Pujas are held three times per month and throughout the year there are weekend courses and retreats. For people with life threatening illnesses healing meditation classes and courses are also held. Tantric initiations and commentaries are given by the resident and visiting lamas from time to time. **Facilities and Services** Facilities at the centre include a bookshop, a library, an indoor theatre, a restaurant and coffee shop, and office space. The residential area contains thirty bedrooms and several dormitories. **Project Description** It is hoped to develop the building through installing central heating, remodelling and expanding the bookshop, and partitioning the dormitory area.

TIBETAN BUDDHIST SOCIETY

Address 1425 Micklehum Road, Yuroke, Victoria, Australia, 3063. **Tel** 613 333 2210. **Distribution Details** The occasional book is published. Some books are only available for limited distribution. **Year Established** 1979. **Founder** Ven. Geshe Acarya Thubten Loden. **Lama/Scholar** Ven. Geshe Acarya Thubten Loden. **General Description** The Tibetan Buddhist Society's aims are threefold: to develop and protect the pure Mahayana Buddhist teachings within Australia; to foster open communication between all spiritual traditions; and to provide community welfare aid to both Tibetan refugees and Australians in need. In pursuance of these objectives, the Society provides both sutra and tantra teachings from the Gelugpa lineage, which are free of charge. It also conducts Tibetan language lessons, and is involved in welfare activities within Australia, and for the Tibetans in India. **Teaching Programme** Classes are conducted on the complete range of Hinayana, Mahayana, and Vajrayana teachings, following the tradition derived from Nagarjuna and Tsong Khapa. There are also introductory lectures and classes giving instruction on relaxation methods, and dealing with stress. Particular emphasis is placed on the practice of the graduated path to enlightenment

(*Lam Rim*). The spiritual director, Ven. Geshe Acarya Thubten Loden, gives initiations into all levels of tantra practice, though he has indicated that no more will be given at the maha-anuttarayoga tantra level. **Facilities and Services** Apart from the centre in Yuroke, the Tibetan Buddhist Society has branches in Dulwich Hill, N.S.W.; East Brisbane, Queensland; North Perth, Western Australia; and Fairfax, in California, USA. Each centre provides meditation rooms; libraries; teachings free of charge; counselling, and is involved in the publication of books derived from the oral commentaries given by the Ven. Geshe Acarya Thubten Loden. **Project Description** The Tibetan Buddhist Society has an ongoing commitment to the support of Tibetan refugees in India, and to looking after the old and sick, and the lonely and poor within the immediate community. Recently, it has been engaged in trying to bring seven Tibetan lamas to live in Australia: Geshe Triyongzin Tulku, Geshe Lharampa Loga, Geshe Kinjo Rinpoche, Geshe Nyalushap Tulku, Geshe Namgyal, Thugse Tulku, and Lama Lhundrup. It is intended to begin the translation and publication of the great Mahayana treatises.

VAJRADHARA GONPA

Address P.O. Box 345, Kyogle, New South Wales, Australia, 2474. **Tel** (02) 653 1762. **Telex/Fax** (02) 653 1762. **Year Established** 1986. **Founder** H.E. Dzongsar Jamyang Khyentse Rinpoche. **Lama/Scholar** H.E. Dzongsar Jamyang Khyentse Rinpoche. **General Description** Vajradhara Gonpa is a non-denominational Buddhist retreat centre in northern New South Wales, situated in 1000 acres of protected natural bushland with spectacular views. The centre has a large temple and a small house for a visiting lama, and offers an idyllic, peaceful and isolated meditative environment. **Teaching Programme** Teachers from all traditions have taught at the centre. **Facilities and Services** The centre has a large kitchen/dining room building and several small builidings. Retreat accommodation is available.

VAJRASATTVA MOUNTAIN RETREAT CENTRE

Address 26 Hathill Road, Blackheath, New South Wales, Australia, 2785. **Tel** 61 47 877 776.

VAJRAYANA INSTITUTE

Address 1 Guthrie Avenue, Cremorne, Sydney, New South Wales, Australia, 2090. **Tel** (02) 909 1330. **Telex/Fax** (02) 904 1247. **Distribution Details** No materials are distributed. **Year Established** 1984. **Founder** Lama Thubten Yeshe/Lama Zopa Rinpoche. **Lama/Scholar** Ven. Geshe Dawo. **General Description** The centre is located in a quiet suburb, close to Sydney Harbour. The centre is run by lay practitioners. A regular programme of evening lectures and public talks, residential and non-residential courses, pujas, and meditation and discussion groups is provided. There is involvement in FPMT tours arranged for lamas, geshes, and experienced ordained and lay scholars. It is a Gelugpa centre and, being a member of the Foundation for the Preservation of the Mahayana Tradition (FPMT), comes under the guidance of its spiritual head, Lama Thubten Zopa Rinpoche. **Teaching Programme** Geshe Dawa teaches *Lam Rim* on Tuesday nights and an advanced subject on Thursday night. There is a weekend course each month as well as initiations and practice days. A discourse is given twice weekly including guided meditation and discussion. A Guru Puja is arranged twice a month, and a Vajrasattva, Medicine Buddha and Tara Puja once a month. Two or three-day courses are held either at the centre, or at a residential country venue. Occasional public talks are given outside the centre, and there are concentrated lecture series and courses when touring teachers are in the area.

Antonio Satta teaches Tibetan language on Monday nights. **Facilities and Services** The centre possesses a library, reading room and bookshop. A bi-monthly newsletter is produced to keep people informed of upcoming events and the spiritual programme.

AUSTRIA

Academic Organisations

UNIVERSITAT WIEN, INSTITUT FUR TIBETOLOGIE UND BUDDHISMUSKUNDE

Address Maria Theresien-Strasse 3, Vienna, Austria, A–1090. **Tel** 34 74 93. **Distribution Details** No materials are distributed. **Year Established** 1973. **Lama/Scholar** Prof Dr Ernst Steinkellner, Dr Torsten Much, Dr Helmut Tauscher, Dr Helmut Krasser, Dr Deborah Klimburg-Salter. **General Description** The institute is concerned with philological and philosophical research and teaching in the fields of Tibetan Studies and Buddhist Studies. Within Buddhist Studies special emphasis is placed on Indian and Tibetan Buddhism, and within Tibetan Studies the emphasis is on the history of religion and philosophy. The main subjects studied in the latter course are Ecclesiastical History (chos 'byung), Pramana and the Madhyamaka philosophical school. **Facilities and Services** The institute's library holds around 8000 volumes on Buddhism and Tibet, and a further 4000 Tibetan texts on microfiche. Religious and philosophical material predominates.

Museums

MUSEUM OF ETHNOLOGY, VIENNA, MUSEUM FUR VOLKERKUNDE

Address Heldenplatz 3, Neue Hofburg, Vienna, Austria, A–1014. **Tel** 0222 93 45 41. **Year Established** 1928. **General Description** The Tibetan collection of the department of Southeast Asia has approximately 3000 items.

MUSEUM OF ORIENTAL ART, VIENNA

Address Burgring 5, Vienna 1, Austria, A–1010.

NATURE HOUSE

Address Museumplatz 5, Salzburg, Austria, A–5020.

Publishing Companies and Journals

OCTOPUS VERLAG

Address Fleischmarkt 16, Vienna, Austria, A–1010. **Tel** 0222/512 71 46. **General Description** Octopus Verlag is a publisher and distributor of books on all forms of Buddhism and an information source for Buddhist teaching facilities in Austria.

Teaching Centres

TASHI RABTEN

Address Letzehof, Feldkirch, Austria, A–6800. **Tel** (05522) 24192. **Distribution Details** Audio tapes of teachings given at Tashi Rabten can be obtained from Verein zur Forderung der Kultur und Weisheit Tibets, in Munich, Germany. **Year Established** 1982. **Founder** Geshe Tadin Rabten. **Lama/Scholar** Geshe Phemba. **General Description** Tashi Rabten offers facilities where people can come to learn more about Tibetan culture, Buddhism, meditation and Tibetan language. The centre possesses a meditation room, capable of holding around 200 people at any one time. **Teaching Programme** Tashi Rabten runs weekend seminars on such subjects as the nature of the mind, and dispelling obstacles to mental development. Pujas and meditation sessions are held every day of the week, except Mondays and Thursdays. **Facilities and Services** One room self-contained apartments are available for those wishing to engage in retreat practices.

BELGIUM

Cultural Organisations and Tibetan Refugee Aid Societies

ROKPA BELGIUM

Address Rue Capouillet 33, Bruxelles, Belgium, B–1060. **Tel** 02 537 5407. **Year Established** 1987. **Founder** H.H. Sixteenth Karmapa.

Museums

ETHNOGRAPHIC MUSEUM, ANTWERP, ASIAN DEPARTMENT

Address Suikerrui 19, Antwerp 1, Belgium, 2000. **Tel** 03/232 08 82. **General Description** The museum has a substantial Tibet/Nepal section. The collection includes a variety of devotional and ritual objects, bronze statues, thangkas and other types of paintings. Several items are quite unique: two Bardo-thangkas in the shape of a stupa; a series of fifty-four miniature paintings depicting the different steps of the meditation on the mandala of Sarvavid Vairocana; a thangka depicting the town of Lhasa, which includes all the important shrines and monasteries in an area up to fifty km around the city; and a large Nepalese Pauba depicting the fully documented (in Newari) story of Sumana. Most of these objects are dated late eighteenth to early nineteenth century.

ROYAL MUSEUM OF ART AND HISTORY

Address Parc du Cinquantenaire 10, Bruxelles, Belgium, B–1040. **Tel** 02–741 72 11. **Telex/Fax** 02–733 77 35. **Lama/Scholar** Prof Dr F. Van Noten. **General Description** The Tibetan collection within the Museum was first started in 1872. Most of the objects came from a Mr Verbert, who lived in China between 1907 and 1935. The collection includes 385 Tibetan and Sino-Tibetan pieces.

Teaching Centres

INSTITUT TIBETAIN

Address Avenue du Paepedelle 91/4G, Bruxelles, Belgium, 1160. **Tel** 02 675 38 05.

INSTITUT YEUNTEN LING

Address Chateau de Fond l'Eveque, 4 promenade Saint Jean l'Agneau, Huy, Belgium, 4500. **Tel** (085) 21 48 20. **Telex/Fax** (085) 23 66 58. **Distribution Details** Distribution of materials is handled by Karma Sonam Gyamtso Ling in Antwerp. **Year Established** 1983. **Founder** Kalu Rinpoche. **Lama/Scholar** Lama Karma Tashi, Lama Tashi Njima, Lama Sopa, Gega Lama. **General Description** Yeunten Ling is situated in a newly reconstructed castle, set in twenty-six acres of forested grounds, and surrounded by a conservation area. It is a peaceful, isolated setting, not far from the city of Huy. The building contains two shrine rooms, study rooms, and accommodation suitable for 150 people at any one time. Three Tibetan lamas, one Tibetan monk, three Western monks, one nun and up to ten lay people are resident there. A seventeen metres high stupa, the 'Stupa of Miracles', modelled on the ancient Indian stupa of Shravasti, was built in the grounds in 1988. Also in the grounds is a three-metre statue of Shakyamuni Buddha. In April 1990 about 2000 people attended the talk 'Buddhism and Science' given by H.H. the Dalai Lama at the institute. **Teaching Programme** Daily meditation sessions are held morning and evening, and teachings are given once a week. Throughout the year, courses and intensive retreats take place. All activities are guided by one of the resident lamas, or by visiting lamas. The lamas can be consulted by any individual seeking advice in their spiritual practice. **Facilities and Services** Excellent facilities exist for short or lengthy retreats. Board and lodging is provided for up to 150 people, and day accommodation for several hundred. A number of retreat cells are currently being completed. A Tibetan monk, Temba Rubgay, the main student of Gega Lama, offers tuition in traditional thangka painting. The Karma Gardri Thangka Painting School, under the guidance of Gega Lama, is scheduled every summer. Courses in Tibetan language and Buddhist philosophy are also offered. In conjunction with Karma Sonam Gyamtso Ling, the Centre produces a quarterly newsletter entitled *Kunchab*, which provides general information concerning the activities of the centre, together with transcripts of important teachings. It is printed in Dutch, French, and English. Details of the other publications can be gained from editions of *Kunchab* available from the centre. **Project Description** Yeunten Ling is engaged in a major project to build an 'International Buddhist Institute' as a place for meetings, research and practice. The building is being carefully designed in the old traditional style of Tibetan architecture. Teachings will also be given at the Institute and include instruction based on the 'five traditional sciences', namely art and craftwork, Tibetan medicine, language, logic and philosophy and inner science. In an interview, Jamgon Kongtrul Rinpoche described the new institute as '... ideal to serve as a venue for inter-faith exchange, conferences on psychology and philosophy, and other disciplines which contribute greatly to spiritual understanding and progress.' Facilities to allow meditators to complete the traditional three-year, three-month retreat are also included in the project. A major fund-raising initiative is currently in progress.

KARMA SHEDRUP GYAMTSO LING
Address Rue Capouillet 33, Bruxelles, Belgium, 1060. **Tel** 322 537 5407. **Founder** Akong Rinpoche.

KARMA SONAM GYAMTSO LING
Address Kruispadstraat 33, Schoten, Belgium, 2900. **Tel** (03) 685 09 19. **Telex/Fax** (03) 685 09 91. **Distribution Details** The centre distributes internationally. Pre-payment is requested. Contact the centre for order forms. **Year Established** 1976. **Founder**

H.H. Gyalwa Karmapa. **Lama/ Scholar** Tsa-Tsa Lama Ogyen, Lama Karma Tashi, Lama Tashi Nyima, Lama Sopa. **General Description** Karma Sonam Gyamtso Ling is located in a four-storey house in a quiet area of the city. It contains a shrine room, a study room, and other rooms to accommodate residents and visitors to the centre. **Teaching Programme** Pujas take place in the centre every night of the week. On Thursdays, teachings are given, either by one of the resident lamas, or by a visiting high lama. In addition, there are occasional longer courses organised. Study groups on the Tibetan language and classic texts, are also held in the centre. **Facilities and Services** The centre possesses a temple, a study room, a library, and rooms for residents and visitors. Every three months a newsletter is produced, entitled *Kunchab*. It is printed in Dutch, French, and English, and includes general information about the activities of the Centre, as well as transcripts of important teachings. Karma Sonam Gyamtso Ling also publish and distribute a number of books, posters, prints, greeting cards, and badges. Past publications have included a traditional Tibetan edition of the *Life and Songs of Milarepa*, and the *Principles of Tibetan Art* (in English and Tibetan), by Gega Lama, an accomplished thangka painter. Kunchab Publications has begun a Tibetan correspondence course available in Dutch, French and German and has published *De meditatie, raadgevingen voor beginners* by Bokar Rinpoche. **Project Description** It is intended to publish the second volume of *Principles of Tibetan Art*. This will deal with the use and meaning of colour in Tibetan thangka painting.

OGYEN KUNZANG CHOLING

Address 111 rue de Livourne/Livornostraat, Bruxelles, Belgium, 1050. **Tel** (02) 648 14 07. **Distribution Details** No materials are distributed. **Year Established** 1972. **Founder** Kangyur Rinpoche. **Lama/Scholar**

Lama Kunzang Cho-Kyi Dorje. **General Description** Ogyen Kunzang Choling is a community of the Nyingmapa lineage tradition, and is headed by Lama Kunzang Cho Kyi Dorje. Lama Kunzang is a Western disciple of H.H. Kangyur Rinpoche. Some 300 people live in the extended community of town and country centres under the direction of Lama Kunzang. The community is self-supporting, running its own wholefood restaurants, shops and other businesses, together with its own medical centre. Ogyen Kunzang Choling was originally established in the province of Kham in Tibet. In recent years it had been guided by the late Kangyur Rinpoche, who in 1968 founded a centre in Darjeeling to continue the teachings in India. Lama Kunzang studied and completed retreats there, and was then asked by Kangyur Rinpoche to establish Ogyen Kunzang Choling in Europe. In 1972 the centre in Brussels was opened, followed by the founding of a monastery (Nyima Dzong) in 1974. The latter is located in southern France, and has been consecrated several times, notably by H.H. Dudjom Rinpoche and H.H. Dilgo Khyentse Rinpoche. In 1978 centres were opened in the cities of Lisbon and Porto in Portugal, and in 1980 another monastery (Hung Cara Dzong) was established in the south of that country. Gyatso Dzong, a centre on the island of Tahiti in the South Pacific, was opened in 1983. More recently H.H. Khyentse Rinpoche has consecrated a stupa (mchod rten) at Nyima Dzong in 1984. **Teaching Programme** Practices undertaken include the ngondro (sNgon 'gro) preliminary practices of Lapur (*Las 'phro gling pa*); the *Khadro Nyingthig* (*mKha 'gro sNying thig*); the *Longchen Nyingthig* (*Klong chen sNying thig*); and the *Pema Samthig* (*Pad ma bSam thig*). There is also study and practice of the *Kunzang Lama'i Shaling* (*Kun bZang bLa ma'i Zhal lung*) of dPal sprul Rinpoche, and the *Rin chen gTer mDzod*, as compiled by Jamgon Kongtrul (Jam-mgon Kong-sprul). **Facilities and Services** The Losar (lo gsar) new year festival and summer seminars may be open to non-members. Please contact the centre for further information. **Project Description** Ongoing work is taking place on the construction and development of rural centres in France (Nyima Dzong), Portugal (Hung Cara Dzong), and Tahiti (Gyatso Dzong). A medical centre is being established and developed, which provides both modern and traditional medicine. A library of classic texts of the tradition is being established.

BHUTAN

Libraries

NATIONAL LIBRARY OF BHUTAN
Address G.P.O. Box 185, Thimphu, Bhutan. **Tel** 2885.

Monasteries and Nunneries

DECHEN CHOELING PALACE
Address P.O. Thimphu, Bhutan.

LEGDRUP DRATSANG KHASAKA MONASTERY
Address P.O. Khasadapchu, Distt Thimphu, Bhutan.

BRAZIL

Teaching Centres

CENTRO DE DHARMA SHI-DE CHOE-TSOG
Address Rua Aimbere 2008, Sao Paulo, Brazil, 01258. **Tel** 011 871 4827. **Founder** Gangchen Rinpoche.

DORJE JIG JE CENTRO
Address Rua Ribeiro de Almeida 50, Laranjeiras, Rio de Janeiro, Brazil, 22240. **Tel** 021 205 0583. **Telex/Fax** 032 4212041. **Founder** Lama Thubten Zopa Rinpoche.

FUNDACAO KARMA TEKSUM CHOKORLING
Address Estrada dos Bandeirantes 10.636, Jacarepagua, Rio Centro, Rio de Janeiro, Brazil, 22700. **Tel** 021 342 8185.

BULGARIA

Academic Organisations

CENTRE FOR TIBETAN AND CENTRAL ASIAN STUDY
Address 65 Chataldja ul, Sofia, Bulgaria, 1504. **Tel** 02 440526. **Telex/Fax** 02 880193. **Lama/Scholar** Dr Georgi Svechnikov (Director).

SOFIA UNIVERSITY, CENTRE FOR ORIENTAL LANGUAGES AND CULTURES

Address Tibetan Department, 79 Naicho Tsanov str., Sofia, Bulgaria, 1303. **Lama/Scholar** Prof Alexander Fedotov. **General Description** The centre offers courses in the study of both Mongolian and Tibetan language and civilisation. Research facilities are also provided.

BYELORUS

Teaching Centres

DZOGCHEN COMMUNITY OF BYELORUS

Address 29–35 Odintsova St., Minsk, Byelorus, 2200–18. **Tel** (0172) 577158.

CANADA

Academic Organisations

UNIVERSITY OF BRITISH COLUMBIA, DEPTS. OF ASIAN AND RELIGIOUS STUDIES

Address, Vancouver, British Columbia, Canada, V6T 1W5. **Tel** (604) 228 3881. **Telex/Fax** (604) 228 5207. **Year Established** 1961. **Lama/Scholar** Dr Ashok Aklujkar, Dr Shotaro Iida, Dr. Daniel Overmyer, Karin Preisendanz, Kenneth E Bryant. **General Description** The Asian Studies Department has three major sections: Chinese, Japanese and South Asian. There are facilities for teaching Sanskrit. Dr Ashok Aklujkar has produced a book on learning Sanskrit for English speaking adults. **Teaching Programme** At undergraduate level, three years of Sanskrit, and two flexible-content courses at the graduate level are offered. Areas of associated strength are: folk religions of China and Korea; Sikkhism. Tibetan instruc-

tion began in 1990. **Facilities and Services** The library has good collections in both Asian and Western languages. **Project Description** Development of printer fonts for Asian scripts.

UNIVERSITY OF CALGARY, DEPARTMENT OF RELIGIOUS STUDIES

Address 2500 University Drive N.W., Calgary, Alberta, Canada, T2N 1N4. **Tel** (403) 220–5886. **Telex/Fax** (403) 284–0848. **Distribution Details** No materials are distributed. **Year Established** 1971. **Lama/Scholar** Dr Leslie Kawamura, Dr A. Barber, Dr Morny Joy, Dr Ronald Neufeldt. **General Description** The Religious Studies Department is non-sectarian and intends to serve both students who have religious affiliations as well as those who do not. The purpose of the department is educational and academic – one of fostering an informed understanding of the varied and important phenomena of religious belief and practice. Since its inception in 1971, rapid growth has moved the enrolment from fifty-two to some 1200 students. Students may focus their studies on either Eastern Religions or Western Religions or The Nature of Religion. **Teaching Programme** Undergraduate courses offered include: Tibetan I and II (Classical Tibetan Language); Sanskrit I and II; The Early Buddhist Tradition; The Mahayana Buddhist Tradition; Tibetan Religious Systems; Readings in Tibetan Literature I and II; Religious Chronicles of Buddhism (chos 'byung); Advanced Studies in Buddhism; Vajrayana Buddhism. The department offers a programme in graduate studies for the Master of Arts degree, allowing for a focus on Eastern Religions. Within the area of Buddhism the courses are: Mahayana Sutras and Shastras; Buddhist Tantra; Yogacara; Madhyamaka; The Buddhist Canon (survey course, mandatory for a graduate student in Buddhism); Buddhist Historical Texts.

Facilities and Services The library contains copies of the *Lhasa Kangyur* (*bKa' 'gyur*), the *Cone Tengyur* (*bsTan 'gyur*), the *Tibetan Tripitaka*, Taipei Edition (complete) and Tokyo University Edition (in part) and the PL–480 collection in micro-fiche form. Included in its reference services, the library offers computer searching of a large number of North American databases.

UNIVERSITY OF TORONTO, DEPT. EAST ASIAN STUDIES
Address, Toronto, Canada, M5S 1A5. **Tel** (416) 978 5928. **Facilities and Services** The Library has a large collection of Tibetan Texts including all text pulished under the PL–480 programme.

UNIVERSITY OF TORONTO, CENTRE FOR RELIGIOUS STUDIES
Address, Toronto, Canada, M5S 1A1. **Tel** (416) 978 1057.

Cultural Organisations and Tibetan Refugee Aid Societies

CANADA-TIBET FRIENDSHIP SOCIETY
Address P.O. Box 6588 Postal Station A, Toronto, Ontario, Canada, M5W 1X4. **Tel** 416 531 3810.

RIGPE DORJE FOUNDATION
Address 120 Le Cavalier, Montreal, Quebec, Canada, H4N 2K2. **Tel** (514) 747 3017. **General Description** Rigpe Dorje Foundation, a registered charitable organisation, is part of an international network of Rigpe Dorje Foundations. Its mandate focuses on initiating, promoting and implementing programmes of social, vocational, educational and medical assistance, and training for Tibetan communities, mainly in India.

TRANS-HIMALAYAN AID SOCIETY
Address 5885 University Blvd., Vancouver, British Columbia, Canada, V6T 1K7. **Tel** (604) 224 5133. **Telex/Fax** (604) 224 4881. **Distribution Details** Quarterly newsletter. **Year Established** 1962. **Founder** Dr George Woodcock. **General Description** The Trans-Himalayan Aid Society is a non-government organisation whose activities are directed towards promoting sustainable development in Northern India and the Himalayan countries. The society was originally founded in 1962 to help Tibetan refugees but that focus has expanded to encompass impoverished villagers of northern rural India. For many years the society worked in close cooperation with the Indian NGO, MYRADA, on a number of large aid projects in many parts of India. **Facilities and Services** There is a quarterly newsletter published by the society which is sent to members giving details and information on project news and update. **Project Description** Current projects include social forestry, community development, promotion of environmental awareness and conservation, vocational training, community health projects, agricultural development and income generating schemes. Sponsorship of children and old people in various refugee communities has been a constant aspect of the society's endeavours.

Museums

NATIONAL GALLERY OF CANADA

Address 380 Sussex Drive, P.O. Box 427, Station A, Ottawa, Ontario, Canada, K1N 9N4. **Tel** 613 990 1985. **Telex/Fax** 613 993 4385. **General Description** The collection of Tibetan art is small but very fine. It comprises sixty-two paintings and thrity-three sculptures from the Heeramaneck collection donated to the National Gallery of Canada by a Toronto collector. Some of the works are part of an exhibition of Tibetan art organised by the Art Gallery of Victoria and circulated in Canada. These works entered the permanent Tibetan collection at the National Gallery of Canada in 1980. Black and white photographs of the collection are available. The works date from the fifteenth to the nineteenth century.

ROYAL ONTARIO MUSEUM

Address Far Eastern Department, 100 Queen's Park, Toronto, Ontario, Canada, M5S 2C6. **Tel** 416 586 5721. **Telex/Fax** 416 586 5863. **Year Established** 1912. **Lama/Scholar** Elizabeth Knox (Research Associate), Dr Dorie Dohrenwend (Associate Curator). **General Description** The Far Eastern Department of the Royal Ontario Museum holds a medium-sized collection of Tibetan material, formed mainly in the first third of the twentieth century, with only occasional later additions, acquired mainly as gifts. It includes around eighty thangkas, a few as early as the sixteenth century but most dating from eighteenth and nineteenth centuries. Figural sculpture also ranges in date from the sixteenth to the nineteenth century, and there is a varied collection of ritual materials. In addition, the Textile Department holds a collection of Tibetan costume and costume accessories.

VANCOUVER MUSEUM

Address 1100 Chestnut Street, Vancouver, British Columbia, Canada, V6J 3J9. **Tel** 604 736 4431. **Telex/Fax** 604 736 5417. **General Description** There are about twenty items in the collection of Tibetan artefacts, including two thangkas, musical instruments, statues, relic boxes, horse saddle blankets, some daily utensils (stove, bowls etc.) and a few ritual items (phurba, bells and banners, prayer wheels and a table prayer wheel).

Publishing Companies and Journals

SHAMBHALA SUN

Address P.O. Box 399, Halifax Central, Halifax, Nova Scotia, Canada, B3J 2P8. **Year Established** 1978. **General Description** *The Shambhala Sun* is a bi-monthly tabloid, founded in 1978 as *The Vajradhatu Sun*. The paper presents teachings and commentary from the Buddhist and other contemplative traditions, with poetry, fiction, portfolio art and news coverage from around the world. *The Sun's* readership includes 10,000 worldwide with two-thirds living in the US. Pass-along readership is significant, with regular copies sent to bookshops, coffee houses, universities, and other centres and interest groups.

Teaching Centres

CHAGDUD GONPA CANADA

Address 2036 Stephens Street, Vancouver, British Columbia, Canada, V6K 3W1. **Tel** (604) 537 4570. **Founder** Chagdud Tulku. **Lama/Scholar** Chagdud Tulku.

DONAG CHOLING

Address c/o Box 5262, Station A, Toronto, Canada, M5W 1N5. **Tel** 416 488 5554. **Year Established** 1983. **Founder** Kyabje Song Rinpoche.

GADEN CHOLING

Address 637 Christie Street, Toronto, Ontario, Canada, M6G 3E6. **Tel** (416) 651 3849. **Distribution Details** Distribution is world-wide. A catalogue is available. Allow up to eight weeks for delivery. **Year Established** 1981. **Founder** Zasep Tulku Rinpoche. **Lama/Scholar** Zasep Tulku Rinpoche. **General Description** Gaden Choling's origins date from when a number of Zasep Rinpoche's students asked him to start a centre in the West, a request that was supported by Kyabje Ling Rinpoche. A small centre was then established, which has grown into a firm base of committed students. Zasep Rinpoche's style has resulted in a very warm, informal atmosphere, in which all individuals share responsibilities and support one another as a 'dharma family'. Zasep Rinpoche attends all meetings and advises the Board of Directors. He devotes a considerable amount of time to giving individuals personal instruction on their meditation practice. Although Rinpoche avoids traditional protocol, he is highly respected and loved by his students. **Teaching Programme** Zasep Rinpoche teaches one evening per week, and conducts occasional weekend retreats and one ten-day retreat annually. On the advice of H.H. the Dalai Lama, Zasep Rinpoche began his teachings at Gaden Choling with an explanation of the two truths of conventional and ultimate reality. Following this, he has focused mainly on the *Lam Rim* teachings. He has also given several empowerments, and occasionally gives initiates instruction into tantric practices, including the anuttarayoga class of tantra. Teachers visit frequently and give empowerments and teachings on all three vehicles of Buddhism (Hinayana, Mahayana and Vajrayana). **Facilities and Services** Gaden Choling is situated in a large downtown semi-detached house in Toronto. The centre houses a collection of books, audio tapes, and video tapes, which are available for in-centre use; members having borrowing privileges. Accommodation is offered to visiting dharma students for up to three days, when there is room. The shrine room is open to individual meditators by arrangement. A bi-monthly newsletter is distributed free of charge to members and others on request (donations towards the cost are always welcome). The shop sells Buddhist literature, audio cassettes, cards, posters, and ritual objects, either by mail order or at the centre itself. **Project Description** Gaden Choling is engaged in raising money to buy land and buildings for a retreat centre in South-East Ontario. It will be located in a rural setting and will have facilities for lay and ordained practitioners. Other fundraising projects are concerned with rebuilding Zuru Monastery in Tibet; coordinating support for Tibetan orphans in Nepal; and in sending medicines to treat Tibetan refugees in India, who are suffering from tuberculosis.

GAMPO ABBEY

Address Pleasant Bay, Cape Breton Island, Nova Scotia, Canada, BOE 2PO. **Tel** 224–2752. **Year Established** 1983. **Founder** Chogyam Trungpa Rinpoche. **Lama/Scholar** Thrangu Rinpoche. **General Description** Gampo Abbey is a monastic centre for the training of western monks, nuns and candidates for ordination. It was founded in 1983 by the late Chogyam Trungpa Rinpoche and is now directed by its Abbot, Thrangu Rinpoche, who resides in Nepal and visits the centre each year. The year is divided into periods of intensive practice and study and periods of work.

This division is for practical reasons in order to accommodate the building work in progress. From May to mid-August, the time of construction work, the atmosphere is less monastic in quality. During this time there is an open invitation for people to come and help and the schedule includes three hours daily for meditation. **Teaching Programme** In mid-August the traditional forty-five-day Rains Retreat (Yarne) is observed. This retreat is open only to monks, nuns and candidates, and is a time of practice, study and learning ritual (such as musical instruments, torma making, etc.) The winter retreat (December-March) is the other time when work ceases and is perhaps the most ideal time for the monks, nuns and candidates. This retreat is open to all interested in experiencing the monastic lifestyle. **Facilities and Services** The centre has four private retreat cabins for solitary practice, as well as group practice rooms. There is also a library. **Project Description** The building project underway is enlarging the existing premises to provide more residential facilities. The centre is also in the process of further developing its library.

KAGYU KUNKHYAB CHULING
Address 4939 Sidley Street, Burnaby, British Columbia, Canada, V5J 1T6. **Founder** Kalu Rinpoche. **Lama/Scholar** Tsewang Gyurme. **Facilities and Services** This centre operator a 3 year Retreat Centre on Saltspring Island near Vancouver.

KAMPO GANGRA DRUBGYUD LING
Address 200 Balsam Avenue, Toronto, Ontario, Canada, M4E 3C3. **Lama/Scholar** Karma Thinley Rinpoche.

KARMA DZONG
Address 1084 Tower Road, Halifax, Nova Scotia, Canada, B3H 2Y5. **Tel** (902) 420–1118. **Telex/Fax** (902) 423 2750. **Year Established** 1980. **Founder** Chogyam Trungpa Rin-

poche. **General Description** Karma Dzong was founded in 1980 by the late Chogyam Trungpa Rinpoche. The centre offers a broad range of activities, programmes and classes to its members. There are also numerous events of an introductory nature for those interested in finding out more about Buddhism and meditation. **Teaching Programme** A quarterly publication entitled *Open Sky* gives details of programmes, events and classes for the coming months. **Facilities and Services** Information on membership and other issues can be obtained from the centre during office hours, 1:30–5:30pm, Monday to Friday. **Project Description** The centre plans to develop its publication *Open Sky* to include stories from the lives of enlightened teachers, poetry, articles on Buddhist arts; and aims to present in each issue various fundamental teachings on Buddhism and the practice of meditation.

KARMA KAGYU CENTRE
Address 503 Huron Street, Toronto, Canada, M5R 2R6.

NAROPA INSTITUTE OF CANADA
Address 5663 Cornwallis Street, Halifax, Nova Scotia, Canada, B3K 2Y5.

ORGYAN OSAL CHO DZONG
Address P.O. Box 68, RR #3, Madoc, Ontario, Canada, K0K 2K0. **Tel** 613 969–2714. **Lama/Scholar** Ven. Lama Jampa Rabjam (Canadian). **General Description** Orgyan Osal Cho Dzong is a centre for the study and practice of Buddhism in the Nyingma and Kagyu lineage traditions. The teachings of Longchen Rabjampa are especially focused on, under the direction of Lama Jampa Rabjam. Lamas are invited to give teachings and visit the centre. In August 1988 H.H. Penor Rinpoche visited the centre and gave teachings on *Longchen Nyingthig* and *Zabmo Yangthig*. Accompanying Penor Rinpoche were lamas, expert dancers and musicians, who performed reli-

gious dances throughout the teachings, such as Vajrakila, The Black Hat and Wrathful Deities dances. **Teaching Programme** Information concerning schedules of teachings and events is available upon request from the centre. **Facilities and Services** The centre has only limited accommodation and catering facilities for visitors during the teaching courses, but camping facilities are available on the grounds. There are several towns nearby with grocery shops and restaurants. Child care is provided during teaching programmes. Further information is available upon request.

RIGPE DORJE CENTRE
Address 4525 Rue St. Jacques West, Montreal, Quebec, Canada, H4C 1K3. **Tel** (514) 931 4384. **Lama/Scholar** H.E. Jamgon Kongtrul Rinpoche. **General Description** This is a centre for the study and practice of the teachings of Tibetan Buddhism from the Kagyu lineage.

SAKYA THUBTEN KUNGA CHOLING,
VICTORIA BUDDHIST DHARMA SOCIETY
Address 1149 Leonard Street, Victoria, British Columbia, Canada, V8V 2S3. **Tel** (604) 385 4828. **Telex/Fax** (604) 598 1210. **Distribution Details** The centre will distribute throughout British Columbia and Alaska. **Year Established** 1975. **Founder** Geshe Tashi Namgyal. **Lama/Scholar** Geshe Tashi Namgyal. **General Description** Sakya Thubten Kunga Choling is located in a large residential house, close to a park and the ocean. The centre takes its inspiration from the resident lama, Geshe Tashi Namgyal, whose regular teachings and accessibility provides a rare opportunity to study all aspects of the Buddha's teachings. Geshe Namgyal's insightful, good natured and witty presence, ably assisted by a resident Western nun, Ani Dechen Drolma, has created a particularly warm atmosphere in which to learn and practise the Dharma. Lama's translated discourses, together with his own teachings in English, present complementary detail, as well as a motivation for comprehensive study. An emphasis is placed on the integration of the teachings into personal life, and a realistic approach stressing the need to study and practise at whatever level allows the student to maintain interest and enthusiasm, is encouraged. Topics covered in the teaching programme include: the practice of stabilising and insight meditation, madhyamaka philosophy, and advice in transcending destructive ways of thinking. Under the gentle guidance of Geshe Namgyal, a small but dedicated group of practitioners strive to realise the teachings and, at the same time, maintain a friendly and welcoming centre to all who have an interest in the Dharma. **Teaching Programme** Geshe Tashi Namgyal teaches Buddhist philosophy and psychology twice a week; one evening through the medium of a translator, and the other, speaking in English. Various practices are performed at the centre, notably the pujas of Shakyamuni Buddha, Avalokiteshvara (Chenrezig) and Green Tara. Other sadhana practices are open only to those who have taken the requisite initiations; these include Manjushri puja and Vajrayogini Tsogkhor (tshogs 'khor). Teachings are given by Geshe Namgyal at the latter

puja, which takes place on the Saturday closest to the twenty-fifth of the Tibetan month. Monday evenings are devoted to the practice of Zen meditation. For those who are interested, private tutoring in the Tibetan language can be arranged with the lama. **Facilities and Services** Sakya Thubten Kunga Choling possesses a meditation/shrine room, capable of seating between forty-five and fifty people. Other facilities include an IBM compatible computer, which is being used for transcription, a tape and book library, and a workshop. A newsletter is distributed to keep members up-to-date with centre developments. Stays of shorter or longer duration can be arranged. **Project Description** A transcription project is underway, making use of the centre's computer. It is hoped to extend the translation facilities that are presently available. A building fund has been started, with the intention of acquiring land in the future. Other involvements of the centre are with a number of community projects, and with therapies that promote better health and concentration.

SAKYA TSECHEN THUBTEN LING, VAJRAYANA BUDDHIST CENTRE

Address 7340 Frobisher Drive, Richmond, British Columbia, Canada, V7C 4N5. **Tel** (604) 271 2651. **Telex/Fax** (604) 273 0922. **Year Established** 1988. **Founder** H.E. Sakya Jetsun Chimey Luding. **Lama/Scholar** H.E. Sakya Jetsun Chimey Luding. **General Description** The centre provides formal instruction, initiations and retreat guidance by its founding lama, H.E. Sakya Jetsun Chimey Luding and visiting lamas. **Teaching Programme** Weekly pujas are held at the centre. **Facilities and Services** The centre publishes a regular newsletter giving details of current news and forthcoming programmes. **Project Description** Since 1991 building work has been in progress to create a retreat centre in California. Its name is Sakya

Dechen Ling and it is located in Napa Valley. A stupa was consecrated on the land in 1989.

TEMPLE BOUDDHISTE TIBETAIN

Address 1870 Avenue de L'Eglise, Montreal, Quebec, Canada, H4E 1G8. **Tel** (514) 765 3515. **Distribution Details** No materials are distributed. **Year Established** 1976. **Founder** Geshe Khenrab Topgyal Gajang. **Lama/Scholar** Geshe Khenrab Topgyal Gajang. **General Description** The resident teacher of Temple Bouddhiste Tibetain, Geshe Khenrab Gajang, gives regular teachings according to the Gelug tradition of Tibetan Buddhism. Emphasis is placed on the *Lam Rim*, or graduated path to enlightenment. The lama is available for individual guidance, and on occasion will give tantric empowerments. He also ministers to the Montreal Tibetan community. The centre is a focus for study, both through the courses that are held there, and as a result of the facilities that support individual learning requirements. Visiting teachers are frequently invited to give teachings on a variety of subjects. Temple Bouddhiste Tibetain's central aim is to provide a graded course of development in both sutras and tantras. **Teaching Programme** Two evenings in the week, lectures are given on the *Lam Rim* (one of which is translated into French), and a further evening is devoted to the Lojong (Blo sbyong) or mind training teachings. Sadhanas practiced at the centre include those of Yamantaka, Vajrayogini, and Vajrasattva. There is also a teaching on the Yamantaka tantra once a month. Group recitation of the *Lam Rim Puja* is performed in conjunction with some *Lam Rim* teachings, and Tsog (tshogs) offerings take place on the tenth and twenty-fifth days of the Tibetan month. Meditation classes occur weekly, and the Mahayana so jong retreat is practised monthly. **Facilities and Services** The centre houses an extensive library of mostly English language books on Buddhism. There are also some Tibetan texts, including the *Complete Works of Je Tsong Khapa*. **Project Description** Work is in progress on the transcription of various audio tapes of teachings.

VAJRADHATU INTERNATIONAL
Address 1084 Tower Road, Halifax, Nova Scotia, Canada, B3H 2Y5. **Tel** 902 425–4275. **Telex/Fax** 902 423–2750. **Year Established** 1972. **Founder** Chogyam Trungpa Rinpoche. **General Description** Vajradhatu International is a world-wide organisation of meditation and study centres based in Halifax, Nova Scotia. It was founded in 1970 by the late Chogyam Trungpa Rinpoche when he settled in the US. Vajradhatu has more than 100 centres, called Dharmadhatus or Dharma Study Groups, throughout the US., Canada, and Europe, offering programmes in the study of Buddhist philosophy and psychology and the practice of meditation. Three rural centres, Karme Choling in Vermont, Rocky Mountain Dharma Centre in northern Colorado, and Gampo Abbey in Cape Breton, Nova Scotia provide the opportunity to study and practise in a contemplative environment. At the present time Vajradhatu International is directed by Sawang Osel Rangdrol Mukpo (the son of Chogyam Trungpa Rinpoche) and the Vajradhatu Board of Directors. Its divisions include Shambhala Training, an international meditation programme, and The Naropa Institute. **Project Description** In 1988, a 100 foot stupa to commemorate the late Chogyam Trungpa Rinpoche was begun at the Rocky Mountain Dharma Centre in Colorado. This project is expected to be completed by 1995.

VAJRADHATU RECORDINGS
Address 1084 Tower Road, Halifax, Nova Scotia, Canada, 80302. **Tel** 902–425–4275. **General Description** Varjadhatu Recordings is a department of Vajradhatu International, a non-profit association of Buddhist meditation centres located throughout the United States, Canada and Europe. Since it was founded in 1972, by the late Chogyam Trungpa Rinpoche, Vajradhatu Recordings has been responsible for the recording of talks, seminars and events given under the auspices of Vajradhatu and the various Nalanda Foundations, including the Naropa Institute. An archive of original recordings from all Vajradhatu centres is maintained by the Recordings Department. **Facilities and Services** A catalogue of the recordings is available and tapes may be purchased.

ZURU LING
Address P.O. Box 15283, Vancouver, British Columbia, Canada, V6B 5B1. **Tel** (604) 874 5323. **Distribution Details** Please contact the centre for more information. **Year Established** 1982. **Founder** Zasep Tulku Rinpoche. **General Description** Zuru Ling is a registered, non-profit, charitable organisation, that was founded in 1982 by Zasep Tulku Rinpoche. Its aim is to provide opportunities for the study and practice of Mahayana Buddhism, and to sponsor visits to Vancouver of qualified Dharma teachers.

Zuru Ling organises a regular teaching and meditation schedule. Several times a year it welcomes visiting Tibetan lamas, as well as teachers from other Buddhist traditions, who give courses, retreats, and initiations at the centre. **Teaching Programme** The centre's founder and spiritual advisor, Zasep Tulku, frequently visits and gives introductory public talks, initiations and weekend workshops or supervises retreats. The centre's regular schedule includes weekly meditation and study classes, and Tsog offerings, taught in part by the more experienced students. A number of other important visitors, such as Tara Tulku and Lati Rinpoche, have visited and taught every year. **Facilities and Services** At present the centre shares a meditation room with three other Vancouver spiritual groups. Some transcipts and tapes of discourses are made available for purchase or loan. A quarterly newsletter is produced. **Project Description** It is intended to move the centre to its own rented house, enabling Zasep Tulku to live at the centre for some time each year. During his absence another lama and translator will reside there. A project to support Zuru monastery in Tibet is underway, together with the Ganden Relief Projects Programme, established by Zasep Tulku to help support Tibetan exiles.

CHILE

Publishing Companies and Journals

EDITORIAL ATISHA
Address Casillo 16039, Santiago, Chile. **Tel** 02 223 8539.

Teaching Centres

DRIKUNG KAGYU LING SANTIAGO
Address P.O. Box 3249, Santiago, Chile. **Tel** 02 221 2614. **Founder** Khenpo Konchog Gyaltsen.

CHINA

Academic Organisations

CENTRAL INSTITUTE OF MINORITIES, MINZU XUEYUAN
Address Bai Xi, Qiao Road 27, Beijing, China.

CHINA CENTRE FOR TIBETOLOGICAL STUDIES
Address, Beijing, China. **Tel** 201 9523 Ext163. **Lama/Scholar** Prof Geleg (Director).

CHINESE ACADEMY OF SCIENCES
Address 5 Jianguomennei Dajie, Beijing, China. **Lama/Scholar** Wu Kunming, Zhu Xi-yuan.

CHINESE MINORITIES LITERATURES INSTITUTE, ACADEMY OF SOCIAL SCIENCES OF THE PRC
Address, Beijing, China. **Tel** 513 8025. **Lama/Scholar** Liu Kui-li (Director).

Ecumenical Centres

CHINESE BUDDHIST ASSOCIATION
Address 25 Fuchengmennei Dajie, Beijing, China, 100034. **Distribution Details** The magazine *Dharmaghosa* is published.

Libraries

MINORITY CULTURAL PALACE LIBRARY, TIBET DIVISION MINORITY
Address Jianguomennei Dajie, Beijing, China. **Lama/Scholar** Prof Sun Wen-qing (Director). **General Description** This library has an extensive Tibetan collection.

COLOMBIA

Teaching Centres

BOGOTA KARMA THEGSUM CHOLING
Address Apt. 250672, Bogota, Colombia.

COSTA RICA

Cultural Organisations and Tibetan Refugee Aid Societies

ASSOCIACIONS CULTURAL, TIBETANO-COSTARRICENSE
Address Apt. 6610, San Jose, Costa Rica, 1000. **Tel** 06 282 439.

CZECH REPUBLIC

Academic Organisations

ACADEMY OF SCIENCES OF CZECH REPUBLIC, ORIENTAL INSTITUTE
Address Department of Far Eastern Studies, Lazenska 4, Prague 1, Czech Republic, 11837. **Tel** 02 533051 53. **Year Established** 1922. **Lama/Scholar** Dr Josef Kolmas, Marta Kiripolska. **General Description** Dr Josef Kolmas specialises in Tibetan history, Sino-Tibetan relations, Tibetan literature and bibliography. Marta Kiripolska is a Mongolist with a basic education in Tibetan and is presently conducting a study of Mongolian folk literature. **Facilities and Services** The Oriental Institute Library houses the complete Derge edition of the *Kangyur* and *Tengyur* (1958), several mss, and blockprints as well as printed books. A catalogue of the collection is available.

CHARLES UNIVERSITY, FACULTY OF PHILOSOPHY
Address Celetna 20, Prague 1, Czech Republic. **Lama/Scholar** Dr Lygzima Chaloupkova (Tibetan language).

LANGUAGE SCHOOL
Address Narodni 20, Prague 1, Czech Republic. **Lama/Scholar** Dr Josef Kolmas. **General Description** Since 1975 Professor Kolmas has conducted Tibetan language courses.

Cultural Organisations and Tibetan Refugee Aid Societies

CZECH-TIBET FRIENDSHIP SOCIETY
Address Pelhrimovska 9, Prague, Czech Republic, 14000. **Tel** 02 692 0738. **Lama/Scholar** Jiri Vobis (Head).

Museums

MUSEUM OF ASIAN CULTURE
Address Stare Mesto, Betlemske namesti 1, Prague 1, Czech Republic.

NAPRSTEK MUSEUM
Address Betlemske nam. 1, Prague 1, Czech Republic. **Lama/Scholar** Dr Zlata Cerna (Curator).

NATIONAL GALLERY, ORIENTAL DEPARTMENT

Address Zamek (Castle), Zbraslav nr. Prague, Czech Republic. **Lama/ Scholar** Dr Nora Jelinkova (Curator).

DENMARK

Academic Organisations

UNIVERSITY OF COPENHAGEN, CENTRE OF INDOLOGY

Address Njalsgade 80, Copenhagen S, Denmark, 2300. **Tel** (31) 542211. **Distribution Details** No materials are distributed. **Year Established** 1845. **Lama/Scholar** Christian Lindtner, Univ. of CPH (professor), Ole H. Pind, Critical Pali Dictionary Office, Jes Asmussen, Univ. of CPH (professor). **General Description** Indian and Buddhist Studies were established at the University of Copenhagen, in 1845 when N.L. Westergaard (1815–1878) was appointed professor. Since then numerous contributions to this subject area have been made by other Danish scholars, notably: Fausboell (1821–1908), C.V. Trenckner (1824–1891), S. Sorensen (1848–1902), Dines Andersen (1861–1940), Poul Tuxen (1880–1955), and many others. **Teaching Programme** The main departmental focus of interest is Buddhism and Indian philosophy, with an historical and philological approach being taken to both. An instructional PhD programme will soon be available. Courses are given in Pali, Sanskrit, and most students are also asked to take Tibetan and/or Chinese. Classes are concerned with the reading of philosophical texts in their original languages. A considerable number of foreign scholars and students attend these courses. **Facilities and Services** The library houses an extensive collection of material on philosophy and Buddhism, particularly Pali texts. There is a good Tibetan collection in the Royal Library, next door to the centre.

Cultural Organisations and Tibetan Refugee Aid Societies

DANISH TIBETAN CULTURAL SOCIETY

Address St. Sohoj, Horsholm Kongevej 40, Horsholm, Denmark, 2970. **Tel** (42) 865 715. **Telex/Fax** (33) 939 382.

STOTTEKOMITEEN FOR TIBET

Address Skyttehaven 10A, Vedbaek, Denmark, 2950. **Tel** (42) 892 475. **Telex/Fax** (31) 563 829.

Libraries

ROYAL LIBRARY DENMARK

Address Oriental Dept, Christians Brygge 8, Copenhagen K, Denmark, DK 1219. **Tel** 33 930 111. **Telex/Fax** 33 329 846. **Year Established** 1665. **Founder** King Frederik III. **General Description** The Tibetan collection of the Royal Library of Copenhagen consists of blockprints, manuscripts, reprinted books and modern books. The subjects covered include: philosophy, literature, art, grammar, medicine, astrology, history, and politics. The blockprint collection includes the *Tibetan Tripitaka*, the Narthang Edition of *Tengyur*, 225 volumes; and the Lhasa Edition of *Kangyur*, 100 volumes. The rest of the blockprints plus the manuscripts amount to about 1200 titles. Among the manuscripts are some very rare Nyingma School texts, on religious as well as historical topics. The collection of reprinted and modern books includes the *Tibetan Tripitaka*, Peking Edition, and other Tibetan works reprinted by Otani University, Kyoto, 168 volumes; the Nyingma Edition of the *Derge Kangyur* and *Tengyur*, reprinted by Dharma Publishing, Berkeley, 117 volumes; and various famous collected works of Tibetan scholars and other books, amounting to about 1000 volumes. The entire collection has been catalogued, and the card catalogue is kept at the Oriental Department of the library.

Teaching Centres

KARMA DRUB DJY LING

Address Svanemolle Vej 56, Copenhagen, Denmark, 2100. **Tel** 31 29 27 11. **Distribution Details** World-wide. Normal procedure: order by letter, the centre will write an invoice and send order upon receipt of payment. **Year Established** 1973. **Founder** H.H. Sixteenth Gyalwa Karmapa.

KARMA THJO PHEL LING

Address Korterupvej 21, Sollested, Denmark, 4920. **Tel** 53 91 61 69. **Telex/Fax** 53 91 60 96. **Distribution Details** The Centre will distribute material worldwide. **Year Established** 1977. **Founder** H.H. Gyalwa Karmapa. **General Description** H.H. Sixteenth Karmapa founded Karma Thjo Phel Ling in 1977, specifically recommending it for meditation retreats. The centre is located in an old farmhouse in the Danish countryside, and due to its isolated position, it provides a tranquil setting for meditation practice. **Teaching Programme** The Avalokiteshvara (Chenrezig) sadhana and various guru yoga practices are emphasised at Karma Thjo Phel Ling. There are also opportunities to practise shamatha (zhi gnas) and vipashyana (lhag mthong) meditation, as well as the lojong (blo sbyong) mind training systems. From time to time visiting lamas give teachings on a wide range of topics. About every month there is a ten-day intensive meditation period for practices such as Dorje Sempa, shamatha etc. **Facilities and Services** There is a stupa and shrine room and a semi-professional layout studio for producing texts and books. The retreat facilities comprise two cabins and a self-enclosed area with six rooms, kitchen and bathroom. Karma Thjo Phel Ling can accommodate visitors for courses both in dormitories and in an extensive camping area. The centre possesses a library with Tibetan texts, and titles in Danish, German, and English. In addition, the tape library contains recordings of many of the teachings that have been given at Karma Thjo Phel Ling and at the Copenhagen centre, Karma Drub Djy Ling. **Project Description** The centre is planning to buy more land and to extend the residential and retreat facilities. Other projects are concerned with the translation of Tibetan texts into Danish, English and German. Past translations have included: the *rDo rje Chang mThong ba* Prayer and the *Bla ma Byang bu*, into Danish; and the Karma Pakshi Tshogs Puja, the Guru Yoga of the Sixteenth Karmapa, and an Avalokiteshvara sadhana, into English.

ESTONIA

Academic Organisations

ESTONIAN ORIENTAL SOCIETY, MAHAYANA INSTITUTE, TARTU UNIVERSITY

Address Department of History, Tiigi 78–117, Tartu, Estonia, EE2400. **Tel** 01434 36949. **Telex/Fax** 01434 35440. **Lama/**

Scholar Prof Linnart Mall. **General Description** The society has a major interest in Tibetan Buddhism. Prof. Mall teaches Tibetan, Sanskrit and Chinese at the university, has translated and published the *Bodhicaryavatara* in Estonian, and publishes a monthly Oriental newsletter/magazine *"Sonumi Tooja"*. The university library has a small Tibetan collection.

Cultural Organisations and Tibetan Refugee Aid Societies

TIBETAN CULTURAL CENTRE IN ESTONIA
Address Trummi Poik 5A–29, Tallinn, Estonia, EE0026. **Tel** 0142 444 107.

Teaching Centres

BUDDHIST COMMUNITY OF ESTONIA
Address 114/3 Pillu St., Tallinn, Estonia, EE0009. **Tel** 0142 596 685. **Year Established** 1988. **General Description** The Buddhist Community of Estonia aims to study all the traditions of Tibetan Buddhism. At present Tibetan language is being studied, texts are being translated, and collective rituals and meditations are practised. The centre has established links with the Buddhist centres of the Kagyu School in Sweden.

FINLAND

Museums

MANNERHEIM MUSEUM
Address Kalliolinnantie 14, Helsinki, Finland, 00140. **Tel** 635–443. **Telex/ Fax** 171–913. **General Description** The Mannerheim Museum is the collection of The Marshal of Finland Baron Gustaf Mannerheim (1867–1951). He had a predilection for the Orient and from his many journeys he brought home furniture, carpets, weapons, ornaments etc. In 1906 he travelled from Russia to China. The collection contains fourteen thangkas, two temple horns of copper and encased silver from Lhasa, and various statues.

FRANCE

Academic Organisations

ECOLE PRATIQUE DES HAUTES ETUDES, CENTRE D'ETUDES SUR LES RELIGIONS TIBETAINES
Address V eme Section (Sciences Religieuses), 22 Avenue du President Wilson, Paris, France, 75116. **Tel** 45537301 Ex 64. **Distribution Details** The E.P.H.E. Section Sciences Religieuses produces a yearly review, (Resume des Conferences). Other publications are also distributed. **Year Established** 1960. **Founder** Prof Rolf A. Stein. **Lama/Scholar** Prof Anne-Marie Blondeau, Dr. Samten Karmay, Dr Yontan Gyatso, Dr Anne Chayet, Dr Yoshiro Imaeda, Dr Francoise Pommaret, Dr Heather Stoddard. **General Description** The C.E.R.T., which is concerned with the study of Tibetan religions, was founded by Prof R.A.Stein. Its principal aim was the collecting of important photographic material on the different aspects of Tibetan religion. A.M. Blondeau succeeded Prof Stein in 1975, as the Director of the centre. Since 1976, the C.E.R.T. has worked in cooperation with the Centre d'Etudes Tibetaines of the College de France. These two centres are solely concerned with research and the cataloguing of material. Since 1986, a research team from the centre National de la Recherche Scientifique, directed by A.M. Blondeau, has been associated with the C.E.R.T. **Teaching Programme** There is no undergraduate teaching at the C.E.R.T. itself. Teaching is carried out within the study programme of the E.P.H.E., by Prof A.M. Blondeau. The research teaching syllabus changes each year. However,

principal themes are: biographies of Padmasambhava; gTer ma and gTer ston; Tibetan rituals; and Bon po studies. Degrees awarded are the Diploma of the E.P.H.E., Sciences Religieuses; and doctorates. **Facilities and Services** There are more than 10,000 photos (prints and negatives) of Tibet, Bhutan, Ladakh, Nepal, and Tibetan refugees, as well as some films and video cassettes. Also available is a library, containing Western specialist works (there is a collection of Tibetan texts at the C.E.T. in the College de France). All documents are catalogued on a card index. In progress is the cataloguing of Tibetan reprints and Tibetan texts held in the libraries of Paris.

INLCO, INSTITUT NATIONAL DES LANGUES, ET CIVILISATIONS ORIENTALES

Address 2 Rue de Lille, Paris, France, 75007. **Tel** 49264200. **Year Established** 1795. **Lama/Scholar** Dagpo Rinpoche, Jampa Gyatso, Ngawang Dakpa, Dr. Fernand Meyer, Nicolas Tournadre, Heather Stoddard-Karmay, Marie-Stella Boussemart, Francoise Pommaret. **General Description** The institut runs a four-year degree course, a masters degree course, a doctorate degree course in Tibetan language, literature or civilisation, and introductory courses on civilisation and Buddhism. The doctorate degree is in collaboration with other research centres in Paris. **Facilities and Services** Library with Tibetan texts and old editions of travellers' accounts, seventeenth to twentieth century. Audio visual centre with tapes for teaching Tibetan language. Catalogue of Tibetan and Western works on Tibet.

INTERNATIONAL ASSOC. OF BUDDHIST STUDIES, UNIVERSITE DE PARIS X

Address Laboratoire D'Ethnologie, Nanterre, Paris, France, 92001. **Tel** 33(1) 40977593. **Telex/Fax** (1) 40977117. **Lama/Scholar** Dr Alexander W. Macdonald. **General Description** The association is devoted to the promotion and strengthening of scholarship in the field of Buddhist Studies and is committed purely to the intellectual treatment of Buddhism. Membership is open to scholars from various disciplines such as philosophy, religion, history, art, archaeology, etc and those who are involved in the promotion of Buddhist Studies. At present there are approximately 670 paying members, individual and institutional, throughout the world. The objectives of the association include inter-disciplinary concern and a comparative outlook in a global perspective of study and research, encourage and support publications of original sources and translations, publish a research periodical and other occasional monographs, hold periodic international conferences and coordinate national/regional conferences. An international conference is planned to be held in Mexico City in October 1994.

UNIVERSITE DE PARIS X, LABORATOIRE D'ETHNOLOGIE

Address Nanterre, Paris, France, 92001. **Tel** 33(1) 40977593. **Telex/Fax** (1) 40977117. **Lama/Scholar** Dr Alexander W. Macdonald. **General Description** The university offers a doctorate programme in ethnology and comparative sociology. Professor

MacDonald teaches a course on the sociology of Tibetan Buddhism.

Cultural Organisations and Tibetan Refugee Aid Societies

FONDATION ALEXANDRA DAVID-NEEL Address Samten Dzong, 27 Avenue du Marechal Juin, Digne, France, 04000. **Tel** 92 31 32 38. **Distribution Details** No materials are distributed. **Year Established** 1977. **Founder** Marie-Madeleine Peyronnet. **General Description** The Alexandra David-Neel Foundation is situated in the former home of the French explorer-writer. Alexandra David-Neel was born in Saint Mandee in 1868, and died in Digne in 1969. Over thirty years of her life was spent travelling and living in Asia. Her house, Samten Dzong, has now become a small museum to which daily guided tours, free of charge, are offered. Opportunities exist to purchase books by Alexandra David-Neel or general works on Tibet at the museum. One may also browse in the Tibetan handicrafts shop, that has a large number of cultural artifacts and carpets, both antique and modern, for sale. The foundation is directed by Alexandra David-Neel's former secretary, Marie-Madeleine Peyronnet. There is no provision for visitors to stay at Samten Dzong. **Teaching Programme** The foundation organises two Dharma courses each year. During the summer they are given by Dagpo Rinpoche or Geshe Losang Thubten from the Guepele Tchantchoup Ling centre in Paris. No charge is made to attend these courses, which are translated into French only. In 1982 and in May 1986, the Foundation received H.H. the Dalai Lama, who taught in a large hall specially rented for the occasion by the municipality of Digne. **Facilities and Services** Courses are held in a hall that can hold between 130 and 150. It is hoped to transfer all Alexandra David-Neel's photographs and Tibetan documents onto video tape. There will then be facilities to show this material to visitors, and if requested make instant prints of any desired document or photograph. All teachings are recorded onto audio tape, though no copies are distributed. The foundation aims to make them available to students following the courses. **Project Description** A video tape of photographs of Tibet, India, Sikkim and Nepal, taken by David-Neel at the beginning of the century, has recently been completed. Several projects are underway to publish David-Neel's writings. In March 1986, Editions du Rocher brought out a work entitled *La Lampe de Sagesse*. A second illustrated biography, including many Tibetan documents, was also published at the end of 1988. Other biographies have been written in the U.S. including *Portrait of an Adventurer* by Ruth Middleton (Shambhala 1989). A fitty-two minute television film has also been produced documenting the journey of Mme. David-Neel through Sikkim, which is available as of early 1993. The foundation is involved in arranging the sponsorship of refugee Tibetan children in India, working in close cooperation with the Tibetan Children's Village and its director. Part of the project has been the provision of a 100-bed dormitory for monks newly arrived from Tibet in Mungod, South India, and a fifty-bed dormitory at the Dharamsala Tibetan Children's Village. In 1989 a second house at the foundation itself was completed, to accommodate visiting lamas and to house the archives and carpets, and for exhibitions.

Ecumenical Centres

CENTRE D'ETUDES BOUDDHIQUES Address 16 Rue Thiers, Grenoble, Isere, France, 38000. **Tel** (76) 46 70 16. **Year Established** 1974. **Lama/ Scholar** Dr P. Stoebner, Lama Tcheukyi, Lama Yeunten. **General Description** The centre runs a large meditation hall in the middle of Grenoble. It is open to all schools of

Buddhism, and hosts Theravada, Soto Zen, Rinzai Zen, Kagyupa (bKa' brgyud pa), and Gelugpa (dGe lugs pa) groups. An important activity of the centre is the editing and distribution of a quarterly journal devoted to Buddhism. It is the only such journal in France, that publishes articles on the diverse traditions of Buddhism. **Teaching Programme** On Monday evenings a beginners meditation class is held. Wednesday evenings are devoted to Avalokiteshvara (Chenrezig) meditation, and Thursday evenings are concerned with the theory and practice of shamatha (calm abiding) and vipassana (insight) meditation. More intensive meditation practice is arranged with visiting lamas on one weekend each month. **Facilities and Services** Apart from providing meditation classes for the local people, the centre runs a library of related material. Intensive meditation retreats are arranged, taking place in the neighbouring centres of Karma Ling and Karma Migyur Ling.

Libraries

BIBLIOTHEQUE DE L'INSTITUT, INSTITUT DE FRANCE
Address 23 Quai de Conti, Paris, France. **Year Established** 1797. **Lama/Scholar** Francoise Dumas (Chief Librarian).

BIBLIOTHEQUE DES LANGUES ORIENTALES, INSTITUT NATIONAL DES LANGUES ORIENTALES
Address Rue de Lille, 4, Paris, France. **Lama/Scholar** Christina Cramerotti (Tibet Collection), Sultana Mohammad (Nepal Collection).

CENTRE D'ETUDES HIMALAYENNES
Address UPR 299, C.N.R.S., 1 place A.-Briand, Meudon, France, 92195.

CENTRE D'ETUDES TIBETAINES, INSTITUTS D'EXTREME-ORIENT
Address 52 rue du Cardinal Lemoine, Paris, France.

ECOLE FRANCAISE D'EXTREME-ORIENT
Address 22 Avenue du President Wilson, Paris, France. **Year Established** 1898. **Lama/Scholar** Sophie Robert (Librarian), Nagwang Dakpa.

MUSEE GUIMET LIBRARY
Address 6 place d'Iena, Paris, France, 75116. **Lama/Scholar** Francis Macouin (Chief Librarian).

Museums

MUSEE DE L'HOMME
Address Place du Trocadero, 75016 Paris 16e, Paris, France.

MUSEE NATIONAL DES ARTS ASIATIQUES, – GUIMET
Address 6 Place d'Iena, 75016 Paris, France. **Tel** 47 23 61 65. **Telex/Fax** 47 20 57 50. **Year Established** 1890. **General**

Description The Muse National des Art Asiatiques – Guimet owns a rich collection of Nepalese and Tibetan art. The collection amounts to about 1550 pieces, including 350 paintings. **Project Description**A catalogue of the thangka collection will be available in 1994.

Teaching Centres

BOUDDHISTE DRUKPA KAGYU
Address 362 rue Lecourbe, Paris, France, 75015. **Tel** 45548317.

DHAGPO KAGYU LING
Address La Sonnerie, Landrevie, Montignac, Dordogne, France, 24290. **Year Established** 1975. **Lama/Scholar** Lama Gendun Rinpoche, Lama Jigme Tsewang. **General Description** Dhagpo Kagyu Ling was founded in 1975 by a group of Tibetan lamas under the instruction of the sixteenth Karmapa. In 1977 the Karmapa came to the Dordogne to consecrate the site. The centre is residential and has about thirty people living on the premises. Lama Gendun Rinpoche and Lama Jigme Tsewang are the resident lamas at the centre and both give regular teachings and spiritual guidance in meditational practice. Visits from other Tibetan lamas are also a regular feature of life at the centre. In the last few years the centre has received visits from Shamar Rinpoche, Situ Rinpoche, Tenga Rinpoche, Bokar Rinpoche, Khenpo Donyo, Lama Thubten, Dr Trogawa Rinpoche, Ponlop Rinpoche and Gyaltrul Rinpoche. **Teaching Programme** Apart from the daily meditation programme, the centre has regular teaching programmes given by the residential and visiting lamas. **Facilities and Services** The centre has facilities to accommodate a considerable number of visitors as well as the regular inhabitants. There are catering facilities, study rooms and a library with books and cassettes available for use. The centre has also published a book called *The Treasury of Knowledge:*

The Stages of Meditation of Shamatha and Vipashyana by Jamgon Kongtrul Lodro Thaye.

DRUK DECHEN LING/ KARMA GYURME LING
Address 3 Route de Rosheim, Boersch, France, 67530. **Tel** (88) 95 87 84. **Telex/Fax** (88) 95 99 98. **Distribution Details** Materials are distributed. **Year Established** 1980. **Founder** Alain Taubert. **General Description** The centre is situated in a small house, located in a rural area. **Teaching Programme** Courses take place every month. They are based on teachings from the Drukpa and Karma Kagyu traditions of Tibetan Buddhism. **Facilities and Services** The centre can accommodate up to five people at any one time. **Project Description** A library is established for Buddhist studies and there is an intention to found a monastery and retreat centre in the vicinity.

DRUK THOUPTEN TCHEUKHOR LING
Address Bel Avenir, Plouray, Brittany, France, 56770. **Tel** 97348265.

DRUKGON JANGCHUB LING
Address Quartier Maura, Route de Ste. Agnes, Menton, Cote d'Azur, France, 06500. **Tel** (93) 57 72 14. **Distribution Details** Copies of the journal *La Nouvelle Revue Tibetaine* are distributed from Paris. **Year Established** 1981. **Lama/Scholar** Ven. Kyabje Thuksey Rinpoche, Ven. Khenpo Rinpoche Yeshe Chodhar, Lama Nyima Gyaltsen. **General Description** Drukgon Jangchub Ling is situated three kms north of the coastal town of Menton, in a quiet wooded region, offering an ideal environment for meditation and other practices. Khenpo Rinpoche Yeshe Chodhar, the director of the centre, gives teachings in the traditional manner, emphasising purity of practice. This has led to a policy of restrained but concentrated development; little effort being made to publicise the cen-

tre's activities widely, but at the same time offering teachings of the highest quality to committed and interested individuals. Drukgon Jangchub Ling is the first permanent Drukpa Kagyu centre in the West. Regular teachings and meditations are conducted at the three levels of practice: Hinayana, Mahayana, and Vajrayana. **Teaching Programme** Normally there are two teachings a week: Wednesdays at 8:30 pm, and Saturdays at 5:30 pm. In addition, there is a Tibetan language class held every Saturday at 4:30 pm. Occasional courses on specific subjects are organised, and individual teachings are given on the request of visiting or local students. The Mahakala puja is performed daily; and on the tenth, fifteenth, and twenty-fifth days of the Tibetan month, Vajradhara, Vajrayogini and Cakrasamvara practices are enacted. Khenpo Rinpoche usually determines the teachings that are given, selecting in accordance with the needs and capabilities of the individual students. **Facilities and Services** Within the Centre there is a shrine room and two other rooms for receiving visitors. Occasional retreats are organised with individual students. A new retreat centre is being developed in Brittany, which Khenpo Rinpoche visits frequently (Centre Bouddhiste Druk Thoupten Tcheukhor Ling, 'Bel Avenir', 56770 – Plouray, Tel: 97 34 82 65). It is hoped to expand this centre beyond its present accommodation limit of forty-five people at any one time. Friends of Drukgon Jangchub Ling publish a quarterly journal entitled, *La Nouvelle Revue Tibetaine*. They can be contacted at 11 Rue Rameau, 75002 – Paris. **Project Description** Due to the limited prospect of further expansion in Menton, all major development projects are being shifted to Thoupten Tcheukhor in Brittany. In order to further this aim, and also provide financial support for the centres, monasteries and monks of the Drukpa Kagyu School, steps are being taken to establish a charitable foundation in Monaco and in Brittany.

GUEPELE TCHANTCHOUP LING

Address Institut Bouddhiste Tibetain, Impasse de la Passerelle, Veneux les Sablons, France, 77250. **Tel** (1) 64 31 14 82. **Distribution Details** Persons interested in acquiring transcripts should write to the centre. **Year Established** 1978. **Founder** Dagpo Rinpoche. **Lama/Scholar** Dagpo Rinpoche, Geshe Yonten Gyatso (occasional). **General Description** Guepele Tchantchoup Ling was founded to make both Tibetan culture and Buddhism in particular, better known in France. Since its establishment, the Institute has developed a number of different activities: the celebration of Buddhist feast days, weekly teachings and intensive seminars, monthly meetings to recite the Six Preliminary Practices, Tibetan language classes, and many other events. The outstanding characteristic of the centre has been the presence of three highly qualified teachers, and the excellence and complementary nature of their teachings. Strong emphasis is put upon teachings of both the *Lam Rim* and philosophy. Buddhist philosophy is taught in order to deepen one's understanding of the *Lam Rim*, and the latter is taught to assure the application of all Buddhist teachings to one's daily life. Techniques of meditation and of philosophical debate are practised, as well as the recitation of texts. Students are encouraged to learn Tibetan in order to receive teachings and read texts directly in that language. Teachings are given in Tibetan and the majority are translated into French; however, at least one weekly class is given in Tibetan alone. The centre has been fortunate in receiving a considerable number of great lamas and geshes, and in being able to request a wide variety of teachings from them. There is no charge for any of the teachings given at the centre. **Teaching Programme** Dagpo Rinpoche has given weekly teachings on the *Lam Rim* over a number of years. In 1991–92 he taught the Perfections of Concentration and Wisdom. He holds yearly a four-day seminar on Tara meditation, sometimes including a long life blessing. During some weekends, he gives instruction on systems of philosophical tenets, currently on the Madhyamika system. **Facilities and Services** For the weekly meetings, on Mondays at 7.00 pm, the centre rents a hall at 102 bis rue de Vaugirand, 75006 Paris. **Project Description** It is hoped to develop the library and cassette lending facilities, and to extend transcription and publication of recorded material. However, the main priorities of the centre remain the giving of teachings, orally and directly to the disciples, and their application in group retreats and otherwise.

INSTITUT KAGYU VAJRADHARA LING
Address Domaine du Chateau d'Osmont, Aubry le Panthou, Vimoutiers, France, 61120. **Tel** 33390044.

INSTITUT MAITREYA DE FRANCE
Address 18 Rue Spontini, Paris, France, 75116. **General Description** The Institut Maitreya de France was founded by Tai Situ Rinpoche in July 1986. Tai Situ Rinpoche is the resident lama at the centre and although he spends a large part of his time travelling, he gives teachings and spiritual guidance on a regular basis at the cen-

tre. The centre organises visits from non-Tibetan speakers to give talks on a wide variety of different subjects, as well as inviting visits from Tibetan lamas. In 1988 the centre received visits from Sogyal Rinpoche and Lama Sherab Dorje. **Teaching Programme** The programme at the institute includes teachings on health, healing, different therapies, psychology, economics, the arts, philosophy, techniques of communication and education. **Facilities and Services** The centre is residential but is limited in accommodation. Various nearby hotels are recommended to guests as an alternative. A list of these is available from the centre.

INSTITUT VAJRAYOGINI
Address Chateau d'En Clausade, Marzens, Lavaur, France, 81500. **Tel** (63) 58 17 22. **Telex/Fax** (63) 58 03 48. **Distribution Details** The centre will distribute throughout Europe and to all Buddhist centres in the world. **Year Established** 1979. **Founder** Lama Thubten Yeshe and Lama Zopa Rinpoche. **Lama/Scholar** Geshe Lobsang Tengye. **General Description** Institut Vajra Yogini is located in a fairly large nineteenth century chateau, about six kilometres from the town of Lavaur, and about forty kilometres from Toulouse, the fifth most populous city in France. It houses between fifteen and twenty Western residents, a Tibetan geshe and two translators. The institute organises many Tibetan Buddhist courses throughout the year, and also retreats including an annual two-month retreat. Twice a year nyung ne fasting practice takes place. Around 400 individuals are on the centre's mailing list, and they receive a programme of events three or four times a year. Institute Vajra Yogini has begun publishing teachings given by the resident lama, the discourse given by H.H. the Dalai Lama in 1982 at the institute, and other teachings given by Lama Zopa Rinpoche and the late Lama Yeshe. The centre also organises

Yoga, Tai Chi, Tibetan medicine, thangka painting, and many other courses. **Teaching Programme** A regular teaching is given every morning by the resident teacher at 8:45 am. The institute invites visiting lamas from time to time, particularly during school holidays. A monthly discourse is given in Toulouse, and also in some other large towns. **Facilities and Services** The institute provides individual retreat facilities. There is a library and a book-shop within the centre. The main building of the Institute has the capacity to welcome about thirty people in single or double room accommodation, and forty in dormitories. There is beautiful park-land around the Institute, and camping and day nursery facilities are available.

INSTITUTE KARMAPA

Address Clos de Girand, Val de Rouse, Caille 06750, France. **Tel** 0033 9360 4874. **Founder** Khenpo Lama Thubten. **Lama/Scholar** Khenpo Lama Thubten.

KAGYU LING

Address Chateau de Plaige, La Boulaye, Toulon-Sur-Arroux, France, 71320. **Tel** (85) 79 43 41. **Distribution Details** The centre distributes world-wide. No pre-payment is required. **Year Established** 1974. **Founder** Kalu Rinpoche. **Lama/Scholar** Lama Tempa Targye, Lama Orgyen Wangdu, Lama Sherab Dorje, Lama Sonam Choepel. **General Description** Kagyu Ling is situated in a chateau set in scenic countryside. There are a num-ber of residents, including four lamas. A shrine room is used for regular meditation practice, pujas, and teachings. Two outlying buildings house an office, printing works, and twenty small retreat and study rooms. A large stupa and a traditionally styled Tibetan temple, which is modelled on the first monastery in Tibet – Samye (bSam yas) – are located nearby. The temple is on three levels, the first level being a large assembly hall. The second level is intended to comprise an extensive library. **Teaching Programme** Teach-ings mainly take place during the school holidays. Instruction is given on various meditative practices, including shamatha (zhi gnas), vipashyana (lhag mthong), and mahamudra. There is also emphasis placed on the four preliminary practices of making pros-trations, Vajrasattva meditation, mandala offerings, and guru yoga. Teachings and initiations are given into the practices of the meditational deities (yidams): Avalokiteshvara, Tara, Kalacakra, and many others. The centre has been blessed by visits from many high lamas including: Shamar Rinpoche, Situ Rinpoche, Kalu Rinpoche, H.H. the Sixteenth Karmapa, Jamgon Kongtrul Rin-poche, Khenpo Tsultrim Gyatso Rinpoche, and the Twelfth Gyal-wang Drukchen Rinpoche. **Facilities and Services** The centre possesses a library, and extensive retreat facilities. In addition to the shrine room already mentioned, there is a large room suitable for those wishing to practice yoga. Kagyu Ling sponsors visits and courses from a wide range of different disciplines, including: doc-tors, astrologers, yoga teachers, philosophers, artists, and pre-emi-nent spiritual teachers. **Project Description** It is anticipated that exhibitions will be held at the temple, devoted to Tibetan cultural affairs, both secular and religious, that will enable visitors to become more familiar with the range of Tibetan culture and arts. There will also be a permanent slide show devoted to Tibet, Bhutan, Sikkim, and the places of pilgrimage in India. A building programme is being planned at Kagyu Ling, that will allow interested individuals to buy self-contained flats in a larger complex, containing a communal dining room. Another project underway is the landscaping of a park to be called 'Dewachen'. A variety of rare trees, flowers and other flora are being planted to enhance its natural beauty.

KAGYU RINCHEN DJOUNGNE LING
Address 24 rue Thiers, La Madeleine, Lille, France, 59110. **Tel**20 55 76 59.

KAGYU RINTCHEN TCHEU LING
Address Route de Mende 2468, Montpellier, France, 34100. **Tel** 67 54 75 40.

KAGYU YIWONG TCHEU LING
Address Mas de Molieres, Saint-Laurent-Le Minier, Surmene, France, 30440. **Tel** 67 73 65 33.

KALACHAKRA CENTRE
Address 6 Rue Paul Fort, Paris, France, 75014. **Tel** 01 45 39 82 71. **Telex/Fax** 01 42 52 50 63.

KARMA LING
Address Chartreuse de Saint Hugon, La Rochette, Arvillard, France, 73110. **Tel** (79) 65 64 62. **Telex/Fax** 79 25 78 08. **Distribution Details** Dharma centres and libraries receive a thirty per cent discount. Postage is additional to catalogue prices. **Year Established** 1981. **Founder** Kalu Rinpoche. **Lama/Scholar** Lama Denis Teundroup, Lama Seunam (Christian Bailly), Ani Zangmo (Brigitte Godart), Neldjorpa Tsering (Xavier Dubois), Neldjorpa Tcheupel (Jean Claude Perrier), Neldjorpa Mingyour (Gil Plazas), Neldjourma Dreulma (Marie Claire Dayot). **General Description** Karma Ling is a centre devoted to study and meditation, located in a former Christian monastery. There are approximately thirty permanent residents, who are occupied with the smooth running of the centre. Work is being carried out on the building in order to accommodate the increasing numbers of visitors, and to expand facilities for Buddhist and other forms of meditation. Conferences are organised in the summer, sometimes attracting 150 people, and concerned with the general theme of communication between different religious traditions and different philosophies. The publishing company, Editions Prajna, distributes those teachings arising from the various seminars that are of particular interest. Two retreat centres have been constructed and, for the last five years, twenty people have been meditating there under the spiritual guidance of Lama Denis Teundroup, a French disciple of Kalu Rinpoche. **Teaching Programme** A typical day at Karma Ling begins with a 7 am rise, followed by a session of shamatha (zhi gnas) meditation. Tibetan classes, at varying levels of instruction, are given during the morning. Individual meditation practice also takes place at this time. Lunch is at 12 am, and the afternoon is given over to work in the Centre. Pujas of Mahakala, Tara and Chod are performed each month. Supper is followed by a meditation session dedicated to the practice of Avalokiteshvara. Teachings are given mostly on the weekends. **Facilities and Services** The centre has individual retreat rooms, and a retreat centre orientated towards those wishing to complete the three-year retreat (both women and men). There are also several individual flats and a communal room. Other facilities include a printing-house, a library, and a shrine room. **Project Description** There is a translation committee (Lotsawa) engaged in translating Tibetan texts, presently the *Dagpo Targyen*.

KARMA MIGYUR LING

Address Centre d'Etudes Tibetaines, Montchardon, Izeron, St. Marcellin, France, 38160. **Tel** (76) 38 33 13. **Telex/Fax** (76) 38 41 91. **Distribution Details** The centre distributes world-wide. A catalogue of the texts produced is available on request. **Year Established** 1975. **Founder** H.H. Gyalwa Karmapa. **Lama/ Scholar** Lama Teunsang, Trinley Tulku, Lama Tsultrim. **General Description** Karma Migyur Ling is a meditation centre of the Kagyu tradition. There are three resident lamas: Lama Teunsang, who has been in France since 1976, Trinley Tulku (resident since 1984) and the Frenchman Lama Tsultrim. Courses are organised throughout the year. Those relating to meditation, Buddhist teachings and spiritual practice are guided by the resident lamas. Other courses (yoga and tai chi for example) are run by visiting teachers. From time to time the centre has hosted the preeminent lamas of the Kagyu tradition, notably: Shamar Rinpoche, Situ Rinpoche, Gyaltsab Rinpoche, Jamgon Kongtrul Rinpoche, Kalu Rinpoche, Tenga Rinpoche, Bokar Rinpoche, Khenpo Deunjeun Rinpoche, and many others. All these lamas have given teachings and initiations at Karma Migyur Ling. In September 1987 a thirteen metre high stupa was completed in the centre grounds, and inaugurated by Shamar Rinpoche and Kalu Rinpoche. **Teaching Programme** Teachings at Kagyu Migyur Ling are drawn from the Kagyupa lineage of Tibetan Buddhism. In addition, there are courses run by visiting teachers on various subjects, including yoga and tai chi. **Facilities and Services** The Centre can accommodate eighty people at any one time. There is a shrine room which is large enough for a hundred people to attend functions. Other facilities available include a library and a shop. Karma Migyur Ling also produce a sadhana manual (translated from Tibetan into French) that contains the spiritual practices of Amitabha and Milarepa, the *Prajnaparamita sutra*, and the eighth Karmapa's '*Guru Yoga of the Four Sessions*' (*thun bzhi bla ma'i rnal 'byor*). **Project Description** It is intended to build a retreat centre for those wishing to complete long retreats. There are also plans to construct a multi-purpose hall for meditation and yoga courses, isolated retreat houses, and a guest house.

MAHA YOGA LING

Address 3 rue de l'Abbaye, Monaco, France. **Tel** 93300281.

NALANDA MONASTERY

Address Rouzegas, Labastide Saint Georges, Lavaur, France, 81500. **Tel** 63 58 02 25. **Telex/Fax** 63 58 03 48. **Year Established** 1981. **Founder** Lama Thubten Yeshe. **Lama/Scholar** Geshe Jampa Tekchok, Geshe Lhundrup Pelbar. **General Description** Nalanda Monastery is a residential community providing opportunity for up to twenty monks to study traditional Buddhist subjects included in the Tibetan Geshe (*dGe bShes*) programme. Such studies are supplemented with general teachings on sutra and tantra. The outstanding features of Nalanda are the unsurpassed qualities of the Abbot, Geshe Jampa Tekchok, and the isolated environment which naturally lends itself to meditation. As

an international community, residents live and work with monks from many Western countries. The main purpose of Nalanda is to help establish the Dharma in the West through educating monks in sutra and tantra teachings, and thereby preparing them to act as teachers. It is also intended to preserve the monastic tradition by providing a monastic environment in which all the ritual practices are performed correctly. **Teaching Programme** A graded course of twelve to fifteen years duration is intended to instil a basic understanding of the five major treatises studied at Sera Je Monastery as part of the geshe's training. These texts are: the *Abhisamayalamkara*, by Maitreya; the *Madhyamakavatara*, by Candrakirti; the *Vinayasutra*, by Gunaprabha; the *Abhidharmakosha*, by Vasubandhu; and the *Pramanavarttika*, by Dharmakirti. Other subjects include: 'The Mind and Mental Factors' (*Blo rig*); 'Signs and Reasonings' (*rTags rig*); 'Buddhist Tenets' (*Grub mtha'*); 'Grounds and Paths' (*Sa lam*); 'Seventy Topics' (*Don bdun cu*); and 'The Graduated Path to Enlightenment' (*Lam Rim*). Extensive commentaries on tantra are also given. All teachings are translated from Tibetan into English. **Facilities and Services** Nalanda is located in a large house set in five acres of forested land with a river frontage. It is an ideal setting for meditation and related studies. There are no special facilities beyond what is necessary to support and run the residential community. There is a library, a photocopier, and an IBM PC XT computer. The experienced Western community is capable of performing all necessary rites of ordination (gelong and getsul), as well as So jong, the rains retreat (yar ne), and the completion of the rains retreat ceremony. **Project Description** It is intended to continue to provide a home for monks, where pure vinaya discipline can be maintained, and monks can be trained to act as teachers of the tradition in the future.

NEHNANG SAMTEN CHOLING

Address Les Tranchats, Plazac, Rouffignac, France, 24580. **Distribution Details** No materials are distributed. **Year Established** 1975. **Founder** Nehnang Pawo Rinpoche. **Lama/ Scholar** Nehnang Pawo Rinpoche (formerly), Lama Karma Tsultrim, Lama Ngadune Chopel. **General Description** Nehnang Samten Choling was founded by H.E. Nehnang Pawo Rinpoche, one of the foremost lamas of the Kagyu Gyalwa Yabse (bKa' brgyud rGyal ba Yab sras) – the fathers and spiritual sons of the Kagyupa Tradition. The centre is situated on a remote hillside, ideally located for secluded retreats. **Teaching Programme** Pujas take place every morning and evening in the meditation room at Samten Choling. There are also special offering ceremonies to Guru Padmasambhava on the tenth of every Tibetan month. On other sacred days, (such as the eighth, fifteenth and thirtieth days of the month), observance of certain vows is undertaken. Both oral and written Tibetan language instruction is offered to those wishing to gain a deeper understanding of the teachings. **Facilities and Services** Nehnang Samten Choling is an ideal location for those intent on retreat. A shrine room is maintained for group practice. **Project Description** To extend the retreat facilities at the Centre in order to accommodate more meditators.

NGOR EWAM KUNZANG LING

Address 8 Cour St. Pierre, Paris, France, 75017. **Tel** (42) 93 48 57. **Distribution Details** The centre will distribute materials throughout Europe. **Year Established** 1980. **Founder** H.E. Ngor Ewam Phende Rinpoche.

NGOR EWAM PHENDE LING

Address 3 Rue du Bout de la Ville, Les Ventes, France, 27180. **Tel** (32) 67 80 63. **Distribution Details** The centre will distribute materials throughout Europe, and in some cases, world-wide. **Year Established** 1974. **Founder** H.E. Ngor Ewam Phende Rinpoche. **Lama/Scholar** H.E. Ngor Ewam Phende Rinpoche. **General Description** The centre is located in several buildings that are in the process of being renovated. It is situated in a small village, and is the main residence of H.E. Phende Rinpoche. Ngor Ewam Phende Ling doubles as a teaching centre and a retreat centre. Teachings are given at all levels of the Buddhist path, and visitors are expected to follow a timetable of study and meditation when staying at the centre. Individual or group retreats under the guidance of Phende Rinpoche can be arranged. A special programme of graduated retreat practice has been set up in accordance with the traditions of the Sakya (Sa skya) school of Tibetan Buddhism. **Teaching Programme** Depending on the teachings, courses are designed to last either for a few days, or a few weeks. They cover all aspects of Buddhist philosophy, but concentrate in particular on topics relevant to the practice of meditation, and the living of a virtuous life. **Facilities and Services** A large building houses the temple, which is decorated with murals, and a statue of the Buddha that stands three metres high. Visitors can be accommodated in ten single and double rooms, as well as several dormitories. All the usual amenities are provided. **Project Description** Ongoing restoration work is concerned with the upkeep of the buildings. A library is being planned that will stock works on Buddhism, both in Tibetan and in Western languages. Help is being given to Tibetan monasteries in India and Nepal, and it is hoped to extend this project.

RIGPA (FRANCE)
Address 22 Rue Burq, Paris, France, 75018.

SAKYA ARCHIVES
Address 28 Chemin de Figuieres Folles, St Remy de Provence, France, 13210. **Tel** 90 92 0506. **Distribution Details** Photographs, Video and Audio tapes are distributed, and a copying service is available. **Year Established** 1987. **Founder** Mark and Patty Rose. **General Description** The Sakya Archives are a video archive documenting complete teachings from the Sakya school of Tibetan Buddhism and the Tshar and Ngor sub-schools in particular. The teachings, which include both the Tibetan and English, include over 800 hours by H.H. Sakya Trinzin recorded in India and teachings by H.E. Chogye Trichen recorded in Nepal. The archive is a privately funded organisation presently centred around the creation of video documents rather than their editing and distribution. Wider availability of the video recordings for distribution is hoped for in the future.

SAKYA TASHI CHOLING
Address Institut De Bouddhisme Tibetain, 14 rue Ancien Champ de Mars, Grenoble, France, 38000. **Tel** 76 87 68 14. **Founder** H.H. Sakya Trizin.

SAKYA TSECHEN LING

Address 5, Rond Point du Vignoble, Kuttolsheim, Marlenheim, France, 67520. **Tel** (88) 87 73 80. **Distribution Details** Please contact the centre for further information. **Year Established** 1978. **Founder** Ven. Geshe Sherab Gyaltsen Amipa. **Lama/ Scholar** Geshe Sherab Gyaltsen Amipa, Lama Dakpa Woeser. **General Description** The Tibetan Buddhist institute, Sakya Tsechen Ling, was opened in May 1978 under the spiritual direction of Ven. Geshe Sherab Gyaltsen Amipa. It was formally inaugurated on 5 November of the same year by H.H. Sakya Trizin, the Head of the Sakya school. The main aim of the institute is to preserve and promote the spiritual, philosophical and cultural traditions of Tibet, with a primary focus being placed on those doctrines associated with the Sakyapa school. Sakya Tsechen Ling sponsors a number of different activities, including: the study of Tibetan canonical texts, the practice of meditation, and the translation of various Tibetan works. **Teaching Programme** Advanced teachings given at the institute derive in large part from the key texts of the Sakyapa tradition, notably the *Lamdre (Lam 'Bras)* and the *Zhenpa Zhidral (Zhen pa bZhi 'bral)*. The study programme followed in relation to Tibetan canonical texts concentrates mainly on Madhyamika philosophy, the *Five Treatises of Maitreya*, and the *Abhidharmakosha* or *Treasury of Manifest Knowledge* of Vasubhandu. A number of weekend courses are arranged throughout the year, featuring discourses given by the centre's founder, the Ven. Lama Sherab. Recent teachings have been concerned with the meditational practices of Green Tara, Vajrapani, Mahakala and Kusali yoga, as well as the *Bodhisattvacaryavatara* of Shantideva – a comprehensive guide to the practices engaged in by beings on the path to enlightenment. It is also possible to study Tibetan language at the institute, on those weekends when courses are not scheduled. **Facilities and Services** A shrine room is maintained at the centre in Kuttolsheim, and there are residential facilities for those attending courses.

URGYEN SAMYE CHOLING

Address Laugeral, St Leon-sur-Vezere, Montignac, Dordogne, France, 24290. **Tel** 53 50 75 29. **Year Established** 1977. **Founder** H.H. Dudjom Rinpoche. **Lama/Scholar** H.E. Shenphen Dawa Rinpoche. **General Description** Urgyen Samye Choling is a Nyingma Buddhist meditation and study centre. Since the death in 1987 of H.H. Dudjom Rinpoche the centre has been directed by his son and successor, H.E. Shenphen Dawa Rinpoche whose European residence is nearby. **Teaching Programme** The teachings and practices of Mahayana and Vajrayana Buddhism are presented. Short courses take place throughout the year. Longer retreat courses usually take place in the summer. Emphasis is on intensive practice according to the nine-yana system of the Nyingma tradition. Personal instruction, oral transmission, initiation, daily practice and retreats are considered essential. Students usually perform the Tantric preliminary (Ngondro) practice and subsequent practices are usually the Terma (visionary revelation, meditative and yogic practices) of Dudjom Rinpoche and Dudjom Lingpa. Transmission and practice of the inner tantras of Nyingma – Mahayoga, Anuyoga and Dzogchen – is authentic and rigorous. Appropriate qualifications for graduated practice are generally required but individual assessment is taken into account. H.E. Shenphen Dawa Rinpoche is bi-lingual in English and Tibetan. **Facilities and Services** Working languages are French and English. Ritual meditative (sadhana) practices are presented in Tibetan with translations. There is a traditional Nyingma Vajrayana temple and grounds. Rooms are available to practitioners or students on request. Camping sites are open in summer season. Self-catering. The village of Le Moustier (between Les Eyzies and Montignac-Lascaux) is fifteen minutes walk from the centre.

GERMANY

Academic Organisations

BAYERISCHE AKADEMIE DER WISSENSCHAFTEN, KOMMISSION FUR ZENTRALASIATISCHE STUDIEN

Address Marstallplatz 8, Munchen 22, Germany, (89) 8000. **Tel** (89) 23031194. **Telex/Fax** (89) 089–23031240. **Distribution Details** Since 1987, the Kommission has produced a series of publications entitled, *Studia Tibetica.* **Year Established** 1954. **Lama/Scholar** Dr Helga Uebach, Dr Jampa L. Panglung. **General Description** The Kommission fur Zentralasiatische Studien is a research institute dedicated to the study of Central Asian civilisation. At present its main project is the compilation of a Dictionary of Written Tibetan. **Teaching Programme** There is no teaching programme. **Facilities and Services** There is a good library accessible to research staff only. **Project Description** The Kommission is primarily engaged in the compilation of a comprehensive reference dictionary of written Tibetan. So far about 200,000 entries have been gathered, and it is anticipated that this phase of the project will take a further ten years. Since 1987, a series of Tibetan texts, from which words for the dictionary have been excerpted, were published, translated and annotated under the title, *Sources and Materials for the Study of Tibetan Lexicography.* Also included in the series were the proceedings of the Fourth Seminar on Tibetan Studies. This conference was convened by the Kommission in 1985, on behalf of the International Association for Tibetan Studies, at Schloss Hohenkammer, near Munich.

GOTTINGEN UNIVERSITY, ETHNOGRAPHICAL INSTITUTE

Address Theaterplatz 15, 3400 Gottingen, Hessen, Germany.

KARL-MARX UNIVERSITAT, DEPT. OF FOLKLORE/ ETHNOGRAPHY OF CENTRAL ASIA

Address Bereich Asien, Karl-Marx Platz 9, Leipzig, Germany. **Lama/Scholar** Dr Manfred Taube (Tibetan specialist).

UNIVERSITY OF BONN, CENTRAL ASIAN SEMINAR, TIBETAN SECTION

Address Regina-Pacis-Weg 7, Bonn, Germany, 5300. **Tel** (0228) 73 74 58. **Telex/Fax** (228) 886657 unibo d. **Distribution Details** A journal is issued annually, entitled *Zentralasiatische Studien.* Other materials are available for research at the university. **Year Established** 1964. **Founder** Walther Heissig. **Lama/ Scholar** Klaus Sagaster (Professor), Jampa K. Phukhang (Lecturer), Sherab Loden Dagyab (Researcher), Pema Tsering

(Researcher), Dieter Schuh (Professor). **General Description** The seminar is a research and teaching establishment engaged in the field of Tibetan and Mongolian studies. It was founded by Walther Heissig, an eminent German scholar, whose speciality was Mongolian culture. Several Tibetan lamas, including H.H. the Fourteenth Dalai Lama, Trijang Rinpoche, and the Thirteenth Shamar Rinpoche, have visited the seminar and participated in seminars into questions of Buddhist philosophy. H.H. the Dalai Lama also gave a lecture on the *Lam Rim* teachings of Je Tsongkhapa, in September 1986. **Teaching Programme** Courses are offered in Tibetan and Mongolian studies, focusing on both the classical and modern expressions of these cultures. Lectures are given on the history, literature, and religious iconography of Central Asia. It is also possible to pursue linguistic studies, both through translation work on classical Tibetan texts, and by training in modern colloquial Tibetan. **Facilities and Services** The seminar possesses a well-stocked reference library, including xerox copies of several foreign Tibetan textual collections (those of Leiden, Dublin and Toyo Bunko for example), together with reprints of Tibetan texts published in India and Bhutan. Also housed here is a collection of audio tape recordings of Tibetan songs and epics. Photocopying facilities are available in the Department.

UNIVERSITY OF HAMBURG, INSTITUTE FOR CULTURE AND HISTORY OF INDIA AND TIBET

Address Tibetological Section, 53 Grindelallee, Hamburg 13, Germany, 2000. **Tel** (40) 4123–3385. **Distribution Details** Publications include: *A History of Drepung Gomang Seminary* by Geshe Gedun Lodro, and three volumes in the series *Tibetan and Indo-Tibetan Studies*. **Year Established** 1919. **Lama/Scholar** Prof Dr. Lambert Schmithausen, Prof Dr. David

Seyfort Ruegg, Prof Dr David Jackson, Dr Felix Erb. **General Description** The institute is an institution for the study of South Asian and Tibetan languages, history and culture. **Teaching Programme** The seminar offers MA and PhD degree level courses in Sanskrit; Tibetan; Pali; Buddhist Philosophy, Religion and Culture; Indian Philosophy, Religion and Culture; and Tibetan Philosophy, Religion and Culture. **Facilities and Services** The seminar houses a large library of Tibetan texts and publications on Tibet. Areas of specialisation include: the transmission and integration of Buddhist teachings into Tibet, the formation of the Tibetan schools, and Indo-Tibetan studies in general.

Cultural Organisations and Tibetan Refugee Aid Societies

DEUTSCH-TIBETISCHE KULTURGESELLSCHAFT EV, GERMAN TIBETAN CULTURAL SOCIETY

Address Fritz-Pullig-Str. 28, Sankt Augustin 2, Germany, D–5205. **Tel** 02241 20 36 10. **Year Established** 1982. **General Description** The German Tibetan Cultural Society (GTCS), based in Koenigswinter near Bonn, was founded by Tibetans and German friends on 27 March 1982. Non-partisan, free of political and religious persuasions, the GTCS is dedicated to promoting understanding and appreciation of Tibetan culture, history and religion. The organisation is non-profit making and has currently over 350 members. **Teaching Programme** The organisation holds two lecture-weekends per year in the spring and autumn.

DEUTSCHE TIBETHILFE E.V., (HAMBURG/MUNCHEN)

Address Wrangelstr. 19, Hamburg 20, Germany, G 2000. **Tel** 040 420 23 33. **General Description** Deutsche Tibethilfe is a non-profit organisation which for thirty years has supported Tibetan refugees in India. This financial support has increased to about DM 2,000,000 per year. In 1991 there were more than 4000 sponsors who personally undertook to finance on a monthly basis Tibetan children, students, monks and old people. All managers and helpers work on an honorary basis.

ECO-TIBET, COORDINATION GERMANY
Address Fritz-Pullig-Str. 28, Sankt Augustin 2, Germany, D–5205. **Tel** 02241 20 36 10. **Telex/Fax** (0228) 26 16 20. **General Description** ECO-TIBET (Environmental Concern Over Tibet) is the Environmental Desk of the Tibet Support Group Germany.

ROKPA HILFSWERK E.V.
Address Magda Wangyal, Arno-Holz Strasse 5, Berlin 41, Germany, D–1000. **Tel** (030) 791 2947. **Year Established** 1988. **Founder** H.H. Sixteenth Karmapa.

TIBET IMAGE BANK
Address Tushita GMBH, Schifferstrasse 170A, Duisburg 1, Germany, D–4100. **Tel** (0203) 33 10 66. **Telex/Fax** (0203) 34 35 71. **General Description** The Tibet Image Bank collects, preserves, and disseminates photographs of Tibet, and chronicles contemporary events. There is an historical archive, and a commercial picture library.

TIBET INFORMATION SERVICE
Address Florastrasse 22, Langenfeld, Germany, D–4018. **Tel** (2173) 75151. **Telex/Fax** (228) 48 54 50.

VEREIN Z. FORDERUNG D. KULTUR TIBETS
Address Gernotstrasse 8, Munchen 40, Germany, 8000. **Tel** 089 300 6386. **Distribution Details** Tapes of discourses recorded at Tashi Rabten (Austria) are distributed.

Libraries

BAYERISCHE STAATSBIBLIOTHEK, ORIENT ABTEILUNG
Address Postfach 34 01 50, Ludwigstr. 16, Munchen 34, Germany, D–8000. **Tel** 089–2198 ex 367. **Telex/Fax** 089 280 9284. **Distribution Details** A very few copies of the catalogue accompanying the 1985 exhibition are still available from the Manuscript Department. **Year Established** 1458. **General Description** Bayerische Staatsbibliothek is the state library of Bavaria. **Facilities and Services** The Orientlesesaal is situated on the second floor of the library. A reading room and reference library is open weekdays. There are 630 manuscripts, 350 xylographs and more than 6000 volumes of modern printed works. Tibetan printed books and blockprints are catalogued on cards, and there is a microfiche catalogue for books published since 1982. Manuscripts can be read in the reading room of the Handschriftenabteilung. Microfilms and xerox-copies can be ordered.

Museums

ETHNOGRAPHY COLLECTION, LUBECK

Address Grosser Bauhof 14, 2400 Lubeck, Schleswig Holstein, Germany. **Tel** 0451 11224340. **General Description** There are about 180 lamaistic objects in the collection, not only from Tibet but also from Mongolia, Nepal and China. They are mostly objects belonging to religious life and include in approximate divisions: 50 paintings, twenty-four tsha-tshas, twenty-one images, fifteen ritualistic objects, writing and printing objects, twelve charms and prayer-wheels, ten musical instruments, and a selection of textiles, utensils (for food, drink, and tobacco), jewellery, and masks.

ETHNOLOGICAL MUSEUM, LEIPZIG

Address Johannisplatz, Leipzig, Germany.

HAMBURGISCHES MUSEUM FUR VOLKERKUNDE

Address Department of South and East Asia, Binderstrasse 14, Hamburg 13, Germany, 2000. **Tel** (40) 44195 527. **Telex/Fax** (40) 441 95 242.

J & E VON PORTHEIM FOUNDATION, ETHNOLOGICAL MUSEUM

Address Haupstrasse 235, 6900 Heidelberg, Baden-Wurttemberg, Germany.

LINDEN-MUSEUM STUTTGART, STATE MUSEUM OF ETHNOGRAPHY

Address South Asian Department, Hegelplatz 1, Stuttgart 1, Germany, D–7000. **Tel** (0711) 123 1242. **Telex/Fax** (0711) 297047. **Lama/Scholar** Prof Dr Peter Thiele (Director), Dr Gerd Kreisel (Curator). **General Description** The collection includes Tibetan and Tibeto-Mongolian art and ethnographic objects (sculptures, paintings, ritual objects, manuscripts, prints etc.). A selection of these are on display in the South Asian Department and published in various issues of *TRIBUS*, the Linden Museum Year-book, the Katalog der tibetischen und mongolischen Sachkultur (H. Roth and V. Ronge, 1989) and in the exhibition guide book.

MUSEUM FUR OSTASIATISCHE KUNST

Address Universitatsstr. 100, Koln 1, Germany, 5000. **Tel** 0049–221–405038. **Telex/Fax** 0049–221–407290. **Lama/Scholar** Dr Adele Schlombs (Director). **General Description** The collection includes a selection of high-quality bronzes, ceramics, lacquer and paintings (China, Japan, Korea) which are also on display at times in other cultural institutions. The museum has a library containing about 15,000 books and special periodicals which are available to the public.

MUSEUM FUR VOLKERKUNDE LEIPZIG, INDIAN DEPARTMENT

Address Schwantesstr 2, Leipzig, Germany. **Lama/Scholar** Heinz Kucharski (Head).

MUSEUM FUR VOLKERKUNDE SMB

Address Abteilung Ostasien, Arnimallee 27, Berlin 33, Germany, 1000. **Tel** 030 8301 352. **Telex/Fax** 030 8315 972. **Year Established** 1873. **General Description** The Tibetan collection of the East Asian Department comprises about 800 items mainly related to nomadic and ritual life. The earliest pieces of some forty ritual and agricultural objects date back to the travels of the brothers Schlagintweit in the Tibetan-Indian border region (1855–56). The main holdings derive from a Tibetan-lamaist sect from the Yellow Temple (Huang-szu) in Peking (thangkas, sculptures, woodblocks, ritual paraphernalia, collected by Eugen Pander in 1883) and from everyday nomadic culture (black tent, saddles, woven and leather bags, butter and tea jars etc.) which were mainly acquired in recent years.

MUSEUM OF ARTS AND CRAFTS

Address 1, Steintorplatz, 2000 Hamburg, Germany.

MUSEUM OF INDIAN ART
Address Takustrasse 40, 1000 Berlin 33, Germany. **Tel** 030 8301361. **Telex/Fax** 4930 8315972. **Year Established** 1963. **General Description** The Museum of Indian Art collection of Tibetan and Tibeto-Nepalese objects covers different groups of artefacts: 283 manuscripts and block prints, 100 paintings on cloth and paper, several of them thangkas, twenty-five terracotta plaques, fifty-nine bronzes and other metalwork, including statues of deities and lamas together with ritual implements, and a variety of miscellaneous objects such as inscribed mani stones, carved wooden book covers, and a bone and textile lama dance costume including headdress, apron, bracelets and necklace. A few objects date back to the sixteenth century, but the majority are from the seventeenth – nineteenth. Approximately twenty artefacts are on display.

MUSEUM OF MUSICAL INSTRUMENTS
Address Bundesalle 1–12, 1000 Berlin 15, Germany.

NIEDERSACHSISCHES LANDESMUSEUM HANNOVER, VOLKERKUNDE-ABTEILUNG
Address Am Maschpark 5, 3 Hannover 1, Niedersachsen, Germany. **Tel** 88 30 51/52. **General Description** The Tibetan collection consists of 379 objects. The most eminent collectors were Hermann and Robert von Schlagintweit (1859), Gordon T. Bowles and Ernst Schafer. There is a published catalogue of the collection available from the Museum.

OVERSEAS MUSEUM
Address Bahnhofsplatz 13, 2800 Bremen, Germany.

PHILIPPS-UNIVERSITAT MARBURG, RELIGIONSKUNDLICHE SAMMLUNG
Address Landgraf-Philipp-Strasse 4, Marburg, Hessen, Germany, D–3550. **Tel** 06421 282480. **Year Established** 1927. **Founder** Professor Rudolf Otto. **Lama/Scholar** Dr Martin Kraatz (Indologist, historian).

ROEMER-UND PELIZAEUS-MUSEUM
Address Am Steine 1–2, Hildesheim, Niedersachsen, Germany, 3200. **Tel** 05121 15979. **Telex/Fax** 05121 35283.

STATE MUSEUM OF ETHNOGRAPHY
Address 22 Maximilianstrasse 42, 8000 Munchen, Bayern, Germany.

VOLKERKUNDLICHE SAMMLUNGEN, IM REISS-MUSEUM
Address Zeughaus C 5, Mannheim 1, Baden-Wurttemberg, Germany, D–6800. **Tel** 0621 293 3783. **Telex/Fax** 0621 10 14 52. **Year Established** 1925. **Founder** City of Mannheim. **Lama/Scholar** Dr Henning Bishof (director), Dr Klaus Born. **General Description** The museum has a collection of about 300 Tibetan objects received from several sources. A few pieces have

come from the Archducal Collection in Karlsruhe, which dates back to the nineteenth century. Others were obtained at auctions in Germany during the 1920s, and there are several that were included in the Gabriel-von-Max Collection, acquired by the city of Mannheim in 1917.

Publishing Companies and Journals

DIAMANT VERLAG
Address Holzhamer Str.5, Arnstorf, Germany, 8382. **Tel** (0049) 87232396. **Year Established** 1980. **Founder** Lama Thubten Yeshe. **General Description** Diamant Verlag is a Buddhist publishing house dedicated to helping preserve and spread Buddhist resources in German speaking countries. The company is a member of the Foundation for the Preservation of the Mahayana Tradition.

EUROPEAN BULLETIN OF HIMALAYAN RESEARCH, SUDASIEN-INSTITUT DER UNIVERSITAT HEIDELBERG
Address Im Neuenheimer Feld 330, Heidelberg, Germany, 6900. **Lama/ Scholar** Prof Richard Burghart, Prof Dr. Andras Hofer, Dr Martin Gaenszle. **General Description** The Bulletin focuses on Nepal, India, Pakistan, Tibet and China, and includes news on forthcoming conferences and funding opportunities for scholars working in the Himalayan region. Information includes descriptions of Himalayan related archives in different countries.

TIBET FORUM
Address Konradstrasse 2A, Munster, Germany, D–4400. **Tel** 0251–230 3860. **Telex/Fax** 0251–833169. **Year Established** 1982. **Founder** Society of the Tibetans in Germany. **Lama/ Scholar** Prof D. Jan Andersson (editor). **General Description** *Tibet Forum* is a German language magazine on all aspects of Tibet and Tibetan culture.

Teaching Centres

ARYATARA CITY CENTRE
Address Lucille Grahnstrasse 47, D–8000, Munchen 80, Germany, D–8000. **Tel** 089 470 1853. **Telex/Fax** 089 272 5022.

ARYATARA INSTITUT
Address Holzhamer Str. 5, Arnstorf, Germany, 8382. **Tel** 8723 2396. **Distribution Details** Aryatara Institut will distribute throughout the world, with a discount being offered to shops and centres. **Year Established** 1980. **Founder** Lama Thubten Yeshe. **Lama/Scholar** Geshe Lobsang Khedrup. **General Description** Aryatara Institut is a country centre with space for between thirty and forty visitors, and up to ten residents at any one time. Geshe Lobsang Khedrup is the resident lama and teaches regularly twice a week. It is located in the former schoolhouse of the village of Jaegerndorf (constructed in 1959). The centre organises some twenty to thirty courses a year that are given by both Tibetan lamas and Western Dharma teachers (men and women). Courses range from those concerned with Tibetan Buddhism exclusively to those drawing parallels between Buddhism and such areas as Christianity, science, psychology, and politics. These latter comparative courses are attended by experts from all the disciplines concerned. Meditation retreats are also arranged by the centre. Aryatara Institut helps in the organisation of courses given in the cities of Munich, Berlin, Vienna and elsewhere. **Teaching Programme** There is no daily teaching programme as such. However, frequent weekend courses take place, and occasionally longer courses, up to one week in length, are held. Courses are given either by Tibetan lamas or Western teachers (monks, nuns or lay) and tend to be commentaries on short texts or meditation practices. Introductory courses to Buddhism are also available. The centre arranges many introductory

courses for the various associated city centres. It also organises regular meditation classes in the area. **Facilities and Services** The centre has eight single rooms and three dormitories that are used to accommodate visitors. There is a gompa or shrine room that is eighty square metres in size. A library contains around 500 books on various subjects, including Buddhism and psychology. There are also a few Tibetan texts, transcripts, and 700 tapes of teachings kept there. Aryatara Institut is associated with the publishing company, Diamant Verlag, that works closely with Wisdom Publications of London. Approximately one book a year is issued (seven have been produced since 1983). The centre also publishes transcripts and pamphlets in German (so far about seventy pamphlets and eight larger commentaries have been printed). **Project Description** The main emphasis of Aryatara Institut's activity is concerned with presenting short introductory dharma courses. Once a year, longer commentaries of textual material are scheduled. Between mid-January and mid-March, the centre is geared to those wishing to complete retreats, either with or without guidance. Ongoing provision is made to rent out facilities to other groups with interest in meditation or alternative therapies. It is intended to continue publishing short meditation guides, transcribed lectures, and spiritual practices. The association with Diamant Verlag is allowing the centre to publish professionally. Amongst the books printed since 1983 are an interview with the Dalai Lama, the life story of the Buddha (*Prince Siddhartha*), and Kathleen McDonald's *How to Meditate*. There are plans to arrange meditation holidays for the general public.

CHODZONG – BUDDHISTISCHES ZENTRUM

Address Hauptstrasse 19, Langenfeld, Germany, D–8531. **Tel** 09164–320. **Telex/Fax** 09164–1494. **Year Established** 1984. **Founder** Regine Leisner. **Lama/Scholar** H.E. Dagyab Kyabgon Rinpoche, Ven. Panglung Rinpoche, Ven. Yiga Rinpoche, Ven. Gyaltzur Rinpoche. **General Description** Chodzong is a Buddhist centre under the direction of H.E. Loden Sherab Dagyab Rinpoche. The principal focus of the centre is the seminar house in Langenfeld, a village in the South of Germany between Nurnberg and Wurzburg. Approximately seven people live there, among them a monk and two nuns. The central theme of Chodzong is the integration of Buddhist practice into everyday Western life. **Teaching Programme** Weekend seminars are held on a regular basis and there is daily group meditation and a meditation evening once a week. Further regular meditation evenings are held in nearby cities, where lectures are also arranged dealing with religious, psychological, social or political themes concerning Tibet and its culture.

DRIKUNG NGADAN CHOLING

Address Auf'm Rain 13, Medelon, Sauerland, Germany, 5789. **Tel** 02982–1667. **Distribution Details** Ferdinand Stange:audio, Ulrike Spitz:published material. Some audio tapes and publications are restricted to those who have received particular initiations. **Year Established** 1981. **Founder** Ayang Rinpoche.

Lama/Scholar Lama Sonam Jorphel, Drubpon Rinpoche. **General Description** Drikung Ngadan Choling was founded in 1981 by Tulku Ayang Rinpoche. In 1982 the centre moved its location to a small village in the hilly landscape of the Sauerland in the middle of West Germany noted for its natural beauty. Six to ten people live in the centre under the spiritual guidance of Lama Sonam Jorphel who is the resident lama. Lama Sonam Jorphel gives initiations, teaches and leads seminars and longer courses at the centre. In 1985, a seven-metre high stupa was constructed at the centre under the guidance of Lama Sonam Jorphel. The centre also invites other teachers from the Drikung Kagyu, as well as from other Buddhist traditions, to visit the centre. **Teaching Programme** The teaching programme at the centre consists of study and practice of Buddhist teachings. These include the study of Buddhist philosophy and Tibetan language, individual practice, and common daily Pujas. The individual practices include: the five-fold profound path of Mahamudra and the Six Yogas of Naropa. The pujas which are performed daily are: Guru puja; short Amitabha puja; Dharmapala puja; and Chod. Other pujas are performed on special religious occasions. Guru Rinpoche, Phowa, and Vajrayogini pujas are performed on the appropriate days of the month. **Facilities and Services** The centre can find accommodation for up to thirty people in the dormitory and there are a few two or three-bedded rooms. Three daily meals are served. Visitors, practitioners and interested people are always welcome. If there is no teaching programme there are possibilities to make retreats in the house. Nearby in the village are some inexpensive boarding houses for alternative accommodation. Camping is possible in the garden of the centre. **Project Description** It is planned to establish a retreat centre and a new Lhakhang (temple) on recently bought land. The centre also wants to invite a thangka painter to live in the centre for one or two years and give courses in Tibetan thangka painting and Buddhist iconography.

KAMALASHILA INSTITUT

Address Schloss Wachendorf, Mechernich, Germany, 5353. **Tel** (02256) 7168. **Distribution Details** Distribution is made world-wide. Only orders worth over DM 50 are accepted. **Year Established** 1981. **Founder** Shamar Rinpoche. **Lama/Scholar** Khenpo Lama Thubten. **General Description** Kamalashila Institut was founded to act mainly as a shedra (shes grva), a college where Buddhist teachings are transmitted in an authentic manner. The centre organises courses given by suitably qualified teachers of all traditions, though those of the Kagyu (bKa' brgyud) lineage predominate, with meditational practice being integrated into the study programme from the beginning. Since 1986, a five-year course has been introduced under the direction of Khenpo Lama Thubten. This aims to review all the basic sutra texts and commentaries, including the *Bodhicaryavatara* of Shantideva and the *Madhyamakavatara* of Candrakirti. In addition, teachings on all the lower levels of tantra are given according to the kam tshang (Karma Kagyu) lineages. These teachings are usually a mixture of empowerments (dbang), textual transmissions (lung), and instructions (khrid), so that students can practice and study at the same time. Many of the teachers at Kamalashila emphasize the mahamudra practise. In particular, Lama Gendun Rinpoche, who is guiding those completing the three-year retreat at Karma Thong Drol Ling, gives teachings on shamatha (zhi gnas), vipashyana (lhag mthong), and mahamudra meditation. **Teaching Programme** Kamalashila Institute offers a range of courses, from introductory talks and meditation classes, to teachings on sutra and tantra. The vajrayana teachings are drawn from the

Karma Kagyu lineages, and are a mixture of empowerments (dbang), textual transmissions (lung), and instructions into the various practices (khrid). Other courses are devoted to the practice of meditation. They are given by qualified teachers of the tradition, and are mainly concerned with shamatha (zhi gnas), vipashyana (lhag mthong), mahamudra, and practices relating to the meditational deities. Green Tara puja is performed in the morning, and Mahakala in the afternoon. There is also regular shamatha (zhi gnas) practice in the evening. Courses from other Buddhist traditions are arranged, notably vipassana meditation and zen sesshins. Every Thursday evening and Sunday morning, za-zen meditation classes take place. Courses are also given on Tibetan medicine and Tibetan language. **Facilities and Services** Located in an old castle, Kamalashila Institut can accommodate up to 100 people at a time (some single rooms are available). There is a large meditation room, a small vajrayana *lha khang* (chapel), and a zen do on the premises. Short retreats can be undertaken in a secluded part of the castle. The library houses audio and video tapes, together with a range of books on Buddhism and Tibetan culture. Tibetan textual holdings include the *Collected Works of the Fifteenth Karmapa (mKha' khyab rDo rje gsun 'bum)*, and the Derge edition of the *Kangyur (bKa' 'gyur)*. A pleasant garden contains a stupa and a small lake. Karma Thong Drol Ling, an affiliated retreat centre, has facilities for those wishing to undertake the traditional three-year retreat. **Project Description** Ongoing projects are concerned with publishing teachings that are given at the centre, and distributing a newsletter. There are also plans to establish a Buddhist university, similar to the Rumtek Shedra in Sikkim, which is affiliated to Benares Sanskrit University. It is hoped to develop the retreat facilities in order to allow mahamudra retreats to take place in the Institute.

KARMA KAGYU VIDEO COLLECTION
Address Landwehr Strasse 83, 8000 Munich 2, Germany. **Tel** (89) 533900. **Founder** Wolfgang Neugebauer.

KARMA TENGYAL LING
Address Albertstrasse 10, Berlin 62, Germany, 1000. **Tel** (030) 782 73 59. **Distribution Details** No materials are distributed. **Year Established** 1977. **Founder** H.H. Gyalwa Karmapa. **Lama/Scholar** Lama Pema Dorje. **General Description** Karma Tengyal Ling was founded in 1977 following the visits to Berlin of Kalu Rinpoche and H.H. the Sixteenth Karmapa, in that year. Since then, many of the pre-eminent lamas of the Karma Kagyu tradition of Tibetan Buddhism have given lectures and courses at the Centre. Karma Tengyal Ling has also hosted teachers from the Drikung Kagyu and Gelugpa schools. **Teaching Programme** Lama Pema Dorje, a highly qualified teacher and meditation master, is the resident lama at Karma Tengyal Ling. Apart from the regular programme of meditation and puja ceremonies, the centre also arranges courses on a variety of subjects connected with Buddhist philosophy, psychology and spiritual practice. **Facilities and Services** Karma Tengyal Ling maintains a shrine room in the

centre. There is also a well-stocked library containing books in English and German, as well as some Tibetan texts. The centre will soon be acquiring copies of the *Kangyur* and *Tengyur*, thanks to the efforts of Lama Pema Dorje.

KARMAPAE CHO LING

Address Harkortstieg 4, Hamburg 50, Germany, 2000. **Tel** 040 389 8702. **Distribution Details** The Centre will distribute throughout Europe. Prepayment is not required. **Year Established** 1972. **Founder** H.H. Gyalwa Karmapa. **Lama/Scholar** Ole Nydahl. **General Description** The Hamburg Karma Kagyu centre, Karmapae Cho Ling, is one of the oldest Tibetan Buddhist centres in West Germany. It has developed continually throughout the last fifteen years, and is now situated in a four-storey house in Hamburg-Altona. The house was extensively renovated and enlarged during 1987. A stupa in the centre's garden was finished in 1989. Three floors are given over to the twenty-two residents, and a further two floors are open to the public. These new premises were formally opened on 17 December 1987, when the Ven. Lama Gendun Rinpoche and the Ven. Lama Jigme Rinpoche presided over the inauguration ceremony. Karmapae Cho Ling aims to provide the opportunity for interested people to come into contact with the wide spectrum of Tibetan Buddhist teachings. To this end regular meditation sessions are arranged during the week, and numerous qualified lamas are invited to give teachings and, when appropriate, initiations. **Teaching Programme** The centre's teaching programme includes three meditation sessions during the week, when the Avalokiteshvara Puja, the Sixteenth Karmapa's Guru Yoga, and the Mandala Ritual of Green Tara are followed. There are also opportunities to study basic Buddhist texts and to practice shamatha meditation. Every first Thursday in the month, a 'Dharma evening' is arranged, that is specifically designed for newcomers. Periodically visiting lamas are welcomed to the centre, to give teachings and initiations. Amongst the many lamas who have visited are: H.E. Shamar Rinpoche, H.E. Tai Situ Rinpoche, H.E. Jamgon Kongtrul Rinpoche, H.E. Gyaltsab Rinpoche, Ven. Thrangu Rinpoche, Ven. Tenga Rinpoche, Ven. Tsecho Rinpoche, Ven. Gendun Rinpoche, Ven. Ponlop Rinpoche, Ven. Garwang Rinpoche, Ven. Lama Jigme Rinpoche, Lama Thubten, Lama Tsewang Choden, and Geshe Thubten Ngawang. A public meeting is held every two to three months when users of the centre can discuss any questions that may have arisen. **Facilities and Services** Two floors of the centre are open to the public. This area includes a large meditation hall, a library, and a spacious room for courses. There is also access to a picturesque garden.

KARME CHOLING, BREMEN

Address Am Hulsberg 121, 2800 Bremen 1, Germany.

MAHAMUDRA RETREAT CENTRE

Address Auf dem Kuppen 7, Windeck-Halscheid, Germany, 5227. **Tel** 02292 7438. **Distribution Details** No materials are distributed. **Year Established** 1986. **Founder** Lama Gendun Rinpoche. **Lama/Scholar** Lama Gendun Rinpoche. **General Description** The Mahamudra Retreat Centre was founded as a retreat centre for those completing the traditional three-year retreat. Since 1990 it has also been open for short retreats and study courses. **Teaching Programme** The teachings and retreats are based on the Karma Kagyu tradition and general Mahayana subjects. **Facilities and Services** There is a shrine room and facilities for about twenty-five people in single and double rooms. There is also a kitchen providing three meals a day. The house is surrounded by gardens and forests. **Project Description** It is intended to continue providing education programmes for those wishing to complete the traditional three-year retreat. There are also plans to extend the retreat facilities to allow individuals to carry out private retreats of different durations and into different practices.

PHUNTSOG RABTEN
Address Hildebeld Str. 1, Munich 40, Germany, D–8000. **Tel** 0049 89 3007778.

TIBETISCHES ZENTRUM
Address Hermann Balk Strasse 106, Hamburg 73, Germany, 2000. **Tel** (040) 644 35 85. **Telex/Fax** (040) 644 35 15. **Distribution Details** All materials are distributed worldwide. **Year Established** 1977. **Founder** Geshe Tadin Rabten/Geshe Gendun Lodro. **Lama/Scholar** Geshe Thubten Ngawang. **General Description** The centre aims to provide an environment conducive to mental development, through listening to, reflecting on, and taking to heart the Buddhist teachings that are given. Training in the graduated path to enlightenment (*Lam Rim*), and strict regard to the principles of moral conduct, are emphasised before individuals are advised to take initiations and practice tantric meditation. Geshe Thubten Ngawang, the resident lama, teaches according to the Kadampa (bKa' gdams pa) and New Kadampa or Gelugpa (dGe lugs pa) traditions, which have their root in the writings and lineages handed down from the Indian masters: Nagarjuna, Shantideva, Atisha, and many others. H.H. the Fourteenth Dalai Lama, the patron, visited the centre in 1982 and 1991. **Teaching Programme** Regular weekly teachings are given on the classic Tibetan and Indian texts, (the *Lam Rim Chen Mo* of Je Tsongkhapa, and the *Abhidharmakosha* of Vasubhandu, for example). Monthly weekend courses have included such titles as: The Right View of Emptiness, The Deeds of a Bodhisattva, and Buddha Nature. Daily recitations and meditations take place in the Centre. During the week, teachings and debates on subjects followed in the Geshe Programme are given. Three courses are provided of a systematic seven-year study programme of Buddhist philosophy, which include the study of translations of major scriptures and examinations. In addition, teachings on pujas, retreats relating to meditational deities and *Lam Rim* subjects, and empowerments are organised by the centre. All teachings are given by Geshe Thubten, and examinations are taken from him. There are also courses in Tibetan language that are arranged by Christof Spitz. **Facilities and Services** Meditation and retreat facilities are offered by the centre. Accommodation is available throughout the year. There is a library and cassette lending facility. The centre also publishes books and distributes a newletter. Buddhist texts may be bought in the bookshop, and ritual implements and other practice materials are on sale in the centre's shop. **Project Description** Tibetisches Zentrum is involved in helping refugees in the re-established monastic college of Sera Je in South India. It is also concerned to raise funds for the Narthang Printing Office Project, and to support the efforts of the 'Buddhist Religious Community of Germany' in campaigning for official recognition

of Buddhism as a religion. The centre is active in promoting inter-faith dialogue, and intends developing its links with Hamburg University. Various translation and publishing projects are being undertaken, including a dictionary of Buddhist terms on database.

VAJRADHATU EUROPE
Address Zwetschenweg 23, Marburg, Germany, W 3550. **Tel** 49 06421 34244. **Telex/Fax** 49 06421 36318. **General Description** A complete list of Vajradhatu centres throughout Europe and North America is available from this centre.

YESHE CHOELING
Address c/o Auwaldstrabe 22, Freiburg, Germany, 7800.

GREECE

Teaching Centres

DO-NGAG ZUNG-JUG LING, RETREAT CENTRE
Address P.O. Box 16, Paros, Greece, 84400. **Tel** 30 284 91 343. **General Description** Do-Ngag Zung-jug Ling is a small quiet retreat centre set in the countryside on an idyllic Greek island. It offers facilities for up to twenty visitors, including special care for up to five individuals and facilities for up to twelve on group retreats, and those participating in seminars and workshops.

KARMA DRUBGYU CHOKOR
Address Sonierou 15-B, Platia Vathis, Athens, Greece, 10438. **Tel** 01 522 0218.

HOLLAND

Academic Organisations

STATE UNIVERSITY OF LEIDEN, INDOLOGICAL INSTITUTE (KERN INSTITUTE)
Address P.O.B. 9515, Leiden, Holland, 2300 RA. **Tel** 071–272503. **Dis-**tribution Details Tibetan published material is currently out of stock. **Year Established** 1925. **Lama/Scholar** Dr T.E. Vetter (Buddhism and Tibetan), Dr H.W. Bodewitz (Sanskrit), Dr D.H.A. Kolff (Modern South Asian History), Dr P.C. Verhagen (Tibetan and Sanskrit). **General Description** Kern Institute was originally established as an Institute for Indian archaeology, but now houses the Department of South and Central Asian Languages and Civilisations. A chair for Buddhist and Tibetan Studies was established in 1956 and has been held by Dr J.W. de Jong, Dr D. Seyfort Ruegg and Dr T.E. Vetter. In the late 1960s and early 1970s Khensur Ngawang Nyima was employed as a lecturer in Buddhist Philosophy and Mongolian. **Teaching Programme** The Kern Institute offers courses in: (1) Indian Philosophy, Buddhism, Tibetan, and Pali; (2) Vedic Sanskrit, Classical Sanskrit, Old and Middle Iranian, and Middle Vedic languages; (3) Modern South Asian history; (4) Modern Indian languages; (5) Art and Material Culture of South Asia. **Facilities and Services** The Kern Institute houses an extensive collection of Tibetan manuscripts and xylographs (*c.* 2100). These have not been extensively catalogued as yet, except for a copy of the Lhasa *Kangyur* (*bKa' 'gyur*) and a large collection of early publications on Buddhism and Buddhist Studies.

Cultural Organisations and Tibetan Refugee Aid Societies

STICHTING ONTMOETING MET TIBETAANSE
Address Postbus 340, Tilburg, Holland, 5000 AH. **Tel** 013 4217201. **Distribution Details** Subscription to *Tibetan Review* available.

TIBETAN AFFAIRS COORDINATION OFFICE, TACO
Address Postbus 1276, Utrecht, Holland, NL 3500 BG.

Ecumenical Centres

DE KOSMOS

Address Prins Hendrikkade 142, Amsterdam, Holland, 1011 AT. **Tel** (020) 267477. **Telex/Fax** 2902480. **Year Established** 1967. Founder Eckart Dissen. **General Description** Kosmos is an adult education centre, which was originally set up in 1967. Up to 1986 it was subsidised by the Dutch government, but it is now in the process of establishing itself as a completely self-sufficient organisation. Its aims are to provide training and educational facilities for the development of consciousness and spirituality. Programmes run at the centre include: yoga, Buddhist meditation, martial arts, esoteric studies, and practical courses in holistic health. **Teaching Programme** All courses at Kosmos are offered on three levels: orientation (beginning), study (advanced) and training (professional education). A wide range of Buddhist teachings and meditation programmes are available. Specifically Tibetan related subjects include weekly classes on *Time, Space and Knowledge*, and on *Kum Nye Relaxation*, according to the systems developed by Tarthang Tulku. A monthly class derived from Nyingma teachings is concerned with mantra recitation, and weekly classes are given by Geshe Lama Konchog Lhundrup on Tibetan Buddhist meditation. Tibetan language instruction is offered weekly, and there are regularly organised lectures and seminars on all aspects of Buddhism. A yearly programme of 'Tibet Days' is scheduled to commemorate the Chinese occupation of Tibet and to draw attention to the Tibetan cultural and religious heritage. Among the many teachers who have visited Kosmos are: H.H. Gyalwa Karmapa (several times), Lama Thubten Yeshe, Lama Thubten Zopa, Chime Rinpoche, Sogyal Rinpoche, Namkhai Norbu Rinpoche, and Gawang Rinpoche. Kosmos have also hosted a number of Tibetan doctors, including Dr Lobsang Dolma, Dr Trogawa Rinpoche and Dr Lobsang Wangyal. **Facilities and Services** A well equipped library is located at the Centre, and there is an extensive tape library which is currently being catalogued. Other facilities include a bookshop, a sauna, and a health food restaurant. Regular exhibitions of photographs, as well as slide and film shows, are arranged. **Project Description** Kosmos intends to continue organising Buddhist related activities and to be involved in both national and international initiatives concerned with the development and preservation of Buddhist culture.

Museums

NATIONAL MUSEUM OF ETHNOLOGY (HOLLAND)

Address Steenstraat 1, P.O. Box 212, Leiden, Holland, 2300 AE. **Tel** (071) 21 18 24. **Telex/Fax** (071) 12 84 37.

RIJKS MUSEUM, DUTCH NATIONAL MUSEUM

Address Department of Asiatic Art, Postbus 50673, 1007 DD Amsterdam, Noord-Holland, Holland. **Tel** 020 73 21 21. **Telex/Fax** 020 79 8146. **General Description** The Department of Asiatic Art of the Rijks Museum has a small collection of eighteenth and nineteenth century Tibetan art objects. These include: one painted clay and four bronze sculptures, and five thangkas.

Publishing Companies and Journals

E.J. BRILL
Address Plantijnstraat 2, PO Box 9000, Leiden, Holland, 2300 PA. **Tel** 0 71 31 26 24. **Telex/Fax** 0 71 31 75 32.

Teaching Centres

KAGYU RINTCHEN GYAMTSO LING
Address Zijlweg 79, Haarlem, Holland, 2013 DD. **Tel** 23 420 955.

KARMA DELEG CHOPEL LING
Address Schoener 14–23, Lelystad, Holland, 8243 TH. **Tel** 03200–52526. **Lama/Scholar** Lama Gawang.

MAITREYA INSTITUUT
Address Heemhoeveweg 2, Emst, Holland, 8166 HA. **Tel** (05787) 1450. **Telex/Fax** 05787 1851. **Distribution Details** Audio tapes are copied and sold for study purposes. Books and transcripts are distributed throughout Benelux. **Year Established** 1979. **Founder** Lama Thubten Yeshe. **Lama/Scholar** Geshe Sonam Gyaltsen. **General Description** Maitreya Instituut is a study and meditation centre, offering courses in Dutch and English. It promotes Mahayana Buddhism in the Netherlands and seeks to integrate Dharma teachings within a contemporary Western setting. **Teaching Programme** The centre sponsors a number of weekend and longer courses that are given by the resident Tibetan lama, Geshe Sonam Gyaltsen, and other visiting teachers. Past courses have been concerned with: the graduated path to enlightenment (*Lam Rim*); death, bardo and rebirth; Buddha nature; and a variety of other topics from sutra and tantra.

The year is divided into three terms, and courses are given in Dutch and/or English. A daily programme of meditations and pujas is maintained. **Facilities and Services** Facilities in the centre include a shrine room; a shop selling Buddhist books and other articles; a coffee bar, dining room and a library containing books and audio tapes of past teachings. Caravans and some rooms are set aside for those wishing to practide retreats and facilities are also rented out to groups. Maitreya Instituut publishes a quarterly newsletter, *Maitreya Magazine*, which is distributed throughout the Netherlands. The centre publishes translations of English-language books on Buddhism in Dutch, as well as a number of sadhanas and prayers. **Project Description** The institute is affiliated to the 'Nederlandse Stichting ter Bevordering van de Tibetaanse Geneeskunde' – an organization that promotes public awareness of Tibetan medicine and the Maitreya Zwolle.

MAITREYA ZWOLLE
Address Steenstraat 5–7, Zwolle, Holland, 8011 TT. **Tel** 038 222471. **Telex/Fax** 038 229302. **General Description** This is the city centre affiliate of the Maitreya Instituut.

SAKYA THEGCHEN LING
Address Laan van Meerdervoort 200a, The Hague, Holland, 2517 BJ. **Tel** (070) 360 66 49. **Distribution Details** Please contact the centre for further information. **Year Established** 1976. **Founder** Geshe Lama Sherab Gyaltsen Amipa. **General Description** Sakya Thegchen Ling was founded in 1976 following the visit of Geshe Lama Sherab Gyaltsen Amipa to the Netherlands. In 1985 the centre's organisational structure was developed and it became formally established as a foundation with the declared aim of furthering 'the study, practice and propagation of Mahayana Buddhism', and 'the preservation and continuation of Tibetan culture'. Over

the years a number of eminent lamas have visited Sakya Thegchen Ling, including H.H. Sakya Trizin in 1978 and 1984, and H.H. Jigdal Dagchen Rinpoche in 1980. Lama Sherab regularly gives teachings at the centre, which are supplemented by study evenings reviewing the range of material covered. **Teaching Programme** On alternate Thursdays, centre members meet to study Buddhist doctrine, and on the remaining Thursdays there are opportunities to work with recorded discourses given by Lama Sherab. A ten-week beginners course is scheduled for Tuesdays. The first seven weeks are concerned with the fundamental principles of Buddhism as described in the *Lamdre (Lam 'bras)*, or Path and its Fruit teachings. The remaining three lessons present an introduction to the practice of meditation. Lama Sherab visits three times a year and has given commentaries to such texts as Nagarjuna's *The Seven Stages for Spiritual Training*, Shantideva's *Bodhisattvacarya-vatara*, Atisha's *The Jewel Ornament of a Bodhisattva*, and *Mahakaruna* by rJe btsun Grags pa rGyal mtshan. Recently, he has given teachings entitled, 'Training of the Mind; the Path of a Bodhisattva', as well as explaining a related thirty-seven part meditational system. **Facilities and Services** Sakya Thegchen Ling maintains a shrine-room where statues of Shakyamuni Buddha, Manjushri and Sachen Kunga Nyingpo, the founder of the Sakya Tradition, can be seen. A newsletter is distributed to keep members informed about centre activities. Buddhist texts, including Lama Sherab's book, *Training of the Mind (De Training van de Geest* – Anhk Hermes, Deventer), can be obtained in the bookshop. **Project Description** An emphasis of the centre is the translation of texts into Dutch.

HONG KONG

Cultural Organisations and Tibetan Refugee Aid Societies

BUDDHIST PERCEPTION OF NATURE
Address 5H Bowen Road, 1st Floor, Hong Kong. **Tel** 523 3464. **Telex/Fax** 869 1619. **General Description** This organisation researches, translates, and publishes Buddhist literature, with environmental themes, with the aim of increasing awareness of the environmental crisis in Tibet and the world.

WISDOM ARCHIVE
Address P.O. Box 98650, TST, Kowloon, Hong Kong. **Tel** (852) 524 4565. **Telex/Fax** (852) 721 2942. **General Description** The Wisdom Archive contains all known tapes, transcripts, and disk versions of teachings by Lama Thubten Yeshe and Lama Thubten Zopa Rinpoche. In addition to the physical and computer disk archive, there is a database listing details of teachings traced, catalogued by date, place, subject, contact people, editor, publisher, language etc. There are now approximately 80Mb of teaching material on disk, 3500 tapes and 30,000 pages of transcripts. 1300 tapes are still to be transcribed. The disk library is on

hard disk and is indexed and cross referenced. The archive spans from 1968 to the present date. It is hoped later to include Geshes, and other teachers.

Teaching Centres

CHAM-TSE LING
Address 546 Nathan Road, 14th floor flat A, Kowloon, Hong Kong. **Tel** 770 7239. **Telex/Fax** 523 3622.

KARMA KAGYU (HK) BUDDHIST SOCIETY
Address 3/F, Wah to Building, 42 Wood Road, Hong Kong. **Tel** 5661123, 8070321. **Telex/Fax** 8876316.

SAKYA CENTRE
Address Flat G YF Cherry Mansion, 27 Oak Street, Kowloon, Hong Kong.

THRANGU VAJRAYANA BUDDHIST CENTRE
Address 29 Station Lane, 3/F, Hung Hom, Kowloon, Hong Kong.

HUNGARY

Academic Organisations

ATTILA JOZSEF UNIVERSITY, DEPARTMENT OF ALTAIC STUDIES
Address Egyetem u.2, Szeged, Hungary, H–6722. **Lama/Scholar** Prof A. Rona-Tas, Dr Arpad Berta. **General Description** The department offers a five-year MA degree course and a three-year PhD in Tibetan Studies. Tibetan studies are facilitated in Szeged by the library of the late Professor Louis Ligeti.

COLLEGE OF EASTERN LANGUAGES, KOROSI CSOMA SOCIETY
Address Izabella u. 46, Budapest, Hungary, 1064. Tel 423 130. Lama/Scholar Prof Jozsef Terjek, Dr Gyorgy Somlai.

ELTA UNIVERSITY, INNER ASIAN FACULTY
Address, Budapest, Hungary. **Lama/Scholar** Prof Jozsef Terjek.

Cultural Organisations and Tibetan Refugee Aid Societies

KOROSI CSOMA SOCIETY
Address 12A Bella, ut 46, Budapest, Hungary, 1064. **Lama/Scholar** Dr Gyorgy Hazai (President), Dr Geza Bethlanfalvy (Secretary). **General Description** The Korosi Csoma Society publishes books and papers on Oriental topics, including Tibet. The society also sponsors the Korosi Csoma Symposiums on academic Tibetan studies, every four years, which alternates every two years with the conferences of the International Association of Tibetan Studies. There is a Korosi Csoma Museum with some Tibetan items.

Ecumenical Centres

BUDDHIST INFORMATION BUREAU, DHARMA PRESS AGENCY
Address 5 Muzeum Street, Budapest, Hungary, H–1088. **Tel** 011 189258. **Telex/Fax** 011 189258. **Lama/Scholar** Dr Ernest Hetenyi (President). **General Description** This is a continuation of the Buddhista Misszio of the Arya Maitreya Mandala of Lama Govinda.

TIBET SOCIETY
Address Ungvar u. 30, Budapest, Hungary, 1142. **Lama/Scholar** Prof Jozsef Terjek (President). **General Description** This is a combination academic and non-sectarian Buddhist centre for those who have studied the Tibetan language.

Libraries

LIBRARY OF HUNGARIAN ACADEMY OF SCIENCES, ORIENTAL COLLECTION
Address V. Arany Janos u. 1, PF7, Budapest, Hungary, 1361. **Tel** 011

224132. **Telex/Fax** 011 31 6954. **Lama/Scholar** Dr Gyorgy
Rozsa (Director General), Dr. Eva Apor (Head of Oriental Dept.),
Elizabeth Toth (Keeper of Tibetan Collection). **General
Description** This library has a Tibetan collection of about 3000
volumes of xylographs and manuscripts, which are all microfilmed.
A catalogue of the Csoma de Koros collection consisting of thirty-
six volumes is available.

Museums

FERENC HOPP MUSEUM

Address Museum of Applied Arts, Ulloi ut 33–37, Budapest IX,
P.O.B 3, Hungary, H–1450. **Tel** 011 17 5635. **Telex/Fax** 361
117 5880. **Distribution Details** Yearbook *Arts Decorativa* and
exhibition catalogue by library exchange. **Year Established** 1919.
Founder Ferenc Hopp. **Lama/Scholar** Dr Maria Ferenczy
(Chief Curator), Bela Kelenyi (Tibetologue), Dr Judit Vinkovics
(Librarian, Mongolist), Gyorgyi Fajcsak. **General Description**
The Tibetan and Nepalese collection of the Ferenc Hopp
Museum includes around 190 objects. The majority of them
(about seventy pieces) are small sculptures and paintings (eighteenth and ninteenth centuries), and there is also jewellery,
weapons, woodcuts, books etc. within the Nepalese material. The
Nepalese figurines form a special feature in the small sculpture
range. **Project Description** The museum plans to hold an exhibition of Lamaist Sculpture and Buddhist Art.

Publishing Companies and Journals

ORIENT PRESS

Address Alkotmany u 83, Budapest XXII, Hungary, 1221.
Lama/Scholar Dr Jozsef Horvath. **General Description** The
Orient Press translate and publish books about Tibet from English
and German into Hungarian.

Teaching Centres

KARMA RATNA LING DARGYE

Address Hunyadi Utca 45, Budapest, Hungary, 1039. **Tel** 011
608 847. **Lama/Scholar** Gyula Steiner (President).

SAKYA TASHI CHOLING

Address Vaci utca 7, Budapest, Hungary, 1052. **Tel** 011 189 115.

INDIA

Academic Organisations

CENTRAL INST. OF HIGHER TIBETAN STUDIES

Address P.O. Sarnath, Varanasi, U.P., India, 221007. **Tel**
42881/45036. **Telex/Fax** 542 45036. **Year Established** 1967.
Lama/Scholar Prof. Ven. Samdhong Rinpoche, Director, Prof.

Geshe Yeshe Thabkhey (Tibetan Studies), Prof. Sempa Dorjee (Sanskrit/Tibetan Studies), Prof. K.N. Mishra (Sanskrit), Prof. R.S. Tripathi (Research Professor). **General Description** The institute is recognised as an independent university and holds courses from undergraduate to postgraduate levels in Buddhology and Tibetology. There are four courses: a 2-year Purva Madhyama course (equivalent to 10th standard); 2-year Uttar Madhyama course (Intermediate); 3-year Shastri course (equivalent to a Bachelor's degree); and a 2-year Acarya course (equivalent to a Master's degree). New course subjects are planned in history, medicine, archeology, astrology, and vocational training. Research in all aspects of Buddhology and Tibetology, Himalayan region studies and Sanskrit studies are also conducted. **Facilities and Services** The institute has an extensive and well catalogued library of Buddhology, Tibetology, Himalayan Region Studies, Sanskrit studies and allied subjects. Several sets of the Buddhist canon in different editions, over 80000 Buddhist text titles in Tibetan including microforms, over 40,000 books in various languages. Documents/materials are available in a variety of formats: manuscripts, zylographs, monographs, printed books, micro documents, audio, video etc. A computerised catalogue database is in progress. **Project Description** Restoration of lost Sanskrit texts from Tibetan sources, translation of Tibetan texts into Sanskrit, Hindi, English. Critical editing and publications of important and rare Buddhist texts. Research into vital areas of Buddhist and Tibetan studies.

NAMGYAL INSTITUTE OF TIBETOLOGY
Address, Gangtok, Sikkim, India.

Cultural Organisations and Tibetan Refugee Aid Societies

DELHI NALANDA INSTITUTE
Address B 19–20, Mehrauli Institutional Area, New Delhi, India, 110016.

Tel 650 767. **Telex/Fax** 332 7527. **Year Established** 1989. **Founder** H.H. Sixteenth Karmapa. **General Description** The Delhi Nalanda Institute of Higher Buddhist Studies was opened in 1989. It was founded to fulfil the late Karmapa's vision of an institution to help preserve Tibetan Buddhism through translation and study of the great Buddhist treatises. The site for the building was donated by the government of India. The building is in the style of a large Tibetan monastery, five stories high and covering over 80,000 square feet in total. There are three residential wings able to accommodate 120 students. It is intended to hold international conferences at the institute, ⏐to publish translated and scholastic works, and to develop the institute into a fully accredited university where students can engage in degree and post-degree level studies. An important part of the institute is the large library, where it is hoped that many thousands of Buddhist texts can be preserved, and around 150,000 books and periodicals will be collected. A microfilm collection of especially rare and fragile Buddhist texts is planned.

INDO TIBETAN CULTURAL INSTITUTE
Address Sadhudhara, Baghdara Road, Kalimpong, Distt Darjeeling, WB, India.

INTERNATIONAL ACADEMY OF INDIAN CULTURE
Address J–22 Haus Khas Enclave, New Delhi, India, 110016. **Tel** 665800. **Founder** Prof Dr Raghuvira. **Lama/Scholar** Prof Lokesh Chandra. **General Description** The academy houses a large collection of rare printed books on Tibet and a rich collection of Tibetan manuscripts and xylographs. Included are the *Peking Kangyur* and *Tengyur*, *Narthang Kangyur*, *Urga Kangyur* in original xylographs and the *Mongolian Kangyur* in original xylographs.

LIBRARY OF TIBETAN WORKS AND ARCHIVES

Address Gangchen Kyishong, Dharamsala, H.P., India, 176215. **Tel** 2467. **Distribution Details** For a catalogue of materials distributed, please contact the secretary. **Year Established** 1972. **Founder** H.H. Fourteenth Dalai Lama. **Lama/Scholar** Geshe Sonam Rinchen, Geshe Dawa, Achok Rinpoche, Geshe Lodro Rinpoche, Tsayul Rinpoche, Sangtsang Rinpoche. **General Description** The Library of Tibetan Works and Archives was founded by H.H. the Dalai Lama in 1970 and officially began to function from 1 November 1971. It was founded with the aim of preserving and propagating the culture of Tibet. The building itself was built according to an authentic Tibetan pattern. There are three resident lamas: Geshe Sonam Rinchen, Geshe Dawa and Achok Rinpoche. The library is run on grant-in-aid received annually from the Department of Culture, Ministry of Human Resources Development, Government of India, volunteer associations and individuals. The governing body has the Dalai Lama as Chairman. There are seven departments each with their own respective heads. These are: Administration; Centre for Tibetan Studies; Publication, Research and Translation; Books and Manuscripts; Foreign Language Reference; Oral History; and Museum and Archives. **Teaching Programme** The department for Tibetan Studies has four sub-departments, each with its own programme of classes. These are: Buddhist Philosophy; Tibetan Language; Thangka Painting; and Woodcarving.

The publications department brings out the four annual issues of *The Tibet Journal* and has published over 300 books in both Tibetan and English since 1971. The books and manuscripts department maintains the library's collection of literary materials in the Tibetan language. The present collection consists of about 60,000 titles. The foreign language section houses books, periodicals and newspaper clippings on all aspects of Tibet and Trans-Himalayan civilisation, in languages other than Tibetan. **Facilities and Services** The books and manuscripts department and the foreign language section are open to the public. Lama-scholars and translators are available to assist scholars and students of Tibetology in their research. The museum and archives department is also open to the visitors where they can view a collection of objects of art. **Project Description** The department of research and translation pursue their own long-term projects of research and translation. Work is in progress on the fourth volume of the *Catalogue of the Library of Tibetan Works and Archives*. The fifth, sixth and seventh volumes will be published in due course and will deal respectively with: works of medicine, Bon, astrology, language and literature; lamas' collected works; and Buddhist philosophy and dialectics. A microfilming project is also in progress, with the aim not only to preserve the library's own manuscripts collection in microfilm form, but especially with the aim of obtaining microfilm copies of rare and important manuscripts and documents held in other collections. A planned catalogue of the museum collection is also in the process of publication.

SANGYE CHOLING TIBETAN ASSOCIATION

Address Sanjoli, Simla 6, H.P., India.

TIBET HOUSE

Address 1 Institutional Area, Lodhi Road, New Delhi, India, 110003. **Tel** 611 515. **Year Established** 1965. **Founder** H.H. Fourteenth Dalai Lama. **Lama/Scholar** Doboom Rinpoche (Director). **General Description** Tibet House is a society established by H.H. the Dalai Lama in 1965, to help promote science, literature and fine arts. The society has been emphasising the promotion of Tibetan and Buddhist studies and culture by organising conferences, seminars, lectures, discourses and dialogues. It endeavours to create awareness of the importance of the art and cultural heritage of Tibet by organising competitions and exhibitions in various fields. It also conducts regular research and publication programmes. **Teaching Programme** The teaching programme details are available direct from Tibet House, and are listed in the twice-yearly issues of the *Tibet House Bulletin*. **Facilities and Services** The Society has a museum containing rare and important pieces: icons, thangkas, jewellery and other art and cultural objects, and a library holding editions of the *Kangyur*, *Tengyur* and some rare manuscripts. It co-ordinates an international Study Group called CO-TACHS (The Circle of Tibetan Art and Cultural Heritage Studies) whose membership is open to individuals and institutions concerned with Tibetan and Buddhist Studies.

TIBETAN BONPO FOUNDATION

Address New Tobgyal, Dolanji Village, P.O. Ochghat, Via Solan, H.P., India.

TIBETAN INSTITUTE OF PERFORMING ARTS

Address P.O. McLeod Ganj, Dharamsala, Distt Kangra, H.P., India, 176219. **Tel** (1892) 2478. **Telex/Fax** (1892) 2357. **Year Established** 1959. **General Description** The Tibetan Institute of Performing Arts was founded in India in August 1959 after the flight into exile of the Tibetan refugees escaping the Chinese occupation. The purpose of the organisation is to preserve the cultural identity of the Tibetan people through the medium of the performing arts. Stories representing the importance of Buddhist thought in Tibetan culture are performed in Tibet's indigenous opera form called Lhamo. A Lhamo performance involves dance, mime and a singing style unique to Tibetan opera. The actors are accompanied by two musicians, a drummer and a cymbalist. While the plot and sung dialogue adhere strictly to classical texts, much topical repartee is interspersed between the scenes. In recent years the opera company has travelled to give performances abroad, visiting Europe, Australia and the USA. **Teaching Programme** Actors are divided into several categories including teachers, junior teachers, general performers, musicians and trainees. A new performer usually trains for one year before he or she begins to take part in opera or folk dance performances. Training involves study of choreography, the playing of musical instruments and voice development, as well as memorisation of traditional opera texts. In addition, TIPA trains instructors in drama and music for the Tibetan schools in India and Nepal.

TIBETAN NUNS PROJECT

Address 119 Khazanchi Mohalla, Dharamsala, H.P., India, 176215. **Tel** 01892 2643. **General Description** The Tibetan Nuns Project aims to provide basic needs, shelter, sustenance and health care, for the recent influx of refugee nuns from Tibet who began arriving in large numbers in early 1991 and continue to arrive on a monthly basis. The project also aims to provide a range of educational facilities. A research programme is envisaged to document the current and historical conditions, lifestyles, demographic details, and biographies of Tibetan nuns. It is hoped that through the project the stature, education, and lifestyle options of the nuns, and of Tibetan women in general, will be increased.

Government Offices

BUREAU OF H.H. THE DALAI LAMA, DELHI
Address 10-A Ring Road, Lajpat Nagar IV, New Delhi, India, 110024. **Tel** (11) 641 4888. **Telex/Fax** (11) 646 1914.

CENTRAL TIBETAN RELIEF COMMITTEE
Address Gangchen Kyishong, Dharamsala, Dist. Kangra, H.P., India, 176215. **Tel** 1892 2214.

COUNCIL FOR RELIGIOUS AND CULTURAL AFFAIRS
Address Gangchen Kyishong, Dharamsala, Distt Kangra, H.P., India, 176215. **Tel** 1892 2685.

EDUCATION DEPARTMENT
Address Gangchen Kyishong, Dharamsala, Distt Kangra, H.P., India, 176215. **Tel** 1892 2572/2721.

KASHAG, TIBETAN COUNCIL OF MINISTERS
Address Gangchen Kyishong, Dharamsala, Distt Kangra, H.P., India, 176215. **Tel** 1892 2457/2598.

OFFICE OF H.H. THE DALAI LAMA
Address Thekchen Choeling, McLeod Ganj, Dharamsala, Distt Kangra, H.P., India, 176219.

OFFICE OF INFORMATION
Address Gangchen Kyishong, Dharamsala, Distt Kangra, H.P., India, 176215. **Tel** 1892 2457/2598. **Telex/Fax** 1892 4357.

Medical Institutions

DEKYI KHANGKAR TIBET MEDICAL CLINIC
Address McLeod Ganj, Dharamsala, Distt Kangra, H.P., India, 176219. **Tel** 2468. **Lama/Scholar** Dr Dolma (formerly).

DR YESHI DONDEN MEDICAL CLINIC
Address Ashoka Niwas, McLeod Ganj, Dharamsala, H.P., India, 176219. **Tel** 2461. **Lama/Scholar** Dr Yeshi Donden.

MAITRI LEPROSY CENTRE
Address P.O. Bodhgaya, Bodhgaya, Bihar, India, 824231. **Tel** 631 20704. **Telex/Fax** 631 23600.

TIBETAN HOLISTIC MEDICAL CENTRE
Address Tshering House, 193 McLeod Ganj, Dharamsala, Distt Kangra, H.P., India, 176219. **Lama/Scholar** Dr Lobsang Rabgay.

TIBETAN MEDICAL AND ASTRO INSTITUTE, DELHI

Address 13 Jaipur Estate, Nizamuddin East, New Delhi, India, 110013. **Tel** 698503. **Lama/Scholar** Dr Tamdin, Dr Kungyur, Dr Choeden Kyizon.

TIBETAN MEDICAL AND ASTROLOGICAL INSTITUTE

Address Khara Danda Road, Dharamsala, Distt Kangra, H.P., India, 176215. **Tel** (1892) 2618. **Lama/Scholar** Dr Tenzin Choedak (Head of Research Dept.), Dr Wangyal, Dr Kelchoe, Dr Dawa Choden. **General Description** The institute has fifty-five branches throughout India and Nepal.

TIBETAN MEDICAL STORE

Address N Division, P.O. Bir, Bir, Distt Kangra, H.P., India, 176077.

YUTHOK INSTITUTE OF TIBETAN MEDICINE

Address Choglamsar, Leh, Ladhak, J and K, India. **Tel** 698503. **Lama/Scholar** Dr Chunglock Younten.

Monasteries and Nunneries

BIR SAKYA LAMA'S SCHOOL

Address P.O. Bir Chowgan, Distt Kangra, H.P., India.

BOKAR MONASTERY

Address Deosey Dara, P.O. Mirik, Distt Darjeeling, W.B., India.

BON MONASTIC CENTRE

Address Dolanji Village, P.O. Ochghat, Via Solan, H.P., India. **Tel** 34.

CHODHE TASHILHUNPO

Address Dickyi Larsoe Tibetan Settlement, Cauvery Valley Project, P.O. Bylakuppe, Distt Mysore, Karnataka, India, 571104.

CHOKLING BUDDHIST MONASTERY

Address P.O. Bir, Distt Kangra, H.P., India.

DAKPO DATSANG

Address Tibetan Settlement, Mainpat, P.O. Kamleshwarpur, Distt Surguja, M.P., India.

DECHEN CHOEKORLING KAGYU MONASTERY

Address Tibetan Settlement, P.O. Clement-Town, Distt Dehra Dun, U.P., India, 248001.

DECHEN CHOEPHEL LING MONASTERY

Address Phuntsok Ling Tibetan Settlement, Lama Camp No. 1, P.O. Chandragiri, Distt Ganjam, Orissa, India, 761017.

DELHI KARMAPAE CHOEDHEY

Address Ladhak Buddha Vihara, Bela Road, New Delhi 54, India. **Tel** 650767.

DHARGYE GON

Address Tibetan Settlement, P.O. Tibetan Colony, Kollegal Taluk, Distt Mysore, Karnataka, India.

DIP TSECHOK LING MONASTERY

Address Camel Track Road, P.O. Mcleod Ganj, Dharamsala, Distt Kangra, H.P., India, 176219.

DODRUP CHEN MONASTERY

Address, Gangtok, Sikkim, India.

DREPUNG GOMANG MONASTERY

Address P.O. Tibetan Colony, Lama Camp No. 2, Mundgod, North Kanara, Karnataka, India, 581411.

DREPUNG LOSELING MONASTERY

Address P.O. Tibetan Colony, Lama Camp No 2, Mundgod, North Kanara, Karnataka, India, 581411. **Tel** 102.

DRIKUNG DHARMA CENTRE

Address Phayang Gonpa, Choglamsar, Distt Leh, Ladakh, J and K, India.

DRIKUNG INSTITUTE

Address P.O. Box 48, Dehra Dun, U.P., India, 248001.

DRIKUNG KAGYU INSTITUTE
Address 0/44 – A Manjuka Tila, Delhi, India.

DRIKUNG KAGYU MONASTERY
Address P.O. Rewalsar, Distt Mandi, H.P., India.

DRUKPA BUDDHIST MONASTERY
Address 23 Sanchal Road, Jore Bungalow, P.O. Ghoom, Distt Darjeeling, W.B., India.

DUDUL RABTEN LING
Address Phuntsok Ling Tibetan Settlement, Camp 2, P.O. Chandragiri, Distt Ganjam, Orissa, India, 761017.

DUNG GON SAMTEN CHOLING
Address P.O. Ghoom, Distt Darjeeling, W.B., India.

DZOGCHEN RUDHAM SAMTEN LING
Address Dhonden Ling Tibetan Settlement, P.O. Tibetan Colony, Kollegal Taluk, Mysore, Karnataka, India.

DZONGKAR CHODE MONASTERY
Address Rabgyeling Tibetan Settlement, P.O. Gurupura, Via Hunsur, Distt Mysore, Karnataka, India, 571105.

DZONGSAR INSTITUTE
Address c/o Royal Bhutanese Embassy, Chanakyapuri, New Delhi, India. **Tel** 292 8036.

DZONGSAR INSTITUTE (BIR BRANCH)
Address P.O. Bir, Distt Kangra, H.P., India, 176077.

EVAM CHOEGAR GYURME LING
Address Tibetan Settlement, P.O. Bir, Distt Kangra, H.P., India.

GADONG BUDDHIST MONASTERY
Address Gangchen Kyishong, Dharamsala, Distt Kangra, H.P., India, 176215.

GANDEN CHOELING NUNNERY
Address P.O. Mcleod Ganj, Dharamsala, Distt Kangra, H.P., India, 176219.

GANDEN CHOEPHELING TIBETAN MONASTERY
Address Upper Lumbering, P.O. Shillong, Meghalaya, India.

GANDEN JANGTSE BUDDHIST MONASTERY
Address P.O. Tibetan Colony, Lama Camp No 1, Mundgod, North Kanara, Karnataka, India, 581411.

GANDEN PHELGYELING MONASTERY
Address P.O. Bodh Gaya, Distt Gaya, Bihar, India.

GANDEN SHARTSE BUDDHIST MONASTERY
Address P.O. Tibetan Colony, Lama Camp No 1, Mundgod, North Kanara, Karnataka, India, 581411.

GANDEN SHEDRUP DHARGYE LING
Address P.O. Sarnath, Varanasi, U.P., India.

GANDEN SHEDRUP DHARGYELING
Address Harianjana, P.O. Bodh Gaya, Distt Gaya, Bihar, India.

GANDEN TASHI CHOELING MONASTERY
Address P.O. Sukhai Pokhari, Distt Darjeeling, W.B., India, 734 101.

GANDEN THARPA CHOELING MONASTERY
Address Tripai, P.O. Kalimpong, Distt Darjeeling, W.B., India, 734 301.

GANDEN THEKCHEN LING
Address Lungsang Samdupling Tibetan Settlement, Camp No. 2, P.O. Bylakuppe, Distt Mysore, Karnataka, India, 571104.

GANDEN THEKCHENLING
Address Norgyeling Tibetan Settlement, P.O. Pratapgarh, Distt Bhandhara, Maharashtra, India.

GANDEN THEKCHOK LING
Address P.O. Manali, Distt Kulu, H.P., India.

GANGTOK BHOSHUNG GURU LHAKANG
Address Nyingmapa Tsechu Association, P.O. Deorali, Gangtok, Sikkim, India.

GOMANG TASHI KHIL MONASTERY
Address Thondup Ling Tibetan Settlement, P.O. Clement-Town, Distt Dehra Dun, U.P., India.

GONJANG SAMTEN CHOEPUG MONASTERY
Address P.O. Ranbull, Distt Darjeeling, W.B., India, 734101.

GYUME TANTRIC MONASTERY
Address P.O. Gurupura, Via Hunsur, Mysore, Karnataka, India, 571188. **Tel** Hunsur 175.

GYUTO TANTRIC MONASTERY
Address Tibetan Settlement, Tenzin Gang, P.O. Kalakthang, Bomdila, Distt Kameng, A.P., India.

HEMIS MONASTERY
Address B.P.O. Changar, Distt Leh, Ladakh, J and K, India, 194101.

HIMALAYAN NYINGMA MONASTERY
Address Khenpo Thupten, P.O. Manali, Distt Kulu, H.P., India.

INSTITUTE OF BUDDHIST DIALECTICS
Address Thekchen Choling, McLeod Ganj, Dharamsala, Distt Kangra, H.P., India, 176219. **Tel** (1892) 2215. **General Description** Courses are offered to foreigners for the study of the traditional Tibetan disciplines of dialectical philosophy, grammar, poetry, etc. There is also a Tibetan language, translation and publication division. **Facilities and Services** An annual newsletter, *Lhagsam Tsegpa*, is published in Tibetan.

JAMYANG CHOLING, BUDDHIST INSTITUTE FOR WOMEN
Address Macleod Ganj, Dharamsala, Distt Kangra, H.P., India, 176219. **Year Established** 1987. **Founder** Karma Lekshe Tsomo. **General Description** Jamyang Choling Institute for Buddhist Women provides monastic training and educational facilities for women of the Tibetan tradition. It is a non-sectarian, non-profit organisation registered as a charity both in California and Himachal Pradesh, seeking to promote the educational development of Buddhist women and to train women teachers in the Tibetan tradition. Students come from Tibet, Nepal, Ladakh, Kinnaur, Spiti and Maharashtra. There are currently twenty-six students, with twenty

in residence. In addition to the Jamyang Choling Institute in Dharamsala there are two other affiliates in Zanskar, Ladakh. **Teaching Programme** The institute offers a full-time training programme in meditation and the traditional Tibetan monastic curriculum, as well as classes in Tibetan grammar, English and Hindi. The daily programme includes group meditation, chanting, debate, and classes in logic, Prajnaparamita (Buddhist philosophy), Tibetan grammar, English and Hindi. The medium of teaching is Tibetan.

JANCHUB CHOLING TIBETAN MONASTERY
Address Dhargyeling Tibetan Settlement, P.O. Tindoling, Via Tezu, Distt Lohit, A.P., India.

JANGCHUB CHOELING
Address Dickyiling Tibetan Settlement, P.O. Kulhan, Sahasdhara Road, Distt Dehra Dun, U.P., India, 248001.

JANGCHUB LING NUNNERY
Address c/o Dhogueling Tibetan Settlement, P.O. Tibetan Colony, Mundgod, N. Kanara, Karnataka, India, 581411.

KACHOE DECHEN LING MONASTERY
Address P.O. Sonada, Distt Darjeeling, W.B., India.

KARMA CHOKOR DECHEN NUNNERY
Address P.O. Rumtek, Via Ranipul, Sikkim, India, 737135.

KARMA DUPGYUD CHOELING
Address T.R. Settlement No 1, Choglamsar, Distt Leh, Ladakh, J & K, India.

KARMA SHEDRUP LING KAGYU MONASTERY
Address Dhoguling Tibetan Settlement, P.O. Tibetan Colony, Mundgod, North Kanara, Karnataka, India, 581411.

KARMA SHEDRUP THARGYE CHOKORLING
Address Vajrayana Buddhist Monastery, P.O. Bodh Gaya, Distt Gaya, Bihar, India. **Lama** H.E. Beru Khyentse Rinpoche.

KARMA THARGYE CHOKORLING KAGYU MONASTERY
Address Tibetan Settlement Mainpat, P.O. Kamleshwarpur, Distt Surguja, M.P., India. **Lama** H.E Beru Khyentse Rinpoche.

KARMAE SHRI NALANDA INSTITUTE
Address P.O. Rumtek, Via Ranipul, Sikkim, India, 737135.

KHAM KATHOK GON MONASTERY
Address Kham Khatok Tibetan Settlement, P.O. Sataun, Distt Sirmour, H.P., India.

KYIRONG TASHI CHOELING
Address P.O. Mcleod Ganj, Dharamsala, Distt Kangra, H.P., India, 176219.

MAHAYANA BUDDHIST NUNNERY, KARMA DRUPGUE DHARGYE LING

Address P.O. Tilokpur, Distt Kangra, H.P., India.

MAHAYANA MONASTERY TASHI CHOLING

Address P.O. Rarang, Distt Kinnaur, H.P., India. **Founder** Karma Thinley Rinpoche

NAMGYAL BUDDHIST MONASTERY

Address P.O. Mcleod Ganj, Dharamsala, Distt Kangra, H.P., India, 176219.

NAMKHA KHYONGZONG

Address Dhoguling Tibetan Settlement, P.O. Tibetan Colony, Mundgod, N. Kanara, Karnataka, India, 581411.

NECHUNG DRAYANGLING MONASTERY

Address Gangchen Kyishong, Dharamsala, Distt Kangra, H.P., India, 176215.

NGAKPA DATSANG

Address Tibetan Colony, Civil Line, Majunu Katilla, Delhi, India, 54.

NGOR AWANG INSTITUTE

Address Dege Division, P.O. Bir, Distt Kangra, H.P., India.

NGOR PAL EWAM CHO DEN

Address P.O. Manduwala, Via Prem Nagar, Distt Dehra Dun, U.P., India.

NEDON GATSAL LING NYINGMA MONASTERY

Address Tibetan Settlement, P.O. Clement-Town, Distt Dehra Dun, U.P., India.

NYINGMAPA MONASTERY

Address Arlikumari P.O. Bylakuppe, Distt Mysore, Karnataka, India, 571104. **Tel** 318.

NYUNG NE LHAKHANG

Address P.O. Mcleod Ganj, Dharamsala, Distt Kangra, H.P., India, 176219.

OGYEN LING MONASTERY

Address Rabgye Ling Tibetan Settlement, P.O. Gurupura, Hunsur Taluk, Distt Mysore, Karnataka, India, 571105.

OGYEN THEKCHOK MONASTERY

Address Phuntsok Ling Tibetan Settlement, Camp No 5, P.O. Chandragiri, Distt Ganjam, Orissa, India, 761017.

PAL SA NGOR TSAR SUM MONASTERY

Address Dhogueling Tibetan Settlement, P.O. Tibetan Colony, Mundgod, North Kanara, Karnataka, India, 581 411.

PALYUL CHOKOR LING NYINGMAPA MONASTERY

Address Tibetan Settlement, P.O. Bir, Distt Kangra, H.P., India. **Lama** Rigu Tulku.

PALYUL NAMDROLING MONASTERY

Address P.O. Bylakuppe, Distt Mysore, Karnataka, India, 571–104. **Lama** H.H. Penor Rinpoche.

PEMA CHOLING MONASTERY

Address Choephel Ling Tibetan Settlement, P.O. Miao, Distt Tirap, A.P., India.

PHENDE LING BUDDHIST MONASTERY

Address P.O. Kamleshwarpur, Distt Surguja, M.P., India.

PHIYANG MONASTERY

Address, Distt Leh, Ladakh, J and K, India, 194106.

PHUNTSOK CHOKORLING KHAMPAGAR MONASTERY, TASHI JONG

Address P.O. Paprola, Distt Kangra, H.P., India.

PHUNTSOK NYAYAB CHOLING

Address Jore Bungalow, Sinchal Road, P.O. Ghoom, Distt Darjeeling, W.B., India, 734101.

PHUNTSOK PEMA CHOKORLING
Address The Tsechu Association, 3/B Mahatab Chand Road, Distt Darjeeling, W.B., India, 734101.

PHURENG SHEDPHEL LING
Address Tibetan Settlement, P.O. Tibetan Colony, Mundgod, N. Kanara, Karnataka, India, 581411.

PURING SAGON DHAMCHOELING
Address Dhogueling Tibetan Settlement, P.O. Tibetan Colony, Mundgod, N. Kanara, Karnataka, India, 581411.

RATO DATSANG
Address Dhogueling Tibetan Settlement, P.O. Tibetan Colony, Mundgod, N. Kanara, Karnataka, India, 581411.

RI GON SAMDUP CHOKORLING
Address Tibetan Settlement, P.O. Tibetan Colony, Kollelgal, Mysore, Karnataka, India.

RIGZIN NAMDROL LING
Address P.O. Mcleod Ganj, Dharamsala, Distt Kangra, H.P., India, 176219.

RUMTEK MONASTERY, DHARMA CHAKRA CENTRE
Address P.O. Rumtek, Via Ranipul, Gangtok, Sikkim, India, 737135. **Tel** 2363.

SA-NGAK CHOKHOR LING MONASTERY
Address Dhogueling Tibetan Settlement, P.O. Tibetan Colony, Mundgod, North Kanara, Karnataka, India, 581411.

SAKYA CENTRE
Address 187 Rajpur Road, P.O. Rajpur, Distt Dehra Dun, U.P., India. **Tel** 84 2286.

SAKYA COLLEGE
Address Mussoorie Road, P.O. Rajpur, Dehra Dun, U.P., India, 248009.

SAKYA GURU BUDDHIST MONASTERY
Address P. O. Ghoom, Distt Darjeeling, W.B., India, 743101.

SAKYA MONASTERY
Address Fair Oaks, 192 Rajpur Road, P.O. Rajpur, Distt Dehra Dun, U.P., India.

SAKYA MONASTERY
Address P.O. Bodh Gaya, Distt Gaya, Bihar, India.

SAKYAPA MONASTERY, BYLAKUPPE
Address Tibetan Settlement, Bylakuppe, Distt Mysore, Karnataka, India, 571104.

SAMDRUP DHARGYE LING MONASTERY

Address Drajur Dzamling Kunkhyab, P.O. Sonada, Distt Darjeeling, W.B., India, 734219. **Lama** Bokar Tulku **Founder** Kalu Rinpoche.

SAMTEN CHOELING MONASTERY

Address Palgon Ritrod, P.O. Manali, Distt Kulu, H.P., India.

SAMTEN CHOELING MONASTERY

Address P.O. Ghoom, Distt Darjeeling, W.B., India, 734101.

SANGYE CHOELING MONASTERY

Address Tibetan Association Sanjoili, Simla 6, H.P., India.

SED GYED DATSANG

Address Pondo Godown, Rishi Road, 10 1/2 Mile, P.O. Kalimpong, Distt Darjeeling, W.B., India.

SERA JE MAHAYANA PHILOSOPHY UNIVERSITY

Address P.O. Bylakuppe, Distt Mysore, Karnataka, India, 571104. **Tel** 135.

SERA ME MAHAYANA PHILOSOPHY UNIVERSITY

Address P.O. Bylakuppe, Distt Mysore, Karnataka, India, 571104. **Tel** 276.

SPITUK MONASTERY

Address, Distt Leh, Ladakh, J and K, India.

TANGYUT GOMPA

Address P.O. Kaza, Lahaul and Spiti, H.P., India.

TASHI CHOELING TIBETAN MONASTERY

Address Dhargyeling Tibetan Settlement, P.O. Tendoling Tezu, Distt Lohit, A.P., India.

TASHI CHOELING TIBETAN MONASTERY

Address P.O. Kurseong, Distt Darjeeling, W.B., India, 734301.

TASHI THONGMON CHODA MONASTERY

Address Dhondup Ling Tibetan Settlement, Clement Town, Distt Dehra Dun, U.P., India.

TASHILHUNPO CULTURAL SOCIETY

Address P.O. Bylakuppe, Distt Mysore, Karnataka, India, 571104.

TATHOK GONPA BUDDHIST MONASTERY

Address P.O. Sakti, Distt Leh, Ladakh, J and K, India.

AWANG MONASTERY, THUPTEN GONPA

Address P.O. Tawang, Distt Kameng, A.P., India.

THEGCHOK NAMDROL LING MONASTERY

Address Camp 4, Lugsung Samdupling Settlement, P.O. Bylakuppe, Distt Mysore, Karnataka, India, 571104.

THODING PEMA TSAL

Address P.O. Tibetan Colony Settlement, Village 5, House 17, Mundgod, N. Kanara, Karnataka, India, 581411.

THUBTEN DHARGYE LING MONASTERY

Address Tibetan Settlement Mainpat, P.O. Kamleshwarpur, Distt Surguja, M.P., India.

THUBTEN SANG-NGAG CHOLING MONASTERY

Address Forest View Villa, West Point, Distt Darjeeling, W.B., India, 734101.

THUPTEN DHARGYE LING

Address Durga Shri Babiya, P.O. Bodh Gaya, Distt Gaya, Bihar, India.

THUPTEN DORJI DRAK NYINGMA MONASTERY

Address Saraswati Garden Estate, P.O. Kusumpti, Simla, H.P., India.

THUPTEN MINDROL LING MONASTERY
Address Phuntsok Ling Tibetan Settlement, Camp No. 4 Jeerang, P.O. Daraha, Via Puramat, Distt Ganjam, Orissa, India, 761017.

THUPTEN SAMPHEL LING KAGYU MONASTERY
Address Tibetan Settlement, P.O. Tibetan Colony, Mundgod, N. Kanara, Karnataka, India, 581411.

THUPTEN SHEDRUP JANGCHUB LING, KAGYU MONASTERY
Address Tibetan Settlement, P.O. Bylakuppe, Distt Mysore, Karnataka, India, 571104.

TIBETAN MONASTERY, SARNATH
Address P.O. Sarnath, Varanassi, U.P., India.

TSANG DOMAR NAMDROL LING, NYINGMAPA MONASTERY
Address Phuntsok Ling Tibetan Settlement, P.O. Malen Dragada, Distt Ganjam, Orissa, India, 761017.

TSECHEN CHOKOR LING SAKYA MONASTERY
Address Lugsung Samdrup Ling Tibetan Settlement, P.O. Bylakuppe, Distt Mysore, Karnataka, India, 571104.

TSO PADMA NYINGMAPA BUDDHIST MONASTERY
Address P.O. Rewalsar, Distt Mandi, H.P., India.

U TSE RITROD
Address c/o Drikung Kagyu Monastery, P.O. Rewalsar, Distt Mandi, H.P., India.

UGYEN CHOLING
Address Dhargyeling Tibetan Settlement, Tibetan Refugee Camp No 1, P.O. Tindoling, Distt Lohit, A.P., India.

URGYEN KUNSANG CHOKOR LING
Address 54, Gandhi Road, Distt Darjeeling, W.B., India, 734101.

YEGA CHOELING
Address P.O. Ghoom, Distt Darjeeling, W.B., India.

ZA MONGYAL BONPO MONASTERY
Address Lingtsang Tibetan Settlement, P.O. Manduwala, via Prem Nagar, Dehra Dun, U.P., India.

ZANGDOK PELRI BUDDHIST MONASTERY
Address Durpin Dara, P.O. Kalimpong, Distt Darjeeling, W.B., India, 734301.

ZEIKAR CHODE
Address Pondo Godown 1 1/2 Mile, Rishi Road, Kalimpong, Distt Darjeeling, W.B., India, 734301.

ZILNON KHAGYE LHAKANG
Address P.O. Mcleod Ganj, Dharam-sala, Distt Kangra, H.P., India, 176219.

Museums

INDIAN MUSEUM
Address Chowringee, Calcutta 13, W.B., India.

NATIONAL MUSEUM OF INDIA
Address 11 Janpath, New Delhi, India.

Publishing Companies and Journals

BIBLIA IMPEX PVT LTD,
BOOKSELLERS AND EXPORTERS
Address 2/18 Ansari Road, New Delhi, India, 110 002. **Tel** 3278034, 3278870. **Telex/Fax** 91 (11) 3282047. **Distribution Details** Suppliers of all types of publication on Buddhism in English and Tibetan.

CHARITRUST TIBETAN HANDICRAFT
EXPORTS
Address 16 Jor Bagh, New Delhi, India, 110 003. **Tel** (11) 623910. **Telex/Fax** 6461914. **General Description** The trust distributes books on Tibet and represents the Library of Tibetan Works and Archives.

CLASSICS INDIA PUBLICATIONS
Address 2484 Nicholson Road, Mori Gate, Delhi, India, 110006. **Distribution Details** Publisher of Tibetan texts.

COUNCIL FOR RELIGIOUS AND
CULTURAL AFFAIRS
Address Gangchen Kyishong, Dharamsala, Distt Kangra, H.P., India, 176215. **Distribution Details** Publishes *Cho Yang*.

DRELOMA
Address Drepung Loseling, Lama Camp 1, Tibetan Colony, Mundgod, North Kanara, Karnataka, India, 581411.

DUPJUNG LAMA
Address c/o Royal Bhutanese Embassy, Chandra Gupta Marg, Chanakyapuri, New Delhi, India, 110021. **Distribution Details** Publisher of Tibetan Texts.

MOTILAL BANARSIDASS PUBLISHERS,
INDOLOGICAL PUBLISHERS AND
DISTRIBUTORS
Address 41 UA Bungalow Road, Jawahar Nagar, Delhi, India, 110007. **Tel** 2918335/2911985. **Telex/Fax** 91112930689. **Distribution Details** Catalogue available. **Year Established** 1903. **General Description** Motilal Banarsidass aims to provide high quality research-oriented works on Indology, especially on Oriental religions, philosophy, culture, history and the arts. The company has branches in Varanasi, Patna, Bangalore and Madras and overseas agents in the UK and USA.

MUNSHIRAM MANOHARLAL
PUBLISHERS PVT.LTD.,
ORIENTAL PUBLISHERS AND
BOOKSELLERS
Address P.O. Box No.5715, 54, Rani Jhansi Road, New Delhi, India, 110 055. **Tel** 7771668, 7773650. **Telex/Fax** 91–11–7512745.

NARTHANG PRESS
Address Central Tibetan Secretariat, Gangchen Kyishong, Dharamsala, Dist. Kangra, H.P., India, 176215. **Tel** (1892) 2457. **Distribution Details** Publishes periodicals and journals, including *Sheja*.

OFFICE OF INFORMATION
Address Gangchen Kyishong, Dharamsala, Distt Kangra, H.P., India, 176215. **Distribution Details** Catalogue available.

TIBET JOURNAL
Address Library of Tibetan Works and Archives, Gangchen Kyishong, Dharamsala, Distt Kangra, H.P., India, 176215.

TIBETAN BULLETIN, OFFICE OF INFORMATION AND INTERNATIONAL RELATIONS

Address Central Tibetan Secretariat, Gangchen Kyishong, Dharamsala, Distt Kangra, H.P., India, 176215. **Tel** (1892) 2457. **Telex/Fax** (1892) 4357. **Distribution Details** Official journal of the Tibetan Administration. Bi-monthly in English.

TIBETAN CULTURAL PRINTING PRESS

Address, Dharamsala, Distt Kangra, H.P., India, 176215. **Tel** (1892) 673. **Distribution Details** Prints Tibetan textbooks for Tibetan educational institutions established in exile. Also restores Tibet's religious texts.

TIBETAN MEDICAL PUBLICATIONS

Address Penrhyn House, W. Rickshaw Road, Kalimpong, Distt Darjeeling, W.B., India, 734 301. **Distribution Details** Publisher of Tibetan texts.

TIBETAN REVIEW

Address c/o Tibetan SOS Youth Hostel, D & SP Area 2, Plot B1, Sector XIV Extn., Rohini, New Delhi, India, 110085. **Tel** 642 5974. **Distribution Details** Monthly English language journal on all aspects of Tibet and Tibetan culture. **Lama/Scholar** Tsering Wangyal (Editor).

Teaching Centres

NGOR EWAM CENTRE

Address P.O. Manduwala, Via Premnagar, Distt Dehra Dun, UP, India.

SHERAB LING INST. OF BUDDHIST STUDY

Address P.O. Upper Bhattu, Distt Kangra, H.P., India, 176125. **Lama/Scholar** Tai Situ Rinpoche. **General Description** Sherab Ling is the seat of Tai Situ Rinpoche and, at present, approximately 150 tulkus, lamas, monks and thrity lay people make up the community. **Facilities and Services** There are separate three-year, three-month retreat centres for nuns and monks. Basic guest house facilities are available with rooms from 15–60 rs daily and retreat cabins in the surrounding forest for visitors from 100–300 rs monthly. The Sherab Ling Newsletter is available free upon request. **Project Description** In 1994 the completion of the new monastery 'Palpung' is planned which will house an extensive library, museum, auditorium and several shrine rooms. The main shrine hall will include a thirty-five foot Maitreya Buddha statue. The whole monastery will be built to traditional Tibetan design.

TUSHITA MAHAYANA MEDITATION CENTRE

Address C–259 Defence Colony, New Delhi, India, 110024. **Tel** 011 462 9562. **Telex/Fax** 011 462 6699.

TUSHITA RETREAT CENTRE

Address McLeod Ganj, Dharamsala, Distt Kangra, H.P., India, 176219. **Tel** 1892 2266.

IRELAND, REPUBLIC OF

Libraries

CHESTER BEATTY LIBRARY AND ART GALLERY

Address 20 Shrewbury Road, Dublin 4, Ireland. **Tel** Dublin 692386. **Telex/Fax** 830985. **General Description** The Tibetan collection at the Chester Beatty Library and Art Gallery consists of the following catalogued items: major canonical works (1701–1728), in-digenous Tibetan works (1729–1757), ritual texts (17581814), thangkas (1816–1837; 1850–1860), mandalas (1815; 1838–1849). Items not appearing in the catalogue are: thangkas (1861–1863), six small paintings on paper mounted on silk (1864), embroidered thangka (1865), text on copper (1866), wooden book covers (1867–1869), painted book cover in glass frame (1899), lamaist ritual objects (1870–1898). A published catalogue of the collection is available.

Teaching Centres

DZOGCHEN BEARA RETREAT CENTRE

Address Garranes, Allihies, Cork, Ireland.

ITALY

Academic Organisations

ISTITUTO ORIENTALE, UNIVERSITARIO NAPOLI, DIPARTIMENTO DI STUDI ASIATICI

Address Piazza S Giovanni Maggiore 30, Napoli, Italy, 80134. **Lama/Scholar** Professor Namkhai Norbu, Professor Ramon Prats. **Teaching Programme** Courses are given on Tibetan and Mongolian language and literature, based on texts by Professor Norbu and other Tibetan and Western scholars dealing with Tibetan culture, secular and religious history and Buddhist doctrine (particularly that of Dzogchen), Tibetan medicine and astrology. Professor Norbu also teaches on the ancient culture and civilisation of Zhangzhung. **Facilities and Services** The department has a library including works relevant to Tibetan culture and Buddhism.

Ecumenical Centres

CENTRO D'INFORMAZIONE BUDDISTA

Address Via Pio Rolla 71, Giaveno, Torino, Italy, 10094. **Tel** (011) 9378331. **Distribution Details** Materials are distributed throughout Italy. **Year Established** 1974. **General Description** Centro d'Informazione Buddista is not a residential centre but rather it is located in a private home. It possesses a reference and lending library of works relating to Buddhism. In addition there is a photographic archive available. The centre has been involved in organising conferences and exhibitions. In particular, it was instrumental in the setting up of the International Congress on Buddhism, that took place in Turin in 1984. **Teaching Programme** Centro d'Informazione Buddista functions mainly in giving out information on other centres' teaching programmes and in assisting in the organisation of conferences that they may arrange. **Facilities and Services** There is a lending and reference library available. The centre offers secretarial help to groups who are organising conferences, exhibitions, slide shows or other educational activities relating to Buddhism. It may also assist in translating if this is required. The centre distributes a Buddhist review entitled *Paramita*. **Project Description** It is hoped to enlarge the library holdings of the centre. Another area where the centre would like to expand its operations is in providing translation facilities, thereby allowing simultaneous translation to take place at conferences. There are also plans to translate textual material.

Museums

NATIONAL MUSEUM OF ORIENTAL ART, ITALY

Address Via Merulana 248, Rome, Italy, 00185. **Tel** (06) 735946. **Telex/Fax** (06) 4870624. **Year Established** 1957. **General Description** The museum was founded in 1957 after an agreement between the Italian Ministry of Education and the Italian Institute for the Middle and Far East. The Tibetan collection of thangkas is one of the most important in Europe, having been collected by the famed Italian scholar Guiseppe Tucci during his travels in the Himalayan regions.

Teaching Centres

CENTRO LAMA TSONG KHAPA

Address Piazza V Emanuele 18, Villorba, Treviso, Venezia-Euganea, Italy, 31050. **Tel** 0422 928 079.

CENTRO MILAREPA

Address Via Saibante 3, 10064 Pinerolo (TO), Italy. **Tel** (0121) 76478. **Distribution Details** Books (in Italian), sadhanas and prints are distributed. **Year Established** 1980. **Founder** Kalu Rinpoche. **Lama/Scholar** Lama Giang Ciub. **General Description** The centre provides weekend programmes of meditation and other courses, and retreats during some holiday periods. Conferences and meditation courses are sometimes arranged at locations outside the centre. There is a library and a newsletter is distributed.

CENTRO RABTEN GHE PEL LING

Address Via Euclide 17, Milan, Italy, 20128. **Tel** 0039 2 2576015. **Founder** Geshe Rabten.

CENTRO SAKYA KUNGA CHOLING

Address V. Marconi 34, Trieste, Italy, 34133.

CENTRO STUDI CENRESIG

Address Via F Acri 2/A, Bologna, Italy, 40126. **Tel** 051 226 953.

CENTRO TERRA DI UNIFICAZIONE, EWAM

Address Via Cortine 98, Barberino Val d'Elsa, Firenze, Italy. **Tel** 055 807 5732. **Telex/Fax** 0577 980552.

COMMUNITA' DZOGCHEN – MERIGAR

Address Archidosso, Grosseto, Italy, 58031. **Tel** 0564 966 837. **Telex/Fax** 0564 966 608. **Distribution Details** Please write to the centre for a current list of distributed materials. **Year Established** 1982. **Founder** Namkhai Norbu Rinpoche. **General Description** The Dzog-chen Community is a non-profit making cultural association with members in many countries throughout the world. The main base or 'Gar' in Europe is Merigar, situated in Tuscany on the slopes of Monte Amiata. Other centres include Tsegyalgar (USA) and Tashigar (Latin America) under the auspices of the Associazione Culturale Communita Dzog-chen. At Merigar on approximately seventy hectars of land, are several buildings including a teaching hall – Gompa, retreat cabins, a specialist library, a publishing house, residential quarters, administrative offices and a barn. **Teaching Programme** Frequent study and practice retreats are organised under the guidance of Chogyal Namkhai Norbu Rinpoche, as well as other Lamas who are invited from time to time. **Facilities and Services** The activities of the Cultural Association Dzog-chen Community can be divided into those of a cultural nature and those mainly linked to the Dzog-chen teachings. At present there are four independent units in Italy affiliated with the Dzog-chen Community. These are: Shang-Shung Editions, a co-operative publishing house, Shang-Shung International Institute for Tibetan Studies, A.S.I.A. Associazione per la Solidarieta in Asia, a non-governmental organisation which directs and co-ordinates projects in the fields of international co-operation in Asia, in particular the preservation of Tibetan culture, and COABIT, a building co-operative for the Dzog-chen Community. **Project Description** Besides several translations of Tibetan texts into many different Western languages, an archive is being made of the oral teachings given by different Masters in the form of transcriptions, audio-cassettes and video-cassettes. There are also plans for future buildings connected with teaching-courses, culture and agriculture etc.

ISTITUTO LAMA TZONG KHAPA
Address Via Poggiberna, 9, Pomaia, Pisa, Italy, 56040. **Tel** 50–685654. **Telex/Fax** 50–685768. **Distribution Details** The institute distributes materials for Wisdom Correspondence Courses worldwide. **Year Established** 1977. **Founder** Lama Thubten Yeshe. **Lama/Scholar** Geshe Jampa Gyatso. **General Description** Istituto Lama

Tzong Khapa, founded in 1977, is the earliest and largest of several FPMT centres in Italy. It is situated in the village of Pomaia in the rolling landscape of Tuscany, near the ancient city of Pisa. A large country villa is home for an international community of thirty, half of whom are monks or nuns. Many of the institute's staff and students reside in the surrounding villages, with the institute becoming an increasingly accepted and respected part of the local community. The institute has a rich programme of events which draws thousands of visitors every year. Most weekends there are courses on a variety of disciplines, including Buddhism, education, psychology and yoga. There are guided study and meditation retreats lasting from ten to fourteen days, and facilities for individuals to engage in their own personal retreats. Some of the most respected Tibetan lamas have blessed the institute with visits lasting weeks or even months. Kyabje Song Rinpoche, Serkong Tsenshab Rinpoche and Venerable Gomo Tulku have all given initiations and substantial teachings at the institute. In 1982, His Holiness the Dalai Lama gave teachings and initiations as well as opening the first international conference on 'Universal Education'. **Teaching Programme** In autumn 1983 the institute embarked on a major new education programme allowing intensive study over a period of years. The programme gives Westerners access to oral teachings on several major texts which were used in Tibetan monastic universities. Lama Yeshe designed a core curriculum of seven subjects, encompassing both sutra and tantra, that culminates in the Degree of Master of Buddhist Philosophy and Meditation. Based on the great Indian and Tibetan Mahayana texts, each course involves as many as 200 lectures over a period of twelve to eighteen months at the institute. Students are awarded certificates for successful examinations in each subject and are entitled to the Master's Degree on completing the whole programme. Sutra texts that are studied in the core curriculum include: the *Lam Rim Chen Mo*, the *Abhisamayalamkara*, the *Madhyamakavatara*, and the *Abhidharmakosha*. In addition, tantric texts are examined on the four classes of Buddhist tantra, and the generation and completion stages of highest yoga tantra (anuttarayogatantra). The institute has developed an extensive range of supplementary courses of thirty to forty lectures that provide a useful introduction to intensive study suitable to newer students. There are also reviews of courses such as Abhisamaya and Madhyamaka, which are beneficial in preparing for examinations. Six of the supplementary courses will be included in the introductory unit of the institute's future Geshe programme. The Geshe programme Introductory Unit comprises: Collected Topics (bsDus grwa); Mind and Cognition (Blo rig); Signs and Reasonings (rTags rig); Tenets (Grub mtha'); Grounds and Paths (Sa lam); and Seventy Topics (Don bdun cu). **Facilities and Services** The main meditation hall is used for lectures and the new library provides space for quiet study. Study and resource materials are steadily increasing giving staff and students access to thousands of cassette recordings and a range of relevant literature in Tibetan, English and Italian. Wisdom Correspondence Courses provide an opportunity for those living at some distance to a teaching centre, to participate in the range of courses offered at the institute.

KARMA DECHEN YANG TSE LING
Address Cooperativa Di Bordo, 128030 Viganella/No, Italy.

MUNI-GHIANA CENTRE
Address Piazza Pallavicino 20, Palermo, Italy, 90146. **Tel** 091 8695102. **Telex/Fax** 091 8695102.

SHINE
Address Via Poggiberna 9, Pomaia, Pisa, Italy, 56040. **Tel** 050 685774. **Telex/Fax** 050 685768.

TAKDEN SHEDRUP TARGYE LING
Address Via Poggiberna 9, Pomaia, Pisa, Italy, 56040. **Tel** 050 685976. **Lama/Scholar** Geshe Jampa Gyatso.

UNIVERSAL EDUCATION-ITALY
Address Via San Bernardino 16, Trento, Italy, 38100. **Tel** 0461 233080.

JAPAN

Academic Organisations

KYOTO UNIVERSITY
Address Yoshida-Homachi, Sakyo-ku, Kyoto, Japan, 606.

Cultural Organisations and Tibetan Refugee Aid Societies

TIBETAN CULTURAL CENTRE IN JAPAN
Address 2–31–22 Nerima, Nerima-ku, Tokyo, Japan. **Tel** (3) 991 5411.

TIBETAN SNOW LION FRIENDSHIP SOCIETY
Address Dotemachi Marutamachi Sagura, Komano-cho 554–3, Kami-gyoo-ku, Kyoto, Japan, 602. **Tel** (75) 256 0859.

Government Offices

OFFICE OF TIBET
Address Celebrity Plaza Shinjuku Bldg. (3F), 1–36–14 Shinjuku, Shin-juku-ku, Tokyo, Japan, 160. **Tel** (3) 3353 4094. **Telex/Fax** 3225 8013.

Teaching Centres

DO NGAK SUNG JUK CENTER
Address 2131 Murakimi, Yachiyo-shi Chibaken, Japan, 276. **Tel** 0474 837906. **Telex/Fax** 0474 837906.

KENYA

Teaching Centres

KARMA THEKSUM CHOLING, BUDDHIST SOCIETY OF KENYA
Address G.T.Z. P.O. Box 41607, Nairobi, Kenya. **Tel** 02 521 501. **Telex/Fax** 02 562 671. **Founder** Akong Rinpoche. **Lama/Scholar** Denise Tomecke, Jim Tomecke.

LATVIA

Ecumenical Centres

BUDDHIST CENTRE OF LATVIA
Address Moskovskaya 279–3, kv 12, Riga, Latvia, 6063. **Tel** 0132 258 117.

Publishing Companies and Journals

UGUNS – PUBLISHING FOUNDATION LATVIAN ROERICH SOCIETY
Address Elizabetes Str. 21A–15, Riga, Latvia, 6010. **Tel** 0132 331 303. **Lama/Scholar** Gvido Trepsha. **Gen-**eral **Description** Uguns publishes Russian translations of various works on Tibetan Buddhism, including some by H.H. the Dalai Lama.

LITHUANIA

Academic Organisations

LITHUANIAN INSTITUTE OF BUDDHIST STUDIES
Address P.O. Box 1183, Vilnius, Lithuania, 2001. **Tel** 0122 771375. **Telex/Fax** 0122 353017. **Lama/Scholar** Vladimir Korobov, Antanas Danielius (President). **General Description** The main subjects studied at the institute are: Prajnaparamita, Lam rim, investigation of various tantric texts, Dzogchen, Tibetan medicine, and Tibetan language.

Cultural Organisations and Tibetan Refugee Aid Societies

PARLIAMENTARY TIBETAN SUPPORT GROUP
Address Gedimino 53, Vilnius, Lithuania, 2026. **Tel** 0122 618291. **Telex/Fax** 0122 614544.

MALAYSIA

Publishing Companies and Journals

CRAZY WISDOM NEWS
Address The Dharma House Society P.J., 3 Jalan 225 46100, Selangor, Malaysia. **Distribution Details** *Crazy Wisdom News* is a newsletter/information service.

Teaching Centres

DZONGSAR MANJUSHRI DHARMA SOCIETY
Address No 21 Lorong Shri Kuantan 53, Kuantan, Pahang Darul Makmur, Malaysia, 25250. **Tel** 09 523490.

KARMA KAGYU DHARMA SOCIETY
Address 4, Tan Sri Datuk William Tan Rd, 93450 Kuching, Sarawak, Malaysia. **Tel** 082 416 363.

SAKYA EWAM LING, KUANTAN BUDDHIST DHARMA SOCIETY
Address No 7 Lorong HJ Ahmad 10, Jalan HJ Ahmad, Kuantan, Pahang Darul Makmur, Malaysia, 25300.

SAKYA KUNGA DELEK LING
Address c/o Tan Chin Hua, 15 Jalan Bunga Kala, Pinji Park, Ipoh, Perak, Malaysia, 31650.

SAKYA LUNGTOG CHOELING
Address 110 Jalan 17/14, Petaling Jaya, Malaysia, 46400.

SAKYA SAMDUP LING
Address P.O. Box 1196, 35 Selangan Rd., Sibu, Sarawak, Malaysia, 90000.

SAKYA TENGYE LING
Address 191 Taman Mutiara, Sungai Petani, Kedah, Malaysia, 08000.

SAKYA TRIYANA DHARMA CHAKRA CENTER
Address Kuil Buddha Siam, Ulu Yam Baru, Ulu Selangor, Malaysia, 44300.

SAKYA TSECHEN SAMPHEL LING
Address 491 Jalan Chong Son, Pokok Assam, Taiping, Perak, Malaysia, 34000.

VAJRAYANA CENTRE
Address 66 Jalan Peace, Kuching, Sarawak, Malaysia, 93740.

MEXICO

Academic Organisations

LATIN-AMERICAN ASSOC OF BUDDHIST STUDIES
Address Apt Postal 19–332, Mexico City (DF), Mexico, 03901. **Tel** (05) 530 0136. **Lama/Scholar** Professor Benjamin Preciado (President).

Cultural Organisations and Tibetan Refugee Aid Societies

CASA TIBET MEXICO, CENTRO DE ESTUDIOS TIBETANOS DE MEXICO A.C.
Address Orizaba 93-A, Col. Roma, Mexico City (DF), Mexico, C.P.067000. **Tel** (05) 514 4290.

MEXICAN-TIBET SUPPORT GROUP
Address Santismo 6, Colonnia San Angel, Mexico City (DF), Mexico, 01000. **Tel** (05) 548 0162.

Publishing Companies and Journals

LATIN-AMERICAN BUDDHIST STUDIES MAGAZINE

Address Apt Postal 19–332, Mexico City (DF), Mexico, 03901. **Lama/Scholar** Sergio Mondragon (Publisher).

Teaching Centres

BUDDHIST INSTITUTE MEXICO, KILNER FOUNDATION

Address Apartado 148, Ajijic, Jalisco, Mexico. **Tel** 5 41 88.

MONGOLIA

Academic Organisations

LANGUAGE & WRITER'S RESEARCH ASSOCIATION

Address Ulan Bator, Mongolia. **Lama/Scholar** T. Tsendsuren (Head of Buddhist Studies).

MONGOLIAN ACADEMY OF SCIENCES, INSTITUTE OF PHILOSOPHY

Address Ulan Bator, Mongolia. **General Description** L. Terbish is a recognised expert on astrology at the Institute of Philosophy.

MONGOLIAN CENTER OF BUDDHIST STUDIES

Address Central Post Office, Box 795, Ulan Bator, Mongolia. **Lama/Scholar** T. Tsendsuren (General Secretary). **General Description** This centre is being given a collection of 2–3,000,000 texts, most of which are Tibetan. The collection was previously stored in a government warehouse.

Ecumenical Centres

ASIAN BUDDHIST CONFERENCE FOR PEACE

Address Ganden, Ulan Bator, Mongolia. **Tel** 53 538, 53904. **Distribution Details** Publish the magazine *Buddhists for Peace*, containing articles on Buddhism. **Lama/Scholar** Bakula Rinpoche (President), Dr G. Lubsantseran (General Sec.). **General Description** The centre has a research programme on Buddhist Studies.

MONGOLIAN ASSOCIATION OF BELIEVERS

Address Priv Post Box 281, Ulan Bator 23, Mongolia. **Tel** 64913. **Lama/Scholar** Bair Tsakhan (President).

Libraries

NATIONAL CENTRAL LIBRARY

Address Ulan Bator, Mongolia. **General Description** The National Central Library has an extensive collection of Tibetan texts.

Medical Institutions

CENTRE OF TRADITIONAL MONGOLIAN MEDICINE

Address Ulan Bator, Mongolia. **Lama/Scholar** Dagbatseren (Director), Bachirlo (Deputy Director). **General Description** The centre has a good collection of Tibetan medical texts.

Monasteries and Nunneries

AMARBAISALAT MONASTERY

Address Amarbaisalat, Mongolia.

ERDENE ZU MONASTERY

Address Kharakhorum, Mongolia.

GANDEN THEKCHOLING MONASTERY

Address Ulan Bator, Mongolia, 51. **Lama/Scholar** Ven. Choji Jamtso (Abbot), Ven. Bulghan (Deputy Abbot). **General Description** The monastery has expanded and revised its five-year training programme, in Mongolian language, for lamas from Mongolia and Burytia, and now includes young lamas from Kalmykia. Yeshe Lodro Rinpoche and Jhado Tulku from India are among its teachers.

Approximately 150 subsidiary monasteries have been restarted all over Mongolia, many of which are in tents erected on the sites of previous monasteries destroyed during the period of Communist rule. **Facilities and Services** The library at the monastery has a substantial collection of mostly Tibetan texts.

Museums

BOGDO KHAN PALACE
Address Ulan Bator, Mongolia.

CHOJI LAMA TEMPLE
Address Ulan Bator, Mongolia.

STATE MUSEUM
Address Ulan Bator, Mongolia.

Publishing Companies and Journals

BUDDHISTS FOR PEACE
Address ABCP Headquarters, Ulan Batar 51, Mongolia. **Tel** 535 38. **Lama/Scholar** Wang chin dorj (Editor-in-Chief).

NEPAL

Cultural Organisations and Tibetan Refugee Aid Societies

SNOW LION FOUNDATION
Address PO Box 1313, Kathmandu, Nepal. **Tel** (977) 521 241. **General Description** The foundation is a welfare fund providing assistance to old and infirm Tibetans.

Government Offices

OFFICE OF TIBET (NEPAL)
Address P.O. Box 310, Lazimpat, Kathmandu, Nepal. **Tel** 11660. **General Description** This is the Bureau of the Representative of H.H. the Dalai Lama for Nepal.

Monasteries and Nunneries

CHUGHAR DUEPHELING
Address c/o Delek Ling Tibetan Settlement, P.O. Box No 1, Chailsa, Solu Khumbu, Nepal.

GADEN CHOEPHEL LING MONASTERY
Address c/o Bodha Handicraft Centre, G.P.O. 908, Kathmandu, Nepal.

GADEN DHARGYELING

Address c/o Pokhara Handicraft Centre (pvt), P.O. Box No 18, Pokhara, Nepal.

GADEN SHEDRUP PHELGYELING

Address Swayambhu Hill, Kathmandu, Nepal.

GADEN TENPAI LING

Address c/o Delek Ling Tibetan Settlement, P.O. Box No 1, Chailsa, Solu Khumbu, Nepal.

GANDEN CHOEKOR LING

Address Tibetan Monastery, Bodhnath, Kathmandu, Nepal.

GANDEN JAMPA LING

Address Maitri Vihar, Swayambu Hill, Kathmandu, Nepal.

JANGCHUB CHOELING BUDDHIST MONASTERY

Address Tashi Palkhil Tibetan Camp, P.O. Box 56, Pokhara, Nepal.

KA-NYING SHEDRUP LING MONASTERY

Address Bodhnath, P.O. Box 1200, Kathmandu, Nepal.

KARMA DHARMA CHAKRA, DWIP MONASTERY

Address Bodhnath, Kathmandu, Nepal. **Lama/Scholar** Dasang Tulku.

KARMA DHUBGYU CHOKORLING

Address Manang Gompa, Matopani, Pokhara, Nepal.

KARMA RAJA MAHA VIHAR

Address Swayambhunath, Box 1094, Kathmandu, Nepal.

KHACHOE GHAKYIL NUNNERY, MAHAYANA BUDDHIST CENTRE

Address P.O. Box 817, Kathmandu, Nepal. **Tel** 00977 1 226717. **Telex/Fax** 00977 1 410992. **General Description** This is the nunnery associated with the Kopan Monastery.

KOPAN MONASTERY, MAHAYANA BUDDHIST CENTRE

Address P.O. Box 817, Kathmandu, Nepal. **Tel** 00977 1 226717. **Telex/Fax** 00977 1 410992. **Year Established** 1969. **Founder** Lama Thubten Yeshe and Lama Thubten Zopa. **General Description** Kopan monastery serves primarily as a training Monastery for Nepalese and Tibetan boys, with a population of some 140 monks and around a dozen teachers. It is also a centre for Western visitors and students of Buddhism with facilities for participating in meditation courses, or private study and retreat. **Teaching Programme** The resident monks study elementary logic and debate. Each year in November a one-month meditation course is held where Western people may become acquainted with Mahayana Buddhism. Other shorter courses (seven to ten days) are offered in March, April, May, June, September and October. The monastery is open all year round for retreat and private study and meditation practise. For resident monks, the full-time study programme includes Buddhist philosophy and debate, English, Tibetan and Nepali languages and some general studies and painting. Monks train to become future teachers and translators. **Facilities and Services** A variety of accommodation is available from dormitory to large, single retreat rooms. There are dining facilities, a library and a large meditation hall. Visitors can participate in scheduled courses or can request private teachings and general instruction from the resident lamas and students.

MONTHANG MONASTERY

Address Mustang, Pokhara, Nepal.

NEPALESE MAHAYANA CENTRE GONPA

Address G.P.O. Box No 17, Kathmandu, Nepal.

NEW BUDDHA MANDIR

Address P.O. Lumbini, Lumbini Zone, Distt Rupandehi 5, Nepal.

NYENANG PHELGYE LING MONASTERY
Address Swayambhu Paduka Panchayat, Dallu, Kathmandu, Nepal.

NYING GON SHEDRUP DOJO LING
Address P.O. Box No 914, Kathmandu, Nepal.

PHULWARY SAKYA MONASTERY
Address P.O. Box 1496, Bodhnath, Kathmandu, Nepal.

POKHARA GYE GON GADEN DHARGYE LING
Address c/o Karma Tsewang Gyurme, Tashi Palkhel Tibetan Camp, P.O. Box 7, Pokhara, Nepal.

POKHARA SHANG GADEN CHOELING
Address c/o Pokhara Handicraft Centre (P), P.O. Box No 18, Pokhara, Nepal. **Lama/Scholar** Ven. Choedring Tulku.

SHECHEN TENYI DHARGYE LING
Address Post Box 136, Bodhnath, Kathmandu, Nepal.

TASHI RABTEN LING
Address P.O. Lumbini, Lumbini Zone, Distt Rupandehi, Nepal, 4504.

TASHI THARTEN LING
Address c/o Tibetan Settlement, P.O. Dhore Patan, Distt Baglung, Daulangin Zone, Nepal.

TEGCHEN LEGSHAY LING
Address, Boudhanath, Nepal. **Year Established** 1988. **Founder** Karma Thinley Rinpoche. **Lama/Scholar** Karma Thinley Rinpoche.

THARLAM MONASTERY
Address P.O. Box 1871, Bodhnath, Kathmandu, Nepal.

THARPA JAMCHEN LHAKANG
Address P.O. Box 4518, Bodhnath, Kathmandu, Nepal.

THARTEN THARGYE LING
Address Dholagiri Zone, Dhor Patan, Baglung, Nepal.

THEKCHOK CHOLING
Address c/o Tibetan Refugee Camp, Folay Gaon, P.O. Gunsa, Distt Anchal, Nepal.

THRANGU TASHI CHOELING
Address Bodhnath, Box 1287, Kathmandu, Nepal.

THUKCHE CHOLING NUNNERY
Address Chokdol Block No.1 873, Swayambu, Kathmandu 4, Nepal. **Lama/Scholar** Ani Yonten Dolma.

THUKJE CHOELING BUDDHIST MONASTERY
Address Saraswati Hill, Swayambu, Kathmandu, Nepal.

TINLEY CHOKORLING MONASTERY, TEMPLE OF THE THOUSAND BUDDHAS
Address New Monastery, Bodhnath, Kathmandu, Nepal.

ZARONG THUPTEN CHOLING
Address c/o Delek Ling Tibetan Settlement, P.O. Box No 1, Chailsa, Solu Khumbu, Nepal.

Museums

NATIONAL MUSEUM OF NEPAL
Address Chhauri, Kathmandu, Nepal.

Publishing Companies and Journals

KAILASH
Address Ratna Pustak Bhandar, Bhotahity, Kathmandu, Nepal.

RANGJUNG YESHE PUBLICATIONS
Address P.O. Box 1200, Kathmandu, Nepal.

RATNA PUSTAK BHANDAR
Address Bhotahity, Kathmandu, Nepal. **Distribution Details** Publisher of Tibetan texts.

Teaching Centres

HIMALAYAN YOGIC INSTITUTE
Address G.P.O. Box 817, Kathmandu, Nepal. **Tel** 413094. **Telex/Fax** 977 1 410992. **Year Established** 1982. **Founder** Lama Thubten Yeshe. **Lama/Scholar** Lama Thubten Zopa Rinpoche. **General Description** The Himalayan Yogic Institute is a member of the Foundation for Preservation of the Mahayana Tradition (FPMT). Day courses and lectures are held every week on Buddhist philosophy and meditation. Other regular courses include Tibetan Medicine, Hatha Yoga, Shiatsu Massage, and Thangka Painting. **Teaching Programme** The centre is closed on Mondays. Details of courses are given in a programme obtainable from the centre. **Facilities and Services** The house includes a meditation room, library and bookshop. Accommodation is available for visitors.

KA-NYING SHEDRUPLING
Address Bodhnath, P.O. Box 1200, Katmandu, Nepal. **Lama/Scholar** Chokyi Nyima Rinpoche.

LAWUDO RETREAT CENTRE
Address P.O. Box 817, Kathmandu, Nepal. **Tel** 1 413094. **Lama/Scholar** Lama Zopa Rinpoche.

MARPA INSTITUTE FOR TRANSLATORS
Address Box 4017, Kathmandu, Nepal.

NAMO BUDDHA RETREAT CENTRE
Address P.O. Box 1287, Kathmandu, Nepal.

NEW ZEALAND

Cultural Organisations and Tibetan Refugee Aid Societies

TIBETAN CHILDREN'S RELIEF SOCIETY
Address 44 Patons Road, Howick, Auckland, New Zealand. **Tel** (9) 534 1436. **Telex/Fax** (9) 437275.

Teaching Centres

DHARGHEY DHARMA CENTRE
Address 22 Royal Terrace, Dunedin, New Zealand. **Tel** 778374. **Distribution Details** The centre intends to distribute materials in the future. **Year Established** 1985. **Founder** Geshe Ngawang Dharghey. **Lama/Scholar** Geshe Ngawang Dharghey. **General Description** The Dharghey Dharma

Centre was founded as an international teaching centre for Geshe Dharghey, who is one of the most highly qualified Gelug lamas alive. His teaching and meditation programme is aimed at building a sound understanding of Mahayana Buddhism. Geshe Dharghey teaches in Tibetan, and so students are encouraged not only to learn 'Dharma', but also to study the Tibetan language. To facilitate this, the class translator also teaches Tibetan language courses. As the only Buddhist centre in this part of New Zealand, Dharghey Dharma Centre acts to encourage harmony and unity amongst the followers of the various Buddhist paths. **Teaching Programme** Teachings are given by Geshe Ngawang Dharghey according to the Gelug tradition of Tibetan Buddhism. The teaching programme is structured in a graded fashion, beginning with the *Lam Rim*, and progressing to the classic texts of Buddhism. Recent teachings have examined Nagarjuna's *Letter to a King* (*Suhrllekha*), and in the future courses will review Shantideva's *A Guide to the Bodhisattva's Way of Life* (*Bodhisattvacaryavatara*), and Candrakirti's *Exposition of the Middle Way* (*Madhyamakavatara*). Tantric teachings and empowerments are given from time to time, when the lama feels that they are appropriate. Weekly meditation classes are also offered by the centre. **Facilities and Services** Located in an historic mansion, the centre possesses a large meditation room. There is no charge for the teachings given there, all costs being funded entirely by donation. Members are kept informed of the centre's activities through newsletters.

DORJE CHANG INSTITUTE

Address P.O. Box 2814, Auckland 1, New Zealand. **Tel** 09 766 509. **Telex/Fax** 09 788 589. **Distribution Details** Materials will be sent anywhere on receipt of reproduction and postage costs. **Year Established** 1976. **Founder** Lama Thubten Yeshe. **Lama/Scholar** Khensur Kalsang Thabkhey, Geshe Thamcho Sangpo (formerly). **General Description** Dorje Chang Institute is located in the inner suburbs of Auckland. It aims to provide a teaching programme suited to the pressures and commitments of urban life, offering regular weekly and weekend courses. It was incorporated as a trust in 1976 under the spiritual direction of Lama Thubten Yeshe and Lama Thubten Zopa Rinpoche, and is a member of the Foundation for the Preservation of the Mahayana Tradition (FPMT). **Teaching Programme** Mahayana teachings are given by visiting Tibetan lamas of all traditions, the resident Gelugpa geshe, and old students. Courses consisting of evening and day lectures, meditations, and retreats are drawn from the vast range of Mahayana Buddhism. They aim to cater for all levels of experience and understanding. **Facilities and Services** Dorje Chang House is situated in its own grounds with pleasant, tranquil gardens, in a quiet suburb of Auckland. The facilities include a library, containing around 700 English language books on Buddhism and associated subjects, as well as a growing number of Tibetan texts. The tape library houses about 200 audio and video cassettes. A good sized meditation hall, suitable for up to seventy people at a time, is situated in the house. There are a few beds available for short term guests, at the discretion of the resident staff. The shop has on sale a wide range of Dharma books, posters, ritual objects and handicrafts. A booklist for mail orders is available. Dorje Chang Institute are also the New Zealand distributors for Wisdom Publications.

KARMA KAGYU THIGSUM CHOKHORLING

Address Bodhisattva Road, Kaukapakapa, New Zealand, R.D.1. **Tel** (0880) 5428. **Distribution Details** Published material is available on receipt of cost and postage. Transcripts and tapes are supplied to Dharma centres. **Year Established** 1978. **Founder** Lama Karma Thinley Rinpoche. **Lama/Scholar** Lama Karma Samten Gyatso. **General Description** Karma Kagyu Thigsum Chokhorling is a shedra (shes grva), or study and retreat centre, located on fifteen hectares of steep to rolling farmland, about thirty-five kilometres north of Auckland. From various high points on the property, views of the Hawaki gulf, and on a clear day some of the offshore islands, may be obtained. The centre is situated at the end of a purpose-built 'no-exit' road, about six kilometres from the nearest highway, yet within easy travelling distance of the city. Karma Choling enjoys considerable natural beauty, and is considered to be a very auspicious place for the development of spiritual insight. **Teaching Programme** Individual instruction is given by the resident lama. Courses take place from time to time, when visiting teachers are staying at the centre. There is a regular programme of morning and evening pujas. **Facilities and Services** Retreat facilities are available at the centre, though prior booking is required. The main shrine room is open to any Buddhist organisation that wishes to use it for retreat courses or teachings. Accommodation facilities include a dormitory, six small 'sleepouts', and a self-contained retreat hut. A new temple is under construction according to traditional Tibetan design. This will be large enough to hold one hundred people in the ground floor shrine hall, and will include rooms for visiting lamas and one room set aside for H.H. the Karmapa, on the top floor. **Project Description** Work is continuing on the construction of the new temple. Various agricultural and light industry/craft development projects are being planned, in order to generate support for the community of practitioners. Such projects include the planting of fruit and nut trees, and the development of garden areas, to provide cash crops and raw materials. Fundraising is taking place to construct a twenty-five foot high concrete statue of Shakyamuni Buddha, on a nearby hill-top. Plans exist to build a crematorium, and to construct a retreat centre for those wishing to complete the traditional three-year retreat.

MAHAMUDRA CENTRE

Address Colville R.D., Coromandel, New Zealand. **Tel** 0843 56851. **Telex/Fax** 0843 56851.

NEW ZEALAND KARMA THEGSUM CHOLING

Address 34, Second Avenue, Whangarei, New Zealand. **Tel** 64–89–481266. **Distribution Details** No materials are distributed. **Year Established** 1981. **Founder** H.H. Gyalwa Karmapa.

NORWAY

Academic Organisations

UNIVERSITY OF OSLO, DEPARTMENT OF RELIGIOUS STUDIES

Address Postboks 1056 Blindern, Oslo, Norway, N–03156. **Distribution Details** No materials are distributed. **Year Established** 1953. **Lama/Scholar** Professor Per Kvaerne, Ass. Professor Jens Braarvig, Research Fellow Hanna Havnevik. **General Description** This is a department offering a general course in comparative religion. **Teaching Programme** The department offers a course in comparative religion entitled 'History of Religion', which is from one to two years in duration. There is also an MA/PhD. programme (three to four years in length, including the introductory course). The department is staffed by four full-time teachers. **Facilities and Services** The department library has no holdings of Tibet-related material, though such holdings are to be found in the Oslo University Library.

Museums

ETHNOGRAPHICAL MUSEUM (OSLO UNIVERSITY)
Address Frederiksgt. 2, Oslo, Norway, N–0164.

Teaching Centres

KARMA TASHI LING
Address Meklenborgveien Sommero, Oslo 12, Norway, 1277. **Tel** (02) 612884. **Distribution Details** Contact the centre for further information. **Year Established** 1975. **Founder** H.H. Gyalwa Karmapa. **Lama/Scholar** Lama Talo. **General Description** Karma Tashi Ling is a centre of the Kagyupa (bKa' brgyud pa) tradition of Tibetan Buddhism. It is situated in a country area of Oslo, surrounded by fields and woods. A separate building houses the shrine room. The centre organises meditation courses for beginners, as well as a regular programme of pujas, preliminary practices, and shamatha meditation. From time to time, visiting lamas give teachings in the centre. **Teaching Programme** Daily ngondro (sngon 'gro) practice is scheduled for the mornings, and evening pujas are devoted to either Avalokiteshvara (Chenrezig) or Mahakala (Nagpo Chenpo). On Sundays, shamatha (zhi gnas) meditation classes take place. There are also meditation courses for beginners and weekend retreats held in the centre. Lama Talo gives individual instruction to his students and visiting lamas of the Kagyupa tradition give occasional courses at Karma Tashi Ling. Some meditation courses are held in the city. **Facilities and Services** There is one retreat hut for individual retreats, and camping facilities are available in the summer. Karma Tashi Ling distributes a newsletter to its members. Interested schools may bring classes to be shown around the centre. **Project Description** There are plans to establish a library in the centre.

PERU

Teaching Centres

KARMA THEKSUM CHOLING LIMA
Address Calle E. Palacios 1125-C, Miraflores, Lima, Peru, 18. **Tel** 014 791 274.

PHILLIPINES

Teaching Centres

KARMA KAGYU D.C.
Address Vajradhara House, 5 Elgin Street, S. Fairview Pk., Quezon City, Phillipines.

POLAND

Cultural Organisations and Tibetan Refugee Aid Societies

POLISH-TIBETAN FRIENDSHIP SOCIETY
Address ul. Bruna 2, m. 10, Warsaw, Poland, 02–594. **Tel** 022–25–4247. **Lama/Scholar** Anna Engelking (President).

Teaching Centres

KARMA KAGYU BUDDHIST CENTER
Address Kuchary 57, Drobin, Poland, 09210. **General Description** This is the country residential centre of the Stowarzyszenie Buddyjskie Karma Kagyu W Polsce. **Facilities and Services** The centre has retreat hut facilities.

STOWARZYSZENIE BUDDYJSKIE KARMA KAGYU W POLSCE
Address ul. Zeblikiewicza 20/3, Krakow, Poland, 31 029. **Tel** 012 22 0484. **Founder** Ole Nydahl. **General Description** This is one of the central branches of this group of Karma Kagyu centres in Poland under the direction of H.E. Shamar Rinpoche. Other main city centres are in Warsaw, Gdansk, Poznan, Lodz, Katowice, Wraclaw, Szchecin, and Olsztin.

ROMANIA

Teaching Centres

KARMA THEKSUM CHOLING ORADEA
Address Str Cosminului Nr 7, Bl X 17, App ll, Oradea, Romania, 3700.

RUSSIA

Academic Organisations

BUDDHIST INSTITUTE, MOSCOW
Address Profsojuznaya 20/9–291, Moscow, Russia, 119292. **Tel** 095 125 0454. **Lama/Scholar** Tom Rabdanov (Executive Director). **General Description** The institute holds courses in Tibetan, Mongolian, Sanskrit, Chinese and Japanese, as well as scholarly aspects of Buddhism. Courses are taught mostly by professors from Moscow University, and held in rooms at the Moscow Technical University.

BURYAT INSTITUTE OF SOCIAL SCIENCES, SIBERIAN BRANCH OF RUSSIAN ACADEMY OF SCIENCES
Address Sakhyanovoi ul. 6, Ulan Ude, Buryatia, Russia, 670042. **Tel** (8) 30122 30136. **Lama/Scholar** Dr. Nikolai Abaev (Head Oriental Studies), Dr. Elbert Bazaron (Inst. of Biology), Dr. Viktor Pupyshev (Tibetologist), Dr. Kseniya M. Gerasinova (Research). **General Description** The Buryat Institute contains one of the best and largest collections of Tibetan blockprints and manuscripts in Buryatia. The research is carried out mainly in the field of ethnology, Tibetan medicine and the history of Buddhism in Buryatia. There is a notable archive collection, and a strong emphasis on research and publishing in the field of Tibetan medicine, Tibetan philology, Buddhist philosophy and practice in India, Tibet, Mongolia, China, Buryatia and Russia.

GEORGE ROERICH MEMORIAL DEPT., INSTITUTE OF ORIENTAL STUDIES
Address Moscow Branch of Academy of Sciences, 12 Rozhdestvenka Ul, Moscow, Russia. **Tel** 095 157 01 79. **Telex/Fax** 095 9752396. **Lama/Scholar** Dr. V.S. Dylykova. **General Description** This collection contains Tibetan manuscripts and blockprints

brought by George Roerich. The institute has a considerable Tibetan library and is the main academic research centre in Moscow. The 10 volume Roerich Tibetan/Russian/English dictionary is published by the institute.

KALMYK INSTITUTE OF SOCIAL STUDIES, ACADEMY OF SCIENCES OF RUSSIA

Address ul. Revolutsionnaya 8, Elista, Kalmyk, Russia, 358000. **Tel** 8 84722 63239. **Lama/Scholar** Dr. Pyotr Bitkeyev (Director). **General Description** The institute has a small museum and library collection. Research is carried out on the local history of Tibetan Buddhism.

ST. PETERSBURG UNIVERSITY, FACULTY OF PHILOSOPHY

Address Room No 130, Mendleev Line 5, St. Petersburg, Russia, 199034. **Tel** 218 94 22. **General Description** The Faculty of Philosophy began a two year course of paid instruction in October 1992. The programme includes studying Chinese, Sanskrit, Buddhist texts and the History of Buddhism.

TUVINIAN RESEARCH INSTITUTE OF LANGUAGE, LITERATURE & HISTORY

Address ul Kochetova 4, Kyzyl, Tuva, Russia, 667000. **Tel** (8) 39422 33190. **Lama/Scholar** Dr. Yury Aranchyn (Director). **General Description** The Tuvinian Institute carries out research on traditional Tibetan Buddhism in this Turkic region of Russian Central Asia.

Ecumenical Centres

ASSOCIATION OF TUVA BUDDHISTS, ALDYN BOGDA

Address Novaya ul. 56, Kyzyl, Tuva, Russia, 667000. **Tel** (8) 39422 21790. **Lama/Scholar** Vladimir Korasal. **General Description** This society has been established in order to revive the study and practice of Buddhism in the area.

BUDDHIST ASSOCIATION OF KALMYK

Address ul. Lermontova 83, Elista, Kalmyk, Russia, 358000. **Tel** 8 84722 63239. **Lama/Scholar** Telo Rinpoche (President). **General Description** This association is to help revive traditional Buddhism throughout Kalmykia. There are Buddhist communities now in almost every village in Kalmykia.

BUDDHIST HOUSE

Address 32–27 Vosstania ul., St. Petersburg, Russia. **Tel** (812) 272 0727.

CENTRAL BUDDHIST BOARD OF RUSSIA

Address Ostojenka 49, Moscow, Russia, 119034. **Tel** 095 245 0939. **Telex/Fax** 248 0264. **Lama/Scholar** Lama Zodpo (Representative). **General Description** The Central Buddhist Board coordinates contact with the Russian Central Government and international relations primarily for the traditional Buryat Buddhist community in Russia. It occasionally holds courses in Tibetan Buddhism with visiting teachers.

Libraries

ARCHIVE OF ACADEMY OF SCIENCES, ARCHIVE OF THE INSTITUTE OF ORIENTAL STUDIES DEPT.

Address Dvortsoyaya Nab 18, St. Petersburg, Russia, 191065. **General Description** This library contains the materials of renowned Russian Tibetologists, amongst whom are: E. Obermiller, Vostrikov and Tubyansky. There are a number of unpublished papers and other materials.

ARCHIVE OF THE GEOGRAPHICAL SOCIETY

Address Grivtsov per. 10, St. Petersburg, Russia. **Tel** (812) 315 6282. **General Description** This library contains all the materials gathered by the Russian expeditions to Central Asia and Tibet during the 19th and 20th centuries. Many of the materials and photographs are as yet unpublished.

INSTITUTE OF ORIENTAL STUDIES LIBRARY, ST. PETERSBURG BRANCH, ACADEMY OF SCIENCES

Address Dvortsovaya Nab 18, St. Petersburg, Russia, 191065. **Lama/Scholar** Prof. Eugene Kychanov (Deputy Director), Dr. V.L. Uspensky (International Relations), Dr. M.I. Vorobyova-Desyatovskaya (Manuscript), Dr. Raisa Krapivina (Sakya Tradition), Dr. Lev S. Savitsky, Dr. Martynov (Law), Dr. Rudoy (Abhidharma). **General Description** This library contains one of the most extensive and valuable collections of Tibetan manuscripts and blockprints in Europe. Included are the collected works of more than 100 leading Tibetan lamas.

TH. STCHERBATSKY ARCHIVE

Address Vasilyersky Ostrov, 5th line, 7, St. Petersburg, Russia. **Tel** 812 213 2860. **General Description** This library contains an extensive collection of materials, texts and papers of Stcherbatsky and other scholars.

Medical Institutions

ALL-RUSSIA INST. OF TRADITIONAL MEDICINE

Address 1st Samotechny Perevlok 17A str. 1, Moscow, Russia, 103473. **Tel** 095 288 6706. **Telex/Fax** 095 288 6706. **Lama/Scholar** Natalya Lukyanova, Dr. Chimed Dorji. **General Description** This institute, in cooperation with the Tibetan Medical and Astro Institute , Dharamsala, India, conducts both clinical and research programmes in Tibetan medicine. It also publishes Russian translations of works on Tibetan medicine, astrology and Buddhism.

Monasteries and Nunneries

AGINSKY MONASTERY

Address Datsan, Aginskoe 1, Aginsky, Chita Region, Russia, 674460. **Tel** (8) 30239 34548. **Lama/Scholar** Ven. Zolto Lama (Abbot). **General Description** The monastery has a good library collection.

IVOLGINSKY MONASTERY

Address Datsan, Ivolginsk, Ulan Ude, Buryatia, Russia, 671210. **Lama/Scholar** Ven. Bandido Khambo, Lama Jamyang (Head Lama), Ven. Dr. Tashi Nyima (Abbot). **General Description** The monastery has a Buddhist School, started in 1991, with two separate programmes, in Buryat and Russian language medium, for training lamas in traditional rituals and monastic subjects of study, and in Tibetan language. A separate course in Tibetan medicine was begun in 1992. The main office of the Central Buddhist Board of Russia is at the monastery. Approximately 20 monasteries have been reopened or refounded throughout Buryatia and the Chita Region.

KHURUL MONASTERY
Address ul. Lermontova 83, Elista, Kalmyk, Russia, 358000. **Lama/Scholar** Ven. Telo Rinpoche (Abbot).

KUNTSECHOINEI DATSAN MONASTERY
Address 91 Primorsky prospect, St. Petersburg, Russia, 197228. **Tel** (812) 239 0341. **Lama/Scholar** Tenzin Khetsun Samayev (Abbot). **General Description** This is the famous St Petersburg Kalacakra Temple. It is primarily a monastery and training centre for young lamas from Buryatia. Public lectures on Tibetan Buddhism and short courses on debate are occasionally held.

TSUGULSKY MONASTERY
Address Datsan, Mogoyty, Chita Region, Russia. **Lama/Scholar** Ven. Jinpa Gyatso Tsybenov (Abbot). **General Description** The lamas at the monastery have good private collections of Tibetan texts.

Museums

CHITINSKY OBLASTNOY KRAYEVEDCHESKY
Address Ulitsa Babushkina 113, Chita, Russia, 672000. **Tel** (8) 30222 32750. **Lama/Scholar** Anna I. Beloborodova (Director). **General Description** This museum contains several hundred Tibetan artefacts, blockprints and manuscripts. There is also a collection of photographs on local Tibetan Buddhism.

ETHNOLOGY MUSEUM OF PEOPLES OF RUSSIA
Address Pl. Iskusstv, St. Petersburg, Russia. **Tel** 812 210 3660. **General Description** The museum has a valuable collection of approximately 2000 sculptures and paintings.

ETHNOLOGY MUSEUM OF PEOPLES OF THE WORLD
Address Universitetskaya nab 3, St. Petersburg, Russia. **Tel** 812 218 0812. **General Description** The museum has a collection of approximately 4000 objects from Tibet and Mongolia. Among these are some interesting bronzes and paintings.

HISTORY MUSEUM OF BURYATIA
Address Ul. Ranjurova 4, Ulan Ude, Buryatia, Russia, 670000. **Tel** 30122 20653. **General Description** The museum has a collection of approximately 10000 Tibetan and Mongolian sculptures, paintings and other artefacts. Some of these pieces are rare and unique. The photo archives contain approximately 7000 negatives and pictures of related material.

MUSEUM OF HISTORY OF RELIGIONS
Address Kazanskaya Pl. 2, St. Petersburg, Russia, 191186. **Tel** 812 271 7426. **Lama/Scholar** Boris Zagumyonny (Librarian), Gorovaya Olga Vasilyevna. **General Description** The museum has a collection of about 10000 Tibetan and Mongolian religious artefacts. There are also approximately 1000 glass negatives and photos.

STATE HERMITAGE

Address Dvortzovaja Nab 34, St. Petersburg, Russia, 19065. **Tel** 812 219 8631. **Lama/Scholar** Gennady Leonov (Tibetan Collection Keeper), Helena Yelihina. **General Description** The museum contains a collection of around 3000 pieces, amongst which are some unique Hara-hoto paintings and rare Tibetan objects of art. This a very highly regarded collection.

STATE MUSEUM OF ORIENTAL ARTS

Address ul Obuha 4, Moscow, Russia. **Tel** 095 227 1113. **Lama/Scholar** Mrs Svetlana Kovalevskaya. **General Description** The museum has a collection of over 2000 Tibetan and Mongolian thangkas and bronzes. The Roerich collection of Tibetan art is housed here.

TUVINIAN AUTONOMOUS REPUBLIC MUSEUM, CALLED AFTER SIXTY HEROES

Address Lenin St., 7, Kyzyl, Tuva, Russia, 667000. **Tel** (8) 39422 23072. **Lama/Scholar** Mongush Kenzin-Lobsan (Director). **General Description** The museum has approximately 2000 artefacts and a substantial collection of blockprints and manuscripts.

Publishing Companies and Journals

MANDAL MAGAZIN: BUDDIZM, TRADIJSH KUL'TURA

Address ul. Revolutsionnaya 8, Elista, Kalmyk, Russia, 358000. **Tel** (8) 84722 63239. **General Description** This Russian language magazine, started in 1992, is published by the Kalmyk Institute of Social Studies of the Academy of Sciences of Russia.

NARTHANG BULLETIN

Address Tavricheskaya 45–82, St. Petersburg, Russia, 193015. **Tel** 812 274 4439. **Lama/Scholar** Andrey Terentyev. **General Description** The *Narthang Bulletin* is a monthly publication, in Russian and English, giving

information on Buddhist communities and activities in Russia. **Facilities and Services** The *Narthang Bulletin* also distribute the book *"The Buddhist Shrine of Petrograd"* by A.I. Andreev, on the history and present situation of the famous Buddhist Temple of St. Petersburg.

NAUKA, GLAVNAYA REDAKTSIYA VOSTOCHNOY LITERATURY

Address Stroyeniye 2, Tsvetnoy boulvard 21, Moscow, Russia. **Tel** 921 0349. **Telex/Fax** 420 2220. **Lama/Scholar** Lev Rozhansky. **General Description** The Novosibirsk branch of this publishing company is especially productive for books on Oriental subjects.

Teaching Centres

KARMA CHOY LING PETERSBURG

Address St. Petersburg Buddhist Centre, 14 Mohovaya St., St. Petersburg, Russia, 191028. **Tel** 812 296 34 68. **Year Established** 1991. **Founder** Ole Nydahl.

MOSCOW NYINGMA DZOGCHEN GROUP

Address Bolshoy Kondratyevsky prospect 10–11, Moscow, Russia. **Tel** 095 254 9748.

RANDOLGAR DZOGCHEN COMMUNITY

Address 25 Tayojnaya St., Novokizhinginsk, Burytia, Russia, 671454. **Year Established** 1992.

ST. PETERSBURG KARMA KAGYU CENTRE

Address 7 Sovetskaya St. 9–14, St. Petersburg, Russia. **Tel** 812 271 7024.

SINGAPORE

Teaching Centres

AMITABHA BUDDHIST CENTRE

Address 494-D Geylang, Singapore, S–1438. **Tel** 745 8547. **Telex/Fax** 741 0438.

KARMA KAKYUD BUDDHIST CENTRE
Address No. 38 Lorong 22, Geylang, Singapore, 1439. **Tel** 7491103/7410935. **Telex/Fax** 7442302.

SAKYA TENPHEL LING, SINGAPORE BUDDHA SASANA SOCIETY
Address Nos 37 & 39, Lorong 25A, Geylang, Singapore, 1438. **Tel** 7494144. **Telex/Fax** 7437681.

SOUTH AFRICA

Publishing Companies and Journals

BUDDHIST BOOK SERVICE
Address PO Box 2674, Pinetown, Natal, South Africa, 3600.

Teaching Centres

CAPETOWN SAMYE DZONG
Address 601 Landcaster, Marlborough Park, Bath Road, Claremont, Cape, South Africa, 7700. **Tel** 021 61 7443. **Founder** Akong Rinpoche.

JOHANNESBURG SAMYE DZONG
Address 31 Streatly Ave, CNR Lothbury, Auckland Park, Transvaal, South Africa, 2092. **Tel** 011 726 7456. **Founder** Akong Rinpoche.

LAM RIM CENTRE JOHANNESBURG
Address 14 Los Angeles Drive, North Cliff, Transvaal, South Africa, 2195. **Tel** 011 673 5688. **Founder** Geshe Damcho Yonten.

NIEU BETHESDA SAMYE DZONG
Address PO Box 15, Nieu Bethesda, Cape, South Africa, 6286. **Tel** 04923 631. **Founder** Akong Rinpoche.

PORT ELIZABETH SAMYE DZONG
Address 6 Sherlock St., Central, Port Elizabeth, Cape, South Africa, 6001. **Tel** 041 55 4334. **Founder** Akong Rinpoche.

SPAIN

Publishing Companies and Journals

EDICIONES DHARMA
Address Apartado 218, 03660 Novelda, Alicante, Spain. **Tel** (96) 560 3200.

Teaching Centres

CET NAGARJUNA (BARCELONA)
Address Rosellon 298, Pral 2A, Barcelona, Spain, 83037. **Tel** 03 4570788. **Telex/Fax** 03 4570788. **Lama/Scholar** Geshe Lobsang Tsultrim.

CET NAGARJUNA (GRANADA)

Address Silencio, 4–5-izqda, Granada, Spain. **Tel** 58 287 404.

CET NAGARJUNA (MADRID)

Address Costanilla de Los Angeles, No.2 escalera izda.,3-dcha, Madrid, Spain, 28013. **Tel** 91 541 3755. **Telex/Fax** 91 429 6708. **Distribution Details** Contact the centre for further information. **Year Established** 1983. **Founder** Lama Thubten Yeshe. **Lama/Scholar** Geshe Thubten Tsering. **General Description** CET Nagarjuna, a member of the Foundation for the Preservation of the Mahayana Tradition (FPMT), is located in a house on the outskirts of Madrid. It is large enough to house a resident lama and two other residents, but does not usually offer accommodation to visitors. The shrine room or gompa (sgom pa) can hold up to fifty people at a time, and can be extended by removing the partition to an adjoining room. There is an extensive collection of books on Buddhism in the library. **Teaching Programme** Monthly courses are given by the different lamas that are resident in Spain. These have included such topics as, *The Graduated Path to Enlightenment* (*Lam Rim*); *Mind Training* or *Lojong* (*Blo sbyong*); and Shantideva's classic text, the *Bodhisattvacaryavatara*. In addition, meditation classes are held twice a week on stabilising meditation ('jog sgom) and analytical meditation (dpyad sgom). Regular pujas are held according to the Tibetan calendar, and there are weekend retreats. **Facilities and Services** The gompa, lecture room, and library are open daily. Courses and lectures on Buddhist philosophy, meditation classes, and weekend retreats, all take place in the centre. There is a bookshop on the premises, and a newsletter is distributed to those who wish to be kept informed about the centre's activities. **Project Description** It is hoped to invite a qualified geshe and translator to become permanently resident in the centre. This will enable CET Nagarjuna to offer a regular graded teaching programme, and allow individuals to seek spiritual guidance.

CET NAGARJUNA (VALENCIA)

Address Calle Joaquin Costa 10-Pta 9, Valencia, Spain, 46005. **Tel** 6 395 1008. **Telex/Fax** 6 383 3043.

DAG SHANG KAGYU, CENTRO DE RETIROS

Address 'Finca El Villero', Panillo-Graus, Huesca, Spain. **Tel** 908 139440. **Founder** Kalu Rinpoche. **Lama/Scholar** Drubgyu Tenpa. **General Description** There is a Tibetan style monastery on 2000 acres of land.

EDICIONES DHARMA (TEACHING CENTRE)

Address Apartado 218, 03660 Novelda, Alicante, Spain. **Tel** (96) 560 3200. **Telex/Fax** (96) 560 4796.

INSTITUTO DHARMA

Address C/Carnisseria, Ciutadella, Menorca, Baleares, Spain, 07760. **Tel** 71 480078. **Distribution Details** Ediciones Amara distribute two Spanish books: *La Esencia del Budismo Tibetano* and *Encuentros en tu Interior*. **Year Established** 1981. **Founder** Geshe Kelsang Gyatso. **Lama/Scholar** Geshe Tamdin Gyatso. **General Description** Instituto Dharma adheres to the Gelugpa school of Tibetan Buddhism. Its main aim is to promote the teachings of the graduated path to enlightenment (*Lam Rim*), as well as other topics from the sutras and tantras, in accordance with the different needs of practitioners. The centre has a membership of around twenty-five, and supports one resident lama, together with a Tibetan translator. It is situated in a holiday resort on the island of Menorca. **Teaching Programme** From October to April, three days in the week are given over to a regular programme of oral commentaries to Tibetan texts. These teachings are translated from Tibetan into English, and then into Spanish. During 1987–88, Geshe Tamdin Gyatso gave an extensive commentary to the tantric practice of Vajrayogini, as well as teachings on Je Tsong Khapa's *Concise Exposition of the Graduated Path* and Thogmed Zangpo's *Thirty-Seven Practices of a Bodhisattva*. From October 1988 to April 1989, the resident lama reviewed the practice of six session guru yoga; a *lojong (Blo sbyong)* text entitled, *The Mind-Training Like the Rays of the Sun*; as well as elucidating the viewpoints propounded by the Prasanghika and Svatantrika Madhyamaka philosophical schools. Twice a year, more general courses on Buddhism are arranged. There is also a weekly guided meditation held in the centre. **Facilities and Services** The centre will help interested students of Buddhism to find accommodation locally. **Project Description** General plans exist to purchase a larger house in order to offer more residential accommodation and to diversify the teaching programme to include group retreats, yoga classes, Tibetan painting courses and other activities.

O SEL LING (RETREAT CENTRE)

Address, Bubion, Granada, Spain, 18412. **Tel** (58) 76 30 88. **Distribution Details** Please contact the centre for further information. **Year Established** 1980. **Founder** Lama Thubten Yeshe. **Lama/Scholar** Geshe Tenpa Dhargye. **General Description** O Sel Ling is a centre dedicated exclusively to retreaters. It is set in the magnificent Sierra Nevada range of mountains in the south east of the country. Close to the little white washed village of Bubion, it was named 'O Sel Ling' – place of clear light – by His Holiness the Dalai Lama. The centre is a member of the Foundation for the Preservation of the Mahayana Tradition (FPMT). The centre also offers introductory courses on Buddhism, in English and Spanish, during the summer months. **Teaching Programme** The resident lama, Geshe Tenpa Dhargye, teaches every day of the week, except Mondays. He is presently giving an extensive commentary to Je Tsong Khapa's classic exposition on the graduated paths to enlightenment, the *'Lam rim chen mo'*. **Facilities and Services** O Sel Ling possesses twelve retreat houses which are available throughout the year. It is possible to do long or short retreats at the centre. **Project Description** The centre intends to build more houses in order to expand its retreat facilities.

THUBTEN LING

Address Aptdo 162, Villena, Alicante, Spain, 03400. **Tel** 6 580 8962. **General Description** This is a retreat centre with facilities for both individuals and groups. In the holiday times the centre organises meditation and introduction to Buddhism courses.

SWEDEN

Cultural Organisations and Tibetan Refugee Aid Societies

SVENSKA TIBETKOMMITTEN

Address Bondegatan 9 A, 5TR, Stockholm, Sweden, S–116 23. **Tel** (8) 714 9102. **Telex/Fax** (8) 718 5316. **Distribution**

Details Publishes a quarterly review newsletter, '*Tibet*'.

SWEDISH TIBET COMMITTEE
Address c/o Kurt Blau, Tiundagatan 52 A, Uppsala, Sweden, S–752 30.

Museums

FOLKENS MUSEUM ETNOGRAFISKA, MUSEUM OF THE PEOPLES
Address Djurgardsbrunnsvagen 34, Stockholm, Sweden, S–11527. **Tel** 08 667 05 60. **Telex/Fax** 08 667 22 44. **General Description** The Folkens Museum Central Asian collections are primarily connected to the research carried out by Dr Sven Hedin and his staff-ethnographer, Dr Gosta Montell, during their travels in the early part of this century and left by Dr Hedin to the museum. The collection brought together between 1929 and 1932 by Dr Montell contains some especially fine pieces. The collection is particularly strong on Tibetan ritual art but also includes everyday household implements. There are about 5000 items collected from Peking, Inner and Outer Mongolia, Tibet and East Turkestan. In addition to the artefacts there is a large collection of photographs of Central Asia/Tibet, also to a great extent left to the museum by Dr Hedin and his colleagues. Further, there are some old films, which are being restored, and a collection of about 5000 drawings by Dr Hedin, which he also left to the museum. Sven Hedin's library relating to China and Central Asia is housed at the museum and runs into several thousand volumes. It covers most material on Central Asia and Tibet published in European languages from the early seventeenth century up to the mid-twentieth century. The museum has some material on Central Asia (including a temple-jurt and a domestic jurt) exhibited. In 1992 there are plans to inaugurate a major permanent exhibition on Central Asia.

Teaching Centres

KARMA SHEDRUP DARGYE LING
Address Hokarvagen 2, 12658 Hagersten, Sweden. **Tel** 08 886 950. **Year Established** 1974. **Founder** Kalu Rinpoche. **Lama/Scholar** Lama Ngawang. **General Description** Karma Shedrup Dargye Ling is the Stockholm centre of the Karma Kagyu tradition. It also acts as a base for the Kagyu Trust, Karma Tenpai Gyaltsen, an organisation representing the Tibetan Buddhist religious community in Sweden. A retreat centre, Karma Dechen Osel Ling, is situated about two hours car journey away, in the country. Here, a group of people are currently completing the traditional three-year retreat. Karma Shedrup Dargye Ling provides an opportunity for members to study and practise Buddhist teachings. Schools may visit as part of their religious education courses. In this way the centre contributes to raising the level of public awareness concerning Buddhism in general and its Tibetan expression in particular. The resident teacher, Lama Ngawang, with his translator, Soenam Tenzin Jamyangling, as well as a number of Western lamas, are all available for consultation. These lamas will also conduct funeral ceremonies, should they be needed. **Teaching Programme** Tara pujas are performed every morning, and the practice of shamatha (zhi gnas) meditation followed by Avalokiteshvara (Chenrezig) and short Mahakala (Nagpo Chenpo, Shadrugpa) pujas, take place in the evenings. On weekends, either Lama Ngawang or a Western lama gives teachings. There are also Tibetan language classes held by Soenam T. Jamyangling and by K. Rinchen, and Lama Chopel gives elementary instruction to a group of children. Courses are held some weekends. These have been on such topics as: The Basic Principles of Buddhism; Seven Point Mind Training or Lojong (Blo sbyongs); the Ngondro (sngon 'gro) preliminary

practices; and shamatha and vipashyana meditation. An annual summer course is held in July on a general topic chosen by Lama Ngawang. Those intending to participate in the next three-year retreat are involved in a preparatory course concerned with learning Tibetan, the Ngondro practices, and various pujas. **Facilities and Services** Karma Shedrup Dargye Ling's library contains an extensive collection of works on Tibetan Buddhism in English, Swedish and Tibetan. Tibetan textual holdings include copies of the *Kangyur (bKa' 'gyur)*, the *Tengyur (bsTan 'gyur)*, Jamgon Kongtrul's *Rin chen gter mdzod* and *Shes bya Kun khyab*, the *rGya chen bKa' mdzod*, the *bKa' brgyud Ngags mdzod*, and the *sNying thig rTsa po*. The centre also houses a bookshop called Snolejonet (Snow Lion). A copier is available to print the considerable amount of Tibetan literature needed for each person in the three-year retreat, and also Swedish translations of various spiritual practices, including those of Avalokiteshvara (Chenrezig), Amitabha, Padmasambhava, Green Tara, the Mahamudra Prayer, the Ngondro Prayer of Noble Conduct (*bzang spyod mon lam*), and Mikyo Dorje's Guru Yoga of the Four Sessions (*Thun bzhi bla ma'i rnal 'byor*). Karma Shedrup Dargye Ling also produce a magazine entitled *Milarepa*, which appears two or three times a year. Facilities exist to accommodate visitors for short retreats. There are also opportunities to practice individual retreats at Karma Dechen Osel Ling under the guidance of Lama Ngawang. The last three-year retreat, the third of its kind, began in 1988. **Project Description** New buildings are being constructed for future three-year retreats and work on a traditional Tibetan temple began in 1990. A number of translations of Buddhist texts into Swedish are being carried out. *The Life of Milarepa*, Chogyam Trungpa's *Meditation in Action* and Kalu Rinpoche's *Foundations of Buddhist Meditation* and other discourses given by him are published by the Centre.

SAKYA CHANGCHUP CHOLING
Address Ingemarsgatan 1B 4tr., Stockholm, Sweden, S–11420. **Tel** (0) 8 15 75 82. **Telex/Fax** (0) 8 660 60 64. **Year Established** 1979. **Founder** Ven. Geshe Sherab Gyaltsen.

SWITZERLAND

Cultural Organisations and Tibetan Refugee Aid Societies

GESELLSCHAFT SCHWEIZERISCH-TIBETISCHE, FREUNDSCHAFT
Address Postfach 1523, Rapperswil, Switzerland, CH–8640.

ROKPA INTERNATIONAL
Address Sonnenhof 5, Benglen, Switzerland, 8121. **Tel** 41 1 825 35 22. **Telex/Fax** 41 1 825 60 12. **Year Established** 1982. **Founder** H.H. Sixteenth Karmapa. **Lama/Scholar** Akong Rinpoche (President). **General Description** Rokpa is an international charitable organisation with its headquarters in Switzerland

and branches in many parts of Europe, North America and Asia. Its original aim was to give aid to sick and destitute Tibetan refugees in India and Nepal, but Rokpa has now extended its activities to help the sick, homeless, aged and mentally distressed throughout many parts of the world regardless of religion, nationality or cultural background. **Project Description** In Tibet, India and Nepal Rokpa arranges sponsorships for the education of children, further education for adults, medical treatment for the sick and support for the elderly. Sponsorship programmes are also run in London, Scotland and Brussels.

Government Offices

OFFICE OF TIBET (SWITZERLAND)
Address Waffenplatzstrasse 10, Zurich, Switzerland, CH–8002. **Tel** 01 201 3336. **Telex/Fax** 01 202 2160. **Lama/Scholar** Gyaltsen Gyaltag (Representative). **General Description** Bureau of the Representative of H.H. the Dalai Lama for Middle and Southern Europe.

Museums

ETHNOGRAPHIC MUSEUM,
UNIVERSITY OF ZURICH
Address Pelikanstrasse 40, Zurich, Switzerland, 8001. Tel 01 2213191. Lama/Scholar Dr Martin Brauen.

ETHNOGRAPHICAL MUSEUM,
GENEVA
Address Boulevard Carl Vogt 65–67, Geneva, Switzerland.

ETHNOLOGICAL MUSEUM, BASEL
Address Augustinergasse 2, Basel, Switzerland.

Teaching Centres

RABTEN CHOELING,
CENTRE FOR HIGHER TIBETAN
STUDIES
Address Ch Du Derochoz, 2, Le Mont-Pelerin, Vaud, Switzerland,

1801. **Tel** (021) 9217798. **Distribution Details** The centre distributes worldwide. A full catalogue is available on request. **Year Established** 1977. **Founder** Geshe Rabten Rinpoche. **Lama/Scholar** Gonsar Rinpoche, Geshe Rabten Rinpoche (formerly), Geshe Thubten Thinley. **General Description** Rabten Choeling aims to preserve the living tradition of Tibetan Buddhism and make it available in the West. To realise this goal it has set up a monastery, where a complete training in all aspects of Buddhism can be undertaken. Incorporated within the monastery is a teaching centre, which is open to all who wish to attend study and meditation courses of both a short and long term nature. Some of the principal activities of Rabten Choeling are the study of philosophical analysis, the practice of meditation, and training in scriptural and colloquial Tibetan. **Teaching Programme** Courses are given in Buddhist philosophy and psychology. There are opportunities to practice meditation, and to learn both classical and colloquial forms of the Tibetan language. Occasional courses are given in the fundamentals of Tibetan art. **Facilities and Services** The centre possesses a shrine room, where teachings and meditation practice take place, and its library contains numerous texts on Buddhism and related subjects, both in Tibetan and in several Western languages. Both these facilities are located in a new part of the centre inaugurated by H.H. the Dalai Lama in 1988. The centre also has accommodation in the form of single and double rooms and dormitory rooms for visitors. **Project Description** It is hoped to extend the study and practice opportunities available at the centre. The centre is a focal point for all Tibetan refugees in Switzerland and a summer course is organised for the Tibetan children in Switzerland, allowing them to learn more of Tibetan language and Buddhism.

RIME JANGCHUP CHOELING
Address Sempacherstrasse 23, Zurich, Switzerland, 8032. **Tel** 41
1 3833442. **Distribution Details** The centre distributes a few
transcripts, video tapes, posters, postcards, and other such materials. **Year Established** 1987.

SAMYE DZONG/KARMA TENPHEL LING
Address Sonnenhof 5, Benglen, Switzerland, 8121. **Tel** (41 1)
825 3522. **Telex/Fax** (41 1) 825 6012. **Distribution Details**
Contact the centre for details. **Year Established** 1980. **Founder**
H.H. Sixteenth Gyalwa Karmapa. **General Description** Samye
Dzong/Karma Tenphel Ling was named by the Sixteenth
Karmapa. The centre has no dedicated building and there are no
organised regular meetings but occasionally high lamas are invited
to give seminars or courses. **Facilities and Services** There is a
very small collection of cassettes and videos available through the
centre contact address.

THUPTEN JANGCHUB LING
Address c/o Via Ruvigliana 11, Viganello, Switzerland, 6962.

TIBET-INSTITUT, MONASTIC TIBETAN INSTITUTE
Address Wildbergstrasse, Rikon, Switzerland, 8486. **Tel** (052) 35
17 29. **Distribution Details** The Institute distributes publications within a series entitled *Opuscula Tibetana*. **Year Established**
1968. **Lama/Scholar** Geshe Geduen Sangpo-Abbot, Geshe
Jampa Lodroe Dahortsang, Datsang Tulku, Sherab Gyaltsen
Amipa, Geshe Rabjampa, Tenzin Phuntsog Jottotshang-Chotse,
Geshe Khedup Thubten Tokhang, Gedun Gyatso Chukha-
Acarya, Losang Tenpa-Novice. **General Description** The
Monastic Tibetan Institute was founded in the 1960s, formally
opening on 28 September, 1968, when the two chief spiritual
tutors of H.H. the Dalai Lama, Yongdzin Ling Rinpoche and
Yongdzin Trijang Rinpoche, presided over a ceremony of dedication. Its aim is threefold: to provide a monastic focal point for
Tibetans living in exile in Switzerland and neighbouring countries,
with the community of monks serving the religious needs of the
exiles both in the private and the liturgical sphere; to be a place for
scientific studies in the field of Tibetological-Buddhology; and
thirdly to spread information in two different ways – firstly by the
teaching of Tibetan children and young people to read and write
and receive religious instruction in their native tongue, and secondly by providing information and teachings to a wider circle of
interested people in the West. Today six monks from both the
Gelugpa (dGe lugs pa) and Sakyapa (Sa skya pa) schools of
Tibetan Buddhism, together with the Abbot, Geshe Geduen
Sangpo, reside in the institute, and work to further these aims.
Teaching Programme Lectures, discussions and seminary sessions are held in the institute and elsewhere on a variety of different topics. The monks of the institute provide instruction to young
Tibetans, thus helping to preserve their cultural heritage. They are
also available to scholars or interested individuals for consultation
on matters relating to the field of Buddhist studies. Having

enjoyed a traditional Tibetan education, they are experts on the classical Buddhist writings and the Mahayana philosophy contained therein, as well as possessing a thorough understanding of the liturgical forms and the symbolism of many ritual practices. They are also qualified to assist in translations from Tibetan into English and German. **Facilities and Services** By means of expert advice and reports the institute is actively engaged in answering questions on such topics as Tibetan textual criticism, religion, history, iconography and sociology; it has also helped many institutions and individual scholars to find answers to questions about Tibetan music, orthography, geography, numismatics, philately, the bestowal of names, calligraphy and bibliography. The institute possesses a large library of western studies on Tibet which is frequently consulted. There is also a film archive and a certain amount of Tibetan textual holdings. A number of publications on Tibetan culture have been produced within the *Opuscula Tibetana* series. Visits to the institute can be arranged. **Project Description** There is an ongoing fundraising project to sustain the institute's present range of activities, as well as extend them.

YIGA CHOZIN
Address Hintere Zunen 6, Zollikon, Switzerland, 8702. **Tel** (05) 01 3918167. **Distribution Details** Tapes are only distributed in exceptional circumstances. **Year Established** 1975. **Founder** Geshe Tadin Rabten/Dora M. Kalff. **General Description** Yiga Chozin is located in the home of Dr Martin Kalff and Sabine Kalff. One room is set aside for teachings which take place regularly. The centre has links with Dora M. Kalff, who is known for her work on 'sandplay therapy'. **Teaching Programme** Yiga Chozin was established to explore connections between Eastern and Western perspectives with regard to religion and psychology. Its emphasis

is on Tibetan Buddhism, but the centre is open to other schools of Buddhism, or indeed other related activities. Yiga Chozin offers regular weekly teachings from the Gelug (dGe lugs) tradition of Tibetan Buddhism by Ven Geshe Jampa Lodro. There are also occasional courses and lectures from other Buddhist schools, as well as talks comparing Eastern and Western viewpoints in related subject areas. **Facilities and Services** No accommodation is available at the centre.

TAIWAN

Teaching Centres

DRIKUNG KAGYU SUTRA TANTRA CENTRE
Address 11 Fl., No. 7, Lane 75, Sec. 1, Ta-An Road, Taipei, Taiwan. **Tel** 02 7713450. **Telex/Fax** 02 7525057. **Lama/Scholar** Ven. Liamchen Gyalpo Rinpoche.

JINGXU FOFA ZHONGXIN
Address 4F No.5 Alley 1 Lane 329, Fulin Road, Shihlin Taipei, Taiwan. **Tel** 2 833 8754. **Telex/Fax** 2 833 8754.

NYINGMA PALYUL DHARMA CENTRE
Address 63/H3 Tsui Gu Chuang, Tu Ku Tsu, Shen Khen Shiang, Taipei, Taiwan, 22205.

SAKYA DHARMA CENTER
Address Fuchin Road Section 2, Yuan Lin Tsang Faa, Taiwan.

SAKYA KUNGA NAMGYAL LING
Address 5FL, No 85–2, Lane 10, Hsin-Hai Road, Section 4, Taipei, Taiwan.

VAJRAYANA SAKYA BUDDHIST INSTITUTE, REPUBLIC OF CHINA
Address 5F No 37, Lane 246, Shing Ming Road, Nuifoo, Taipei, Taiwan.

THAILAND

Cultural Organisations and Tibetan Refugee Aid Societies

BUDDHIST PERCEPTION OF NATURE, WILDLIFE FUND THAILAND
Address 255 Asoke Road, Sukhumvit 21, Bangkok, Thailand, 10110. **Tel** 258 9134. **Telex/Fax** 20477 GAZOIL TH.

THAI-TIBET CENTER
Address 4753 3 Soi Wat Thong Nappakhum, Domejchaopraya Rd. Klong-sarn, Bangkok, Thailand, 10600.

UK

Academic Organisations

SCHOOL OF ORIENTAL AND AFRICAN STUDIES, LONDON UNIVERSITY
Address Thornhaugh Street, Russell Square, London, UK, WC1H OXG. **Tel** 071–637 2388. **Lama/Scholar** Philip Denwood (Far East/Art and Archaeology), Dr Tadeusz Skorupski (Religious Studies), Prof Thupten Nyima (Tibetan Dict. Project), Dr Gyurme Dorje (Tibetan Dict. Project). **General Description** SOAS is the only university college in the UK dedicated entirely to the study of Asian and African cultures. **Teaching Programme** The Far East and Religious Studies departments offer undergraduate MA and postgraduate teaching and research programmes in Tibetan language and literature, Buddhist studies and Tibetan art. **Facilities and Services** The library has a unique UK collection of Asian literature. Tibetan texts in book form include the *Peking Kangyur* and *Tengyur*, *Sakya Kabum* and assorted publications from China and India. On microfiche part of the PL 480 series is available. There is also a rare collection of secondary language sources on Tibetan history, geography, religion and philosophy and arts. **Project Description** In progress is a four-year Tibetan Dictionary project funded by the Leverhulme Trust. This involves a translation of the three-volume *Greater Tibetan-Chinese Dictionary*, published in 1984, to which additions will be made on the basis of reference material derived from previously published dictionaries and unpublished word lists. Specialists will be invited to contribute to the dictionary in its later stage of development. The aim is to produce an on-line electronic dictionary as well as a printed copy. The project has inspired the development of computerised Tibetan fonts for use in a multiscript environment.

UNIVERSITY OF BRISTOL, DEPARTMENT OF THEOLOGY AND RELIGIOUS STUDIES
Address 36 Tyndall's Park Road, Bristol, Avon, UK, BS8 1PL. **Tel** (0272) 303412. **Distribution Details** No materials are dis-

tributed. **Year Established** 1965. **Lama/Scholar** Dr Paul Williams, Dr Rupert Gethin. **General Description** This is a general department of theology and religious studies. In religious studies the emphasis is on Indian studies, and in particular Buddhism. Dr Paul Williams works in the field of Tibetan and Mahayana Buddhism; Dr Rupert Gethin's area of study is Pali Buddhism. The university library holds the collection of the late Edward Conze, and the department offers an Edward Conze Memorial Prize, each year, for work in Buddhist Studies. **Teaching Programme** Undergraduate degrees in Theology and Religious Studies, Theology and Sociology or Politics, Philosophy and Theology, History of Art and Theology, and Religion with Literature are offered. Theology and Religious Studies degree students may specialise in Indian Studies. At present first year students take Philosophy of Religion, an Introduction to the study of Religions, Indian Civilisation, Biblical Studies, and Christian History and Thought. Second year choices include Dimensions of Hinduism, Modern Hinduism, Buddhism, and Sanskrit or Pali Language. Third year choices include Further Buddhist Studies, Pali Buddhist Texts, Tibetan Religions and Indian Society. Postgraduate specialities are Pali and Indo-Tibetan Buddhism. An MA is available in Buddhist Studies with Elementary Sanskrit, Pali or Tibetan. Full details available from the department. **Facilities and Services** The department houses a large private collection of Tibetan texts, mainly on microfiche. Included is the *Lhasa Kangyur (bKa' 'gyur)*; *Cone Tengyur (bsTan 'gyur)*; the complete works of Tsong kha pa and his principal disciples; Bu ston; Shakya mChog ldan; and 'Jam dbyangs bzhad pa; all the Madhyamaka Text Series, Madhyamaka works of Mi pham, Mi bskyod rDo rje and others. There is also a complete Pali canon (PTS edition). All may be made available to research scholars.

Cultural Organisations and Tibetan Refugee Aid Societies

DHARMA THERAPY TRUST

Address 12 Victoria Place, Bedminster, Bristol, UK, BS3 3BP. **Tel** 0272–231138. **Distribution Details** A list of tapes and books available may be obtained by contacting the centre. **Founder** Tsultrim Zangmo. **General Description** Dharma Therapy Trust is a registered charity founded by an English Tibetan Buddhist nun, Tsultim Zangmo, to promote the Buddhist faith and the relief of suffering through education and complementary medicines, including Tibetan medicine. Dharma Therapy Trust works in close cooperation with Lam Rim Buddhist Centre in Bristol, having the same spiritual director, Geshe Damcho Yonten. Visits from Tibetan doctors are arranged by the trust as often as possible, often co-sponsored by the Tibet Foundation in London and the Dutch Foundation for Tibetan Medicine. The trust is establishing more regular visits to the UK by Tibetan doctors. The trust plans to further its aims through the sponsorship of refugee Tibetan monks in India. **Teaching Programme** Visits by Tibetan doctors include, when possible, talks, seminars and workshops on Tibetan medicine, as well as individual consultations. Three visits took place in 1990 in April, July and October. In April 1989, Dr Wangyal and Dr Namgyal spent nearly three weeks in Bristol giving talks, seminars and workshops. Dr Wangyal spoke about the causes of illness as seen in Tibetan medicine and Dr Namgyal led a seminar on Diagnostic Techniques. In July 1989 Dr Dorjee visited briefly enabling those who had consulted Dr Wangyal in April to follow up treatment. In October 1989 Dr Ngarongshar, the Senior Physician at the Delhi Branch Clinic of the Tibetan Medical and Astro. Institute, visited the centre for a few days in order to give private consultations. **Facilities and Services** The centre publishes its own newsletter on a regular basis giving information on past and future events and visits as well as general news about the trust. The Lam Rim Bristol centre also has a selection of taped talks and workshops by Dr Rabgay, Dr Choedhak, Dr Wangyal, and Dr Namgyal and a few small books by Dr Rabgay on topics of Tibetan medicine.

MERIDIAN TRUST

Address 330 Harrow Road, London, UK, W9 2HP. **Tel** 071 289 5443. **Telex/Fax** 071 286 4739. **Distribution Details** All orders must be prepaid. Send remittance payable in pounds sterling, specify home video format, and allow twenty-eight days for delivery. **Year Established** 1982. **Founder** Geoff Jukes. **General Description** The aim of the Meridian Trust is to provide both the Buddhist and general audience with a wider access to teachings from all traditions of Buddhism as practised in the world today, while at the same time to assist in the assimilation of its underlying principles in a manner that is relevant to a Western cultural background. This is to be achieved primarily through the media of film and television. To date, a major activity of the Trust has been to videotape the Buddhist transmission of knowledge as taught by masters from the Tibetan traditions. In the future, projects will examine Buddhism from other traditions such as the Theravadin, Zen and Chinese schools. In addition, parallels that exist between the modern discoveries of science, psychology, medicine, education, the arts and religious enquiry, and the ancient wisdom of the East will be explored. **Facilities and Services** The Meridian Trust distributes a wide range of material on video and film. Topics recorded include explanations of the fundamental principles of Buddhist philosophy and meditation, such as teachings on the condition of existence, death and rebirth, the attainment of happiness and the avoidance of suffering, and developing the human potential to the full. In addition, more advanced aspects of Buddhist meditation and psychology, as found in the teachings on emptiness and those on the general principles of Buddhist tantra, are available on a restricted basis. A number of programmes have also been prepared on the cultural and historical tradition of Tibet. The Meridian Trust provides advice and assistance in arranging teaching programmes based on these video recordings. This is done either through workshops, in which a combined video and lecture service is provided, or through guidance in developing and integrating the use of videos into a teaching programme. This facility is open to small groups as well as larger educational organisations. The trust has full editing facilities run by its subsidiary Meridian Film and Video Ltd. These include two editing suites: Edit I is a broadcast standard three-machine High Band S.P., or two machine Low Band to High Band S.P. suite; Edit II is a Low Band off-line suite which also has VHS to Low Band capabilities. Full sound mixing facilities as well as duplicating facilities and equipment rental (professional and domestic) are offered. These facilities are available to outside agencies on a commercial basis – all profits going towards the funding of The Meridian Trust. **Project Description** An important priority of the Meridian Trust is to maintain and develop its project of film and video documentation. While programmes are prepared for those with a specialised interest, the trust is also developing ways of making Buddhism accessible to a wider Western audience by sponsoring public talks, seminars and related events, and serving as a resource to the academic community from the primary to the university levels. A major project is concerned with documenting the teachings of many of the remaining older Tibetan lamas, living in India and the West, as a resource for Buddhist scholars in the future. To this end the 'Lama Project' was set up by donating further video equipment and video tapes to the Tibetan communities in India and providing the facilities to train Tibetans in all aspects of video production. The project includes the teachings of masters of the four Tibetan Buddhist traditions both in India and the West and also masters of the ancient Bon tradition.

OCKENDEN VENTURE

Address 6 Glisson Road, Cambridge, UK. **General Description** The Ockenden Venture is a cultural centre which has offered courses on meditation and Buddhism taught by Khensur Jampa Donyo Rinpoche, and courses on Tibetan language taught by Kalden Lodoe. There are also occasional talks by visiting speakers and some other events such as Tibetan celebrations. **Teaching Programme** Programmes beginning at 7:30 pm have been held on four evenings a week. For 1990 the schedule was: Spoken Tibetan classes held on Mondays, basic meditation on Tuesdays, study for non-beginners on Thursdays, and videos and readings of H.H. the Dalai Lama's talks on Fridays. Further details of these and other programmes are available from the centre. **Facilities and Services** The centre has facilities for holding study groups and classes, a library of books and video tapes on Tibet, Buddhism and related topics.

ORIENT FOUNDATION

Address Queen Anne House, 11, Charlotte Street, Bath, Avon, UK, BA1 2NE. **Tel** (0225) 336 010. **Telex/Fax** (0225) 311 362. **Year Established** 1982. **Founder** Graham Coleman. **General Description** The Orient Foundation is an educational non-profit organisation in the USA (501 C3) and a registered charity in Great Britain. Four of the founding trustees of the foundation worked together between 1976 and 1981 to produce and distribute the four-hour feature documentary 'Tibet: A Buddhist Trilogy', widely regarded as the most definitive documentary film to date on Tibetan culture. Since 1982, the foundation has through its film production and film distribution activities and through the initiation of the Tibetan Cultural Resources Project, been dedicated to the preservation of the artistic, philosophical and cultural traditions of Tibet and classical India and to the development of an appreciation for this rich and sophisticated cultural heritage. **Facilities and Services** A priority of the foundation since the early 1980s has been to assist the exiled Tibetan communities in their efforts to preserve the oral lineages of Tibet. To date, the foundation has traced and catalogued in excess of 30,000 hours of oral commentarial material, as given by Tibet's leading cultural figures, covering all aspects of Tibet's rich cultural heritage. A database and a printed reference guide have been prepared to this material, both of which also include a guide to Tibetan related facilities world-wide, biographies of key contemporary cultural figures and an extensive glossary of Tibetan and Sanskrit terms. The entire Tibetan Cultural Resources Database is available on disc from the Orient Foundation. The database can be run on any IBM compatable machine with a minimum twenty MB hard disc. The facilities and biographies sections of the database have been published under the title *Handbook of Tibetan Culture*

1993 by Random House. **Project Description** Currently the foundation is administering an extensive oral history recording programme within the exiled Tibetan communities focusing on the recording of oral commentaries in the fields of philosophy, medicine, history and the arts. Priority will be given to those subject areas whose oral commentarial lineages have been revealed by the database to be so far unrecorded. Simultaneous with the above the foundation plans to assist all those who already possess recordings of oral commentarial material to preserve these on suitable long term archival media.

ROKPA TRUST U.K.

Address Samye Ling, Eskdalemuir, Nr. Langholm, Dumfriesshire, UK. **Tel** 03873 73232. **Founder** H.H. Sixteenth Karmapa.

TIBET FOUNDATION

Address 43 New Oxford Street, London, UK, WC1 1BH. **Tel** 071 379 0634. **Telex/Fax** 071 405 3814. **Distribution Details** A catalogue of publications and cassettes is available. **Year Established** 1985. **Founder** Phuntsog Wangyal. **General Description** The Tibet Foundation is a registered charity started in 1985 to work to create a greater awareness in the world of all aspects of Tibetan culture and the needs of Tibetan refugees. The patron is H.H. the Dalai Lama. The foundation is engaged in raising funds to provide help for the various welfare agencies of the Tibetan administration, working in a wide range of relief and care programmes for Tibetan refugees. In addition, the foundation attempts to create a general awareness of the needs of the refugees and seeks to provide up-to-date information on their plight. The foundation also works towards raising money to make available audio, visual and written materials, including the works of the Dalai Lama, and to facilitate and develop activities such as publication, translation, research and seminars. It seeks financial support to promote and assist in visits to the West from representatives of Tibetan Buddhism and culture. **Teaching Programme** The foundation has a wide range of relief and care programmes for Tibetan refugees which includes: the resettlement of refugees, medical care, education and training, and providing for the elderly. A comprehensive sponsorship programme for Tibetan refugees in India and Nepal is one of the principle ways in which the foundation helps the refugees to become self-sufficient. There are also various sponsorship schemes for other sectors of the Tibetan refugee community including young adults who have come to the settlements, old people and young monks in exile. The foundation also organises cultural events in London and in various parts of the country, and co-ordinates visits by Tibetans to the UK. **Facilities and Services** A comprehensive collection of books and tapes about Tibet and Tibetan Buddhism is available for purchase and a newsletter is published twice a year detailing news and information about the foundation.

TIBET INFORMATION NETWORK

Address 7 Beck Road, London, UK, E8 4RE. **Tel** (081) 533 5458. **Telex/Fax** (081) 405 3814. **Distribution Details** Regular information bulletins are distributed.

TIBET SOCIETY AND
RELIEF FUND OF THE UK

Address Olympia Bridge Quay, 70 Russell Road, Kensington, London, UK, W14 8JA. **Tel** 071–603 7764. **Telex/Fax** 071–603 7764. **Year Established** 1959. **Founder** Francis Napier Beaufort Palmer. **General Description** The society was founded in June 1959 in order to give expression to the widespread interest and deep concern aroused in the UK by the Chinese occupation of Tibet. The objects are: to promote the cause of Tibetan independence, to bring before the world the sufferings of the oppressed people of Tibet, to assist those Tibetans who had fled from Tibet to India and elsewhere and to promote understanding of Tibetan history, culture and religion. **Facilities and Services** Members receive periodical newsletters giving the latest information about the Tibetan situation in general and the society's activities. The latter include lectures, film shows, exhibitions and social events.

Ecumenical Centres

BUDDHIST SOCIETY

Address 58 Eccleston Square, London, UK, SW1V 1PH. **Tel** 071 834 5858. **Distribution Details** The Society publishes a quarterly journal entitled *The Middle Way*. **Year Established** 1924. **Lama/Scholar** Ven. Sumedho Bhikkhu. **General Description** The Buddhist Society was established in 1924; it is one of the oldest Buddhist Societies in Europe. The object of the society is to publish and make known the principles of Buddhism and to encourage the study and application of these principles. The society adheres to no one Buddhist school, and aims to give the newcomer an impartial introduction to the many branches of Buddhism practised in Britain today. **Teaching Programme** A comprehensive programme of all classes, lectures and special events held at the Society is

printed in the quarterly journal *The Middle Way*. **Facilities and Services** The Society's premises are open to both members and non-members between 2 and 6pm every day except Sunday. Public lectures and classes are mostly held from 6:30pm. Members are entitled to use the society's General Lending and Reference Libraries, the former either by direct borrowing or by post.

Government Offices

OFFICE OF TIBET (UK)

Address Linburn House, 342 Kilburn High Road, London, UK, NW6 2QJ. **Tel** 071 328 8422. **Telex/Fax** 071 624 4100. **General Description** Bureau of the Representative of H.H. the Dalai Lama for the UK and Scandanavia.

Libraries

BRITISH LIBRARY OMPB

Address Great Russell Street, London, UK, WC1 3DG.

INDIA OFFICE LIBRARY AND
RECORD NEWS, DEPT. ORIENTAL MSS
AND PRINTED BOOKS

Address British Library, 197 Blackfriars Road, London, UK, SE1 8NG.

WELLCOME INSTITUTE, FOR THE
HISTORY OF MEDICINE

Address 183 and 200 Euston Road, London, UK, NW1 2BP. **Tel** 071 383 4414. **Telex/Fax** 071 388 3164. **Year Established** 1913. **Founder** Sir Henry Wellcome. **General Description** The Wellcome Institute for the History of Medicine is a reference library and contains manuscripts, xylographs, books, paintings and drawings chiefly connected with the history of medicine. The institute has acquired prior to 1970:seventy-seven Tibetan manuscripts, fifty-four Tibetan xylographs, one modern print in Tibetan script, a mani stone, twenty-eight thangkas, eighteen banners, ten other paintings and drawings and eight printing blocks. Museum objects are on indefinite loan to the Science Museum.

Museums

ASHMOLEAN MUSEUM

Address Department of Eastern Art, Ashmolean Museum, Oxford, Oxfordshire, UK, OX1 2PH. **Tel** 0865 278071. **Telex/Fax** 0865 278018. **Year Established** 1683. **Founder** Elias Ashmole. **General Description** The Department of Eastern Art holds a collection of several hundred Tibetan artefacts, some being on longterm loan from the Bodleian Library and a private collection. Bronze and other metal images and various ritual objects and vessels predominate. There are also over 100 thangkas at present in the collection; the majority of which are on loan. A selection from the collections is on permanent display in the department's galleries.

BRITISH MUSEUM, DEPARTMENT OF ORIENTAL ANTIQUITIES

Address Great Russell Street, London, UK, WC1B 3DG. **Tel** 071 636 1555. **Telex/Fax** 071 323 8480. **Year Established** 1753. **General Description** The British Museum was founded by an Act of Parliament in 1753. The material from Tibet includes objects in the following categories: religious and ritual equipment of all kinds, costumes, arms and armour, banner paintings, inscriptions, bookcovers, sculpture in most media, and some categories of domestic equipment.

GLASGOW MUSEUMS AND ART GALLERIES

Address Department of Archaeology and Ethnography, Kelvingrove, Glasgow, Strathclyde, Scotland, UK, G3 8AG. **Tel** 041 357 3929. **Telex/Fax** 041 357 4537. **Year Established** 1870. **General Description** The Tibetan collection consists of about 200 items. Best represented are a great variety of religious items: images, printed prayers, offering utensils, amulets, rosaries and musical instruments. There are eight Buddhist images in metal, including a spectacular gilded image of Avalokiteshvara, standing about a metre high on a pedestalled lotus base. This was presented in 1905; most of the other smaller images were acquired in 1929 as part of the Boyd collection of Asian Hindu and Buddhist figures. The collection also includes: eight thangkas, a full size standing prayer wheel, a stupa mould, and a stupa made in such a mould. In addition there are thirty examples of musical instruments, some Tibetan costumes, various food consumption utensils, a few weapons and some miscellanea.

LEEDS CITY MUSEUM

Address Municipal Buildings, Leeds, West Yorkshire, UK, LS1 3AA.

LIVERPOOL MUSEUM,
NATIONAL MUSEUMS AND GALLERIES ON MERSEYSIDE

Address William Brown Street, Liverpool, Merseyside, UK, L3 8EN. **Tel** 051 207 0001. **Telex/Fax** 051 207 3759. **General**

Description The Liverpool Museum has a Tibetan collection comprising approximately 2000 items covering a wide range of Tibetan culture. The collection has been put together over the last 100 years from a variety of bequests and purchases. **Project Description** Work will be continuing on this collection over the next few years.

MUSEUM OF ARCHAELOGY AND ANTHROPOLOGY

Address Downing Street, Cambridge, Cambridgeshire, UK, CB2 3DR. **Tel** 333511.

NUNEATON MUSEUM

Address Riversley Park, Nuneaton, Warwickshire, UK, CV11 5TU. **Tel** (0203) 350595. **Year Established** 1917. **Founder** Edward Melly. **General Description** The Nuneaton Museum Tibetan collection of approximately seventy items includes: prayer wheels, relic boxes, tea bowls and pots, knives, swords, a portable shrine, apron and horns/trumpets. The material is poorly documented but in good condition. The items are available for study.

ORIENTAL MUSEUM

Address University of Durham, Elvet Hill, Durham, Durham, U.K., DH1 3TH. **Tel** 091 374 2911. **Year Established** 1960. **General Description** The collection of about 100 items of Tibetan artefacts includes: about twenty to twenty-five thangkas, a number of figurines, two wooden book covers and a few items of daily life. A photographic record was made of the entire collection in 1982, and prints are available on request at the museum.

PITT RIVERS MUSEUM

Address Parks Road, Oxford, Oxfordshire, UK, OX1 3PP. **Tel** 0865 270927. **Year Established** 1884. **Founder** General Augustus Henry Lane Fox Pitt-Rivers. **General Description** The museum holds a moderately large collection of Tibetan artefacts including religious objects, clothing, and jewellery, most of them dating from the late nineteenth century or early twentieth century. In addition, there is an important photographic collection in the archives, in particular the original negatives of photographs taken by Sir Charles Bell in 1920–21.

ROYAL MUSEUM OF SCOTLAND

Address Chambers Street, Edinburgh, Lothian, UK, EH1 1JF. **Tel** 031 225 7534. **Telex/Fax** 031 220 4819. **General Description** The Royal Museum of Scotland has a large Tibetan collection of about 1000 objects, mainly acquired during the late nineteenth and early twentieth centuries. It consists of Buddhist paintings and religious items such as altar vessels, butter lamps, prayer wheels, talismans etc. equipment used in everyday life, costumes, jewellery and armour. Much of the collection was acquired through missionaries such as Annie Ross Taylor, the Rev J. Innes Wright, and from members of the Younghusband expedition of 1904.

VICTORIA AND ALBERT MUSEUM

Address Cromwell Road, South Kensington, London, UK, SW7 2RL. **Tel** 071 938 8290. **Telex/Fax** 071 938 8661. **Year Established** 1852. **Lama/Scholar** John Guy, John Clarke. **General Description** The Victoria and Albert Museum collection of Tibetan cultural objects comprises: 130 thangkas including two fifteenth century Sino-Tibetan pieces and a fifteenth century western Tibetan painting of Padmasambhava; approximately 200 sculptures including a small group of wooden images and reliefs; approximately 900 ritual and domestic objects, mostly of metal including: musical instruments, masks, dough moulds, bookcovers, libation vessels, butterlamps, prayer-wheels, teapots, boxes and jewellery; a small collection of Himalayan textiles including complete costumes of a monk, an abbot and a masked dancer.

WELLCOME COLLECTION (SCIENCE MUSEUM)

Address The Science Museum, Exhibition Road, London, UK, SW7 2DD. **Tel** 071 938 8000. **Telex/Fax** 071 938 8118. **Distribution Details** Written requests only. **Year Established** 1913. **Founder** Sir Henry Wellcome. **General Description** The Science Museum houses the Wellcome Museum of the History of Medicine. This is a collection of about 100,000 artefacts recording medical practice world-wide. Within the collection are about 3000 Tibetan and Sino-Tibetan artefacts covering mostly the ritual and religious aspect of Tibetan medicine. The majority of the collection was acquired between 1920 – 1940 and most is nineteenth century. In 1976 the Wellcome Collection was transferred to the Science Museum. Material is displayed in two permanent galleries, Glimpses of Medical History and The Science and Art of Medicine. A small proportion (about four per cent) of the Tibetan material is on display in the second gallery. The reserve collection is available to scholars. Access is by written appointment at least one month in advance.

Publishing Companies and Journals

ELEMENT BOOKS LIMITED

Address Old School House, Bell St, Shaftesbury, Dorset, UK, SP7 8BP. **Tel** 0747 51448. **Telex/Fax** 0747 51394.

GANESHA PRESS

Address 27 Lilymead Avenue, Knowle, Bristol, UK, BS4 2BY. **Tel** 0272 712961. **Lama/Scholar** Ngakpa Jampa Thaye (David Stott).

MIDDLE WAY

Address The Buddhist Society, 58 Eccleston Square, London, UK, SW1V 1PH. **Tel** 071 834 5858.

PENGUIN BOOKS LTD.

Address 27 Wrights Lane, London, UK, W8 5TZ. **Tel** 071 416 3000. **Telex/Fax** 071 416 3099.

RIDER BOOKS

Address Random Century House, 20 Vauxhall Bridge Road, London, UK, SW1V 2SA. **Tel** 071 973 9690. **Telex/Fax** 071 233 6057.

SERINDIA PUBLICATIONS

Address 10 Parkfields, Putney, London, UK, SW15 6NH. **Tel** 081 788 1966. **Telex/Fax** 081 785 4789.

THARPA PUBLICATIONS

Address 15 Bendemeer Road, London, UK, SW15 1JX. **Tel** 081 788 7792. **Telex/Fax** 071 589 9611. **Distribution Details** A publisher of Buddhist books by Geshe Kelsang Gyatso providing a comprehensive presentation of essential sutra and tantra practices of Mahayana Buddhism. **Year Established** 1984.

WISDOM BOOKS
Address 402 Hoe Street, London, UK, E17 9AA. **Tel** (081) 520 5588. **Telex/Fax** (081) 520 0932. **Distribution Details** major distributor of books on all aspects of Buddhism and Tibetan culture. A comprehensive catalogue is produced. Materials are distributed world-wide. **Year Established** 1989.

Teaching Centres

AMRITA DZONG,
THE LONDON KAGYU CENTRE
Address c/o 86 Handside Lane, Welwyn Garden City, Herts, UK, AL8 6SJ. **Tel** (0707) 320782. **Lama/Scholar** Lama Chime Rinpoche. **General Description** Amrita Dzong is a centre for the practice and study of Buddhism as taught through the Kagyu-Benchen tradition, under the spiritual direction of Lama Chime Rinpoche.

BIRMINGHAM KARMA LING
Address 41 Carlyle Road, Egbaston, Birmingham, UK, B16 9BH.

JAMYANG MEDITATION CENTRE
Address 10 Finsbury Park Road, Finsbury Park, London, UK, N4 2JZ. **Tel** 071 359 1394. **Distribution Details** No materials are distributed. **Year Established** 1978. **Founder** Lama Thubten Yeshe. **Lama/Scholar** Geshe Namgyal Wangchen. **General Description** Jamyang Meditation Centre, formerly known as the Manjushri London Centre, was started under the direction of Lama Yeshe and has continued as a member of the Foundation for the Preservation of the Mahayana Tradition (FPMT). It is a city centre geared to meet the needs of both those in full-time work and the unemployed. The centre is non-residential, except for occasional resident teachers, a spiritual programme coordinator and housekeeper. The Jamyang Meditation centre aims to provide the opportunity for meditation and study, based on the methods of Je Tsongkhapa. It is therefore a centre within the Gelug (dGe lugs) tradition of Tibetan Buddhism. Teaching is given on a variety of levels, from the general and introductory, through to advanced Buddhist philosophy. Preserving the pure tradition is emphasised, although methods of presentation that reach out to Londoners and visitors are attempted. **Teaching Programme** Teachings are mostly held in the evenings and weekends. The programme ranges from instruction in general meditation techniques, which are not specifically Buddhist, through to teachings on the *Lam Rim*, or graduated path to enlightenment, traditional Buddhist meditation and more advanced Buddhist philosophy. Visits from qualified lamas of the tradition are arranged several times a year. **Facilities and Services** The centre possesses a shrine room where the teachings and meditation classes take place. There is also one room upstairs used for visiting teachers. A small bookshop offers a range of Buddhist texts together with some ritual implements, greeting cards, and thangka posters.

KAGYU SAMYE LING
Address Eskdalemuir, Nr. Langholm, Dumfriesshire, UK, DG13 0QL. **Tel** 03873 73232. **Telex/Fax** 03873 73223. **Year Established** 1967. **Founder** Trungpa Rinpoche/Akong Rinpoche. **Lama/Scholar** Akong Rinpoche. **General Description** Kagyu Samye Ling has as its focus a monastery building constructed in the Tibetan style. It is a large centre providing study, retreat and meditation facilities for Buddhists and non-Buddhists alike. Its aim is to increase the mental and spiritual well-being of its residents and also to preserve the cultural and spiritual heritage of Tibet. Study is under the guidance of well-qualified teachers. The centre was founded in 1967 by Trungpa Rinpoche and Akong Rinpoche. Visiting teach-

ers, often the most eminent lamas of the Kagyu tradition, lead study courses at Christmas, Easter and Tibetan New Year and also during the summer from July to September. Qualified teachers from other spiritual traditions also visit the centre to give instruction. Meditation instruction and advice is available most of the year. The courses given at the centre cover a wide range of Buddhist and non-Buddhist subjects. In recent years there have been courses in massage, healing, herbalism and homeopathy, Tai Chi Chuan, and Tibetan art. **Teaching Programme** Visitors are entirely free to make their own daily programme, taking part in study, prayer or work activities as they feel most appropriate. There are many craft activities, such as statue-making and pottery, in which visitors may participate. Visitors are asked to give a few hours help daily with the household and farm chores, printing and building work, although this is not obligatory. There is a daily programme beginning with a rising bell at 5:45am and ending with a 10:00pm bedtime. **Facilities and Services** The Temple, containing many beautiful religious articles, is open from early morning until late at night. Solitary retreat facilities are also available. The library contains more than 2000 books on various topics with a special section on Tibetan and Asian studies. Books, prayers, photographs, religious objects, Tibetan refugee products, craftwork, toiletries and confectionery are available in the centre shop open daily except on new and full moon days.

KAMPO GANGRA SHEDRUP LING

Address 25 Hollybank Road, Mossley Hill, Liverpool, U.K., LI8 1H. **Tel** 051 733 2336. **General Description** Shedrup Ling belongs to the Karma Kagyu tradition of Buddhism and is one of a number of Kagyu and Sakya centres founded in the U.K., by Karma Thinley Rinpoche and Ngakpa Jampa Thaye (David Stott), which comprise the Dechen Community. The centre itself is situated in a converted house close to the centre of Liverpool. There is an on-going practice programme comprising meditation on Chenrezig, Amitabha and Guru Rinpoche in addition to basic meditation. **Teaching Programme** The teaching programme is based around teachings given by Ngakpa Jampa Thaye, which include both textual teachings and Vajrayana initiations and instructions. Karma Thinley Rinpoche gives teachings during his visits to England. In addition there are weekly open classes suitable for newcomers.

LAM RIM BRISTOL

Address 12 Victoria Place, Bedminster, Bristol, U.K., BS3 3BP. **Tel** 0272– 639089. **Year Established** 1986. **Founder** Lam Rim Bristol Trust. **Lama/Scholar** Geshe Damcho Yonten. **General Description** The Lam Rim Bristol Buddhist Group was begun in 1982 by a small group of people, interested in Tibetan Buddhism, who invited Geshe Damcho Yonten of the Lam Rim Buddhist Centre, Wales to give teachings in Bristol. Both centres are under the spiritual guidance of Geshe Damcho Yonten and work together to provide opportunities for daily practice and teachings in the city, complemented by retreat facilities and intensive study

in the countryside. In 1986, the Lam Rim Bristol Trust was formed and charitable status was granted. The centre has developed on its premises a "Centre for Whole Health", in liasion with the Dharma Therapy Trust. The Centre for Whole Health began in 1988 and was developed as a means of giving active expression to the Buddhist principles of care and concern for others, and as a means of support to the Buddhist Centre. **Teaching Programme** The Lam Rim Bristol Buddhist Group has weekly meetings for meditation, discussion, puja and study as well as regular teachings given by Geshe Damcho. The teachings follow the Gelugpa school. Visiting teachers often give weekend courses; and the centre hopes to host regular visits by teachers from India. Alongside a programme of Buddhist teachings and meditation, the Centre for Whole Health offers individual therapies and an ongoing programme of talks, courses and workshops. A quarterly programme is published giving details of both the Buddhist Centre and the Centre for Whole Health activities. **Facilities and Services** The top floor of the centre is dedicated to the Lam Rim Bristol Buddhist Group and provides a Shrine Room and accommodation for a teacher and resident. The Centre for Whole Health has rooms for group activities and also provides individual consulting rooms for practitioners of complementary therapies. There is also an expanding library of books and tapes, a small shop selling books and Buddhist artefacts and a refreshment area.

LAM RIM BUDDHIST CENTRE

Address Pentwyn Manor, Penrhos, Raglan, Gwent, U.K., NP5 2LE. **Tel** (060 085) 383. **Distribution Details** Occasional transcripts are produced. Copies of some spiritual practices are available. Please contact the centre for more information. **Year Established** 1978. **Founder** Geshe Damcho Yonten. **Lama/Scholar** Geshe Damcho

Yonten. **General Description** The Lam Rim Buddhist Centre is a charitable trust founded in 1978. Its aim is to maintain an educational programme of Buddhist teachings based on the finest principles of meditation, human growth and personal development. The Spiritual Director is the Ven. Geshe Damcho Yonten, formerly Abbot of Samtenling Monastery in Norba, Ladakh, and graduate of Drepung Monastic University, Lhasa. The centre is situated in beautiful countryside in South Wales. Pentwyn Manor is a well built, nicely appointed, mock-Tudor style house which stands in eight and a half acres of field garden and coppice, amid rolling farmland close to the Black Mountains. This delightful setting provides a peaceful atmosphere which is highly conducive to meditative reflection. In order to preserve an environment which is calm and conducive to a contemplative life, visitors as well as residents are requested to observe the five Buddhist precepts undertaken by all lay Buddhists: avoidance of killing, stealing, sexual misconduct, lying and the taking of intoxicants. **Teaching Programme** The programme of weekend courses presented by the centre is both interesting and varied, extending beyond a purely Buddhist theme to include courses in Yoga, Tai Chi and Alternative Therapies. Meditative training of several types is also available according to a carefully constructed programme. In particular, Geshe Damcho Yonten teaches every Sunday and Tuesday on the graduated path to enlightenment. From time to time Lam Rim and its residents and friends are blessed by the presence of visiting high lamas who have come to Europe from India in order to give teachings and initiations into the practices of Tibetan Buddhism. **Facilities and Services** Accommodation is available for groups or individuals, either in dormitories or in a limited number of single rooms. Everyone is welcome whether their interest is to attend a course, to make a meditation retreat, or just to visit the centre for a quiet weekend or to find out more about what's going on. Delicious vegetarian food is provided which is much appreciated as one of the highlights of a weekend at Lam Rim. Many of the vegetables are grown in the centre's own garden. Lam Rim is particularly reknowned for its retreat facilities. **Project Description** Lam Rim is presently raising money for a general refurbishment of the shrine room. Aid is given to the re-established Drepung Loseling monastic settlement in India whenever possible. In particular, interested sponsors can help support the education of young Tibetan monks at Loseling. Contact the centre for further information.

LONDON DHARMADHATU
Address 27 Belmont Close, Clapham, London, U.K., SW4. **Tel** 071–720 3207. **Distribution Details** Mostly talks by Chogyam Trungpa and his principal students are distributed, usually to members only. **Year Established** 1985. **Founder** Chogyam Trungpa Rinpoche. **General Description** Dharmadhatu is a part of the larger organisation of Vajradhatu, an association of meditation and study centres founded in 1970 by the late Chogyam Trungpa Rinpoche. The centre offers meditation instruction on an individual basis at no charge. All of the meditation sessions are open to the general public, including all-day practice periods held on the first Sunday of every month. In Europe and the U.K. Vajradhatu offers courses in meditation and Buddhist Studies. In the Republic of Ireland, a rural retreat called "Dao Shonu" has been established to provide an environment conducive to more extensive periods of meditation practice. Further information on Vajradhatu centres is available on application to the Dharmadhatu London centre. **Teaching Programme** Dharmadhatu offers a variety of study courses, both weekly and, occasionally, on weekends. These courses present the Buddhist teachings and provide ways to examine and understand the personal experience of meditation practice. Classes are taught on a range of subjects from beginning to advanced levels. Topics include all the traditional stages of the Buddhist path as well as relating our experience on this path to life in the present-day world. Open meditation session are held on Monday and Wednesday evenings and Sunday mornings. Classes are held on Wednesdays. Programme details are available from the centre.

LONGCHEN FOUNDATION
Address 30 Beechey Avenue, Old Marston, Oxford, Oxfordshire, U.K., OX3 OJU. **Tel** (0865) 72 55 69. **Distribution Details** Brochure and details of Introductory Courses available. **Year Established** 1976. **Founder** Dilgo Khyentse Rinpoche & Chogyam Trungpa. **Lama/Scholar** Khenpo Tsultrim Gyatso, Michael Hookham (Director), Dr Shenpen Hookham. **General Description** The Longchen Foundation was established in 1976 in accordance with the wishes of the Patron, Dilgo Khyentse Rinpoche, and the Director, Chogyam Trungpa Rinpoche. The purpose of the foundation is to train students in all aspects of the

Buddhist tradition in general and the Nyingma tradition in particular. In 1982, under Chogyam Trungpa Rinpoche's direction, it set up the Nitartha School. This latter organisation promotes the study, practice and contemplative life of Buddhism by providing a systematic and detailed training in each of these aspects of the teaching. The principal teacher of the foundation is Michael Hookham, with Dr Shenpen Hookham as assistant teacher. Both the Longchen Foundation and the Nitartha School are registered charities. **Teaching Programme** The Longchen Foundation's chief areas of activity at present are the Nitartha School which meets for weekend courses in London or Oxford and local groups that meet weekly in London, Oxford, Leigh-on-sea, Aylesbury, Worcester and Whitstable. A series of teaching and practice weekends are held every eight weeks, in Oxford. Every alternate weekend is devoted to meditation, the others to study with some meditation sessions. Extra classes providing for study of Buddhist primary and secondary sources in greater depth (including Tibetan language courses) are also available. Various other events are organised including introductory weekends, retreats and courses by Khenpo Tsultrim Gyatso Rinpoche and his student Dzogchen Ponlop Rinpoche. **Facilities and Services** The Longchen Foundation has a small library and an extensive cassette library for use by members. Its main resources are its teachers and the various books, articles, pamphlets and hand-out materials produced by them. The foundation also publishes a newsletter. **Project Description** Currently Shenpen and the students of the Nitartha School are developing an Open Learning, Spiral Curriculum programme. Its core theme is the Indestructible Heart Essence (Buddha Nature) and the key concept areas are Openness, Clarity and Sensitivity.

MADHYAMAKA BUDDHIST CENTRE
Address Centres under the direction of Geshe Kelsang Gyatso, requested not to be listed.

MANJUSHRI INSTITUTE
Address Centres under the direction of Geshe Kelsang Gyasto, requested not to be listed.

NEZANG BUDDHIST MEDITATION GROUP
Address 5 Sedley Taylor Road, Cambridge, U.K., CB2 2PW. **Year Established** 1986. **Founder** Ato Rinpoche. **General Description** The Nezang Buddhist Meditation Group was founded by Ato Rinpoche in 1986. The group meets monthly (except in August and December) on a Saturday afternoon when there is usually a Dharma talk followed by chanting and meditation. There is no formal membership and meetings are open to all.

RIGPA UK
Address 330 Caledonian Road, London, U.K., N1 1BB. **Tel** 071 700 0185. **Telex/Fax** 071 609 6068. **Distribution Details** Rigpa distribute in the U.K. and overseas. A publications list is available on request. **Year Established** 1981. **Founder** Sogyal Rinpoche. **Lama/Scholar** Sogyal Rinpoche. **General Description** The London Rigpa Centre was founded in 1981 by the Ven. Lama Sogyal Rinpoche. The overall aim of the Centre is to encourage a true understanding of the teaching of Buddha, to provide facilities for its practice, and at the same time to make possible a real exchange between the Buddhist approach and that of related Western disciplines. It is a member of the Rigpa Fellowship, an international association of Buddhist meditation centres under the direction of Sogyal Rinpoche. **Teaching Programme** The programme of the Rigpa Centre offers a complete introduction to the teaching and practice of 'Buddha-dharma', while at the same time providing the continuity and graduated presentation necessary for successful study. There are courses led by Sogyal Rinpoche throughout the year on subjects such as: Meditation, Training the Mind in

Compassion, Vajrayana Preliminaries, Healing, Buddhist Psychology, Death and Dying, and Dzogchen (rDzogs chen). There are also, in the spirit of the Rime (Ris med) tradition, seminars arranged from visiting teachers of all Buddhist lineages. In addition, ongoing courses on meditation, compassion, and the preliminary practices (sngon 'gro), are led by senior students of Sogyal Rinpoche. **Facilities and Services** Rigpa's focus is the maintenance of a traditional shrine room where Buddhist teachings and practice can take place in an inspiring setting. The centre also acts as the base from which the international schedule of teachings, retreats and conferences conducted by Sogyal Rinpoche are coordinated. **Project Description** Editing of Sogyal Rinpoche's teachings is currently in progress with a view to eventual publication. Another project is concerned with the translation and publication of Buddhist prayers and texts. To date the *Longchen Nyingthig Ngondro (Klong chen sNying thig sNgon 'gro)* and the *Rigdzin Dupa* sadhanas have been translated. Rigpa is active in support of the re-established Dzogchen Monastery in South India.

SAKYA CHOGYAL SECHEN DZONG
Address 348 Woodvale, London, U.K., SE23 3D4.

SAKYA THINLEY RINCHEN LING
Address 27 Lilymead Avenue, Knowle, Bristol, U.K., BS4 2BY. **Tel** 0272 712961. **Year Established** 1977. **Founder** Karma Thinley Rinpoche. **Lama/Scholar** Ngakpa Jampa Thaye (David Stott). **General Description** Sakya Thinley Rinchen Ling is the oldest and most well established Sakya centre in the U.K. and is the main Sakya centre of a group of centres throughout Europe collectively known as the "Dechen Community". Regular meditation classes and teachings on Tibetan Buddhism are offered. Visiting Lamas have included H.H. Sakya Trizin, Lama Karma Thinley Rinpoche and Phende Rinpoche. **Teaching Programme** There is an introductory meeting every Thursday evening and Ngakpa Jampa Thaye teaches regularly at the centre, usually one weekend in every two months. Over the past fifteen years he has given teachings and oral transmissions from many texts of the Sakya tradition. In addition to regular teachings and personal guidance, Ngakpa Jampa Thaye also gives Vajrayana empowerments. **Facilities and Services** The centre has a publishing company, the Ganesha Press, and publishes an annual journal of the Dechen Community called the *Dechen Review*. There is also Ganesha Fine Arts who are importers of high-quality Tibetan thangkas, and Ganesha Tapes stock a wide selection of tapes by Ngakpa Jampa Thaye. **Project Description** The Thinley Rinchen Ling Trust owns a property in France, Chang-lo-chen, which is planned as the future retreat centre of the Dechen Community.

THRANGU HOUSE
Address 76, Bullingdon Road, Oxford, Oxfordshire, U.K., OX4 1QL. **Tel** (0865) 241555. **Distribution Details** Tapes and books are available to those attending meetings at the centre. **Year Established** 1980. **Founder** Thrangu Rinpoche. **General**

Description Thrangu House offers facilities to those wishing to practice meditation and pujas or engage in study. Study is often based on teachings that have been given at other centres and which have been recorded on audio or video tapes. Tibetan lamas are invited to the centre, usually at weekends, to give teachings, meditation instruction, empowerments, and private interviews. **Teaching Programme** There is no set teaching programme but occasional courses are arranged when Tibetan lamas visit the centre. The centre also begun in 1988 to organise an annual Namo Buddha Summer Seminar in Worcester College, Oxford. The seminar offers an opportunity for Buddhist practitioners at all levels to receive teachings, study, discuss and practise meditation and Buddhism in the beautiful and peaceful surroundings of Worcester College. **Facilities and Services** The centre houses a library of books and audio tapes. There is also a shrine room open for group and private meditation practice.

U.S.A.

Academic Organisations

AMHERST COLLEGE, DEPARTMENT OF RELIGION
Address, Amherst, Massachusetts, U.S.A., 01002. **Tel** (413) 542 2000. **Distribution Details** No materials are distributed. **Year Established** 1821. **Lama/Scholar** Janet Gyatso (Amherst College), Tai Uno (Smith College), Dennis Hudson (Smith College), Jamie Hubbard (Smith College), Jay Garfield (Hampshire College), Indira Pederson (Mt Holyoke College). **General Description** The Amherst College Religion Department works in association with the religion departments at Smith College, Mount Holyoke College, Hampshire College, and one faculty at UMASS Amherst.

Courses are offered in Eastern and Western Religions, as well as Religious Ethics, Philosophy of Religion, Social Scientific Studies, Comparative Studies and Textual Studies (primarily in Greek and Latin). Buddhist Studies are primarily taught by Professor Gyatso at Amherst, and Professors Uno, Hubbard and Hudson at Smith College. Various visiting professors have given courses in the Department, including Tara Rinpoche in 1983, and Professor George Dreyfus in 1990. **Teaching Programme** Amherst College offers an introductory class which surveys Asian religions. Course Religion 29, deals with the Indo-Tibetan religious tradition. There are also courses on The Poetry of Enlightenment, Buddhist Scriptures, and a senior level course entitled, "Issues in Buddhist Philosophy". At Smith College, there are a series of survey courses (Buddhism I, Buddhism II etc.), as well as a number of higher level seminars. Students are encouraged to study pertinent foreign languages. In addition, there are usually some excellent comparative programmes each year. Past courses have included Buddhist and Christian monasticism and a seminar on compassion in Buddhism and Christianity. **Facilities and Services** The Department is housed in a building on Amherst Campus, occupying a suite of classrooms and offices. There is access to other lecture rooms, as well as campus audio-visual material. The Department produces a course booklet, detailing the various programmes in five associated colleges. It is also involved in liaising with outside organisations to arrange visits from lecturers and to host seminars.

ANTIOCH COLLEGE, BUDDHIST STUDIES PROGRAM
Address Antioch Education Abroad, Yellow Springs, Ohio, U.S.A., 45387. **Tel** (513) 767 6366. **Telex/Fax** (513) 767 1891. **Distribution Details** No materials are distributed. **Year Established** 1979. **Founder** C. Robert Pryor

and Tara Doyle. **Lama/Scholar** Ven. Chokyi Nyima Rinpoche (Guest scholar), Rev. Syunko Horiuchi (Guest scholar), Sri Anagarika Munindra (Guest scholar). **General Description** Antioch Education Abroad offers a three-month study tour to Bodhgaya, India. This is intended primarily for undergraduates and takes place each autumn. Emphasis is placed on a comparative approach to both theory and practice, so that participants may reach their own understanding of that essence which is common to all the varieties of Buddhism, while learning to appreciate the many cultural and historical environments in which it has flourished. In Bodhgaya, participants may take courses in Buddhist Philosophy, Ancient Indian History, Contemporary Buddhist Culture, Hindi, Tibetan, and Meditation as well as design their own independent research project. Credit for this work will then be transferred to degree programmes at their home-base college or university. **Teaching Programme** The programme consists of four components: core courses; language; meditation practicum; and field research. Buddhist Philosophy focuses on the Abhidharma, Madhyamaka, and Yogacara traditions. Ancient Indian History students enquire into the social, economic and political forces relevant to Buddhism from approximately 600 B.C.E. to 1200 C.E. Contemporary Buddhist Culture presents an analysis of the diverse social patterns through which Buddhism influences Asian people today. Beginning Tibetan places emphasis on developing the oral proficiency necessary to converse with Tibetan teachers and pilgrims in Bodhgaya and the written proficiency necessary to translate simple Buddhist texts. **Facilities and Services** Participants benefit from the diverse resources of Bodhgaya. Classes are taught by Antioch faculty and guest scholars. Lodging and vegetarian meals are provided at the guest house of the Burmese Vihar.

BATES COLLEGE, DEPARTMENT OF PHILOSOPHY AND RELIGION
Address 301 Hathorn Hall, Lewiston, Maine, USA, 04240. **Tel** 207–786–6311. **Distribution Details** No materials are distributed. **Year Established** 1855. **Lama/Scholar** John Strong. **General Description** The religious studies section of the Department consists of four lecturers, three teaching Western religions and one Eastern. **Teaching Programme** There is a Tibetan element in all of the courses that include Buddhism. In addition, a seminar on Tibetan Buddhism is held approximately every three years. **Facilities and Services** The library houses approximately sixty volumes in English on Tibetan religions, mostly on Tibetan Buddhism.

CALIFORNIA INSTITUTE OF INTEGRAL STUDIES, PROGRAM IN PHILOSOPHY AND RELIGION
Address 765 Ashbury Street, San Francisco, California, USA., CA 94117. **Tel** 415 753 6100. **Distribution Details** No materials are distributed. **Year Established** 1970.

CARLETON COLLEGE, DEPARTMENT OF RELIGION
Address One North College Street, Northfield, Minnesota, USA, MN 55057. **Tel** (507) 663 4232. **Distribution Details** No mate-

rials are distributed. **Year Established** 1955. **Lama/Scholar** Bardwell Smith (Chinese/Japanese studies), Roger Jackson (Tibetan studies), James Fisher (Nepal studies), Eleanor Zelliot (Indian studies). **General Description** The College is concerned with undergraduate liberal arts education. The Department of Religion offers courses in Western and Eastern religions as well as the methodology of religious studies. **Teaching Programme** The undergraduate course allows for a degree of specialization in Eastern religions. Areas of study include; The Religions of India, Chinese Religious Thought, Japanese Religion and Culture, Theravada Buddhism in South and Southeast Asia, and Tibetan Buddhism. **Facilities and Services** The College Library has an extensive collection of books on religion, with a number relating to Buddhism and the religions of Asia. Holdings on Tibet include many English language works, and the Taipei edition of the *Derge Tibetan Tripitaka*. Other Tibetan works are available via Interlibrary Loan.

CASE WESTERN RESERVE UNIVERSITY, DEPT OF ANTHROPOLOGY/CENTER FOR RESEARCH ON TIBET

Address Mather Memorial Building 238, Cleveland, Ohio, U.S.A., 44106. **Tel** (216) 368 2264. **Telex/Fax** (216) 368 5334. **Distribution Details** 2 tapes to accompany Essentials of Modern Literary Tibetan: a reading course and reference grammar, by M.C. Goldstein Univ. of Calif Press, 1991. **Lama/Scholar** Prof Melvyn C. Goldstein, Dr Paljor Tsarong, Prof Cynthia M. Beall. **General Description** The department's newly founded Center for Research on Tibet is coordinating, in collaboration with the Tibetan Academy of Social Sciences, a series of studies over the next decade. These will examine critical questions regarding the nature of social, physiological and ecological adaptation to Tibet's

unique environment. Graduate students can specialise in Tibet. **Teaching Programme** The Asian Civilisations Programme encourages students to take courses in a variety of different disciplines, thus exposing them to the many facets of Asian culture. Specific courses include: Tibet and the Himalayas – an introduction to the society, culture and history of Tibet and the Himalayan areas of Nepal, Ladakh, Sikkim and Bhutan; Buddhism – a general course taught by the Department of Religion – and several courses on Chinese history taught by the history department. **Facilities and Services** The department possesses a Macintosh computer programmed for typing, word-processing, and printing in Tibetan script. There are also micro-computer laboratories and a mainframe computer available for the storage and manipulation of research data. A Tibetan modern history, a Tibetan-English dictionary and a Tibetan phrasebook have been produced. Professor Goldstein has a large personal collection of audio taped interviews with leading Tibetan political figures, which has been used in the development of his book on modern Tibetan history. **Project Description** Among present projects are research into Tibetan large-scale monasticism, Tibetan grammar, Tibetan pastoral nomadism and the adaption of Tibetans to high altitude.

COLUMBIA UNIVERSITY, DEPARTMENT OF RELIGION

Address Kent Hall, New York, New York, USA, 10027. **Tel** (212) 854 5924. **Distribution Details** No materials are distributed. **Year Established** 1780's. **Lama/Scholar** Prof Robert Thurman (Buddhist Studies), Prof Matthew Kapstein. **General Description** The programme in Buddhist studies, administered by the interdepartmental committee of the University Committee on Oriental Studies, is offered jointly by the departments of Religion, East Asian

Languages and Cultures, and Middle East Languages and Cultures. Study in the programme is carried out in conjunction with work for the PhD degree in one of these departments, and students should refer to the appropriate department for further information or should consult Professor Thurman direct.

COLUMBIA UNIVERSITY,
DEPARTMENT OF MIDDLE EAST LANGUAGES

Address 602 Kent Hall, New York, New York, USA, 10027. **Tel** (212) 854 2556. **Distribution Details** No materials are distributed. **Year Established** 1780s. **Lama/Scholar** Prof Robert Thurman, Prof Matthew Kapstein, Prof Alex Wayman (retired). **General Description** Undergraduate and graduate courses in colloquial and classical Tibetan language, and Buddhist philosophy are offered. **Teaching Programme** Courses available within the graduate programme in the past include: Tibetan Language (elementary, intermediate and supervised readings); Indian Philosophy; Hindu and Buddhist Tantra; the Indic Studies Spring Seminar (this is thematic in content – e.g., Goddesses, Philosophy, Role of Art etc.); Himalayan Civilisations; Indian Art (includes early Buddhist and Tibetan art, primarily in the period seventh to eleventh centuries AD); Oriental Humanities (includes Tibetan selections). **Facilities and Services** There is an extensive library collection, which includes the Narthang edition of the *Kangyur (bKa' 'gyur)* and *Tengyur (bsTan 'gyur)*, and the *Derge Kangyur*. The Library of Congress procurement service for Tibetan works is also available.

DICKINSON COLLEGE, DEPARTMENT OF RELIGION

Address Carlisle, Pennsylvania, USA, 17013–2896.

FAIRFIELD UNIVERSITY, DEPARTMENT OF RELIGIOUS STUDIES

Address Fairfield, Connecticut, USA, 06430. **Tel** (203) 254–4000.

HARVARD UNIVERSITY,
CENTRE FOR THE STUDY OF WORLD RELIGIONS

Address 42 Francis Avenue, Cambridge, Massachusetts, U.S.A., 02138.

HARVARD UNIVERSITY,
DEPARTMENT OF EAST ASIAN LANGUAGES AND LITERATURE

Address 2 Divinity Avenue, Cambridge, Massachusetts, U.S.A., 02138.

INDIANA UNIVERSITY,
DEPARTMENT OF URALIC AND ALTAIC STUDIES

Address 157 Goodbody Hall, Bloomington, Indiana, USA, 47405. **Tel** (812) 855 2233. **Distribution Details** An annual subscription to *The Journal of the Tibet Society* is included in the membership fee of the Tibet Society. **Year Established** 1966. **Lama/Scholar** Christopher Beckwith (Tibetan Studies), Thubten Jigme Norbu (Tibetan Studies), Elliot Sperling (Tibetan

Studies), George Kara (Mongol Studies), Michael Walter (Tibetan Studies), Jan Nattier (Religious Studies). **General Description** The Department of Uralic and Altaic Studies is concerned with the languages and cultures of peoples from the Eurasian heartland. The departmental programme offers formal courses and interdisciplinary studies in nearly all the recognised fields of these cultures. There are various fields in which major or minor work is possible – Finnic, Hungarian, Turkish, Uzbek, Mongolian and Tibetan. The comprehensiveness of the programme is unique in the United States and it enjoys an international reputation. Its importance is recognized by the US Department of Education which has established the Inner Asian and Uralic National Resource Center at Indiana University. **Teaching Programme** Although the department does not offer an undergraduate major, numerous undergraduate courses are available which satisfy the Arts and Humanities Distribution Requirement. Specifically, there are courses in introductory and advanced Tibetan and Selected Readings of Tibetan Texts, which are open to undergraduates. In addition a Certificate in Inner Asian Studies, with a concentration on Tibetan studies, may be obtained. The Tibetan field is one of the major fields leading to advanced degrees in the department. A thorough grounding in the Tibetan language, both modern and classical, is the basis for extensive individualized training in the student's particular interest. Students in Tibetan are trained to study Tibetan culture in connection with other areas and fields. **Facilities and Services** The Tibetan Collection in the Indiana University Library includes approximately 4000 titles. Among these are about 300 Bon po titles, the Peking edition of the *Kangyur* (*bKa' 'gyur*) and *Tengyur* (*bsTan 'gyur*), and two other editions of the *Kangyur*. Also at the University is the Antoinette Gordon Collection of Tibetan Art. At the Indiana University Museum is a collection consisting of some 2500 colour slides and eighty hours of sound recordings.

NAROPA INSTITUTE, DEPARTMENT OF BUDDHIST STUDIES Address 2130 Arapahoe, Boulder, Colorado, USA, 80302. **Tel** (303) 444 0202. **Telex/Fax** (303) 444 0410. **Distribution Details** Contact Vajradhatu Recordings for audio tapes, and Vajradhatu Press for transcripts. **Year Established** 1974. **Lama/Scholar** Dr Reginald Ray, Dr Judith Simmer-Brown, Dzigar Kongtrul Rinpoche, Sarah Harding. **General Description** The Naropa Institute is a private, non-sectarian, accredited upper-divisional college and graduate school which offers baccalaureate and master's degrees in the arts, humanities and social sciences. Founded in 1974 in Boulder, Colorado, its educational philosophy is rooted in the Buddhist contemplative tradition. In the BA and MA Buddhist Studies programmes, Buddhism is studied as a living tradition from both historical and doctrinal perspectives. Included are the examination of root texts, commentaries, and the oral tradition of Buddhist masters as well as the study and practice of meditation. In addition, Buddhism is studied within the context of the great religious traditions of the world. **Teaching Programme** The Buddhist studies programme is inspired both by the scholar-practitioner traditions of Tibetan Buddhism and by the critical methods of modern Western scholarship. Specific subjects offered within the program include advanced courses on Tantric Thought and the History of Early Buddhism in Tibet. Dzigar Kongtrul Rinpoche teaches Buddhist studies and annually offers courses in the *Bodhisattvacaryavatara*, chapter IX, and *Uttaratantra*, as well as advanced Tibetan language study and meditation training. Also Ven Thrangu Rinpoche annually teaches a week long course on selected Mahayana and Vajrayana topics. Introductory courses are available in Tibetan language, thangka painting and calligraphy. One semester's study in Nepal is offered with lamas of all major lineage traditions. **Facilities and Services** The institute possesses a well-stocked library, including an extensive collection of catalogued material from the *Kangyur* (*bKa' 'gyur*) and the *Tengyur* (*bsTan 'gyur*). **Project Description** The institute is located on a small campus adjacent to the University of Colorado in the heart of the city of Boulder. It has a new library, conventional classrooms and studio spaces, and meditation halls. There are no residence halls, but housing is available nearby.

OHIO STATE UNIVERSITY, DEPARTMENT OF HISTORY OF ART
Address 100 Hayes Hall, 108 North Oval Mall, Columbus, Ohio, USA, 43210–1318. **Tel** (614) 292 7481. **Distribution Details** No materials are distributed. **Lama/Scholar** John C. Huntington. **General Description** The Department of History of Art offers courses to undergraduate and graduate students on selected topics in Tibetan Art. **Teaching Programme** The lecture course, History of Art 674, is open to upper division undergraduates and to graduate students, and is concerned with Tibetan art. In the past, topics covered have included: Styles of Tibetan Painting, Iconography of the Four Major Tibetan Sects, and Nepali and Tibetan Religious (Buddhist) Architecture. Most recently the course has concentrated on painting styles and the iconography contained in the paintings. Graduate level courses offered include studies and seminars in Buddhist art, Inner Asian art, and Chinese art. There are opportunities to specialise in Tibetan art and focus on questions of Tibetan cultural influence in Central Asia. **Facilities and Services** The university library has an extensive collection of Western language works on Buddhist Art, Art History and Tibetan culture generally. **Project Description** The university is involved in the Huntington Photographic Archive project of Buddhist and related art which will eventually contain nearly 250,000 photographs of Buddhist art. About 40,000 are Himalayan Tibetan material. *The Encyclopedia of Buddhist Iconography* is a long-term, multi-volume project that will include material related to Tibet in the categories: Indic Buddhism; Nepal, Tibet and Mongolia; and Later China.

RICE UNIVERSITY, DEPARTMENT OF RELIGIOUS STUDIES
Address P.O. 1892, Houston, Texas, USA, 77251. **Tel** 7135278180x2710. **Year Established** 1989. **Lama/Scholar** Anne Klein. **General Description** The department has a well established programme in medical ethics, and an MA in Asian religions including Tibetan Buddhism is available (possibly to be developed into a PhD programme). There are some scholarships available both to foreign and domestic students. Tibetan students with the necessary qualifications are encouraged to apply to this or any other department of Rice University. There are opportunities for PhDs to apply for Rockefeller post doctoral positions if the project is interdisciplinary (contact Rice Inst. for Cultural Studies, attn. Michael Fischer).

SMITH COLLEGE, EAST ASIAN STUDIES PROGRAM

Address Smith College, Northampton, Massachusetts, USA, 01063. **Tel** (413) 584 2700. **Distribution Details** No materials are distributed. **Year Established** 1982. **Lama/Scholar** Prof Marilyn M. Rhie (Art and E.Asian Stud.), Prof Tai Uno (World Religions – Budd.). **General Description** Smith College has established a major and a minor in East Asian Studies. Tibetan studies are offered under the E.A.S. program, primarily in the art/culture subject area at present. Tibetan art is also taught in seminars, on an irregular basis, in the Art Department, and is taught in the course entitled, The Art of India. A new chair in Religion/East Asian Studies will hopefully attract eminent teachers of Tibetan Buddhism in the future. **Teaching Programme** One regular course, entitled The Art and Culture of Tibet, is presently offered and is taught in alternate years. Sections of The Art of India course are concerned with Tibetan art, (this too is taught in alternate years within the Department of Art). A major and a minor are currently available in East Asian Studies. **Facilities and Services** There is an excellent library with many holdings in ancient and contemporary Tibetan art and history, religion, and travel books. It also contains a good archive collection of Tibetan art, and about 4000 slides of Tibetan art.

STANFORD UNIVERSITY

Address Dept. of Religious Studies Building, Stanford, California, USA, 94305-2089. **Lama/Scholar** Elizabeth Napper.

STATE UNIVERSITY OF NEW YORK, INSTITUTE FOR ADVANCED STUDY OF WORLD RELIGIONS

Address 5001 Melville Memorial Library, Stony Brook, New York, USA., 11794-3383. **General Description** The institute provides information and facilities for researchers into the teaching, study and practice of religions. It maintains a library, produces various publications and makes available microfiche copies of rare material. **Teaching Programme** Lawrence Research Fellowships are granted to researchers into various fields, among them Tibetan religion and culture. **Facilities and Services** The institute has a large library with an extensive collection of Tibetan works. A great number of titles are available on microfiche, including the entire *Kangyur* in Lhasa, Derge and Narthang editions, the *Choney Tengyur*, and the PL-480/SFC collection of the Library of Congress. The institute also publishes various periodicals. **Project Description** There is a programme to translate some of the most important Buddhist texts, among them Gampopa's *Jewel Ornament of Liberation*.

SYRACUSE UNIVERSITY, DEPARTMENT OF ANTHROPOLOGY

Address 500 University Place, Syracuse, New York, USA, 13244-4300. **Tel** (315) 423 4822. **Distribution Details** No materials are distributed. **Year Established** 1961. **Lama/Scholar** Dr Agehananda Bharati. **General Description** Syracuse University is one of the six national resource centres for South Asian research. Its department of anthropology is a well rounded one, with an emphasis on cultural anthropology and South Asian studies. Prof Bharati is the only faculty member concerned with Tibetan or Tibetological studies. **Teaching Programme** The only Tibet-related teaching is a course given by Prof Bharati every other academic year, entitled Peoples and Cultures of the Himalayan Region. The other department members are strictly South Asianists, and the only Asian language actually taught is Hindi. **Facilities and Services** The library is on PL-480, and obtains all monographs published in India and Nepal. All Tibetan materials published in India and Nepal will consequently be available.

UNIVERSITY OF CALIFORNIA, DEPT. OF EAST ASIAN LANGUAGES
Address 104 Durant Hall, Berkeley, California, USA, 94720. **Tel**
(510) 642 3480. **Lama/Scholar** Prof Lancaster, Prof Bosson.
General Description Courses on literary and spoken Tibetan
language at undergraduate level only are offered.

UNIVERSITY OF CHICAGO, OFFICE OF INFORMATION
Address Administration Building, 5801 South Ellis, Chicago, Illi-
nois, USA, 60637. **Distribution Details** No materials are distributed. **Year Established** 1965. **Lama/Scholar** Frank
Reynolds (History of Religions), Gary Ebersole (History of Religions), Joseph Kitagawa (Emeritus Prof in H. of R.), Wendy D.
O'Flaherty (History of Religions). **General Description** The
Department offers MA and PhD programmes for those specialis-
ing in the arts, literatures, philosophies and religions of South
Asia. An interdisciplinary programme of great flexibility awarding
both MA and PhD degrees, and allowing for Tibetan Buddhist
studies, is available from the Dept. of South Asian Languages and
Civilisations in the Division of the Humanities. The programme in
History of Religions in the Divinity School encourages historical
and interpretive research with a major focus on Buddhism. The
Department of Anthropology encourages the pursuit of field
research relating to Tibet and adjacent Himalayan areas. The
Department of Linguistics allows for research into Tibetan lan-
guage. **Teaching Programme** Areas of linguistic concentration:
Sanskrit, Bengali, Urdu, Hindi, and Tamil. The department fac-
ulty includes a member with primary interest in Buddhism, Frank
Reynolds (a joint appointment with History of Religions). Stu-
dents interested in Indian Buddhism are encouraged to apply.
Tibetan language is not regularly taught at the University of
Chicago. **Facilities and Services** The university libraries are
amongst the finest in North America in all areas of South Asian,
Far Eastern and Tibetan literatures, and include the complete
PL–480 collections in Tibetan and the major Indian languages.
The Field Museum of Natural History in Chicago is nearby and
has an exceptional collection of Tibetan artefacts of all kinds.

UNIVERSITY OF COLORADO,
DEPARTMENT OF RELIGIOUS STUDIES
Address Box 292, Boulder, Colorado, USA, 830309.

UNIVERSITY OF MICHIGAN, ASIAN LANGUAGES AND CULTURES
Address ALC 3070 Frieze Bldg., Ann Arbor, Michigan, USA,
48109–1285. **Tel** (313) 764 0376. **Telex/Fax** (313) 747 0157.
Distribution Details No materials are distributed.
Lama/Scholar Donald S Lopez Jr, Luis O. Gomez, T. Griffith
Foulk. **General Description** The department is focused primarily on East Asian languages and literatures, though it has offered
courses in South and Southeast Asian and Tibetan languages as
well as Buddhist Studies. **Teaching Programme** The department offers courses in the following fields: (1) Modern and classical languages and literatures – Chinese, Japanese, Indonesian; (2)
Modern languages – Hindi, Tagalog, Thai; (3) Classical languages

and literature – Sanskrit and Tibetan; (4) Thought – Classical Chinese Philosophy, Buddhist Philosophy, and Religious Thought; and also a PhD in Buddhist Studies. **Facilities and Services** The library has an extensive collection of material on Buddhism in all major relevant languages.

UNIVERSITY OF NORTHERN CAROLINA, DEPT. OF PHILOSOPHY AND RELIGION

Address, Wilmington, North Carolina, USA, 28403–3297.

UNIVERSITY OF NORTHERN IOWA, DEPARTMENT OF PHILOSOPHY AND RELIGION

Address, Cedar Falls, Iowa, USA, 50614–0501. **Tel** (319) 273 6221. **Distribution Details** Introductory materials on Tibetan Buddhism are available on request from Prof Robinson. **Year Established** 1969. **Lama/Scholar** James Burnell Robinson, Shivesh C. Thakur. **General Description** The department has eight people on the teaching staff, divided between specialists in philosophy and specialists in religion. It is engaged primarily in undergraduate courses, with majors in philosophy, religion, and a combined philosophy and religion major. There is also considerable teaching in the general education programme of the university. Professor James Robinson teaches a cycle of advanced courses in Asian religion. Tibetan Buddhism is taught as a unit within a larger course on Hinduism and Buddhism. Professor Shivesh Thakur has on-going research interests in classical Indian philosophy, including Buddhism, but has not worked specifically on Tibet. **Teaching Programme** The department offers courses on: Religions of the World, "Philosophy: basic Questions", and contributes to the Humanities sequence – an overview of Western civilisation with occasional looks at Asia as the inclination of the instructor permits. Several sequenced courses are

run: the history of Western Philosophy; the development of Christianity; and the great living religions outside Western Christianity. There are also courses in ethics, aesthetics, Women in Christianity, and other subjects. Tibetan Buddhism is currently a unit in the course Hinduism and Buddhism. Specific aspects of Tibetan Buddhism and tantra have been utilised in the Meditation and Mystical Experience course, and in Psychology of Religious Experience. **Facilities and Services** The department has responsibility for the Josef Fox Seminar Room, 72 Baker Hall. The university museum has a few Tibetan artifacts but is developing its collection in other directions. There is a quite reasonable selection of books on Asian religion generally in the library.

UNIVERSITY OF SOUTH FLORIDA, DEPARTMENT OF RELIGIOUS STUDIES

Address 4202 E. Fowler Avenue, CPR 304, Tampa, Florida, USA, 33620–5550. **Tel** (813) 974 2221. **Telex/Fax** (813) 974 5911. **Year Established** 968. **Lama/Scholar** Nathan Katz. **General Description** The Department of Religious Studies offers baccalaureate and masters degrees in the study of religion. Authorised in 1968, the department comprises seven full-time faculty, approximately twenty undergraduate majors and twenty graduate students. Instruction is offered in all major religious traditions and in thematic and methodological issues. A masters degree programme commenced in 1980, and about 1200 students study in the department each year. **Teaching Programme** As well as a general undergraduate major in religious studies, the department has offered since 1980 a Master of Arts degree designed to meet the needs of a variety of people interested in the academic study of religion. As well as providing students with basic research skills, the course stresses the changing roles and functions of religion in the modern secular world. The core seminars include a study of Religion and Culture of the East. Professor Katz offers instruction in Buddhism, Tibetan language and Asian traditions. **Facilities and Services** The departmental library contains a good range of Western language material on Tibet. In addition, Prof Katz's personal library, which includes a variety of works in Tibetan, is made available to his students.

UNIVERSITY OF VIRGINIA, DEPARTMENT OF RELIGIOUS STUDIES

Address Center for South Asian Studies, 125 Minor Hall, Charlottesville, Virginia, USA, 22903. **Tel** (804) 924 3741. **Distribution Details** No materials are distributed. **Year Established** 1973. **Lama/Scholar** Prof Jeffrey Hopkins (Indo-Tibetan Buddhism), Prof Paul S. Groner (East Asian Buddhism), Prof Karen C. Lang (Indian/Theravada Buddh.), Mr William A Magee (Tibetan Language), Prof Richard B. Martin (Bibliographer), Dr David F. Germano (Indo-Tib. Buddh, Lang). **General Description** The Department of Religious Studies caters for Buddhist studies at both undergraduate and graduate levels. Courses are scheduled within a programme of history of religions, with subject areas being divided into Indo-Tibetan, Indian/Theravada, and East Asian Buddhism. The Center for South Asian Studies arranges regular extended visits from Tibetan scholars, who give lectures on a variety of topics drawn from the traditional monastic syllabi. **Teaching Programme** The Buddhist Studies programme offers MA and PhD degrees in Indo-Tibetan, Indian/Theravada, and East Asian Buddhism. In the PhD programme, the Indo-Tibetan track requires a minimum of three and a half years of Tibetan; since 1988 an Introductory Intensive Summer Tibetan Language Institute has been taught by William A. Magee, in conjunction with an indigenous Tibetan scholar, to prepare students to enter second year Tibetan in the autumn. Two years of Sanskrit and a semester of Pali are also required. Students also take a course in Buddhist bibliography and seminars in Tibetan, Indian, Chinese, and Japanese Buddhism. They are required to attend seminars in related fields, such as philosophy, anthropology, history, and art. Also required in the PhD programme are seminars and courses in two other religions, the history of religions, and other scholarly methods. Descriptions of the Indian/Theravada and East Asian tracks in Buddhist studies can be obtained from the university's Center for South Asian Studies. **Facilities and Services** The Alderman Library's Tibetan collection contains extensive holdings of Tibetan texts, well catalogued and kept up to date by its bibliographer, Professor Richard B. Martin. Through the Center for South Asian Studies, the Buddhist Studies programme participates in an outreach programme through which PhD candidates teach part-time at neighbouring colleges. The center also arranges Buddhist Studies colloquia, film screenings, and South Asia seminars. **Project Description** Mr Magee has been developing proficiency-based guidelines and teaching materials for Tibetan language, as well as a Tibetan Oral Proficiency Examination.

UNIVERSITY OF WASHINGTON, DEPARTMENT OF ASIAN LANGUAGES AND LITERATURE

Address Gowen Hall, DO–21, Seattle, Washington, USA, 98195. **Tel** (206) 543 4996. **Distribution Details** Further information can be obtained from the Materials Collection of the Instructional Media Services. **Year Established** 1969. **Lama/Scholar** Geshe Ngawang L. Nornang, Prof Leonard W. J. van der Kuijp, Prof Ter Ellingson, Dr Lawrence Epstein. **General Description** The Department of Asian Languages and Literature was established as a separate department in 1969. However, the teaching of Asian languages predates this by many years. The Tibetan language programme was formally established in 1960 by Turrell V. Wylie, who died in August, 1985. Literary Tibetan is presently taught by Dr Leonard W. J. van der Kuijp, and Colloquial Tibetan by Geshe N.L Nornang. In addition faculty members from other departments (Prof Ellingson from Ethnomusicology and Dr Epstein from Anthropology), are involved in the Tibetan studies programme. **Teaching Programme** A comprehensive array of Tibetan language courses are offered in the department. These include: colloquial Tibetan at beginner, intermediate and advanced levels; Literary Tibetan and Advanced Literary Tibetan; and Buddhist Tibetan. Furthermore, there are courses entitled Readings in Tibetan and Readings in Tibetan Literature. Undergraduate research in this subject area is also catered for. **Facilities and Services** The Far Eastern Library has the entire Special Currency Program (PL–480) *Tibetan Collection* (approximately 5000 titles). The library also includes its own *Tibetan collection* of approximately 230 titles; also a large number of Tibetan titles are available on microfilm. The Ethnomusicology Archive contains an extensive collection of audio and videotape recordings of Tibetan and other Buddhist ritual and music.

UNIVERSITY OF WISCONSIN, DEPARTMENT OF SOUTH ASIAN STUDIES

Address 1242 Van Hise Hall, 1220 Linden Drive, Madison, Wisconsin, USA, 53706. **Tel** (608) 262 3012. **Distribution Details** All materials are for sale internationally. Please contact the department for further information. **Year Established** 1961. **Lama/Scholar** Geshe Lhundrup Sopa, Frances A. Wilson, Manindra K. Verma, David M. Knipe, Muhammad U. Memon. **General Description** The department is concerned with both research and teaching in the social and humanistic disciplines. Its area of study is the South Asian subcontinent, including the countries: India, Sri Lanka, Pakistan, Bangladesh, Nepal, Afghanistan and Tibet. **Teaching Programme** The department offers both a Bachelor and Master of Arts degree in South Asian Studies. It is also possible to obtain a doctorate by majoring either in South Asian Language and Literature or in Buddhist Studies. The former option allows for a specialisation in South Asian Civilisation and Culture or alternatively in South Asian Religions. **Facilities and Services** The principal collections of all areas of South Asian Studies are housed in the memorial library and are extensively catalogued.

WESLEYAN UNIVERSITY, DEPARTMENT OF RELIGION

Address Wesleyan University, Middletown, Connecticut, USA, 06457. **Tel** (203) 3479411E25. **Distribution Details** No materials are distributed. **Year Established** 1831. **Lama/Scholar** Prof Janice D. Willis, Prof Stephen D. Crites, Assoc. Prof. Eugene M. Klaaren, Assoc. Prof Jerome H. Long, Assoc Prof James H. Stone. **General Description** The department offers a cross-cultural, interdisciplinary programme which explores the variety of religious experiences and expressions. In addition to courses which demonstrate the power and limits of various critical disciplines in the study of religion, the department provides opportunities to analyse: systems of belief and patterns of religious behaviour; the history of religious traditions; the functions of religion in society; and various forms of religious expression such as myth, ritual, sacred story, scripture, liturgy, theological and philosophical reflection. **Teaching Programme** The department offers three categories of courses through which students can organise a curriculum of studies appropriate to their needs. These are: access courses, which serve as a foundation for more advanced studies; text and traditions courses that examine the scriptures, histories, structures, and rituals of the major world religions; critical disciplines courses that review and critically analyse methodologies, theories, and strategies employed by scholars of religion. Specific courses include: Introduction to Buddhism; Tibetan Buddhism, investigating Mahayana Buddhism as practised in the Tibetan context; and Buddhist Theories of Knowledge. **Facilities and Services** The Olin Library houses a large number of volumes, some of which relate to Tibet.

Cultural Organisations and Tibetan Refugee Aid Societies

ASIAN CLASSICS INPUT PROJECT

Address Washington Area Office, 11911 Marmary Road, Gaithersburg, Maryland, USA, 20878–1839. **Tel** (301) 948 5569. **General Description** The project has been organised for the purpose of preserving and furthering the study of important examples of Asian literature, through the creation and distribution of computer disks containing these works in a simple and accurate digital form. There are at present completed in digital form seven major texts from the *Kangyur* and *Tengyur* collections of classical Sanskrit literature in Tibetan translation, three native catalogues to the *Kangyur* and *Tengyur*, and selected errata to the Delhi edition of the *Derge Kangyur* and *Tengyur*. The seven texts are: *Abhisamayalamkara*; *Mulaprajna*; *Madhyamakavatara*; *Uttaratantra*; *Abhidharmakosha*; *Vinayasutra*; and *Pramanavarttika*.

BODHI US

Address P.O. Box 7000-GRD, Redondo Beach, California, USA, 90277. **Tel** (310) 378 0260. **Telex/Fax** (310) 378 4282. **General Description** The Benevolent Organisation for Development, Health and Insight (BODHI) US is involved in two major projects among Tibetan refugees in India: health education for monks and wild dog sterilization. It is hoped that the success of these projects will contribute indirectly to TB eradication. The organisation is also developing proposals for an environment project to reduce the problem of deforestation. A periodical newsletter '*The Bodhi Times*' is published.

BUDDHIST PERCEPTION OF NATURE

Address 1518 K St., Suite 410, Washington, District of Columbia, USA, 20005. **Tel** (202) 628 4123. **Telex/Fax** (202) 347 6825.

FPMT CENTRAL OFFICE

Address P.O. Box 1778, Soquel, California, U.S.A., 95073. **Tel** 408 476 8435. **Telex/Fax** 408 476 4823. **Distribution Details** A Journal, *Mandala*, dealing with news of the FPMT centres around the world, is distributed.

ORIENT FOUNDATION

Address 261 Madison Avenue South, Suite 103, Bainbridge Island, Washington, USA, 98110. **Tel** (206) 842 1114. **Telex/Fax** (206) 842 5472. **Year Established** 1982. **Founder** Graham Coleman. **General Description** The Orient Foundation is an educational non-profit organisation in the USA (501 C3) and a registered charity in Great Britain. Four of the founding trustees of the foundation worked together between 1976 and 1981 to produce and distribute the four hour feature documentary 'Tibet: A Buddhist Trilogy', widely regarded as the most definitive documentary film to date on Tibetan culture. Since 1982, the foundation has through its film production and film distribution activities and through the initiation of the Tibetan Cultural Resources Project, been dedicated to the preservation of the artistic, philosophical and cultural traditions of Tibet and classical India and to the development of an appreciation for this rich and sophisticated cultural heritage. **Facilities and Services** A priority of the foundation since the early 1980s has been to assist the exiled Tibetan communities in their efforts to preserve the oral lineages of Tibet. To date, the foundation has traced and catalogued in excess of 30,000 hours of oral commentarial material, as given by Tibet's leading cultural figures, covering all aspects of Tibet's rich cultural heritage. A database and a printed reference guide have been prepared cataloguing this material, both of which also include a guide to Tibetan related facilities world-wide, biographies of key contemporary cultural figures and an extensive glossary of Tibetan and Sanskrit terms. The entire Tibetan Cultural Resources Database is available on disc from the Orient Foundation. The database can be run on any IBM compatable machine with a minimum twenty MB hard disc. The facilities and biographies sections of the database have been published under the title *Handbook of Tibetan Culture* 1993 by Random House. **Project Description** Currently the foundation is administering an extensive oral history recording programme within the exiled Tibetan communities focusing on the recording of oral commentaries in the fields of philosophy, medicine, history and the arts. Priority will be given to those subject areas whose oral commentarial lineages have been revealed by the database to be so far unrecorded. Simultaneous with the above the foundation plans to assist all those who already possess recordings of oral commentarial material to preserve these on suitable long term archival media.

PRISON DHARMA NETWORK

Address P.O. Box 987, Bloomfield, Connecticut, USA, 06002.

PROJECT TIBET

Address 403 Canyon Road, Santa Fe, New Mexico, USA, 87501. **Tel** (505) 982 3002. **Distribution Details** Project Tibet distributes newsletters and a pamphlet. **Year Established** 1980. **Lama/Scholar** Paljor Thondup (Administrator). **General Description** Project Tibet was founded in 1980 by Tibetan refugees in the United States and their friends and sympathisers. Its purpose is to maintain the customs and traditions of Tibet for refugees who fled Tibet after the 1950s Chinese takeover. It helps Tibetan refugees establish handicraft centres and farms as a means of becoming self-sufficient. It also raises money for educational, religious, medical and vocational needs, until the goal of self-sufficiency has been reached.

Adoption of Tibetan pen friends is arranged, and there is a corre-
spondence/aid programme that encourages Western people to
send a letter and a small donation each month to a Tibetan
refugee. **Teaching Programme** Project Tibet conduct seminars
and lectures on Tibetan-related subjects. It also offers a film and
slide show about Tibet. **Facilities and Services** A shop operates
as a retail and wholesale outlet for Tibetan refugee handicrafts.
The project also maintains a compound in Santa Fe that serves as
quarters for visiting Tibetans and a location for special events.
Newsletters and a pamphlet are published to keep interested individuals informed about the activities of Project Tibet. **Project
Description** It is hoped to establish a compound in Phoenix, Ari-
zona, in the near future.

RIGPE DORJE FOUNDATION

Address 328 North Sycamore Ave., Los Angeles, California,
USA, 90036. **Tel** (213) 934 5002. **Distribution Details** *Tibetan
Buddhist Calendar.* **General Description** Rigpe Dorje Foundation
is a charitable organisation formed to help the poor and underpriv-
iledged; to provide education and educational facilities; and to preserve cultural and traditional heritage primarily for the people of
Tibet living in exile. **Project Description** Sponsorship programmes for children of Tibetan refugee families, elder Tibetans,
and Tibetan Buddhist monks. Each sponsorship provides basic
necessities and educational fees; development and construction of
educational facilities for young Tibetan children and young
Tibetan monks; development of health facilities for Tibetan communities; the construction of spiritual structures for the monastic
community of Tibetan Buddhist monks such as monasteries, stupas, and higher Buddhist institutions; also the preservation of art,
culture, traditions and spiritual beliefs of Tibet and Tibetan people.

SAKYADHITA,
INTERNATIONAL ASSOCIATION OF BUDDHIST WOMEN

Address 400 Hobron Lane, #2615, Honolulu, Hawaii, USA,
96815. **Year Established** 1987. **General Description** This
international organisation with representation in Australia,
Canada, UK, Germany, India, Japan, Sri Lanka, Thailand and the
US was founded at the conclusion of the first International Conference on Buddhist Nuns held in Bodhgaya, India, in February
1987. It seeks to unite Buddhist women of the various countries
and traditions, to promote their welfare, and to facilitate their
work for the benefit of humanity. **Teaching Programme** The
organisation publishes a newsletter entitled *Sakyadhita.* **Facilities
and Services** Information is available on Buddhist teaching programmes, meditation courses and issues of particular interest to
women in Buddhism. Also available is information and counselling for women interested in ordination and monastic training.
Local meditation support groups, retreats and international conferences are organised for Buddhist women.

SAMAYA FOUNDATION

Address 75 Leonards Street, New York, New York, USA, 10013.
Tel 212–219–2908. **Telex/Fax** 212–941–9639. **General Descrip-**

tion The Samaya Foundation was formed in 1976 as an educational and cultural foundation committed to the practice and preservation of Tibetan arts and sciences. The foundation offers ongoing programmes contributing to the expanding dialogue between Eastern and Western civilisation and houses an extensive video archive. The Samaya Foundation's primary emphasis is the creation of television projects concerning Tibetan culture. **Teaching Programme** The foundation issues a newsletter detailing some of the events of the past and coming year. **Facilities and Services** In 1988, the Samaya foundation began broadcasting *Window on Tibet*, the first weekly television series dedicated exclusively to Tibetan culture, and a number of other television programmes are currently in development. Museum projects have included the creation of a sand mandala in New York and Los Angeles, and currently video documentation of the extensive Tibetan art collection at the Newark Museum is being made. Two books have been scheduled for publication by the foundation: *Cancer & Consciousness* and *Journey Through the Wheel of Time*. The foundation administers the Time and Space fund, supporting Tibetan monks and nuns in exile.

SCHOOL FOR INTERNATIONAL TRAINING

Address Kipling Road, Brattleboro, Vermont, USA, 05301. **Tel** (802) 257 7751. **Telex/Fax** (802) 257 9274. **General Description** The school organises a College Abroad Semester Program for US undergraduate students in Dharamsala, India; Nepal; and Tibet. Studies encourage understanding of Tibetan life and culture, fluency in Tibetan language, and focused, independent study on a topic of importance within the field of Tibetan studies.

SEATTLE TIBETAN CULTURAL CENTER

Address 5042 18th Ave. N.E., Seattle, Washington, USA, 98105. **Tel** (206)

522 6967. **Year Established** 1985. **Founder** H.H. Jigdal Dagchen Sakya. **Lama/Scholar** H.H. Jigdal Dagchen Sakya. **General Description** The centre is a subsidiary educational organisation of Sakya Monastery. The centre's goal is to preserve and share Tibetan culture with the community at large. To that end, the Cultural Center houses a Tibetan exhibition, offers lectures on Tibetan culture, classes on Tibetan language and history, sponsors an annual Tibetan New Year Festival, and provides rooming facilities for those interested in learning about Tibet. The Cultural Advisor to the centre is Mrs Jamyang Dagmola Sakya who is also author of **Princess from the Land of the Snow**. **Facilities and Services** The centre has eight residents of various nationalities, including Tibetan. It has a conference room. Activities include Tibetan Losar Celebrations, hosting lamas and dignitaries, hosting Tibetan language and culture classes that are sponsored by the Tibetan Women's Association, and occasional social activities.

TIBET CENTER

Address 359 Broadway, New York, New York, USA, 10003. **Lama/Scholar** Khyongla Rato Rinpoche.

TIBET HOUSE, NEW YORK

Address 3rd Floor, 241 East 32nd St., New York, New York, USA, 10016. **Tel** (212) 213 5592. **Telex/Fax** (212) 213 6408. **Year Established** 1987. **Founder** Richard Gere. **General Description** Tibet House in New York City is a cultural centre dedicated to preserving the full spectrum of Tibet's cultural and religious heritage; to present to the West Tibet's ancient traditions of philosophy, art and science. The vital culture of Tibet is presented through a wide range of special events and public programmes produced with leading museums, educational institutions, performing arts centres, television stations, and book publishers. Tibet House organises travelling exhibitions of Tibetan arts and artefacts, presents seminars of Tibetan history, culture and religion by Western and Tibetan scholars, and co-ordinates major conferences on all aspects of Tibet. **Teaching Programme** Tibet House programmes take place in New York City and nationwide.

TIBETAN COMPUTER CO.

Address 1113 Spruce St., Boulder, Colorado, USA, 80302. **General Description** The company produces Tibetan word-processing software for IBM compatibles. Tibetan fonts for laser and dot matrix printers and Sanskrit diacritic fonts have been created.

TIBETAN CULTURAL CENTER (TIBET SOCIETY)

Address 3655 South Snoddy Road, Bloomington, Indiana, USA, 47401. **Tel** (812) 855 8222. **Distribution Details** The Tibet Society publishes a periodical known as *The Journal of the Tibet Society*. **Year Established** 1967. **Founder** Thubten Jigme Norbu. **General Description** The Tibetan Cultural Center and the Tibet Society were established in Bloomington, Indiana, in order to preserve Tibetan culture and heritage. In 1987 a traditional Tibetan Stupa was dedicated in a ceremony at the twenty-acre site in Bloomington. The Tibetan Cultural Center plans to develop the site to include a library, visitors' centre, gardens, a museum and an assembly hall. The Tibet Society celebrated its twentieth anniversary in September, 1987. It has recently established its home at the Tibetan Cultural Center. The Tibet Society sponsors charitable, cultural and educational acitivities that are intended to aid Tibet's cultural heritage. Special support is given to the study and publication of works on Tibet and Tibetans. **Project Description** The Tibetan Cultural Center is seeking funding for the development of a Lekhang or workshop. This will be a 5000 sq ft building containing offices, visitor's accommodation, kitchen facilities and an assembly room, all in the distinctive architectural style of Tibet. The Lekhang/workshop will enable the Tibetan Cultural Center to provide facilities for conferences, exhibitions, seminars, and a variety of community activities.

TIBETAN CULTURAL STUDY CENTER

Address 316 Center Street, Old Town, Maine, USA, 04468. **Tel** (207) 827 6212. **Distribution Details** Newsletter published quarterly, *Maine TCC*.

TIBETAN NUNS PROJECT

Address P.O. Box 40542, San Francisco, California, USA, 94140. **Tel** (804) 295 5533.

Ecumenical Centres

BUDDHIST PEACE FELLOWSHIP

Address P.O. Box 4650, Berkeley, California, USA, 94704. **Tel** (415) 525 8596. **Distribution Details** Publishes a newsletter three times a year. **General Description** The Buddhist Peace Fellowship campaigns for the support of human rights and assists refugees. Public talks, workshops, and retreats are organised. **Facilities and Services** The BPF publishes a newsletter three times a year.

Government Offices

INTERNATIONAL CAMPAIGN FOR TIBET, US TIBET COMMITTEE

Address 1518 K. Street NW, Suite 410, Washington, District of Columbia, USA, 20005–1401. **Tel** 202 628 4123. **Telex/Fax** 202 347 6825. **Year Established** 1988. **Founder** Kalon Tenzin Namgyal Tethong. **Lama/Scholar** Lodi Gyari (director). **General Description** Established in 1988, the International Campaign for Tibet (ICT) promotes human rights and democratic freedoms in Tibet. The organisation publishes a report, six times a year, called *Tibet Press Watch*. The ICT also publishes a comprehensive resource directory of the Tibetan offices, human rights organisations and Tibet support groups etc. around the world.

OFFICE OF TIBET (NEW YORK)

Address 241 East 32nd Street, New York, New York, USA, 10016. **Tel** (212) 213 5010. **Telex/Fax** (212) 779 9245. **Distribution Details** Publishes the journal *News Tibet*. **Lama/Scholar** Rinchen Dharlo (Representative). **General Description** Bureau of the Representative of H.H. the Dalai Lama.

Libraries

ALDERMAN LIBRARY

Address University of Virginia, Charlottesville, Virginia, USA, 22903. **Tel** (804)924–4981. **General Description** The Alderman Library has an extensive Tibetan collection of more than 5000 volumes, including the PL–480 *Tibetan Comprehensive*, a reference collection of catalogues, iconographic works, together with secondary historical and cultural materials. The library is considered to have one of the largest Tibetan collections in existence and has an extensive and easily accessible card filing system.

AMERICAN ORIENTAL SOCIETY LIBRARY

Address Sterling Memorial Library, Yale Station, New Haven, Connecticut, USA, 06520.

ASIAN LIBRARY, UNIVERSITY OF ILLINOIS

Address 325 Main Library, 1408 W. Gregory Drive, Urbana, Illinois, USA, 61801. **Tel** 217 333 1501. **Telex/Fax** 217 244 0398.

CENTER FOR RESEARCH LIBRARIES

Address 6050 S. Kenwood Avenue, Chicago, Illinois, USA, 60637. **Tel** 312 955 4545. **Distribution Details** Loans to non-members available on a limited basis for a fee. **General Description** The Center for Research Libraries has a collection of Tibetan monographs received through the PL–480 Program. There are no reference services available.

CHARLES PATTERSON VAN PELT LIBRARY, UNIVERSITY OF PENNSYLVANIA

Address 3420 Walnut Street, Philadelphia, Pennsylvania, USA, 19104 6206. **Tel** 215 898 7460. **Telex/Fax** 215 898 0559. **General Description** The University of Pennsylvania Library has a collection of over 7,000 volumes, most of which were acquired between 1962 and 1985. It includes important multivolume sets, such as the *Encyclopedia Tibetica* (150 volumes); the *Kangyur* (103 volumes); and *Complete works of Tsongkhapa* (28 volumes). In addition the library has a few Tibetan manuscripts. **Facilities and Services** The Tibetan collection is a non-circulating collection but is open to scholars for research on premises. Arrangements for use must be made in advance. Xerox copies of the texts will be supplied on cost basis when needed.

CLEVELAND PUBLIC LIBRARY, JOHN G. WHITE COLLECTION OF ORIENTALIA

Address Fine Arts & Special Collections Dept., 325 Superior Avenue, Cleveland, Ohio, USA, 44114. **Tel** 216 623 2818. **Telex/Fax** 216 623 6987. **Year Established** 1869. **Founder** John G. White. **General Description** The library holds 2452 volumes pertaining to Tibetan studies, including 1052 in Tibetan. Emphasis is on literary and religious texts and translations. Numerous facsimile editions of manuscripts are included, such as chapters from the *Mahayana Sutra* and the *Tibetan Tripitaka*, Peking edition, reprinted under the supervision of the Otani University, Kyoto. A separate catalogue of main entries for titles in Tibetan is maintained.

CORNELL UNIVERSITY LIBRARY

Address Olin Hall, Cornell University, Ithaca, New York, USA, 14853. **Tel** 607 256 4247. **General Description** The Cornell University Library has a Tibetan collection of more than 2000 PL-480 texts. Some of the manuscripts are catalogued.

EAST ASIA LIBRARY

Address University of Washington, Gowen Hall, DO–27, Seattle, Washington, USA, 98195. **Tel** 206 543 4490. **Telex/Fax** 206 474 0096. **Lama/Scholar** Professor L.W.J. van der Kuijp, Geshe Nornang. **General Description** The East Asian Library was one of the recipients of the Tibetan materials which were acquired by the Library of Congress through their PL-480 Program. There are 8455 volumes of books, 2975 sheets of microfiches, and 223 reels of microfilm in the Tibetan language. **Teaching Programme** The Department of Asian Languages and Literature at the University of Washington offers an excellent Tibetan Studies Programme leading to the Master of Arts and Doctor of Philosophy degrees.

EAST ASIAN LIBRARY, UNIVERSITY OF CHICAGO

Address 1100 East 57th Street, Chicago, Illinois, USA, 60637. **Tel** 312 702 8432. **Telex/Fax** 312 702 0853. **General Description** The East Asian Library houses a collection of Tibetan books acquired mainly by Berthold Laufer during his travels in India, Sikkim and Peking. The collection was previously kept in the Newberry Library.

EAST ASIATIC LIBRARY, UNIVERSITY OF CALIFORNIA

Address Room 208 Durant Hall, Berkeley, California, USA, 94720. **Tel** 415 642 2556.

FRANKLIN D. ROOSEVELT LIBRARY

Address, Hyde Park, New York, USA, 12538. **Tel** 914 229 8814. **General Description** The Tibetan collection was presented to President Roosevelt by Colonel Tolstoy who had been given the items by the Dalai Lama in 1943. Included in the collection are four silk hand-sewn thangkas.

GEST ORIENTAL LIBRARY

Address Princeton University, 317 Palmer Hall, Princeton, New Jersey, USA, 08544. **Tel** 609 258 3182. **Telex/Fax** 609 258 4105.

Year Established 1926. **General Description** The Gest Oriental Library has four or five rare Tibetan books, as yet unidentified.

HARVARD-YENCHING LIBRARY
Address Dept. of East Asian Languages, Harvard University, 2 Divinity Avenue, Cambridge, Massachusetts, USA, 02138. **General Description** The Harvard-Yenching Library has in its Tibetan collection five different editions of the *Tibetan Tripitaka* and various collected writings of the Sakya Buddhist tradition.

INDIANA UNIVERSITY LIBRARIES
Address Bloomington, Indiana, USA, 47401. **General Description** The Tibetan collection consists of the Peking edition of the *Tripitaka*, 168 volumes, works from the Sakya tradition, and approximately 3500 volumes from the Special Foreign Currencies Program. The collection is fully catalogued.

KALAMAZOO PUBLIC LIBRARY
Address 315 South Rose Street, Kalamazoo, Michigan, USA, 49006.

LEHMAN LIBRARY,
COLUMBIA UNIVERSITY
Address Columbia University, Lehman Library 2nd Floor, New York, New York, USA, 10027. **Tel** 212 854 8046. **General Description** This library, in conjunction with the other Columbia University Libraries, houses several thousand Tibetan-language books, manuscripts, and xylographic reproductions from Tibet, India, Nepal and Bhutan. It is one of the largest Tibetan language collections in the United States. There is also a large, active collection of material in other languages on Tibetan culture, history, Buddhism, and current affairs.

LIBRARY OF CONGRESS
Address Asian Division, Washington, District of Columbia, USA, 20540. **Tel** 202 707 5600. **Telex/Fax** 202 707 1724. **General Description** The Tibetan collection at the Library of Congress (LC) can be described in three categories: 1) various redactions of the *Kangyur* and *Tengyur*: original xylograph sets of the *Derge Kangyur*, *Narthang Tengyur*, and *Cone Kangyur* and *Tengyur*; and reprint editions of the *Peking Kangyur* and *Tengyur*, and *Derge Kangyur* and *Tengyur*. 2) approximately 300 original xylographs and manuscripts which were acquired for LC between 1900–28 by William Rockhill, Berthold Laufer, and Joseph Rock; and 3) reprints acquired for LC and other participating US libraries through the Library's Special Foreign Currency Program administered through the New Delhi Field Office from the early 1960s to the present (about 3000 separate bibliographic entries, over 5000 volumes). **Project Description** The Library's New Delhi Field Office plans to re-institute its Tibetan acquisitions programme through which Tibetan books in category three were acquired.

LOS ANGELES PUBLIC LIBRARY
Address 630 W 5th Street, Los Angeles, California, USA, 90071. **Tel** 213 626 7555.

MEMORIAL LIBRARY
Address University of Wisconsin-Madison, 728 State Street, Madison, Wisconsin, USA, 53706. **General Description** The main section of the Tibetan collection of works in the Memorial Library comprises of several thousand volumes of the PL–480 *Tibetan Comprehensive*. There is also a reprint of the 168-volume Peking edition of the *Tibetan Tripitaka* and a microfiche copy of 209 volumes of the *Cone Kangyur*.

NATIONAL GEOGRAPHIC SOCIETY
Address 16th and M Street N.W., Washington, District of Columbia, USA, 20036. **General Description** The National Geographic Society library has one Tibetan manuscript.

NEW YORK PUBLIC LIBRARY

Address Oriental Division, Fifth Avenue and 42nd Street, New York, New York, USA, 10018. **Tel** (212) 930 0721. **Telex/Fax** 212 921 2546. **Year Established** 1895. **General Description** At present the majority of holdings in the Tibetan collection consist of material acquired through the Library of Congress: the Public Law 480 Program and the Library of Congress Special Foreign Currency Program. For material in the library before 1972, there are more than 1000 items listed in the Dictionary Catalogue of the Oriental Collections, 1960, and its Supplement, 1976, as well as in various shelf lists. These represent holdings in the Oriental Division as well as other parts of the library.

ORIENTAL LIBRARY

Address University of California, Los Angeles, California, USA, 90024. **Tel** (213)825 4923. **General Description** The Oriental Library at the University of California has 1125 volumes in its collection including a 168 volume photo-reproduction of the Peking Edition of the Tibetan Tripitaka.

PIERPONT MORGAN LIBRARY

Address 29 East 36th Street, New York, New York, USA, 10016. **Tel** 212 685 0008. **General Description** The library has a collection of three Tibetan manuscripts.

UNIVERSITY OF CALIFORNIA GENERAL LIBRARY

Address East Asiatic Library, University of California at Berkeley, Berkeley, California, USA, 94720. **Tel** 415 642 2556. **General Description** The East Asiatic Library of the University of California at Berkeley has a collection of more than 6000 volumes in Tibetan as well as some Tibetan language works on microfilm and microfiche. Most of the Tibetan language books, over 5000 volumes, were acquired through the PL–480 Program of the Library of Congress. In addition to the PL–480 material, the library owns nearly 500 dpe-chas, including the Narthang *Kangyur*, the *Rinchen gter mdzod*, a number of works by Gelug authors, Tibetan translations of various sutras, and some miscellaneous works. The library also has some 350 Tibetan volumes, mostly paperback, published in the People's Republic of China, as well as the 168-volume *Tibetan Tripitaka*, Peking Edition, published in Japan.

UNIVERSITY OF HAWAII LIBRARY

Address Asia Collection, 2550 The Mall, Honolulu, Hawaii, USA, 96822. **Tel** 808 956 8116. **Year Established** 1907. **General Description** The Tibetan language collection is based primarily on the materials acquired through the Special Foreign Currency Program (formerly the PL–480 Program), a co-operative acquisition programme administered by the Library of Congress in New Delhi. The library also acquires materials concerning Tibet in other languages at a level which supports the courses offered by the various academic departments of the university.

YALE UNIVERSITY LIBRARY

Address Beinecke Rare Book and Manuscript Library, Box 160A Yale Station, New Haven, Connecticut, USA, 06520. **General Description** The Tibetan collection includes: the Lhasa edition of the *Kangyur* in 100 volumes, a gift of the Fourteenth Dalai Lama in 1950; 409 block-printed volumes which include the collected works and biographies of former Dalai Lamas and the writings of other lamas of the principal monastic orders, also twelve volumes of medical texts and thirty-three monastic manuals; six manuscript texts on various subjects – original and canonical; over 1000 volumes relating to Tibetan Buddhism composed by lamas of the five principal orders, also volumes of the non-Buddhist Bon-po religion, all lithographed from Tibetan texts available in India. Texts acquired under the PL–480 Tibetan Comprehensive are in the collection. A detailed description of the holdings is available in *The Tibetan Collection at Yale* by W.E. Needham, Yale University Library Gazette, Vol.34 No.3, (January 1960). The library also has a museum collection which includes: 124 prints, seven woodblocks, fifty-four thangkas, three dorjes, eight bronzes, one needlework banner and various ritual objects.

Medical Institutions

MIND/BODY MEDICAL INSTITUTE

Address New England Deaconess Hospital, 110 Francis St., Boston, Massachussetts, USA, 02215. **Tel** (617) 732 9530. **Distribution Details** Cassette tapes are available of annual symposia. **Lama/Scholar** Dr Herbert Benson. **General Description** The institute is part of a Harvard Medical School project researching advanced meditation techniques, used by Tibetan and Buddhist monks, to learn how controlled relaxation and self-regulation may activate the body's healing mechanisms. The research also involves comparisons between Western

and Buddhist psychology.

Museums

AMERICAN MUSEUM OF NATURAL HISTORY

Address Department of Anthropology, AMNH, Central Park West at 79th Street, New York, New York, USA, 10024. **Tel** 212 769 5886. **Telex/Fax** 212 769 5233. **General Description** The American Museum of Natural History has a substantial collection of Tibetan material, comprising mostly religious objects. The collection includes about 300 thangkas, more than 500 statues and various manuscripts.

AMERICAN NUMISMATIC SOCIETY

Address Broadway and 156th Street, New York, New York, USA, 10032. **Tel** 212 234 3130. **Telex/Fax** 212 234 3381. **Year Established** 1858. **General Description** The American Numismatic Society has over 2000 Tibetan coins acquired over the years from various sources. These are available for study by appointment with the curator. There is an excellent library, open to the general public, and a catalogue which has about 100 cards for books and articles on Tibetan coinage. Books may not be loaned outside the building, but a limited photocopy service is available. There are also many coins of Nepal, Sikkim, Bhutan and India. **Facilities and Services** The society publishes *Numismatic Literature*, a semi-annual survey of all numismatic publications.

ANTOINETTE K. GORDON COLLECTION

Address Goodbody Hall 157, Indiana University, Bloomington, Indiana, USA, 47405. **Tel** 812 337 2233. **General Description** The Antoinette K. Gordon Tibetan collection comprises approximately 70 artefacts including thangkas; and other paintings, bronzes, ritual objects, and various domestic items.

ASIAN ART MUSEUM OF SAN FRANCISCO

Address The Avery Brundage Collection, Golden Gate Park, San Francisco, California, USA, 94118. **Tel** 415 668 8921. **Telex/Fax** 415 668 8928. **Year Established** 1966. **Founder** Avery Brundage. **General Description** There are about 250 objects in the Tibetan collection, among which 140 are thangkas, the rest consist of sculptures, ritual objects and jewellery. The collection is particularly strong in Sino-Tibetan art. There is a permanent gallery of Himalayan objects (Tibet, Nepal, and Bhutan), and a library which has a good collection of books on Tibetan art in English and Chinese. Black and white photographs and slides of most of the collection are available.

BALTIMORE MUSEUM OF ART

Address Art Museum Drive, Baltimore, Maryland, USA, 21218. **Tel** 301 396 7101. **Telex/Fax** 301 396 6562. **Year Established** 1914. **General Description** The Baltimore Museum of Art collection of Tibetan material contains: twelve Sino-Tibetan gilt bronze votive figures, which range in date from the fifteenth to the eighteenth century, and four thangkas, in very poor condition, which range from the eighteenth to early nineteenth century. The gilt bronzes were examined by John Ford, of Baltimore, in 1989; and the thangkas by John Pope, of the Freer Gallery, in 1958.

BROOKLYN MUSEUM

Address 200 Eastern Parkway, Brooklyn, New York, USA, 11238. **Tel** 718 638 5000. **Telex/Fax** 718 638 3731. **General Description** Founded in 1823, the Brooklyn Museum today holds over 1,000,000 works of art housed in seven curatorial departments. The museum is an institution devoted to public education and is regarded as one of the ten largest and most prominent museums in the United States. The Tibetan art collection includes: twenty-eight thangkas, twenty-five sculptures, eight bronzes, four costume-related pieces, four rugs, four wooden objects, three silver objects, one mast and a pair of eighteenth century earrings. The museum's Art Reference Library contains seventy-one books pertaining to Tibetan art, civilisation, history, and religion. Objects from the Tibetan Collection are featured in **Masterpieces in the Brooklyn Museum** (Brooklyn 1986) which highlights a twelfth or thirteenth century seated Maitreya and a fourteenth century mandala of Vajrasattva. These objects are also depicted in the article '*Art of the Himalayan Region*' by Amy G. Poster published in the April 1982 edition of *Apollo* (a special issue devoted to The Brooklyn Museum).

BUSH COLLECTION OF RELIGION AND CULTURE, COLUMBIA UNIVERSITY

Address Department of Religion, Kent Hall, New York, New York, USA, 10027. **Tel** (212) 280 3218. **General Description** The Bush Collection includes of a small but varied Tibetan collection.

CINCINNATI ART MUSEUM

Address Eden Park, Cincinnati, Ohio, USA, 45202. **Tel** 513 721 5204. **General Description** The Tibetan collection includes seven paintings, seven bronzes and various ritual objects.

CLEVELAND MUSEUM OF ART

Address 11150 East Boulevard at Univ. Circle, Cleveland, Ohio, USA, 44106. **Tel** 216 421 7340. **General Description** The Cleveland Museum of Art has a small collection of Tibetan items including thangkas, bronzes, ritual objects and one wooden shrine.

DAYTON ART INSTITUTE

Address Forest and Riverview Avenues, P.O. Box 941, Dayton, Ohio, USA, 45401. **Tel** 513 223 5277. **Telex/Fax** 513 223 3140. **Year Established** 1919. **General Description** The Dayton Art Institute has a small Tibetan collection with eleven paintings, seven sculptures (bronze, painted wood, silver, and gilt bronze), and a few ritual objects (lamps, vajras etc.)

DENVER ART MUSEUM

Address 100 West 14th Avenue Parkway, Denver, Colorado, USA, 80204. **Tel** 303 640 2203. **Telex/Fax** 303 640 2030. **Year Established** 1893. **General Description** The museum has forty Tibetan objects in its collection. These include: eleven thangka paintings, six sculptures, thirteen ritual objects, and ten textiles. In addition, the collection includes related objects from Nepal and China.

DETROIT INSTITUTE OF ARTS

Address Department of Asian Art, 5200 Woodward Avenue, Detroit, Michigan, USA, 48202. **Tel** 313 833 1718. **Telex/Fax** 313 833 2357. **General Description** The museum has a small collection of Tibetan artefacts which include: eight thangkas, a sculpture of Tara, and two turquoise and gold-over-silver Tibetan Buddhist ornaments.

EVANSVILLE MUSEUM OF ARTS AND SCIENCE

Address 411 S.E. Riverside Drive, Evansville, Indiana, USA, 47713. **Tel** 812 425 2406. **General Description** The museum has a small but varied collection of Tibetan artefacts some of which are on display. The remainder may be viewed by prior arrangement.

FIELD MUSEUM OF NATURAL HISTORY

Address Asian Archaeology and Ethnology, Roosevelt Road at Lake Shore Drive, Chicago, Illinois, USA, 60605. **Tel** 312 922 9410. **General Description** The Tibetan collection at the Field Museum of Natural History was mostly bought by Dr Berthold Laufer in Eastern Tibet and Beijing between 1908–1910. The remaining pieces were purchased in Calcutta in 1962. There are a total of 3884 items catalogued in the collection and approximately 500 uncatalogued books and manuscripts. Items include: transportation (wicker straps, boats and equipment); animal equipment, such as stirrups, saddles, yak nose rings, whips etc.; weapons; tools; firemaking equipment and candlesticks, lamps etc.; containers; household furnishings; ornaments; games and toys; musical instruments; costumes; personal accessories; religious artefacts; paintings etc.; prints and woodcuts; writing materials; and money.

FOGG ART MUSEUM

Address Oriental Department, Harvard University, 32 Quincy Street, Cambridge, Massachusetts, USA, 02138. **Tel** 617 495 2391.

FOWLER MUSEUM OF CULTURAL HISTORY, UCLA

Address University of California, 405 Hilgard Avenue, Los Angeles, California, USA, 90024–1549. **Tel** (213) 825–4923. **Year Established** 1963. **General Description** The Museum's Tibetan holdings consist of 418 various artefacts.

FREER GALLERY OF ART, SMITHSONIAN INSTITUTION
Address Jefferson Drive at 12th St., S.W., Washington, District of Columbia, USA, 20560. **Tel** (202) 357 2104. **Telex/Fax** (202) 357 4911.

GRAND RAPIDS PUBLIC MUSEUM
Address 54 Jefferson Avenue, S.E., Grand Rapids, Michigan, USA, 49503. **Tel** 616 456 3977. **General Description** The Grand Rapids Public Museum has a small collection of Tibetan artefacts.

JACQUES MARCHAIS CENTER OF TIBETAN ART
Address 338 Lighthouse Avenue, Staten Island, New York, USA, 10306. **Tel** 212 987 3478. **Year Established** 1945. **Founder** Mrs Harry Klauber (Alias Jacques Marchais). **General Description** The Jacques Marchais Center of Tibetan Art was founded in 1945 to foster, promote and encourage interest, study and research in the culture, art and literature of Tibet and other oriental countries. To this end, the centre collects objects, books and photographs and makes them available to the public through exhibitions, publications and other interpretive means. Designed in the Tibetan architectural style, one building is used as a library and the other, which contains the permanent exhibition, closely resembles a Tibetan Buddhist mountain temple. The Tibetan museum is unique in displaying its art in a setting especially conducive to its understanding and enjoyment. **Facilities and Services** The centre is open to the general public Wednesday to Sunday from 1 to 5 pm April until the end of November. From December until the end of March, museum hours are by appointment only. The museum shop stocks a variety of unusual gift items, books, and jewellery from the Orient.

LOS ANGELES COUNTY MUSEUM OF ART
Address 5905 Wiltshire Boulevard, Los Angeles, California, USA, 90036. **Tel** 213 857 6091. **Telex/Fax** 213 931 7347. **Year Established** 1965. **General Description** The Los Angeles County Museum of Art has a significant and comprehensive collection of Tibetan art. A catalogue of the complete collection is available through the museum shop.

LOWIE MUSEUM OF ANTHROPOLOGY
Address University of California, 103 Kroeber Hall, Berkeley, California, USA, 94720. **Tel** 415 642 3681. **Telex/Fax** 415 643 8557. **Year Established** 1901. **Founder** Regents of the University of California. **General Description** The Tibetan collection contains between 120–150 objects, mostly religious in nature, although there are also some secular household items and textiles.

MATHERS MUSEUM OF WORLD CULTURES
Address 601 East Eighth Street, Bloomington, Indiana, USA, 47405. **Tel** 812 855 6873. **Year Established** 1963. **General Description** The Mathers Museum holds a Tibetan collection of masks, musical instruments, ritual objects and some garments.

METROPOLITAN MUSEUM OF ART
Address Fifth Avenue at 82nd Street, New York, New York, USA, 10028. **Tel** 212 879 5500.

MONTCLAIR ART MUSEUM
Address 3 South Mountain Avenue, Montclair, New Jersey, USA, 07042. **Tel** 201 746 555. **General Description** The museum has a small Tibetan collection comprising thangkas, ritual items and a manuscript.

MUSEUM OF CULTURAL HISTORY
Address University of California, 55A Haines Hall, Los Angeles, California, USA, 90024. **Tel** 213 825 9341. **General Description** The Museum of Cultural History has a Tibetan collection of approximately 200 objects. These include: thangkas, blocks for printing textiles, musical instruments (bells, trumpets, drums), incense burners, charm boxes, temple cornices and knives.

MUSEUM OF FINE ARTS
Address Huntington Avenue, Boston, Massachusetts, USA, 02115. **Tel** 617 267 9300. **General Description** The Museum of Fine Arts has a Tibetan collection of approximately 154 thangka paintings and fifty sculptures.

MUSEUM OF INTERNATIONAL FOLK ART
Address Museum of International Folk Art, P.O. Box 2087, Santa Fe, New Mexico, USA, 87501. **Tel** 505 827 8350. **Telex/Fax** 505 827 8349. **Year Established** 1953. **Founder** Florence Dibell Bartlett. **General Description** The Tibetan holdings at the Museum of International Folk Art are small but include several very fine ritual objects (conch shell, tea bowl, etc.), one eighteenth century painting depicting the Wheel of Life, one woman's costume from the 1960s, one man's coat from the 1920s, and several prayer boxes. The number of items held in the collection is approximately twenty-four.

NEBRASKA UNIVERSITY STATE MUSEUM
Address Division of Anthropology, W–436 Nebraska Hall, Lincoln, Nebraska, USA, 68588–0514. **Tel** 402 472 5044. **Year Established** 1871. **General Description** The museum has about twenty-five Tibetan artefacts including prayer boards, jewellery, weapons, bells and containers.

NELSON-ATKINS MUSEUM OF ART
Address Oriental Department, 4525 Oak Street, Kansas City, Missouri, USA, 64111. Tel 816 561 4000. **Telex/Fax** 816 561 7154. **Year Established** 1933. **Founder** Trustees of the Nelson and Atkins trusts. **General Description** The museum possesses a small collection of Tibetan objects, consisting of twenty-seven metal images, two stucco votive tablets, twenty-eight thangkas, five pieces of jewellery, sixteen ritual objects, and one woodblock. The objects range in age from the fifteenth to the twentieth century, with the majority dating from the nineteenth to the twentieth century. The material originated primarily from Central Tibet, with a small number of images and thangkas from Eastern Tibet. Some photos and slides of the collection are available.

NEWARK MUSEUM
Address 43–49 Washington Street, P.O. Box 540, Newark, New Jersey, USA, 07101. **Tel** 201 596 6550. **Telex/Fax** 201 642 0459. **Year Established** 1909. **General Description** The Newark Museum's Tibetan collection is one of the largest and most comprehensive in the world. It was formed from items collected by American missionaries working in Kham and Amdo between 1911 and 1948. This original group of pieces consists of paintings, sculpture, manuscripts, ritual objects, textiles, and ethnographic materials. Between 1959 and the present objects from Tibetan refugees, primarily from the

Central Tibetan regions have been collected, including an important group of official costumes and documents. Some 10,000 objects and 2000 archival photographs and films now constitute the holdings. Eight permanent display rooms specially designed for the Tibetan Collection were opened in November 1989, and a complete Buddhist altar consecrated in September, 1990. A five-volume catalogue is available.

NORTON SIMON MUSEUM OF ART AT PASADENA
Address Colorado and Orange Grove, Pasadena, California, USA, 91105. **Tel** 213 449 6840. **Telex/Fax** 818 796 4978. **General Description** The museum has a Tibetan collection of about forty-five items. These include: about thirty statues in bronze, gilt bronze, gilt bronze with inlay, iron, and lacquered wood; seven carved wood book covers; one painted fabric; five ritual daggers (one wood, four bronze); and one copper box.

PARRISH ART MUSEUM
Address 25 Job's Lane, Southampton, New York, USA, 11968. **Tel** 516 283 2118. **Telex/Fax** 516 283 7006. **Year Established** 1898. **General Description** The Parrish Art Museum has a small collection of six Tibetan thangkas from the nineteenth century. The subjects of these thangkas are Amitayus, Ushnisha Vijaya, Yamaraja, Gesar, and two of Vajrapani.

PEABODY MUSEUM (MASS)
Address Department of Ethnology, East India Square, Salem, Massachusetts, USA, 01970. **Tel** 508 745 1876. **Telex/Fax** 508 744 6776. **General Description** The Ethnology department of the Peabody Museum of Salem maintains a collection of 350 Tibetan ethnographic objects. These include both religious and secular materials, ie., ritual implements, thangkas (including a fine, rare dated Ming dynasty thangka), statues, musical instruments, altar objects, jewellery and prayer beads, apparel and household objects. The department also holds over 300 Bhutanese objects, religious and secular, with a fine collection of Bhutanese textiles. A small Nepalese collection is also present.

PEABODY MUSEUM OF NATURAL HISTORY
Address Division of Anthropology, Yale University, 170 Whitney Avenue, New Haven, Connecticut, USA, 06511. **Tel** 203 436 3770. **General Description** The museum has a substantial Tibetan collection of approximately 230 items. The collection is well catalogued and includes a varied selection such as textiles, weaving and basketwork, paintings and prints, metalwork, leatherwork, jewellery, musical instruments, household items, writing materials, sculptures, and costumes. In addition there are four photographs of Tibetan scenes. **Teaching Programme** Courses are taught through the affiliated Department of Anthropology at Yale University.

PEABODY MUSEUM. OF ARCHAEOLOGY AND ETHNOLOGY
Address Harvard University, 11 Divinity Avenue, Cambridge, Massachusetts, USA, 02138. **Tel** 617 495 2248. **Telex/Fax** 7535.

Year Established 1867. **General Description** The museum Tibetan collection consists of approximately 385 objects, including objects relating to both monastic and lay religious practices. Among these objects are monks' clothing, prayer wheels, thangkas, objects identified as 'charms' or 'amulets', bells, drums and a thigh-bone trumpet. The photographic collection includes photographs of monks and a series from the Wulsim expedition.

PHILADELPHIA MUSEUM OF ART
Address 26th Street and Ben Franklin Parkway, Philadelphia, Pennsylvania, USA, 19103. **Tel** 215 763 8100. **Telex/Fax** 215 236 4465. **Year Established** 1876. **General Description** The Museum's Tibetan collection comprises approximately thirty-six sculptures, four manuscripts, thirty-five paintings, three wood book covers, eight silver objects, eleven secular metal objects, twenty ritualistic objects of various media and some costumes and textiles. There are also some Tibetan objects on loan.

PUTMAN MUSEUM
Address 1717 West 12th Street, Davenport, Iowa, USA, 52804. **Tel** 319 324 1933. **General Description** The Tibetan collection at the Putman Museum was given to the museum after being bought in Darjeeling in 1905. It comprises a variety of artefacts including prayer boxes, jewellery, bronzes and ritual objects.

ROSE ART MUSEUM
Address Brandeis University, P.O. Box 9110 (415 South St.), Waltham, Massachusetts, USA, 02254-9110. **Tel** 617 736 3434. **Year Established** 1961. **Founder** Edward and Bertha Rose/Nettie and Louis Horch. **General Description** The Rose Art Museum, Brandeis University, houses the Riverside Collection of Tibetan Art which includes approximately 200 objects of Tibetan origin. The majority of works were acquired by Nettie and Louis L. Horch, founders of the Master Institute of United Arts, Inc., which sponsored expeditions into Tibet during the years 1924–28. The Master Institute, including the Riverside Museum, was established in New York in 1922, and Mr and Mrs Horch were its principal benefactors throughout its fifty year history. The entire collection of the Riverside Museum was given to Brandeis University, in honour of Mr and Mrs Horch, in 1971. Many aspects of Tibetan art and culture are represented in the collection in the form of paintings, sculptures and ritual objects.

SAN DIEGO MUSEUM OF ART
Address Balboa Park, P.O. Box 2107, San Diego, California, USA, 92112. **Tel** 619 232 7931. **Telex/Fax** 883594. **General Description** The San Diego Museum of Art Tibetan collection comprises twenty items. These include: seven thangka paintings; two watercolour paintings; one lamaist thigh-bone trumpet; one coin purse; one metal knife with scabbard; and eight sculptures (two brass, six bronze).

SANTA BARBARA MUSEUM OF ART
Address 1130 State Street, Santa Barbara, California, USA, 93101. **Tel** 805 963 4364. **Telex/Fax** 805 966 6840. **Year Established** 1941. **General Description** The Santa Barbara Museum of Art holds a collection of approximately thirty Tibetan artworks, almost equally divided – ten bronze sculptures, ten ritual objects and ten thangka paintings. Most of the works date from the eighteenth to twentieth centuries.

SEATTLE ART MUSEUM
Address Volunteer Park, 1400 E. Prospect, Seattle, Washington, USA, 98112 3303. **Tel** 206 625 8970. **Telex/Fax** 206 625 8913. **Year Established** 1933. **Founder** Dr Richard E. Fuller. **General Description** The Seattle Art Museum collec-

tion of Tibetan artefacts comprises forty-two various items. These include: three pieces of bone carving; one bronze stupa; five pieces of jewellery; four pieces of metalwork; one conch shell horn; five paintings; twelve sculptures; nine pieces of silver; and two textiles.

SMITH COLLEGE MUSEUM OF ART
Address, Northampton, Massachusetts, USA, 01063. **Tel** 413 585 2770. **Telex/Fax** 413 585 2075. **Year Established** 1879. **Lama/Scholar** Edward Nygren (Director). **General Description** The museum has a small collection of Tibetan objects, including a few thangkas and some metal pieces, two nineteenth century prayer boxes, an eighteenth century prayer wheel, and an early nineteenth century skull cup.

SMITHSONIAN INSTITUTION, HUMAN STUDIES FILM ARCHIVES, DEPT. OF ANTHROPOLOGY
Address Museum of Natural History, Rm. E307, Smithsonian Institution, Washington, District of Columbia, USA, 20560. **Tel** (202) 357 3349. **Distribution Details** No materials are distributed. **Year Established** 1981. **Lama/Scholar** Dr John Homiak. **General Description** The Smithsonian Institution established the Human Studies Film Archives in October 1981 to collect and preserve ethnographic film and video materials. Through study of these rich visual resources of non-western and western cultures, the Film Archives wish to promote increased understandings of the social complex of human life. It works with social scientists, film-makers and other interested parties in acquiring and preserving visual documents of past and contemporary cultural groups. **Facilities and Services** There are film and video screening facilities for researchers. Research services are offered and there is an automated cataloguing system. The archives act as a clearing-house for information on anthropological film. There are public programming facilities at the Museum of Natural History. Film holdings include 800 feet (edited) of the investiture of the Dalai Lama and some 360,000 feet of traditional Tibetan life and culture shot from 1976–1983, with supplementary research.

ST. LOUIS ART MUSEUM
Address Forest Park, St. Louis, Missouri, USA, 63110. **Tel** 314 721 0067. **Telex/Fax** 314 721 6172. **General Description** The St. Louis Art Museum has a Tibetan collection comprising eighteen sculptures and a complete set of thirteen thangkas depicting a Jataka tale.

TEXTILE MUSEUM
Address 2320 S. Street N.W., Washington, District of Columbia, USA, 20008. **Tel** 202 667 0441. **General Description** The Textile Museum's collection includes fourteen rugs, classified as Tibetan, and ten such textiles (six of which are Bhutanese). Under the heading of 'textiles' there is also a spinning wheel. **Teaching Programme** There are occasional lectures, publications and exhibitions on related subjects.

THOMAS BURKE MEMORIAL MUSEUM
Address University of Washington, Ethnology Division, Seattle, Washington, USA, 98195. **Tel** 206 543 5590. **General Description** The museum has a Tibetan collection of approximately 190 artefacts including: ninety thangkas, various religious objects, musical instruments, statues, masks, jewellery and everyday utensils. An extensive and thorough inventory of the collection is available from the Museum.

TOLEDO MUSEUM OF ART
Address Monroe Street at Scottwood Avenue, Box 1013, Toledo, Ohio, USA, 43697. **Tel** 419 255 8000. **Telex/Fax** 419 255 5638. **General Description** The Toledo Museum of Art holds a collection of seventeen Tibetan items. These include: one woodblock; three pieces of jewellery; four pieces of metalwork; six paintings; two sculptures; and one bronze ceremonial dagger.

UNIVERSITY MUSEUM OF ARCHAEOLOGY, AND ANTHROPOLOGY
Address University of Pennsylvania, 33rd and Spruce Streets, Philadelphia, Pennsylvania, USA, 19104. **Tel** 215 243 4000. **Telex/Fax** 215 898 0657. **General Description** The museum has a collection of approximately 300 Tibetan artefacts. The majority are religious and include items such as prayer wheels, prayer beads, charm boxes, phurbas, vajras, bells, bowls, musical instruments, ritual hats and aprons, statuettes and thangkas. The secular items include some jewellery, swords, snuff boxes and textiles.

UNIVERSITY OF MICHIGAN MUSEUM OF ART
Address Alumni Memorial Hall, 525 S. State St., Ann Arbor, Michigan, USA, 48109–1354. **Tel** 313 764 0395. **Telex/Fax** 313 764 3731. **Year Established** 1946. **General Description** The collection of Tibetan artefacts at the museum total nineteen items. These include: two ivory/bone plaques; three pieces of metalwork (one conch shell trumpet, two prayer wheels); seven paintings; three woodblock prints; and four sculptures (two stone, one gilt bronze with inlays, and one copper and wood).

VIRGINIA MUSEUM OF FINE ARTS
Address 2800 Grove Avenue, Richmond, Virginia, USA, 23221. **Tel** 804 367 8253. **Telex/Fax** 804 367 9393. **Year Established** 1936. **General Description** The museum has a small but significant collection of Tibetan art including twenty-four thangkas of the thirteenth to nineteenth centuries and metal sculpture from the fourteenth to nineteenth centuries. Many of the thangkas were originally owned by G. Tucci; several of them are key monuments in the history of Tibetan painting. There is also a small selection of Sino-Tibetan works.

WALTERS ART GALLERY
Address 600 North Charles Street, Baltimore, Maryland, USA, 21201. **Tel** 301 547 9000. **General Description** The Asian collection at the Walters Art Gallery possesses nine Tibetan objects and six Tibetan paintings.

WASHINGTON COUNTY MUSEUM OF FINE ARTS
Address P.O. Box 423 City Park, Hagerstown, Maryland, USA, 21740. **Tel** 301 739 5727. **General Description** The museum holds ten Lamaist paintings which were included in the collection of paintings and sculpture presented to the Museum for its opening in 1931 by Mrs Anna Brugh Singer. These Lamaist paintings, dating from about the middle of the nineteenth century, originate from Mongolia or Tibet and came to Mrs Singer from the collection of the Dutch artist Willem Dooyewaard. A number of drawings of Mongolian and Tibetan subjects by Willem Dooyewaard are also included in the permanent collection of the Museum.

Publishing Companies and Journals

DENSAL
Address 352 Mead Mountain Road, Woodstock, New York, USA, 12498. **Tel** 914 679 2487.

DHARMA PUBLISHING
Address 2425 Hillside Ave, Berkeley, California, USA, 94704. **Tel** (415) 548 5407.

HIMALAYAN RESEARCH BULLETIN
Address Southern Asian Inst, Columbia Univ, 420 West 118th Street, New York, New York, USA, 10027.

INTERNATIONAL ASSOC. OF BUDDHIST STUDIES
Address Dept. of Oriental Languages, University of California, Berkeley, California, U.S.A., 94720. **Lama/Scholar** Prof Lewis Lancaster (Treasurer).

JEWEL PUBLISHING HOUSE
Address P.O. Box 146, New York, New York, USA, 10002.

JOURNAL OF THE TIBET SOCIETY
Address PO Box 1968, Bloomington, Indiana, USA, 47402. **Distribution Details** The journal and a Tibet Society newsletter are distributed.

KAGYU DRODEN KUNCHAB PUBLICATIONS
Address Karma Dawa Tashi Books, 3476 21st Street, San Francisco, California, USA, 94110.

LOTSAWA PRESS
Address 175 San Marin Dr., Suite 108, Novato, California, USA, 94947.

MAHAYANA SUTRA AND TANTRA PRESS
Address 216A West Second Street, Howell, New Jersey, USA, 07731. **Tel** (201) 364 3458. **Distribution Details** MSTP distribute worldwide. Please write to the Mahayana Sutra and Tantra Press, NJ, for a current publications list and ordering information.

NAMO BUDDHA PUBLICATIONS
Address 1390 Kalmia Avenue, Boulder, Colorado, USA, 80304. **Tel** 303 449 6608. **Distribution Details** Ten books by Thrangu Rinpoche have been published.

PARALLAX PRESS
Address P.O. Box 7355, Berkeley, California, USA, 94707. **Tel** (415) 548 3721. **Telex/Fax** (415) 548 1692.

POTALA PUBLICATIONS
Address 241 East 32nd Street, New York, New York, U.S.A., 10016. **Tel** 212 213 5010. **Year Established** 1977. **General**

Description Potala publishes and distributes books on Tibet and related subjects.

SHAMBHALA PUBLICATIONS

Address Horticultural Hall, 300 Massachusetts Avenue, Boston, Massachusetts, USA, 02115. **Tel** (617) 424 0030. **Telex/Fax** (617) 236 1563. **Year Established** 1969. **Founder** Samuel Bercholz. **General Description** Shambhala is a publisher of books on Buddhism and East-West/New Age themes.

SNOW LION PUBLICATIONS

Address P.O. Box 6483, Ithaca, New York, USA, 14851. **Tel** 607 273–8506. **Telex/Fax** 607 273–8508. **General Description** Snow Lion is a major publisher of books on Tibet and is producing the textbooks necessary for a five-year degree programme at Namgyal Monastery in Ithaca, New York.

STATE UNIVERSITY OF NEW YORK PRESS

Address State University Plaza, Albany, New York, USA, 12246.

TRICYCLE: THE BUDDHIST REVIEW

Address 163 W. 22nd St., New York, New York, USA, 10011. **Distribution Details** Quarterly public forum for Buddhists from all traditions.

WISDOM PUBLICATIONS

Address 361 Newbury Street, Boston, Massachusetts, USA, 02115. **Tel** (617) 536 3358. **Telex/Fax** (617) 536 1897. **General Description** Wisdom is a non-profit publisher and distributor of books on Buddhism, Tibet, and related East-West themes. Titles are published and selected in appreciation of Buddhism as a living philosophy and with the commitment to preserve and transmit important works from all the major Buddhist traditions. Book sponsorship programmes are offered which allow the publication of titles which otherwise could never have been published. **Facilities and Services** A comprehensive catalogue is available.

Teaching Centres

AMERICAN INSTITUTE FOR BUDDHIST STUDIES, DEPARTMENT OF RELIGION

Address 623 Kent Hall, Columbia University, New York, New York, USA, 10027. **Tel** (212) 854 5154. **Telex/Fax** (212) 854 5922. **Year Established** 1973. **Founder** Geshe Ngawang Wangyal. **Lama/Scholar** Prof Robert Thurman (Buddhist Studies). **General Description** The American Institute for Buddhist Studies (AIBS) is a tax-exempt, non-profit, educational corporation. Its central philosophy asserts the essential harmony between the Buddhist approach to understanding and the Western liberal arts ethos in that both uphold the authority of reason, the value of pure science, and the efficacy of compassionate action. The institute is involved in a major research and translation project, primarily centred on the *Tengyur* (*bsTan 'gyur*). It co-sponsors conferences, notably the Inner Science Conference with H.H. the Dalai Lama at Amherst College, and the Green Gulch Monasticism Conference. Teaching programmes have included extensive seminars given by Tara Tulku Rinpoche and many other Tibetan lamas as well as teachers from Zen, Pure Land and other Buddhist schools. Tibetan language courses are given and programmes have been organised at such establishments as the Omega Institute, The Open Center, and Minneapolis Zen Center. AIBS functions to broaden awareness of Buddhist Asia, to assist professionals to access the resources of the Buddhist Tradition, and to encourage the participation of Buddhist philosophers in inter-religious and inter-cultural dialogue. **Teaching Programme** AIBS helps organise teachings and conferences throughout the world. The institute acts as co-sponsors in such events and assists in the translating of discourses. Periodically it hosts visiting lamas, and other Buddhist teachers for extended teachings. Tibetan language classes can be arranged on request. AIBS is also involved in giving talks at colleges, churches and other institutions on matters relating to Buddhism and Tibetan culture. It has participated in a number of conferences, including one on Nishitani's work, the Inner Science Conference, and one at Green Gulch on Monasticism. **Project Description** To assist the translation project, arrangements have been made to acquire desk top publishing materials, and it is intended to begin publication over the next few years. Texts presently being prepared for publication are the *Mahayanasutralamkara*, the *Samodhinirmoccana Sutra*, the *Mahayanasangraha*, and the *Abhidharmasamuccaya* (all from the *bsTan 'gyur*). The Institute has been involved in the establishment of Tibet House in New York and has helped in arranging a tour of museums displaying Tibetan art work. Another project with which AIBS is linked is the creation of a multi-language Buddhist dictionary that will cross-reference Chinese, Tibetan, Sanskrit, Japanese and Western language terms. AIBS is also involved in the Society of Tibetan Medicine, helping to expose Western culture to Tibetan medicine.

BUDDHAYANA
Address P.O. Box 580, Marion, Massachusetts, USA, 02738. **Tel** 508 748 0800. **Telex/Fax** 508 748 0806. **Lama/Scholar** Dodrup Chen Rinpoche, Tulku Thondup Rinpoche. **General Description** Buddhayana was founded in 1975 to ensure the continuation of the Tibetan Buddhist tradition, to facilitate the translation of Tibetan scriptures into English and to sponsor original writings on Tibetan Buddhism. Tulku Thondup Rinpoche is a writer and translator supported by Buddhayana. Tulku Thondup's many works are published in India, the United States and in England. **Facilities and Services** Publications include Buddhist texts in booklet form and books by Tulku Thondup Rinpoche.

BUDDHIST INSTITUTE SAN FRANCISCO
Address 19125 Overlook Road, Los Gatos, San Francisco, California, USA, 95030. **Tel** 408 947 6160.

CHAGDUD GONPA FOUNDATION, RIGDZIN LING
Address P.O. Box 279, Junction City, California, USA, 96048. **Tel** (916) 623 2714. **Telex/Fax** (916) 623 6709. **Distribution Details** Please contact the centre for further information. **Founder** Chagdud Tulku. **Lama/Scholar** Chagdud Tulku. **General Description** Rigdzin Ling is the principal residence of Chagdud Rinpoche and the headquarters of the Chagdud Gonpa Foundation and Padma Publishing. Its facilities are being developed to provide for group and individual retreats. A central temple on traditional Buddhist lines is being constructed. **Teaching Programme** It is planned to offer instruction on Vajrayana Buddhism, Tibetan language and meditation. **Project Description** A school of Nyingma studies is being planned. Other projects include the Mahakaruna Foundation, a charity to raise funds to

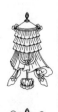

help Tibetan refugees in India and Nepal, and a Tibetan library to purchase and preserve Tibetan texts.

CHAGDUD GONPA, ATI LING
Address P.O. Box 90, Oakville, California, USA, 94562. **Tel** (707) 944 1907. **Lama/Scholar** Tulku Jigme Tromge.

CHAGDUD GONPA, LOS ANGELES.
Address 2503 W. 117th Street, Hawthorne, California, USA, 90250. **Tel** (213) 754 0466. **Founder** Chagdud Tulku Rinpoche.

CHAGDUD GONPA, WILLIAMS RETREAT CENTER.
Address 1960 E. Fork Road, Williams, California, USA, 97544. **Tel** (503) 846 6942. **Founder** Chagdud Tulku Rinpoche.

CHAKPORI LING FOUNDATION
Address P.O. Box 370, Forestville, California, USA, 95432. **Tel** 707 527 7363. **Telex/Fax** 707 869 3111.

DAGSHEN NYAMJA
Address 4063 N. Kenmore 2nd Floor, Chicago, Illinois, USA, 60613. **Tel** 312 5251088.

DECHEN LING
Address 198 North River Road, Cottage Grove, Oregon, USA, 97424. **Tel** (503) 942 8619. **Founder** Chagdud Tulku Rinpoche. **Lama/Scholar** Lama Sonam Tsering.

DEER PARK BUDDHIST CENTER
Address 4548 Schneider Drive, Oregon, Wisconsin, USA, 53575. **Tel** (608) 835 5572. **Distribution Details** Please contact the centre for further information. **Year Established** 1975. **Founder** Geshe Lhundrup Sopa. **Lama/Scholar** Geshe Lhundrup Sopa, Geshe Lobsang Donyo. **General Description** Deer Park was founded by Geshe Lhundrup Sopa to help preserve and transmit traditional Buddhist thought and practice so that this and future generations could continue to reap the benefits that these have to offer. Named after the grove in Benares, India, where the Buddha Shakyamuni first taught, Deer Park provides an opportunity for the continuous and uninterrupted exposition of Hinayana, Mahayana and Vajrayana teachings. These teachings are given by highly respected lamas of the Tibetan tradition. Two eminent geshes reside in the centre and teach throughout the year, while visiting teachers provide special instructions during weekend and month-long programmes. Deer Park is dedicated to cultivating an environment in which individuals with a sincere interest in a religious life centred around Buddhism can develop a well-directed practice based upon a profound and mature inner faith which, in turn, is based upon knowledge and compassion. Teachers and students at Deer Park realise that this is not easy to achieve but none-the-less are steadily working towards to that goal. **Teaching Programme** As of 1986, the regular classes consisted of three one-to-two-hour sessions a week during the fall, winter, and spring. On Sundays Geshe Lhundrup Sopa translated and gave an extensive commentary on an expanded compendium of the steps of the Buddhist path, the *Lam Rim Chen Mo* by Je Tsong Khapa. Geshe Lobsang Donyo taught on Tuesday nights, offering a commentary on a shorter version of the steps of the path, the '*De Lam*'. Geshe Donyo also gave a commentary on the tantric practice of Vajrayogini, on Thursday nights, to those students who had received this empowerment. The weekend programmes are either a number of discourses on a particular subject of importance to a Buddhist practitioner, or a two- to three-day retreat. Such programmes occur three or four times a year. During the summer, Deer Park invites distinguished Buddhist teachers who, together with the resident geshes, provide intensive teachings on both sutra and tantra.

These programmes are usually about four weeks long. **Facilities and Services** Deer Park occupies a thirteen-acre site in rural Wisconsin, close to Madison, the state capital. Presently there are two buildings on the land. One is the residence of Geshe Sopa, Geshe Donyo, and the other monks associated with the centre. The other is the temple where teachings and other religious functions are held. The temple was initially built in 1981 for the visit of H.H. the Dalai Lama, when he performed the Kalacakra ceremony for the first time outside Asia. The monks' residence houses a fairly extensive library of assorted Buddhist works. There is also a newly finished office as well as a conference room used for meetings, child care during Sunday classes, and other centre activities. **Project Description** In order to fulfil the goals of preserving and transmitting Buddhism, Geshe Sopa and the others at Deer Park feel it is essential to have an established community of ordained men and women. Thus, the centre's major efforts are aimed at further developing Evam Gatsel, the monastery consisting of the monks of Deer Park, and to the eventual establishment of a convent. Other projects include the building of a small school for serious students of Buddhism and the construction of a stupa.

DHARMA FRIENDSHIP FOUNDATION
Address 4945 145th Avenue S.E., Bellevue, Washington, USA, 98006. **Tel** (206) 641 5469. **Distribution Details** Please contact the Foundation for current ordering information. **Year Established** 1985. **Founder** B. Alan Wallace (Ven. Jhampa Kelsang). **Lama/Scholar** Gen Lamrimpa, Jampal Tenzin (formerly). **General Description** Dharma Friendship Foundation is a non-profit educational and religious organisation. Its primary purpose is to provide public talks, lecture series, retreats, and seminars on Buddhist philosophy, psychology, ethics, meditation, and cognitive sciences as presented by highly qualified teachers of the Tibetan tradition. Additionally, efforts are directed towards the preservation of the written, oral, and meditative traditions of Mahayana Buddhism. Membership is open to all, with a voting membership being confirmed by a contribution in any amount to the Foundation. Meetings are held informally once a month in a member's home. **Teaching Programme** Classes have been conducted under the Foundation's auspices by the Venerable Gen Lamrimpa, a highly accomplished Tibetan teacher and practitioner. He has given a series of lectures on the gradual stages of the path to awakening, and throughout 1988 led a one-year intensive meditation retreat for the cultivation of mental quiescence (shamatha). The Spiritual Director of the Foundation, Alan Wallace, shared the leadership of the retreat with Gen Lamrimpa and is an accomplished public speaker in his own right. Apart from giving lectures on Shantideva's *Bodhisattvacaryavatara* and other traditional Buddhist texts, he also taught on the role of Buddhism in contemporary Western society. Group meditation classes are scheduled by the Foundation on a regular basis. Gen Lamrimpa's translator, Thubten Jampa, offered beginners classes in Tibetan language. **Facilities and Services** Public lectures and classes are given at a number of rented halls and centres throughout Seattle. Retreats

are located at the Cloud Mountain Meditation Center, set in the beautiful and peaceful surroundings of Washington's woodlands. The foundation coordinates the provision of transcripts, books and audio/video reproductions of pertinent material. **Project Description** Dharma Friendship Foundation intends to continue their programme of one-year and three-month retreats. It is hoped to ensure the continued presence of a Tibetan lama to give personal guidance and instruction to retreaters.

DORJE KHYUNG DZONG
Address P.O. Box 131, 288 County Rd 626, Gardner, Colorado, USA, 81040. **Tel** 303 939 9698. **Year Established** 1971. **Founder** Chogyam Trungpa Rinpoche. **General Description** Dorje Khyung Dzong is a Buddhist solitary retreat center set in 400 acres of alpine meadows and woods, 8500 feet up the slopes of Mt. Greenhorn, looking across Huerfano Valley at Mt. Blanca and the Sangre de Cristo Range in southern Colorado. The centre is part of the Vajradhatu organisation. **Teaching Programme** There are two meditation instructors in residence. The centre is a retreat centre for the use of Vajradhatu members undertaking solitary retreats. Retreat facilities are open to individuals not affiliated to Vajradhatu on a case by case basis. Information can be obtained by contacting the retreat coordinator in Boulder, Colorado. **Facilities and Services** Eight fully equipped cabins are available for solitary retreats of any duration (from a weekend to a year or more). Each cabin has a wood stove, a propane cooking stove and heater, fuel, kitchen utensils, lamps, a bed, pillow, meditation cushion, mat, etc. A refrigerator containing ice packs is in the showerhouse and an outhouse and water pump are nearby. Food is not provided but may be purchased through the caretakers.

DRIKUNG DHARMA CENTER
Address 1515 State St, Santa Barbara, California, USA, 93101.

DUNGKAR GONPA SOCIETY
Address HCR #1, Box 169, Lew Beach, New York, USA, 12753. **Tel** (914) 439 5542. **Telex/Fax** (914) 439 5542.

EWAM CHODEN
Address 254 Cambridge Avenue, Kensington, California, USA, 94708. **Tel** (415) 527 7363. **Year Established** 1971. **Founder** Lama Kunga, Thartse Rinpoche. **Lama/Scholar** Lama Thartse Kunga. **General Description** Ewam Choden Tibetan Buddhist Center was established in order to provide an opportunity for the practice and study of Tibetan religion and culture. The integration of method and wisdom, indicated by the word, 'Ewam', is emphasised by the centre as an especially relevant practice for this time. Ewam Choden was founded by Lama Kunga, Thartse Rinpoche, who was trained at Ngor Monastery, a branch of the Sakya (Sa skya) School of Tibetan Buddhism. He is a reincarnated lama, his line of succession originating in Sevan Repa, a heart disciple of the illustrious Milarepa. A range of activities is offered by the centre, including meditation classes, seminars, and Tibetan language instruction. **Teaching Programme** On Sunday evenings, regular meditation practice takes place. Classes and seminars are given on various subjects. Other functions include the ceremonial observation of lunar holy days and religious holidays, as well as Tibetan language classes. Private interviews with the resident lama can be arranged. **Project Description** It is hoped to continue to expand the centre's activities on numerous levels. Many students are involved in the work of translating Tibetan texts in English under the direction of Lama Kunga. Several centre members have been developing skill in creating traditional Buddhist ritual

objects and images. The centre is also extremely interested in maintaining close relations with the Tibetan community in India, both in the sense of sending students to study there with the few remaining great teachers and in the sense of lending sorely needed aid to refugees.

EWAM CHOKHOR LING
Address SR 5601, Keaau, Hawaii, USA, 96749. **Tel** (808) 966 8843.

GANDEN FOUNDATION
Address 823 Don Diego, Santa Fe, New Mexico, USA, 87501. **Tel** 505 989 9590. **Telex/Fax** 505 989 9519. **Year Established** 1980. **Founder** H.H. Ganden Tripa, Jampel Shenpen. **General Description** The Ganden Foundation was founded by Ganden Tri Rinpoche. The foundation organises the sponsorship of lamas and scholars visiting the US and offers monthly lectures and teachings on Buddhism. The scope of the foundation has recently expanded to include the sponsorship of cultural exchanges, and has sponsored the Drepung, Namgyal and Gyuto monk tours. The foundation has also funded a cultural exchange between the Tibetan Childrens' Village and the Santa Fe Indian school. **Teaching Programme** A programme of forthcoming lectures and teachings is available on written application to the foundation. **Facilities and Services** The foundation has no actual centre but organises its programme of events to take place in various premises. A newsletter is published to give details of forthcoming teachings and events. **Project Description** The foundation plans to establish a school of dialectics with resident monks.

GYALWA GYATSO CENTER
Address 168 West 86th St, #9A, New York, New York, USA, 10026. **Tel** 212 580 0094.

KAGYU CHANGCHUB CHULING
Address 73 NE Monroe, Portland, Oregon, USA, 97212. **Tel** (503) 284 6697. **Distribution Details** Audio tapes are distributed mainly in the Portland area, but the Center will send them elsewhere upon request. **Year Established** 1976. **Founder** Kalu Rinpoche. **Lama/Scholar** Lama Tsangtsing. **General Description** Kagyu Changchub Chuling encourages the traditional practice of Tibetan Buddhism, according to the Karma and Shangpa Kagyu (Shangs pa bKa' brgyud) lineages. Over the years it has hosted a number of great teachers, thereby allowing many people in the Portland area to come into contact with the Dharma. Lama Tsangtsing, who oversees the centre, lives in Eugene, Oregon. He guides members of the centre in methods of meditation and the tenets of Vajrayana Buddhism. The practices of Avalokiteshvara (Chenrezig), ngondro (sngon 'gro), and shamatha (zhi gnas) meditation, are emphasised. Chanting involved in the pujas is in Tibetan, using books which contain transliteration and translation of the Tibetan. **Teaching Programme** The programme follows the traditional teaching and practice of the Karma and

Shangpa Kagyu lineages. Two scheduled meditation sessions are held at the centre weekly, with chanting in Tibetan. A study group meets twice monthly for discussion of Dharma texts. Lama Tsangtsing, as well as advanced Western disciples of Kalu Rinpoche, make regular visits to the centre to teach and lead short retreats. The centre also sponsors other visiting lamas, sometimes several times a year. **Facilities and Services** Kagyu Changchub Chuling owns a four-bedroomed house with a shrine room and a small bookstore, stocking approximately 150 titles, as well as posters, incense, and ritual implements. In addition to accommodating several residents, there is an extra room available for visitors or short-term residents.

KAGYU DRODEN KUNCHAB

Address 1892 Fell Street, San Francisco, California, USA, 94117. **Tel** (415) 752 5454. **Distribution Details** The centre will distribute worldwide. A catalogue of listings and prices is available. **Year Established** 1974. **Founder** Kalu Rinpoche. **Lama/ Scholar** Lama Lodro Chophel. **General Description** Nineteen residents live in the centre and around 500 attend its functions. Instruction is given on Hinayana, Mahayana and Vajrayana teachings by the resident lama, Lama Lodro, and by many visiting teachers. Occasionally Tantric empowerments are performed, and retreats take place regularly. The centre owns 160 acres of land in Mendocino County, California, where weekend retreats and some empowerments take place. A facility for three-year retreats is under construction. **Teaching Programme** Teachings are given on all aspects of Buddhism, though a specific focus is Tantric meditation. There is a daily schedule of Avalokiteshvara (Chenrezig) and Mahakala sadhanas, and each month there is an opportunity to practice nyung ne meditation. On weekends Ngondro, Green Tara and Chod prac-

tices are performed. Meditation retreats for larger groups are conducted at the Mendocino retreat centre. **Facilities and Services** The centre is located in a three-storey house, containing two shrine rooms and a meditation hall. An extensive library is available, including a large tape collection. **Project Description** It is planned to build facilities for three-year retreats and develop the lamas' residence at the retreat centre in Mendocino County. There is a continuing commitment to increasing the library holdings on Tibet and Buddhism and to extend the tape collection of recorded teachings of eminent Kagyu (bKa' brgyud) lamas, puja recitations, and sadhana commentaries. A number of translations are taking place of various sadhana texts.

KAGYU SHENPEN KUNCHAB

Address 751 Airport Road, Santa Fe, New Mexico, USA, 87501. **Tel** (505) 471 1152. **Distribution Details** Contact the bookstore for further information. **Year Established** 1975. **Founder** Kalu Rinpoche. **Lama/ Scholar** Lama Karma Dorje. **General Description** Kagyu Shenpen Kunchab supports a continuous programme of teachings and meditation and in particular provides a location to which visiting lamas can be invited, thus allowing for a wide range of contact between teachers and students. The centre hosts a resident lama and has facilities to house up to ten other residents. A sixty-foot Bodhi Stupa and temple at the centre acts as a place of pilgrimage to Buddhists from all over the country. **Teaching Programme** The regular programme consists of Avalokiteshvara (Chenrezig) meditation, Tuesday, Wednesday and Sunday, weekly meditation instruction and Tara puja, and monthly pujas in English or Tibetan. There is also a weekly study group covering various topics such as: mind training (blo sbyong), compassion, visualisation, and the preliminary practices (sngon 'gro). In addition to these courses, special teaching programmes are arranged when visiting teachers are at Kagyu Shenpen Kunchab. Lama Karma Dorje is available for personal consultation. Sunday morning is devoted to Tara Puja and instruction and practice of Vipassana Meditation. **Facilities and Services** A sixty foot stupa, containing a shrine room decorated with traditional Tibetan wall paintings, a statue and altar, provides the focal point for the centre. Three houses, together with three complete apartment units, serve as accommodation for the community of residents and the resident teacher. There are retreat facilities available on land approximately forty miles from the centre. During special events, camping is permitted on the two acres of land surrounding the main buildings. **Project Description** A comprehensive Buddhist bookshop has recently been opened and acts as a focal point for Buddhist studies. The centre is in the process of constructing living quarters for visiting lamas.

KAGYU THEGCHEN LING

Address 2327 Liloa Rise, Honolulu, Hawaii, USA, 96822. **Tel** (808) 941 8561. **Distribution Details** No materials are distributed. **Year Established** 1974. **Founder** Kalu Rinpoche. **Lama/Scholar** Lama Karma Rinchen. **General Description** Kagyu Thegchen Ling is a teaching centre located in the city of Honolulu. It houses a number of people including the resident teacher, Lama Karma Rinchen. Kagyu Thegchen Ling was instrumental in organising the Kalacakra Ceremony given by the Venerable Kalu Rinpoche in 1987. **Teaching Programme** The centre has a regular programme of morning and evening pujas. Nyung ne practice retreats take place twice a year. Frequent meditation classes for beginners and more experienced practitioners are taught by the resident lama and visiting teachers. In addition, regular visits are made by high lamas of the tradition, giving various teachings. **Facilities and Services** A shrine room provides the setting for regular teachings and meditation practice. There is also a bookstore and a small library.

KAGYU THUBTEN CHOLING

Address 127 Sheafe Road, Wappingers Falls, New York, USA, 12590. **Founder** Kalu Rinpoche. **Lama/Scholar** Lama Norlha.

KARMA RIMAY O SAL LING

Address P.O. Box 1029, Paia, Maui, Hawaii, USA, 96779. **Tel** (808) 579 8076. **Distribution Details** Tapes are distributed locally to centre members and associates. Tape information is published in the newsletter. **Year Established** 1974. **Founder** Kalu Rinpoche. **Lama/Scholar** Lama Tenzin. **General Description** Karma Rimay O Sal Ling (Maui Dharma Center) is located on the island of Maui in the Hawaiian Islands. The centre maintains practices within the Vajrayana tradition of Tibetan Buddhism, remaining non-sectarian in its views and inviting guest teachers from all Buddhist traditions. **Teaching Programme** The resident teacher, Ven. Lama Tenzin, teaches Buddhist philosophy and practice on a regular basis. There are daily group practices of meditation and prayers recited in Tibetan and English. Throughout the year retreats and seminars are taught by Lama Tenzin and various visiting teachers. The Buddhist holidays are observed with special events. **Facilities and Services** The centre possesses a large shrine room and accommodation for residents and some guests. Other facilities include a bookstore and library. The centre's retreat facility has rooms for individual retreat, located at Huelo on the north shore of Maui. The centre distributes a regular newsletter. **Project Description** The centre's plans revolve around activities which will help to provide for continued stability and expansion of the centre.

KARMA THEGSUM CHOLING
Address P.O. Box 8059, Santa Cruz, California, USA, 95061. **Lama/Scholar** Lama Dudjom Dorje.

KARMA TRIYANA DHARMACHAKRA
Address 352 Meads Mountain Road, Woodstock, New York, USA, 12498. **Tel** (914) 679 5906. **Distribution Details** K.K.I. Bookstore distributes worldwide. Write for a tape and book list as well as ordering information. **Year Established** 1978. **Founder** H.H. Gyalwa Karmapa. **Lama/Scholar** Khenpo Karthar Rinpoche, Bardor Tulku Rinpoche. **General Description** Karma Triyana Dharmachakra is the North American seat of H.H. the Gyalwa Karmapa, head of the Karma Kagyu school of Tibetan Buddhism. Founded in 1978, it offers traditional teachings as transmitted by the Kagyu lineage meditation masters since the tenth century. The centre is located on a twenty-acre site in the Catskill Mountains above Woodstock, New York, surrounded by forests, meadows and streams. Venerable Khenpo Karthar Rinpoche, Abbot of Karma Triyana Dharmachakra, and Venerable Bardor Tulku Rinpoche are the distinguished resident lamas appointed by H.H. Karmapa. Seminars on Buddhist philosophy, psychology and meditation practice are offered by resident and guest teachers throughout the year. All are welcome to take advantage of the rare opportunity to study and practice Buddhism in a traditional environment. **Teaching Programme** Weekend seminars are given regularly, both by the resident lama, Khenpo Karthar Rinpoche, and numerous visiting lamas of the Karma Kagyu tradition. Recent courses have been concerned with the practice of meditation, the *"Four Dharmas of Gampopa"*, and *"The Four Sessions of Guru Yoga"* (given by H.E. Tai Situ Rinpoche). H.E. Jamgon Kongtrul Rinpoche visited in 1987, giving empowerments and also teachings on *Showing the Essence*, a text by the Third Karmapa Rangjung Dorje, with commentary by Jamgon Kongtrul the Great. During 1988, Karma Triyana Dharmachakra was fortunate to host the Venerable Ponlop Rinpoche, who gave a series of weekend seminars on the '*Three Yanas*'. From time to time, intensive Tibetan language courses are offered. A number of spiritual practices are undertaken at the centre, including the pujas of Green Tara, Mahakala and Avalokiteshvara. The two-day fasting ritual of 1000-armed Avalokiteshvara (Chenrezig), takes place some weekends, and an annual ngondro (sngon 'gro) retreat is scheduled for the month of January. **Facilities and Services** Karma Triyana Dharmachakra offers extensive accommodation facilities to people attending seminars or those simply wishing to visit or to practice a meditation retreat. A quarterly newsletter, *Densal*, is distributed containing a mixture of edited teachings, general articles about Tibetan Buddhism, and news of Karma Kagyu activities. Karma Kagyu Institute bookstore stocks a wide range of dharma tapes and books on Buddhism, which are available by mail order. A number of religious artefacts are also obtainable from the centre, including: photographs, thangka reproductions,

malas and incense. Karma Triyana Dharmachakra has a number of affiliated centres located throughout the United States. They are called 'Karma Thegsum Choling', and have been established under the auspices of H.H. the Sixteenth Gyalwa Karmapa to further the transmission of the teachings of the Kagyu Lineage. **Project Description** Over the last few years, the centre has had as its major emphasis the construction of a monastery, in accordance with the wishes of H.H. Sixteenth Gyalwa Karmapa, and more recently at the request of H.E. Jamgon Kongtrul Rinpoche that it be completed in time for the enthronement of the Seventeenth Karmapa.

KARME CHOLING

Address Star Route, Barnet, Vermont, USA, 05821. **Tel** 802 633–2384. **Telex/Fax** 802 633–3012. **Year Established** 1970. **Founder** Chogyam Trungpa Rinpoche. **General Description** Karme Choling was founded by the late Chogyam Trungpa Rinpoche. The centre, located in northern Vermont, offers programmes in the practice of meditation, study, and instruction on how Buddhist teachings can be applied to daily life situations. Regular courses are organised when lamas are invited to give instruction and lead meditation groups. In addition to the programmes offered, visitors may come for any length of time and participate in the daily schedule, which includes four hours of meditation, two hours of staff-guided independent study, three and a half hours of work, and evening classes. **Teaching Programme** The centre publishes a leaflet outlining details of the forthcoming programme for the season. Introductory weekends are held on a regular basis and combine four hours of group meditation practice each day with a series of talks, tapes, and discussions focusing on either meditation or Buddhist psychology. Advanced programmes are available for authorised students. Dathun (month-long session) or Weekthun (week-long session) consists of nine to ten hours of group meditation daily. Shambhala training, a programme of study and meditation practice based on the principles presented in *Shambhala: The Sacred Path of the Warrior* by Chogyam Trungpa, is available. Each of the five weekend programmes consists of lectures, meditation instruction, group discussions, and extended periods of meditation. **Facilities and Services** All programmes include meals and informal accommodation. Bedding is not provided. Many attractive retreat cabins are located throughout the 540-acre property, and are available year-round for practitioners who wish to undertake solitary practice for periods of ten days or longer. Childcare is available for a limited number of children.

KHYENTSE FOUNDATION

Address 230 West 79th St, New York, New York, USA, 10024. **Tel** 212 595 6543.

KUNZANG ODSAL PALYUL CHANGCHUB CHOELING

Address 18400 River Road, Poolesville, Maryland, USA, 20837. **Tel** 301 428–8116. **Telex/Fax** 301 972 8846. **Year Established**

1982. **Founder** Tulku Ahkon Norbu Lhamo (Catherine Burroughs). **Lama/Scholar** Ahkon Lhamo (Catherine Burroughs). **General Description** Kunzang Odsal Palyul Changchub Choeling was founded in 1982 by Jetsunma Ahkon Norbu Lhamo, who is the present director. Visiting lamas are invited to give teachings at the centre. In 1988 Penor Rinpoche, the Supreme head of the Nyingma Tradition, came to the centre to give teachings on the Rinchen Terdzod. During his visit to the centre in August 1988, Penor Rinpoche consecrated a thirty-five foot stupa which had been completed in time for the occasion. Since that time a sixty-five-acre peace park has been created which has meditation gardens, walking paths, and a stupa park which will contain nine stupas on completion in autumn 1992. **Facilities and Services** The centre will supply a list of inexpensive hotels in the nearby town. There is camping available a short drive away from the centre. There is a shop called the Mani Jewel Gift Store which sells Buddhist items, books, jewellery, crystals and assorted gifts. **Project Description** A site is being prepared for construction of a seventy-five foot statue of Buddha Amitabha.

KUNZANG PALYUL CHOLING
Address 18400 River Road, Poolesville, Maryland, USA, 20837. **Tel** 301 428 8116.

KURUKULLA CENTER
Address P.O. Box 67262, Chestnut Hill, Massachusetts, USA, 02167. **Tel** 617 421 9668. **Telex/Fax** 617 536 1897. **Distribution Details** Publishes *Lotus Arrow* newsletter. **Founder** Lama Thubten Yeshe. **Lama/Scholar** Geshe Tsultrim Chophel. **General Description** This centre is affiliated to the Foundation for the Preservation of the Mahayana Tradition (FPMT) under the spiritual direction of Lama Thubten Zopa Rinpoche.

LAND OF MEDICINE BUDDHA
Address 5800 Prescott Road, Soquel, California, USA, 95073. **Tel** 462 8383. **Telex/Fax** 462 8380.

LIGMINCHA BON INSTITUTE
Address P.O. Box 7182, Richmond, Virginia, U.S.A., 23221. **Tel** (804) 730 4653. **Telex/Fax** (804) 730 0020. **Lama/Scholar** Geshe Tenzin Wangyal.

MAHASIDDHA NYINGMAPA CENTER
Address P.O. Box 87, East Mountain Road, Charlemont, Hawley, Massachusetts, USA, 01339. **Tel** 413 339 8339. **Year Established** 1973. **Founder** Dodrup Chen Rinpoche. **Lama/Scholar** Dodrup Chen Rinpoche, Tulku Thondup Rinpoche. **General Description** The centre has a temple where members and visitors practice and study together. There is also a Tibetan stupa and two retreat cabins **Teaching Programme** The Mahasiddha Nyingmapa Center follows mainly the practices of the Longchen Nyingthig tradition of the Nyingma school of Tibetan Buddhism. Students occasionally get together to study and practise in groups and also receive individual teachings or enter into retreats. **Facilities and Services** The temple has a shrine, rooms for the teachers, a kitchen and dining room.

MAHAYANA SUTRA AND TANTRA CENTER, DC.
Address P.O. Box 44275, Washington, District of Columbia, USA, 20026. **Tel** (301) 585 4575. **Distribution Details** Printed publications are available at the centre, but for mail order contact Mahayana Sutra and Tantra Press, N.J. **Year Established** 1975. **Founder** Geshe Lobsang Tharchin. **General Description** Affiliated to the Mahayana Sutra and Tantra Center of New Jersey, the centre in Washington D.C. shares its aims to preserve and disseminate Buddhist knowledge. The centre's teaching programme includes classes on Buddhist philosophy, sutra and tantra, and

Tibetan language. It is also involved with various translation and publication projects, liaising with the Mahayana Sutra and Tantra Press to this end. Regular Buddhist ceremonies are scheduled, and the centre participates in a number of aid projects to assist Sermey Monastic University in India. **Teaching Programme** The centre organises monthly classes, instruction being given by Geshe Lobsang Tharchin. Teachings are given on Tibetan texts, with Geshe Tharchin giving oral commentaries in English. The range of subjects followed includes: the *Lam Rim*, debate, logic, abhidharma, the *Abhisamayalamkara*, madhyamaka philosophy, and some tantric practices. Tibetan language instruction is also available. Meetings for group study and practice are held weekly. An annual retreat is held in August at the affiliated centre in New Jersey. **Facilities and Services** Please write or telephone the centre for details concerning location of classes. Mahayana Sutra and Tantra Press publications are available for borrowing and purchase. **Project Description** The Washington D.C. Center participates in the audiotaping and transcribing of teachings for eventual publication by the Mahayana Sutra and Tantra Press. It also helps in the sponsorship of scholars and orphaned monks of Sermey Monastic University and also the various aid projects that have been organised.

MAHAYANA SUTRA AND TANTRA CENTER, NJ.
Address 216A West Second Street, Howell, New Jersey, USA, 07731. **Tel** (201) 364 1824. **Distribution Details** MSTP distribute worldwide. Please write to the Mahayana Sutra and Tantra Press, NJ, for a current publications list and ordering information. **Year Established** 1975. **Founder** Geshe Lobsang Tharchin. **Lama/Scholar** Geshe Lobsang Tharchin. **General Description** The Mahayana Sutra and Tantra Center of New Jersey was established in 1975 and incorporated as a non-profit religious organisation dedicated to the preservation and dissemination of Buddhist knowledge in 1980. It provides an opportunity for all to gain an appreciation for the high level of scholarship and the living tradition of practice contained within the Tibetan Buddhist lineages. The centre's teaching programme includes classes on Buddhist philosophy, the sutras and tantras, and both Tibetan and Sanskrit languages. MSTC is active in translating textual material into English and, through the Mahayana Sutra and Tantra Press, producing and distributing publications. Regular Buddhist ceremonies and services are organised and a number of different welfare projects are being carried out with the aim of assisting Sermey Monastic University in India. Close links exist between the Centre in New Jersey and the Mahayana Sutra and Tantra Center of Washington D.C. **Teaching Programme** Classes are held at the facilities of Rashi Gempil Ling (the 'First Kalmuk Buddhist Temple'). Instruction is given there by Sermey Geshe Lobsang Tharchin, following Tibetan texts and explaining in English. Subjects studied include: the *Lam Rim* (basic Buddhist philosophy); Buddhist debate and logic; and readings from the Sutras, Abhidharma, *Abhisamayalamkara*, Madhyamaka, and the Tantras. Other courses are held on Tibetan language, Sanskrit language, and there is also Buddhist instruction for children. An annual

retreat, which usually includes an intensive week of teachings, takes place in August. Regular classes are given throughout the year, on Sundays and weekday evenings. **Facilities and Services** All classes and religious services are held at Rashi Gempil Ling. The centre maintains a library of English, Sanskrit and Tibetan books on Buddhism. This collection includes the IASWR microfiche edition of the *Cone Tengyur (bsTan 'gyur)*, and Rashi Gempil Ling possess the complete Shol Parkhang edition of the *Lhasa Kangyur (bKa' 'gyur)*. The Mahayana Sutra and Tantra Press are active in producing and distributing a number of publications. Recently it has developed a Tibetan text processing system for creating reproduction-quality Tibetan typesetting with an IBM-PC or compatible computer and certain dot matrix printers. The programme and manual are available for a nominal charge. **Project Description** Work is continuing on the audiotaping and transcribing of instructional classes, and the translation of Buddhist texts into English. These transcripts and translations are then published and distributed by Mahayana Sutra and Tantra Press. Other projects include an 'Asian Classics' input project, the videotaping of ceremonies, and the development of computer software programmes for printing Tibetan. It is hoped to extend the number of classes and projects on Buddhism for children and young adults. A scholarship fund has been set up to support Tibetan debate scholars and orphaned monks at Sermey Monastic University in India. The centre is also active in helping with building and self-sufficiency work projects, as well as medical and health programmes for the monks at Sermey.

MAITREYA INSTITUTE
Address 3315 Sacramento Street, Suite 622, San Francisco, California, USA, 94118. **Tel** (415) 668 5920. **Year Established** 1985. **Founder**

H.E. Twelfth Tai Situ. **General Description** The Maitreya Institute was established by H.E. Tai Situ Rinpoche originally in Hawaii. Further centres have since been established in San Francisco and most recently in France. The Maitreya Institute is non-profit, non-sectarian, and community oriented. It provides multidisciplinary lectures, conferences, performances, workshops and classes. Visiting speakers are invited, giving classes and workshops on a variety of subjects focusing on such subjects as music/psychology/philosophy/healing arts/spiritual resources and new economics. **Teaching Programme** Information on forthcoming workshops and classes is available from the centre.

MANJUSHRI CENTER
Address 57 N. Prospect St., Amherst, Massachusetts, USA, 01002. **Tel** (413) 253 5074. **Lama/Scholar** Prof A.F. Thurman. **General Description** Classes are held in Buddhist philosophy and Tibetan language by visiting teachers.

MILAREPA CENTER
Address Barnet Mountain, Barnet, Vermont, USA, 05821. **Tel** (802) 633 4136. **Telex/Fax** (603) 638 2119. **Founder** Lama Thubten Yeshe. **Lama/Scholar** Geshe Tsultrim Chompel. **General Description** Located in Vermont's scenic Northeast Kingdom, the 270-acre Milarepa Center is one of over sixty Buddhist centres of the worldwide Foundation for the Preservation of the Mahayana Tradition (FPMT), under the spiritual guidance of Thubten Zopa Rinpoche, teacher of Buddhist philosophy and meditation for thousands of students. Milarepa Center hosts qualified Buddhist teachers who provide instruction in meditation and philosophy, and provides facilities for individual and group retreats. An integrated schedule of meditation, study and work enables residents to apply the Buddha's teachings to daily life. **Teaching Pro-**

gramme Although the centrer is open the whole year for teachings, meditation classes, individual and group retreats, most of the teaching programme activity occurs between April and October. A three-month Vajrasattva retreat is held annually January to March. Each month we celebrate Tsog, practise appropriate pujas, and Mahayana Precepts are observed on the new and full moons. Students are welcome as residents on a work-study basis, especially to help build individual retreat huts. **Facilities and Services** The facilities available include a twelve-room house, garage-work-shop and barn. There is also a Dharma book-audio/video tape library, and a newsletter is distributed regularly. **Project Description** It is hoped that Geshe Tsultrim Chompel, from Sera Monastery in India, will come to live and teach at Milarepa Center in the near future.

NAMGYAL MONASTERY, INSTITUTE OF BUDDHIST STUDIES
Address P.O. Box 127, Ithaca, New York, U.S.A., 1481. **Tel** 607 273 0739. **Telex/Fax** 607 273 8508. **Year Established** 1992. **General Description** Founded by Namgyal Monastery, the personal monastery of H.H. the Dalai Lama, in 1992 as the North American branch of the monastery. The Institute is staffed by Tibetan Buddhist monks and Western scholars and provides an opportunity for the systematic study in English of Tibetan Buddhism in a traditional monastic setting. There is a wide range of programmes on offer open to both women and men. Emphasis is on Tibetan language courses as well as special workshops on the arts, debating, etc. During the Summer an Intermediate Colloquial Tibetan Language 6-week Intensive and various retreats are available. Guest speakers are invited to visit. The monastery, which is famous for its exquisite sand mandalas, also provides monks for museum and gallery sand mandala exhibitions.

NAMO BUDDHA SEMINAR
Address 1390 Kalmia Avenue, Boulder, Colorado, U.S.A., 80304. **Tel** 303 449 6608. **Distribution Details** Ten books by Thrangu Rinpoche have been published. **General Description** The centre is a non-profit organisation set up to promote the activities of Thrangu Rinpoche, a khenpo of the Kagyu school. A yearly six-week seminar in Nepal, a three-week seminar in England and a Mahamudra retreat in California are offered.

NECHUNG DORJE DRAYANG LING
Address Wood Valley Temple and Retreat Center, P.O. Box 250, Pahala, Hawaii, USA, 96777. **Tel** (808) 928 8539. **Telex/Fax** (808) 928 6271. **Distribution Details** The centre distributes worldwide. **Year Established** 1973. **Founder** Nechung Rinpoche. **Lama/Scholar** Lama Lozang Tonden. **General Description** Nechung Drayang Ling is a non-sectarian Buddhist teaching and retreat centre in the Tibetan tradition but open to other Buddhist and non-Buddhist programmes and cultural exchanges. It was founded by a master of the Nyingma and Sarma traditions, Nechung Rinpoche, who integrated practices and teachings from all the lineages of Tibetan Buddhism. Located on

the island of Hawaii, the centre is at the crossroads of both Eastern and Western cultures and has a wide base of ethnic influences and peoples from all over the world. **Teaching Programme** Nechung Drayang Ling has a wide range of programmes and an open schedule consisting of discourses given by visiting lamas, daily meditations, and various ritual ceremonies. Talks are also given in Honolulu and on the other islands. Due to the centre's country location, seminars are usually organised at weekends. All programmes are announced in the newsletter and advertised in local newspapers. **Facilities and Services** Wood Valley Temple is a renovated Japanese temple, built at the turn of the century in a plantation community five miles above the town of Pahala, in the district of Ka'u on the island of Hawaii. It is surrounded by forest and sugar cane fields at an elevation of 2000 feet, with a cool temperate climate. Presently it consists of two complexes: the original temple, lamas' quarters, library, and dining hall, are on a small hill overlooking the Pacific. The retreat centre, dedicated to Tara, is also a renovated Japanese temple, moved from the town of Pahala. The upper storey has a meditation hall and two residences; the lower storey consists of a library, dining hall, two dormitory rooms for ten people each, two private rooms, and a dining hall. When not in use for Temple activities, they are available for other groups or individuals, at a nominal fee. There is also a small book and gift store. **Project Description** Nechung Drayang Ling is expanding and improving its facilities in order to make the best use of its potential. Several translation and publishing projects are in progress. There are also plans to transcribe some of the most important teachings that have been given at the centre. Plans to construct a library/research area, a larger meditation/activity hall, and guest/retreat bungalows are currently in progress.

NYINGMA INSTITUTE
Address 1815 Higland Place, Berkeley, California, USA, 94704. **Tel** (510) 843 6812. **Distribution Details** Dharma Publishing distribute worldwide. Write for current catalogue and order form. **Year Established** 1973. **Founder** Tarthang Tulku Rinpoche. **Lama/Scholar** Tarthang Tulku Rinpoche. **General Description** The Nyingma Institute was founded in 1973 by Tarthang Tulku. The institute is a teaching and retreat centre as well as a working community. The institute classes and programmes offer a secular, non-dogmatic approach to the knowledge traditions of Tibetan Buddhism, open to anyone. **Teaching Programme** In addition to programmes in traditional Buddhism and Buddhist culture, there are classes and programmes in psychology, philosophy, meditation, relaxation and art. A study by mail series of programmes is also provided with guidance from the institute faculty. A catalogue of programmes for the year is available from the centre. **Facilities and Services** The centre is residential and has retreat facilities and accommodation for guests. Personal retreats can be arranged as well as group retreats. A list of audio cassette tapes available for purchase is printed at the back of the centre catalogue.

ORGYEN CHOGYE CHONDZO LING
Address 735 SE Tacoma, Portland, Oregon, USA, 97202. **Tel** (503) 234 1573.

OSEL SHEN PHEN LING
Address 338 West Alder St., Missoula, Montana, USA, 59802. **Tel** 406 721 3155. **Year Established** 1987. **Founder** Lama Thubten Zopa Rinpoche. **General Description** Osel Shen Phen Ling was founded in 1987 by Lama Thubten Zopa Rinpoche. The centre is set in a residential district. Guests and participants are always welcome and accommodation is available for visitors wishing to use the

facilities any time for their own meditation, take part in a guided retreat, or simply to stay and enjoy the peaceful environment. Most of the weekend retreats are at the introductory level, and anyone is welcome to participate. **Teaching Programme** Meditation sessions are conducted weekly at two different venues. Details of teaching programmes and retreats are available from the centre. A newsletter is published giving information on forthcoming events and centre news. **Facilities and Services** The centre has a meditation room with an altar, a library, and kitchen. The centre is developing its collection of cassette and video tapes. The cassettes may be listened to on the premises or purchased. Books on Tibetan Buddhism and other Buddhist items are available for purchase from the centre. **Project Description** The centre has established a sponsorship programme with a state prison. This involves leading weekly meditation and discussion sessions at the prison and providing a fund for books etc. Also planned is the development of a counselling referral service. To help give financial stability, the centre is organising and leading Buddhist and general Himalayan and Tibetan tours; local backpacking tours in the Montana and Idaho wilderness; and selling Nepali and Tibetan import items. Cultural programmes are presented at the centre and at universities and colleges in Montana and Idaho. The centre also assists with a Tibetan refugee sponsorship programme.

PADMA SHEDRUP LING
Address P.O. Box 117, Fairfax, California, USA, 94930. **Tel** 415 485 1356. **Lama/Scholar** Ven. Chhoje Rinpoche.

PALDEN SAKYA CENTER
Address 1807 Glasco Turnpike, Woodstock, New York, USA, 12498. **Tel** (914) 679 2560. **Lama/Scholar** Lama Pema Wangdak.

PALDEN SAKYA CENTER
Address P.O. Box 1603, Cathedral Station, New York, New York, USA, 10025. **Tel** (212) 459 4112.

PALDEN SAKYA DHARMA STUDY GROUP
Address 7 Sister Wool Farm, 114 White Church Lane, Brunswick, New York, USA, 12180.

PANDU BHUMA VIHARA
Address Tibetan Cultural Center, 5042 18th Avenue N.E., Seattle, Washington, USA, 98105. **Tel** (206) 522 6967. **Distribution Details** No materials are distributed. **Year Established** 1984. **Founder** H.H. Jigdal Dagchen Sakya. **Lama/Scholar** H.H. Jigdal Dagchen Sakya, H.H. Ngawang Trinly Sakyapa.

RANGRIG YESHE CENTER
AddressP.O. Box 1167, Stockbridge, Massachusetts, USA, 01262. **Tel** 413 298 5141.

RIGPA FELLOWSHIP
Address P.O. Box 7866, Berkeley, California, USA, 94707. **Tel** (510) 664 3922. **Telex/Fax** (510) 644 9517. **Distribution Details** Payment is in US dollars or International Money Orders.

Transcripts are only available to Rigpa students. **Year Established** 1980. **Founder** Sogyal Rinpoche. **General Description** Rigpa Fellowship comprises an international network of centres and groups of students who follow the teachings and practices from the Nyingma and Dzogchen traditions of Tibetan Buddhism under the guidance of Sogyal Rinpoche. Centres exist in the United States, Britain, France, Germany, Ireland and Australia with two long-term retreat centres, in the south of France and Ireland. Groups of students also meet in Switzerland and Holland. In the US study groups exist in the following cities: New York, Washington D.C., Boston, Chicago, Dayton, OH, Seattle, Portland, OR, and in California: Berkeley, Santa Rosa, Santa Cruz and San Diego. Yearly retreats are held in Britain at Easter, in France in the Summer, in Germany after Christmas, in the US in June and Thanksgiving and in Australia in late January. Rigpa sponsors teachings from eminent visiting masters from all Buddhist traditions. **Teaching Programme** Sogyal Rinpoche's students throughout the world follow an integrated programme of retreats, intensive courses and special study groups under his personal guidance. A teaching programme exists in Berkeley, CA, as well as in the other centres internationally. Rigpa offers a graduated series of courses, both for the general public as well as for more advanced practitioners. The introductory classes include an overview of the principal themes of Buddhist teaching, in particular of the practice of meditation and its integration into everyday life and training the mind in compassion. Other courses are offered on the care of the dying. **Facilities and Services** A shrine room and office are maintained in Berkeley, CA. 'Sound of Dharma' distributes audio tapes, and video tapes are available from Rick New at 1805 38th Avenue, Seattle, WA 98122 [Tel. (206) 328 2694]. **Project Description** Continuing the development of the Lerab Ling retreat facility in the South of France, which serves as a centre for group as well as individual long-term retreats. Development of services and courses based on the shared insights between Buddhism and modern Western disciplines, such as psychotherapy, healing, the study of death and care of the dying, the arts and sciences.

RIME DAKSHANG KAGYU
Address 1102 South Edith Ave, Alhambra, California, USA, 19803.

ROCKY MOUNTAIN DHARMA CENTER
Address Red Feather Lakes, Colorado, USA, 80545. **Tel** (303) 881 2530. **Year Established** 1971. **Founder** Chogyam Trungpa Rinpoche. **General Description** This is a retreat centre, established to provide year-round retreat facilities for members of the Vajradhatu organisation and others. It is situated in 350 acres of Colorado highland forest, with mostly dormitory accommodation (for course participants), a few single rooms, and cabins for those involved in long solitary retreats. All accommodation is heated. **Teaching Programme** Various meditational retreat courses are held during each year.

SAKYA CHOKHOR YANGTSE
Address Pleasant Road, Barre, Massachusetts, USA, 01005. **Tel** (508) 355 2092. **Lama/Scholar** Lama Migmar Tseten.

SAKYA JAMPAL CHOLING CENTRE
Address 61 Grove St, Apt 4A, New York, New York, USA, 10014. **Tel** 212 989 1829.

SAKYA KACHOD CHOLING
Address 5050 B Hannah Road, Friday Harbor, Washington, USA., 98250. **Tel** (206) 378 3490. **Founder** H.E. Sakya Jetsun Chimey Luding. **Lama/Scholar** H.E. Sakya Jetsun Chimey Luding. **General Description** Sakya Kachod Choling is a retreat facility founded by H.E. Sakya Jetsun

Chimey Luding, the sister of His Holiness Sakya Trizin. It is situated on San Juan Island in Puget Sound, Washington State. The centre helps to sponsor students wishing to enter retreat under the direction of Lamas of the Sakya Tradition and in particular those under the direction of H.E. Sakya Jetsun Chimey Luding who is the spiritual director.

SAKYA KUNGA DZONG
Address 1024 NE 144th Street, Miami, Florida, USA, 33161. **Tel** (305) 945 7315.

SAKYA MONASTERY OF TIBETAN BUDDHISM
Address 108 N.W. 83rd Street, Seattle, Washington, USA, 98117. **Tel** (206) 789 2573. **Telex/Fax** (206) 789 2573. **Distribution Details** Sakya Monastery distributes worldwide. **Year Established** 1974. **Founder** H.H. Jigdal Dagchen Sakya. **Lama/Scholar** H.H. Jigdal Dagchen Sakya, H.H. Ngawang Trinly Sakyapa, H.E. Dezhung Rinpoche (formerly). **General Description** Sakya Monastery is a focal point for Dharma teachings in the United States, attracting visits from many of the great lamas of Tibetan Buddhism. The monastery serves as the shrine, library, and spiritual home for the community of practitioners studying with H.H. Jigdal Dagchen Rinpoche. There are five residents who have either monastic or lay vows. The central practice of the monastery is meditation on the Bodhisattva Avalokiteshvara (Chenrezig). Sakya Monastery embraces a non-sectarian approach, in the past having welcomed pre-eminent lamas from all four major traditions of Tibetan Buddhism. Specifically, Kalu Rinpoche of the Kagyu tradition, H.H. Dudjom Rinpoche of the Nyingma, the Gelug Geshe Ngawang Dharghey, as well as H.H. the Dalai Lama and many of the most renowned lamas of the Sakya school have visited. **Teaching Programme** Various regular practices occur in the Monastery. These include Chenrezig meditations, which take place twice a week; once according to the practice described by Thangtong Gyalpo (Thang stong rGyal po) and Jamgon Kongtrul ('Jam mgon Kong sprul), and once according to that delineated by Ngorchen Konchog Lhundrup (Ngor chen dKon mchog Lhun grub). Discourses are given by the Monastery's resident lamas, H.H. Jigdal Dagchen Sakya and Ngawang Trinly Sakyapa, and occasionally by Ven. Geleg Rinpoche and Ven. Migyur Rinpoche, who visit from Nepal. Tibetan language classes can be scheduled by arrangement. Additionally, special observances are held each month according to the Tibetan lunar calendar, open only to those with the necessary empowerment: on the tenth day a tsog (tshogs) composed by Jamgon Mipam ('Jam mgon Mi pham) is made to Padmasambhava, Green Tara is practised on the fifteenth day, a Vajrayogini tsog in the tradition of Tsarchen Losal Gyatso (Tshar chen Blo gsal rGya mtsho) on the twenty-fifth, and on the twenty-ninth a Mahakala Ritual in the Sakya tradition of Yabchen Kunga Lodro (Yab chen Kun dga' Blo gros). Also, Buddhist holidays and lama memorials are celebrated. **Facilities and Services** When the main ''du khang' has been completed it will have the capacity to sit 275 at

any one time. There are five rooms for the residents, who caretake the main shrine and the protectors' shrine. The Monastery possesses a large book and audio-tape library of 1000 books and 200 tapes. Textual holdings contain over 200 Tibetan language books, including the *Nyingma Gyubum* (*rNying ma rGyud 'bum*), the fourteen volume *Druptap Kundu* (*sGrub thabs Kun btus*), Jamgon Kongtrul's *Sheja Kunkyap* (*Shes bya Kun khyab*), the Sakya Kabum (*Sa skya bKa' 'bum*), and a recent copy of the *Derge Kangyur* (*sDe dge bKa' 'gyur*) printed in Derge. A newsletter is sent out to all monastery members. **Project Description** The monastery is engaged in extensive remodelling of its building in order that it may more closely resemble the traditional Tibetan design for monasteries. A permanent shrine room is being prepared which will include painted mandalas, frescos, a double life-size statue of the Buddha, and life-size statues of Padmasambhava and Sachen Kunga Nyingpo. There are also plans to construct a 'mgon khang', dedicated to Mahakala. The library is in the process of becoming a branch of the Library of Tibetan Works and Archives, Dharamsala, India. A stupa is being built on the monastery grounds in memory of His Eminence, the late Dezhung Rinpoche.

SAKYA PHUNTSOK LING
Address 608 Ray Drive, Silver Spring, Maryland, USA, 20910. **Tel** (301) 589 3115. **Year Established** 1987. **Founder** Dezhung Rinpoche. **Lama/Scholar** Lama Kalsang Gyaltsen.

SAKYA SHEIDRUP LING
Address Sakya Center, P.O. Box 391042, Cambridge, Massachusetts, USA, 02139. **Tel** (617) 492 2614. **Distribution Details** Some transcripts have been reproduced for distribution. **Year Established** 1980. **Founder** Dezhung Rinpoche. **Lama/Scholar** Lama Migmar Tseten. **General Description** Sakya Shei-drup Ling was founded on the occasion of Dezhung Rinpoche's first visit to Cambridge in June, 1980. Since that time the centre has had a continuous meditation and study programme and has hosted a number of visiting teachers of the Sakya tradition. An emphasis on meditation retreats has impelled the group towards founding a country retreat center. In the fall of 1984, Dezhung Rinpoche encouraged the purchase of land in Barre, Massachusetts, which has since developed into the Sakya Chokhor Yangtse Retreat Center. Although Sakya Shei-drup Ling does not currently possess a permanent place for Dharma activities in the city, efforts are being directed towards the re-establishment of such a centre. In the meantime, group meditations and a regular teaching programme are continuing in members' homes and in rented halls. **Teaching Programme** Each Sunday night a group meditation of the sixteen Arhats puja takes place. On full and half moon days, qualified members perform Hevajra practice from the *Lamdre*. The resident teacher, Lama Migmar Tseten, teaches various classes at introductory and advanced level on Buddhist philosophy and meditation, and there is a Tibetan language class. Various special teaching programmes are arranged when eminent lamas of the Sakya lineage tradition visit the centre. **Facilities and Services** Retreat facilities are available at Sakya Chokhor Yangtse, a country centre located in several buildings on a remote and beautiful hilltop overlooking the Nashoba Valley. A newsletter, *The Sakya Satellite*, keeps members informed about the weekly meditation schedules and classes. **Project Description** A major emphasis for the group is in continued development of the retreat centre, Sakya Chokhor Yangtse. Further projects include the building of a stupa, dormitories and retreat cabins, and a new temple.

SAKYA THUBTEN DARGYE LING
Address P.O. Box 13477, Dinkytown, Minneapolis, Minnesota, USA, 55414. **Tel** (612) 738 2738. **Lama/Scholar** Lama Pema Wangdak.

SAKYA TSECHEN KUNKHYAB CHOLING,
TIBETAN SAKYA BUDDHIST CENTER OF OLYMPIA
Address 2508 Mitchell Ave. NE, Olympia, Washington, USA, 98506. **Tel** (206) 352 2426. **Year Established** 1980. **Founder** H.H. Jigdal Dagchen Sakya. **Lama/Scholar** H.H. Jigdal Dagchen Sakya, Geshe Jamyang Tsultrim. **General Description** Sakya Tsechen Kunkhyab Choling is a branch Tibetan Buddhist Center of Sakya Monastery, Seattle, Washington. **Teaching Programme** Weekly mediation classes are held and various courses taught throughout the year.

SAKYA TSECHEN THUBTEN LING
Address 1709 Myrtle Street, Oakland, California, USA, 94607. **Tel** (510) 452 0354. **Lama/Scholar** H.E. Sakya Jetsun Chimey Luding. **General Description** Jetsun Chimey Luding gives teachings several times a year at the centre.

SAPAN INSTITUTE
Address 137 N.W. 205th Street, Seattle, Washington, USA, 98177. **Tel** 206/526–0942. **Year Established** 1987. **Founder** Tanpi Gyaltsen Dhongthog Rinpoche. **General Description** The Sapan Institute was founded in 1987 by Tanpi Gyaltsen Dhongthog Rinpoche and is dedicated to preserving, disseminating, and practising Tibetan Buddhism, particularly in the Sakya tradition. The institute is administered by a Board of Directors and an executive committee. The chairman of the Board of Directors is Dhongthog Rinpoche. In addition to providing religious services in the Sakya tradition, the centre hosts visiting teachers, provides public lectures, language classes, and the translation of Buddhist texts. **Teaching Programme** The programme of the Sapan Institute includes weekly teachings on a text selected by Dhongthog Rinpoche, a weekly class in Tibetan language and literature, public lectures on Buddhist practice and Tibetan culture, and a yearly seminar on Buddhist philosophy. **Facilities and Services** The Institute currently operates from the home of Dhongthog Rinpoche and plans to have a separate building in the future. **Project Description** The institute intends to publish a periodical of Buddhist practice and cultural activities, a glossary of Buddhist terms, and translations of Tibetan texts into English. A translation of a history book by Dhongthog Rinpoche is also in progress. The institute also intends to develop and maintain a library of works, in Tibetan and English, on Buddhism and Buddhist culture.

SARNATH PROJECT, THE PADMASAMBHAVA SOCIETY
Address Box 6036, West Palm Beach, Florida, USA, 33405. **Lama/Scholar** Khenpo Palden Sherab.

SHANTIDEVA CENTER

Address HCR 4660, Keaau, Hawaii, USA, 96749. **Tel** 808 966 6877. **Year Established** 1989. **Founder** Lama Thubten Yeshe. **General Description** The Shantideva Center is a member of the Foundation for the Preservation for the Mahayana Tradition (FPMT). The centre hosts regular teachings by eminent Tibetan Buddhist teachers. **Teaching Programme** Details of the teaching programme and other news is available in the Shantideva newsletter publication. **Project Description** A project to build a stupa is in progress.

THEKCHEN CHOLING

Address 60933 Main St., Jones, Michigan, USA, 49061. **Tel** 616 244 8484 **Lama/Scholar** Ven. Gomang Khensur Rinpoche. **General Description** Thekchen Choling is set in two and a half acres of woods, buildings and land. The centre emphasises that its main focus is the establishing of a Buddhist-owned and operated cottage industry that will support its projects of assisting Tibetan refugee youths and young adults in obtaining vocational and educational skills. Visits from Buddhist teachers and intercultural events will also take place at the centre, and there are plans for the building of a shrine room, library and stupa.

THUBTEN DHARGYE LING

Address 2658 La Cienega Avenue, Los Angeles, California, USA, 90034. **Tel** (213) 839–8057. **Distribution Details** Write to Geshe Gyaltsen for permission. **Year Established** 1979. **Founder** Geshe Tsultrim Gyaltsen. **Lama/Scholar** Geshe Tsultrim Gyaltsen. **General Description** Thubten Dhargye Ling was founded in 1979 by Geshe Tsultrim Gyaltsen. He gives weekly classes on beginning and advanced Buddhist studies in the Gelugpa tradition and leads various retreats during each year. The centre hosts visits from various Buddhist teachers and in the past hosted the Dalai Lama, who gave the centre its name, in 1979 and 1984. In 1989 it organised the Kalacakra initiation given by the Dalai Lama in Los Angeles. The centre is active in the cause of Tibetan human rights and is closely affiliated with the L.A. regional office of the US Tibet Committee and International Campaign for Tibet. **Teaching Programme** Geshe Gyaltsen gives introductory Buddhist teachings every Sunday morning at 10:30–12:00 and covers advanced topics on Wednesday evenings, 7:30–9:00pm. This schedule is interrupted when visiting lamas teach or when retreats take place. Group Tsog offerings are held twice a month for those with the appropriate initiations. **Facilities and Services** Thubten Dhargye Ling has a large meditation hall and a library of Buddhist texts, both in English and Tibetan. There are no accommodation facilities for guests at present. Also a newsletter is distributed. **Project Description** Thubten Dhargye Ling and Geshe Gyaltsen sponsor monks who study at Ganden Shartse Monastery in south India. They also have a building fund to help the monks of Lhopa Khangtsen at Ganden Shartse to build a prayer hall and dormitories. Transcription is in progress of various teachings which Geshe Gyaltsen has given at Thubten Dhargye Ling. The centre is sponsoring the building of a 'Peace Temple' in Malibu, California.

THUBTEN DHONDRUP LING

Address 938 South Berendo, Los Angeles, California, USA, 90006. **Tel** (213) 388 5992. **Distribution Details** Prepayment is required. Rush orders cannot be easily accommodated due to copying limitations. **Year Established** 1981. **Founder** Jetsun Kushola. **Lama/Scholar** Lama Lobsang Drakpa. **General Description** Thubten Dhondrup Ling is a centre of the Sakya tradition. It promotes meditation and Tibetan Buddhist studies in general.

The centre has been visited several times by various lamas, notably: Jetsun Kushola, Dezhung Rinpoche, and Ludhing Khen Rinpoche. All have given extensive teachings and numerous empowerments. The resident teacher is Lobsang Drakpa, who teaches Tibetan language and on the Path and its Fruit, or Lamdre (*Lam 'Bras*). **Teaching Programme** Students meet once a week to practise meditation when no special function has been arranged. Core attendance ranges from six to twelve people which rises to around fifty when visiting lamas are present. Teachers can both teach and live at the centre during their stay. **Facilities and Services** The centre is orientated towards visits made by travelling lamas. These visits number about two per year and can last from a few days to a few weeks in duration.

TIBETAN BUDDHIST LEARNING CENTER

Address Labsum Shedrub Ling, R.D. 1 Box 306 A, Washington, New Jersey, USA, 07882. **Tel** (201) 689 6080. **Distribution Details** No materials are distributed. **Year Established** 1958. **Founder** Geshe Ngawang Wangyal. **Lama/Scholar** Geshe Thubten Gyatso, Geshe Lobzang Tsetan, Ven. Thupten T. Taikhang. **General Description** The Tibetan Buddhist Learning Center was founded by the Venerable Geshe Wangyal in 1958, in the Kalmuck-Mongolian community of Freewood Acres, Howell, New Jersey. Originally called the Lamaist Buddhist Monastery of America, it was re-named in 1986 to reflect better the present activities of the centre. It is a non-profit, tax-exempt religious organisation and has over the years supported many Kalmucks in maintaining their traditional Buddhist worship, as well as laying the groundwork for the spread of Buddhist teachings in North America. The Learning Center's facilities are now all located in Washington, New Jersey. Its main aim is to promote and extend understanding of Tibetan Buddhism in the West. To achieve this, the centre sponsors the study of Tibetan Buddhism, translation of Buddhist texts, and provides an environment which is conducive to religious practice. **Teaching Programme** Classes are open to the general public on the second and fourth Sundays of each month. They deal with the stages of the path to enlightenment (*Lam Rim*) and follow prayer and meditation in the temple. In addition, three-day seminars are held two or three times a year, allowing for an in-depth study of various religious subject matters. They are taught by the resident geshes, visiting lamas, and American scholars. In 1979, 1981, 1984, 1987, 1989 and 1990 H.H. the Fourteenth Dalai Lama visited, giving teachings on each occasion. The Learning Center has also hosted Kyabje Ling Rinpoche, Senior Tutor to H.H. the Dalai Lama and Ganden Throne Holder (Head of the Gelugpa School of Tibetan Buddhism), who taught in 1980. Opportunities exist for scholars to stay at the centre, and to make use of the research facilities. During July and August, summer classes are arranged, taking place on weekends. **Facilities and Services** The Tibetan Buddhist Learning Center is located in North-western New Jersey, on sixteen acres of land. There are three buildings on the property. The rectory is inhabited by the Executive Director of the centre, Joshua Cutler and his wife

Diana. The school house accommodates the resident monks and includes accommodation for students to stay. A large temple contains permanent quarters reserved exclusively for H.H. the Fourteenth Dalai Lama, Spiritual Head of the centre, together with apartments for his attendants. In the middle of the property stands a large stupa that was completed in 1984. It contains the remains of the founder of the Learning Center, the late Venerable Geshe Wangyal, along with many treasured relics that have been given through the years. The library houses an extensive collection of books on Buddhism, including a bequest of an entire library of Oriental books, and a large number of Tibetan texts recently purchased in India. **Project Description** In the past the centre has sponsored many lamas and geshes to come and develop their skills in the English language. In consultation with H.H. the Dalai Lama, the project was begun in 1962, and geshes were invited in 1966, 1972, 1974, 1978, 1982, and 1984. Subsequently, many have left to teach around the world, while others continue to reside at the centre. The late Geshe Wangyal supervised the studies of a number of American students and with their help translated several Tibetan texts. The centre is also sponsoring a complete translation of *The Great Exposition of the Stages of the Path to Enlightenment*, a treatise of 500 Tibetan folios written in the fifteenth century by Je Tsong Khapa.

TIBETAN MEDITATION CENTER Address 9301 Gambrill Park Road, Frederick, Maryland, USA, 21702. **Tel** 301 473 5750. **Distribution Details** Materials can be obtained on request. Please contact the Center for a list of available texts and tapes. **Year Established** 1979. **Founder** His Holiness the thirty-seventh Drikung Kyabgon. **Lama/Scholar** Khenpo Konchog Gyaltsen, Lama Konchog Samten. **General Description** The Tibetan Meditation centre serves as

the North American headquarters of the Drikung Kagyupa ('Bri gung bKa' brgyud pa) school of Tibetan Buddhism. Through its regular teaching programme, the centre provides an opportunity for Western people to become acquainted with the Dharma and thereby generate an appreciation for one of the great cultures and religions of the world. As a particular emphasis, the Tibetan Meditation Center seeks to preserve those practices and insights that are specific to the Drikung Kagyupas. **Teaching Programme** A weekly lecture is given by the resident lama, Khenpo Gyaltsen, who is also available for private consultation. Once a week a discussion group meets to review and examine a previously chosen topic or book. There are also Tibetan language classes for those interested in learning to read, write, and speak Tibetan. Meditations at the centre include: the sadhanas of Amitabha and Avalokiteshvara (Chenrezig), the Guru Yoga of Jigten Sumgon (founder of the Drikung Kagyu lineage), and shamatha meditation. A Sunday afternoon retreat provides for longer group meditation on these practices. Opportunity exists after scheduled events, to perform tsog (tshogs) offerings and to engage in the practices of the Dharma Protectors and Chod (gcod). Every two weeks, Phowa ('pho ba) practice is held for those with the appropriate teachings. Periodically, visiting lamas give initiations and specially arranged courses. The centre celebrates the New Year Festival, Losar (lo gsar), and also holds an annual Tibetan cultural evening. **Facilities and Services** The centre includes a shrine room and a library of texts relating to Buddhist philosophy and culture. Rooms are rented on a monthly basis to practising Buddhists. **Project Description** There is a commitment to further the upkeep of the three-year retreat centre in Ladakh and to help the Drikung Kagyu Institute in Dehra Dun. This centre will comprise a monastery, retreat centre for Westerners, a Tibetan medical centre, a general dispensary, schools and a library. Whenever possible support is given to the Tibetan refugees, in particular those around the Drikung Kagyu monasteries in India. There is also a scheme to provide aid to individual Tibetan refugee children on a person-to-person basis.

TSE GYAL GAR DZOGCHEN COMMUNITY

Address P.O. Box 277, Conway, Massachusetts, USA, 01341. **Tel** (413) 369 4466. **Distribution Details** Contact the centre for further information on the catalogued tape collection. A catalogue can be obtained for $7.00 **Year Established** 1983. **Founder** Namkhai Norbu. **General Description** The centre is located in two wood-frame houses, situated on several acres of land, surrounded by the rolling hills of Central Massachusetts. One house is a private residence, while the other contains a teaching hall and residential facilities. An area is maintained to allow closed retreats to take place. **Teaching Programme** Retreats are held several times each year. **Facilities and Services** The centre can accommodate individuals and offers closed retreat facilities. There is also a teaching hall. **Project Description** An ongoing project is concerned with translating Tibetan textual material of the Dzogchen tradition into Western languages. Transcriptions are also being made from the oral discourses of Namkhai Norbu Rinpoche.

TSECHEN LING

Address 4469 23rd Street, San Francisco, California, USA, 94114. **Tel** 415 6410671. **Telex/Fax** 415 6414145.

UDIYAN MAITREYA KOSHA

Address 2525 Grape, Denver, Colorado, USA, 80207. **Tel** 303–355–2767. **Founder** Lucille Schaible. **General Description** Udiyan Maitreya Kosha is a Nyingma lineage centre founded by Lucille Schaible, a teacher of the Nyingma lineage tradition recognised by H.H. Dudjom Rinpoche. The centre name was given by H.H. Dudjom Rinpoche. Lamas are invited frequently to visit the centre. Khenpo Palden Sherab, Tsewang Dongyal, and Shenpen Dawa Rinpoche have all made several visits to the centre. **Facilities and Services** The centre has a collection of taped recordings of visiting Lamas, although none of Shenpen Dawa Rinpoche.

UNFETTERED MIND

Address 11600 Washington Place, Suite 210, Los Angeles, California, USA, 90066. **Tel** (310) 397 1656. **Telex/Fax** (310) 397 1656. **Distribution Details** The centre distributes worldwide, by mail order. **Year Established** 1975. **Founder** Kalu Rinpoche. **General Description** This is a non-profit organisation offering individual guidance, group practice/instruction, seminars and retreats. Topics covered in the teaching programme include meditation, philosophy and ethics. Emphasis is placed on the resolution of the personal and emotional issues which arise in the course of meditation practice. **Teaching Programme** Specific areas which are studied and developed in both individual guidance and group

work are basic meditation (shamatha/vipashyana), the three marks of existence (impermanence, suffering, and non-self), compassion (the four immeasurables and taking and sending), nonself and emptiness (using a sequence of meditations based on the historical development of philosophical schools). In addition, the application of these different methods to psychological and personal issues is strongly emphasised. Vajrayana is generally taught only on an individual basis after the student has completed approximately two to three years study and practice. Programmes are being developed for specific professional groups to use in the conduct of their professional lives. **Facilities and Services** The centre rents space for practice, classes, retreats, and workshops. At this time, it does not maintain a shrine room. **Project Description** Unfettered Mind is interested in developing approaches to practice and spiritual development which are accessible and effective for people in a modern urban setting. The courses and teachings offered by the centre are aimed principally at providing an adequate foundation of theory and practice for the development of understanding and experience. In particular, the complementary relationship between psychological development and spiritual understanding is being actively explored in classes, counselling, and small groups.

VAJRADHUTU USA

Address 1345 Spruce Street, Boulder, Colorado, USA, 80302. **Tel** 303 444–0190. **Distribution Details** Contact for information. **Year Established** 1973. **Founder** Chogyam Trungpa Rinpoche. **General Description** Vajradhatu USA is the administrative headquarters in the USA for all its affiliates within the United States. The organisation was founded in 1973 by the late Chogyam Trungpa Rinpoche. Vajradhatu has more than 100 centres, called Dhar-

madhatus or Dharma Study Groups, throughout the US, Canada, and Europe, offering programmes in the study of Buddhist philosophy and psychology and the practice of meditation. Three rural centres, Karme Choling in Vermont, Rocky Mountain Dharma Centre in northern Colorado, and Gampo Abbey in Cape Breton, Nova Scotia provide the opportunity to study and practise in a contemplative environment. The international organisation, Vajradhatu International, has its headquarters in Nova Scotia, Canada. **Project Description** Construction of a stupa to commemorate the late Chogyam Trungpa Rinpoche is underway at the Rocky Mountain Dharma Center.

VAJRAPANI INSTITUTE

Address P.O. Box I, Boulder Creek, California, USA, 95006. **Tel** (408) 338 6654. **Telex/Fax** (408) 338 3666. **Distribution Details** Transcripts and tapes of courses, will be duplicated on request. **Year Established** 1975. **Founder** Lama Thubten Yeshe. **General Description** Vajrapani Institute is composed of a group of students practising the teachings of Lama Thubten Yeshe and Lama Thubten Zopa Rinpoche. Over the past fifteen years, the group has been building a retreat centre in the forested hills ˙the Santa Cruz mountains. In the process, Vajrapani residents have developed qualities of self-reliance, trust and mutual cooperation, functioning very much as a family. Lack of certain basic amenities at the Retreat Center have fostered attitudes of perseverance, selfsufficiency and enjoyment of physical labour. During the winter, the centre is fairly inaccessible, providing the opportunity for long personal retreats. In the warmer months of the year, many eminent lamas of the Gelugpa Tradition, as well as Western teachers, stay, giving weekend and longer courses on all aspects of sutra and tantra. **Teaching Programme**

Annual summer programmes are arranged to cover a variety of different subjects. Recent courses have ranged from general introductions to Buddhist meditation and psychology, through teachings on the *Lam Rim* or Graduated Path to Enlightenment, to an initiation and commentary on the anuttarayogatantra practice of *Guhyasamaja*. The institute was fortunate to welcome H.H. Gaden Tri Rinpoche, the head of the Gelugpa School of Tibetan Buddhism, to give this latter initiation. During his stay he also taught on the practice of shamatha (zhi gnas) meditation and gave the Bodhisattva vows. Geshe Tsultrim Gyaltsen, spiritual head of Thubten Dhargye Ling in Los Angeles, is a frequent visitor and has recently given commentaries on the *Yellow Tara sadhana* and the purification practices of Heruka Vajrasattva and the thirty-five Confessional Buddhas. In October 1989 H.H. the Dalai Lama blessed the centre and gave teachings to 600 people. **Facilities and Services** The main building at Vajrapani Retreat Center is a large 'gompa-kitchen'. On the top floor is a shrine room that seats 100 and a smaller room where a library is to be housed. Other buildings include a smaller gompa, a self-contained house for visiting teachers, and a partially completed dormitory for twenty people. Visitors can be accommodated either in the dormitory or on the numerous camping sites that are available. Retreat facilities, in several self-contained retreat cottages are offered throughout the year to those who require minimal support. In the grounds of the centre stands a fifteen foot high stupa, erected in memory of Lama Thubten Yeshe. **Project Description** Vajrapani Institute's main project is to complete the building programme at the Retreat Center. Plans exist to build twelve retreat huts, and work continues on the existing buildings.

VAJRAYANA FOUNDATION

Address 2013 Euraka Canyon Road, Watsonville, California, USA, 95076. **Tel** 408 761 6266. **Telex/Fax** 408 761 6265. **Lama/Scholar** Lama Tharchin Rinpoche.

YESHE NYINGPO (LOS ANGELES)

Address 12021 Wilshire Blvd, Los Angeles, California, USA, 90025. **Tel** 213 452 3511.

YESHE NYINGPO (NEW YORK)

Address 19 West 16th Street, New York, New York, USA, 10011.

YESHE NYINGPO (OREGON)

Address Box 124, Ashland, Oregon, USA, 97520. **Lama/Scholar** Gyaltrul Rinpoche. **General Description** The centre is one of a group of Yeshe Nyingpo centers on the West Coast of the USA Visiting lamas come and give teachings and empowerments. A retreat center, Tashi Choling, is being established outside Ashland, with a four-storey temple and a forty foot Vajrasattva statue with gardens.

UKRAINA

Academic Organisations

**SCHOOL OF RELIGIOUS STUDIES,
DONETSK OPEN UNIVERSITY**
Address Universitetskaya 2, Donetsk,
Ukraina, 340000. **Tel** 0622 931815.
Lama/Scholar Igor Kozlovsky (Dean).
General Description The school
offers general courses on Buddhism
and Oriental religions.

Ecumenical Centres

**BUDDHIST COMMUNITY OF
CHERNIGOV**
Address 61–1 Desnyaka St.,
Chernigov 8, Ukraina, 250008.

VENEZUELA

Teaching Centres

CARACAS KARMA THEKSUM CHOLING
Address Apt 60.961, Caracas,
Venezuela, ZP-A–1060. **Tel** 02 93
7647. **Founder** Khenpo Karthar Rin-
poche. **Lama/Scholar** Rafael Ortiz
(President).

DZOGCHEN COMMUNITY CARACAS
Address PB.A. Res Pedernales, Ave.
Paez, Montalban 11, Caracas,
Venezuela, 1021. **Tel** 02 10584.

DZOGCHEN COMMUNITY MERIDA
Address Apt Postal 483, Merida,
Venezuela, 5101.

ZIMBABWE

Teaching Centres

KARMA THEKSUM CHOLING HARARE
Address 22 Harris Road, Highlands,
Harare, Zimbabwe. **Tel** 04 48394.
Founder Akong Rinpoche.

BIOGRAPHIES
OF CONTEMPORARY LAMAS
AND SCHOLARS

NOTES TO THE BIOGRAPHIES

The criteria for inclusion in the biographies section relates to the compilation of the Tibetan Cultural Resources Database. The database contains descriptive records to 30,000 hours of oral commentary given by leading Tibetan lamas and scholars, which has been recorded on audio/video tape since the early 1960's. Also catalogued are the commentarial writings of Tibetans published in Western languages since 1959. Those lamas or scholars that have taught extensively or published in the West are therefore the most likely to be represented.

Between 1988 and the present, the Foundation wrote to each of the lamas/scholars (or their representatives) whose written/oral commentaries are catalogued in the Tibetan Cultural Resources Database, inviting them to provide a short biography, with an emphasis on their scholastic history. These biographies were then edited, entered into the database and returned to each lama or scholar for proofing. Only in a very few cases have the biographies been compiled from secondary sources.

The biographies are presented according to the tradition with which the lama or scholar is historically or most commonly linked. Since lamas often study within a variety of traditions and become affiliated with the manifest structures of differing traditions or sub-schools, this categorisation should not be regarded too inflexibly.

Within each tradition or school, the biographies are presented in alphabetical order. The length of each entry is dependent on the detail of the biographical material sent to the Foundation for inclusion and does not in any way relate to status.

Every care has been taken in the compilation of the following biographies. However, since in most cases each individual or their representative composed the biography, this leads to inconsistencies in the phoneticisation of Tibetan and Sanskrit terms. These have been standardised as much as possible and where applicable, the Tibetan transliteration, in a Wylie derived standard, and Sanskrit transliteration, with diacritics, can be found in the glossary.

We apologise sincerely for any errors or omissions. We invite all participating individuals to inform us as they wish to update their entries.

SPIRITUAL AND TEMPORAL LEADER OF TIBET

H.H. the Fourteenth Dalai Lama

HIS HOLINESS THE FOURTEENTH DALAI LAMA

The present Dalai Lama, Jampel Ngawang Lobsang Yeshe Tenzin Gyatso, was born in Taktser, Amdo into a humble farming family on 6 July 1935. When he was two years old he was recognised as the reincarnation of the late Thirteenth Dalai Lama, the location of the young child being just as predicted and his body marked in the traditional way. In 1939 he was brought to Lhasa where he was enthroned in 1940. He began his education, in the Potala and Norbulingka palaces, under the guidance of his chief tutor, the ex-abbot of Gyuto monastery Ling Rinpoche and his junior tutor the Sera Je scholar Trijang Rinpoche. He began with the usual range of subjects – Logic, Prajnaparamita, Madhyamaka, Abhidharma and Vinaya, together with history, poetry, astrology and, later, extensive studies of tantra. The great scholar Kunu Lama Tenzin Gyaltsen was also significant in his education. He obtained the degree of Lharampa Geshe at the age of twenty-four. In his early teens he made efforts to begin learning English. At the age of sixteen he was obliged to assume the full temporal responsibility and functions of his position as Dalai Lama, owing to the problems created in Tibet by the advancing Chinese occupation. At the invitation of Mao Tse Tung he visited China in 1954. No reconciliation being possible between the Tibetan people and the Chinese army, the Dalai Lama left Lhasa on 17 March 1959, seven days after the civil uprising against the Chinese. He was given sanctuary in India, where he remains today in exile at the small northern town of Dharamsala. More than 100,000 of his compatriots were able to follow him into exile, most of them resettling in India and Nepal. In India, he remains as spiritual leader of the Tibetan people and formal head of their government-in-exile. Since 1959 he has campaigned for the peaceful return of Tibet to independence, work for which he was awarded the Nobel Peace Prize in 1989. He conducts a wide range of teaching activities, giving empowerments and discoursing on Buddhist texts to large audiences in Bodhgaya, Dharamsala and various other places in India and travelling frequently around the world to lecture on Buddhism and world peace. He has studied extensively in all four traditions of Tibetan Buddhism, receiving transmissions and commentaries from their major scholars and lineage holders. His published works include two autobiographies, *My Land and My People* and *Freedom in Exile*, together with *Opening the Eye of New Awareness* (a survey of Tibetan Buddhism); A *Human Approach to World Peace*; *Kindness, Clarity and Insight* (a collection of lectures) and *The Kalacakra Tantra*.

BON

Scholastic Biographies

H.H. the Thirty-third Menri Trizin

H.H. XXXIII MENRI TRIZIN

H.H. XXXIII Menri Trizin, Lungtog Tenpei Nyima, the 33rd abbot in the line of the Menri (sMan ri) abbatial lineage, was born in Kyangthang, Amdo, in the Earth Snake Year 1929. At age eight he entered Kyangthang monastery and studied reading, writing and the daily recitations of the monastery. From 12 to 17 he studied Tibetan Medicine under Zhuwo Tanpa Luhundrup. He also learned to perform the rituals of the Secret Tantras and did full length preliminary practice under the guidance of Sherap Tenpey Gyaltsen, the head lama of the Kyangthang monastery. From 18 to 26 his principal teacher was Geshe Tenzin Lodro Gyatso from whom he received further empowerments, instructions and reading transmissions and studied Dialectics, Tantra and Dzogchen together with other related subjects. At 27 he received his Geshe degree, and travelled throughout the eighteen Bon regions. On his return he was asked to become abbot of Kyangthang monastery. However, he soon left the monastery and embarked on a pilgrimage to China after which he returned to Menri and Yungdrung Ling, where he remained until 1959. Following the Chinese invasion he left for Nepal and India where he began collecting important Bon texts. Whilst on such a search in Dolpo, Nepal, he met Prof David Snellgrove and later while publishing texts in Delhi he was invited by Prof Snellgrove, together with Lobpon Tenzin Namdak and Samten Karmay, to the School of Oriental and African Studies, London University, under the sponsorship of the Rockefeller Foundation. During the three years spent in the UK he visited several monasteries of the Benedictine and Cistercian orders and took a great interest in their religious life. In July 1964, he had a private audience with Pope Paul VI. Then for two years, he worked as assistant professor at Oslo University with Prof Simonsson. In 1969 he was appointed successor to the late Menri abbot and was requested by all the monks and lay Bonpos to return to India. Since then he has remained primarily at Dolanji, where Menri Monastery has been re-established and more than 300 Bon refugees are re-settled.

LOBPON TENZIN NAMDAK

Lobpon Tenzin Namdak was born in Kyungpo, Kham in 1926. As a young boy, until the age of eleven, he was a member of Tingchen monastery, where he learnt to read and write, and studied various monastic rituals. Following this he spent some time in the study of Thangka painting and other arts, and at the age of fifteen he joined Yungdrung Ling monastery in Central Tibet, a monastery of the Bon tradition, as an artist. He embarked on a pilgrimage to Nepal when aged seventeen, and on his return he began to study with Tsultrim Gyaltsen Rinpoche of Yungdrung monastery, with whom he stayed for eight years on an island in Lake Namtso. From Tsultrim Gyaltsen he received all the important doctrines of Bon, including transmissions of Dzogchen. He also studied tantra, grammar, poetry, and history. From the age of twenty-three onwards he undertook a number of retreats, including the dark retreat of Dzogchen. Later he studied with Ponlop Sangye Tenzin at Menri monastery, where he gained the title of geshe at the age

of twenty-seven. After this he was requested to become the lobpon or main teacher at Menri monastery, a request he accepted after receiving all the remaining transmissions of Bon from Gyaltsab Yungdrung Gyaltsen. He left Tibet in 1959 due to the Chinese occupation, fleeing to India where he stayed first in Calcutta and then in Darjeeling. At the end of 1961 he was invited to the University of London, where he worked with Prof Snellgrove on *The Nine Ways of Bon*. He returned to India in 1964 and in 1967 set up, with Menri Trizin, the Bon Foundation at Dolanji, the settlement which has become the centre of the Bon tradition in exile. He re-established Menri monastery there, and in 1977 added the Bon Dialectic School to the monastery. He returned to Tibet in 1986, visiting Bon monasteries and communities. In 1989 he established the Bon Educational Foundation in Kathmandu, and undertook a teaching tour of some Western countries.

SAMTEN GYALTSEN KARMAY

Samten Gyaltsen Karmay was born in Amdo Province, Tibet. From the ages of eight to fourteen he attended a local Bonpo monastery before following the three-year course of Dzogchen meditation at Kyangthang monastery. At twenty he obtained the geshe degree and travelled to Drepung monastery for further studies. During the 1959 Chinese invasion of Tibet he and his family left Tibet to settle briefly in India. From 1961 to 1964 he was a visiting scholar at the School of Oriental and African Studies, London University, from where he obtained the MPhil degree for a thesis on Bon history and later a PhD for his thesis on the origin and development of Dzogchen in Tibetan Buddhist traditions. At present Dr Karmay is Charge de Recherche at the Centre National de la Recherche Scientific and a member of the Laboratoire d'Ethnologie et de la Sociologie Comparative at the University of Paris. He is engaged in research on symbolism, mythology and ritual in Tibetan popular religion, and the Gesar epic. He is the author of *The Treasury of Good Sayings: A Tibetan History of Bon* (1969) and editor of *Secret Visions of the Fifth Dalai Lama* (1988).

NYINGMA

H.H. Dudjom Rinpoche

H.H. Dilgo Khyentse Rinpoche

Scholastic Biographies

CHAGDUD TULKU

Chagdud Rinpoche was born in 1930 in Kham, Eastern Tibet. His mother was a famous practitioner. He was recognised as the reincarnation of the previous Chagdud Tulku when aged three. When still a child he studied in a monastery of the Drukpa Kagyu tradition, learning the Six Yogas of Naropa and other methods and performing a three-year retreat at the age of eleven. After this he entered the monastery of his predecessor, Chagdud Gompa in the Nyarong part of Kham (said to be the second oldest monastery in Kham). His training continued under the guidance of the previous Jamgon Kongtrul, by whom he was introduced to the Dzogchen practice, Jamyang Khyentse Chokyi Lodro, and many others. His root lama was the Nyingma lama Khenpo Dorje, whom he met in the early 1950s. He later received empowerments and instruction from Dudjom Rinpoche and Dilgo Khyentse Rinpoche. He left Tibet following the unrest due to the Chinese occupation, becoming a refugee in India where he worked in various Tibetan refugee camps, making use of his medical knowledge and instructing people particularly in the practice of phowa. In 1979 he was requested by his American acquaintances to go to the USA, where he first lived for a year in San Francisco. He is now the resident teacher at the Chagdud Gonpa Foundation, California, from where he oversees a group of centres in the US and Canada. His published works include *Life in Relation to Death*.

DODRUP CHEN RINPOCHE

Dodrup Chen Rinpoche was born in 1927 in Golok, Kham. He is the fourth incarnation of Dodrup Chen Jigme Thinley Ozer. At the age of four he was enthroned at Dodrup Chen monastery in Kham. From an early age he studied with teachers such as Jamyang Khyentse Chokyi Lodro, the Sixth Dzogchen Rinpoche, Zhechen Kongtrul and Gyarong Namtrul Rinpoche. His particular instructors in the Dzogchen practice were Yukhok Chatralwa and Apang Terton. When he was nineteen he went on pilgrimage to Central Tibet and undertook a retreat at Tsering Jong. He later established a college at Dodrup Chen monastery and initiated the reprinting of the collected works of Longchenpa. Due to the Chinese occupation of Tibet he left for Sikkim in 1957, settling at Gangtok where he has established a thriving monastery and college. Since 1973 he has often visited Western countries, teaching at various Buddhist teaching centres in Europe and the USA, and he has established the Maha Siddha Nyingmapa Center in Massachusetts.

H.H. DILGO KHYENTSE RINPOCHE

Dilgo Khyentse Rinpoche was born in 1910 in Kham Derge, Eastern Tibet. He was Head of the Nyingma School of Tibetan Buddhism, and one of the principal lineage holders of the Dzogchen Longchen Nyingthig tradition. He was recognised as an incarnation whilst still in his mother's womb by Mipham Rinpoche, who foresaw his exceptional destiny. At the age of eleven he entered Zhechen Monastery in Kham, one of the six principal monasteries of the Nyingma tradition, and was formally recognised and enthroned by his teacher, Zhechen Gyaltsab Rinpoche, as the wisdom-mind emanation of Jamyang Khyentse Wangpo (1820–92) a renowned nineteenth century lama closely associated with the Rime tradition, who was in turn believed to be an emanation of Manjushri. Khyentse Rinpoche spent many years at Zhechen with his teacher who imparted to him all the essential instructions and empowerments of the Nyingma tradition. He also studied intensively with many other great masters and scholars from all four lineage traditions, including

Dzongsar Khyentse Chokyi Lodro, Umdze Tenzin Dorje of Palpung and Zhenga Rinpoche, practising for years in remote caves and solitary hermitages. When in his early twenties he discovered several Terma – texts hidden previously by Padmasambhava. Whilst in Tibet he spent in all more than twenty years in retreat. Following the Chinese occupation of Tibet and the resulting civil unrest he went into exile, establishing the Zhechen Tenyi Dhargye Ling monastery in Nepal and becoming spiritual advisor to the royal family of Bhutan. He also built a new stupa at Bodhgaya, and prepared plans for the construction of seven other stupas in each of the great pilgrimage places associated with the life of the Buddha. He travelled extensively throughout India, Southeast Asia and the West, including France, the UK and the USA, and during the 1980s twice visited Tibet. He was appreciated as one of the most outstanding Nyingmapa masters, and was especially renowned for his accomplishment of Dzogchen or Atiyoga practice. He composed many commentaries, meditation texts and poems, and became famous for his outstanding scholarship and wisdom. He also played an important part in preserving Tibet's rich spiritual heritage by collecting and publishing many rare Buddhist texts which otherwise would have been lost forever. He passed away in Bhutan on 28 September 1991.

H.H. DRUBWANG PENOR RINPOCHE

H.H. Drubwang Penor Rinpoche, the eleventh throne holder of the Palyul lineage, was born in 1932 in Tibet, as prophesied by the great Thubten Chokyi Dorje, the Fifth Dzogchen Rinpoche. He entered the Palyul monastery in 1936 and took his vows of refuge from the great Khenpo Ngaga Rinpoche. From early in his life he received transmissions from a number of great masters, notably the second Tarthang Chogtrul Rinpoche (1894–1959). He took his ordination from Chogtrul Rinpoche and received the name Thubten Lekshed Chokyi Drayang. At Dago monastery, he received the Nam Cho Great Perfection one month preliminary practice of Buddha in the Palm of the Hand. He also studied poetry, astrology and medicine. In 1944, when he was twelve, he received the *Kagye Do Wang Chenmo* (Great Empowerment of the Eight Herukas) and the *Rinchen Ter Dzod* (Precious Terma Treasury) empowerments, transmissions and secret sealed protector empowerments from the second Tarthang Chogtrul Rinpoche. From the Fourth Karma Kuchen Rinpoche, Thegchog Nyingpo, he received the *Nam Cho*, Ratna Lingpa's *Ter Cho* and the *Kagye Sang Dzog Drubwang Chenpo Bum Gya Chen* (Eight Herukas Accomplishment Empowerment of the Perfected Secret Sealed Vase) with simultaneous commentary. Also, from the Fourth Karma Kuchen Rinpoche, he received, in twelve consecutive days, the *Gongdu Drubwang Chenmo* (Great Accomplishment Empowerment of the Condensed Enlightened Mind) according to Jamgon Kontrul's Empowerment Index. At thirteen he took his novice ordination whilst at the Dago retreat centre, and received the name Do Ngag Shedrub Tendzin Choglay Namgyal, meaning Doctrine Upholder of the Teachings and Practices of Sutra and Tantra Victorious in all Directions. From Khenpo Legshed Jordan he received the Kham tradition of Mogton Dorje Palzang's Empowerment text *Wang Chod Drangtsi Chu Gyun* (A Continuous Flow of Nectar) on two occasions, making him a holder of the earlier Kathog tradition. Khenpo Legshed Jordan also gave him all the empowerments, transmissions and teachings on the *Dam Ngagdzod* (Treasury of Essential Instruction); Terton Dorje Lingpa's revelation *Lama Kadu* (Condensed Utterance of the Lama); *Hung Kor Nying Thig* (Hung Kor's Heart Essence); *Ngari Kagyed Yongdu* (Ngari's Completely Condensed Eight Herukas); Lerab Lingpa's revelation *Tendrei Ney Sel Kor* (Clarification of Negative Omens) and many others. From the Fourth Karma Kuchen Rinpoche, Thegchog Nyingpo, Penor Rinpoche received many transmissions, including the *Dupa'i Do Wang* (Anu Yoga empowerment) of the *Rinchen Trengwa* tradition, written by Nyalpa Deleg. In the Tarthang monastery, he received all the transmissions of the *Kangyur* and *Tengyur*, as well as completing a Vajrakila retreat. He then entered into retreat with his teacher, Chogtrul Rinpoche, for four consecutive years. With Khenpo Nuden, Khenpo Sonam Dondrub, Khenpo Dondrub and others, he studied the sutras and afterwards travelled on a pilgrimage to Central Tibet. He returned to Palyul monastery in 1956, and renovated the nearby Dago monastery. Here he gave all the empowerments, transmissions and teachings of the *Nam Cho* and Ratna Lingpa's revelations. In 1959, during the Chinese occupation, he fled to Nepal eventually settling in Bylakuppe, Mysore, South India. In 1963, he built the new Thekchog Namdrol Shedrub Dargye Ling Monastery and a Scholastic College. All the major lineage-holding Tulkus and Lamas of the Palyul tradition are in residence at the Namdroling monastery, directly under the guidance of Penor Rinpoche. He has travelled extensively, and in 1982 visited

Tibet, where he has played a major part in the reconstruction of the original Palyul. Since the passing away of H.H. Kheyntse Rinpoche, Penor Rinpoche, at the request of the Nyingma Lamas, has become head of the Nyingma School

H.H. DUDJOM RINPOCHE

The late H.H. Dudjom Rinpoche, Jigdral Yeshe Dorje, was born on 10 June 1904, into a noble family in the S.E. Tibetan province of Pemako. He was recognised as the incarnation of Dudjom Lingpa (1835–1904), a famous discoverer of many concealed teachings (Terma), particularly those related to the practice of the yidam Vajrakila. Dudjom Rinpoche studied with many of the most outstanding lamas of his time, beginning his studies with Khenpo Aten in Pemako. At the age of eight, he began to study with Orgyen Chogyur Gyatso, a personal disciple of the great Patrul Rinpoche. In his teens he attended the great monasteries of Central Tibet such as Mindroling, Dorje Drak and Tarje Tingpoling, as well as those of East Tibet, like Kathog and Dzogchen. It was to Mindroling that he returned to perfect his understanding of the Nyingma tradition. Foremost amongst his many teachers were Phungong Tulku Gyume Ngedon Wangpo, Jedrung Thinle Jampa Jungne, Gyume Phende Ozer and Minling Dordzin Namdrol Gyatso. Dudjom Rinpoche's main area of activity was in Central Tibet, where he maintained the Mindroling tradition, and especially at Lamaling and his other seats in the Kongpo and Puwo regions, south-east of Lhasa. Unique in having received the transmission of all the existing teachings of the Nyingma tradition, Dudjom Rinpoche was famous in particular as a great terton, whose Termas are now widely taught and practised, and as a leading exponent of Dzogchen. A master of masters, he was acknowledged by the leading Tibetan lamas as possessing the greatest power in communicating the nature of mind, and it was to him that they sent their students when prepared for this 'mind-direct' transmission. He was also famous as a very prolific author and a meticulous scholar. His writings are celebrated for the encyclopaedic knowledge they display of all the traditional branches of Buddhist learning, including poetics, history, medicine, astrology and philosophy. A writer of inspirational poetry of compelling beauty, he had a special genius for expressing the meaning and realisation of Dzogchen with a crystal-like lucidity. His *Collected Works*, published recently in India and numbering forty volumes, do not include his complete output. Amongst the most widely-read of his works are the *Fundamentals of the Teaching of Buddha*, and *History of the Nyingma School*, which he composed soon after his arrival in India as an exile, and which have been published in English. At the invitation of H.H. the Dalai Lama, Dudjom Rinpoche also wrote a political history of Tibet. Another major part of his work was the revision, correction and editing of many ancient and modern texts, including the whole of the Canon Teachings (*bKa' ma*) of the Nyingma School. Upon leaving Tibet, he established a number of vital communities of practitioners in India and Nepal such as: Zangdok Palri in Kalimpong, Dudul Rabten Ling in Orissa, and the monasteries at Tsopema and Boudhnath. Latterly, he founded several major centres in the West, including Urgyen Samye Choling, in France, and the Yeshe Nyingpo centers in America. He passed away in France on 17 January 1987.

KHENPO PALDEN SHERAB

Khenpo Palden Sherab was a member of Riwoche monastery in Kham, where he undertook extensive study of Buddhist philosophy and practice. After coming into exile to escape the Chinese occupation of Tibet, he became the scholar in charge of Nyingma Studies at Varanasi University in India. Since 1982 he has been a visiting teacher at the Udiyan Maitreya Kosha Buddhist teaching centre in Colorado, USA.

KHETSUN SANGPO RINPOCHE

Khetsun Sangpo Rinpoche was born in 1921 in Central Tibet. He studied with various teachers from the traditions of Nyingma, Sakya and Gelug, amongst them a woman held to be an incarnation of Machig Labdron, and whilst still in Tibet he studied at Drepung Gomang monastery near Lhasa. After coming into exile to escape the Chinese occupation of Tibet, at the request of the Dalai Lama he taught in Japan for ten years from 1961 to 1971. He was a visiting scholar at the University of Virginia during 1974–75 and also during the summer of 1986. He is at present head of a school in Boudnath, Nepal known as the Nyingma Wish Fulfilling Centre. He has written the *Biographical Dictionary of Tibet and Tibetan Buddhism* in eight volumes, and *Tantric Practice in Nyingma* (Translated by J. Hopkins).

LAMA GOMPO TSETEN

The late Gompo Tseten Rinpoche was born in 1905 in Amdo. At the age of eight he entered a monastery, and in time became abbot of the Sangye Mingye Ling monastery in Labrang, Amdo. Obliged to leave Tibet by the Chinese occupation, he resided in exile in India, where he held the post of abbot at various monasteries. He is renowned as one of the few living masters fully accomplished in Dzogchen and in Tsalung (the practices focusing on the inner channels and winds). He visited the USA on several occasions, beginning in 1979, to teach. He returned to returned to his monastery, Sangye Mingye Ling in Labrang Tibet to teach and passed away there in 1990.

NAMKHAI NORBU RINPOCHE

Professor Namkhai Norbu was born in 1938 in the village of Ge-ug in the Chongra part of Derge, Kham. At the age of two he was recognised as the reincarnation of Adzom Drugpa – a great nineteenth century master of Dzogchen and a Terton (discoverer of hidden texts) – and later was confirmed as the mind emanation of the seventeenth century lama Lhodrag Zhabdrung. As a child he was taught the *Dzogchen Sangwa Nyingthig* and *Longchen Yabshi* by Dzogchen Khen Rinpoche and two of his uncles. From Negyab Chotrul Rinpoche he received the transmissions of the *Nyingma Kama*, *Longsal Dorje Nyingpo* and Migyur Dorje's *Namcho*. From Khen Palden Tsultrim Rinpoche he received the transmission of the Sakya *Gyude Kundu*. From the ages eight to twelve he studied at the Wonton college of Derge Gonchen monastery under Khyenrab Chokyi Ozer Rinpoche, studying eight texts by Indian masters and the five texts of Maitreya, various tantras and commentaries including the four medical tantras, the Sakya *Drubtab Kundu*, and astrology. At the same time, until the age of fourteen, at Kuse Serjong college he studied the *Prajnaparamita sutras*, *Abhisamaya-lamkara* and various tantric texts. Under the guidance of Dzongsar Khyentse Rinpoche at the Dzongsar monastery he studied the Sakya *Zab-*

cho Lamdre and various tantric texts. At the Khamdre college he studied logic and Sakya Pandita's *Tsema Rigter* with Khen Minyag Damcho. At Sengchen Namdrag he performed a retreat with his uncle Togdan Urgyen Tenzin, and at that time was able to receive the cycles of *Dorje Drolo* and *Gongpa Zangtal* and the *Longchen Nyingthig* from the son of his former incarnation. In 1951, he visited the solitary hermit Ayo Khadro Dorje Paldon, said to be a living embodiment of Vajrayogini and 113 years old, and received from her the *Khadro Sangdu* terma of Jamyang Khyentse Wangpo, the *Khadro Yangthig* and *Longchen Nyingthig*, and also some mind-Termas of her own. In 1954, as the Chinese occupation of Eastern Tibet was accelerating he was invited to China as a representative of Tibetan youth. He briefly taught Tibetan language at the Southwestern University of Minor Nationalities in Szechuan. In China he met the lama Gankar Rinpoche from whom he received instruction on the Six Yogas of Naropa, Mahamudra, *Konchog Chidu* and Tibetan medicine. He also learnt to speak Chinese and Mongolian. When he was seventeen he met his root lama, Nyala Rinpoche Rigzin Jangchub Dorje, who lived in the Khadro Gar valley to the east of Derge. From him he received initiation and transmission of the Semde, Longde and Mengagde teaching of Dzogchen. After a year he set out on a pilgrimage to Central Tibet, Nepal, India and Bhutan. On his return he decided to leave Tibet for exile, due to the Chinese occupation, and from 1958 to 1960 he was in Gangtok, Sikkim working as author and editor of Tibetan textbooks for the government. In 1960 he was invited to Italy by Prof G. Tucci and became a research associate at the Inst Italiano per il Medio ed Estremo Oriente. From 1964 he has been a full professor at the Istituto Orientale, University of Naples, teaching Tibetan language and history and

Mongolian language. Amongst his research projects has been an investigation of Bonpo literature. He has guided retreats on Dzogchen in Italy, England, various other European countries and the USA, also teaching Yantra Yoga, medicine and astrology. His students form various 'Dzogchen Communities' to help consolidate his teaching. He has published several books in Tibetan, Italian and English.

NECHUNG TULKU

The late Nechung Tulku, Thubten Konchok Tenzin Pal Sangpo was identified, as a very young boy, by the Thirteenth Dalai Lama as the reincarnation of the incarnate lama of Nechung monastery, south of Lhasa. He entered Nechung monastery at the age of five, and by the age of seven had begun his formal studies of the elementary subjects with the lama Dordrag Rigzin Chenmo and the Nechung abbot. Later he studied under Yeshe Gyatso, a teacher from Mindroling monastery, staying with him in his apartment at the Potala palace in Lhasa. Additionally he was able to study the Lamrim and other subjects with a variety of well respected scholars. Following his exile from Tibet due to its occupation by the Chinese, in 1962, he lived in India until he moved to Hawaii in 1975. There he became the teacher at the Nechung Dorje Drayang Ling Buddhist temple and retreat centre.

SOGYAL RINPOCHE

Sogyal Rinpoche was born in the early 1950s in the Trehor part of Kham, Eastern Tibet. As a young child he was brought up mostly at Dzongsar monastery in the care of the renowned lama Jamyang Khyentse Chokyi Lodro who recognised him as the reincarnation of Terton Sogyal, a discoverer of many hidden texts (Terma) and master of the practice of Dzogchen. When old enough for formal study he learnt poetry, drama, logic and various Buddhist texts from private tutors. Due to the growing Chinese occupation of Kham encroaching from the east Sogyal Rinpoche was taken in 1954 to Central Tibet in the party of Jamyang Khyentse Rinpoche, and from there they soon proceeded to Sikkim as the situation worsened all over Tibet. Following the death of Jamyang Khyentse Rinpoche, his root lama, he continued his studies with Dudjom Rinpoche and Dilgo Khyentse Rinpoche, also beginning to study English in 1959. He later attended a university in Delhi studying Indian philosophy, and took up a visiting scholarship to Cambridge University in England where he studied comparative religion. Following this, for a number of years he served as translator and aide to Dudjom Rinpoche, who was the inspiration behind his work in the West. Sogyal Rinpoche has established a number of Buddhist teaching centres in Europe and North America, the Rigpa Fellowship, which practise the Buddhist path under his guidance. He now spends most of his time travelling and teaching around the world, specialising in presenting the Tibetan views on death and dying, and Dzogchen. He is the author of *View, Meditation and Action, Dzogchen and Padmasambhava*, and the recently published *The Tibetan Book of Living and Dying*.

TARTHANG TULKU

Tarthang Tulku Kungaleg was born at Archung in the Golok region of Amdo in 1935. He was educated at Tarthang monastery in Eastern Tibet, studying various Buddhist texts. He left for Sikkim in 1958. Arriving in India, he taught Buddhist philosophy at the Sanskrit University, Varanasi, for nearly seven years. In 1968 he went to America, establishing the Tibetan Nyingma Meditation Center in California. He established the Dharma Press and Dharma Publishing in 1970, the Nyingma Institute in 1973, the Odiyan Retreat Center in 1975, the Tibetan Aid Project, and the Tibetan Nyingma Relief Foundation. He served as general editor of the Nyingma edition of the Tibetan *Kangyur* (in 120 volumes, Dharma Publishing, 1981); he has written many books, among them *Sacred Art of Tibet*; *Kum Nye Relaxation* (vols 1 & 2); *Mother of Knowledge* (on the life of Yeshe Tsogyal); *Crystal Mirror* (vols 1–5), *Gesture of Balance* and *Time, Space and Knowledge*. He has worked to support the reconstruction of Tarthang monastery in Tibet, and in 1988 founded the Nyingma Institute of Nepal.

THINLEY NORBU

Thinley Norbu is the eldest son of the late H.H. Dudjom Rinpoche, former head of the Nyingma lineage tradition. He is an incarnation of Tulku Drime Oser, son of Dudjom Lingpa and held to be an emanation of Longchenpa. As a young man he studied for nine years at the Mindroling monastery in Tibet. Since coming into exile after the Chinese invasion of Tibet, he has written a number of books, among them *The Small Golden Key*, on Buddhist practice; *Magic Dance – the Display of the Self-Nature of the Five Wisdom Dakinis*, on the manifestation of phenomena; and a translation of Patrul Rinpoche's *Practice of the Essence of the Sublime Heart Jewel, The Propitious Speech from the Beginning, Middle and End*.

TSERING LAMA JAMPAL ZANGPO

Tsering Lama, Jampal Zangpo, was born in the village of Mugsang Pedra in Derge, Kham. Many of his family were famous for their scholarship. In his youth he entered the Mugsang monastery where he received elementary education in reading, writing and recitation. He then went to Palyul monastery where he studied with many renowned masters of the Palyul tradition of the Nyingma lineage, receiving transmissions from his main teacher, Drubwang Penor Rinpoche, and from Khenpo Ngaga Rinpoche, the Fourth Karma Kuchen Rinpoche, the Second Tarthang Chogtrul Rinpoche and others. These studies included the *Nyingma Kama*, *Rinchen Terdzod* and *Namcho* transmissions. He was able to study Sanskrit, Tibetan grammar, poetry, logic and astrology, and performed a three-year retreat at the Palyul retreat centre. Following this he became the teacher of the reincarnation of his late teacher (ie., the Third Drubwang Penor), the Second Dzonang Rinpoche, Tulku Thubten Palzang, and various government officials of the Derge district. His book on the Palyul tradition of Nyingma has been published in English as *A Garland of Immortal Wish-fulfilling Trees*.

TULKU THONDUP RINPOCHE

Tulku Thondup was born in Golok in Amdo in 1939. He was recognised at the age of four as the reincarnation of a famous scholar of the Dodrup Chen monastery, Konme Khenpo. Thondup Rinpoche entered Dodrup Chen monastery and studied various Buddhist texts, becoming the monastery's ritual master (Dorje Lobpon). In 1958 he moved to India, teaching from 1967–76 at Lucknow University and from 1976–80 at Visva-Bharati University. In 1980 he went to the USA, and was a visiting scholar at Harvard University. He now works at translation of and research into Tibetan Buddhist texts, especially those of the Nyingma lineage tradition, under the auspices of the Buddhayana Foundation, and has published various books, among them *Hidden Teachings of Tibet* (on Terma); *Buddhist Civilisation in Tibet*; *Buddha Mind* (Longchenpa on Dzogchen), and *Enlightened Living* (on ethical conduct).

TULKU URGYEN RINPOCHE

Tulku Urgyen Rinpoche was born in Kham in 1920. He is the reincarnation of the former Guru Chowang Tulku. Until the age of twenty-one he studied with his father Tsangsar Chime Dorje, a very learned lay practitioner, receiving from him a transmission of the Kangyur, and the Chokling Tersar, which he also received from his uncle, Tulku Samten Gyatso. His family are the main lineage holders of Baram Kagyu, which stems from Gampopa's disciple Baram Darma Wangchuk. From Kyungtrul Karjam he received the transmission of *Dam Ngag Dzod*, the Chowang Gyatso empowerments of Chod, and various other instructions, including the *Lamrim Yeshe Nyingpo* which he also studied with Jogya Rinpoche. His uncle Tersey Rinpoche also gave him instruction on Dzogchen. He received the *Rinchen Terdzod* from Kasey Kongtrul, the son of the Fifteenth Karmapa. He received the Gyachen *Kadzod* from his uncle Sangngag Rinpoche, the Kagyu *Ngagdzod* from the Sixteenth Karmapa and the Sheja Kunkyab from Tana Pema Rinpoche. He was able to give the transmission of *Dzogchen Desum* to the Sixteenth Karmapa and to Dudjom Rinpoche and has transmitted the *Chokling Tersar* to numerous lamas of both Kagyu and Nyingma traditions. Whilst still in Eastern Tibet he spent a period of three years in retreat, and later he again spent three years in retreat at Tsurphu in Central Tibet. After leaving Tibet due to the Chinese occupation he spent a further three years in retreat in Sikkim. At present he resides at Nagi Gonpa Hermitage, a nunnery above the Kathmandu valley. He has established several monasteries and retreat centres in Nepal. He is the author of *Vajra Heart*, a book on Dzogchen, and in recent years has given instruction to numerous Western students. He has two sons residing at Ka-Nying Shedrup Ling monastery in Boudhnath, Tulku Chokyi Nyima and Chokling Migyur Dewey Dorje.

VEN YUDUL TROGYAL

Ven Yudul Trogyal was born in 1935 in Tagtsal, Dongkar Dzong, Central Tibet. From the ages of thirteen to eighteen he studied astrology at the Tse Mindroling monastery, and acquired proficiency in the Tibetan almanac. He also studied with Rawa Chodrag Rinpoche at Drikung, practised the art of weather control at Tagtsal and received the complete *Rinchen Terdzod* transmission from Dudjom Rinpoche. He mastered the skill of hail-storm control through the practice of the wrathful aspects of Guru Rinpoche, and underwent the full course of retreat and rituals. He then became weather controller for the Tagtsal, Ganden, Phenpo and Phari areas of Tibet.

KAGYU

Drikung Kagyu

H.H. the Thirty-seventh Drikung Kyabgon

Scholastic Biographies

H.H. THIRTY-SEVENTH DRIKUNG KYABGON

Konchog Tenzin Kunsang Thinley Lhundrup, the Thirty-seventh Drikung Kyabgon, was born on 4 June 1947 in Lhasa to the well-known Tibetan family of Tsarong. In 1950 he was recognised as the incarnation of the previous Drikung Kyabgon. At the age of five he received ordination from the Fourteenth Dalai Lama, at Drikung Monastery, the seat of the Drikung Kagyu tradition. In 1959, at the time of the Chinese military takeover, he was forced to leave his monastery and live in Lhasa with one of his former tutors. From 1960 to 1969 he was a student in Chinese schools and then worked in communes in Central Tibet. In 1975 he escaped to India and later that year visited the USA, where his parents were living. In 1976, he returned to India and resumed his spiritual training in the Drikung Kagyu lineage. His studies included the practices of Phowa, Mahamudra, and the Six Yogas of Naropa. Since 1976 he has travelled to more than 100 monasteries outside Tibet, such as Lamayuru and Phiyang in Ladakh. He has toured extensively in the USA, Canada, and the Far East.

KHENPO KONCHOG GYALTSEN

Khenpo Konchog Gyaltsen was born in Tsari, Chosam, southeastern Tibet in 1946. From 1962–67 he attended the Central School for Tibetans in Darjeeling. Then from 1967–76 he attended the Central Institute for Tibetan Higher Studies at the Sanskrit University, Varanasi, India, where he studied Buddhist philosophy, history and poetry. He graduated with distinction and was awarded the acarya degree. From 1978–81 he undertook a three-year, three-month meditational retreat at Lamayuru Monastery in Ladakh, studying and practising the Five Profound Paths of Mahamudra and the Six Yogas of Naropa under the guidance of Kyunga Rinpoche. Upon completion of these studies, he was awarded the position of Khenpo by all Drikung Kagyu Monasteries. From 1981 to 1982 he taught Buddhist philosophy and meditation to both Eastern and Western students at Almora and Lamayuru Monastery in Ladakh. In 1982 he began teaching at the Tibetan Meditation Centre in Washington, D.C., at the request of H.H. the Drikung Kyabgon, head of the Drikung Kagyu tradition. In 1985 he made a brief visit to Tibet to study under Pachung Rinpoche at Drikung Til Monastery, returning to the USA in March 1986. He regularly visits Europe, South America and Southeast Asia and has established three centres in Chile and several centres in the USA. His publications include: *Prayer Flags*, the *Dharma Songs of Lord Jigten Sumgon*; *In Search of the Stainless Ambrosia*; *Garland of Mahamudra Practices*; and *Great Kagyu Masters*. Several unpublished meditation instructions have also been translated.

TULKU CHOKYI NYIMA

Tulku Chokyi Nyima Rinpoche was born in Tibet in 1951 into the Tsangsar family, which for many generations has been the holder of the Baram Kagyu lineage. He is the eldest son of Tulku Urgyen Rinpoche. At eighteen months he was recognised by the sixteenth Karmapa as the seventh reincarnation of the renowned Gar Drubchen. In 1959, during the Chinese military takeover, Chokyi Nyima left Tibet and went to India and Nepal. Until he was thirteen he studied at the Young Lamas School in Dalhousie, then continued his education at Rumtek monastery in Sikkim, the seat of the Karmapa in exile, where he spent eleven years studying under the guidance of the Karmapa. His studies at Rumtek included the *Abhidharmakosha* by Vasubandhu; the five texts of Maitreya; *Pramanavarttika* by Dharmakirti; *Bodhisattvacaryavatara* by Shantideva; *Madhyamakavatara* by Candrakirti; and various commentaries and other texts. In 1975 he joined his father and younger brother, Chokling Rinpoche, in Boudhanath, Nepal, where at the request of the Sixteenth Karmapa they established Ka-Nying Shedrup Ling monastery. He now resides there and supervises the monastery. Since 1977 he has been instructing Western students in meditation. In 1983 he founded the Rangjung Yeshe Institute for Buddhist Studies, where he conducts yearly seminars in English, every October. He accompanied his father in 1980 on a world tour, visiting Europe, USA and Southeast Asia and teaching on Dzogchen and Mahamudra. He established Rangjung Yeshe Publications in 1985, from which transcripts of his discourses and other books may be obtained. His works include *The Union of Mahamudra and Dzogchen* and *Rise, Never Set*.

KAGYU

Drukpa Kagyu

H.H. the Twelfth Gyalwang Drukchen Rinpoche

Scholastic Biographies

KHENPO YESHE CHODHAR

Khenpo Yeshe Chodhar was born in 1928 in Lhathok, Kham. He began his spiritual education at the age of eight, becoming a monk at twelve. He went to Central Tibet, under the guidance of an abbot of Drepung Loseling monastery, and studied for three years at Drepung monastery, near Lhasa. He then returned to Kham to study at Zigar monastery in Derge district. After graduating, Khenpo Yeshe Chodhar entered the Druk Sangag Choling Monastery in Southern Tibet where he stayed for one year pursuing further studies. After leaving Tibet at the time of the Chinese military takeover, he stayed for two years in Buxador monastic refugee camp in Bengal. Khenpo Yeshe Chodhar has received empowerments and transmissions from many of the lineage holders of all major Tibetan traditions. He has studied in the five higher subjects of Logic, Prajnaparamita, Abhidharma, Madhyamaka and Vinaya. He has also extensively studied Tantra, and possesses the Mahayana Pranidhicitta and Prasthanacitta Bodhisattva vows in two lineages: that of Manjushri, emphasising profundity of view, and the tradition of Maitreya, emphasising extensiveness of conduct. In 1967, he became a professor at the Central Institute of Higher Tibetan Studies at Varanasi. In 1972, the Dalai Lama, the sixteenth Karmapa and the Twelfth Gyalwang Drukchen Rinpoche unanimously appointed him as chief abbot of the entire Kagyu lineage. In 1983 he visited the West to give spiritual guidance and instruction, having already taught in Bhutan, Ladakh, and many parts of India. He is also responsible for overseeing the Drukpa Kagyu Monastery in Darjeeling – Thubten Sang Ngag Choling, the new Zigar Monastery in India, and the Meditational Retreat Centre in Rewalsar. Primarily he now lives and teaches at Drukgon Jangchub Ling in Menton, France.

KAGYU

Karma Kagyu

H.H. the Sixteenth Karmapa

H.H. the Seventeenth Karmapa

Scholastic Biographies

AKONG RINPOCHE

Akong Rinpoche was recognised by the Sixteenth Karmapa as the reincarnation of the former chief abbot of Tsawa Gang Drolma Lhakhang – a monastery in Eastern Tibet. He received the monastic training of an incarnate lama, and also studied medicine. From Zhechen Kongtrul Rinpoche he received the transmission of Mahamudra. In 1963, Akong Rinpoche travelled to Britain, and in 1967 he co-founded, together with Chogyam Trungpa Rinpoche, the teaching centre Kagyu Samye Ling, in Scotland. Since 1970 he has been the administrator at Kagyu Samye Ling and has established many other centres and groups in Europe, America and Africa. Since 1984 he has visited Tibet regularly and is involved in a programme for rebuilding or instituting monasteries, schools and medical centres there. He is the director of the international charity organisation Rokpa, which aids Tibetans within and outside of Tibet. He has written one book Taming the Tiger based on his therapy programmes.

ATO RINPOCHE

Ato Rinpoche was born in 1933 at Ato Shokha, Gatod (Upper Ga), in the Kham region of Tibet. He is the eighth incarnation of the Tenzin Tulku of Nezang monastery in Gatod. He was identified as a tulku by the Eleventh Tai Situpa, and confirmed in his position by the Sixth Panchen Lama. At the age of eight he was formally enthroned, and received in the course of his education empowerments and instructions from the Second Jamgon Kongtrul of Palpung monastery, (to which tradition Nezang monastery belongs). Other teachers to whom he is indebted are his uncle, Dilgo Khyentse Rinpoche, Benchen Khenpo Yaga, Dargye Khenpo Jamlo, as well as to Nezang Tulku Damtsig and Lama Karma Thubten Thinley, between 1950 and 1953, together they guided him through a three-year retreat during which he practised the Six Yogas of Naropa in the traditional way, ie., preliminary practices (ngondro), three levels of Guruyoga, and main practices associated with four meditational deities, Chod and Mahakala. In subsequent retreats in Tibet he further developed his practice of Vajrayogini and the six yogas of Naropa. In 1957 he spent a year at Tsurphu and received teachings and empowerments from the Sixteenth Karmapa. In 1958 he attended Sera Monastery in Lhasa but his studies were interrupted by the events of March 1959 and he left for India. Between 1960 and 1963 he was the Kagyupa representative in Dharamsala on the Tibetan Government in Exile's Council for Religious and Cultural Affairs. From 1963 to 1966 he was assistant to Sister Palmo at the Young Lamas' School which she founded in Dalhousie; in 1966 he was put in charge by the Dalai Lama of a new monastery with members and teachers of all four lineage traditions that was created out of the school. In 1967 he married and came to live in Cambridge, UK. He worked as a nurse at Fulbourn Psychiatric Hospital until his retirement in

1981. He teaches privately, or by invitation to groups in the UK, Europe and North America. In 1986 he founded the Nezang Buddhist Meditation Group which meets monthly in Cambridge.

BARDOR TULKU

Bardor Tulku Rinpoche was born in Eastern Tibet. After the Chinese military takeover in 1959, he left Tibet for Rumtek monastery, Sikkim, the seat of the Sixteenth Karmapa in exile. At Rumtek monastery he studied all the methods of the Kagyu lineage tradition. He was instructed by the Karmapa to establish Karma Triyana Dharmachakra teaching centre in the USA in 1978, and he now resides there as a teacher of Buddhist philosophy.

BERU KHYENTSE RINPOCHE

Beru Khyentse Rinpoche was born in Tibet in 1946. He began his philosophical studies at the age of ten and spent two years memorising texts and doing a short ngondro preliminary retreat. At age fourteen he began study of the *Bodhisattvacaryavatara* and Madhyamaka, with Khenpo Chime Tenzin as his teacher. Then until he was eighteen he continued his studies with: Madhyamaka; poetry; grammar; vocabulary; Prajnaparamita; Vinaya; *Uttaratantra* by Maitreya; *Jewel Ornament of Liberation* by Gampopa; and *Letter to a Friend by Nagarjuna*. Also, Kalu Rinpoche gave him the empowerments of and instruction on the Chikshe Kundrol. In 1967, when he was twenty-one, he received Lamdre and Chokhor teachings from H.H. Sakya Trizin and from Kalu Rinpoche he received the empowerments and instructions of the Karma Kagyu Mahamudra. After this Beru Rinpoche began a three-year and three-month retreat in Mainpat, M.P., India, which he completed in 1971. In 1972, at the age of twenty-six, he was invited by the Karmapa to Rumtek monastery, Sikkim, the Karmapa's seat in exile, where he remained for

two years and studied rituals, mudras and dance. He also studied Rangjung Dorje's *Zabmo Nangdon* with Khenpo Thrangu Rinpoche. In 1973 he received the Kalacakra initiation from the Dalai Lama, and in 1975 he received the *Kagyu Ngagdzo* empowerments from the Karmapa. He has established Karma Shedrup Thargye Ling monastery at Bodhgaya, which was officially opened by the president of India in 1989. His commentary to the Ninth Karmapa's *Mahamudra Eliminating the Darkness of Ignorance* has been published under the same name.

CHOGYAM TRUNGPA RINPOCHE

Chogyam Trungpa Rinpoche was born in Kham, Tibet in 1939. At the age of eighteen months he was recognised as the eleventh throneholder of the Trungpa lineage. When he was five he was enthroned as the supreme abbot of the Zurmang group of monasteries in Eastern Tibet. In addition to the traditional monastic disciplines, he studied calligraphy, thangka painting and monastic dance. In 1948 he received ordination as a novice monk and in 1958, at the age of nineteen, he received the qualification of Kyorpon (Doctor of Divinity) and Khenpo. He was then ordained as a full monk. In 1959, at the time of the Chinese military takeover, he escaped to India and was appointed by the Dalai Lama to serve as spiritual advisor at the Young Lamas' School in Dalhousie, India. In 1963 he received a Spaulding sponsorship to attend Oxford University, where he studied comparative religion, philosophy and fine art. In 1968 he co-founded – together with Akong Rinpoche, and became director of Samye Ling meditation centre in Dumfriesshire – Scotland. In 1969 he relinquished his monastic vows and in 1970 married a Scottish woman, Diana Mukpo. He then moved to the US and founded the Karme Choling Buddhist Meditation and Study Centre in Vermont.

He also established Vajradhatu, an international Tibetan Buddhist association of about 100 meditation and study centres in the U.S., Canada and Europe. In 1974 he established the Nalanda Foundation, a non-sectarian educational organisation; its divisions include Shambhala Training, a secular meditation programme, and the Naropa Institute, an innovative liberal arts college. He was a poet and the author of many books on Tibetan Buddhism in English, the better known of which are: *Born in Tibet* (his autobiography, 1966), *Meditation in Action* (1969), *Cutting Through Spiritual Materialism* (1973), *First Thought, Best Thought* (1974), *The Dawn of Tantra* (1975), *The Myth of Freedom* and *The Way of Meditation* (1976). Trungpa Rinpoche died on 4 April 1987, in Halifax, Nova Scotia.

H.E. GYALTSAB RINPOCHE

The Twelfth Gyaltsab Rinpoche, Drakpa Tenpei Yaphel, was born in 1954 in Nyemo, near Lhasa. He was recognised by the Sixteenth Karmapa, and was enthroned at the Tsurphu monastery. At the time of the Chinese military takeover in 1959 he was brought out of Tibet by the Karmapa, and is now the regent of the new Rumtek monastery, Sikkim, the Karmapa's seat in exile. In the early 1960s he studied for a time with the Karmapa in the older Karma Kagyu monastery which had been built at Rumtek, during the time of the Ninth Karmapa. During this time Rinpoche received several important empowerments from the Karmapa. Following this, for a brief time he studied at a conventional secular school. He soon returned to Rumtek, where he began to study the complete range of the Karma Kagyu lineage. These studies included: *Abhidharmakosha* by Vasubandhu; the five texts of Maitreya; *Pramanavarttika* by Dharmakirti; *Bodhisattvacaryavatara* by Shantideva; *Madhyamakavatara* by Candrakirti; together with various commentaries and other texts. Gyaltsab Rinpoche is one of the Regents heading the Karma Kagyu lineage tradition until the late Karmapa's reincarnation is reinstated.

H.E. JAMGON KONGTRUL RINPOCHE

The late, third incarnation of Jamgon Kongtrul Rinpoche was born in 1954 in Central Tibet. He was recognised by the Sixteenth Karmapa at the age of three. The Karmapa recommended that he be taken to Kalimpong, India, along with his parents. The family soon left for India, as the situation in Tibet had worsened due to the Chinese military takeover. In 1959 he was brought to join the Karmapa at Rumtek, in Sikkim, the Karmapa's seat in exile. The Karmapa gave him novice ordination, giving him the name of Karma Lodro Chokyi Senge. That same year, on the auspicious occasion of Lhabab Duchen, the Karmapa ceremonially enthroned him at Rumtek. He then began extensive studies in Buddhist philosophy and practice. The training at Rumtek includes study of the *Abhidharmakosha* by Vasubandhu; the five texts by Maitreya; *Pramanavarttika* by Dharmakirti; *Bodhisattvacaryavatara* by Shantideva; *Madhyamakavatara* by Candrakirti; together with various commentaries and other texts.

Eventually the Karmapa transmitted to him the complete teachings of the Karma Kagyu lineage. In addition, he later received instruction from other distinguished masters, including the *Kalacakra* empowerment from Kalu Rinpoche. Since his twenties he travelled extensively in North and South America, Europe, Australia and Asia in an effort to preserve and disseminate Buddhist teachings. He is the author of a biography of the Sixteenth Karmapa. He was one of the four Regents heading the Karma Kagyu lineage tradition until the late Karmapa's reincarnation is reinstated. Tragically Jamgon Kongtrul Rinpoche died in a car accident on 26 April 1992.

H.E. SHAMAR RINPOCHE

The thirteenth incarnation of Shamar Rinpoche was born in 1952 in Derge, a province of Kham, into the Atub family. He is a nephew of the Sixteenth Karmapa. When he was nine years old he was recognised by both the Karmapa and the Dalai Lama. He was formally enthroned in 1964 in Rumtek, Sikkim, the Karmapa's seat in exile. Having already begun studies with the Karmapa in Tsurphu monastery whilst still in Tibet, Shamar Rinpoche continued to study under his direction in Sikkim. His studies at Rumtek included the *Abhidharmakosha* by Vasubandhu; the five texts of Maitreya; *Pramanavarttika* by Dharmakirti; *Bodhisattvacaryavatara* by Shantideva; *Madhyamakavatara* by Candrakirti; together with various commentaries and other texts. In addition to Tibetan Buddhist philosophy and practice, his studies have also included learning English. In recent years he has been involved in supervising the development of the School for Buddhist Studies at his monastery near Kathmandu, Nepal, as well as touring America and Europe and establishing the Nalanda Institute in New Delhi. He is one of the Regents heading the Karma Kagyu lineage tradition until the late Karmapa's reincarnation is reinstated.

H.E. TAI SITU RINPOCHE

The Twelfth Tai Situ Rinpoche, Pema Dongak Nyingshe Wangpo, was born in 1954 in Palyul in Derge, Eastern Tibet. The circumstances of Situ Rinpoche's birth and the signs accompanying it were exactly as predicted by H.H. the Sixteenth Karmapa, enabling him to identify the child as the reincarnated Situ tulku. He was enthroned at the age of eighteen months by the Karmapa at Palpung monastery. When he was six years old, due to the Chinese occupation of Tibet he was obliged to leave for Bhutan, and from there he travelled to Sikkim, where after a period of illness he was able to join the newly refurbished Rumtek monastery in Sikkim, established as the seat in exile of the Karmapa. As a young man he was able to receive the full range of empowerments from the Sixteenth Karmapa, and to undertake the monastery's rigorous programme of study of Buddhist treatises. In addition to this he trained in the arts closely associated with Tibetan Buddhism. In 1975 he assumed in full his traditional responsibilities. In the early 1980s he founded the monastery of Sherab Ling in Bir, North India, establishing his headquarters there. Since 1980 he has toured extensively in Western countries, and in 1984 returned on a visit to Tibet. He founded the Maitreya Institute in the USA in 1984, and this now has branches in Honolulu, San Francisco and France. He is the author of *Way to Go* an introduction to Buddhist philosophy and practice, and *Tilopa*, on the tenth century yogi and translator. He also organises and participates in various conferences internationally. He is one of the Regents heading the Karma Kagyu tradition until the new Karmapa is instated.

H.H. SIXTEENTH GYALWA KARMAPA

Rangjung Rigpe Dorje, the Sixteenth Karmapa was born in 1924 on the fifteenth day of the sixth lunar month, at Denko, Kham. His father's name was Tsewang Paljor and his mother was Kelsang Chodon. As a child he displayed tremendous intelligence and when he was seven years old the previous Situ and Jamgon Kongtrul Tulkus visited his birth place and performed his novice ordination, and a ceremonial empowerment of the meditational deity Vajravarahi. During the same year he was taken to Palpung monastery at the invitation of the previous Situ Rinpoche where his formal enthronement ceremony took place. Situ Rinpoche then accompanied the Karmapa to Tsurphu monastery, the traditional seat of the Karmapas. Halfway between Kham and Tsurphu, at Gyina Gon monastery, the Black Hat ceremony was performed. At Lhasa the Thirteenth Dalai Lama performed his 'hair-cutting' ceremony. Karmapa returned to Tsurphu monastery where a second enthronement ceremony was performed by Drukchen Mipham Chokyi Wangpo and Situ Rinpoche. He then studied with Kangkar Rinpoche for four years. After visiting various monasteries on a journey to Kham, Situ Rinpoche took the Karmapa to Palpung monastery, where he received the full Kagyupa Treasury teachings and the oral transmissions. Also at Palpung he took the empowerments and initiations of *Drubtab Kundu* and studied the *Vinaya Sutra, Prajnaparamita, Abhidharmakosha* by Vasubandhu, the *Cakrasamvara Tantra*, the *Kalacakra Tantra* and various commentaries and other texts, under the guidance of Situ Rinpoche and Khyentse Rinpoche. Later whilst at Tsurphu monastery, Karmapa received further instruction from Jamgon Kongtrul Rinpoche, including the Six Yogas of Naropa and the remaining oral transmissions. In 1959 the Karmapa escaped to India after the Chinese military takeover of Tibet. In 1962, at the invitation of the royal family of Sikkim, he established Rumtek Monastery, Sikkim, as his principal seat in exile. He first visited the USA and Europe in 1974, a visit which led to the founding of many Kagyu Buddhist teaching centres. The Karmapa died on 5 November 1981.

KARMA THINLEY RINPOCHE

Karma Thinley Rinpoche was recognised by Sakya Trizin, Dakshul Thinley Rinchen as the reincarnation of Beru Shaiyak Lama Kunrik. He was subsequently recognised by the Sixteenth Karmapa as the fourth Karma Thinley Rinpoche. He studied with many leading contemporary teachers including Zhechen Kongtrul, Dilgo Khyentse Rinpoche and Ling Rinpoche. In addition to his learning in the Kagyu and Sakya traditions, he has also studied the Nyingma and Gelugpa traditions. In 1974, the Karmapa appointed Karma Thinley Rinpoche a 'Choje Lama' of the Karma Kagyu lineage. An accomplished artist and an expert on the Kalacakra Tantra, Karma Thinley has also written *The History of the Sixteen Karmapas of Tibet*, published in 1980 by Prajna Press, USA. Karma Thinley Rinpoche teaches in Toronto at Kampo Gangra Drubgyud Ling.

KHENPO CHODRAK TENPHEL

Khenpo Chodrak Tenphel was born in 1951 in Derge, Kham, Eastern Tibet. In 1959, at the time of the Chinese military takeover, he left Tibet with his family, arriving in India in 1960. When he was ten, he went to Sikkim, to study under the Sixteenth Karmapa at Rumtek monastery, the Karmapa's seat in exile. Under Topga Rinpoche, who later became the general secretary at Rumtek, he studied Tibetan grammar, poetry, *Letter to a Friend* by Nagarjuna, and *The Jewel Garland* by Gampopa. With Khenpo Khedrup he studied *Treasury of Reasoning on Valid Cognition*, and *Ascertainment of the Three Vows* by Ngari Pandita Pema Wangyal. At seventeen he took the vows of a noivce monk. After a visit to Bhutan with the Karmapa, Khenpo Chodrak Tenphel began studies with his root guru, Khenpo Thrangu Rinpoche. He studied Mipham's *Introduction to Knowledge* together with many texts of the sutra tradition. After studying in this way for seven years with Thrangu Rinpoche, he then studied commentaries to tantra, including *The Profound Inner Meaning* by Rangjung Dorje and *Moonlight: Meditational Stages of Mahamudra*. He then received from the present Karmapa the three great instructions on Mahamudra of the Ninth Karmapa. He later also received from him the Chagchen Dashung, the collected teachings of Gampopa, the Gyachen Kadzo, and the Chikshe Kundrol. From H.H. Khyentse Rinpoche, he received from among the *Seven Treasures* of Longchenpa *The Treasury of the Wish-Fulfilling Jewel* and *The Treasury of the Dharmadhatu*. He also received the transmission and instruction on *The Treasury of Knowledge*. From Kalu Rinpoche, he received the cycle of the Shangpa Kagyu teachings. When he was twenty-one, he took full ordination from the Karmapa. In 1976, he received the transmission of *The Treasury of the Kagyu Mantrayana Teachings*, after which his teacher, Thrangu Rinpoche left Rumtek for Nepal. In 1977, he studied two chapters of *The Extensive Commentary* on Valid Cognition (Pramanavarttika) under Khenpo Tsultrim Gyatso. In 1978, the Karmapa appointed him as an assistant abbot and he began to teach. In 1979, together with Khenpo Tsultrim Gyatso, he started a small monastic college (Shedra) called the Karma House of Manjushri, within Rumtek monastery. At present Khenpo Chodrak Tenphel lives and teaches at Rumtek monastery.

KHENPO KARTHAR RINPOCHE

Khenpo Karthar Rinpoche was born in Kham, Eastern Tibet in 1925. At the age of twelve he joined Thrangu monastery where he began preliminary studies of Buddhist philosophy. After taking full ordination from the previous Situ Rinpoche he began a series of retreats. After this he continued more advanced studies within Thrangu monastery, studying for five years until the age of thirty. The next six years he spent travelling with Thrangu Rinpoche, and in 1958 left Kham altogether to avoid the Chinese communist domination of Eastern Tibet, going to Tsurphu monastery near Lhasa, from where he soon left Tibet for exile in India. He stayed at first in the monastic refugee camp at Buxador in West Bengal, remaining there for eight years. In 1967 he was sent to teach at Rumtek monastery in Sikkim, the seat in exile of the Karmapa, and then within two years was appointed visiting abbot of Tashi Choling monastery in West Bhutan. After teaching there for six months he spent another fifteen months at the convent at Tilokpur in Himachal Pradesh. He was then able to receive the *Damngag Dzod* empowerments from Dilgo Khyentse Rinpoche at the nearby Tashi Jong monastery. He then returned to Rumtek, staying there until 1975 when he was sent to another monastery named Tashi

Choling, in East Bhutan. In that same year he was given the title of *Choje Lama* by the Karmapa. In 1976 he was appointed abbot of Karma Triyana Dharmachakra teaching centre in the USA, and he teaches there and regularly visits affiliated teaching centres throughout North America.

KHENPO LAMA THUBTEN

Khenpo Lama Thubten studied in Sarnath, at the Institute for Higher Tibetan Studies, where he obtained the acarya degree. He is the founder and resident teacher of the Institute Karmapa teaching centre in Caille, France.

KHENPO THRANGU RINPOCHE

Khenpo Thrangu Rinpoche was born in Kham in 1933. At the age of five he was formally recognised by the Sixteenth Karmapa and the previous Situ Rinpoche as the incarnation of the great Thrangu tulku. Entering Thrangu monastery, from the ages of seven to sixteen he studied reading, writing, grammar, poetry, and astrology, memorised ritual texts, and completed two preliminary retreats. At sixteen under the direction of Khenpo Lodro Rabsel he began the study of the three vehicles of Buddhism, spending some time in retreat. At twenty-three he received full ordination from the Karmapa. When he was twenty-seven he left Tibet for India at the time of the Chinese military takeover and was called to Rumtek, Sikkim, where the Karmapa had his seat in exile. At thirty-five he took the geshe examination before 1500 monks at Buxador monastic refugee camp in Bengal, and was awarded the degree of Rabjam. On his return to Rumtek he was named Khenpo (teacher) at Rumtek and all other Kagyu monasteries, and became the abbot of Rumtek monastery itself and of the Nalanda Institute for Higher Buddhist studies within Rumtek. He has been the personal teacher of the four principal Karma Kagyu tulkus: Shamar Rinpoche, Situ Rinpoche, Jamgon Kongtrul Rinpoche and Gyaltsab Rinpoche. Thrangu Rinpoche has travelled extensively throughout Europe, the Far East and the USA; he is the abbot of Gampo Abbey, Nova Scotia, Canada, of Thrangu House, Oxford, in the UK. In 1984 he spent several months in Tibet where he ordained over 100 monks and nuns and visited several monasteries. He has also founded his own monastery, Thrangu Tashi Choling in Boudhnath, a retreat centre and college at Namo Buddha, east of the Kathmandu Valley, and has established a school in Boudhnath for the general education of lay children and young monks. He has begun the building of a nunnery in Boudhnath and a college at Sarnath. His published works include *Buddha Nature, Showing the Path to Liberation* and *Opening the Door to Emptiness*. He is engaged in a project to publish a collection of all the Tibetan texts necessary to undertake retreats in accordance with the Karma Kagyu lineage teachings.

KHENPO TSULTRIM GYATSO

Khenpo Tsultrim Gyatso was born in Eastern Tibet in 1934. In his mid to late teens he practised under Lama Zopa Tarchin, a yogin from Dilyak monastery in Eastern Tibet. He stayed with him for several years, living in an adjacent cave to Lama Zopa's, until he had completed his training. He then went to Dilyak monastery to study Mahayana texts with Teya Drubpon and at about age twenty he received the Lam Rim Yeshe Nyingpo from H.H. Dilgo Khyentse Rinpoche when this was being given to the king of Bhutan. At this time he set off to spend about five years roaming the charnel grounds and caves of Central Tibet practising Chod. Eventually he arrived at Tsurphu where he met Dilyak Drupon Rinpoche whom H.H. Karmapa had appointed as Drupon of Tsurphu (the main seat of the Karmapa in Tibet). Tsultrim Gyatso received Mahamudra, pointing out instructions from H.H. Karmapa; stayed in charnel grounds and caves around Tsurphu for a year or so continuing his Chod practice and receiving various teachings from Dilyak Drupon, including the *Zab mo nangdon* and *Hevajra Tantra*. While visiting Nyemo a group of nuns asked for his help in coping with the Chinese situation and he subsequently led them out of Tibet. In India he spent nine years at the refugee camp at Buxador where he gained his Khenpo degree from H.H. Karmapa. He later received the Geshe Lharampa degree from H.H. Dalai Lama. As well as having studied the Gelug and Kagyu lineages, he received extensive Sakya teachings from the former Dzongsar Khyentse Rinpoche. He also received the *Rinchen Terdzo* from H.H. Dilgo Khyentse in Bhutan where he built a small nunnery, a nun's retreat centre and a temple to Tara. In 1975, he was asked by H.H. Karmapa to be the abbot of his seat in the Dordogne, but he requested to be allowed instead to serve by training translators in depth in the study of the Tibetan texts. To this end he set up the Thegchen Shedra in 1976, where over the years he has trained many Westerners to translate orally and produce translations and other works mainly in English. He established the Marpa Translator's Institute in Nepal in 1985 and has a number of students in retreat near Milarepa's cave in Yolmo. Together with Thrangu Rinpoche he has been responsible for training the new generation of Karma Kagyu Khenpos who graduated in 1991 in Sikkim, at the Nalanda Institute, founded by H.H. Karmapa. He is well known in all the Kagyu centres in the US, the Far East and Europe and is famous for his skill in debate and his ability to defend the controversial Shentong doctrine in the face of its detractors. His book *Progressive Stages of Meditation on Emptiness* is regarded as an important text book by many Buddhist groups and educational institutions.

LAMA GANGA

The late Lama Ganga was born on 26/27 February 1933, at Ga Yul in Jyekundo, Kham. He entered Thrangu Monastery at the age of thirteen, where he memorised various Buddhist texts and rituals, and began to study Buddhist philosophy. He received monk's ordination when aged eithteen from the Sixteenth Karmapa. For ten years he meditated in retreat on the Six Yogas of Naropa. After leaving Tibet for India, at the time of the Chinese military takeover, he attended the Seminary for the Four Schools of Tibetan Buddhism, and furthered his practical knowledge at Thimpu in Bhutan and at Rumtek Monastery in Sikkim, the seat of the Karmapa in exile. In 1976 he went to the USA with Khenpo Karthar Rinpoche, and later was appointed to be Karma Triyana Dharmachakra's representative in California. In the early 1980s, Lama Ganga travelled to Kagyu Samye Ling in Scotland to instruct students in a three-year retreat there, and subsequently he divided his activities between California and Scotland. He visited Tibet in 1986 and 1987, accompanying Thrangu Rinpoche. Lama Ganga passed away in Tibet, during his third visit, on 18 July 1988.

LAMA GENDUN RINPOCHE

Lama Gendun Rinpoche was born in 1918 in Nangchen, Kham. At the age of seven he began his studies at Kyodrag monastery. At seventeen he became fully ordained, and when aged twenty-one he entered the Karma Kamtsang retreat centre in the monastery, undertaking a retreat of three years, three months on the Six Yogas of Naropa. His main teacher at Kyodrag monastery was Lama Tulku Tenzin. After several more years' study he went on a pilgrimage, visiting the holy places of Tibet and Nepal, and meditating in different caves blessed by great siddhas of the past such as Guru Rinpoche and Milarepa. In 1959, at the time of the Chinese military takeover, Gendun Rinpoche left Tibet for India where the Sixteenth Karmapa gave him the directorship of a newly established monastery in eastern Bhutan. After three years in this position he went to Kalimpong and remained in semi-retreat for a further twelve years. Each year, he visited Rumtek monastery, Sikkim, the Karmapa's seat in exile, where he received instructions from the Karmapa. In 1975, on the advice of the Karmapa, he went to France and took up residence in the Dordogne at Dhagpo Kagyu Ling monastery. Gendun Rinpoche has since visited many of the Buddhist centres in Europe, and since 1986 has also directed the three-year retreat centre of Thong Drol Ling in Germany.

LAMA KARMA RINCHEN

Lama Karma Rinchen was born in 1931 in Kham, Eastern Tibet. At the age of eleven he entered Palpung monastery. In the first five years he learned basic meditation, and began his studies of Buddhism, and astrology. At sixteen, he entered a three-year, three-month retreat, practising the Six Yogas of Naropa and studying the ritual practices of Tibetan Buddhism. At nineteen he moved to Tsurphu monastery near Lhasa to further study meditation for another year. Then at the Gelugpa monastery of Drepung, near Lhasa, he studied logic and debate. In 1959, at the time of the Chinese military takeover, Lama Rinchen left Tibet and travelled to Sonada Monastery in Darjeeling, India where he studied under Kalu Rinpoche until 1976, when he moved to Hawaii. In Hawaii, he established Kagyu Thegchen Ling Dharma Centre, and in 1982, Situ Rimay Chuling Retreat Centre located in Hauula, Hawaii.

LAMA LODRO CHOPHEL

Lama Lodro Chophel was born in Sikkim in 1942. From the ages of eight to thirteen he pursued preliminary studies at the Rumtek Monastery in Sikkim. He also received training in the tantric tradition of the Kagyu lineage, such as sadhana, ritual, music and dance. From the age of thirteen he studied with Tenzin Rinpoche and with Thrangu Rinpoche, abbot of Rumtek. He began a solitary retreat when he was sixteen, but was obliged to stop due to illness in the third year. Upon his recovery, when he was eighteen Lama Lodro finished the traditional three years three months retreat. He then embarked on a three-year retreat in Bhutan. He has received the teachings of the Karma and Shangpa Kagyu

Schools, the Longchen Nyingthig of the Nyingma lineage and the transmission of the Chod lineage. He was the leader of a solitary retreat for two years at the Pangang Caves and then for the next seven years was the ritual master at Sonada Monastery, Darjeeling, the monastery of Kalu Rinpoche. From 1974–76 Lama Lodro resided in Sweden, and taught in Belgium, Denmark, Germany, Holland and Norway. In 1976 the Karmapa and Kalu Rinpoche decided that Lama Lodro should go to America as resident lama at Kalu Rinpoche's centre Kagyu Droden Kunchab in San Francisco. Lama Lodro is the author of *The Quintessence of the Animate and Inanimate: A discourse on the Holy Dharma*; *Bardo Teachings – The way of Death and Rebirth*; *Attaining Enlightenment*; *Maintaining Bodhisattva Vows*; *Mahakala Booklet*; and has translated many discourses and sadhanas.

LAMA TENPA GYATSO

Lama Tenpa Gyatso began his studies at the Nenang monastery near Lhasa. Leaving Tibet for India in 1959 at the time of the Chinese military takeover, he went to Sonada monastery, near Darjeeling, where he studied under the guidance of Kalu Rinpoche, and completed two three-year retreats. Since 1976 he has lived and taught at the Kagyu Ling retreat centre in France.

LAMA THUBTEN NAMGYAL

Lama Thubten Namgyal was born in 1918 and entered Tai Situpa's Palpung monastery at the age of five. Following his three-year retreat he was sent to head a group of monasteries in Powo near the Assamese border, from where he escaped into India in 1959. Some years later he took charge of the Bhotia Busty monastery in Darjeeling until 1976 when the sixteenth Karmapa sent him to Denmark. In 1979 he travelled to England and was resident teacher at the Birmingham Karma Ling centre. He acted as the

assistant retreat-master for the Kagyu Samye Ling four-year retreat from 1984 to 1988. He died in Birmingham in 1989.

PONLOP RINPOCHE

Ponlop Rinpoche was born on 24 June 1965 at Rumtek monastery in Sikkim. His father was Damcho Yongdu, the General Secretary to H.H. Karmapa. Less than one month after his birth, he was officially recognised by H.H. Karmapa and H.H. the Dalai Lama. The Dzogchen Ponlop Tulku is one of the three main tulkus of the great Dzogchen monastery in Eastern Tibet. Ponlop Rinpoche was enthroned at Rumtek monastery on 29 February 1968. At at early age, he received refuge vows and novice monk's vows from H.H. Karmapa. He received the Bodhisattva vow from Karmapa at the temple of Swayambhu Stupa, Kathmandu. He has received most of the Kagyu and Nyingma teachings and empowerments from H.H. Karmapa, H.H. Dilgo Khyentse, Kalu Rinpoche, and other great teachers. At fourteen, he began studying Buddhist philosophy at Karme Jamyang Khang Primary School in Rumtek. He entered the monastic college of Rumtek, Karma Shri Nalanda Institute for Higher Buddhist Studies, as soon as it was opened in 1981. Since then, he has been engaged in the traditional Buddhist curriculum of philosophy, psychology, logic, and debate. The main teachers at the Institute were Thrangu Rinpoche and Khenpo Tsultrim Gyatso Rinpoche. Ponlop Rinpoche has been one of the most outstanding students of the institute and became one of its main teachers even before he had graduated. He gained his Rabjampa degree at the end of 1991. He teaches widely on Mahayana texts and practices in the USA. and Europe.

TENGA TULKU

Tenga Rinpoche was born in 1932 in the vicinity of Benchen monastery,

Kham. He was recognised as the incarnation of Lama Tenzin Chogyal by the previous Tai Situ Rinpoche at the age of eight, and he then began his studies at Benchen, the abbot, the Ninth Sangye Nyenpa Rinpoche, becoming his root lama. When aged eighteen he received full ordination and the name Karma Tenzin Thinley Pal Sangpo from Situ Rinpoche. When he was twenty-two he began a three-year retreat, after the successful completion of which he took on a teaching role at Benchen monastery. He had to leave Benchen due to the Chinese invasion. First he travelled to Lhasa, then on to Tsurphu in the company of Sangye Nyenpa Rinpoche. From there he escaped to Bhutan, and accompanied the late Karmapa to Rumtek monastery in Sikkim, where the Karmapa established his seat in exile. He remained there for seventeen years, becoming Dorje Lobpon of the monastery. A feature of his extensive learning is his knowledge of mandala painting and sculpture. In 1974 he accompanied the Karmapa on his first tour of Western countries. In 1976 he settled in Kathmandu, establishing a retreat centre and a monastery there. Since 1980 he has regularly visited Karma Kagyu teaching centres in Europe.

TRALEG KYABGON RINPOCHE

Traleg Kyabgon Rinpoche was born in 1955 in Eastern Tibet. At the age of two, he was recognised by H.H. the Gyalwa Karmapa as the ninth incarnation of the Traleg tulkus, and enthroned as the abbot of Thrangu Monastery in Kham where he began his studies. He left Tibet in 1959 at the time of the Chinese military takeover, and went to Dungse Rinpoche's monastery, Sang Ngag Choling, in Darjeeling. At Sang Ngag Choling he studied under Khenpo Sogyal: the *Abhidharmakosha*, the Six Treatises of Nagarjuna, the *Bodhisattvacaryavatara* by Shantideva, the *Pramanavarttika*, the *Sutralamkarakosha*, the *Abhidharmasamuccaya* by Asanga, the *Madhyantavibhanga* by Vasubandhu, and the *Mahayanottaratantra* by Maitreya. Under the instruction of Khenpo Noryang he studied the *Hevajra tantra*, the *Guhyasamaja tantra* and the *Zabmo Nangdon*. After leaving Sang Ngag Choling, Traleg Kyabgon Rinpoche spent five years at the Institute of Higher Tibetan Studies at Sarnath, where under Khenpo Tsondru and Khenpo Palden Sherab he studied the history of Buddhism, Sanskrit, Hindi, English, the *Ngalso Korsum* by Longchenpa, the *Longchen Nyingthig*, *Longchen Dzod Dun*, and *Rangdrol Korsum*. He also spent several years at Rumtek in Sikkim, the main seat of the Karma Kagyu lineage. Traleg Rinpoche has received the complete teachings of the Karma Kagyu tradition of Vajrayana Buddhism, and he is well acquainted with the practices and philosophy of the Drukpa Kagyu school of the Kagyu lineage, having spent nine years studying with the regent of the Drukpa Kagyu school, the late Dungse Rinpoche, at his monastery in Darjeeling. In 1980, he moved to Melbourne, Australia, as the official representative of the Kagyu lineage and established the Kagyu Evam Buddhist Institute where he regularly conducts courses in the practice and theory of Buddhism. He is also extending his own scholarship interests through the study of Western philosophy and psychology at Trobe University, where he is preparing his MA thesis in comparative philosophy.

<u>KAGYU</u>

Shangpa Kagyu

Kalu Rinpoche

Scholastic Biographies

BOKAR RINPOCHE

Bokar Rinpoche, Karma Shedrup Yongdu Pal Zangpo, was born in 1939 not far from the Bokar Monastery, seat of his previous incarnation. He was recognised as a tulku at the age of four by the Sixteenth Karmapa. Initially he studied at Bokar monastery and from ages twelve to fourteen he studied at the Karmapa's main seat, Tsurphu monastery in central Tibet. In 1959, when the Karmapa fled Tibet at the time of the Chinese military takeover, Bokar Rinpoche joined him at Rumtek monastery, in Sikkim. From 1967 Bokar Rinpoche stayed in retreat for a period of three years practising the Six Yogas of Niguma, and subsequently undertook another three-year retreat on the Six Yogas of Naropa. He underwent these retreats under the direction and guidance of Kalu Rinpoche at Sonada, Darjeeling. Bokar Rinpoche later became the retreat master of the retreat centre at Sonada, and was also appointed, by the Karmapa, master of the three-year retreat facility at Rumtek. He has founded a retreat centre at Mirik, in Darjeeling, India.

KALU RINPOCHE

The late Kalu Rinpoche was born in the Trehor region of Kham, Eastern Tibet, in 1905. His father, Karma Lekshe Drayang, the Thirteenth Ratak Palzang Tulku, was a noted doctor, writer and Buddhist practitioner. Both his parents were students of Jamgon Kongtrul Lodro Taye, Jamyang Khyentse Wangpo and

Mipham Rinpoche, all founders and leaders of the Rime move-ment. He began his formal studies at Palpung monastery at the age of thirteen. The Eleventh Tai Situ Rinpoche gave him the ordained name Karma Rangjung Kunkyab. After two years of studying the sutras and tantras, and receiving instruction and empowerments from many of the great lamas at Palpung and other monasteries in Kham, Kalu Rinpoche gave a profound and instructive discourse on the three vows before an assembly of 100 monks and lay people. At sixteen he entered the traditional three-year retreat under the direction of his root lama, Lama Norbu Dondrup from whom he received the complete transmission of the Karma Kagyu and Shangpa Kagyu traditions. At twenty-five, he departed for an extended twelve-year solitary retreat in the moun-tains of Kham wandering without possessions, until Situ Rinpoche sent word for him to return and teach. Kalu Rinpoche then assumed the duties of director of three-year retreats at Palpung, and he was recognised at this time by the sixteenth Karmapa as the activity emanation of Jamgon Kongtrul Lodro Taye. In the 1940s he began visiting monasteries of many schools and lineages, all over Tibet, and on a visit to Lhasa taught the Regent. In 1955, he visited the Karmapa at Tsurphu, who asked him to leave Tibet in order to prepare the ground in India and Bhutan for the proba-ble impending exile. Kalu Rinpoche first went to Bhutan, where he established two retreat centres and ordained 300 monks. In 1965 he established his own monastery at Sonada in Darjeeling, Samdrub Dhargye Ling, and established a three-year retreat facil-ity there. He then founded other such facilities in India. Since 1971, Kalu Rinpoche has travelled many times to Europe and North America, establishing teaching centres and facilities for the traditional three-year retreat. In 1983 he gave the great cycle of empowerments, *Rinchen Terdzod*, one of the Five Great Treasures gathered by Jamgon Kongtrul Lodro Taye, to the four regents of the Karmapa, as well as to thousands of lamas, monks, nuns and lay people. He is the author of *The Dharma That Illuminates All Beings* and *The Gem Ornament Of Manifold Oral Instructions*. Kalu Rinpoche died on 10 May 1989 at his monastery in Sonada, India. His reincarnation (b.1990) was recognised by Tai Situpa at Sonada in 1992.

LAMA NORLHA

Lama Norlha was born in Kham, Tibet in 1935. At the age of eight he entered a monastery and began his education. In 1961, two years after the Chinese military takeover in Tibet, he left for India and spent seven years in the Samdrub Dhargye Ling Monastery in Darjeeling. In 1976 he left India for the USA, where he is at present the resident teacher at the Kagyu Thubten Choling teaching centre.

LAMA ORGYEN WANGDU

Lama Orgyen Wangdu was born in 1937 in Bhutan at Jangchub Choling. At the age of twelve he entered Jangchub Choling monastery where he began study of Buddhist philosophy, includ-ing the practice of chanting, monastic dance, torma making and

mandala painting. He progressed through the monastic curriculum until forced to flee Tibet after the Chinese occupation. In 1971, at the age of thirty-four, whilst at Kalu Rinpoche's monastery at Sonada, Darjeeling, he began a three-year retreat on the Six Yogas of Naropa and the Six Yogas of Niguma. Lama Orgyen Wangdu is at present living and teaching at Kagyu Ling in France.

LAMA SHERAB DORJE

Lama Sherab Dorje was born in Bhutan in 1941. He spent twenty years studying the main texts of the Kagyu lineage at Jangchub Choling monastery in Bhutan and further studied at Samdrub Dhargye Ling in Darjeeling, India, where he performed a three-year retreat on the Six Yogas of Niguma under the direction of Kalu Rinpoche. Lama Sherab is currently a resident teacher at Kagyu Ling in France. He is particularly skilled in painting, sculpture and architecture.

LAMA SONAM WANGCHEN

Lama Sonam Wangchen was born in 1961 in Darjeeling in India. At the age of five he entered Samdrub Dhargye Ling, the monastery of his uncle, Kalu Rinpoche, at Sonada, Darjeeling. As a young monk he travelled extensively accompanying Kalu Rinpoche on his visits all over the world. At the age of seventeen, Lama Wangchen began a three-year retreat at Samdrub Dhargye Ling. In 1983, upon completion of his retreat, he took part in the six months *Rinchen Terdzod* empowerments given by Kalu Rinpoche. He has received all the teachings and empowerments of the Kagyu lineage, as well as those of the Shangpa Kagyu from Kalu Rinpoche. He came to Europe to direct Kalu Rinpoche's teaching centres in Belgium, together with Lama Ogyen, and has since taught in Belgium, the Netherlands, France and Germany. Lama Wangchen has a good command of English.

LAMA TENZIN

From the ages of six to twenty-one Lama Tenzin studied at Tashilhunpo monastery in Shigatse, Tibet, the seat of the Panchen lamas. Whilst at Tashilhunpo he began intensive studies of Logic, Prajnaparamita, Madhyamaka, Abhidharma and Vinaya, the subjects leading to the qualification of geshe in Gelug monasteries. In 1959, before he could complete these studies, he was compelled to leave Tibet due to the Chinese military takeover. He went to Sonada monastery in Darjeeling, where he continued his studies under the guidance of Kalu Rinpoche and Bokar Rinpoche, also completing a three-year retreat.

KAGYU

Taglung Kagyu

Scholastic Biographies

TAGLUNG TSETRUL RINPOCHE

Taglung Tsetrul Thubten Gyaltsen was born in 1944 in Namru, Tibet. He is regarded as one of the high ranking lamas of the Taglung Kagyu tradition, and is at present a member of the Ecclesiastical Department of Tibet in Lhasa.

<u>SAKYA</u>

H.H. Sakya Trizin

H.H. Jigdal Dagchen Sakya Rinpoche

Scholastic Biographies

DEZHUNG RINPOCHE

Dezhung Rinpoche was born in the Fire-Horse Year, 1906, in the Ga region of East Tibet, into a family famous for its skilled physicians. At the age of five, he appealed to his parents to be sent to a monastery so that he could devote his life to the Buddhist path. He was sent to live and study with his uncle, Ngawang Nyima, a monk who spent most of his life in retreat at Tharlam monastery. At ten years old, he met the great Sakya lama, Jamgon Ngawang Legpa Rinpoche, who had just emerged from a fifteen-year retreat. Dezhung Rinpoche regarded Ngawang Legpa as his root guru and subsequently became his chief disciple, receiving novice monk's vows from him in 1921. His early education included instructions in etymology, versification, and rhetoric. He received basic teachings on Hinayana, Mahayana and Vajrayana treatises, and in particular on the Madhyamaka, or the Middle Way school. Among his teachers at this time were the Gelugpa lama, Lobsang Chokyi Gawa, and a Nyingmapa lama, Zhenga Chokyi Nangwa. At eighteen, he was enthroned as the third incarnation of Dezhung Lungrig Nyima, the incarnate lama of Dezhung monastery, having previously been recognised as his incarnation by Jamgon Ngawang Legpa. Respect for his root guru led Dezhung Rinpoche to choose as his personal practice the development of compassion through meditation on Chenrezig. Following the guidance of his lama, he received extensive instruction and empowerments from over forty lamas including the renowned Rime master, Jamyang Chokyi Lodro. These teachings included the Sakya *Lam 'bras Tshogs bshad, Lam 'bras slob bshad*, and the s*Grub thabs Kun btus* (Compendium of Sadhanas), a fourteen-volume collection of meditational texts on 1000 deities. He also

completed over ten years of retreats and travelled widely throughout Tibet teaching and giving empowerments. At the time of Legpa Rinpoche's passing, he appointed Dezhung Rinpoche to succeed him as abbot of Tharlam monastery. However, soon after that, Dezhung Rinpoche was forced to flee the country. In 1960, he accompanied H.H. Jigdal Dagchen Sakya and his family to the United States to participate in a research project on Tibetan culture and religion at the University of Washington in Seattle. During his more than twenty-year stay in America, he taught and gave empowerments extensively at teaching centres across the USA and Canada, and founded centres in New York City, Minneapolis, Boston, Los Angeles, and Seattle. In 1986, Dezhung Rinpoche went to live at Tharlam Monastery in Nepal, in order to teach and oversee the construction work. It was there that he passed away on 16 May 1987.

GESHE SHERAB GYALTSEN

Geshe Sherab Gyaltsen Amipa was born in 1931 at Sakya town in the region of Sakya. Amipa is his family name. At the age of seven he joined Sakya Thubten Lhakhang Chenmo, the main seat of the Sakya tradition. He began elementary studies of reading, memorisation and debate, followed by five years study of logic, five years devoted to the paramitas following the *Five Texts of Maitreya* and the *Bodhisattvacaryavatara* of Shantideva. During this time his principal teacher was Khenpo Sangye Tenzin. At the age of seventeen he received the Lamdre instruction from the renowned Sakya Trizin Ngawang Tutob Wangchuk, and performed a number of retreats. He passed the *bKa' bcu* (first stage) examination aged eighteen. At this time he led the dancing of the various protectors at the annual four-day festival during which the entire *Kangyur* was read at the Sakya monastery. He next studied Abhidharma, Madhyamaka, and the three vows (pratimoksha, bodhi-sattva vows and tantric vows). He finally took and gained the degree of Geshe Dungrabjampa. He began teaching students of his own, and took additional instruction on *The 13 Golden Dharmas of Sakya* and other texts. In 1956 he attended as a representative of the Sakya government a series of meetings called by the occupying Chinese officials in Lhasa. When the civil situation deteriorated, he left Tibet in early 1960 for exile in India. There he stayed for two years at the Sakyaguru monastery in Darjeeling. Following this he resided at the Young Lamas' school in Dalhousie. In 1967 he was sent to the newly established Tibet Institut in Rikon, Switzerland. He visited England, Germany, Holland and Italy founding and teaching at many Buddhist teaching centres. In 1974 he spent six months preparing an exhibition of Tibetan items at the University of Zurich. In 1978 he founded the Sakya Tsechen Ling centre (European Institute of Tibetan Buddhism) in France. He has written a textbook for colloquial Tibetan language available in English and French, *A Waterdrop from the Glorious Sea* (a history of the Sakya lineage tradition), and *The Opening of the Lotus* (on Mahayana Buddhism) available in English, French, Dutch, Italian and Czechoslovakian.

GESHE TASHI NAMGYAL

Geshe Tashi Namgyal was born in Sakya, Tibet in 1922. At the age of eight he entered the Sakya monastery of Thubten Llakhang Chenmo (founded in the twelveth century by Chokya Pagpa), took full monk's vows at twenty-one, and when aged twenty-five obtained the geshe degree of Dungrabjampa. For many years he taught at the monastery as 'Parchin Lobpon' and at thirty-four was appointed abbot of Jashong monastery and its nearby convent. In 1960, after having been imprisoned by the Chinese occupation army, he fled to India and joined Sakyaguru monastery in Darjeeling. At the instigation of the Dalai Lama, together with a select group of geshes, he worked for one year at the College for Lamas, in Musoorie, compiling new teaching materials. Upon completion of the project he moved to Benares and spent the next three years at Varanasi Sanskrit University where he obtained the acarya degree. In 1972, at the request of the Dalai Lama, he volunteered to accompany a group of Tibetan refugees to Canada as one of four spiritual leaders. In 1974 he founded Sakya Thubten Kunga Choling in Victoria, BC, where he continues to be the resident lama, and in 1988 Tashi Choling in Anchorage, Alaska. He lectures every week at his centre in Victoria, is a regularly invited teacher at centres throughout the USA and Canada, and is actively involved in community projects. He is the author of two books.

H.E. CHOGYE TRICHEN

H.E. Chogye Trichen was born in 1920 at Shalu, Tsang, into the ancient noble and religious family of the Shalu Ce. It was intended that he should join the Khangsar Labrang at Ngor, but the Thirteenth Dalai Lama decreed that he was in fact the incarnation of a lama of the great Phenpo Nalendra monastery north of Lhasa. His main teachers were his uncle, the previous Chogye Trichen at

Nalendra, Rinchen Khyentse Wangpo (1869–1927), Nalendra Simog Rinpoche Nawang Kunga Tenzin Trinlay (c 1884–1963), and Ngor Khangsar Dampa Rinpoche (1876–1953). In 1959 he left Tibet for Mustang, Nepal, after the Chinese invasion. After having worked for six years as the General Secretary of the Religious and Cultural Affairs Dept. of H.H. the Dalai Lama, he built the first Tibetan monastery at Lumbini. He has taught extensively in Nepal, India, Southeast Asia and the USA. In addition to being one of the main teachers of H.H. Sakya Trizin, he has given teachings to leading masters of all Tibetan traditions, including H.H. the Dalai Lama. He has also written numerous works, several of which have been translated into English, including a manual of monastic culture, *Gateway to the Temple* (Kathmandu, Ratna Pustak Bandhar, 1979) and *The History of the Sakya Tradition* (Bristol, Ganesh Press, 1983), and a history of Lumbini, which includes an account of his founding of a temple there. He has also founded the new Jamchen Lhakang monastery, near Boudnath Stupa, Kathmandu and a retreat centre. At present he lives at Jamchen Lhakang.

H.E. LUDING KHEN RINPOCHE

His Eminence Luding Khen Rinpoche, Sharchen Luding Jamyang Nyima, is the seventy-fifth throneholder of the Ngor tradition of the Sakya lineage. He was born in the village of Yeru, in Tsang Province, Tibet, in 1931, into the noble family of Sharchen, from which many outstanding Buddhist scholars have come. He began his studies at the age of seven. He was ordained as a monk at the age of ten, and received a thorough education in the Buddhist arts, sciences, sutras, and tantras from many of the foremost lamas of this century, especially from his own root lama, Jamyang Thubten Lhungtok Gyaltsen, the former Ngor abbot. He

studied Prajnaparamita, Vinaya, Madhyamaka, Abhidharma, Logic and Epistemology. In addition, he has made extensive studies of the Tibetan medical system. After completing these philosophical trainings, he went on to receive extensive tantric empowerments and instruction. In particular, he studied the entire corpus of the *Path and its Fruit*, or *Lamdre*, system of meditation. He has received the complete Sakya *Lamdre* teachings three times and has spent several years in retreat meditating on all four classes of tantric practices. In 1954 he was enthroned, by request of the Sakya Trizin, as the Seventy-fifth Throneholder of Ngor Ewam Choden. As supreme head of the Ngor tradition, he has conferred full ordination on over 3000 monks and nuns in Tibet, India, and Nepal. He has established monasteries and taught extensively throughout Tibet, India, Nepal, Southeast Asia, and the USA.

H.E. NGOR EWAM PHENDE RINPOCHE

H.E. Ngor Ewam Phende Rinpoche was born in Tharlam, Kham, in 1934. He was recognised as the reincarnation of a past abbot of Ngor Ewam Choden in the province of Tsang. Subjects he studied with his first root lama, Jamgon Ngawang Legpa, included: *Lamdre Loshe*; *Lamdre Toshe*; empowerments of Hevajra, Vajrayogini, Vajrabhairava, and the Seven Mandalas of the Ngor tradition; and many teachings concerning Dharma Protectors. With his second root lama, Phende Khen Rinpoche Ngawang Khedrub Gyatso, he studied the *Collection of All Tantras* (*Gyude Kundu*), and the *Collection of All Sadhanas* (*Drubtab Kundu*). With his third root lama, Tampa Rinpoche, he received empowerments and instruction including the Seven Mandalas of Ngor; the Cycle of the Three Red Deities; Vajrakila; Vajrayogini; and various Protectors. With a renowned Ngagpa of Jyekundo he studied the six different categories of treatises according to the Sakyapa. He has also studied astrology and completed many retreats. Whilst still in Tibet, he visited all twenty-one Ngorpa monasteries of the Gaba province and other places in Kham. Altogether he taught and gave empowerments at more than sixty monasteries. At the time of the Chinese military takeover in 1959, he left Tibet for exile in India where he remained for eleven years. He then left India, eventually living in France and establishing two teaching centres, Ngor Ewam Phende Ling, where he now resides, and Ngor Ewam Kunzang Ling. He also teaches in other parts of Europe and Asia, and visited Tibet in 1988.

H.E. SAKYA JETSUN CHIMEY LUDING

H.E. Sakya Jetsun Chimey Luding was born in Tibet in 1938, the year of the earth tiger. She was born into the noble family of the Khon lineage, the leading family of the Sakya lineage tradition. She was trained alongside her brother, who became head of the Sakya lineage, and has been teaching and giving empowerments since the age of eleven. She is one of three women in the history of Tibet to have transmitted the *Lamdre* (*Path and its Fruit*) teachings, the system of contemplative and meditative practice special to the Sakya lineage. She is also renowned for her teaching on Vajrayogini. At the request of the Sakya Trizin and other lineage holders, she began teaching in the West. At present she is the resident lama at the teaching centre Sakya Tsechen Thubten Ling in Canada.

H.H. JIGDAL DAGCHEN SAKYA RINPOCHE
H.H. Jigdal Dagchen Sakya Rinpoche was born in 1929. He is the forty-second generation holder of the Sakya Khon lineage. He is regarded as the incarnation of Ngor Ewam Luding Khenchen Jamyang Chokyi Nyima. As future successor to the Sakya throne, his early education included classical literature; Buddhist philosophy and the four classes of tantra. He was taught by Khenchen Sangye Rinchen, the abbot of the south monastery of Sakya, and Wangdu Tsering, secretary of the Sakya government. He also learned various ritual practices of the Sakya tradition from Ponlop Shakya of the north monastery. His first root lama was his father, Sakya Trichen Ngawang Thuptop Wangchuk, who gave him the unbroken Sakya Khon lineage transmission of the Vajrakila empowerments and the complete *Lamdre Tsogshe* transmission. In Kham he studied with thirty-five different lamas, including his two additional root lamas, Dzongsar Khyentse Rinpoche and Dilgo Khyentse Rinpoche. From them he received initiations and instruction on *Lamdre Lhoshe*, Sakya *Druptab Kuntu*, and the *Damngag Dzod*. He also completed various retreats. In 1960, he moved to the USA where he founded the Sakya Monastery from where he oversees a group of Sakya teaching centres.

H.H. SAKYA TRIZIN
H.H. Sakya Trizin was born in Tsedong, Southern Tibet in 1945. He is descended from the Khon royal family, one of the most ancient Tibetan spiritual families, and is the forty-first in an

unbroken lineage of lamas that stretches back to 1073 AD. He is the head of the Sakya tradition, and the title 'Sakya Trizin' means 'Holder of the Throne of Sakya'. He became the head of the Sakya at the age of seven upon the death of his father, and has received an intensive training in the study and practices of the Sakya tradition. Whilst still a child, he completed a seven-month retreat. Amongst his main teachers were: Jamyang Khyentse Chokyi Lodro, Ngawang Lodro Shenpen Nyingpo, Chogye Trichen Rinpoche, and Khenpo Appey Rinpoche. In 1959, at the age of fourteen, he left Tibet during the Chinese military takeover and went to India. He then studied with H.E Chogye Trichen Rinpoche, who instructed him on the Rime collections, the *Gyude Kundu* (*Collection of Tantras*), and the *Lamdre*. As well as holding the three main Sakya lineages of Sakya, Tsar and Ngor, H.H. Sakya Trizin holds the complete teachings of both the Iron Bridge and Great Perfection lineages of Nyingma, given by Drupchen Rinpoche and Jamyang Khyentse Rinpoche respectively. He is also holder of the *Lamdre* teachings, which cover the Hinayana, Mahayana and Mantrayana paths. He has founded numerous monasteries throughout India and East Asia, and established his seat in exile at Rajpur, U.P., India, near to which he founded Sakya College, the school of higher philosophical studies where training is given in logic, philosophy and psychology. He is fluent in English, and since 1974 he has made several world tours teaching in Europe, the USA and Southeast Asia.

KHENPO APPEY RINPOCHE

Khenpo Appey Rinpoche was born in the Kutse district near Dege, in Kham, Tibet. He studied mainly at Dzongsar monastery, and his main teachers were Dzongsar Khyentse Rinpoche and the Dzongsar seminary khenpo, Dragyab Lodro. He left Tibet in the 1950s and worked for a brief time at the Namgyal Institute of Tibetology, Sikkim. He was then appointed tutor to H.H. Sakya Trizin, and later, at the latter's urging, founded the Sakya College. After retirement from his duties as head of the Sakya College he spent long periods in retreat at Pharphing, Nepal, and has also taught extensively in Southeast Asia.

KHENPO MIGMAR TSERING

Khenpo Migmar Tsering was born in 1956 in Dopta Tayling, Central Tibet. He left Tibet with his family in 1959 following the Chinese occupation. He received elementary education at a Tibetan primary school in exile in South India. In 1970 he joined the Tibetan Institute at Sarnath, where he studied Sutrayana Buddhist philosophy, principally under the late Khenpo Rinchen, together with Sanskrit, English and history. In 1972 he joined the Sakya College where he studied all the aspects of Hinayana, Mahayana and Vajrayana under Khenpo Appey Rinpoche. In 1982 he received the Lobpon degree (equivalent to M.A.) from Sakya College. He served for a while as a translator in the Translation Bureau of the Library of Tibetan Works and Archives, Dharamsala. From 1983 to 1989 he taught at the Central Institute of Higher Tibetan Studies at Sarnath as a lecturer in Sakya philosophy. Whilst in those posts he continued his studies, receiving transmission such as the *Lamdre* from H.E. Sakya Trizin, Chogye Trichen Rinpoche and Luding Khen Rinpoche. In August 1989 he was appointed head of the Sakya College, Rajpur, and was enthroned as its abbot.

LAMA MIGMAR TSETEN

Lama Migmar Tseten was born in 1955 in Gyangtse, Central Tibet. He left Tibet with his family in 1959 following the Chinese occupation. He received elementary education at a Tibetan primary school in exile in

India, then in 1970 he joined the Tibetan Institute at Sarnath, where he studied Sutrayana Buddhist philosophy, principally under the late Khenpo Rinchen, together with Sanskrit, English and history. In 1980 he received the acarya degree and was appointed director of the Sakya Centre and the Sakya Institute in 1981. Whilst serving as director he continued his studies, receiving transmissions such as the *Lamdre* from H.H.Sakya Trizin, H.E. Chogye Trichen Rinpoche and H.E. Luding Khen Rinpoche. In 1989 he became the teacher at the Sakya Chokhor Yangtse, the US seat of H.H Sakya Trizin in Massachusetts, USA.

LAMA THARTSE KUNGA

Thartse Zhabdrung Kunga Rinpoche was born into the family of Shukapa which has close links to the Thartse Labrang of Ngor. He was the younger brother of the late Ngor Thartse Khenpo Sonam Gyatso (1933–1987). He received training as a "candidate" (zhab-drung) to the Ngor abbacy. He came to the U.S. in 1962, and in 1971 he established the Ewam Choden Tibetan Buddhist Center in Kensington, California. He has several publications, including translation collaborations.

LAMA THUBTEN CHOEDAK

Lama Thubten Choedak was born in 1954 in northern Tibet. He is one of the main disciples of H.E. Chogye Trichen Rinpoche. After eight years of monastic training he completed three and a half years solitary meditation retreat on the *Lamdre* and Hevajra practices of the Sakya tradition in Lumbini, the birth-place of Buddha. He has served as a translator for many prominent teachers from all the four traditions including H.H. Ling Rinpoche, the late senior tutor to H.H. the Dalai Lama. He has taught in various Buddhist centres, temples, universities and colleges in Malaysia, Singapore, New Zealand and Australia. He has also graduated from the Australian National University in Canberra and has written a thesis on the origin of the *Lamdre* tradition in India. Recently he established the Drogmi Tibetan Translation Services and has begun a major project to undertake the translation of selected *Lamdre* works.

T.G. DHONGTHOG RINPOCHE

T.G. Dhongthog Rinpoche is one of the prominent Sakya scholars of his generation. He was born in the Trehor district of Kham, and was recognised when young to be the reincarnation of the Dhongthog Tulku. He left Tibet in the 1950s and lived for about twenty years in India, mainly in New Delhi, before travelling to Seattle, USA. Whilst in India he worked as librarian at Tibet House. In recent years he has founded a small institute of Sakya studies and practices in north Seattle, the Sapan Institute. He studied under a great many Sakya, Nyingma and Rime lamas, including Dzongsar Khyentse, Khangsar Dampa Rinpoche, and H.H. Dudjom Rinpoche. He is a noted poet and grammarian and has numerous publications to his credit including works of history, lexicography, and doctrine. His most recent major work was the biography of Gaton Ngawang Legpa which he wrote in collaboration with Dezhung Rinpoche.

<u>GELUG</u>

Kyabje Yongdzin Ling Rinpoche

Kyabje Yongdzin Trijang Rinpoche

Scholastic Biographies

ACHOK TULKU

Achok Rinpoche Lobsang Thubten Khenrab Gyatso was born in 1944 in the Choktse region of Amdo. At the age of three he was identified by the Panchen Lama as the reincarnation of the head lama of the monastery Achok Tsenyi Gonpa; ie., as the fourth Achok Tulku. He joined this monastery at the age of five and stayed there until aged thirteen under the tutelage of Yongdzin Chinpa Gyatso and Gangwa Rinpoche, and was given the ordained name of Lobsang Thubten Khenrab Gyatso. During this time he was required to perform the functions of a high lama, such as bestowing blessings, performing divinations and rites for the dead, etc. In 1957 he joined Ganden Shartse monastery near Lhasa, but was soon forced to leave Tibet following the civil troubles due to the Chinese occupation. He went to the monastic refugee camp at Buxador, Bengal, and for the next ten years continued his study of the five great subjects – Logic, Prajnaparamita, Madhyamaka, Abhidharma and Vinaya, leaving the camp in 1969 to study for three years at Varanasi. After a brief period at the newly reestablished Ganden Shartse monastery in South India he was appointed abbot of the recently reestablished Tashikyil monastery near Dehra Dun in 1973. In 1977 he resigned the post of abbot and took the Lharampa Geshe degree. After this he began to study English, and started working at the Library of Tibetan Works and Archives on its catalogue, where he now remains. During this period he also began work on a thesis on the logic text *Pramanavarttika (Tshad ma rnam 'grel)* by Dharmakirti. In 1980 he visited the University of Vienna in Austria.

DAGPO RINPOCHE

Dagpo Rinpoche, also know as Bamcho Rinpoche, was born in 1932 in the Kongpo region south east of Lhasa. Having been recognised as the reincarnation of the previous Dagpo Lama, Jamphel Lhundrup, by the Thirteenth Dalai Lama, he entered the Bamcho monastery in the nearby region of Dagpo where he began initial studies of calligraphy, reading, and various rituals. When aged thirteen he moved to the monastery of Dagpo Shedrupling and began the study of the five great subjects – Logic and the texts of Prajnaparamita, Madhyamaka, Abhidharma and Vinaya – and tantra; he made special study of *Lamrim*, in which this monastery was especially strong. After thirteen years he left to complete his studies at Drepung Gomang monastery, principally under Khenzur Ngawang Nyima, having in all some thirty-four teachers including Phabongkha Rinpoche, Trijang Rinpoche, Ling Rinpoche and the Dalai Lama. He was able to undertake several retreats and additionally studied astrology, grammar, poetry and history. He remained at Drepung Gomang until 1959, when he left Tibet due to the Chinese occupation. He arrived in France in 1960 and settled there, teaching at the INLCO university and writing, in collaboration, several books on Tibet and Buddhism. In 1978 he founded the Centre Boudhiste Tibetain Guepele Tchantchoup Ling in France and at present he teaches there and at other Buddhist teaching centres in France, Italy, Switzerland, Holland, Belgium, Germany, Singapore and Indonesia. He often returns to India to meet his spiritual masters and to teach.

DAGYAB LODEN SHERAB

Dagyab Loden Sherab, the ninth Dagyab throneholder, was born in Menya in Amdo in 1939. He was recognised as the reincarnation of the previous Dagyab Rinpoche at an early age, and began basic reading, writing and memorisation in 1946, studying at the Ma Gon and Bu Gon monasteries in Dagyab province. In 1955 he began studies at Drepung monastery near Lhasa, studies which were interrupted when he was forced to leave Tibet owing to the Chinese occupation. In exile in India, he continued to study until 1964 when he obtained the Lharampa Geshe degree. Studying principally under Tsonsang Tulku, Pema Gyaltsen Rinpoche (then the abbot of Loseling monastery), and Nyima Gyaltsen Rinpoche (then abbot of Shagkor college of Loseling), he covered the five great subjects of Logic, Prajnaparamita, Madhyamaka, Abhidharma and Vinaya. He later took up residence in West Germany, where he is presently a member of the University of Bonn Central Asian Seminar. He serves as spiritual guide to the Chodzong Buddhist centre, and travels extensively around Germany and to other countries, including occasionally India and Tibet, to teach. He is the author of a number of books, articles and translations, including *Buddhism in the West* and several important works on art and iconography, and is fluent in German and English.

DENMA LOCHO RINPOCHE

Locho Rinpoche was born in 1927 in the Nangchen district of northernwestern Kham. He was recognised at the age of four as the reincarnation of a famous scholar, Geshe Lobsang

Choyin, who was active in Mongolia and Kham and had four times given a transmission of the entire *Kangyur*. He was installed as head of the Sekar monastery where his predecessor had spent his last years. When aged twelve Locho Rinpoche departed for Drepung Loseling monastery near Lhasa. He began the curriculum of detailed study of the five great subjects – Logic, Prajnaparamita, Madhyamaka, Abhidharma and Vinaya – studying under Geshe Tongpon Rinpoche amongst others. At the age of twenty-six he took the degree of Lharampa Geshe, gaining first place. Following this he joined Gyume monastery, in order to further study tantra, remaining there for five years until forced to leave Tibet to escape the Chinese occupation. During this time he served a period as Gekyo (disciplinarian) of the monastery. In exile in India he first stayed at a monastery near Varanasi, engaged in recitation of the Vinaya, and then between 1963 and 1965 he spent two years in research work at Calcutta University. The following six years he spent as principal of the school of Buddhist philosophy at Leh in Ladakh. In 1972 he moved to Dharamsala, North India, staying in semi-retirement, and during 1977 – 78 acted as a visiting scholar at the University of Virginia. He was appointed abbot of Namgyal monastery in Dharamsala in 1985, and in 1986 undertook a teaching tour of various Western countries, also visiting Korea in 1988. He is the author (together with Lati Rinpoche) of *Meditative states in Tibetan Buddhism*.

DOBOOM TULKU

Lobsang Tenzin Doboom Tulku was born in a nomad family at Gasheu Do in Kham in 1941. He was recognised as the Doboom Tulku at the age of three, and was taken care of at the residence of his predecessor, where he undertook preliminary studies until the age of eleven, when he moved to Dhargye monastery and began the study of Logic. He soon transferred to Drepung Loseling monastery near Lhasa, where for the next six years he studied the earlier part of the curriculum leading to the qualification of geshe – detailed analysis of Logic, Prajnaparamita, Madhyamaka, Abhidharma and Vinaya. In 1959 he was forced to leave the monastery and Tibet for exile in India following the Chinese occupation of Tibet. He spent some nine years at the monastic refugee camp at Buxador in Bengal, continuing his education. For three years from 1969 he attended Varanasi University and attained the acarya degree. Following this he was appointed librarian at Tibet House in New Delhi. He edited some forty-seven volumes of the works of Bodong Chogle Namgyal at this time. In 1973 he became a librarian at the newly established Library of Tibetan Works and Archives in Dharamsala, responsible for cataloguing the Tibetan material and also giving some discourses. In 1976 he became assistant secretary at the Private Office of H.H. the Dalai Lama. At the present time he is director of Tibet House, Delhi.

GELONG RINCHEN KONCHOG

Gelong Rinchen Konchog was born in 1919 in Gang, near Lhasa, Tibet. From the ages of six to sixteen he studied at Drepung Loseling monastery, also near Lhasa. In 1925 he became a member of the great prayer festival committee, and at the same time became a member of the Drepung monk police association. He trained for six years to become a fully qualified monk policeman (rDob rDob).

GESHE DAMCHO YONTEN

Geshe Damcho Yonten was born in 1931. He became a monk at the age of six, joining the Gya Khangtsog (house) of Drepung Loseling monastery near Lhasa. After elementary studies, he studied in depth the major subjects of Logic, Prajnaparamita, Madhyamaka, Abhidharma and Vinaya. He was obliged to leave Tibet in 1959 due to the Chinese occupation, fleeing first to Bhutan, then to Assam, finally reaching the Tibetan refugee camp at Buxador in Bengal. From there he moved to Ladakh, studying Abhidharma with Khenzur Jampa Tsampel at Ridzong monastery. Whilst in Ladakh, he served as abbot of Samten Ling monastery for four years. He returned to central India in 1966, and in 1970 gained the Lharampa Geshe degree. Having met many Western people, he was invited to Europe in 1976, and in July 1978 was a founder of the Lam Rim Buddhist Centre in Wales, where he remains resident teacher.

GESHE GEDUN LODRO

The late Geshe Gedun Lodro was born in Lhasa in 1924. He entered Drepung Gomang monastery, studying the five great subjects of Logic, Prajnaparamita, Madhyamaka, Abhidharma and Vinaya and eventually teaching students of his own. He fled Tibet in 1959, and attained his Lharampa Geshe degree in exile in India in 1961. In 1969 he began lecturing at Hamburg University, a post he held until his death in 1979. He was a visiting professor at the University of Virginia from January to August 1979.

GESHE JAMPA GYATSO

Geshe Jampa Gyatso was born in the Dam region of central Tibet on 15 December 1931. Having met Purchog Jamgon Rinpoche of Sera monastery and received from him the elementary vows and the name Jampa Gyatso when aged seven, he left home at thirteen and joined Sera Je monastery near Lhasa. At the age of sixteen he began intensive study of the five great subjects – Logic, Prajnaparamita, Madhyamaka, Abhidharma and Vinaya. He was forced to flee Tibet in 1959 following the Chinese occupation, and then spent two years in hospital in Rajastan. In 1961 he resumed his studies at the temporary monastic refugee camp at Buxador, Bengal. He began the acarya course at the Sanskrit University, Varanasi in 1967, receiving the acarya degree in 1970. During 1971 he attended Gyume monastery, studying tantra. He received his Lharampa Geshe degree in 1972, returning after the examination to Gyume monastery, and was soon asked to take part in a research programme at the Institute for Higher Tibetan Studies in Varanasi, investigating the interpretation of subjects dealt with by the Prajnaparamita sutras from the viewpoints of various Buddhist tenets. Part of 1975 he spent at Gyume monastery, where he served as Gekyo (disciplinarian) and was awarded the Ngagrampa Geshe degree. In 1976 he was invited to Kopan monastery in Nepal to teach the *Abhidharmakosha* to some thirty Western monks and nuns; he stayed there for four years, until he was requested to become resident teacher of the Istituto Lama Tzong Khapa, where he has been since 1980.

GESHE JAMPA LODRO

Geshe Jampa Lodro Dahortsang was born in Lhasa on 12 February 1927. He learnt from his grandfather how to read and recite scripture. At the age of seven he was able to attend school in Lhasa, where he learnt to write. At

eight years old he joined Sera Je monastery, near Lhasa, and began study of Logic, Prajnaparamita, Madhyamaka, Abhidharma and Vinaya. He remained at Sera until forced to flee Tibet with many of his fellow monks in 1959 following the Chinese occupation. He fled at first to Dalhousie in North India, and was later able to sit and attain the Lharampa Geshe degree. He studied mainly under Khenzur Lobsang Wangchuk. He went on to join Gyume monastery for further study of tantra, where he became Gekyo (disciplinarian). He left for Switzerland in 1970, where he worked for seven years in a factory. After this he was invited to teach at the Yiga Chozin Buddhist teaching centre, and he continues to teach there now.

GESHE JAMPA TEKCHOK

At the age of eight Geshe Jampa Tekchok entered Sera Je monastery near Lhasa, and for the next twenty-one years he studied the monastic curriculum of Logic and Prajnaparamita, Madhyamaka, Abhidharma and Vinaya texts. In addition to his studies he gained students of his own. After the Chinese invasion he served as one of the principal teachers at the Buxador Tibetan monastic refugee camp in West Bengal, India. He later studied at the Sanskrit University in Varanasi and gained the acarya degree; after that he spent he spent seven years as lecturer at the Institute for Higher Tibetan Studies in Sarnath. He spent 1979 to 1982 at the Manjushri Institute in Cumbria, England as director of the 'Geshe Studies' programme, moving from there to Nalanda monastery, France, where he serves as abbot.

GESHE KHENRAB GAJANG

Geshe Khenrab Tobgyal Gajang was born in 1928 in Kham. He joined Ganden Jangtse monastery near Lhasa, studying the five great subjects of Logic, Prajnaparamita, Madhyamaka, Abhidharma and Vinaya. Having fled Tibet in 1959 to escape the Chinese occupation he continued his studies in exile in India, attaining the degree of geshe. In 1978 he founded the Temple Bouddhiste Tibetain in Quebec, Canada, where he remains as teacher and director.

GESHE KONCHOK TSEWANG

Geshe Konchok Tsewang was born in Tibet in 1926. As a youth he joined Sedru monastery in Kham, and later moved to Drepung Loseling monastery near Lhasa where he embarked on the extensive course of study for the qualification of geshe, involving study of Logic, Prajnaparamita, Madhyamaka, Abhidharma and Vinaya. Following the exodus resulting from the Chinese occupation of Tibet in 1959, he spent some years at the monastic refugee camp in Buxador, West Bengal where he was able to complete his studies. Here he attained the Lharampa Geshe degree. Following this he spent three years at the Institute of Higher Tibetan Studies at Varanasi, and then eleven years at the Gyuto monastery in Assam, where he was able to further study tantra. In 1982 he joined the Manjushri Institute in Cumbria, England where he became spiritual director of Buddhist studies. In 1991 he retired, to Gyuto monastery in Assam.

GESHE LHUNDRUP SOPA

Lhundrup Sopa was born in the region of Tsang in 1923. He entered the nearby Ganden Chokor monastery in 1932, beginning the study of logic and debate in 1936. He moved to Sera Je monastery near Lhasa in 1941, where he studied in depth the subjects of Prajnaparamita, Madhyamaka, Abhidharma and Vinaya. At the same time he also had many students of his own. He fled Tibet in 1959 following the Chinese occupation, and stayed until 1962 in a refugee camp at Buxador in Bengal. In 1962 he was awarded the Lharampa Geshe degree, the best of his year. Later that year he moved to America. He was appointed tutor to three young lamas at Geshe Ngawang Wangyal's monastery in New Jersey, and became president of this monastery. Since the late 1960s he has been a professor of Tibetan Buddhist Studies at the University of Wisconsin, and has spent many between-term breaks teaching in Europe. In 1975 he founded the Deer Park Buddhist Center in the USA., and remains there to the present day as main teacher and abbot of Ewam monastery. He has written a number of authoritative articles and books on Mahayana Buddhism, including *Practice and Theory of Tibetan Buddhism* in collaboration with Prof Jeffrey Hopkins, and *Wheel of Time: The Kalacakra in Context.*

GESHE LOBSANG DOGA

Geshe Lobsang Dorje Doga was born in the village of Kanze, in the region of Kham, in July 1935. In 1942 he joined Kanze monastery, a monastery of the Gelugpa tradition with some 3 000 monks. He remained there for ten years, before entering Sera Je monastery near Lhasa and taking ordination as a novice monk. There he studied principally under Geshe Ngawang Dhargyey, covering the subjects of Logic, Prajnaparamita and Madhyamaka.

He was obliged to flee Tibet in 1959 following the Chinese occupation, and he spent the years until 1967 at Buxador refugee camp studying Abhidharma and Vinaya under the ex-abbot of Gyume monastery, Khensur Urgyen Tseten. In 1967 he was selected to be sent to study Sanskrit at Varanasi University, from which he was awarded the acarya degree in 1976. The next two years were spent at the reestablished Sera Je monastery in South India; then in 1978 he began three years as teacher at the Kopan monastery in Nepal. In March 1982 he was awarded the Lharampa Geshe degree, and following this he spent 1983 touring Australia teaching at Buddhist teaching centres of the FPMT organisation. In 1984 he joined the Tara Institute in Melbourne as its resident teacher, where he remains today.

GESHE LOBSANG DONYO

Geshe Lobsang Donyo was born in the region of Tsang, central Tibet. As a youngster he joined Lhartse monastery in Tsang, and later moved to Sera Je monastery near Lhasa. He left Tibet following the Chinese occupation, and in exile in India gained an acarya degree from the Sanskrit University at Varanasi. After this he went back to Sera Je – reestablished in South India – and gained his geshe degree. He then began further study of tantra at Gyume monastery, serving a period as Gekyo (disciplinarian). In 1979 he took the position of resident teacher at the Deer Park Buddhist Center in Wisconsin, USA.

GESHE LOBSANG GYATSO

Geshe Lobsang Gyatso was born in 1932 in the Kongrak region of Kham. From the age of eight he began receiving instruction in Buddhism, and when aged twelve he entered the Dhondup Ling monastery in Kham where he pursued elementary studies of memorisation, writing etc. At the age of fifteen he joined Sera Je monastery near Lhasa, where for the next twelve years he studied in depth the five great subjects of Logic, Prajnaparamita, Madhyamaka, Abhidharma and Vinaya. In 1959 he fled to exile in India with many of his compatriots, following the occupation of Tibet by China. He spent eight years at the monastic refugee camp at Buxador in Bengal, where he was able to continue his studies in preparation for the geshe examination. In 1968 he undertook a three-year course of study at the Institute for Higher Tibetan Studies in Varanasi, receiving the acarya degree. Following this he took the geshe examination, gaining the first position Lharampa degree. In 1970 he entered Gyuto monastery in order to pursue detailed study of tantra. During this time he served a period as Gekyo (disciplinarian) of the monastery. He remained there for ten years, and was able to study all the rituals, methods of mandala construction and stages of the tantras of Guhyasamaja, Heruka, Yamantaka etc. He was the resident teacher at Vajrapani Institute in California from 1981 to 1984. At present he lives and teaches at Pacific Grove, California.

GESHE LOBSANG TENGYE

After twenty-five years of study at Sera Je monastery both in Tibet and in exile in India, Lobsang Tengye qualified as a geshe after examinations in the five main subjects – Logic, Prajnaparamita, Madhyamaka, Abhidharma and Vinaya. In 1969 on the instruction of the Dalai Lama he was sent to Thailand for eight years to study on a scholarship awarded by the Thai government. Following that he went to France in June 1978, staying first for two years at the Linhson Vietnamese Monastery in Paris, and then in 1980 joining the Institute Vajra Yogini Buddhist teaching centre as resident teacher.

GESHE LOBSANG THARCHIN

Geshe Lobsang Tharchin was born in Lhasa in 1921. He joined Sera Me monastery in 1929, and began study of elementary subjects and the more profound course leading to the geshe degree – comprising detailed study of Logic, Prajnaparamita, Abhidharma, Madhyamaka, and Vinaya. He gained the Lharampa Geshe degree in 1953, in the first rank. Following this he pursued further study of tantra at Gyume monastery until 1959, when he was obliged to flee Tibet following the Chinese occupation. During the years 1959 – 1970 he served on the textbook committee of the Tibetan Government in Exile, in India, publishing books for use in the Tibetan schools established in exile. At the same time he served in the administration of Gyume monastery following its reestablishment in India, and spent some time teaching in the Tibetan schools. In 1972 he was invited to the USA where he began to lecture on Buddhism and undertook various translation projects. From 1974 he has served as the abbot of the Rashi Gempil Ling Kalmuk Buddhist Temple in New Jersey. In 1975 he finished a course in English language at Georgetown University and also established the Mahayana Sutra and Tantra Centers in New Jersey and Washington DC. He was appointed a permanent director of the reestablished Sera Me monastery in South India in 1983. He has translated and written a number of books, including a translation of Vasubandhu's *Abhidharmakosha*, and was editor of *Medical Vocabulary* by B. Gould and Sir H. Richardson.

GESHE NGAWANG DHARGYEY

Geshe Ngawang Dhargyey was born in 1925. He joined the Dhargyey monastery in the Trehor region of Kham at the age of seven, and began elementary study. At sixteen he moved to Sera Je monastery near Lhasa, continuing his study of Logic, Prajnaparamita, Madhyamaka, Abhidharma and Vinaya. By the time he was nineteen he was teaching students of his own. When aged twenty-one he took full ordination, and soon after this was obliged to flee Tibet owing to the Chinese occupation, in 1959. He gained his Lharampa Geshe degree while still in the Buxador refugee camp in Bengal in India. He was requested by the Dalai Lama in 1971 to give traditional Tibetan instruction on Buddhism to Western students at the newly established Library of Tibetan Works and Archives in Dharamsala, North India, a position he retained until 1984. At that time the LTWA published a number of his books on Mahayana Buddhism, including *Tibetan Tradition of Mental Development, Anthology of Well Spoken Advice, Advice From a Spiritual Friend* (with Geshe Rabten), and *A Commentary to the Kalacakra Tantra*. He was appointed a visiting lecturer at the University of Washington in 1982, teaching for a semester on Tibetan iconography, and later that year toured Buddhist teaching centres in the USA, Canada, Europe, Australia and New Zealand, arriving back in India in 1983. He undertook a six-month tour of Australia in 1984, after which he took up residence in New Zealand, establishing the Dharghey Dharma Centre and taking a post as its resident teacher.

GESHE NGAWANG LEGDEN

Geshe Ngawang Legden was born in 1914, and at the age of seven joined a monastery of the Gelugpa tradition in the region of Kham. In 1933 he transferred to Sera Je monastery near Lhasa where he studied *Lamrim* and the five great subjects of Logic, Prajnaparamita, Madhyamaka, Abhidharma and Vinaya, gaining his Lharampa Geshe degree in 1957. He fled Tibet with many of his countrymen in 1959, going to Dalhousie in North India where he spent the next two years in retreat. In 1961 he began teaching at the temporary monastic refugee camp at Buxador, Bengal. Then between 1965 and 1973 he taught at the Nalanda Sanskrit University. He is one of the few people alive who hold the entire lineage of the sutra and tantra works of Lama Tsong Khapa. He was selected in 1975 as abbot of the reestablished Sera Je monastery in Mysore, South India. He spent 1980 to 1981 in Australia teaching at the Chenrezig Institute, Queensland.

GESHE NGAWANG NORNANG

Geshe Nornang was born in 1927. He joined Dagpo Shedup Ling monastery in 1936 and began to study the curriculum leading to the geshe qualification: Logic, Prajnaparamita, Madhyamaka, Abhidharma and Vinaya, under the guidance of Khenpo Lobsang Jignyen. He passed the geshe examination in 1958. In 1940 he was appointed Drungyig (secretary), dealing with the monastery's business affairs, a post he held until 1959. Since coming into exile he has been co-author of a book on language with Prof M Goldstein, *Modern Spoken Tibetan: Lhasa Dialect*, and collaborated on *Manual of Spoken Tibetan* and four volumes of *Spoken Tibetan Texts* with Chang and Sheft. He now teaches colloquial Tibetan at the University of Washington, Seattle.

GESHE NGAWANG WANGYAL

The late Geshe Ngawang Wangyal was born in Astrakhan, USSR, in 1901 of Kalmuck-Mongolian parents. At the age of six he joined a monastery, beginning his elementary studies, and by the age of eleven he began translating Tibetan texts into Mongolian. He studied under the guidance of Ngawang Lobsang Dorjieff, who advised him in 1922 to continue his training in Tibet. After travelling for one and a half years, Geshe Wangyal reached Lhasa and entered the nearby Drepung Gomang monastery. He continued detailed study of Logic, Prajnaparamita, Madhyamaka, Abhidharma and Vinaya, receiving his geshe degree in 1938. He spent the years 1935 to 1936 researching in Peking, China, comparing various editions of the *Kangyur* and *Tengyur*. In 1951 he left Tibet for India, moving on from there to the USA, where he arrived in February 1955. Upon arrival in America he taught at Columbia University in New York, and in 1958 founded the Lamaist Buddhist Monastery of America, Labsum Shedrub Ling (renamed the Tibetan Buddhist Learning Centre in 1986). He remained there as head teacher and director until his death in January 1983. In 1973 he founded the American Institute of Buddhist Studies, in Massachusetts. He translated and published several books on Mahayana Buddhism, including *The Door of Liberation*; *The Prince Who Became a Cuckoo*; and published posthumously, *The Jewelled Staircase*.

GESHE PALDEN DRAKPA

Geshe Palden Drakpa was born in Dagko, in the Trehor region of Kham in 1933. At the age of thirteen he joined Dagko monastery and began preliminary studies. At eighteen he entered Drepung Loseling monastery near Lhasa. He began detailed study of the five great subjects, beginning with Logic, Prajnaparamita, and Madhyamaka. He had to leave Tibet, following its occupation by the Chinese, in 1959, and stayed at the monastic refugee camp at Buxador, where he was able to continue his studies of Vinaya and Abhidharma. Between 1969 and 1973 he studied at the Central Institute for Higher Tibetan Studies at Varanasi, and gained the acarya degree. In 1975 he received the Lharampa Geshe degree. Whilst at Drepung monastery, which was reestablished in India, during the latter parts of his study and also after gaining his geshe degree he was a teacher of various Buddhist texts, Tibetan grammar and poetry. From 1978 to 1988 he was resident teacher and spiritual instructor at Tibet House in Delhi, during which time he attended various seminars and conferences in India and elsewhere, and was a visiting professor at Choglamsar Buddhist Institute. In 1986 he spent four months at the Central Institute of Tibetan Studies in Ladakh, and in 1988 three months as a full visiting professor at the University of Virginia, USA. At the request of the monastery, he returned to Drepung Loseling in 1988 to resume teaching there. He has written three books, *Enchanting Groves of Logical and Scriptural Citations* (an analysis of Vinaya); *Lamp Dispelling Mental Darkness* (a guide to daily Buddhist practice); and *Elegant Explanation of Ornamentation to Faith*, all in Tibetan.

GESHE PUNTSOK THINLEY
The late Geshe Puntsok Thinley was born in Northern Tibet in 1929. He joined Sera monastery near Lhasa in 1937 and began to study first the elementary subjects and then the more profound curriculum leading to the geshe degree – Logic, Prajnaparamita, Madhyamaka, Abhidharma and Vinaya. He took full ordination in 1949. Following the civil upheavals after the Chinese occupation he left Tibet in 1959, and continued his studies at the reestablished Sera Je monastery in South India. He became a Lharampa Geshe in 1979. He was invited to become a resident teacher at the Chenrezig Institute in Queensland, Australia in 1980, remaining there until his death in 1987.

GESHE RABTEN
The late Geshe Rabten was born in 1920. At an early age, he joined Sera Je monastery near Lhasa, studying and teaching there for some twenty years up to the time of his exile, together with many of his colleagues, in 1959. He trained in the normal curriculum of Logic, Prajnaparamita, Madhyamaka, Abhidharma and Vinaya leading to the geshe qualification. Upon completion of this study he was appointed as a personal assistant to the Dalai Lama. From 1969 onwards, Geshe Rabten counted among his students many Westerners, and in 1977 he founded the Tharpa Choling Centre for Higher Buddhist Studies (now called Rabten Choeling) in Switzerland. He remained there as spiritual director until his death in 1986. He is the author of a number of authoritative books on Mahayana Buddhism, including *The Essential Nectar* and *Treasury of Dharma* on *Lamrim* texts; *Advice From a Spiritual Friend* (with Geshe Ngawang Dhargyey); and *Echoes of Voidness* on the Heart Sutra.

GESHE SONAM GYALTSEN

Geshe Sonam Gyaltsen was born in 1926 near the Kongpo – Kham border. At the age of five he became a monk and began elementary studies at the local monastery. To pursue his studies further he transferred to Ganden Jangtse monastery near Lhasa when he was eighteen, remaining there until fleeing Tibet in 1959. In India at the reestablished Ganden Jangtse he completed his study of the five great subjects and obtained the highest Lharampa Geshe degree. Subsequently he entered the lower tantric college, Gyume monastery, where he obtained the Ngagrampa degree. He served a term as Gekyo (Disciplinarian) of Gyume monastery, before moving on to the Institute for Higher Tibetan Studies at Varanasi in order to take the acarya degree and a doctorate in Buddhist studies. In 1977 he was appointed tutor to Phara Tulku by Trijang Rinpoche and returned to Ganden, where he was able to teach many other students also. In 1980 he moved to France and taught at Guepele Tchantchoup Ling and other teaching centres in France and Italy until 1990 when he was appointed Umdze (leader of ritual) at Gyume monastery, and returned to India.

GESHE SONAM RINCHEN

Geshe Sonam Rinchen was born in 1933 in Dhargyey, in the Trehor region of Kham. Eager to be a monk, at the age of twelve he ran away to the nearby Dhargyey monastery, and persuaded his parents to let him stay there. He began preliminary studies, and was encouraged to continue with higher philosophical study. At the age of nineteen he joined Sera Je monastery near Lhasa, and embarked on the detailed study of Logic, Prajnaparamita and Madhyamaka texts. He was forced to flee Tibet for India in 1959 after the Chinese occupation, and in the Buxador monastic refugee camp in West Bengal was able to continue his study of Madhyamaka,

Vinaya and Abhidharma. He entered the Sanskrit University at Varanasi in 1967, gaining the degrees of shastri and acarya and remaining there until 1976. He then moved to the Library of Tibetan Works and Archives in Dharamsala, where he is currently a resident scholar, and regularly teaches extensive courses on Buddhist philosophy and meditation. In 1980 he passed the examination of Lharampa Geshe. At the end of 1982 he spent three months in Japan as a guest lecturer at Nagoya University and Kyoto University. In 1986 he undertook a five-month tour of Australia, teaching at various Buddhist teaching centres there.

GESHE TAMDIN GYATSO

Geshe Tamdin Gyatso was born in Drayab in the province of Kham around 1922. When aged eleven he joined a local monastery and began elementary studies. At nineteen he moved to Ganden Shartse monastery near Lhasa and started detailed study of the five great subjects of Logic, Prajnaparamita, Madhyamaka, Abhidharma and Vinaya. Whilst in Tibet he studied under Lobsang Puntsok, Lobsang Tsultrim and others, his studies being interrupted in 1959 when he fled into exile to escape the Chinese occupation. In India in 1976 he took the Lharampa Geshe degree, and following this he served as a teacher of Buddhism and Tibetan language in three Tibetan schools. He then spent seven years in Dharamsala, further studying sutra and tantra. In 1987 he was asked to join the Instituto Dharma on Minorca, Spain as the resident teacher; he remains there, occasionally visiting other Buddhist teaching centres in Spain and, in 1989, visiting England on a teaching tour.

GESHE THUBTEN DAWO

Geshe Thubten Dawo was born in the village of Galob in Eastern Tibet. At the age of nine he joined the nearby

Labcho Do monastery where he began elementary studies. When aged twenty-one he entered Sera Je monastery near Lhasa, where he began intensive study of the five great subjects of Logic, Prajnaparamita, Madhyamaka, Vinaya and Abhidharma. Following the Chinese invasion of Tibet he fled to India in 1959, continuing his studies at the monastic refugee camp at Buxador, West Bengal, and at Sera Je monastery after its reestablishment in exile in South India. He joined the Sanskrit University in 1973, gaining the acarya degree in 1977. By 1979 he had also received the Lharampa Geshe degree. During the 1980s he taught at various Tibetan Buddhist teaching centres in Australia.

GESHE THUBTEN GYATSO
Geshe Thubten Gyatso was born on 1 June 1925 at the town of Gome in the province of Amdo. In 1931 he joined Ganden Tashi Dorje Ling monastery, and in the following years studied also at Labrang Tashikyil, becoming fully ordained in 1945 at the Amdo Gome Choge monastery, under the guidance of Kashar Rinpoche. He remained there until 1959, teaching Buddhist philosophy. Upon his escape from the Chinese occupation of Tibet in 1959 he stayed at the monastic refugee camp in Buxador, Bengal in India until 1968, where he was able to continue his study of the five great subjects of Logic, Prajnaparamita, Madhyamaka, Abhidharma and Vinaya. He then moved to the reestablished Drepung Gomang monastery in South India. There he taught, and also became general manager and treasurer of Gomang. In 1980 he left for the Tibetan Buddhist Learning Centre in New Jersey, USA, where he remains as a teacher. He also acts occasionally as a visiting professor at the University of Virginia.

GESHE THUBTEN LODEN
Geshe Thubten Loden was born around 1925. He became a monk in 1931. In 1939 he joined the Sera Je monastery near Lhasa, beginning his study of the five great subjects of Logic, Prajnaparamita, Madhyamaka, Abhidharma and Vinaya. He left Tibet in 1959 due to civil turmoil following the Chinese occupation, and went on to study at the Sanskrit University in Varanasi where he gained the acarya degree. It was at this time that he also obtained his geshe degree. Following that he held several senior positions at the reestablished Sera monastery in South India. He began to work as the principal teacher at the Chenrezig Institute Buddhist teaching centre in Queensland, Australia in 1976, remaining until 1979. In 1980 he established his own Buddhist teaching centre in Melbourne, the Tibetan Buddhist Society.

GESHE THUBTEN NGAWANG
Geshe Thubten Ngawang was born on 10 March 1931 in the To region of Western Tibet. He became a monk at the age of eleven, joining Sera Je monastery. Soon after this he went to the Dhargyey monastery in Kham, eastern Tibet to study Tsong Khapa's *Lamrim*, Shantideva's *Bodhisattvacaryavatara* and various other works under the guidance of Jampa Khedrup Rinpoche. He also began there the curriculum leading to the geshe qualification – study of

Logic, Prajnaparamita, Madhyamaka, Abhidharma and Vinaya, continuing this after rejoining Sera monastery at the age of twenty-five. Fleeing Tibet with a great many of his fellow monks in 1959, he stayed for ten years at the Buxador refugee camp in Bengal where he continued his studies. He transferred to Sera Je monastery upon its reestablishment in South India. In 1979 he gained the Lharampa Geshe degree, and soon after this was requested to become resident teacher at the Tibetisches Zentrum in Hamburg, Germany, where he has remained ever since.

GESHE THUBTEN THINLEY

Geshe Thubten Thinley was born in Trehor, Kham in 1933. Between the ages of nine and fifteen he studied elementary subjects at a nearby monasery. He joined Sera Je monastery near Lhasa at the age of fifteen and began the study of the five great subjects of Logic, Prajnaparamita, Madhyamaka, Vinaya and Abhidharma. He left Tibet for exile in India in 1959 following the Chineses occupation of Tibet. He continued his studies and at the age of thirty-eight, gained a first division acarya degree from Varanasi University. He then spent twelve years in retreat at Dharamsala, North India, concentrating on Lamrim practices. In 1983 he became a teacher at the teaching centres Tashi Rabten in Austria and Rabten Choeling in Switzerland. He is also the founder of Rabten Champa Ling in Munich, Germany.

GESHE THUPTEN JINPA

Geshe Thupten Jinpa was born in Dzongkar, Tibet in 1958. He received his elementary education at the Central School for Tibetans in Simla, India. At the age of eleven he joined Dzongkar Chode Monastery, South India, where he began his initial monastic training. In 1978, he joined Shartse College at Ganden Monastic University for higher studies. At Ganden he studied Buddhist logic, epistemology, psychology, phenomenology, Madhayamaka ontology, and religion, culminating in his obtainment of the Lharam Geshe degree in 1989. Lharam is equivalent in the Tibetan monastic tradition to a Doctor of Divinity. Whilst still a student he also taught at Shartse College. Since 1986 he has been the principal translator to H.H. the Dalai Lama on philosophy, religion and science, and has in that capacity travelled extensively to various Western countries. In 1989 he entered Cambridge University, UK, to study Western philosophy, and received his honours degree in 1992. He has translated and edited *Union of Bliss and Emptiness* and *Path to Bliss: Guide to the stages of Meditation*, both by H.H. the Dalai Lama, published by Snow Lion, USA. His published works also include papers on topics such as the Buddhist perspective on the nature of philosophy, a comparative study of Nietzschean perspectivism and the philosophy of emptiness, and the role of subjectivity in Tibetan Vajrayana art. He is also a co-author of *Fluent Tibetan*, the forthcoming Tibetan language textbook of the University of Virginia, Charlottesville, to be published by Snow Lion, USA.

GESHE TSULTRIM GYALTSEN

Geshe Tsultrim Gyaltsen was born in Chamdo in Kham. He joined Ganden Shartse monastery near Lhasa where he studied the five great subjects of Logic, Prajnaparamita, Madhyamaka, Abhidharma and Vinaya. He gained the degree of Lharampa Geshe and then joined Gyuto monastery, also near Lhasa. After leaving Tibet for exile, he spent many years teaching Tibetan grammar, history and Buddhism to Tibetan students in England. He has also taught at the University of California, Santa Barbara and the University of Oriental Studies, Los Angeles. In 1979 he founded the Thubten Dhargye Ling Buddhist teaching centre in Los Angeles, where he remains as resident teacher. He has also founded the Thubten Rinchen Ling Tibetan Buddhist Centre in Houston, Texas; the Gaden Thubten Ling Tibetan Buddhist Centre in Portsmouth, England; and the Mahakaruna Tibetan Buddhist Centre in Fairbanks, Alaska. He gives lectures and seminars on Buddhism and Tibetan culture in Canada, Mexico and various other countries. He has had one book published in the USA, *Keys to Great Enlightenment*.

GESHE YESHE WANGCHUG

Geshe Yeshe Wangchug was born in Kongpo, Tibet. He studied for fourteen years at Sera Me monastery near Lhasa. His studies were not completed, due to the Chinese occupation in 1959. At present he works as a staff member at the Lhasa Academy of Social Sciences.

GESHE YONTEN GYATSO

Geshe Yonten Gyatso was born in 1933 in the province of Amdo. When he was seven years old he began elementary study at the local monastery of Lhamo Dechen, moving on to Labrang Tashikyil monastery when he was sixteen. Here he was the foremost student in his class, excelling especially in the study of Pramana. When aged twenty-four he moved to the Drepung Gomang monastery near Lhasa where he continued his study of the five great subjects – Logic, Prajnaparamita, Madhyamaka, Abhidharma and Vinaya – principally under Khenzur Ngawang Nyima. Having fled Tibet with many of his fellow monks, he became a teacher in the monastic Tibetan refugee camp at Buxador in Bengal. He was invited to France in 1964, where he still resides, performing research and teaching at Guepele Tchantchoup Ling and at other teaching centres in France. He is the author of numerous works on Tibetan political and religious history and on Buddhist philosophy.

GOMO TULKU

The late Gomo Tulku was recognised at an early age as the reincarnation of his predecessor, and he entered Sera Je monastery near Lhasa. There he studied the curriculum of Logic, Prajnaparamita, Madhyamaka, Abhidharma, Vinaya, and was able to receive instruction on all aspects of the Gelugpa tradition. Having attained the degree of Lharampa Geshe, he spent some time at Gyume monastery near Lhasa pursuing further study of tantra. He went into exile in India after the occupation of Tibet by the Chinese. He settled and began teaching at Mussoorie, in North India. He gave up his monastic robes and is now married. He has undertaken some teaching tours abroad, particularly to Switzerland.

GONSAR RINPOCHE

Gonsar Rinpoche Tenzin Khedup Jigme Namgyal was born to an aristocratic family in Lhasa in 1949. When aged three he was recognised by the Dalai Lama as the reincarnation of a lama of Sera monastery, Gonsar Tulku Lobsang Dondup Rabgye, who was in turn an incarnation of Yongdzin Ngawang Dondup, lineage holder of the Tamdin tradition and tutor to the Seventh Dalai Lama. At the age of six Gonsar Rinpoche joined Sera Je monastery, near Lhasa, and began to study under the guidance of the late Geshe Rabten. In 1959, due to the civil unrest following the Chinese occupation, he accompanied Geshe Rabten on his flight to India, staying first at the Buxador refugee camp in Bengal, then moving to Dharamsala, where the Dalai Lama had established his seat. He accompanied Geshe Rabten to Switzerland in 1974, to reside at the Tharpa Choling monastery (re-named Rabten Choeling). He is now abbot of that monastery and director of its accompanying teaching centre. He has collaborated in the translation of many books on Mahayana Buddhism.

GUNGBAR CHETSHANG RINPOCHE

Gungbar Chetshang Rinpoche Thubten Ngodrub Thinley Rabgye was born in the village of Tsiphu in the Derge region of Kham in 1942. He is the elder of two incarnate lamas of the Gungbar Labrang and was recognised at the age of four. He entered the Gungbar Labrang (or residence) at Barda monastery and began to study elementary subjects under the previous incarnation of the present (younger) Gungbar Chungtshang. In 1957 he joined Drepung Loseling monastery near Lhasa, where he began the study of logic. Following the Chinese occupation of Tibet in 1959 he escaped to India, staying for the next ten years in the monastic refugee camp at Buxador in Bengal. There he was able to continue study of the five great subjects – Logic, Prajnaparamita, Madhyamaka, Abhidharma and Vinaya – taking the Lharampa Geshe examination in 1979. In 1980 he entered Gyuto monastery for further study of tantra, subsequently returning to Drepung. He undertook a world tour during 1988–89, heading a group giving public performances of various rituals.

GYALTZUR RINPOCHE

Lobsang Palden Gyaltzur Rinpoche was born in the Gyalthang region of Kham on 30 January 1938. Recognised as a reincarnated lama at a young age, he stayed at the nearby Gyalthang monastery as a boy, moving to Drepung monastery near Lhasa in 1953. He remained there studying the monastic curriculum of Logic, Prajnaparamita and Madhyamaka, principally under the two Drepung-Loseling scholars Pema Gyaltsen and Nyima Gyaltsen, until 1959 when he and many of his fellow monks and countrymen were forced to flee Tibet due to the Chinese occupation. After arriving in exile in India he spent some years at the reestablished Gyuto monastery in India. He now lives in Switzerland, and regularly teaches at European teaching centres such as Chodzong in Germany.

H.H. GANDEN TRIPA, JAMPEL SHENPEN

Ganden Tripa Jampel Shenpen was born in 1921 in the province of Kham. At the age of twelve he became a monk, joining Ganden Jangtse monastery near Lhasa. After intensive study of the five great subjects – Logic, Prajnaparamita, Madhyamaka, Abhidharma and Vinaya – he gained the degree of Lharampa Geshe in 1956. Following this he entered Gyume monastery, also near Lhasa, for further study of tantra, remaining there until his escape from Tibet in 1959 following the Chinese occupation and the resultant civil unrest. Upon its reestablishment in India he became the abbot of Gyume monastery. During 1980 – 81 he was a visiting scholar at the University of Virginia. He was appointed Ganden Tripa, the head of the Gelug lineage tradition and the ninety-eighth successor to Tsong Khapa, in 1984.

JHADO TULKU

Jhado Tulku Tenzin Jungne was born in 1954, near the monastery of the previous Jhado Tulku, Jhado Samten Ling on the shore of the holy lake Namtso north of Lhasa, known in Mongolian as Tengri Nor. At the age of three he was recognised as the reincarnated Jhado Tulku and entered the monastery. In 1959 following the Chinese occupation of Tibet he was taken into exile in India. He studied (mainly English language) for one year at the Young Lamas' School in Dalhousie in North India, then stayed in Dharamsala and began monastic studies under an ex-abbot of Gyume monastery, the Sera scholar Kelsang Namdol. From 1972–73 he was at the Bhandara settlement for Tibetan refugees; then he continued his study of the monastic curriculum – Logic, Prajnaparamita, Madhyamaka, Abhidharma and Vinaya – at the reestablished Sera Je monastery in South India. He was a student of Khenzur Lobsang Wangchug until the latter's death in 1979. Since 1991, he has been teaching at Ganden Thekcholing Monastery, Ulan Bator, Mongolia.

KACHEN DRUBGYAL

Kachen Drubgyal was born in 1902 in Sumling, Spiti, Himachal Pradesh, in India. At an early age he went to Tibet and studied at the Tashilhunpo monastery, Shigatse. He was ordained by the Panchen Lama Chokyi Nyima at the age of eighteen. When aged thirty-three he gained the qualification of Kachen, and proceeded to study at the Drepung monastery, Lhasa. He studied extensively the five major subjects of Logic, Prajnaparamita, Madhyamaka, Vinaya and Abhidharma, together with tantra, and received an oral transmission of the Kangyur from Khangsar Rinpoche at Sera monastery. He is at present the abbot of Tabo monastery at Spiti.

KACHEN LOBSANG ZOPA

Kachen Lobsang Zopa was born in 1922 in Syagngo, Ladakh. At an early age he entered the Tashilhunpo monastery where he engaged in the study of logic and other subjects, gaining the qualification of Namdrel Kachen. He completed three years of intensive retreat, and later was appointed as a Tibetan teacher to the Chinese. He is at present in exile in India, where he is the abbot of the reestablished Tashilhunpo monastery at Bylakuppe, Mysore.

KHENZUR LOBSANG THUBTEN RINPOCHE

Khenzur Lobsang Thubten Rinpoche was born in 1925 in Eastern Tibet. At the age of seven he entered the monastery in his home town. In 1945 he continued his study of the five great subjects of Logic, Prajnaparamita, Madhyamaka, Vinaya and Abhidharma at Sera Je monastery near Lhasa. Due to the Chinese occupation of Tibet he fled to India in 1959. He was able to continue studying at the monastic refugee camp at Buxador, West Bengal. During that time he gained the Lharampa Geshe degree. In 1960 he moved to Dharamsala where he gave oral transmissions and taught on the *Kangyur*. In 1979 he began a three year retreat on Vajrayogini. He was elected Abbot-Chancellor of the reestablished Sera Je monastery in South India in 1983, a position he held until becoming the resident teacher at Buddha House in Adelaide, Australia in 1988.

KHENZUR NGAWANG NYIMA

Khenzur Ngawang Nyima was born in 1907 near Ude in Buryat (Inner Mongolia, part of the former USSR). When aged seven he began his elementary studies at Cholede monastery (Ganden Dhargyey Ling). When he was sixteen he left Buryat for Tibet, and after a year travelling he joined Drepung Gomang monastery near Lhasa. Here he began detailed study of Logic, Prajnaparamita, Madhyamaka, Abhidharma and Vinaya. At the age of twenty-two he took full ordination from the Thirteenth Dalai Lama, and he began teaching students of his own while still in the Madhyamaka class. He obtained his geshe degree when aged thirty-seven, and was then chosen as tutor to the Fourteenth Dalai Lama's elder and younger brothers, Taktser Rinpoche and Ngari Rinpoche. In 1948 and 1956 he left Tibet briefly on pilgrimages to India and Nepal, and he finally left Tibet in 1958 following the Chinese occupation. He taught at the Sanskrit University in Varanasi from 1960 to 1967, and then worked as a research assistant in Holland at the Leiden University until 1972, when he retired to Switzerland. He returned to India in 1977 as abbot of the reestablished Drepung Gomang monastery in South India, staying in this post until 1980. He now lives in Switzerland but returns frequently to India to teach. He has visited and taught in Buddhist teaching centres in Italy, France and Switzerland, and his collected works take up six volumes including commentaries on sutra, logic, Madhyamaka, Prajnaparamita, tenets, and history.

KHENZUR PEMA GYALTSEN

The late Khenzur Pema Gyaltsen Rinpoche was born in the Ba region of south-eastern Tibet in 1906. As a child he was unusually proficient at memorisation of scripture. He joined Drepung Loseling monastery near Lhasa when he was nineteen. Here he studied

intensively the normal curriculum of Logic, Prajnaparamita, Madhyamaka, Abhidharma and Vinaya, and appeared for his final examination at the age of forty-two, gaining the highest place Lharampa Geshe degree of that year. He then entered Gyume monastery for further study of tantra, after which he was appointed abbot of the Jepa college of Loseling monastery. In 1954 he was appointed abbot of all Loseling, remaining until forced to flee to India with a great many of his fellow monks following the Chinese occupation, in 1959. At the temporary monastic refugee camp at Buxador in Bengal he was able to continue as abbot of Drepung Loseling, giving up the post in 1970 when the monastery was reestablished in South India. From then on until his death in 1985 he served, at the request of the monastery, as overall head abbot of Drepung. He undertook tours of Europe, the USA and Canada in 1976 and 1983. He is the author of a number of important commentaries in use at Loseling and other monasteries.

KHENZUR YESHE THUBTEN

Khenzur Yeshe Thubten was born in Chashe in the province of Kham on 15 October 1915. He joined the nearby Sedru monastery in 1928, moving on to Drepung Loseling monastery near Lhasa in 1931. There he undertook rigorous study of the five great subjects – Logic, Prajnaparamita, Madhyamaka, Abhidharma and Vinaya – until 1959, when he left Tibet with many of his compatriots following the Chinese occupation. He gained the degree of Lharampa Geshe at the first examination held in exile in India, at Bodhgaya in 1961, in which he was ranked first. Following this he was posted to Ladakh, serving as principal of the newly established school of dialectics at Leh. In 1967 he became principal of the Institute of Higher Tibetan Studies at Varanasi, remaining there until 1972. In 1974 he was appointed abbot of Drepung

Loseling monastery, reestablished in South India, serving as abbot for seven years. In 1982 he visited the USA, lecturing for one month at Middlebury College and for seventeen months at the University of Virginia as a visiting lecturer in the Buddhist Studies programme. He returned to the USA in 1984, spending one year as temporary director of the Tibetan Buddhist Learning Center in New Jersey. He again visited the University of Virginia from August to October 1985, and in the autumn of 1987. In addition he visited several European countries to teach at various Buddhist teaching centres. He died in 1989.

KYABJE SONG RINPOCHE

The late Song Rinpoche Lobsang Tsondru Thubten Gyaltsen was born in the town of Songgo in the district of Nangzang, Kham, in 1905. As a child he was taught by Gyal Khangtse Rinpoche, and was exceptionally good at memorisation. When he was eleven years old he joined Ganden Shartse monastery near Lhasa. Under the principal guidance of Trijang Rinpoche and Geshe Ngawang Lobsang he studied intensively the five great subjects of Logic, Prajnaparamita, Madhyamaka, Abhidharma and Vinaya, finally appearing for the Lharampa Geshe examination in 1929, gaining second place overall. He subsequently entered Gyuto monastery, also near Lhasa, for further study of tantra. Then in 1937 he was appointed abbot of Ganden Shartse, and served in this post until 1946. He then began travelling around Tibet performing various religious functions until he was obliged to leave for exile in India in 1959 following the Chinese occupation. In India he stayed at the Buxador monastic refugee camp, and taught the refugees from Sera Me monastery. Following that he was appointed principal of a Tibetan teacher training college at Mussoorie in North India, then principal of the Institute of Higher Tibetan Studies at Varanasi. Upon his retirement he took up residence at the newly established Ganden Shartse monastery in South India. He embarked on a teaching tour of Western countries in 1978, visiting America, Canada, England, France, Italy and Switzerland. Rinpoche died in 1984 and his reincarnation, born in 1985, was discovered in 1990 in Kulu, India.

KYABJE YONGDZIN LING RINPOCHE

The late Ling Rinpoche Jetsun Thubten Lhungtok Namgyal Thinley Palzangpo, was born at dawn on the sixth day of the eleventh month of the Tibetan Water-Rabbit year (1903), at Yaphu northwest of Lhasa. He was the sixth in his series of reincarnations, a lineage perceived as the human manifestation of Vajrabhairava. The Sixth Ling Rinpoche was discovered and recognised by the Thirteenth Dalai Lama and the state oracles of Nechung and Gadong, and formally enthroned at the age of seven. While residing at his retreat monastery, Garpa Ritro, during his early years, he followed basic training in reading, writing, memorisation and other preliminary studies. In 1912, when he was ten years old, he joined Drepung Loseling monastery near Lhasa, where he began intensive study of Logic, Prajnaparamita, Madhyamaka, Abhidharama and Vinaya. He revceived novice ordination from the

Thirteenth Dalai Lama in 1913, and full ordination in 1923. In 1924 he was awarded the Lharampa Geshe degree at the annual Great Prayer Festival in Lhasa. From the age of twelve, he received many discourses on all aspects of sutra and tantra, receiving empowerments from thirty great lamas, including the Thirteenth Dalai Lama, his root lama Phabongkha Dechen Nyingpo, Buldu Rinpoche, the regent Kyabgon Sikyong Tadrag Rinpoche, Khangsar Rinpoche, Chone Lama Rinpoche, Yongdzin Trijang Rinpoche and many others. In 1936 he was appointed abbot of Gyuto monastery by the ruling Regent, Reting Rinpoche, having previously served a term as Gekyo (disciplinarian). In 1940, the present Dalai Lama was enthroned. Having served as his assistant tutor earlier while abbot of Gyuto, Ling Rinpoche was now appointed junior tutor. Later, in 1949 he was appointed Sharpa Choje, the second highest position in the Gelug tradition next to the Ganden throneholder, and subsequently he became the Dalai Lama's senior tutor. Along with the junior tutor, Trijang Rinpoche, he continued to offer the Dalai Lama the unbroken and undegenerated lineage of transmission of both sutra and tantra. In 1959, following the Chinese invasion of Tibet, Ling Rinpoche accompanied the Dalai Lama into exile in India, residing with him first at Mussoorie and later in Dharamsala. Following the death of the ninety-sixth Ganden throneholder, Ling Rinpoche ascended to the Ganden throne on 6 March 1965, also becoming abbot of Ganden Phelgyeling monastery in Bodhgaya. He remained in this position until his death on 25 December 1983. His reincarnation, born in 1984, was discovered in 1987 in Dharamsala, North India.

KYABJE YONGDZIN TRIJANG RINPOCHE

The late Trijang Rinpoche Lobsang Yeshe Tenzin Gyatso was born in 1901 in the small village of Tsel Gungthang near to Lhasa. He was recognised when four years old as the reincarnation of the second Trijang Rinpoche, a former Ganden throneholder. He entered Ganden monastery near Lhasa, living in the house of his predecessor, and began studies with a private teacher, Lobsang Tsultrim. His root lama was Phabongkha Rinpoche. He then embarked on the profound study of Logic, Prajnaparamita, Madhyamaka, Abhidharma and Vinaya leading to the degree of geshe, which he obtained at the age of nineteen, receiving the third position Lharampa degree. Following this he joined Gyuto monastery for further study of tantra, remaining there for some years. When he was twenty-four he journeyed to Kham to his predecessor's monastery, Sampel Ling, where he taught extensively. In 1953 he was appointed junior tutor to the young Dalai Lama (the senior tutor being Ling Rinpoche), and he accompanied the Dalai Lama on his visit to China in 1954. In 1959, following the unrest due to the Chinese occupation of Tibet, he accompanied his student into exile in India. He settled in a house at Dharamsala, the northern town where the residence of the Dalai Lama in exile was established, and continued to teach until his death in November 1981. He undertook various tours of North America, Europe and Australia, teaching in Buddhist centres there, and had many Western devotees. His works consist of eight volumes which include the famous *Liberation in the Palm of Your Hands*. In 1985 his reincarnation, born in 1983, was discovered in Dalhousie, North India.

LAMA THUBTEN YESHE

The late Lama Thubten Yeshe was born in 1935 at Tolung Dechen near Lhasa. At the age of six he joined Sera Je monastery, where after elementary subjects he began the study of the five

great subjects of Logic, Prajnaparamita, Madhyamaka, Abhi-
dharma and Vinaya. He left Tibet in 1959 following the Chinese
occupation, and stayed at the Buxador monastic refugee camp
until 1969. It was at the refugee camp that he became tutor to
Thubten Zopa Rinpoche, with whom he founded the Nepal
Mahayana Gompa Centre in Nepal after leaving the camp. Lama
Yeshe and his student quickly acquired many pupils from Western
countries; their organisation expanded to include in 1973 the
Kopan monastery in Kathmandu, the Kopan International
Mahayana Institute, and from then on an increasing number of
Buddhist teaching centres in various countries around the world,
managed by the Foundation for the Preservation of the Mahayana
Tradition, of which Lama Yeshe was head until his death in
March 1984 (a post to which Zopa Rinpoche succeeded). The
FPMT founded by Lama Yeshe now has more than sixty teaching
centres in Australasia, USA, Europe, India and Nepal. He is the
author of several books, including *Wisdom Energy* (I & II), *Silent
Mind, Holy Mind,* and many of his discourses have been published
as transcripts. In 1986 a Spanish boy born in 1984 was identified
as his reincarnation, named Tenzin Osel.

LAMA THUBTEN ZOPA
Thubten Zopa Rinpoche was born in 1946 at Solo Khumbu in
Nepal. He was recognised at the age of four as the reincarnation of
a famous meditator who had lived nearby, the Laudo Lama. He
entered the Dungkar monastery in Tibet where he studied until
1959, when he fled into exile following the Chinese occupation.
He studied for some time at the Young Lamas' School in
Dalhousie, then at the Buxador monastic refugee camp where he
came under the tutelage of Lama Thubten Yeshe. Together they
founded the Nepal Mahayana Gompa Centre in Nepal in 1969, a
project which developed with the help of Western students into
Kopan Monastery in Kathmandu, and the worldwide FPMT
organisation. In 1984 following the death of Lama Yeshe he took
over the position of spiritual head of the FPMT, which directs
over sixty Buddhist teaching centres around the world. He tours
extensively, teaching at these centres.

LATI RINPOCHE
Lati Rinpoche Jangchub Tsultrim was born in the province of
Kham in 1923. At an early age he was identified as an incarnate
lama, and he first attended a local monastery, Dagyab, from the
age of nine to fifteen, then moved on to Ganden Shartse
monastery near Lhasa. There he began elementary studies, and
detailed study of the five great subjects – Logic, Prajnaparamita,
Madhyamaka, Abhidharma and Vinaya. He studied under Khenzur Lobsang Chopel, among others. In 1956 he gained the degree
of Lharampa Geshe, and the following year joined Gyuto
monastery for further study of tantra. He remained there until
1959 when he had to flee Tibet following the Chinese occupation.
After spending one year at the monastic refugee camp at Buxador,
Bengal, he went to Dharamsala to assist in the religious affairs of
the Dalai Lama, remaining for the next fifteen years at Namgyal

monastery in Dharamsala. In 1976 he visited the USA, lecturing at the University of Virginia as a visiting professor for fourteen months. Following that he toured Europe, teaching in France, Switzerland and Germany. He was appointed abbot of Ganden Shartse monastery in 1977, serving in the post until 1984. He has written and co-written a number of books, including *Mind in Tibetan Buddhism* (with E. Napper); *Buddhism of Tibet and the Key to the Middle Way*; *Death, Intermediate State and Rebirth in Tibetan Buddhism*; *Meditative States in Tibetan Buddhism* (with Locho Rinpoche); and *The Precious Garland and the Song of Four Mindfulnesses*.

LOBSANG CHODRON (MRS)

Mrs Lobsang Chodron was born in 1915 in Dagyab, Kham, Tibet. She was the wife of Demo Rinpoche Ngawang Lobsang Thinley Rabgye. She studied widely, including the Chod practice, with the previous Mogchok Rinpoche, the twenty-eighth Lhatsun Rinpoche and Geshe Dondon, a celebrated master of the Chod practice. Between the ages of twenty-one and thirty she extensively performed the Chod commitments, involving journeying to 108 cemeteries and springs.

NGAWANG GELEK RINPOCHE

Nyare Khentrul Rinpoche, Ngawang Gelek Demo, was born in 1939 in Lhasa, into the family of an ex-regent of Tibet. At an early age he joined Drepung Loseling monastery near Lhasa, studying the elementary subjects and then the more detailed analysis of Logic, Prajnaparamita, Madhyamaka, Abhidharma and Vinaya, under the guidance of Gyungdung Rinpoche and Lhatsun Rinpoche among others. He escaped from Tibet in 1959 following the Chinese occupation, and after a brief spell at the refugee camp at Buxador in Bengal he went to Dharamsala to study with a group of incarnate lamas. In

1963 he became a layman. He married in 1969 and since then has been living in Delhi where he is a publisher and editor of Tibetan scripture, working in association with Tibet House.

NGAWANG NAMGYAL

Ngawang Namgyal was born in 1929 in Dab Yangten Gon, Tibet. At the age of fourteen he began his studies, joining Sera monastery near Lhasa. At present he lives in the Pomra college of the reestablished Sera monastery at Bylakuppe, Mysore, in India.

NGAWANG TENZIN

Ngawang Tenzin was born in 1906 in Jyangkhog, Lithang, in Kham. At the age of seven he became a monk and at present lives in retirement in exile at the reestablished Sera monastery in Bylakuppe, Mysore, in India.

NYALUSHA RINPOCHE

Nyalusha Rinpoche Jampa Kelsang Thubten Wangchuk was born in 1942 near De Gonpa, a temple in Kanze, Kham. At the age of six he was recognised and enthroned at the monastery of his predecessor, Tawu Nyitso Gonpa. During 1950 he was favoured with a number of empowerments including the *Rinchen Gya Tsa* and *Tsepag Lha Gu* cycles, given by the Sera lama Kutsang Rinpoche. In 1952 he entered Ganden Jangtse monastery near Lhasa. He began studies of Logic and Prajnaparamita, but was forced to leave Tibet following the Chinese occupation in 1959. In exile in India, he stayed at the Buxador monastic refugee camp in Bengal until 1965, continuing his studies in such subjects as Madhyamaka, Abhidharma and Vinaya. In 1965 he went to Dharamsala in North India where he was able to study Tibetan grammar, poetry and religious history as well as some Western subjects including English. He was a teacher at the Tibetan Children's Village in Dharamsala from 1968 to 1972, when he became secretary and accountant at the Tibetan Medical

Centre, also in Dharamsala. From 1978 he has been resident at the reestablished Ganden monastery in South India where he is a teacher. He received the degree of Lingtse Geshe in 1979.

PANCHEN LAMA, THE TENTH

The late Tenth Panchen Lama, Panchen Chokyi Gyaltsen, was born on 3 February 1938 in the village of Karang Bidho, Amdo, Eastern Tibet. The Panchen Lamas were second highest in the Gelug spiritual hierarchy, next only to the Dalai Lamas. In 1941 the previous Panchen Lama's attendants, who had escaped with him to China, unilaterally recognised Gonpo Tseten, the three-year-old son of Gurgon Tseten and Sonam Dolma, as the Tenth Panchen Lama. The Tibetan government withheld its approval of the child. Soon after the birth of Gonpo Tseten, Alak Jigme Trinley Gyatso, a high lama of Tashikyil monastery in Amdo, told the boy's parents that he was the reincarnation of the Panchen Lama. He subsequently took the child under his tutelage and ordained him into the monkhood under the spiritual name of Lobsang Thinley Lhundrup Chokyi Gyaltsen. Alak Gyatso taught him to read and write and gave him extensive spiritual teachings, particularly on the Kalacakra Tantra, as this was a special practice of the Ninth Panchen Lama. He also appointed Gyalak Lobsang Tenpai Gyaltsen, his favourite pupil, as the boy's private spiritual tutor. In 1951, the Panchen Lama was invited to Peking to coincide with the arrival of the Tibetan delegation which went there to discuss the so-called 17-Point Agreement with the Chinese. During the negotiations surrounding the acceptance of the 17-Point Agreement the representatives of Tashilhunpo monastery met the Dalai Lama and he gave the recognition to the new Panchen Lama under the title of Tenzin Trinley Jigme Chokyi-Wangchuk. Following this the Panchen Lama left for Lhasa and from there travelled on to Tashilhunpo where he resumed his monastic education. He received all the special teachings of the Tashilhunpo monastery from Gyayag Rinpoche. In addition, he took a hermit-practitioner, named Kachen Angnyima from the southern Tibetan region of Dzonga, as his tutor. When Angnyima passed away, he turned to Kachen Nyulchu Rinpoche Lobsang Cheophel, from whom he received extensive teachings in Buddhism. From the age of three until his death on 28 January 1989, the Panchen Lama's life and activities were strictly controlled by the Chinese government. After the flight of H.H. the Dalai Lama to India, the Panchen Lama was appointed by the Chinese as the acting head of Tibet. In 1960, he was appointed the vice-chairman of the National People's Congress. During 1964, he was subjected to criticisms by Chinese officials and was accused of being anti-Party, anti-socialism, and anti-people. He was ousted from the post of the Committee's chairmanship and taken to Peking and placed under house arrest until 1965. He was formally imprisoned from August 1965 until the end of 1975. In 1980 he was reinstated as the vice-chairman of the National People's Congress. Immediately on his release from prison he asked for permission to visit Tibet which was finally granted in June 1982. He managed to visit Lhasa, with permission, seven more times. He also visited various parts of Amdo in Eastern Tibet and with the approval of the Chinese government also visited Nepal, Japan, and Australia. On 9 January 1989 he left Peking for Shigatse where he was to renovate and rebuild the Tashilhunpo monastery. He died, in what has been considered by some as mysterious circumstances, a short while later on 28 January 1989, at the Tashilhunpo monastery.

PANCHEN OETUL RINPOCHE

Panchen Oetul Lobsang Thubten Gelek Wangchuk Pal Zangpo was born in 1939 in Kham, and recognised as one of the four oetul or alternative emanations of the late Seventh Panchen Lama. He entered Drepung Gomang monastery near Lhasa in 1951, and began study of the monastic curriculum – Logic, Prajnaparamita, Madhyamaka, Abhidharma and Vinaya. In 1959 the Chinese, having invaded Tibet, put him in a prison camp. He escaped to India in 1960, joining the Sanskrit University at Varanasi where he read Sanskrit and Hindi and gained the acarya degree. He completed his formal Tibetan education, gaining the Lharampa Geshe degree, and completed tantric studies at Gyume monastery. He then resided at the reestablished Drepung Gomang monastery in South India, and in 1987 was sent by the Dalai Lama to pursue an inter-faith dialogue with various Christian monasteries and nunneries in Great Britain. During this tour, in addition to staying at Christian monasteries he taught at various Buddhist teaching centres, and resided for a while at the Samye Ling centre, in Scotland. In 1990 he settled in Ireland, where he now lives at Tashi Kyil centre in County Down. In addition to Tashi Kyil centre he has established Jampa Ling, a teaching centre in County Cavan.

RAKRA TETHONG RINPOCHE

Rakra Tulku Thubten Chodar was born in 1924 in Derge, Kham. He was recognised as the seventh in the Rakra line of incarnations by the Thirteenth Dalai Lama at the age of four. In 1931 he spent one year at the Tashilhunpo monastery in Shigatse, then moved back to Kham upon his father's appointment to an official post, staying at the Pasho monastery until 1935 when he joined Drepung Gomang monastery near Lhasa. He intensively studied the five great subjects – Logic, Prajnaparamita, Madhyamaka, Abhidharma and Vinaya – leading to the qualification of geshe. He received the degree of Lharampa Geshe at the age of twenty, then spent the years 1944 – 49 at Gyume monastery pursuing further studies of tantra. He served as Gekyo (disciplinarian) of the monastery for a period of six months. He received the qualification of Geshe Ngagrampa. During this time he became friends with the famous non-conformist Gelugpa scholar Gendun Chopel, and also studied religious painting. In 1950 he gave up monastic life and moved to India, first to study Sanskrit in Kalimpong with Professor Roerich. He later attended Tagore University in Calcutta, and also studied with Professor Basudev Gokkale in Poona from 1954 – 56. Following this he worked for three years for All India Radio in Delhi, at the same time researching at Delhi University. He married in 1959, and moved to Switzerland, where he presently lives in the town of Trogen, supervising the education of Tibetan children there and teaching privately.

SEMPA DORJI

Sempa Dorji was born in 1933 in Kunu Dribling, Himachal Pradesh, India. At an early age he went to Tibet to study at Tashilhunpo monastery. In 1961 he returned to India and continued his studies at the Central Institute for Higher Tibetan Studies at Sarnath, Varanasi. At present he is reading Classical Indian Buddhist Texts at Sarnath.

SERKONG RINPOCHE

The late Serkong Rinpoche was born in 1914 in the region of Lhoka in southern Tibet. He is held to be an incarnation of Dharma Dodey, a son of the great translator Marpa. He entered Ganden Jangtse college where after just fourteen years of study he received the Lharampa Geshe degree. Following this he spent nine years at the Gyume monastery, where he served a period as disciplinarian. In 1948 he was appointed one of the debating partners (Tsenshab) of the young Dalai Lama, a position he held until his death. He studied extensively in all four traditions of Tibetan Buddhism. He accompanied the Dalai Lama on his visit to Peking in 1954, and also into exile in India in 1959 following the uprising against the Chinese occupation of Tibet. In exile he helped to establish the Office of Religious and Cultural Affairs of H.H. the Dalai Lama, and he undertook several teaching tours of Western countries. He emparted many initiations and lineages to H.H. the Dalai Lama and was His Holiness' main Kalacakra teacher. He died in 1983 and his reincarnation, born in 1984, was discovered in 1988 in Spiti, India.

TARA TULKU

From an early age the late Tara Tulku studied at Drepung Loseling monastery near Lhasa. In 1956 he was awarded the Lharampa Geshe degree. He then joined Gyuto monastery for further study of tantra, becoming abbot of that monastery. Following the Chinese occupation of Tibet he fled into exile in India with many of his compatriots. He was later appointed abbot of the Ganden Phelgyeling monastery at Bodhgaya. During 1982 he undertook a tour of North America lecturing at various Buddhist teaching centres there.

THOMTHO TULKU

Thomotho Tulku Lobsang Damcho Gyatso was born in 1950 in Lithang, Kham. At the age of five he was recognised as the reincarnation of the Twelfth Thomtho Tulku, and was enthroned at Jamchen Ling monastery in Lithang. In 1957 he joined Sera Je monastery near Lhasa, embarking on the intensive study of Logic, Prajnaparamita, Madhyamaka, Abhidharma and Vinaya leading to the qualification of geshe. He left Tibet in 1959 due to the Chinese occupation, and stayed for the next ten years at the Buxador monastic refugee camp continuing his studies. In 1970 he moved to the reestablished Sera Je monastery in South India, where he remains today.

THUBTEN GYALTSEN

Thubten Gyaltsen was born in 1932 in India. At the age of thirteen he entered the monastery of Kyi at Lahul Spiti, in Himachal Pradesh. In 1957 he went to Tibet for further study and returned to India in 1959. He now lives at Kyi monastery, Spiti.

THUBTEN TULKU

Thubten Tulku Jampa Thubten was born in a village south of Lhasa in 1941. He was recognised as the reincarnation of the previous Thubten Rinpoche in 1943. From 1944 to 1957 he stayed at the Dza Samdrub monastery where his predecessor had lived, in Dzakho, a part of Kham. He studied under Rinchen Tseten; first, preliminary subjects such as reading, writing and debate, then beginning detailed study of Logic, Prajnaparamita, Madhyamaka, Abhidharma and Vinaya. He joined Sera Je monastery in 1957, studying under Geshe Ngawang Dhargyey. In 1959 he was obliged to flee Tibet due to the Chinese occupation, staying until 1962 in Kalimpong, Darjeeling and then moving to Dalhousie where he studied under Geshe Dhargyey again, also learning English. In 1966 he was awarded a diploma from the Teachers' Training College, and from 1968 to 1970 taught Tibetan children in Kalimpong. He then spent some time teaching at each of the Tibetan refugee settlements of Bylakuppe, Orissa and Mundgod, and has been at Mundgod since 1976, teaching at the Central School for Tibetans.

YESHE PHENDEY

Yeshe Phendey was born in 1939 in Phenpo, north of Lhasa. He joined Drepung Loseling monastery near Lhasa. He now lives as a resident monk at Dagyab Labrang monastery in the Tibetan settlement at Bylakuppe, Mysore, India.

ZASEP TULKU

At the age of five Zasep Tulku was installed as the abbot of Zuru Gompa in the Lharog Gedun Dorje Jungpug region of Nangchen Kham, having been recognised as the reincarnation of the previous abbot. From the age of seven he spent some time studying at the nearby Tashi Lhapug Monastery, obtaining an empowerment of Yamantaka, returning to Zuru to study one of Lama Tsong Khapa's *Lamrim* texts. He also visited the Sakya monastery of Nalanda for three months, gaining an initiation of Ami-

tayus. When he was ten he began studies at Sera Je monastery near Lhasa, receiving instruction on Prajnaparamita and Madhyamaka. He was able to perform preliminary retreats at Sera and Mt Kailash, and later at Mustang on the border with Nepal. Having left Tibet due to the dangers following the Chinese occupation, he took full ordination from Trijang Rinpoche in Dharamsala in India, and studied under Trijang Rinpoche's guidance for three years. After this he spent ten years in Dalhousie studying under Geshe Ngawang Wangyal. In 1972 he began the acarya course at Varanasi University, receiving his degree in 1975. Following this he spent eighteen months in Thailand, meditating and also studying the Hinayana system with Achaan Bhuddhadhassa. In Australia in 1976 he was translator for Geshe Loden, and subsequently went on to establish the Ganden Choling and Zuru Ling centres in Canada in 1979, where he continues to teach regularly.

ZIMEY RINPOCHE LOBSANG PALDEN

Zimey Rinpoche was born in 1927 in Yangteng, in Eastern Tibet. Following his recognition as the reincarnation of the previous Zimey Rinpoche at the age of four, he was formally installed as the head of Tangten monastery where he then began his religious training. At eleven he left for Lhasa to join Shartse College at Ganden Monastic University. There he successfully completed his studies in Buddhist logic, epistemology, ethics, phenomenology, Madhyamaka ontology, and religious studies. His monastic college rewarded his unusual scholarship by conferring on him the Geshe Lharam degree at the young age of twenty-two. The same year he joined the Gyuto Tantric college where he studied tantra for five years. During these years he developed a close relationship with two great Gelug masters of his time, Kyabje Trijang Rinpoche (who later became a tutor to H.H. the Dalai Lama) and Kyabje Song Rinpoche. This enabled him to become the heir to many of the lineages of Tsongkhapa's precious oral tradition. In the mid 1950s he was a member of the entourage of H.H. the Dalai Lama when His Holiness visited Peking and India. During this time he also served as a senior Tibetan teacher in the first modern school opened in Lhasa. During the 1960s in India he was actively involved in the restoration of Tibetan education and culture in the exile community in India. He composed and edited the first Tibetan textbooks for Tibetan schools, and also trained the first two groups of Tibetan teachers. Later he served as rector at various Tibetan schools within India. In addition to his stature as a high lama, he is also respected as one of the highest authorities on Tibetan literature, poetry, and lexical studies. His writings in Tibetan cover wide areas of scholarship such as philosophy, meditative practices, biographies, and poetry. After resigning from active public life in 1974, he undertook a series of retreats during which he engaged in various meditative practices. In 1979, at the request of Ganden Shartse College, he moved his residence to Mundgod, South India, and began teaching at the monastery. Since moving to Ganden he has been devoting most of his time to travelling within India and Nepal teaching at various Tibetan communities and leading an academic and monastic life at Shartse College in Mundgod.

DOCTORS

Khyenrab Norbu (Principal of Mentsekang)

Scholastic Biographies

DR DHADON

Dr. Dhadon escaped from Tibet into exile in India after the Chinese occupation, in 1959. She later graduated from the Tibetan Medical and Astro College in Dharamsala, North India, and has gained extensive experience of the practice of Tibetan medicine. She has taught both in India and abroad, and has undertaken consultation/teaching trips to the USA and Europe. At present she is in charge of a Tibetan medical clinic in Dharamsala.

DR LOBSANG DOLMA KHANGKAR

The late Dr. Lobsang Dolma Khangkar was born on 6 July 1934 in the Khangkar family, in Kyirong, Western Tibet, in a line of physicians going back for thirteen generations. At the age of fourteen she began her medical training at the Khangkar Tibetan Medical School. She spent ten years in intensive study of theory and practice of Tibetan medicine, astrology and related Buddhist philosophy. In 1959, she took over as head of the Khangkar Hospital following the imprisonment by the Chinese and subsequent death of her father. Her practical training came principally from her father, Dr Tsering Wangdu, but all her textual study was made under the supervision of Geshe Lhungtok Nyima. After coming into exile, she practised medicine in Nepal from 1960 to 1962. She then went to India in order to join the Tibetan refugee community that had been formed under the guidance of the exiled Dalai Lama. She spent several years working in an orphanage for Tibetan refugee children in Kangra before opening her own private medical clinic in Dalhousie. In 1972, she was appointed Chief Medical Officer of the Tibetan Medical Institute. In 1978, she opened her own clinic, Dekyi Khangkar, in Dharamsala. She was a member of the Council of the International Association for the Study of Traditional Asian Medicine (Harvard Medical School, USA), and a member of the Board of Directors for PhD students in Tibetan Medicine at Visva-Bharati University, Calcutta. She has received honorary doctorates from several American universities and has delivered extensive lectures and conducted workshops in universities of the USA, UK, Switzerland, Australia, Italy and Holland. She is the author of a book entitled *Lectures on Tibetan Medicine*, which is mainly compiled from her lectures during a tour of Australia and Holland. Dr Dolma has devised several new Tibetan medicines. These include a contraceptive pill, medicines for painless child delivery, for curing baldness, barrenness in women and sterility in men. She passed away at her residence in Dharamsala on 15 December 1989 after a prolonged illness. She is survived by her husband and two daughters, both practitioners of medicine. Her elder daughter succeeded her as head of the Dekyi Khangkar clinic in Dharamsala.

DR LOBSANG RABGAY

Dr Lobsang Rabgay studied as a monk in the Gelug tradition and spent eight years training as a Tibetan physician. He received a PhD in Tibetan Medicine and Buddhist Psychology from Visva-Bharati University, and studied under many doctors. According to the traditional training of a Tibetan doctor, his studies included the memorisation of the *Four Medical Tantras* (*rGyud bzhi*), followed by a study of the eleven principal subject divisions, including: embryology, anatomy, metabolic function, the signs of death, pathology, and diagnosis. He has held the post of a religious secretary to the Dalai Lama and more recently has been a research associate at the New York Heart Research Foundation. Dr Rabgay is fluent in English.

DR LOBSANG WANGYAL

Dr Lobsang Wangyal was born in 1922 in Chonye, Central Tibet. In 1939, he began his medical studies and entered the Medical and Astrological Institute (Mentsekang) in Lhasa in Tibet. According to the traditional training of a Tibetan doctor, his studies began with the memorisation of the *Four Medical Tantras (rGyud bzhi)* and were followed by a detailed study of the eleven principal subject divisions, including: embryology, anatomy, metabolic function, the signs of death, pathology, and diagnosis.

DR TENZIN CHOEDAK

Dr Tenzin Choedak was born in 1924 at Ringpung Dzong near Shigatse, Tibet. At the age of ten he joined the nearby monastery of Nyepo Chode, and when he was seventeen he left for medical education and training at the Mentsekang in Lhasa. There he engaged in prolonged study of Tibetan medicine, under the supervision of the famous physician, Ven. Khyenrab Norbu, the founder of the Institute. According to the traditional training of a Tibetan doctor, he first memorised the *Four Medical Tantras (rGyud bzhi)*, before embarking on a detailed study of the eleven principal subject divisions, including: embryology, anatomy, metabolic function, the signs of death, pathology, and diagnosis. Dr Choedak returned to his native monastery at the age of thirty, with a first class diploma in both the theory and practice of Tibetan medicine. In 1954, he went to Phari, Rechung Phutok, to experiment in the involved process of detoxifying mercury for use in medicinal compounds. After considerable success in Phari, Dr Choedak was summoned by the Tibetan Government to Lhasa in 1955. From 1953 he had held the position of personal physician to the Gyalyum Chenmo, the mother of the Dalai Lama, and in 1956 was appointed personal physician to H.H. the Dalai Lama. Following the unsuccessful popular uprising against the Chinese occupation in 1959, Dr Choedak was imprisoned for seventeen years. In 1973, whilst still in prison, he successfully cured several prison officials. As a result, his status improved and he was allowed to practice medicine in the prison infirmary. When his seventeen-year prison sentence had been served in full, he was released and appointed head of a state funded medical research team. In 1980 the Chinese authorities permitted him to leave Tibet. In India, he took up his former post as personal physician to the Dalai Lama and joined the Tibetan Medical Institute in Dharamsala as chief medical officer and head of the research department. Since 1984 he has visited Europe and the USA to participate in conferences exploring the role of Tibetan medicine in global medicine. More recently he has been engaged in research programmes, one of which is in association with the Harvard Medical School, under Dr Herbert Benson, into the treatment of diseases such as asthma, cancer, hepatitis, multiple sclerosis and AIDS. He is also concerned to recreate the Tibetan medical texts, which have been lost in recent years, by re-writing them from memory.

DR TROGAWA RINPOCHE

Dr Trogawa Rinpoche was born in 1931 in central Tibet. He was recognised as the incarnation of a famous lama and physician. At the age of twelve he entered the Mindrol Rabten Ling (Gyangtse) Monastery and from ages sixteen to twenty-four studied Tibetan medicine as apprentice to Dr Nang Nongshag in Lhasa. Since leaving Tibet in 1954, he has practised medicine throughout the Himalayan region. He has taught at the Tibetan Medical and Astrological Institute in Dharamsala in India, and was one of the principal speakers at the First International Conference on Tibetan Medicine in Italy in 1983.

DR YESHI DONDEN

Dr Yeshi Donden was born in 1929 in the village of Namro, near Lhasa. At the age of six he was ordained as a novice monk in the local monastery of Shedrup Ling. His talent for memorisation caused him to be selected to represent his monastery at the Mentsekang, the larger of Lhasa's two state-run medical colleges. From the age of eleven, he began his medical training by memorising all 156 chapters of the *Four Medical Tantras* (*rGyud bzhi*). At the age of thirteen he moved on to a detailed examination of the eleven divisions of study. This comprised a familiarisation with the traditional diagrammatic exposition of Tibetan medicine – the illustrated Tree of Medicine – together with its points of correspondence with the *Four Tantras*; recognition of the three bodily humours; and then, in succession, the study of embryology, anatomy, metabolic function, the signs of death, pathology, treatment and finally diagnosis. After four years he was sent by Khyenrab Norbu (mKhyen rab nor bu, 1882–1962), Mentsekang's principal, to undertake a four-year internship with a master

physician practising in Lhoka. There he became fully experienced in the prescription of herbal medicines, emetics and purgatives, and the practice of moxibustion, cauterisation and acupuncture. Concurrently, he developed an encyclopaedic knowledge of Tibetan medicine's vast pharmacopoeia, through assisting in the yearly expeditions of the Medical College to collect medicinal plants. This knowledge was confirmed when he passed first in herbal identification examinations, at the age of twenty. In 1951 Dr Donden received his medical diploma, and spent the next few years travelling throughout Tibet treating numerous patients. He left for India in 1959, during the Chinese military takeover, and helped to treat the refugees in Dalhousie. In 1960 he was appointed personal physician to the Dalai Lama, a post he held until 1980. Dr Donden became the Founder-Director of the Tibetan Medical Centre in Dharamsala in 1963, establishing a seven-year curriculum for the training of Tibetan doctors. He resigned in 1969, opening a private practice in McLeod Ganj. In recent years he has been instrumental in acquainting the Western medical community with Tibetan medicine, and was a visiting lecturer at the University of Virginia in 1980. His lectures have been published by Snow Lion Publications under the title *"Health Through Balance"*.

JAMPAL KUNKHYAB

Jampal Kunkhyab was born in 1946 in Riwoche, Kham, Tibet. He studied Tibetan Medicine and is at present the resident doctor at the Tibet Sports Academy in Lhasa.

GLOSSARY OF KEY TIBETAN, BUDDHIST AND SANSKRIT TERMS

NOTES TO THE GLOSSARY

The glossary was co-written between 1990 and 1993 by Geshe Thupten Jinpa (translator to H.H. The Dalai Lama) and Dr Gyurme Dorje (a Tibetologist based at the School of Oriental and African Studies, University of London) and edited, at each stage of preparation, by Graham Coleman.

The criteria for selection of the terms was a computer search of the descriptive records to a large proportion of all the oral commentaries given by leading Tibetan lamas and scholars, which have been recorded on audio/video tape or published in English, since the early 1960's. More than 30,000 hours of such recordings are catalogued in the Tibetan Cultural Resources Database. A great many of the most common key terms which a reader will encounter when reading material relating to Tibetan culture have therefore been included. The reader should note, however, that given the open nature of the criteria for selection, these terms do not necessarily reflect the preferred terminology of the authors of this glossary.

Within each glossary entry, the transliteration and phoneticisation of Tibetan and Sanskrit terms has been standardised as much as possible. It has, unfortunately, not been possible to include diacritical marks for the Sanskrit, and instead, an anglicised phonetic version has been provisionally given. However, with the immanent creation of Tibetan and Sanskrit fonts which will run efficiently in IBM configured relational databases, we hope, in the future, to include Sanskrit diacritics and Tibetan and Sanskrit script within the bodies of the entries themselves and throughout the database.

As far as the headings for each of the individual entries are concerned, currently, the word as it appears in the database and Handbook is given first, followed by the Tibetan word in Tibetan script, the Tibetan word in standard transliteration, and the Sanskrit word with diacritics.

The Tibetan script and Sanskrit diacritic font settings are courtesy of Peter Lofting, LaserQuill, Windsor, UK.

GLOSSARY OF KEY TIBETAN, BUDDHIST AND SANSKRIT TERMS

Words in bold type can be referenced elsewhere in the glossary; Tibetan and Sanskrit words are given in italics and text names in small caps / italics.

Abbot མཁན་པོ་ mkhan po *upādhyāya*

The **abbot** of a Tibetan monastery is either appointed by a high *lama*, such as the *Dalai Lama*, or elected by the senior members of the monastery. However, the Tibetan word *mkhan-po* (pronounced *khenpo*), though popularly used to denote an **abbot** of a monastery, actually refers to the senior master or preceptor who presides in the ordination ceremony of new monks. In some traditions, the word '*khenpo*' is used almost in the same sense as '*geshe*' to indicate a professor of Buddhist philosophy.

Abhidharma (skrt.) ཆོས་མངོན་པ་ chos mngon pa *abhidharma*

Etymologically, *abhi* means 'manifest', '**realised**' or 'experienced' and *dharma*, '**knowledge**', '**reality**', '**truth**' or 'phenomenon'. In its original philosophical usage, it refers to the phenomenological states of the **direct perception** of the ultimate nature of **reality** as experienced by the *Arya* (sublime or superior beings). The word later acquired a rather broad application encompassing such subjects as phenomenology, psychology, **knowledge** and **cosmology**. This later usage most probably evolved due to the classification of the literatures dealing with the above topics under the category of *abhidharma* in the threefold division of the Buddhist canon (known as *Tripitaka*). Therefore, *abhidharma* is often translated as 'manifest **knowledge**' or just '**knowledge**', and sometimes also as 'phenomenology' or 'metaphysics'. The most popular works on *abhidharma* in the Tibetan Buddhist tradition are *Asanga's* ABHIDHARMASAMUCCAYA and his brother *Vasubandhu's* ABHIDHARMAKOSHA. The systems which evolved from the two books differ in their metaphysical premises and they are known as the 'upper *abhidharma*' and the 'lower *abhidharma*'.

ABHIDHARMAKOSHA (skrt.) ཆོས་མངོན་པ་མཛོད་ chos mngon pa mdzod *Abhidharmakoṣa*

One of the most important classical Indian works on the study of Buddhist *abhidharma*. Written by the fourth century Indian philosopher *Vasubandhu*, the book is divided into eight chapters covering a wide range of topics of great scholastic prominence in ancient Indian thought, namely: the nature and divisions of the **aggregates**, **elements**, and sense-fields (Ch.1); the specific functions of the sensory faculties (Ch.2); **cosmology** and evolution

(Ch.3); **karma** (Ch.4); primary and secondary **dissonant emotions** or *klesha* (Ch.5); paths and individuals (Ch.6); attainment of the result (Ch.7); and the sequence of the meditative **concentrations** (Ch.8). The discussion of the above topics is approached mainly from the philosophical perspectives of the Kashmiri *Vaibhashika* school of thought. See **Abhidharma** and **Vasubandhu**.

ABHIDHARMASAMUCCAYA (skrt.) མངོན་པ་ཀུན་བཏུས་ mngon pa kun btus
Abhidharmasamuccaya

One of the principal works of the fourth century Indian *Pandita Arya Asanga* on the study of *abhidharma*. The title of the text can be translated as THE COM-PENDIUM OF **KNOWLEDGE**; it deals extensively with the Buddhist description of the processes of **mind** and the division into primary **mind** and secondary **mental factors**, together with the phenomenological aspects of the latter. *Asanga's* treatment of the subject is based on the idealist philosophical position of the *Cittamatra* school of thought.

ABHISAMAYALAMKARA (skrt.) མངོན་རྟོགས་རྒྱན་ mngon rtogs rgyan
Abhisamayālaṃkāra

Considered one of the greatest commentarial discourses on the collection of *sutras* known as *Prajnaparamita*, the PERFECTION OF **WISDOM/DISCRIMINATIVE AWARENESS SUTRAS**. Although the work is divided into eight chapters, corresponding to the eight main subject-matters of the **WISDOM/DISCRIMINATIVE AWARENESS SUTRAS**, it is relatively short, and written in verse. It is used as the root text by all the major monastic colleges in the Tibetan tradition for their study of the main philosophical topics of the *sutra* system and their related practices. Along with four other major works, it forms what later became known as the *FIVE WORKS OF MAITREYA*. The name of the text can be translated into English as *THE ORNAMENT OF CLEAR REALISATION* or *THE ORNAMENT OF EMERGENT REALISATION*.

Abhisheka (skrt.) དབང་བསྐུར་ dbang bskur *abhiṣeka*

A ritual ceremony performed by eminent *lamas* to empower prospective trainees into the practice of *tantra*. It consists primarily of ritual processes which are meant to activate the potentials inherent within the mental continuum of the trainee. These serve to perfect the body, speech and **mind** of the trainee, thus making him/her eligible to engage in the specific practices of *tantra*. Such an **empowerment** ceremony is an essential prerequisite for the practice of *tantra* in the Buddhist tradition.

Acarya (skrt.) སློབ་དཔོན་ slob dpon *ācārya*

The original meaning of the term is similar to that of *geshe* and is usually translated as 'master'. In contemporary Indian universities, it is the equivalent of a Master of Arts degree. See **Geshe**.

Activities of the Buddha སངས་རྒྱས་ཀྱི་ཕྲིན་ལས་/མཛད་པ་ sangs rgyas kyi phrin las/mdzad pa *kṛtyakriyā*

The principal activity of the *buddhas* (fully **enlightened** beings) is to bring about the welfare of all **sentient beings**, an aim which initially motivated their aspiration to attain the fully enlightened state. Traditionally, a *buddha's* activities are spoken of either in terms of body, speech and **mind**; or in terms of the **skilful means** employed in working for the benefit of others, e.g., the **fourfold**

activities of pacification, enrichment, influence and force. See the **Twelve Deeds of the Buddha** and **Fourfold activities**.

Aggregates སྤུང་པོ་ phung po *skandha*

A general philosophical term referring to the principal faculties which constitute a **sentient being**. Buddhist literature speaks of five such faculties, technically known as the five **aggregates** or components, namely: those of form, feeling, perception/discrimination, conditioning/motivational factors, and **consciousness**. The Tibetan term *phung-po*, like its **Sanskrit** counterpart *skandha*, literally means 'heap' or 'pile', an aggregate of many parts. Our physical body is composed of its material parts and the mental aggregate is composed of the processes or the instances which form a mental event. Thus, the idea of an aggregate is inherent within the concepts of both body and **mind**. **Sentient beings** in the **desire** and **form realms** manifestly possess all the five **aggregates** and those in the **formless realm**, only the four mental **aggregates**.

Akshobhya (skrt.) མི་བསྐྱོད་པ་ mi bskyod pa *Akṣobhya*

The **Buddha** of one of five **enlightened-families** corresponding to the perfected states of an individual's five **aggregates**. *Akshobhya* is the perfected state of our faculty of consciousness, or alternatively, our **aggregate** of form, and is the manifestation of either the *buddha's* **pristine cognition** of **reality**'s expanse, or the mirror-like **pristine cognition**, visualised in the aspect of an embodied **deity**. *Akshobhya* is usually depicted as dark blue in colour. *Akshobhya* literally means the 'Immutable One'. **See Enlightened-Families** for alternative correspondences.

Amdo (tib.) ཨ་མདོ་/མདོ་སྨད་ a mdo/mdo smad

The North-eastern part of Tibet and one of the three traditional provinces, the other two being *Kham* (South-eastern Tibet) and *Utsang* (Central and Western Tibet).

Amitabha (skrt.) འོད་དཔག་མེད་ 'od dpag med *Amitābha*

The **Buddha** of one of five **enlightened-families** corresponding to the perfected states of an individual's five **aggregates**. *Amitabha* is the perfected state of our faculty of perception/discrimination, and is the manifestation of the *buddha's* **pristine cognition** of discernment visualised in the aspect of an embodied **deity**. Although *Amitabha* is usually depicted as red in colour, his appearance varies according to the different practices of *tantra* in relation to which he is visualised. *Amitabha* literally means 'limitless' or 'boundless light'.

Amitayus (skrt.) ཚེ་དཔག་མེད་ tshe dpag med *Amitāyus*

A **meditational deity** particularly associated with longevity practices. *Amitayus* is regarded as the **Buddha Amitabha** appearing in the aspect of a **deity** of longevity and together with white *Tara*

and *Ushnishavijaya*, forms a trinity of **meditational deities** associated with life and longevity. Practices centred on *Amitayus* often belong to the *Kriya* class of *tantra*, although *Anuttarayogatantra* forms also occur (e.g., *tshe-lha rigs-lnga*). *Amitayus* literally means 'limitless life'.

Amoghasiddhi (tib.) དོན་ཡོད་གྲུབ་པ་ don yod grub pa *Amoghasiddhi*

The *Buddha* of one of five **enlightened-families** corresponding to the perfected states of an individual's five **aggregates**. *Amoghasiddhi* is the perfected state of our faculty of conditioning and motivational factors and is the manifestation of the *buddha's* **pristine cognition** of accomplishment, visualised in the aspect of an embodied **deity**. *Amoghasiddhi* is usually depicted as green in colour. *Amoghasiddhi* literally means 'All Accomplishing One'. See **Enlightened-Families.**

Ani (tib.) ཨ་ནེ་ a ne

A colloquial term for nuns, often suffixed by the honourific 'la'. *(lags)*.

Antigod ལྷ་མ་ཡིན་ lha ma yin *asura*

See **Six Realms.**

Anuttarayogatantra (skrt.) རྣལ་འབྱོར་བླ་ན་མེད་པའི་རྒྱུད་ rnal 'byor bla na med pa'i rgyud *anuttarayogatantra*

The *Anuttarayogatantra* is the highest of the **four classes of** *tantra*, the other three being, in their proper order: *Kriya, Carya,* and *Yoga tantra. Anuttara* means 'unsurpassed' or 'highest'. There were two distinct phases in the dissemination of these *tantras* in Tibet, which are reflected in two different ways of classifying this class of *tantras*. According to the *Nyingma* school, which represents the earlier phase of dissemination, they are classified into *Mahayoga, Anuyoga* and *Atiyoga*, whereas the later schools (*Sarma*) classify them into Father, Mother and Non-dual or Indivisible *tantras*. The differences between the **four classes of** *tantra* are based on the different emphases which the texts place on external ritual practices (*Kriya*), visualisation (*Carya*), internal *yoga* practices (*Yoga*), and techniques for manifesting the *buddha-body* (*Anuttara*). *Anuttaratantra* is especially distinguished from the other three classes of *tantra* by its treatment of the main *tantric* subject matters such as **'clear light'** and **'illusory body'**. Representative of the *anuttarayoga* class of *tantras* according to the earlier dissemination are: *GUHYAGARBHA* and *GUHYASAMAJA* (*Mahayoga*), MDO DGONGS-PA 'DUS-PA (*Anuyoga*), and KUN-BYED RGYAL-PO (*Atiyoga*); or *GUHYASAMAJA* and *YAMARI* (Father *Tantras*), *CAKRASAMVARA* and *HEVAJRA* (Mother *Tantras*), and *KALACAKRA* (Non-dual or Indivisible *Tantras*) according to the later dissemination.

Arhat (skrt.) དགྲ་བཅོམ་པ་ dgra bcom pa *arhat*

A being who has attained freedom from the **cycle of existence (***samsara***)** by eliminating the *karmic* tendencies and the **dissonant emotions** which give rise to compulsive existence in a cycle of death and **rebirth**. *Arhat* is interpreted to mean either "worthy one" or "foe-destroyer", the foe in this context being the **dissonant emotions** which are at the root of our conditioned existence. The status of an *arhat* is the ideal goal to which practitioners of the *Hinayana* aspire. An individual person who has become an *arhat* has still not become a fully **enlightened** *buddha*. This is because the attainment of *Buddhahood* requires, in addition to the elimination of the **dissonant emotions**, a total overcoming of all the habitual tendencies imprinted upon our mental continuum by our long association with deluded states of **mind**. In other words, the attainment of full **enlightenment** requires the total overcoming of all personal limitations, which can be achieved only through a path that possesses the unification of the **skilful means** of universal **compassion**, together with the **discriminative awareness** directly perceiving the true nature of **reality**, at the most profound level.

Arya (skrt.) འཕགས་པ་ 'phags pa *ārya*

A being who has attained a direct **realisation** of the true nature of **reality**, in other words, the lack of **self-identity** of both oneself and phenomena. *Arya* literally means 'sublime' or 'superior', and those who have achieved the above feat are sublime and superior in the sense that their perception of **reality** is direct, i.e., transcendent of our conceptually conditioned ordinary perception of the world. The first level of the *Arya* experience is called the path of insight, which is the third of the **five paths** to **enlightenment**. The **five paths** are those of accumulation, preparation, insight, **meditation**, and no more learning. The *Arya* level includes the last three of these paths.

ARYAMAITRIPRANIDHANARAJA (skrt.)
འཕགས་པ་བྱམས་པའི་སྨོན་ལམ་གྱི་རྒྱལ་པོ་ 'phags pa byams pa'i smon lam gyi rgyal po *Āryamaitripraṇidhānarāja*

A poetic *sutra* written in verse and recounting the aspirational prayers of the **bodhisattva Arya Maitreya**. The reading of this beautiful prayer is very popular among Tibetans and is often known by heart. It is also commonly referred to simply as 'the Aspirational Prayer of **Loving Kindness**' *(byams smon)*.

Aryashura (skrt.) འཕགས་པ་དཔའ་བོ་ ('phags pa) dpa' bo *Āryaśūra*

An alias of the Indian *Pandita Ashvagosha*. See *Ashvagosha*.

Asanga (skrt.) ཐོགས་མེད་ thogs med *Asaṅga*

A fourth century Indian philosopher and saint accredited with the founding of the Indian Buddhist school of thought known as *Cittamatra* or *Vijnanavada*, also sometimes known as *Yogacara*. His works include the ***ABHIDHARMASAMUCCAYA***, the *MAHAYANASAM-GRAHA*, and the famous collection known as the *FIVE **BHUMI***. *Asanga* is also responsible for the conversion to **Mahayana** Buddhism of his brother *Vasubhandu*, the famous Indian *abhidharma* scholar, who originally represented the *Vaibhashika* school of thought. Along with *Nagarjuna*, *Asanga* is considered one of the two most important personalities in the development of the *Mahayana* Buddhist schools of ancient India. Their works are still respected as the most authoritative in this field.

Ashvaghosha (skrt.) རྟ་དབྱངས་ rta dbyangs *Aśvaghoṣa*

Also known as *Viracarya* or *Aryashura*, *Ashvagosha* was a celebrated first century Indian Buddhist scholar and poet known for

his dialectical skills. He was formerly a non-Buddhist and was later converted to Buddhism as a result of having lost in a philosophical debate with *Aryadeva* at **Nalanda** university. His works include the famous SEVENTY VERSES ON ASPIRATION and the BUDDHACARITA, one of the most poetic extant descriptions of the life of the **Buddha Shakyamuni**.

Astrology རྩིས་ rtsis *jyotiṣa*

Tibetan **astrology** is a combination of two independent astrological systems, one which developed in India, mainly based on the **KALACAKRA TANTRA**, and the other which originated in ancient China. The former (*dkar-rtsis*) focuses on the position of the constellations and lunar mansions, while the latter (*nag-rtsis/'byung-rtsis*) is concerned primarily with geomantic observations.

Asura (skrt.) ལྷ་མ་ཡིན་ lha ma yin *asura*

See **Six Realms**.

Atisha (skrt.) ཨ་ཏི་ཤ་ A ti sha *Atiśa*

An eleventh century Indian Buddhist scholar from *Vikramashila* university in ancient Bengal, who came to Tibet at the invitation of the king of *Ngari* (Western Tibet), *Lhalama Yeshe-o*, and his nephew *Jangchub-o*. **Atisha**, also known as *Dipamkara-shrijnana*, was a key figure in the revival of Buddhism in Tibet, following its persecution by the Tibetan king *Langdarma* in the ninth century. **Atisha's** works include the celebrated text entitled BODHIPATHAPRADIPA, **LAMP FOR THE PATH OF ENLIGHTENMENT**. Together with his most famous disciple *Dromtonpa*, **Atisha** is accredited with the founding of the Tibetan Buddhist school known as **Kadam**.

Atiyoga (skrt.) ཤིན་ཏུ་རྣལ་འབྱོར་ shin tu rnal 'byor *atiyoga*

The highest of the **nine yana** according to the **Nyingma** school's ninefold **yana** classification, known in Tibetan as *shin-tu rnal-'byor* or *rdzogs-pa chen-po*. For a brief explanation, see **Nine Yanas** and **Dzogchen**.

Attachment འདོད་ཆགས་ 'dod chags *rāga*

In Buddhist psychology, **attachment** (or mental attraction) is usually perceived as one of the principal **dissonant emotions** which afflict the **mind** of an individual, thus perpetuating a chain of constant **rebirth** in the **cycle of existence**. **Attachment**, **hatred** (or mental aversion), and **delusion** are known as the 'three poisons' and together with pride, mundane ambition/envy, and distorted views, constitute the six root **dissonant emotions**.

Avalokiteshvara (skrt.) སྤྱན་རས་གཟིགས་དབང་ཕྱུག་ spyan ras gzigs dbang phyug *Avalokiteśvara*

An embodiment of the **compassion** (*mahakaruna*) of all the **buddhas** (the fully enlightened **mind**), as visualised in the form of a **meditational deity**. **Avalokiteshvara** is considered to be the "patron **deity**" of Tibet and has many different aspects. The most popular aspects of **Avalokiteshvara** are the 'Thousand-armed' *Mahakarunika*, *Padmapani* and *Khasarpani*. **Avalokiteshvara's** sacred **mantra** is the famous six-syllable **mantra** of Tibet: *OM MA-NI PAD-ME HUM*.

Bardo (tib.) བར་དོ་ bar do *antarābhava*

Equivalent to the *Sanskrit* term *antarabhava*, *bardo* indicates an interval or intermediate period of experience between death and **rebirth** and, as expounded particularly in texts of the *Nyingma* and *Kagyu* lineages, between the various important phases of life, death and rebirth. Although some of the early *Hinayana* schools speculated on the presence or absence of such an **intermediate state** between death and **rebirth**, a developed view of *bardo* emerged in the context of *Mahayana* thought and the esoteric teachings of the *Vajrayana* tradition. According to the *Nyingma* perspective, *bardo* is explained in terms of a six- or fourfold division. Here, according to the fourfold division, the **cycle of existence** is divided into the following phases: life itself (*rang-bzhin bar-do*), the time of death or *chikai bardo* (*'chi-kha'i bar-do*), actual **reality** or *chonyi bardo* (*chos-nyid bar-do*), when the **peaceful and wrathful deities** manifest, and the process of **rebirth** or *sidpa bardo* (*srid-pa'i bar-do*). During each of these phases, the **consciousness** of a **sentient being** is said to undergo an experiential transition, and corresponding to these experiences, there are specific meditative techniques conducive to **liberation** from **cyclic existence**. The less elaborate view of Indian *abhidharma* regarding *bardo* is based on two classical sources: the *ABHIDHARMASAMUCCAYA* by *Asanga* and the *ABHIDHARMAKOSHA* by *Vasubandhu*.

Benares བྷཱ་རཱ་ཎ་སཱི་ vā rā ṇa sī *Vārāṇasī*

An historically important place in the state of *Uttar Pradesh*, north-central India, also known as *Varanasi*. It is at *Sarnath*, on the outskirts of *Benares*, that the *Buddha Shakyamuni*, after his attainment of *buddha*hood, gave his first public discourse on the topic of the **Four Noble Truths**. The first discourse is traditionally known as the 'First **Turning of the Wheel** of the *Dharma*'. See **Dharmacakra**.

Bhagavan (skrt.) བཅོམ་ལྡན་འདས་ bcom ldan 'das *bhagavān*

Often translated as 'transcendent lord' or 'blessed lord', this is an honorific term indicating a *buddha* who: 1) has subdued **dissonant emotions** (*klesha*) and **obscurations**; 2) possesses the diverse **enlightened attributes**; and 3) has passed beyond *samsara* and *nirvana*.

Bhavaviveka (skrt.) ལེགས་ལྡན་འབྱེད་ legs ldan 'byed *Bhāvaviveka*

A fifth century Indian scholar whose criticism of *Buddhapalita's* interpretation of *Nagarjuna's* philosophy of **emptiness** led to the split in the *Madhyamaka* school of *Mahayana* Buddhism. He is accredited with the founding of the *Svatantrika* school of *Madhyamaka* philosophy. His principal works include the *PRAJNAPRADIPA* and *MADHYAMAKAHRIDAYA*.

Bhikshu (skrt.) དགེ་སློང་ dge slong *bhikṣu*

A fully ordained monk. See **Pratimoksha Vows**.

Bhumi (skrt.) ས་ sa *bhūmi*

Bhumi literally means 'earth', 'soil', 'land', 'ground' or 'level'. Within the context of the Buddhist path it refers to the progressive levels of **realisation** through which individuals pass as they journey towards full **enlightenment**. *Mahayana* literature speaks of ten such *bhumi*s known as the 'ten *bodhisattva* levels or grounds' (*dashabhumi*), while the *tantras* speak of thirteen or sixteen levels, adding three or six *buddha*-levels to those of the *bodhisattvas*. See **Grounds of a Bodhisattva**.

Bindu (skrt.) ཐིག་ལེ་ thig le *bindu*

Translated as 'seminal point' or 'drop' of energy, the term *bindu* conveys a wide range of meanings. It refers to: a) the pure essence of the white/male and red/female generative or seminal fluids of the body which, along with the energy **channels** and **winds** (flowing through the **channels**), form an important aspect of human physiology according to Buddhist medical theory and *tantra*; b) a synonym for *Dharmakaya*, known as the 'unique seminal point' (*thig-le nyag-gcig*); and c) the seminal points of light which appear during the *thod-rgal* practices of *atiyoga* when the *rupakaya* becomes manifest.

Black hat ཞྭ་ནག་ shva nag

This is a name for the black *vajra* crown associated with the **lineage** of the *Karmapas*. The *Karmapas* are known as the '**Black Hat**' *Karmapas* on account of this famous '**black hat**' which, in one view, was originally presented by the Mongol princes to *Karmapakshi*, the Second *Karmapa*. The celebrated '**black hat**' worn by recent *Karmapas* was given to the fifth *Karmapa*, Tezhinshekpa, by the Ming emperor Yunglo, and it has been worn ceremonially by his subsequent incarnations. The *Karmapas* are contrasted with the *Shamarpas* (or 'Red Hat' *Karmapa*). See **Karmapa**. The term **black hat** also refers to a large circular hat decorated on top with a trident, a skull and peacock feathers, which is worn by monks during certain ceremonial dances. The **black hat** dance is symbolically associated with the assassination of the despot king *Langdarma* by *Lhalung Palgyi Dorje* in the seventh century AD. *Lhalung Palgyi Dorje* was believed to have dressed in a similar costume with broad sleeves from which he drew a bow and arrow and shot at *Langdarma* while the king was reading an announcement from a stone column.

Blessing བྱིན་རླབས་ byin rlabs *adhiṣṭhāna*

In a Buddhist context, the word **blessing** relates to the sense of inspiration, (received from an external source) which transforms the potentials inherent within the individual's mental continuum. The Tibetan term which is commonly translated into English as **blessing** is *byin-rlabs* (pronounced *'jinlap'*). *Byin* means 'magnificence', 'excellence' and 'brilliance', and *rlabs* 'transformed', 'overwhelmed' and 'enveloped'. Thus together the two syllables mean: 'to be transformed through inspiring magnificence'.

Bodhgaya རྡོ་རྗེ་གདན། rdo rje gdan *Vajrāsana*

An historical place in the state of *Bihar*, north-central India, where Prince

Siddhartha (**Buddha Shakyamuni**) attained **buddha**hood while meditating under the shade of a fig tree, which became known as the 'tree of **enlightenment**' or '*Bodhi* Tree'. The classical Buddhist name for this place is *Vajrasana*, so-called because there is said to be a '*vajra* seat' indicative of the indestructible nature of **buddha**hood under the tree. However, the modern name, *Bodhgaya*, which has gained universal usage, is derived from the name of the nearest major town, G*aya*. The city of *Patna* (*Pataliputra*), capital of *Bihar* state, lies not far to the north.

Bodhicitta (skrt.)  བྱང་ཆུབ་ཀྱི་སེམས་ byang chub kyi sems
bodhicitta

An altruistic aspiration to attain full **enlightenment** for the benefit of all beings. *Bodhicitta* is cultivated on the basis of certain mental attitudes, principal among them being the development of **love** and great **compassion** towards all beings equally. The Tibetan tradition speaks of two major systems for training one's **mind** in the generation of *bodhicitta*: the first is *Atisha's* 'seven-point **cause and effect**' and the second is *Shantideva's* 'equality and exchange of oneself with others'. A genuine generation of *bodhicitta* is attained only when, through the training of the **mind**, the aspiration to attain full **enlightenment** becomes spontaneous and no longer requires any deliberate exertion. At that stage the individual becomes a *bodhisattva*. Literally, *bodhi* means 'enlightenment', and *citta*, 'mind'. *Mahayana* literature speaks of two types of *bodhicitta*: the conventional *bodhicitta* and the ultimate *bodhicitta*. The former refers to that aspect of *bodhicitta* defined above, whereas the latter refers to the **discriminative awareness** *(prajna)* directly realising **emptiness** which is induced by the altruistic motivation of *bodhicitta*. In a *tantric* context *bodhicitta* also refers to the white/male and red/female seminal fluids of the body.

Bodhisattva (skrt.) བྱང་ཆུབ་སེམས་དཔའ་ byang chub sems dpa'
bodhisattva

A spiritual trainee who has generated the altruistic **mind** of *bodhicitta* and is on the path to full **enlightenment**. *Bodhisattvas*, literally meaning 'heroes of enlightenment', are courageous individuals who dedicate their entire being towards a single goal, i.e., to bring about the welfare of all **sentient beings**. An essential element of this commitment to work for others is the determination purposely to remain within the **cycle of existence** instead of simply seeking freedom from **suffering** for oneself.

BODHISATTVACARYAVATARA (skrt.) སྤྱོད་འཇུག spyod 'jug
Bodhisattvacaryāvatāra

One of the most celebrated expositions in classical Indian literature on the *bodhisattva* doctrine of *Mahayana Buddhism*, written by the eighth century Indian poet and saint *Shantideva*. The text is written in verse and has ten chapters. It deals extensively with the stages of training one's **mind** in the generation of

bodhicitta, and also with the essential practices of the **bodhisattva's** conduct or way of life. It is considered one of the most authoritative texts on the study and practice of the **bodhisattva** ideals within the Tibetan tradition.

Bodhnath (skrt.) བྱ་རུང་ཁ་ཤོར་ bya rung kha shor *Bodhnāth*

Name of the great **stupa** at *Boudha,* north-west of *Kathmandu,* said to contain relics of the previous **Buddha** *Kasyapa,* and associated in Nepalese chronicles with the sixth century king *Manadeva.*

Bon (tib.) བོན་ bon

An ancient spiritual tradition, considered by scholars to be of Zoroastrian or Kashmiri Buddhist origin, which was widespread in Tibet, particularly in the western region of **Zhangzhung** prior to the official introduction and establishment of Buddhism. Although its literature appears to distinguish it from both the indigenous beliefs of Tibet and the Buddhist traditions, it has over the last several hundred years assimilated many of the teachings of the **Buddha Shakyamuni** and developed a neo-Buddhist theoretical foundation. The **Bon** tradition is particularly strong in the *Shang* region of **Tsang,** in *Kongpo, Khyungpo* and the *Ngawa* region of **Amdo.**

Bonpo (tib.) བོན་པོ་ bon po

A follower of **Bon.** See **Bon.**

Buddha (skrt.) སངས་རྒྱས་ sangs rgyas *buddha*

Buddha literally means 'awakened', 'developed' and '**enlightened**'. The Tibetan equivalent *sangs-rgyas* (pronounced *'sang-gye'*) is a combination of two words *sangs-pa* (awakened or purified) and *rgyas-pa* (developed). The two words in this context denote a full awakening from **ignorance** in the form of the two **obscurations** and a full **realisation** of true **knowledge** or the **pristine cognition** of *buddha-mind.* A fully awakened being is therefore one who, as a result of training the **mind** through the spiritual paths, has finally realised the full potential for complete **enlightenment** and has eliminated all the **obstructions** to true **knowledge** and **liberation.** *Buddhas* are characterised according to diverse modes of *buddha*-body (*kaya*), *buddha*-speech (*vak*), *buddha*-mind (*citta jnana*), attributes (*guna*) and activities (*karmakriya*). See also **Buddha-nature, Buddhahood, Kayas, Shakyamuni, Tathagata** and **Jnana.**

Buddha-Body སྐུ་ sku *kāya*

The various aspects of the bodies of a **buddha.** See **Kayas.**

Buddha/Enlightened-Families རིགས་ rigs *kula*

See **Enlightened-Families.**

Buddha-Mind (སངས་རྒྱས་ཀྱི་) ཐུགས་ (sangs rgyas kyi) thugs *jñāna/citta*

The five aspects of a **buddha's pristine cognition.** See **Jnana.**

Buddha-Nature (སངས་རྒྱས་ཀྱི་) ཁམས/ རིགས་ (sangs rgyas kyi) khams/ rigs (*buddha*)*dhātu/gotra*

The seed of **enlightenment** which is inherent within the mental continuum of all

sentient beings. It is this potential which makes it possible for every individual to realise the true nature, given the application of appropriate methods. The notion of **buddha-nature** is intimately linked with the Buddhist concept of the essential nature of **mind**, which according to Buddhism is considered to be pure, knowing and luminous. **Dissonant emotions** such as **desire**/attraction, **hatred**/aversion and jealousy, etc., which perpetually afflict our **mind** and give rise to **suffering**, are not the essential elements of our **mind** but **karmically** conditioned tendencies. Moreover, these **dissonant emotions** are all rooted in an ignorant state of **mind** which misapprehends the true nature of **reality**. Hence, through gaining genuine insights into the true nature of **reality**, misconceptions can be dispelled, thus cutting the root of all our **delusions** and allowing the **buddha-nature** within to manifest. The **buddha-nature** is also known as **Tathagatagarbha**, the 'nucleus of the **tathagata**', which is a synonym for this essence of **buddha**hood. It has two aspects, namely the **buddha-nature** which naturally abides *(prakrtishthagotra)* and the **buddha-nature** which is deliberately cultivated *(samudanitagotra)*.

Buddha-Speech (སངས་རྒྱས་ཀྱི་) གསུང་ (sangs rgyas kyi) gsung *vāk*

The various aspects of the speech of a **buddha**. See **Mantra** and **Enlightened Attributes..**

Buddhahood (སངས་རྒྱས་ཀྱི་) གོ་འཕང་/སངས་རྒྱས་ཉིད་ (sangs rgyas kyi) go 'phang/sangs rgyas nyid *buddhatva*

The attainment of a **buddha,** who has not only gained total freedom from **karmically** conditioned existence and overcome all the tendencies imprinted on the **mind** as a result of long association with **delusion,** but also fully realised or manifested all aspects of **Buddha-body, speech, mind, attributes and activities**. See **Buddha.**

Buddhist Cosmology ནང་པའི་ལུགས་ཀྱི་འཇིག་རྟེན་འདོད་ཚུལ་ nang pa'i lugs kyi 'jig rten 'dod tshul

There are two main systems of **Buddhist cosmology**, one emerging from *abhidharma* texts such as **Vasubhandu's** ABHIDHARMAKOSHA and the other from the KALACAKRA TANTRA. In both cases there is an acceptance of multiple world systems and of our own as just one amongst these. In a large part, **Buddhist cosmology** is a metaphorical extrapolation of the nature of **mind**.

Burnt Offering སྦྱིན་སྲེག་ sbyin sreg *homa*

A *tantric* ritual involving the burning of many substances, such as wheat, sesame seeds, mustard etc. in a fire lit on a specifically designed hearth. There are different types of **burnt offering** corresponding to the **fourfold activities** of peace, development, influence and force. The peaceful **burnt offering** is the most commonly practised, and it is performed normally as a supplement to the **deity** *yoga* practices at the end of a long *tantric* **retreat.**

Cakra (skrt.) འཁོར་ལོ།/ཙ་འཁོར་ 'khor lo/rtsa 'khor *cakra*

Cakra literally means a 'wheel' or 'circle'. In a *tantric* context, *cakra* refers to the energy centres within a person's body. Buddhist *tantric* physiology speaks of three primary parallel *nadi*, subtle energy **channels**, existing within the human body and running from the crown down to the groin. At certain points within the body the two side **channels** loop around the central **channel**, thus forming knots which obstruct the flow of subtle energy within the central **channel**. It is the branching off of several **channel** spokes, in the region of the knots, that forms a *cakra*. The principal *cakras* are said to be located at the crown, throat, heart, navel and secret organ of a person.

Cakrasamvara (skrt.) འཁོར་ལོ་སྡོམ་པ་ 'khor lo sdom pa *Cakrasaṃvara*

Also known as *Heruka*, **Cakrasamvara** is a **meditational deity** of the *Anuttarayogatantra* class. There are many different aspects of the **deity** deriving from the various traditions established by the Indian masters who propagated this practice. The principal among the traditions are those of the Indian *tantric* meditators *Luipa*, *Krishnacarya* and *Ganthapada*. The study and practice of this *tantra* is widespread in the *Kagyu*, *Sakya* and *Gelug* traditions of **Tibetan Buddhism**, while related forms known as *Buddhasamayoga* and *Shriheruka* are well-known within the *Nyingma* tradition.

Calm abiding ཞི་གནས་ zhi gnas *śamatha*

A state of **mind** which is characterised by the stabilisation of attention on an internal object of observation, conjoined with the calming of external distractions to the **mind**. In addition 'calm abiding' is characterised by the suppleness of **mind** and body which is attained by training one's **mind** through the **nine stages of mental development**. *Shamatha*, which can also be translated as 'tranquil abiding' or 'tranquillity', is an essential basis for training one's **mind** in the generation of *Vipashyana*, a true (analytical) insight into the more profound aspects of the chosen object, such as its **emptiness** or its ultimate nature. See **Mental Pliancy** and the **Nine Stages of Mental Development**.

Candrakirti (skrt.) ཟླ་བ་གྲགས་པ་ zla ba grags pa *Candrakīrti*

A seventh century Indian scholar of the *Madhyamaka* school of thought. His defence of *Buddhapalita* against *Bhavaviveka* and the consequent strong criticism of the latter's acceptance of autonomous **syllogism** led to the emergence of a new school of *Madhyamaka* known as *Prasangika* (Consequentialist). *Candrakirti's* works include the *PRASANNAPADA* (his highly acclaimed **commentary** on *Nagarjuna's* MULAMADHYAMAKAKARIKA), and the *MADHYAMAKAVATARA* (his supplement to *Nagarjuna's* text) and its auto-**commentary**. The *MADHYAMAKAVATARA* is used as the main sourcebook by most of the Tibetan monastic colleges in their studies of **emptiness** and the philosophy of the *Madhyamaka* school.

Caryatantra (skrt.) སྤྱོད་པའི་རྒྱུད་ spyod pa'i rgyud *Caryātantra*

The second among the **four classes of *tantra***. One of the distinguishing characteristics of this class of *tantra* is that in its practice an equal emphasis is placed on both the internal **meditation** (and visualisation) and the external rituals. The principal *tantra* in this class is known as the *AWAKENING OF GREAT VAIROCANA (MAHAVAIROCANABHISAMBODHITANTRA)*, which features the four-faced form of

Tara *(Green)*

Nagarjuna

Vairocana called *Kunrig Nampar Nangze* (*Sarvavid **Vairocana***).

Cause and Effect རྒྱུ་འབྲས་ rgyu 'bras *hetuphala*

In the context of Buddhist philosophy the term refers to the natural law that exists between a cause and its effect. Some of the principal features of the law are: 1) nothing evolves uncaused; 2) any entity which itself lacks a process of change cannot cause any other event; and 3) only causes which possess natures that accord with specific effects can lead to those effects. '**Cause and effect**' is often used to translate the ***Sanskrit*** word ***karma*** which literally means 'action'. The concept of ***karma***, however, not only involves a notion of 'action' but also the psychological tendencies and imprints built up within one's **mind** by the execution of both physical and mental actions. It is also worth bearing in mind that the idea of ***karma*** or '**cause and effect**' in Buddhism cannot be equated with the notion of causality as understood in a strictly deterministic sense.

Chamdo (tib.) ཆབ་མདོ་ chab mdo

Name of a large city at the confluence of two ***Mekong*** tributaries in ***Kham***, the South-eastern part of Tibet, and also an administrative name for the surrounding region. See map.

Channels རྩ་ rtsa *nāḍī*

Energy **channels** are the vein-like passages through which flow the subtle energies that sustain life and which also give rise to various conceptions within the individual's **mind**. According to Buddhist medicine and ***tantric*** physiology a human body contains 72,000 such **channels**, all of them branching off from three main **channels** which run from the crown down to the level of the groin. See **Cakra**.

Chenrezig (tib.) སྤྱན་རས་གཟིགས་ spyan ras gzigs *Avalokita*

The Tibetan equivalent of *Avalokita*. See **Avalokiteshvara**.

Chikai Bardo (tib.) འཆི་ཁའི་བར་དོ་ 'chi kha'i bar do

One of the four (or sometimes classified as six) **intermediate states,** expounded largely in texts of the ***Nyingma*** school. Within this fourfold or sixfold division of ***bardo***, the ***chikai bardo*** (*'chi-kha'i bar-do*) specifically refers to the period beginning from the onset of the definitive signs of death and lasting up to the moment when the **consciousness** leaves the body. This state is said to begin with the gradual dissolution of **five** physical **elements** and their associated modes of **consciousness** prior to death, and to end before the **peaceful and wrathful deities** appear to the **consciousness** of the deceased during the **intermediate state** of actual **reality** (*chos-nyid bar-do*). It is during this period that the basic luminosity or **inner radiance** of the ground (*gzhi'i 'od-gsal*) is experienced, enabling the deceased to realise the nature of ***Dharmakaya***. Accordingly, many techniques have been developed

to effect this **realisation** at the moment of death, including the four ways of dying known to superior **yogins**, the three ways of dying for mediocre **yogins**, and the instructions on '**consciousness transference**' (*'pho-ba*) for inferior **yogins**.

Chod (tib.) གཅོད་(ཡུལ་) gcod (yul)

A set of unique **meditational** practices known as *chodyul (gcod-yul)*, or 'object of cutting'. Based on the ***Prajnaparamita*** tradition, these practices seek to overcome both a **self**-cherishing attitude and the apprehension of an **inherently existing self-identity**, which two kinds of **obscuration** lie at the root of all our **delusions** and **suffering**. These **obscurations** in the form of the **yogin's** own body are symbolically turned into an 'object of cutting' and **compassion**ately offered as a **feast-offering** to unfortunate spirits, often in the awesome surroundings of a charnel ground. The **lineage** of ***Chod*** practice originated in Tibet from the Indian **yogin** *Phadampa Sangye* and the **yogini** *Machik Labkyi Dronma*. The texts of ***Chod*** are sung in melodious verses, accompanied by the rhythmic playing of large hand-drums and bells.

Chonyi Bardo (tib.) ཆོས་ཉིད་བར་དོ་ chos nyid bar do

One of the four (or sometimes classified as six) **intermediate states,** as expounded largely in the texts of the ***Nyingma*** school. Accordingly, the **intermediate state** of 'actual **reality**' or '***chonyi bardo***' (*chos-nyid bar-do*) arises after the ***chikai bardo*** and before the **intermediate state** of the process of **rebirth** (*srid-pa'i bar-do*). 'Actual **reality**' is a synonym for **emptiness** (***shunyata***), **ultimate truth** (*paramarthasatya*), the coalescence of pure appearance and **emptiness** (*snang-stong zung-'jug*) and so forth. The moment of 'actual **reality**' refers to the time at which the **peaceful and wrathful deities** indicative of the ***buddha*-body** of perfect resource (***sambhogakaya***) appear to the **consciousness** of the deceased in their coloured light forms, which correspond to the primordial, purified natures of the five **aggregates**, the five elemental properties, etc. Simultaneously the deceased experiences the dull lights of the impure **aggregates** and **obscurations**, which cloud recognition of 'actual **reality**'. Therefore there exist diverse meditative techniques which enable the **yogin** or **yogini** to recognise the **peaceful and wrathful deities**.

Cintamani Tara (skrt.) སྒྲོལ་མ་ཙིནྟ་མ་ནི་ sgrol ma tsi nta ma ni *Cintāmaṇitārā*

A specific **meditational** practice of the female **deity** Green ***Tara***. Normally Green ***Tara*** is associated with the ***Kriya tantras***, but ***Cintamani Tara*** belongs to the ***Anuttarayogatantra*** class, and so includes both the **generation**/creation stage and the **completion/perfection stage** of *tantric* **meditation**. This particular **lineage** of ***Tara*** originated from the early nineteenth century Tibetan master *Tagpu Dorje Chang* who was inspired by the mystical experiences which arose in association with his visions of Green ***Tara***. This practice is popular mainly in the ***Gelug*** tradition of **Tibetan Buddhism**. ***Cintamani*** literally means the 'jewel of the heart'.

Cittamatra (skrt.) སེམས་ཙམ་ sems tsam *Cittamātra*

One of the four major Buddhist philosophical schools of ancient India, also known as *Vijnanavada*, and sometimes identified with the term *Yogacara*. Founded by the fourth century Indian scholar and saint ***Asanga***, this school of thought propounds a phenomenalistic view of the world. Its main tenet is that all phenomena are either actual mental events or extensions of the **mind**. In addition, the school propounds that there exists no atomically composed material world which is external to, or independent of, our perceptions. The *Cittamatra* school possesses one of the most complex and comprehensively argued metaphysical and epistemological theories among the four major Buddhist philosophical schools. *Citta* means '**mind**' and *matra* 'only'.

Cittamatrin (skrt.) སེམས་ཙམ་པ་ sems tsam pa *Cittamātrin*

An adherent of the *Cittamatra* school. See **Cittamatra**.

Clear Light འོད་གསལ་ 'od gsal *prabhāsvara*

Also known as '**inner radiance** of **mind**-as-such' (*prabhasvaracitta*), this term refers, in the context of the **completion** or perfection stage of **Anuttarayogatantra**, to the subtlest level of **mind** (which is the fundamental, essential nature of all our cognitive events). Though ever present within all **sentient beings**, this **inner radiance** becomes manifest only when the gross **mind** has ceased to function. Such a dissolution is experienced by ordinary beings, naturally, at the time of death, but can also be experientially cultivated through **Anuttarayogatantra** techniques in **meditation** and specifically through yogic techniques applied during the interval between the dream and waking states of **consciousness**. *Tantric* literature speaks of different degrees of subtlety in one's experience of '**clear light**', which are of vital importance for understanding the true nature of **mind**. A basic distinction is made between the 'mother' **clear light** (which occurs at death but may not necessarily be accompanied by an awareness of its nature) and the 'son' or 'off-spring' **clear light** (which is an awareness of lack of **inherent existence**, i.e., the nature of the mother **clear light**, developed in **meditation**).

Collected Topics བསྡུས་རྭ་ bsdus rva

Known as *dura* in Tibetan, the '**COLLECTED TOPICS**' include the elementary study of debate and dialectics in Tibetan monastic education. The topics are extracted mainly from *Dharmakirti's* classic work on Buddhist logic and **epistemology** the *PRA-MANAVARTTIKA* and are divided into three levels: the initial, the middling and the advanced. The books dealing with **Collected Topics** are written specifically as introductions to logic and the art of reasoning for students at the beginner's level. The evolution of such a systematic and phased training in logic and debate is accredited to the tenth century Tibetan logician *Chapa Chokyi Senge* who is believed to have also written the first book on **Collected Topics**. See **Tarig**.

Commentary འགྲེལ་པ་/ འཁྲིད་ 'grel pa/'khrid *vrtti*

A **commentary** on a text can take the form of either an oral or a written elucidation. Two basic types therefore occur, namely: 'guidance' (*khrid*, pronounced '*tri*'), which is usually associated with oral instructions, and 'exposition' ('*grel-pa*, pronounced '*drelwa*'), which is usually associated with written works. The

former type comprises the exegesis (*bshad-khrid*), the guidance which lays bare the oral teachings (*dmar-khrid*), and the experiential guidance of meditative development (*nyams-khrid*). The latter category includes the literal interpretation of a text (*tshig-'grel*), the exposition of the intended themes of a text (*don-'grel*), the explanatory treatment of the most difficult points of a text (*bka'-'grel*), and the extensive **commentary** (*rgya-cher 'grel*).

Compassion ཉིང་རྗེ་ snying rje *karuṇā*

In Buddhist literature the term is often used as a short form for 'great **compassion**' which refers to a totally unbiased **mind** that aspires to the **liberation** of all **sentient beings** from **suffering**, equally. **Compassion** is said to become 'great' only when, through proper training of the **mind**, such an altruistic aspiration becomes spontaneous and no longer requires any conscious effort for its arisal. The measure of having realised such a state is that one spontaneously feels a sense of intimacy and **compassion** towards all others, with the same degree of commitment that one feels towards one's most beloved. It is worth bearing in mind that in Buddhism, **compassion** should not be understood in terms of pity, which implies a feeling of superiority toward the object of **compassion**.

Completion Stage རྫོགས་རིམ་ rdzogs rim *sampannakrama*

The **completion** or perfection **stage** of *Anuttarayogatantra*, which is contrasted with the **generation** or creation **stage** in which the visualisation of the **deity** is developed and refined. Following the meditative generation of the form and an approximation of the **pristine cognition** of the **deity** during the **generation stage**, the **completion stage** employs techniques for controlling the **winds** and seminal fluids within the **energy channels** of the *yogin's* transmuted body. The purpose is to make manifest the **inner radiance** induced by the ever deepening **realisation** of the four kinds of '**emptiness**' or 'dissolution stages' (*stong-pa bzhi*) and of the coemergent **pristine cognition** induced by the four kinds of delight or joy (*dga'-ba bzhi*). The factor which marks the transition from generation stage to completion stage is the *yogin's* ability to draw the **winds** (*prana*) into the central channel.

Concentration བསམ་གཏན་ bsam gtan *dhyāna*

Meditative **concentration** has various meanings depending on the context. In *abhidharma* literature it is numbered among the series of **mental events or factors**, where it indicates the faculty of single-pointedness and stability (one of the five **mental factors** of ascertainment, faculties present during a veridical cognitive event). In *Hinayana* **meditation** it refers to the **four concentrations**, through which **sentient beings** are said to attain birth in the **form realm**. In the *Mahayana* tradition, it is the fifth of the **six perfections** cultivated by a *bodhisattva*. Among examples of meditative **concentration** (*dhyana* in *Sanskrit*) are '**calm abiding**' (*shamatha*) and *samadhi* (*ting-nge-'dzin*), which in its Buddhist usage indicates a true grasp of the profound nature of **reality** acquired through powerful contemplation. See **Four Concentrations** and **Mental Factors**.

Confession བཤགས་པ་ bshags pa *deśanā*

A spiritual practice which involves the disclosure and **purification** of one's accumulation of negative actions. A successful practice of **confession** must be undertaken within the framework of what are known as the four powers: 1) the power of repentance; 2) the power of reliance; 3) the power of the actual antidote; and 4) the power of resolve never to indulge in the act again. See **Four Opponent Forces**.

Conflicting Emotion ཉོན་མོངས་ nyon mongs *kleśa*

See **Dissonant Emotions**.

Consciousness ཤེས་པ་/ རྣམ་ཤེས་ shes pa/rnam shes *vijñāna*

In Buddhism, consciousness is defined as 'an awareness which is knowing and luminous'. It is not physical and thus lacks any resistance to obstruction. It has neither shape nor colour; it can be experienced but not externally perceived as an object. In short, it is the agent through which we know and perceive the world. There are six types of consciousness: the five sensory consciousnesses and mental consciousness. Some schools of thought accept, in addition to the above six, *Alayavijnana*, a fundamental store consciousness, and *Klishthamanovijnana*, a deluded consciousness, thus making an eightfold division. In either case, the original *Sanskrit* term *vijnana* or its Tibetan equivalent *rnam-shes* (pronounced *'namshe'*) not only includes the conscious cognitive events, but also the subconcious aspects of the **mind** as well. Hence, consciousness has a much broader application in the Buddhist context.

Consciousness Transference འཕོ་བ་ 'pho ba *saṃkrānti*

See **Phowa**.

Consequence ཐལ་འགྱུར་ thal 'gyur *prasaṅga*

A form of reasoning which principally reveals internal inconsistencies within the argument of an opponent. Such a form of reasoning forces opponents either to give up their original position or to maintain it at the cost of a self-contradiction. Although employed by all schools of Buddhist thought, it is the *Madhyamaka Prasangika* school which employs consequential arguments the most vigorously. See **Pramana** and **Syllogism**.

Conventional Truth ཐ་སྙད་བདེན་པ་ tha snyad bden pa *vyavahārasatya*

All Buddhist philosophical systems of thought expound their metaphysical views within the framework of **two truths**: the '**conventional truth**' and the '**ultimate truth**'. However, the definition of the **two truths** differs within the Buddhist philosophical schools based on each school's epistemological theories. According to the *Mahayana* schools of thought, which place greatest emphasis on the concept of the **two truths**, the **conventional truth** can be defined as the empirical aspect of **reality** conventionally experienced through our perceptions. Such an aspect of **reality** is true only within the relative framework of our own veridical experiences. **Conventional truth** is also known as 'relative **truth**' or 'deceptive **truth**'. See **Ultimate Truth**.

Copper (Coloured) Mountain བཟང་མདོག་དཔལ་རི་ bzang mdog dpal ri

The **copper** coloured **mountain** of *Camaradvipa (rnga-yab gling)* is the name of the **pure realm** of *Padmasambhava* where he is said to reside in an awesome rainbow-light form.

Cosmology འཇིག་རྟེན་འདོད་ཚུལ་ 'jig rten 'dod tshul

See **Buddhist Cosmology**.

Cyclic Existence འཁོར་བ་ 'khor ba *saṃsāra*

A state of existence, conditioned by one's **karmic** tendencies and imprints from past actions, i.e., recurring habitual patterns, which is characterised by a cycle of life and death and by **suffering**. Buddhist literature explains the process of how an individual rotates in such a cycle in terms of what are known as the '**twelve links of dependent origination**', the first link in the chain being **ignorance**. See **Twelve Links of Dependent Origination**.

Dagpo Kagyu (tib.) དྭགས་པོ་བཀའ་བརྒྱུད་ dvags po bka' brgyud

A generic name for the various *Kagyu* lineages descended from *Dagpo Lharje Gampopa*, one of *Milarepa*'s foremost students.

Daka (skrt.) མཁའ་འགྲོ་ mkha' 'gro *ḍāka*

The male counterpart of a *Dakini*. See **Dakini**.

Dakini (skrt.) མཁའ་འགྲོ་མ་ mkha' 'gro ma *ḍākinī*

A *yogini* who has attained either mundane or supermundane accomplishments (*siddhi*), the latter referring to the **realisations** of the fully enlightened **mind**. She can be a human being who has achieved such attainments or a manifestation of the **enlightened mind** of the **meditational deity**. *Dakini* also refers to someone born in the '**pure realm**' of the *Dakinis*. The Tibetan equivalent '*Khandro*' literally means 'space voyager', the term space here being used metaphorically to imply **emptiness** (the ultimate nature of **reality**) and 'voyager' meaning someone immersed in its experience.

Dalai Lama (tib.) ཏཱ་ལའི་བླ་མ་/རྒྱལ་བ་རིན་པོ་ཆེ་ tā la'i bla ma/rgyal ba rin po che

The temporal and spiritual leader of Tibet. The *Dalai Lama's* temporal reign began at the time of the Fifth *Dalai Lama* in the seventeenth century. Since then Tibet has been ruled, periodically, by the succession of *Dalai Lamas*, until China's invasion in the 1950s. The *Dalai Lamas* are chosen according to a strict traditional procedure of observation and examination initiated following the death of the previous *Dalai Lama*. The present *Dalai Lama* is the fourteenth in the succession of this **reincarnation lineage**. The title *Dalai Lama* was originally offered to *Sonam Gyatso*, the Third *Dalai Lama*, by the then Mongol prince, *Altan Qan*. The Mongol word *Dalai*, *Gyatso* in Tibetan, means 'ocean (of **wisdom**)'.

Damtsig Dorje (tib.) དམ་ཚིག་རྡོ་རྗེ་ dam tshig rdo rje *Samayavajra*

A **meditational deity** specifically related to the practice of restoring broken commitments and pledges of the *tantric* path, by those holding *tantric* **vows**.

Dedication of Merit དགེ་བ་སྔོ་བ་ dge ba sngo ba *puṇyapariṇāma*

An important element of Buddhist practice enacted normally in the form of a recitation of certain verses of dedication at the conclusion of a spiritual practice. In all Buddhist practices, the motivation at the beginning and the dedication at the end are regarded as highly significant. The most popular objects of the dedication are: the flourishing of the *dharma* throughout the universe and the attainment of full **enlightenment** by all **sentient beings**. Dedicating one's positive potential in this way ensures the stability of the potential, which could otherwise be vulnerable to destruction by anger and other adverse conditions.

Deity ལྷ་ lha *deva/devatā*

See **Meditational Deity**.

Deity Yoga ལྷའི་མངོན་རྟོགས་/བསྐྱེད་རིམ་ lha'i mngon rtogs/bskyed rim *devatābhisamaya/utpattikrama*

See **Generation Stage**.

Delusion གཏི་མུག་ gti mug *moha*

One of the six primary '**dissonant emotions**' and '**three poisons**' of the **mind**, which along with attraction and aversion, arises from **fundamental ignorance** at the onset of cyclical existence. It is characterised by a misunderstanding of the nature of **reality**. Although **delusion** is generally defined as a **mental factor** which obscures one's **mind**, thus obstructing the individual from generating **knowledge** or insight, Buddhist schools differ as to whether or not this process of **obscuration** is active or inactive. Those such as *Nagarjuna* and *Dignaga* who maintain that it is an active process, define **delusion** as a distorted mental state which misapprehends the actual nature of **reality**. However, Asanga and some of his followers define **delusion** as a passive state of obscuration. Some translators have used the term **delusion** to refer to '**dissonant emotions**' in general. See **Dissonant Emotions**.

Demigod ལྷ་མ་ཡིན་ lha ma yin *asura*

See **Six Realms**.

Demon གདོན་འགེགས་/འབྱུང་པོ་ gdon 'gegs/'byung po *vighna/bhūta*

The Tibetan *don geg* is a general term referring to all types of malevolent forces, while *jung po* (*bhuta*) indicates a class of elemental spirits. References to the variety and nature of demonic forces appear mainly in Tibetan medical literature, where certain illnesses are described as being 'demonically caused', and also in *tantric* texts where specific rituals to overcome them are prescribed. Although such literature often describes these forces in animistic terms, ascribing to them personalities of their own etc, in a Buddhist context they are regarded as subtle physiological and

psychological forces which obstruct the well-being of the individual. Such forces are perceived as manifestations of one's own deluded, negative **mind** and not autonomous separate beings.

Dependent Origination རྟེན་འབྲེལ་ rten 'brel *pratītyasamutpāda*

Also translated as 'dependent arising' this term refers to the dependent nature of all phenomena. The concept of **'dependent origination'** can be said to be one of the most fundamental metaphysical views of Buddhist thought and it is intimately linked with the Buddhist notion of causation. The principle of **dependent origination** asserts that nothing exists independently of other factors, the reason for this being that things and events come into existence only by dependence on the aggregation of multiple causes and conditions. There are various levels of subtlety in the meaning of **dependent origination**, depending on the interpretation of this principle by different philosophical schools of thought. The Tibetan tradition maintains that the most profound understanding of **dependent origination** is that found in the **Madhyamaka Prasangika** school. Here, **dependent origination** is equated with the **Madhyamaka Prasangika** view of **emptiness**. See **Twelve Links of Dependent Origination**.

Desire འདོད་ཆགས་ 'dod chags *rāga*

In Buddhist literature, **desire** is defined as a **'mental factor'** that is attracted towards mundane objects, both external and internal, and aspires to possess them. It is one of the six primary **dissonant emotions** and the term is used mainly with a negative connotation in Buddhist writings. See **Attachment**.

Desire Realm འདོད་ཁམས་ 'dod khams *kāmadhātu*

Buddhism speaks of the nature of an individual's **rebirth** in **cyclic existence** within the framework of three realms: the **desire realm**, the **form realm** and the **formless realm**. The **desire realm** refers to a state of mundane existence where an individual's life is dominated by sensual experiences, particularly the sensations of **suffering** and pleasure. It includes the human realm, animal realm and also some *deva* (**god**) realms.

Deva (skrt.) ལྷ་ lha *deva*

See **Six Realms** and **Gods**.

Dharma (skrt.) ཆོས་ chos *dharma*

A very broad term with a wide range of usage, derived from the **Sanskrit** *dhri* (to hold) and rendered in Tibetan as *chos* (pronounced '*cho*'), which literally means 'change' or 'transformation', and refers both to the process of spiritual transformation and the transformed result. Ten classical definitions of *dharma* are given by **Vasubandhu** in his *VYAKHYAYUKTI*, namely: knowable phenomena, path, *nirvana*, object of **mind**, **merit**, life, scripture, material object, regulation and doctrinal tradition. In terms of the doctrinal tradition of Buddhism in particular, *dharma* includes: the **realisation** (*adhigama*) of the **buddhas**, both of the state of cessation and the paths leading to it, and the **transmission** of authoritative texts (*agama*) and their oral commentarial **lineages** which expound the path to **buddha**hood.

Dharmacakra (skrt.) ཆོས་ཀྱི་འཁོར་ལོ་ chos-kyi 'khor lo *dharmacakra*

A metaphorical word referring to the spiritual **realisations** on the path to

enlightenment and also the original teachings of the *Buddha Shakyamuni* which outline such paths. '*Dharmacakra*' literally means the 'wheel of *dharma*'. Its association with the concept of a wheel derives from a comparison with the '**Wheel of Sharp Weapons**' said to be held in the hand of a universal emperor. Within the context of this comparison, *dharma* is composed of the central axis of ethical discipline, the sharp spokes of analytic **discriminative awareness** (*prajna*), and the stabilising perimeter of meditative **concentration** (*dhyana*). Like the mythological wheel, *dharma* is regarded as swift in its transformative passage and as having the capacity to overcome its adversaries. The three great discourses which the *Buddha Shakyamuni* gave at *Sarnath*, *Rajagriha* and *Shravasti* respectively are also known as the 'three turnings of the wheel of *dharma*' or the three *Dharmacakrapravartana*. See **Sutra**.

DHARMADHARMATAVIBHAGA (skrt.) ཆོས་དང་ཆོས་ཉིད་རྣམ་འབྱེད་ chos dang chos nyid rnam 'byed *Dharmadharmatāvibhāga*

One of the FIVE WORKS OF *MAITREYA*. Like its counterpart the *MADHYANTAVIBHAGA*, it deals mainly with the philosophical views associated with the *Tathagatagarbha* doctrine, as well as with the *Cittamatra* school of thought.

Dharmadhatu (skrt.) ཆོས་དབྱིངས་ chos dbyings *dharmadhātu*

As the 'expanse' of actual **reality**, *dharmadhatu* refers to the **emptiness** which is the dimension of the *Dharmakaya*. It also indicates the **pristine cognition** of **reality**'s expanse (*dharmadhatujnana*), which is the aspect of *buddha*-**mind** associated with *Vairocana* or *Akshobhya*. See **Emptiness**.

Dharmakaya (skrt.) ཆོས་སྐུ་ chos sku *dharmakāya*

According to *Mahayana* Buddhism, the *buddha*-**nature** is fully enlightened in a presence comprising three, four or five **buddha**-bodies (*kaya*). Among these the *Dharmakaya* refers to the ultimate nature of the fully enlightened **mind**, a coalescence or union of pure appearance and **emptiness**. As **emptiness** it is: non-dualistic, pure and free of all levels of conceptuality and can only be directly experienced; and as pure appearance it is: the underlying pristine nature of **mind**, a non-dualistic and subtle **inner radiance**, present as an uncultivated seed in unenlightened beings and fully developed as the resultant **Buddha**hood from which the diverse *Sambhogakaya* and *Nirmanakaya* manifestations of *buddha*-**body** arise. On its **realisation** at the moment of death, see **Chikai Bardo**.

Dharmapala (skrt.) ཆོས་སྐྱོང་ chos skyong *dharmapāla*

See **Protector**.

Dharmarakshita (skrt.) ཆོས་སྲུང་ chos srung *Dharmarakṣita*

The eleventh century Indian author of an important text on the

practice of **Lojong** entitled *THE WHEEL OF SHARP WEAPONS*.

Dharmata (skrt.) ཆོས་ཉིད་ chos nyid *dharmatā*

In **Mahayana** Buddhism, 'actual **reality**' is a synonym for **emptiness** or **ultimate truth**. The actual **reality** (*chos-nyid*, Skrt. *dharmata*) or **ultimate truth** of phenomena is contrasted with the apparitional or apparent **reality** of phenomena (*chos-can*, skrt. *dharmin*). The word **dharma** in the sense of knowable phenomena is considered to be neutral in terms of these **emptiness** and apparitional aspects.

Dhyana (skrt.)

See **Meditative Concentration**.

Dhyani Buddhas རྒྱལ་བ་(རིགས་ལྔ་) rgyal ba (rigs lnga) *(pañcakula) jina*

See **Enlightened-Families**.

Direct Perception མངོན་སུམ་ mngon sum *pratyakṣa*

A perceptual state which is non-conceptual and direct in its cognition of the object. '**Direct perceptions**' can be either sensory or mental. '**Direct mental perceptions**' refer to our intuitive **direct perceptions** which arise spontaneously without any reliance on conceptual processes. According to the **Sautrantika** school (the main Buddhist epistemologists) **direct perception** is also defined as being pure and non-deceptive. In any case, all Buddhist philosophical schools commonly agree that **direct perceptions** must be true, as opposed to perceptual illusions.

Discriminative Awareness ཤེས་རབ་ shes rab *prajña*

See Prajna.

Dissonant Emotions ཉོན་མོངས་ nyon mongs *kleśa*

Psychological defilements which afflict our **mind** and obstruct the expression of its essentially pure nature. **Abhidharma** literature mentions six primary **dissonant emotions** and their derivatives, the twenty secondary **dissonant emotions**. At the root of all these psychological defilements lies a **fundamental ignorance** (*avidya*),which misapprehends the true nature of **reality**. The original **Sanskrit** word *klesha* is also translated as 'conflicting emotion', 'afflictive emotion', 'defilement', or 'negative emotion and cognitive events'. The Tibetan equivalent *nyon-mongs* (pronounced '*nyonmong*') is defined as a mental event whose arisal causes psychological afflictions within the **mind**, thus destroying its peace and composure. In addition to the three **dissonant emotions** or 'poisons', namely **delusion**, **attachment** and **hatred**/aversion, there is another enumeration of five, including pride and mundane ambition/envy, and yet another of six which adds wrong **view**.

Divination བརྟག་པ་/མོ་ brtag pa/mo *parīkṣā*

A practice of divining possible future circumstances through the interpretation of certain observations or, in some cases, through possession by **protective deities**. The most popularly practised forms of **divination** in Tibet were *mo* (observations performed on the basis of throwing dice or using rosaries), *phra* (pronounced '*tra*'; a ritual in which the practitioner reads from a mirror), and *lung* (consultation with **oracles**). These practices have been continued in the Tibetan tradition, following the introduction of Buddhism into Tibet, as aspects of **skilful means** in helping others.

Doha (skrt.) ད་ཧ་ do ha *dohā*

A category of poetic songs inspired by the **meditator's** mystical experiences. A classic example of such *doha* is the collection of songs by the Indian *Mahasiddha Saraha*.

Dorje (tib.) རྡོ་རྗེ་ rdo rje *vajra*

In the sense of *rdo-rje pha-lam* (pronounced '*dorje phalam*'), this term means the diamond, literally 'the sovereign among all stones'. In Buddhism however *rdo-rje* indicates the indestructible **reality** of *buddhahood*, which is defined as both imperishable (*mi-gshigs*) and indivisible (*ma-phyed*). The emblem symbolic of this indestructible **reality** is also known as *rdo-rje* or *vajra*. This is a sceptre-like *tantric* ritual object which is held in the right palm when playing a ritual bell. The sceptre symbolises **skilful means** and the bell, **discriminative awareness**. Holding these together in the two palms represents the perfect union of **discriminative awareness** and method/**skilful means**.

Dorje Lobpon (tib.) རྡོ་རྗེ་སློབ་དཔོན་ rdo rje slob dpon *vajrācārya*

The 'master of indestructible **reality**' (*Vajracarya*) who presides over elaborate *tantric* rituals including **empowerment** ceremonies, embodying the central **deity** of the *mandala*.

Dorje Naljorma (tib.) རྡོ་རྗེ་རྣལ་འབྱོར་མ་ rdo rje rnal 'byor ma *Vajrayoginī*

See **Vajrayogini**.

Dorje Trolo (tib.) རྡོ་རྗེ་གྲོད་ལོད་ rdo rje gro lod

One of the eight manifestations of *Guru Rinpoche*. See **Guru Rinpoche**.

Dorje Zhonu རྡོ་རྗེ་གཞོན་ནུ་ rdo rje gzhon nu *Vajrakumāra*

Also known as *Vajrakumara*, this is a well-known form of *Vajrakila*.

Dream Yoga རྨི་ལམ་ (གྱི་རྣལ་འབྱོར་) rmi lam (gyi rnal 'byor) *svapna(yoga)*

One of the **six yogas of Naropa** specifically involving meditative techniques for utilising and transforming dream **consciousness** within **Anuttarayogatantra**. See **Six Yogas of Naropa**.

Drepung (tib.) འབྲས་སྤུངས་ 'bras spungs

One of the three great *Gelug* monastic universities of Tibet. Founded by *Jamyang Choje Tashi Palden* in 1416, *Drepung* was reputed to be the largest monastery in the world before 1959. Much of the original monastery was destroyed consequent to the suppression of the **Lhasa** uprising in 1959, although the assembly hall and some of the college buildings are currently undergoing restoration. A new monastic institute named after the original **Drepung** has been re-established by the exiled Tibetan community and is now flourishing in *Mundgod*, south India. Although the original **Drepung** in Tibet had six colleges, currently in India there are two, namely **Loseling** and **Gomang**.

Drikung Kagyu (tib.) འབྲི་གུང་བཀའ་བརྒྱུད་ 'bri gung bka' brgyud

The branch of the **Kagyu** tradition established at *Drikung Til* Monastery in the upper *Kyichu* valley in 1179 by *Kyopa Jigten Gonpo Rinchenpel*.

Drukpa Kagyu (tib.) འབྲུག་པ་བཀའ་བརྒྱུད་ 'brug pa bka' brgyud

The branch of the **Kagyu lineage** descended from *Lingje Repa* and *Tsangpa Gyare*. It has three divisions - upper, lower and central, which correspond to its geographical dispersal throughout the Tibetan plateau.

Dualism གཟུང་འཛིན་གྱི་ལྟ་བ་ / གཉིས་སྣང་ gzung 'dzin gyi lta ba/gnyis snang *grahyagrahakadarśana*

Any level of perception of **duality**. Buddhist thought describes various forms of **dualism**, principal amongst these being: 1) a dualistic perception of subject and object; 2) all appearances of **inherent existence**; 3) all appearances of conventionalities; and 4) all forms of conceptuality. A genuine direct **realisation** of **emptiness** is non-dual, in that it is free from all the above forms of **dualism**.

Duality གཟུང་འཛིན་ / གཉིས་སྣང་ gzung 'dzin/gnyis snang *grahyagrahaka*
See **Dualism**.

Dura (tib.) བསྡུས་ར་ bsdus rva
See **Collected Topics**.

Dzambala (skrt. read Jambhala) ཛམ་བྷ་ལ་ dzam bha la *Jambhala*
See **Jambhala**.

Dzogchen (tib.) རྫོགས་ཆེན་ rdzogs chen *mahāsandhi/mahāsampanna*

A synonym for **Atiyoga**, the highest of the **nine yana** according to the **Nyingma** tradition. **Dzogchen** is rendered in English as 'Great Perfection', and is defined as the practice in which the **generation** and **completion stages** are effortlessly present. It is known as 'perfection' (*rdzogs*) because all the **enlightened attributes** of the three **kaya** are effortlessly perfected in the stabilisation of intrinsic awareness (*rang-gi rig-pa*): the **Dharmakaya** which is the essence or **emptiness**, the **Sambhogakaya** which is its natural expression and radiance, and the **Nirmanakaya** which is its all-pervasive unimpeded **compassion** expressed in physical form. It is called 'great' (*chen*) because this perfection is the underlying nature of all things. The **tantra** texts and instructions of **Dzogchen** are divided into three classes: the mental class (*sems-sde*) which emphasises the radiance of **mind**-as-such (*sems-nyid*), the spatial class (*klong-sde*) which emphasises the **emptiness** of **reality**'s expanse, and the esoteric instructional class *(man-ngag-gi-sde)*, in which these aspects are given equal emphasis and in which the meditative techniques of Cutting through Resistance *(khregs-chod)* and All-Surpassing **Realisation** *(thod-rgal)* lead respectively to the manifest **realisation** of the *Dharmakaya* and the *Rupakaya*.

Eightfold Noble Path འཕགས་ལམ་ཡན་ལག་བརྒྱད་ 'phags lam yan lag brgyad *aṣṭāṅgamārga*

One of the **four noble** or sublime **truths** taught by the *Buddha* during his first sermon at *Sarnath*, and also the culminating category among the seven categories which subsume the **thirty-seven aspects of the path to enlightenment**. The **eightfold noble path** is thus the means by which **sufferings** are destroyed or the conclusive path by which the **enlightenment** of the *bodhisattvas* is cultivated. It comprises correct **view**, correct analysis, correct speech, correct action, correct livelihood, correct effort, correct mindfulness, and correct contemplation or meditative stabilisation *(samadhi)*.

Eight Mahayana Precepts (ཐེག་ཆེན་གྱི་)

གསོ་སྦྱོང་ཡན་ལག་བརྒྱད་པའི་ཁྲིམས་ (theg chen gyi) gso sbyongs yan lag brgyad pa'i k *aṣṭāṅgaposadhā*

See **Mahayana Ordination**.

Eight Practice Lineages སྒྲུབ་པའི་ཤིང་རྟ་ཆེན་པོ་བརྒྱད་ sgrub pa'i shing rta chen po brgyad

Also known as the 'eight great conveyances' *(shing-rta chen-po brgyad)* as described in *Jamgon Kongtrul's* SHES-BYA KUN-KHYAB and other eclectic anthologies, these are the **lineages** of the following eight traditions: *Nyingma, Kadam, Sakya, Kagyu, Shangpa Kagyu, Kalacakra* Shadangayoga, *Chod* & *Zhiche*, and *Orgyen Rinchenpel's* tradition of *Sevasadhana*.

EIGHT VERSES OF THOUGHT TRANSFORMATION
བློ་སྦྱོང་ཚིག་བརྒྱད་པ་ blo sbyong tshig brgyad pa

One of the most celebrated works of the Tibetan *Kadampa* master and **meditator** *Langri Thangpa*. Although very short and succinctly expressed, it outlines the essential aspects of the training of one's **mind** in the conduct of a *bodhisattva* . Its main emphasis is on the altruistic practices of the *bodhisattva's* way of life. Particularly highlighted are the skilful ways in which a true practitioner can transcend adverse circumstances and transform these into conditions which will enhance spiritual progress. This text forms part of a tradition which evolved in ancient India and later developed, in Tibet, as a distinct category of practices known as *blo-sbyong* (pronounced '**l***ojong'*), often translated as '**Thought Transformation**' or '**Mind Training**'. See **Lojong**.

Ekajati (skrt.) (སྔགས་སྲུང་མ་)ཨེ་ཀ་ཛ་ཏི་ (sngags srung ma) e ka dza ti *Ekajaṭī*

A protectress of the secret *mantra* tradition, particularly of *Atiyoga*. She has a ferocious appearance, with one hair-knot, one eye, one tooth and one breast.

Ekavira (skrt.) དཔའ་བོ་གཅིག་པ་ dpa' bo gcig pa *ekavīra*

Literally meaning a 'solitary hero', the term is often used to refer to **meditational deities** which are normally visualised as solitary, i.e., without a consort. A popular **deity** among the *Ekavira* class is a solitary aspect of *Vajrabhairava*.

Elements ཁམས་ khams *dhātu*

See **Five Elements**.

Eleven Round Contemplation དམིགས་སྐོར་བཅུ་གཅིག་ dmigs skor bcu gcig

A synthesis of the two main systems for generating **bodhicitta**, namely the method of *Atisha*, known as 'the seven point **cause and effect**' and the method developed by *Shantideva*, which is called 'equality and exchange of oneself with others'. The eleven steps in the **meditation** are: 1) cultivating **equanimity**; 2) recognising all beings as intimately connected with oneself; 3) recollecting their kindness 4) repaying their kindness; 5) developing a special sense of **equanimity** cultivated on the basis of empathy with others; 6) reflecting on the short-comings of **self**-cherishing; 7) reflecting on the benefits of cherishing the welfare of others; 8) **meditation** on 'giving'; 9) **meditation** on 'taking'; 10) generating the unusual attitude of taking upon oneself the responsibility to help others; and 11) the **realisation** of actual **bodhicitta**, which is the culmination of the above practices.

Empowerment དབང་བསྐུར་ dbang bskur *abhiṣeka*

See **Abhisheka**.

Emptiness སྟོང་པ་ཉིད་ stong pa nyid *śūnyatā*

The ultimate nature of **reality** which is the total absence of **inherent existence** and **self-identity** with respect to all phenomena. See **Inherent existence** and **self-identity**. Its synonyms include '**ultimate truth**' (*paramarthasatya*), 'actual **reality**' (*chos-nyid/dharmata*), and 'suchness' (*tathata*). Although the term is known also in *Hinayana* Buddhism, it is in the philosophical tenets of the *Mahayana* schools and particularly the *Madhyamaka* school that the different interpretations of **emptiness** were greatly elaborated. The *Madhyamaka* school is named after the 'Middle Way' (*madhyamapratipad*) between the extremes of **eternalism** and **nihilism**, which was expounded by *Shakyamuni Buddha*, in the earliest *sutras*. There exist different philosophies of **emptiness** within the *Madhyamaka* school: that of the *Svatantrika* who emphasise the use of independent **syllogisms** in proof of **emptiness**, and that of the *Prasangika* who emphasise the consequentialist logic of negation and *reductio ad absurdum* to destroy conceptual elaborations concerning **emptiness**. There is also the tradition known as the **Great** *Madhyamaka*, which in the course of meditative insight distinguishes between the intrinsic **emptiness** of phenomena (*rangtong*) and the extrinsic **emptiness** of pure **enlightened attributes** (*shentong*). Based on different ways of classifying phenomena, the *Mahayana sutras* list either twenty, sixteen, four or two kinds of **emptiness**. There is also a variant usage of

Shantideva

Candrakirti

the term in *tantra* where the concept of the 'four **emptinesses**' or 'four dissolutions' is introduced. See **Madhyamaka, Reality, Eternalism** and **Nihilism**.

Enjoyment Body ལོངས་སྐུ་ longs sku *saṃbhogakāya*

More accurately rendered in English as '*buddha*-**body** of perfect resource' or '*buddha*-**body** of perfect rapture', the *Sambhogakaya* among the three *kaya,* refers to the pure light forms of the *buddha*-**body** endowed with the perfect resource of the major and minor marks (such as the hundred **peaceful and wrathful deities**) which have the power to manifest as an emanational *buddha*-**body** (*nirmanakaya*) and thereby serve the diverse dispositions of **sentient beings**. It is said in *Mahayana* literature that the *Sambhogakaya buddha*-forms manifest in and of themselves at very high levels of **realisation**; that is to say that they appear at a point at which the duality between subject and object dissolves. Such a form is not materially composed and is devoid of any resistance to obstruction. It is characterised as being spontaneously or effortlessly present (*lhun-grub*) and manifest in and of itself (*rang-snang*). According to *tantra*, the *Sambhogakaya* is cultivated on the basis of the **seed-syllables** of the **peaceful and wrathful deities**. See **Dharmakaya, Nirmanakaya** and **Rupakaya**.

Enlightenment བྱང་ཆུབ་ byang chub *bodhi*

In the Buddhist context, '**enlightenment**' refers to an individual's awakening to the **mind's** true nature, *bodhi*, in **Sanskrit**. The Tibetan equivalent *byang-chub* (pronounced '*jangchup*') has the sense of **purification** (*byang*) of **obscurations** and perfection (*chub*) of **omniscience**. The process of '**enlightenment**' therefore proceeds in conjunction with the dispelling of the **dissonant emotions** which obscure the perception of **reality**. A fully-enlightened one is a *bodhisattva* or *buddha* who is totally free from all obstruction to true **knowledge** and the state of **liberation,** and is hence **omniscient** in the **knowledge** of **reality**. See **Bodhisattva, Buddhahood** and **Omniscience**.

Enlightened Attributes (སངས་རྒྱས་ཀྱི་) ཡོན་ཏན་ (sangs rgyas kyi) yon tan *(buddha) guṇa*

The **enlightened attributes** or **qualities of the *buddhas*** (*yon-tan*) are categorised in the commentarial literature of classical Buddhism, particularly by *Maitreya* in Ch. 8 of his *ABHISAMAYA-LAMKARA* and in Pt. 3 of his *MAHAYANOTTARATANTRASHASTRA*. The former refers to the diverse **enlightened attributes** associated with the four *kaya* of the *buddhas*, while the latter categorises sixty-four specific attributes. These comprise: the ten powers of the *buddhas*' **pristine cognition** (*dasabala*), the four fearlessnesses (*caturvaisaradya*), the eighteen distinct characteristics of the *buddhas* (*astadasavenikabuddhadharma*), and the thirty-two major marks on the *buddhas*' body (*dvatrimsanmaha-purusalaksana*), along with the eighty minor marks. These

attributes may also be classified in terms of the specific attributes of a *buddha's* body, speech and **mind**. The attributes of *buddha*-**body** are the thirty-two major marks and eighty minor marks. Those of exalted *buddha*-**speech** are known as the 'sixty melodies of *Brahma*', which implies that *buddha*-**speech** is soothing, gentle, firm, audible from a great distance, and so forth. The attributes of *buddha*-**mind** are threefold: **compassion, omniscience**, and power. In *tantric* literature, a classification of five resultant **enlightened attributes** is given, namely: 1) the pure *buddha*-field; 2) the dimensionless celestial palace; 3) the radiant and pure rays of light; 4) the exalted thrones of the deities; and 5) the possession of desired resources. See also **Activities of the Buddha**.

Enlightened Families རིགས་ rigs *kula*

The five '**Enlightened-Families**' are the perfected, purified states of our five **aggregates, elements,** sense-organs, and sensory perceptions. Since all **sentient beings** possess these faculties, either in their potential or fully manifest forms, any individual who attains *buddha*hood realises their perfected state. Each of the five **enlightened families** comprises a central male *buddha*, representing one of the purified **aggregates**, and a female *buddha* representing one of the purified **elements**. In addition, four of the five **enlightened families** are surrounded by peripheral *bodhisattvas*, representing the purified sense-organs, and sensory perceptions. The five are as follows: 1) the *buddha*-**family** headed by the male *buddha* **Vairocana** (the purified aspect of our **aggregate** of con-sciousness/form), 2) the *vajra* family headed by the male *buddha* **Akshobhya** (the purified aspect of our **aggregate** of **consciousness**/form); 3) the *ratna* family, headed by the male *buddha* **Ratnasambhava** (the purified aspect of our **aggregate** of feeling); 4) the *padma* family, headed by the male *buddha* **Amitabha** (the purified aspect of our **aggregate** of perception/discrimination); and 5) the *karma* family, headed by the male *buddha* **Amoghasiddhi** (the purified aspect of our **aggregate** of conditioning and motivational factors). The correlation between the '**enlightened-families**' and the **aggregates** can vary according to differing *tantric* systems, particularly in the case of *Vairocana* and *Akshobhya* who may alternately be known as the purified aspect of **consciousness** or of form.

Epistemology བློ་རིག་གི་སྐོར་ blo rig gi skor

The branch of philosophy concerned with the theory of **knowledge**. The main questions discussed in Buddhist **epistemology** are the nature of **knowledge**, the divisions of **knowledge**, the various means to **knowledge**, the distinctions between true opinion and **knowledge**, theories of perception, and the various divisions of awareness into **mind** and **mental factors**. The principal sources for these studies are to be found in the literature on *abhidharma*, and pre-eminently in the works of Buddhist logicians such as *Dignaga* and his famous student *Dharmakirti*.

Equanimity བཏང་སྙོམས་ btang snyoms *upekṣā*

One of the essential preliminary meditative perspectives cultivated when training one's **mind** in the development of the altruistic **mind** of *bodhicitta*. It is a state of **mind** in which the practitioner cultivates an unbiased attitude towards all **sentient beings,** regarding them as being completely equal and thus overcoming any sense of partiality towards them. Normally one's attitude towards other persons, for example, is strongly prejudiced by one's classification of others into seemingly incompatible groups of friends, enemies or those regarded with indifference. See **Bodhicitta**.

ESSENCE OF REFINED GOLD གསེར་ཞུན་མ་ gser zhun ma

A text on **Lamrim** practice written by the Third **Dalai Lama**, *Sonam Gyatso*. It is a **commentary** on **Tsong Khapa's** text entitled *SONGS OF SPIRITUAL EXPERIENCE*, a succinct work on the gradual path *(lam-rim)* written in verse. **Tsong Khapa's** text is also known as his short version of the **Lamrim**.

Eternalism རྟག་ལྟ་ rtag lta *nityavāda*

One of the two extremes that one must avoid when seeking an insight into **emptiness**, the true nature of **reality**, the other extreme being **nihilism**. Along with synonyms such as 'absolutism' and 'eternalistic extremism', the term in general Buddhist usage refers to the four so-called eternalistic schools of ancient India, namely *Samkhya, Vaishnavism, Shaivism* and *Jainism*. However, since the definition of the extreme of '**eternalism**' varies according to the subtlety of the philosophical perspective on **emptiness**, the **Hinayana** philosophical traditions and some **Mahayana** schools are also classed as extremist by the **Madhyamaka Prasangika**, to whom all apprehensions of **inherent existence** constitute falling into the extreme of '**eternalism**', and a total denial of existence constitutes falling into **nihilism**. It is in this context that an understanding of **emptiness** is described as the genuine 'Middle Way' *(madhyamapratipad)*. See **Nihilism**.

Ethics ཚུལ་ཁྲིམས་/བླང་དོར་ tshul khrims/blang dor *śīla*

In Buddhist philosophy the term '**ethics**' is used mainly in its practical sense, referring primarily to the ethical principles according to which genuine practitioners of the Buddhist path must live their lives. A morally disciplined life is regarded as an essential foundation without which it is impossible to embark on any valid spiritual path.

Exchanging Self with Others བདག་གཞན་མཉམ་བརྗེས་ bdag gzhan mnyam brjes

A specific method for training the **mind** in the generation of the altruistic **mind** of **enlightenment** (*bodhicitta*), systematised by the seventh century Indian poet and accomplished master **Shantideva**. An extensive treatment of this topic can be found in his celebrated book the **BODHISATTVACARYAVATARA** (*INTRODUCTION TO THE CONDUCT OF A BODHISATTVA*), although some aspects of these practices can be also found in earlier Buddhist works such as **Nagarjuna's** *RATNAVALI* (*JEWEL GARLAND*).

Feast Offering ཚོགས་ tshogs *gaṇa*

See **Tsog**.

FIFTY VERSES OF GURU DEVOTION བླ་མ་ལྔ་བཅུ་པ་ bla ma lnga bcu pa

An important text, written by the Indian scholar **Ashvagosha**, which outlines the proper perspectives and procedures through which **tantric** practitioners should relate to their spiritual teacher. Also described are the qualifications of an appropriate **tantric** master.

Fire Offering སྦྱིན་སྲེག་ sbyin sreg *homa*
See **Burnt Offering**.

Five Elements འབྱུང་བ་ལྔ་ 'byung ba lnga *pañcabhūta*

The **elements** of earth, water, fire, wind, and space. These **five elements** refer to both the components of external phenomena and to the five internal components of the human body. The internal **elements** are the physical properties of solidity, fluidity, heat, movement and energy and the vacuities within our bodies. A proper understanding of both external and internal **elements** and their relationship is very important in the practice of Buddhist **tantra**.

Five (Mahayana) Paths (ཐེག་ཆེན་གྱི་) ལམ་ལྔ་ (theg chen gyi) lam lnga *pañcamārga*

See **Grounds and Paths**.

FIVE WORKS OF MAITREYA འབྱམས་ཆོས་སྡེ་ལྔ་ 'byams chos sde lnga

These **five works** accredited to the **bodhisattva Maitreya** are: *ABHISAMAY-ALAMKARA (ORNAMENT OF CLEAR/EMERGENT REALISATION)*, *MAHAYANOT-TARATANTRASHASTRA (SUPREME CONTINUUM OF THE GREATER VEHICLE)*, *MAHAYANASUTRALAMKARA (ORNAMENT OF THE MAHAYANA SUTRAS)*, *MADHYA-NTAVIBHAGA (DISTINCTION BETWEEN THE MIDDLE AND EXTREMES)*, and *DHARMA-DHARMATAVIBHAGA (DISTINCTION BETWEEN PHENOMENA AND ACTUAL REALITY)*.

Fivefold Path of Mahamudra ཕྱག་ཆེན་ལྔ་ལྡན་ phyag chen lnga ldan

An entire practice of the path to **buddha**hood based on the **Mahamudra** system of the **Kagyu** school. The five paths are: **meditation** on **bodhicitta** (*byang-sems sgom-pa*), **deity yoga** (*lha'i rnal-'byor*), **guruyoga** (*bla-ma'i rnal-'byor*), the actual path of **Mahamudra** (*phyag-rgya chen-po lam-dngos*), and the concluding **dedication of merit** (*sngo-ba*).

Form Body གཟུགས་སྐུ་ zugs sku *rūpakāya*

In **Hinayana** Buddhism the term **Rupakaya** refers to the thousand **buddhas** of the aeon, including **Shakyamuni**. In **Mahayana**, however, the term is used to refer to both the **Sambhogakaya** and **Nirmanakaya** aspects of manifestation. In **Vajrayana** Buddhism the notion of **kaya** is expressed in terms of the ground, path and result. In the context of the ground, the **Rupakaya** arises from the nondual expanse of **Dharmakaya**. In the context of the path, it spontaneously arises out of great unimpeded **compassion**, naturally in accordance with the potential of **sentient beings**; and in the context of the result, it is the ultimate fruit of the successful accumulation of **merit**. See **Two Accumulations** and **Dharmakaya**.

Form Realm གཟུགས་ཁམས་ gzugs khams *rūpadhātu*

One of the three realms or divisions of **cyclic existence**, contrasted with those of

desire and formlessness. The **form realm** is characterised as a realm of existence in which the level of **consciousness** is comparatively subtle and is temporarily devoid of gross sensations of pain and pleasure. It is a state beyond ordinary human existence and inhabited only by non-humans. Birth in such a realm requires the attainment of one or all of the four meditative **concentrations** in past lives. *Abhidharma* literature mentions twelve ordinary realms of form and five 'pure abodes' (*shuddhanivasa*) above them, where birth can be taken consequent on these **four concentrations**. See **Four Concentrations**.

Formless Realm གཟུགས་མེད་ཁམས་ gzugs med khams *ārūpyadhātu*

Among the three realms or divisions of **cyclic existence**, the **formless realm** is regarded as the highest level at which one can be reborn within the **cycle of existence** and a state where an individual is said to exist only at the level of **consciousness**. Here, all of the individual's physical faculties exist only as potencies. *Abhidharma* literature mentions four levels of t'₁e **formless realm** corresponding to the **four formless absorptions** of meditation. See **Four Absorptions**.

Four Absorptions སྙོམས་འཇུག་བཞི་ snyoms 'jug bzhi *catuḥ samāpatti*

In contrast to the four meditative **concentrations** which effect birth in the **form realms**, the **four formless absorptions** lead progressively to the summit of cyclical existence with increasing subtlety. According to *abhidharma* literature, the four are: infinite space, infinite **consciousness**, nothing-at-all, and neither cognition nor non-cognition.

Four Classes of Tantra རྒྱུད་སྡེ་བཞི་ rgyud sde bzhi

1) *Kriyatantra* (Action *Tantra*); 2) *Caryatantra* (Performance *Tantra*); 3) *Yogatantra* (Union *Tantra*); and 4) *Anuttarayogatantra* (Unsurpassed Union *Tantra* or **Highest Yoga Tantra**). These four kinds of *tantric* literature can be defined either in terms of the relative emphasis which they place on internal **meditation** and external ritual, or in terms of the intensity of afflictive cognitive and emotional states (**attachment** in particular) which can be transformed into a blissful experience conjoined with the **realisation** of the true nature of **reality**. In *Kriyatantra*, greater emphasis is placed on the ritual, i.e., the external activities; in *Caryatantra*, there is an equal emphasis on both internal **meditation** and external ritual; in *Yogatantra*, a greater emphasis is placed on the internal **meditations;** and in, *Anuttarayogatantra* not only is the greatest emphasis placed on the internal **meditations** but also, at a certain stage, external rituals are dissuaded.

Four Common Preliminaries ཐུན་མོངས་ཀྱི་སྔོན་འགྲོ་བཞི་ thun mongs kyi sngon 'gro bzhi

1) The cultivation of an appreciation for the potentials and the

opportunities of human existence; 2) reflection on death and **impermanence**; 3) reflection on **karma**; and 4) reflection on the unsatisfactory nature of life in **cyclic existence**. These four considerations are regarded as key subjects of contemplation in a practitioner's quest to overcome **attachment** to the attractions of worldly life. Successfully undertaken, they lay a firm foundation for spiritual growth.

Four Concentrations བསམ་གཏན་བཞི་ bsam gtan bzhi *caturdhyāna*

These states of meditative **concentration** are conducive to birth in the seventeen levels of the **form realm**. The four states are characterised, in their proper order, by a temporary sojourn from: 1) physical sensations of pain; 2) from mental unhappiness; 3) from mental excitements related to pleasure; and 4) from mundane experiences of joy as a whole. The main source for the study of these meditative states is the literature on *abhidharma*.

Four Dharmas of Gampopa དྭགས་པོའི་ཆོས་བཞི་ dvags po chos bzhi

These teachings expounded by *Gampopa Dagpo Lharje* are: 1) turning one's **mind** to the spiritual path; 2) engaging in meditative practices; 3) overcoming misconceptions through the understanding of **emptiness**; and 4) transforming misconceptions into essentially pure awareness.

Fourfold Activities ལས་བཞི་ las bzhi *catuḥ kriyā*

More usually known as the 'four rites' (*las bzhi*), these are specific ritual functions based on the dynamic modes of a *buddha*'s activity, namely: pacification, enrichment, subjugation/influence and **wrath**/force. Along with spontaneous or effortless activity, these comprise the aspects of *buddha*-activity. In *tantric* practice, their application is usually effected in the context of a **burnt offering** ritual (*homa*).

Four Guardians (Guardian Kings) རྒྱལ་ཆེན་བཞི་ rgyal chen bzhi *caturmahārāja(kāyika)*

Also known as the 'Four Great Kings' (*Caturmaharajakayika*), they are: *Virudaka*, *Virupaksha*, *Dhritarashtra* and *Vaishravana*, who respectively guard the east, west, south and north, protecting the doctrine and its practitioners from interfering forces. They are often depicted in the murals either side of the main door of a temple or monastic assembly hall.

Four Hallmarks of Correct View ལྟ་བ་བཀའ་རྟགས་ཀྱི་ཕྱག་རྒྱ་བཞི་ lta ba bka' rtags kyi phyag rgya bzhi

The four principles which constitute the fundamental insights of the Buddhist path to **enlightenment**. They are: 1) all conditioned existence is **impermanent**; 2) all **deluded** experiences are **sufferings**; 3) all things are **empty** and lack **self-identity**; and 4) *nirvana/liberation* is true peace. These four principles are also often referred to as the 'four seals', the '**four views**' or the 'four axioms' of Buddhism.

Four Immeasurables ཚད་མེད་བཞི་ tshad med bzhi *catvāry apramāṇāni*

Immeasurable **compassion**, **love**, joy and **equanimity**. The cultivation of the four immeasurable wishes, which is normally accompanied by recitation of the short prayer below, is a common preliminary to daily practice. This contemplation establishes correct motivation and provides a strong impetus to cultivate the altruistic aspiration of **bodhicitta**. The **four immeasurables** are the deeply felt sincere wishes: 1) may all **sentient beings** be free from **suffering** and its causes; 2) may all beings enjoy happiness and accumulate its causes; 3) may all beings abide forever in bliss; 4) may all beings remain ever in **equanimity**, free of **attachment** and aversion caused by the prejudices of nearness and distance with respect to others.

Four Limits མུ་བཞི་/མཐའ་བཞི་ mu bzhi/mtha' bzhi *catuṣkoṭi*

Usually these are listed as: the extremes of production and cessation (*skye-'gag*), **eternalism**/absolutism and **nihilism** (*rtag-chad*), existence and non-existence (*yod-med*), and appearance and **emptiness** (*snang-stong*). In the context of the **Madhyamaka** dialectic they may also refer to the fourfold system of dialectical negation (*catuṣkoṭi*), namely: negation of the positive, negation of the negative, negation of both, and negation of neither.

Four Mindfulnesses དྲན་པ་ཉེར་བཞག་བཞི་ dran pa nyer bzhag bzhi *catuḥsmṛtyupasthāna*

Also known as the 'four foundations of **mindfulness**' or 'four recollections', these are: **mindfulness** of body, feeling, **mind** and phenomena, which together form the basis of the **thirty-seven aspects of the path to enlightenment**.

Four Noble Truths འཕགས་པའི་བདེན་པ་བཞི་ 'phags pa'i bden pa bzhi *catvāri āryasatyāni*

The teaching on the **four noble** or sublime **truths** forms the basis of the first promulgation of Buddhism, since it is the very first formal discourse given by **Buddha Shakyamuni** in **Sarnath** following his attainment of **buddha**hood at **Bodhgaya**. The **four truths** are: the **truth** of **suffering**, the **truth** of its origins, the **truth** of cessation, and the **truth** of the path leading to such cessation. The understanding of these **four truths** is an indispensable basis for a successful practice of the Buddhist path. The doctrine of **four truths** lays the foundation upon which the entire structure of the path to **enlightenment** is built. The first **two truths** constitute one inter-relationship of **cause and effect** and the remaining two, another. Without proper insight into the first inter-relationship no genuine aspiration to seek freedom from **cyclic existence** will arise. Similarly, without insight into the second, no genuine release from the bondage of **karmically** conditioned existence can be achieved. In fact, the entire Buddhist path can be seen as an elaboration on the theme of these **four truth**s.

Four opponent forces སྟོབས་བཞི་ stobs bzhi *catvāri balāni*

In Buddhism, a successful practice of **confession** and **purification** must consist of what are known as the **four opponent forces** or, more commonly, the 'four antidotal powers'. The four powers are: 1) the power of repentance with regard to the negative acts committed; 2) the power of reliance, i.e., the **confession** must be

complemented by the reinforcement of seeking **refuge** in the **three jewels** and the generation of the altruistic **mind** of *bodhicitta*; 3) the power of the actual antidote, which can be either a **meditation** on **emptiness**, the recitation of certain *mantras*, or **meditation** on **love** and **compassion**, etc.; and 4) finally, the power of resolve, which is the determination never to indulge wilfully in such negative acts again.

Four Preliminaries (སྔོན་འགྲོའི་) བློ་ཟློག་རྣམ་བཞི་ (sngon 'gro'i) blo zlog rnam bzhi

See **Four Common Preliminaries** and **Four Uncommon Preliminaries**.

Four Principles of Buddhism

See **Four Hallmarks**.

Four Session Guruyoga ཐུན་བཞིའི་བླ་མའི་རྣལ་འབྱོར་ thun bzhi'i bla ma'i rnal 'byor

'*Guruyoga*' is an important preliminary **meditation** in which the practitioner visualises the *guru* as inseparable from the **meditational deity**, thus enabling the aspirant to cultivate an ideal perception of the *guru*. A correct relation to one's main *guru* is considered vital in the Tibetan tradition, as this lays a successful foundation for progress on the spiritual path. This factor becomes all the more important in *tantra* for here, receiving spiritual inspiration as transmitted through an unbroken **lineage**, from a living *guru*, is considered indispensable. However, it must be pointed out that it is vital that the person who is taken as the *guru* must possess the minimum qualifications of a teacher as prescribed in the authoritative literature. The 'four sessions' refer to an intensive undertaking of meditative practice, such as the cultivation of right attitude towards one's *guru*, within the framework of four sessions. The recommended time for the practice of the four sessions is: 1) early morning till dawn; 2) after sunrise till just before noon; 3) from afternoon till just before sunset; and 4) from sunset till late evening.

Four Uncommon Preliminaries ཐུན་མོང་མ་ཡིན་པའི་སྔོན་འགྲོ་བཞི་ thun mong ma yin pa'i sngon 'gro bzhi

1) Taking **refuge**; 2) *Vajrasattva* **meditation** and recitation of the *mantra*; 3) making *mandala* **offerings**; and 4) practice of *guruyoga*. These four practices are prerequisites for a successful practice of *tantra*, hence the name **uncommon preliminaries**.

Four Views ལྟ་བ་བཞི་ lta ba bzhi *caturdṛṣṭi*

See **Four Hallmarks**.

Fundamental Ignorance མ་རིག་པ་ ma rig pa *avidyā*

The source of all **dissonant emotions** (*klesha*) including **desire**/attraction, **hatred**/aversion and **delusion**. **Fundamental ignorance** is the source of the **twelve links** of **dependent origination**. This **ignorance** is of two types: **ignorance** with respect to the nature of **reality** and **ignorance** with respect to the principles of karmic causation, i.e., the inter-relationship between actions and their consequences. The first is said to arise in three inter-related aspects: 1) **consciousness** of individual **self**hood (*bdag-gnyis gcig-pu'i ma-rig-pa*); 2) the co-emergent ignorance which is the implicit habitual misapprehension of actual

reality (*lhan-cig skyes-pa'i ma-rig-pa*); and 3) the conditioned **ignorance** of the imaginatory process (*kun-brtags-pa'i ma-rig-pa*) through which individual perception discerns its object.

Gampopa (tib.) སྒམ་པོ་པ་ sgam po pa

A great Tibetan scholar of the twelfth century (1079-1153) and one of the closest disciples of the *yogin* and poet *Milarepa*. Also known as *Nyame Dagpo Lharje*, he was the founder of the *Dagpo Kagyu* sub-school of the *Kagyu* tradition. His works include, among others, the famous *JEWEL ORNAMENT OF LIBERATION* (*dvags-po thar-rgyan*).

Ganden (tib.) དགའ་ལྡན་ dga' ldan

One of the three great *Gelug* monastic universities of Central Tibet. *Ganden* was founded by the Tibetan philosopher saint *Tsong Khapa* in 1409, and is also known as *Geden*. It soon became one of the foremost centres of philosophical development in Tibet, giving rise to a whole new tradition, the *Gelug*, which came to be named after it. *'Gelug'* literally means the followers of the *Geden* tradition. *Ganden* has two main colleges, *Jangtse* and *Shartse*, and was the third largest monastery in the vicinity of *Lhasa* before 1959, with over 4000 resident monks. Like the other two monastic universities, *Sera* and *Drepung*, *Ganden* is now re-established amongst the exiled Tibetan community re-settled in south India.

Gar (tib.) གར་ gar *nāṭya*

A ceremonial dance often performed as a part of a *tantric* ritual such as *Kalacakra*. The dancers are dressed in elaborate costumes and represent various *tantric* **deities**. Such dances are normally characterised by precisely choreographed rhythmic steps performed in conjunction with specific beats of the accompanying drums and cymbals.

Garuda (skrt.) ཁྱུང་ / མཁའ་ལྡིང་ khyung/mkha' lding *garuḍa*

A mythological bird normally depicted with an owl-like sharp beak, often holding a snake, and with large and powerful wings. Reference to this bird can be also found in Hindu literature, where it is often mentioned as the flying mount of powerful *deva* (mundane **gods**). In *tantric* Buddhism, the *Garuda* is associated with *Vajrapani* and certain **wrathful** forms of *Padmasambhava*, and may symbolise the transmutative power which purifies certain malevolent influences and pestilences etc. In the *Terma* tradition, the *Garuda* is sometimes revered as a guardian of treasures (*gter-bdag*) or even as a repository of treasures (*gter-ka*).

Gautamiputra (skrt.) གོ་ཏ་མའི་བུ go ta ma'i bu *Gautamīputra*

See **King Gautamiputra**.

Gelong དགེ་སློང་ dge slong *bhikṣu*

See **Bhikshu**.

Gelug (tib.) དགེ་ལུགས་ dge lugs

One of the four main traditions of **Tibetan Buddhism**. Founded by the great fourteenth century philosopher *Tsong Khapa* and his foremost students, it quickly established itself as a dominant tradition of **Tibetan Buddhism** with its monasteries extending from the far west of Tibet to *Chamdo*, *Dartsedo*, and *Amdo* in the east. Following the Third *Dalai Lama*'s visit to Mongolia, it became the state religion in Mongolia and the Buriat regions of the Russian Federation, and during the seventeenth century its hierarchy became the dominant political force in Central Tibet when the Fifth *Dalai Lama* assumed both spiritual and temporal power with the assistance of Mongol armies. '*Gelug*' literally means 'the followers of the virtuous path' and is named after the monastery called *Geden* or *Ganden* founded by *Tsong Khapa* in 1409.

Gelugpa དགེ་ལུགས་པ་ dge lugs pa

The followers of *Gelug* tradition of **Tibetan Buddhism**. See **Gelug**.

Generation Stage བསྐྱེད་རིམ་ bskyed rim *utpattikrama*

In contrast to the **completion** or perfection **stage** of *tantric* practice, the **generation** or creation stage is a **meditation** in which mundane forms, sounds and thoughts are meditated upon as natural expressions of **deities**, **mantras**, and **pristine cognition** (*jnana*), respectively. The **generation stage** is characterised by the meditative processes of the practitioner's gradual identification with the form and **pristine cognition** of the **meditational deity**, and it is during this stage that the elaborate visualisation of the **deity** is gradually constructed. This process, known as **self**-generation, which is a simulacrum of bringing the three *kaya* onto the path, is composed of three principal aspects: dissolution into **emptiness** (*dharmakaya*), arising into a subtle form such as a **seed syllable** or emblem (*sambhogakaya*), and full emergence into the **deity's** form (*nirmanakaya*). Generally speaking, **generation** or creation **stage** practices are seen as means of cultivating the qualities of the enlightened **mind** using *mantra* (sound) and visual imagery, in preparation for the more subtle experiences of the **completion stage** practices.

Gesar (tib.) གེ་སར་ ge sar

A king of a legendary empire called '*Ling*' within Tibet and associated with a whole series of fantastic stories and epic poems often referring to ancient warfare with neighbouring countries and grand mythic exploits. The stories are known collectively as the stories of *Ling (gling sgrung)* and are extremely popular throughout Tibet, from *Ladakh* in the far west to *Golok* and *Amdo* in the northeast, and even further afield in Mongolia. They are normally sung by professional bards in melodious tunes with specific tones and cadences for different characters. The historical placing of *Gesar* is unclear, and the modern Tibetan historian *W.D. Shakabpa* says in his *A POLITICAL HISTORY OF TIBET* that the legend might originate from an historical person by the name of *Gesar Norbu Dradul*. However, the royal family of *Lingtsang* in *Kham* claims descent from *Gesar*, and several pilgrimage sites are associated with him in the *Amnye Machen* mountain range, where his **protector** rituals are popular.

Geshe (tib.) དགེ་བཤེས་ dge bshes *kalyāṇamitra*

'*Geshe*' is an abbreviation of *dge-ba'i bshes-gnyen* (pronounced '*gewai shenyen*') which is a direct translation of the **Sanskrit** word *kalyanamitra*, literally meaning a 'spiritual friend or benefactor'. In other words, this term was originally employed with reference to a spiritual teacher or **guru**, who could contribute to an individual's progress on the spiritual path. Subsequently, however,. it came to have an academic usage, particularly in the Gelug school, where a '**geshe**' is identified as a scholar with a doctorate in traditional Buddhist studies. A **geshe** degree normally requires fifteen to twenty years of rigorous study and is the highest academic degree obtainable in the **Gelug** monastic educational system. The subjects studied are divided into five major topics: **Pramana** (logic and **epistemology**), **Prajnaparamita** (perfection of **wisdom**), **Madhyamaka** (the Middle Way philosophy), **Abhidharma** (phenomenology and Buddhist psychology), and **Vinaya** (Buddhist **ethics**). **Geshe** degrees were in the past obtainable only from the large monastic universities of the **Gelug** tradition.

Giving and Taking གཏོང་ལེན་ gtong len

An important element in the training of one's **mind** whilst generating the altruistic aspiration of **bodhicitta**. '**Giving**' refers to the visualisation practice of giving one's wealth, success, prosperity and even the future consequences of one's positive actions to others; '**taking**' is the taking upon oneself of the **suffering**, pain, unhappiness and misfortunes of others. The first practice is related to the generation of loving kindness and the second to unbiased **compassion** for all beings.

Gods ལྷ་ lha *deva*

This term is used by translators to refer to beings existing in realms higher than the human realm. They can be either mundane as in the case of the beings of the **deva** realms (**gods** within the confines of **cyclic existence**) or supermundane in the case of the **meditational deities** of a *tantric mandala*.

Gompa དགོན་པ་ dgon pa *araṇya*

An isolated place or monastic site situated remote from urban settlements, generally rendered in translation as 'monastery'.

Graduated Path to Enlightenment བྱང་ཆུབ་ལམ་གྱི་རིམ་པ་ byang chub lam gyi rim pa *bodhipaṭhakrama*

The stages of the path leading to full **enlightenment**. Known as **Lamrim** in Tibetan, the texts dealing with this theme outline the entire path to **enlightenment** within the framework of what are known as the three levels of the path, corresponding to the trainees of initial, middling and great capacities. Although the sources for such writings can be traced to the original **Mahayana sutras**, the first text to be explicitly associated with this '**three scope**' approach was **Atisha's** LAMP FOR THE PATH TO ENLIGHTEN-MENT. Based on this work, an entire corpus of literature emerged in Tibet which became collectively known as **Lamrim**. These writings later became the dominant manuals on practice among

the followers of the *Kadam* and *Gelug* traditions. Other traditions also incorporate *Lamrim* within them, as, for example, in the elaborate exposition of the nine *yanas*; and the salient tenets of *Lamrim* are synthesized within the preliminary practices of *tantric* meditation according to all schools.

Great Bliss བདེ་བ་ཆེན་པོ་ bde ba chen po *mahāsukha*

See **Mahasukha**.

Great Madhyamaka དབུས་མ་ཆེན་པོ་ dbus ma chen po *mahāmadhyamaka*

See **Shentong**.

Great Perfection

See **Dzogchen**.

Grounds and Paths ས་དང་ལམ་ sa dang lam *bhūmimārga*

More usually rendered in English as 'levels and paths', the term denotes the progressive levels and paths of spiritual **realisation** through which an aspiring *bodhisattva* journeys towards full **enlightenment**. On the levels, see **Grounds of a Bodhisattva**. The paths are five in number, namely those of: 1) accumulation; 2) preparation; 3) insight/seeing; 4) **meditation**; and 5) no more learning, also known as the 'final path'. This fivefold progression of the spiritual path is pursued both by the *bodhisattva* who moves towards full **enlightenment** and the adherent of *Hinayana*, who is restricted to a personal search for freedom from the **sufferings** of **cyclic existence**. See **Sutrayana**.

Grounds of a Bodhisattva བྱང་ཆུབ་སེམས་དཔའི་ས་ byang chub sems dpa'i sa *bodhisattvabhūmi*

Mahayana literature speaks of ten levels or grounds of *bodhisattva* **realisation**. These are, in their proper sequence: 1) the joyful; 2) the stainless; 3) the luminous; 4) the radiant; 5) the difficult to overcome; 6) the manifest; 7) the far-reaching; 8) the immovable; 9) the excellent intelligence; and 10) the clouds of doctrine. In the context of the **five paths**, these ten levels start from the third path, i.e., the path of insight/seeing, which commences with the initial experience of a direct **realisation** of **emptiness**. Hence the name, path of insight/seeing. The principal sources for the discussion of the ten levels are: *Nagarjuna's* RATNAVALI, *Candrakirti's* MADHYAMAKAVATARA and *Asanga's* BODHISATTVA-BHUMI. These texts are based on the *DASABHUMIKASUTRA*. See **Bhumi**.

GUHYAGARBHA (skrt.) གསང་བའི་སྙིང་པོ་ gsang ba'i snying po *Guhyagarbha*

The primary and most important *tantra* text of the *Mahayoga* class, according to the ninefold *yana* of the *Nyingma* tradition. It is the primary literary source for the *mandala* of the hundred **peaceful and wrathful deities**, and a text which received the attentions of many Indian and Tibetan commentators, such as *Padmasambhava*, *Indrabhuti*, *Vimalamitra*, *Rongzompa*, *Yungtonpa*, *Longchen Rabjampa*, and *Lochen Dharmasri*, who have interpreted the text according to both *Mahayoga* and *Atiyoga*.

GUHYASAMAJA (skrt.) གསང་བ་འདུས་པ་ gsang ba 'dus *Guhyasamāja*

Name of a principal **meditational deity** and *tantra* text, representative of *Mahayoga*, according to the *Nyingma* school, and of the father *tantra* class of

Anuttarayogatantra, according to the **Sarma** schools. This **deity** is normally depicted as dark blue in colour with three faces and six arms. The study and practice of this *tantra* was prevalent among Indian Buddhist masters, and over twenty **lineages** of Indian origin have been identified based on the different interpretations of the root *tantra*. The two most established systems in Tibet are the so-called *Arya* system, which has *Akshobhya* in the central form of *Guhyasamaja (bsang-'dus 'phags-lugs mi-bskyod rdo-rje)* and the system of *Buddhajnanapada* which has *Manjuvajra* as the central form of *Guhyasamaja (bsang-'dus 'jam-pa'i rdo-rje'i lugs)*.

Gunaprabha (skrt.) ཡོན་ཏན་འོད་ yon tan 'od *Guṇaprabhā*

A seventh century Indian scholar and one of the most learned students of *Vasubandhu*. His greatest achievements were in the field of *Vinaya* (Buddhist monastic discipline) and his knowledge in this subject is said to have been even greater than that of his teacher. His works include the celebrated text the *Vinayasutra*, which later became the primary text for the study and practice of *Vinaya* according to the *Mulasarvastivadin* school. The *Vinaya* tradition of this school became the official system in Tibet, and the *VINAYASUTRA* is now used as the standard textbook by all the major monastic universities of Tibet.

Guru (skrt.) བླ་མ་ bla ma *guru*

A spiritual teacher or mentor. The *Sanskrit* word *'guru'* literally means 'heavy' or 'weighty', and by extension a 'venerable teacher'. The Tibetan equivalent *'bla-ma'* (pronounced *'lama'*) means 'unsurpassed' or 'supreme', indicating that the **guru** is unsurpassed in terms of being the perfect object toward which **meritorious** activity can be directed. However, it is important to note that specific qualifications are necessary on the part of the teacher in order to be considered as a **guru**. These qualifications differ according to the level of spiritual practice at which the **guru** is adopted as teacher. Ultimately, the **guru** is one's own **buddha-nature**. See **Meditational Deity**.

Guru Devotion བཤེས་གཉེན་བསྟེན་ཚུལ་ bshes gnyen bsten tshul

Tibetan Buddhism emphasises the maintenance of a proper relationship between a practitioner and the **guru**. 'Devotion' in this context refers to reliance on a constructive and sincere attitude on the part of the student. In the *Nyingma* tradition, for example, there are texts describing three different ways of delighting the **guru**, namely through actions of body, speech and **mind**. *Guru* **devotion** is also the first stage in the practice of *Lamrim*, where it includes the cultivation of right attitudes and engaging in right actions towards the **guru**. *Lamrim* literature speaks of such twofold practice as 'a proper reliance on a **guru** through both **mind** and action.' See *FIFTY VERSES OF GURU DEVOTION*.

Guru Rinpoche (tib.) གུ་རུ་(སློབ་དཔོན་) རིན་པོ་ཆེ་ gu ru (slob dpon) rin po che *Ratnaguru (ie. Padmasambhava)*

A title of **Padmasambhava**, the master from *Oddiyana* who, along with **Shantarakshita** and King **Trisong Detsen**, formally established Buddhism in Tibet during the eighth century. In particular he is renowned for his suppression and conversion of malevolent spirits and hostile non-Buddhist forces, as well as for introducing to Tibet many oral **transmissions** and texts of **Mahayoga** and **Atiyoga**. To practitioners of the **Nyingma** school and all those who follow the practices of **Mahayoga** and **Atiyoga**, he is revered as a 'second **buddha**', and there are many systems of **meditation** based on the visualisation of his rainbow-like form. Tibetan literature contains a number of biographical accounts, which describe his life in the form of eight or twelve different manifestations.

GURUPANCASHIKA (skrt.) བླ་མ་ལྔ་བཅུ་པ་ bla ma lnga bcu pa *gurupañcaśikā*

See *FIFTY VERSES OF GURU DEVOTION*.

Guruyoga (skrt.) བླ་མའི་རྣལ་འབྱོར་ bla ma'i rnal 'byor *guruyoga*

See **Four Session Guruyoga**.

Gyaltsab Je (tib.) རྒྱལ་ཚབ་རྗེ་ rgyal tshab rje

Gyaltsab Je *Darma Rinchen* (1364-1431) was one of the two chief disciples of **Tsong Khapa** and the immediate successor as the head of the **Gelug** school after **Tsong Khapa's** death. Among his many works, his detailed and analytical **commentary** on *Dharmakirti's* **PRAMANAVARTTIKA** is considered to be one of the most authoritative texts on the subject of Buddhist logic and **epistemology** in Tibetan literature.

Gyalwa (tib.) རྒྱལ་བ་ rgyal ba *jina*

Literally meaning 'conqueror' or 'victor', *rgyal-ba* (pronounced '**gyalwa**') is an epithet for '**buddha**', indicating the victory attained by a **buddha** over **cyclic existence**. In particular the **Sambhogakaya** forms of the **buddha-body** are described as the 'five **enlightened families** of conquerors' *(rgyal-ba rigs-lnga)*, in which case the five **buddhas**, **Vairocana** and so forth, are known as the five conquerors, appearing in either peaceful or wrathful form. The primordial **buddha Vajradhara,** 'lord of the sixth **enlightened-family**', who represents the **Dharmakaya**, is also known by the title **Gyalwa**. Moreover, in the Tibetan language *gyalwa* may be used as an honorific title before the names of highly venerated beings, e.g., *Gyalwa Yeshi Norbu* (for H.H. **Dalai Lama**), or *Gyalwa* **Karmapa**.

Haribhadra (skrt.) སེང་གེ་བཟང་པོ་ seng ge bzang po *Haribhadra*

An eighth century Indian scholar considered one of the greatest authorities on **Prajnaparamita** studies. His works include the highly respected **commentary** on the *ABHISAMAYALAMKARA* entitled *THE ELUCIDATION OF MEANINGS*, which is still used as one of the key Indian works in the study of **Prajnaparamita** in all of the major Tibetan monastic universities.

Hatred ཞེ་སྡང་ zhe sdang *dveśa*

One of the '**three poisons**' of the **mind** and also one of the 'six primary **dissonant emotions**', it is the gross form of aversion. In Buddhist literature, **hatred** is

Virupa

Tilopa

often used interchangeably with anger. See **Attachment**.

Hayagriva (skrt.) རྟ་མགྲིན་ rta mgrin *Hayagrīva*

Literally meaning "horse-necked", **Hayagriva** or *Tamdrin*, in Tibetan, is the name of a wrathful **meditational deity**, often red in colour, with a green horse's head protruding from amongst the hair on his head. The teachings and texts associated with **Hayagriva** belong within the **sadhana** class of **Mahayoga**, as practiced by the **Nyingma** school, where they are known as the **tantras** of **buddha- speech**. **Hayagriva** is considered to be a **wrathful** manifestation of **Avalokiteshvara**, the **deity** of infinite **compassion**, and one of his most revered images is to be found in the **protector** shrine at **Sera Je** college in **Lhasa**. More generally, he is also found alongside *Acala* as a gate **protector** inside sacred shrines or temples.

Hearer ཉན་ཐོས་ nyan thos *śrāvaka*

See **Shravaka**.

HEART OF WISDOM/DISCRIMINATIVE AWARENESS SUTRA
ཤེས་རབ་སྙིང་པོའི་མདོ་ shes rab snying po'i mdo
Prajñāpāramitāhṛdayasūtra

Also known in its short form as the '**HEART SUTRA**', it is one of the most important **Maho·· ·na sutras** belonging to the collection of the **Prajnaparamiiu sutras**. The explicit subject matter of the **sutra** is the doctrine of **emptiness**, and it is written in the form of a dialogue between *Shariputra* (one of the two principal disciples of the **Buddha Shakyamuni**) and the **bodhisattva Avalokiteshvara**. The **sutra** is extremely popular among all traditions of **Tibetan Buddhism**; so much so that many people recite it by heart, and, because of its brevity, use it as a basis for **meditation** on **emptiness**.

Heavens ལྷ་ཡུལ་ lha yul *devaloka*

This term, more accurately rendered as 'god-realms', refers to the higher levels of existence assumed by *devas* in the **desire** and **form realms**. See **Desire Realm** and **Form Realm**.

Hell དམྱལ་བ་ dmyal ba *naraka*

States of existence within the **karmically** conditioned cycle of **rebirth** where the experience of **suffering** is most intense and extended. *Abhidharma* literature mentions two main types of such **hell**-like existences, characterised by the dominance of either freezing cold or burning heat. These two are in turn divided into several different sub-categories. See **Six Realms**.

Heruka (skrt.) ཁྲག་འཐུང་དཔའ་བོ་ khrag 'thung dpa' bo *heruka*

In general, this epithet comprises all wrathful **meditational deities** and is interpreted in Tibetan as 'blood-drinker' (*khrag-'thung-pa*) or 'blood-drinking hero' (*khrag-'thung-dpa'*). Specifi-

cally, it refers to the **deity** *Shriheruka* and his other later forms, such as *Cakrasamvara* or *Paramasukha*. See **Cakrasamvara** and **Wrath**.

HEVAJRA (skrt.) ཀྱེ་རྡོ་རྗེ་ kye rdo rje *Hevajra*

One of the principal **meditational deities** and *tantra* texts of the mother class of *Anuttarayogatantra*, the practice of which is dominant in the *Sakya* school of **Tibetan Buddhism**.

Highest Yoga Tantra བླ་ན་མེད་པའི་རྒྱུད་ bla na med pa'i rgyud *anuttarayogatantra*

See **Anuttarayogatantra**.

Hinayana (skrt.) ཐེག་པ་དམན་པ་ theg pa dman pa *Hīnayāna*

Buddhism is often categorised according to the so-called two *yanas* or vehicles, the *Hinayana* and the *Mahayana*. Of these, the system of Buddhism which mainly emphasises an individual's **liberation** from **cyclic existence** is called *Hinayana*, the 'lesser' or 'smaller' vehicle. It is important to bear in mind the difference between *Hinayana* as a practical system of conduct on the path and *Hinayana* as a philosophical school of thought. Generally speaking the distinction between the two *yana* is made on the basis of the primary motivations of the practitioners, i.e., in the case of *Hinayana* the primary motivation is the individual's own liberation from *samsara*, whereas in the *Mahayana* the motivation is the altruistic intention to attain enlightenment for the benefit of others. In terms of path, the former emphasises the practice of the **Four Noble Truth**s and the **twelve links of dependent origination**, while the latter emphasises the practice of the **six perfections**. In contrast, the distinction between the *Hinayana* and *Mahayana* schools of thought is made on the basis of the differences in philosophical positions. The principle philosophical schools of *Hinayana* are *Vaibhashika* and *Sautrantika*. See **Mahayana** and **Theravada**.

Humours ཉེས་པ་ nyes pa *doṣa*

The **three humours** - wind, bile and phlegm, the analysis of which forms the basis of both *Ayurveda* (traditional Indian medicine) and Buddhist medicine which evolved in both ancient India and Tibet. Diagnosis is often made on the basis of the balance or imbalance of these **three humours**.

Hungry Ghost ཡི་དྭགས་ yi dvags *preta*

Also translated as 'tormented spirit', the *Sanskrit* term *preta* refers to one of the six classes of living beings within the **karmically** conditioned cycle of **rebirth**, the other five being: *deva, asura,* human, animal, and **hell**-like beings. The tormented spirits are characterised as being in a state of existence which, in terms of the degree of **suffering**, is intermediate to the animal and **hell**-realms. See **Six Realms**.

Identity རང་མཚན་ rang mtshan *svalakṣaṇa*

In its philosophical usage, '**identity**' refers to the nature or the essence which makes something a particular thing or event and not something else. It is also the factor which serves as the basis for our identifying the particular object or event. However, depending upon one's metaphysical view, the grounds for establishing the **identity** of a phenomenon may vary. A realist may argue for the existence of objective criteria which are independent of our conceptuality, whereas a nominalist may argue that to speak of **reality** independent of our conceptuality is meaningless. See **Selflessness** and **Self-identity**.

Ignorance མ་རིག་པ་/རྨོངས་པ་ ma rig pa/rmongs pa *avidyā*

See **Fundamental Ignorance**.

Illusory body སྒྱུ་ལུས་ sgyu lus

Illusory body *(sgyu-lus)* is a **completion stage** practice associated with a number of important *tantra*-texts such as the *GUHYASAMAJA*, and meditational cycles such as the *SIX YOGAS (OR DOCTRINES) OF NAROPA*. In general seven kinds of **illusory body** have been enumerated, namely: 1) the symbolic *(dpe'i sgyu-ma)*; 2) the apparitional *(snang ba sgyu-ma)*; 3) the dream-like *(rmi-lam sgyu-ma)*; and those which are associated with 4) the **intermediate states** after death *(bar-do'i sgyu-ma)*; 5) **inner radiance** *('od-gsal sgyu-ma)*; 6) emanation *(sprul-pa sgyu-ma)* and; 7) **pristine cognition** *(ye-shes sgyu-ma)*. In the context of the **completion stage**, there is both a pure practice of the **illusory body** and an impure practice of the **illusory body**. The former is a **meditation** focusing on the *mandala* of the **deities** who embody **pristine cognition**, visualised according to the so-called twelve similes of illusion *(sgyu-ma'i dpe bcu-gnyis)*. By contrast, the latter is a **meditation** which establishes that all material worlds and their sentient contents appear but lack **inherent existence**. See **Subtle Body**.

Impermanence མི་རྟག་པ་ mi rtag pa *anitya*

One of the three marks of causally conditioned phenomena, the other two being **suffering** and the lack of **self-identity**, as expounded by the *Buddha Shakyamuni*. Although Buddhist literature mentions various degrees of **impermanence**, in general it can be defined as the momentarily changing nature of all things. Nothing endures through time without change, and the process of change is dynamic and never ending, reflecting the nature of flux and fluidity in **conditioned existence.** This fundamental quality of **impermanence** extends to both the external world and the perceiving **mind**.

Indian Buddhism འཕགས་ཡུལ་གྱི་ནང་པའི་གྲུབ་མཐའ་ 'phags yul gyi nang pa'i grub mtha'

Buddhism evolved as a system of thought and practice in India, probably (in the view of most traditional writers) from the sixth century BC onwards, and on the basis of the discourses of the *Buddha Shakyamuni*. Although there are diverse methods of classification, **Indian Buddhism** in general came to comprise two main philosophical systems of practice - *Hinayana* (the lesser vehicle) and *Mahayana* (the greater vehicle). Tibetan authors recognise four major philosophical perspectives within **Indian Buddhism**, namely those of the *Vaibhashika*, *Sautrantika*, *Cittamatra*, and *Madhyamaka*.

Inherent Existence རང་བཞིན་གྱིས་གྲུབ་པ་ rang bzhin gyis grub pa *svabhāvatā*

An ontological status of phenomena which accords to phenomena the nature of their existing in their own right, inherently, in-and-of themselves, objectively, and independent of any other phenomena such as our conception and labelling. The **Madhyamaka** school of thought refutes such a nature of existence and argues that nothing exists inherently, for nothing can be found to exist independent from conceptuality and labelling when scrutinised through an ultimate analysis. The **Madhyamika** hold that things and events exist only conventionally, and their existence can be validated only within a relative framework of conventional **reality**. Absence of such an ontology, i.e., absence of the **inherent existence** of all phenomena, is defined as the true nature of **reality**, **emptiness**, by the **Madhyamaka** schools.

Initiation དབང་བསྐུར་ dbang bskur *abhiṣeka*

A frequent mistranslation of **abhisheka,** the **'empowerment'** ceremony through which a practitioner is introduced to the practice of t**antra**. See **Abhisheka.**

Inner Radiance འོད་གསལ་ 'od gsal *prabhāsvara*

See **Clear Light.**

Intermediate State བར་དོ་ bar do *antarābhava*

See **Bardo**.

Jambhala (skrt.) ཛམ་བྷ་ལ་ dzam bha la *Jambhala*

A **tantric deity,** normally depicted seated and with a bulging belly, who is mainly associated with wealth and prosperity.

Jangtse (tib.) བྱང་རྩེ་ byang rtse

One of the two colleges of **Ganden** monastic university founded by *Netan Rinchen Gyaltsen.* *'Jangtse'* literally means 'North Point' or the 'Northern Summit'. See **Ganden.**

JATAKA (skrt.) སྐྱེས་རབས་ skyes rabs *Jātaka*

The '**Jataka** Tales', recounting the past lives of the **Buddha Shakyamuni,** form one of the twelve traditional divisions of the **Buddha**'s discourses. In particular, they illustrate how the **Buddha**, in his past lives, dedicated himself to the **bodhisattva's** way of life, worked for the benefit of others, and thereby enhanced his motivation of **bodhicitta**. While this literature is represented most voluminously in the Pali recension of the Buddhist canon, the Tibetan tradition reveres a shorter anthology of these tales, translated from the stylised **Sanskrit** verse of *Ashvagosha's JATAKAMALA, THE ROSARY OF JATAKA TALES.*

Je Rinpoche (tib.) རྗེ་རིན་པོ་ཆེ་ rje rin po che

An honourific title normally used to refer to **Tsong Khapa**, the founder of the **Gelug** school of **Tibetan Buddhism**. See **Tsong Khapa.**

Jenang (tib.) རྗེས་གནང་ rjes gnang *anujñā*

A **tantric** ceremony which, though comparable to an **empowerment**, is not a full **empowerment** ceremony, but rather a promissory rite. *'Jenang'* or *anujna*, in **Sanskrit**, literally means 'a giving of permission'. This authorises the practitioner to **meditate** on and recite the *mantra* of a specific **meditational deity**.

Jetsun (tib.) རྗེ་བཙུན་ rje btsun *bhaṭṭāraka*

An honorific title often used as a prefix to the names of high *lamas* and **meditational deities**. *'Jetsun'* literally means someone who is an object of veneration or reverence, having an ability to guide beings on the path to **liberation**. The term may also indicate great purity, or excellence of ethical or monastic discipline.

JEWEL ORNAMENT ཐར་པ་རྒྱན་ thar pa rgyan

An abbreviation of the title of *Gampopa's* famous text *THE JEWEL ORNAMENT OF LIBERATION*.

JEWEL ROSARY རིན་ཆེན་ཕྲེང་བ་ rin chen phreng ba *Ratnāvali*

An abbreviation of the title of a text on the practice of *Lojong* or **'Thought Transformation'** written by *Atisha*. The full title of the book is *THEGPA CHENPOI LOJONG JANGCHUP SEMPA NORBUI TRENGWA* which translates literally as *THE MAHAYANA TRANING OF THE MIND ENTITLED 'A JEWEL ROSARY FOR BODHISATTVAS'*.

Jinasagara (skrt.) རྒྱལ་བ་རྒྱ་མཚོ་ rgyal ba rgya mtsho *Jinasāgara*

An aspect of the **meditational deity** *Avalokiteshvara*. The practice of this particular *tantra* belongs to the *Anuttara-yogatantra*. Note that in some translations, the **Sanskrit** form has sometimes been reconstructed as *Jinasamudra*.

Jnana (skrt.) ཡེ་ཤེས་ ye shes *jñāna*

Pristine cognition or **mind** of a *buddha*, often loosely translated into English as **'wisdom'**. Although all **sentient beings** possess the potential for actualising *jnana* within their mental continuum, the psychological confusions and deluded tendencies which defile the **mind** obstruct the natural expression of these inherent potentials. Buddhist literature mentions five types of *buddha*-**mind** which are the quintessential perfected states of our own mental faculties, and which correspond to the five **enlightened families**. These are: 1) the **pristine cognition** of **reality's** expanse (*dharmadhatujnana*); 2) the mirror-like **pristine cognition** (*adarshajnana*); 3) the **pristine cognition** of sameness (*samatajnana*); 4) the **pristine cognition** of discernment (*pratyavekshanajnana*); and 5) the **pristine cognition** of accomplishment (*krityupasthanajnan*a). See five **Enlightened-Families**. The main characteristics of a *buddha*'s **pristine cognition** are: 1) that it is **omniscient**; 2) it is infinitely **compassionate**; and 3) it is fully capacitated, i.e., it is free from all personal limitations.

Kachen (tib.) ཀ་ཆེན་ ka chen *mahāstambha*

An academic title awarded to scholars at the completion of their

philosophic and other studies at the monastery of *Tashilhunpo*. It is *Tashilhunpo's* equivalent of the title *Geshe*. See **Geshe**.

Kadam (tib.) བཀའ་གདམས་ bka' gdams

A school of **Tibetan Buddhism** founded by the eleventh century Indian scholar and saint *Atisha* and his Tibetan disciple *Dromtonpa*. This school is particularly known for its great emphasis on the practical application of the ideals of a *bodhisattva* within the practitioner's daily life and is responsible for the development in Tibet of a specific collection of writings known as *Lojong* or 'Thought Transformation'. The *Kadam* school later evolved into three sub-divisions *Lamrimpa, Shungpawa,* and *Mengagpa,* each founded by one of the three *Kadam* brothers, whose names were *Potowa, Chekawa* and *Phuljungwa*. Although there is no existing school of **Tibetan Buddhism** now explicitly known as *Kadam,* the teachings of this school are highly respected by all the four major traditions, and in particular by the *Gelug* school, which is also sometimes known as the 'New *Kadam*' school. See **Atisha**.

Kadampa (tib.) བཀའ་གདམས་པ་ bka' gdams pa

Followers of the *Kadam* school of **Tibetan Buddhism**.

Kagyu (tib.) བཀའ་བརྒྱུད་ bka' brgyud

One of the four major traditions of **Tibetan Buddhism**, this **lineage tradition** stems from the Indian *mahasiddhas* such as *Tilopa, Naropa* and *Maitripa* through to *Khyungpo Naljor* who founded the *Shangpa Kagyu* **lineage** and *Marpa Lotsawa* who formed the *Dagpo Kagyu* **lineage**. The latter comprises four major sub-schools, namely the *Karmapa,* the *Tshalpa,* the *Barampa* and the *Phagmodrupa,* the last of which is further divided into the branches of the *Drikungpa, Taglungpa, Drukpa,* Yazang, Trophu, Shugseb, Yelpa, and *Martshang*. These traditions integrate practices derived from both the *sutras* and the *tantras*. There is particular emphasis on the *Mahamudra* system of practice and on yogic practices such as the *SIX YOGAS OF NAROPA*.

Kailash (skrt.) གངས་རིན་པོ་ཆེ་/གངས་ཏི་སེ་ gangs rin po che/gangs ti se *Kailāśa*

A sacred snow mountain in the western part of Tibet associated with the Buddhist *tantric* **meditational deity** *Cakrasamvara*. *Hindus* consider the mountain and the lake *Manasarovar* (which is below the mountain) as the sacred abode of Lord *Shiva*. *Kailash* is the summit of a mountain known as Gang-ti-se in Tibetan literature. It is 6656 metres above sea level and lies to the north of *Purang* district, in the western province of Tibet.

Kalacakra (tib.) དུས་ཀྱི་འཁོར་ལོ་ dus kyi 'khor lo *Kālacakra*

One of the most well-known **meditational deities** of *Anuttarayogatantra*. *Kalacakra* is associated with the salvific myth of *Shambhala* and this **deity** is highly venerated amongst the laity. Most Tibetans try to receive the **empowerment** of *Kalacakra* at least once during their life since there is a popular folk belief that attending this **empowerment** will ensure a birth in the mythical land of *Shambhala* in the future. However, on a more serious level this *tantra* is one of the richest sources for the study of the Buddhist systems of **cosmology**, **astrology**, astronomy, subtle energy systems, **mind**/body relationships and various other related topics. The *Kalacakra tantra* and its commentaries also include profound explanations of the practice of **Kalacakra** and its theoretical foundations.

Kalon (tib.) བཀའ་བློན་ bka' blon

A cabinet minister in the Tibetan government.

Kalpa (skrt.) བསྐལ་པ་ bskal pa *kalpa*

The aeon (skrt. *kalpa*) is a concept of fundamental importance for the traditional Indian and Buddhist understanding of cyclical time. According to **Abhidharma** literature, a great aeon (*mahakalpa*) is divided into eighty lesser or intervening aeons (*antarakalpa*). In the course of one great aeon, the external universe and its sentient life-forms unfold and disappear. During the first twenty of the lesser aeons, the universe is in the process of creation and expansion (*vivartakalpa*); during the next twenty it remains created; during the third twenty, it is in the process of destruction or contraction (*samvartakalpa*); and during the last series of the cycle, it remains in a state of destruction.

Kamalashila (skrt.) ཀ་མ་ལ་ཤི་ལ་ ka ma la shī la *Kamalaśīla*

An eighth century Indian scholar and student of **Shantarakshita** who was invited to Tibet by King **Trisong Detsen**. In order to resolve the doctrinal dispute between the philosophical views propounded by **Shantarakshita** and a Chinese *Hoshang* (Buddhist monk) called *Mo-ho-yen*, the king staged a formal debate during which *Mo-ho-yen* and **Kamalashila** each argued for the validity of their own positions. **Kamalashila** is said to have defeated the Chinese in debate and his refutation of *Mo-ho-yen's* views later evolved into a trilogy called BHAVANAKRAMA, THE STAGES OF MEDITATION.

KANGYUR (tib.) བཀའ་འགྱུར་ bka' 'gyur

The **Tibetan Buddhist** canon which contains a large number of original **sutras** and **tantras** translated from Indian sources. The **KANGYUR** as we now know it was formally compiled as a complete collection by the great fourteenth century Tibetan scholar and encyclopaedist *Buton Rinchen Drup. Buton* was also responsible for the compilation of the **TENGYUR**, the canonical collection containing translations of authoritative Indian commentarial works. Many manuscript versions of these anthologies were prepared over the centuries, and important xylographic editions were published at *Narthang, Derge, **Lhasa**, Cho-ne, Beijing*, and also in *Ladakh*. '**KANGYUR**' literally means the translated sacred words or transmitted **precepts** of the **buddhas**, and '**TENGYUR**', the translated commentaries.

Karma (skrt.) ལས་ las *karma*

The doctrine of actions and their causal consequences. The concept of **karma** includes in its causal aspect both the actual actions (physical, verbal and mental) and the psychological imprints and

tendencies created within the **mind** by such actions. After the performance of an action a causal chain is maintained within the mental continuum which continues through successive **rebirths**. Such a *karmic* potential is later activated when it interacts with appropriate circumstances and conditions, thus leading to the fruition of its effects. The doctrine of **karma** has two main features: 1) one never experiences the consequences of an action not committed; and 2) the potential of an action once committed is never lost unless obviated by specific remedies. See **Cause and Effect**.

Karma Kagyu (tib.) ཀརྨ་བཀའ་བརྒྱུད་ karma bka' brgyud

One of the four sub-schools of the **Dagpo Kagyu lineage**, descended from **Gampopa**, whose student *Dusum Khyenpa* (1110-1193) established important monasteries at *Karma Gon* in **Kham** and *Tsurphu* in Central Tibet, giving rise to a distinct **lineage tradition**. His successor *Karmapakshi* is said to have been the first *tulku* to be formally recognized in Tibet, and sixteen successive emanations had been recognized until the death of **Karmapa** *Rigpe Dorje* in 1981. The seventeenth **Karmapa** was recognised in Tibet in 1992.

Karmapa (tib.) ཀརྨ་པ་ karma pa

The title of the seventeen successive incarnations, beginning with **Karmapa** *Dusum Khyenpa* who have presided over the **Karma Kagyu** school since its inception. **Karmapa** is also an alternative name for the school itself. The most important hierarchs of the school, in addition to the '**black hat**' **Karmapa**, are the *Shamarpa* of *Yangpachen*, the *Tai Situpa* of *Palpung*, and the *Gyaltsab* of *Tsurphu*.

Kashag (tib.) བཀའ་ཤག་ bka' shag

The official name of the Tibetan cabinet.

Kaya(s) (skrt.) སྐུ་ *kāya*

The 'body' of a **buddha**. The word body is used in this context to refer not only to the physical body of a **buddha**, but also to the differing 'dimensions' in which the embodiment of fully **enlightened attributes** occurs. The **buddha-body** can be categorised in different ways, corresponding to the different levels of the teaching. **Hinayana sutras** speak of the **Dharmakaya** (**buddha-body** of **reality**) and **Rupakaya** (**buddha-body** of form), while the **Mahayana sutras** in general have elaborated the threefold division into **Dharmakaya**, **Sambhogakaya** and **Nirmanakaya**. **Mahayana sutras** of the **tathagatagarbha** class, and their related treatises such as the *Mahayanottaratantrashastra* speak of four **buddha-bodies**, namely **Dharmakaya**, **Sambhogakaya**, **Nirmanakaya** and **Svabhavikakaya**, the last of which is interpreted either as an active/passive distinction in **Dharmakaya**, or (especially in *tantric* literature) as the underlying indivisible essence of the **kayas**. Higher **tantras**, however, speak of five **kayas**, including the *Abhisambodhikaya* and *Vajrakaya* as the expressive and indivisible aspects of **Dharmakaya** respectively; and in **Atiyoga**, yet other names may be employed for the **Dharmakaya** and **Rupakaya** at the time of their realisation.

Kham (tib.) ཁམས་/ མདོ་སྟོད་ khams/mdo stod

One of the three main traditional provinces of Tibet, covering the south-eastern part of the country, particularly the region known as the 'four rivers and six ranges' which includes the watersheds of the *Salween, Mekong, Yangtze, Yalung,* and *Gyarong* rivers. See map.

Khenpo (tib.) མཁན་པོ་ mkhan po *upādhyāya*

The Tibetan word for monastic preceptor or **abbot**. See **Abbot**.

Khensur (tib.) མཁན་ཟུར་ mkhan zur

A former **abbot** of a monastery. When an **abbot** retires from his post he automatically acquires the title of *Khensur*. See **Abbot**.

King Gautamiputra (skrt.) རྒྱལ་པོ་གོ་ཏ་མིའི་བུ་ rgyal po go ta mi'i bu *Rāja Gautamīputra*

The recipient of *Nagarjuna's* LETTER TO A FRIEND. See *LETTER TO A FRIEND*.

Knowledge ཤེས་བྱ་ shes bya *jñeya*

The English word '**knowledge**' may represent a number of Tibetan terms. As 'culture' or 'science' (*rig-gnas*), it comprises the ten branches of traditional science - visual arts or crafts, medicine, grammar, logic, inner science/Buddhist philosophy, **astrology**, poetry, composition, drama and synonymics. As an 'object of **knowledge**' (*shes-bya*) it may include the entire encyclopaedic range of **knowledge**, including the study of the higher levels of Buddhist philosophy. Similarly, in *abhidharma* it refers to all 'knowable phenomena' including the various aspects of form, the primary **mind** and **mental factors**/events, relational or disjunct entities, and uncompounded entities like space. In *Mahayana* literature, **knowledge** also refers to the **emptiness** or lack of **inherent existence** which is the true nature of knowable phenomena. A *Madhyamika's* notion of **truth** for conventional **knowledge** (e.g., our empirical **knowledge** of the world) is a provisional one, whose validity can only be coherently ascertained within the relative framework of our conventional experience. For **knowledge** as an epistemological state of knowing, see **Pramana**.

Kriyatantra (skrt.) བྱ་བའི་རྒྱུད་ bya ba'i rgyud *Kriyātantra*
See **Four Classes of Tantra**.

Kumbum (tib.) སྐུ་འབུམ་ sku 'bum

Literally meaning 'hundred thousand images', *sku-'bum* (pronounced '*kumbium*') often refers to a *stupa*, a sacred monument, containing many thousands of clay images. It is also the name of a large *Gelug* monastery founded in 1588 by the Third *Dalai Lama* at the birth place of *Tsong Khapa*, in *Amdo* province. The full name of the monastery is *Kumbum Jampa Ling*.

Kusali (skrt.) ཀུ་ས་ལི་ ku sa li *kuśālin*

Literally meaning the 'virtuous one' or also a 'wanderer', the word is used to refer to serious **meditators** who have renounced the

conventional way of life and chosen to lead a life pursuing their meditative practices freed from the fetters of social conditioning.

Kyabgon (tib.) སྐྱབས་མགོན་ skyabs mgon

Literally meaning the '**refuge** and **protector**', it is a honorific title often used as a prefix to the names of high *lamas*, e.g., *Kyabgon Yeshi Norbu* for H.H.*Dalai Lama*.

Kyabje (tib.) སྐྱབས་རྗེ་ skyabs rje

An honorific title, meaning 'lord among **refuges**', which is used to address a high *lama*, e.g., *Kyabje Dudjom Rinpoche*, the late head of the *Nyingma* school, or *Kyabje Ling Rinpoche*, the senior tutor of H.H. the Fourteenth *Dalai Lama*. '*Kyabje*' literally means 'lord of **refuge**'.

Labrang (tib.) བླ་བྲང་ bla brang

Household or residence of a high **reincarnate** *lama*.

Lam Rim (tib.) ལམ་རིམ་ lam rim *paṭhakrama*

See **Lamrim**.

Lama (tib.) བླ་མ་ bla ma *guru*

See **Guru**.

LAMA CHOPA (tib.) བླ་མ་མཆོད་པ་ bla ma mchod pa

A text on *guruyoga* practice, taking *Lama Tsong Khapa* as the *guru*, written by the Fifth *Panchen Lama*, Lobsang Chokyi Gyaltsen. It is written in verse and is one of the most popular *guruyoga* practices in the *Gelug* tradition. '*LAMA CHOPA*' literally means 'making **offerings** to the *guru*'. See **Guruyoga**.

Lamdre (tib.) ལམ་འབྲས་ lam 'bras *mārgaphala*

A unique collection of meditative practices related to the *tantric* **deity** *Hevajra*, which are pre-eminent in the *Sakya* school of **Tibetan Buddhism**. *Lamdre* instructions outline the entire theory and practice of the *Mahayana* path as presented in the contemplative tradition of the *Sakyapas*. The origins of the *Lamdre* **lineage** are traced to the Indian *tantric yogin Virupa*, from whom the **lineage** continued to *Krishnacarya* and *Dombipa*. The *Lamdre* **lineage** was introduced to Tibet by the Tibetan translator *Drokmi Lotsawa*, who imparted the **transmission** to the great *Sakya* master *Kunga Nyingpo*.

LAMP FOR THE PATH བྱང་ཆུབ་ལམ་སྒྲོན་ byang chub lam sgron *Bodhipaṭhapradīpa*

An influential text on the practice of *Lamrim* written by the eleventh century Indian master *Atisha*. See **Atisha**.

Lamrim (tib.) ལམ་རིམ་ lam rim *paṭhakrama*

Literally meaning 'the gradual path' or 'the stages of the path', the word is used to refer both to the **graduated path to enlightenment** and also the texts which outline such a systematic path. See **Graduated Path to Enlightenment**.

Lay Precepts དགེ་བསྙེན་གྱི་སྡོམ་པ་ dge bsnyen gyi sdom pa *upāsaka samvara*

The five **precepts** of a **lay** practitioner who has taken the *Upasaka* **Vows** (lay person's **vows**). The **precepts** are the abstinence from the following five acts: killing, stealing, sexual misconduct, telling lies and drinking intoxicants.

LETTER TO A FRIEND བཤེས་སྤྲིངས་ bshes springs *Suhṛllekha*

A letter of instruction written by **Nagarjuna** to one of his disciples, **King Gautamiputra**, outlining the essential points of **Mahayana** practice and their relevance to daily life.

Lhagthong ལྷག་མཐོང་ lhag mthong *vipaśyanā*

Commonly translated as 'higher insight', 'special insight' or '**penetrative insight**', this is an analytical meditative state, penetrating the nature, characteristics or function of the chosen object of **meditation**, which is accompanied by physical and mental suppleness and generated on the basis of mental tranquility or **calm abiding**. The object of such an insight can be mundane, such as the topics of **impermanence** and **suffering**, or supermundane, such as **emptiness**, the **ultimate** nature of **reality**. This higher insight can be attained only in union with **calm abiding** and many **meditation** manuals state that the **realisation** of **calm abiding** is an essential prerequisite for the cultivation of higher insight. However, in *Anuttarayogatantra*, there exist advanced techniques which enable practitioners to attain **calm abiding** and higher insight simultaneously. Generally speaking, all **meditations** can be categorised as either genuine examples of, or similitudes of, **calm abiding** or higher insight; for all forms of **meditation** must be either absorptive or analytic in their approach to the **meditation** object. '*Lhag*' means 'higher' or 'special', and '*thong*' a 'vision' or 'insight'. See **Calm Abiding** and **Meditation**.

Lhamo Opera ལྷ་མོ་ lha mo

Traditional Tibetan opera based on popular Tibetan stories such as *KING DAWA SANGPO*, *LADY NAGSA*, and *TWO BROTHERS DONYO AND DONCHUNG*, etc. It is believed that *lhamo* as a performing art was initiated by *Thang-tong Gyalpo*. The operas are usually performed in colourful silk costumes and the libretto sung in a unique attenuated high pitched voice, accompanied by precise movements of the body, performed in time with an instrumental background of drums and cymbals. Operas often last an entire day and include spoken dialogue and comic sketches.

Lharampa (tib.) ལྷ་རམས་པ་ lha rams pa

One who holds the title of *Lharam* **Geshe**, the highest ranking degree among the various *geshe* titles. See **Geshe**.

Lhasa (tib.) ཧ་ས་ lha sa

The capital city of all Tibet during the seventh to ninth centuries when Tibet was governed by a series of Buddhist kings. *Lhasa* was subsequently reinstated as a capital city by the Fifth *Dalai Lama* in 1641, and from that time, until 1951, spiritual and temporal power were unified there.

Liberation ཐར་པ་/གྲོལ་བ་ thar pa/grol ba *mokṣa/mukti*

In a Buddhist context, the word refers specifically to freedom from **cyclic existence**, the karmically conditioned cycle of death and **rebirth**, and consequently to freedom from all forms of physical and mental **suffering**. Such a **liberation**, *moksha*, can be attained only through the total elimination of all the **dissonant emotions** which afflict the **mind** and which perpetuate the cycle of existence. Primary amongst these **dissonant emotions** are: **delusion** (misapprehension of the nature of **reality**), **attachment**, and **hatred**/anger. A person who has attained such a **liberation** is known as an *arhat*, a 'Foe Destroyer'. See **Arhat**.

Lineage བརྒྱུད་པ་ brgyud pa *paramparā*

An unbroken line of successive masters through which is transmitted the oral instructions on particular texts or practices. As far as the oral **transmission** itself is concerned, three types of **lineage** are recognised, namely: intentional, symbolic and aural which correspond respectively to the mode of **transmission** of *buddhas*, *vidhyadharas* and human beings. However in the case of revealed teachings or treasures (*gter-ma*), there are three additional **lineages** or modes of **transmission**.

Lineage Tradition ཆོས་ལུགས་ chos lugs *dharmaparamparā*

This term is sometimes used in the context of the glossary to translate the Tibetan word *cho lug*, which refers to specific spiritual traditions or schools.

Lithang (tib.) ལི་ཐང་ li thang

Name of a town and its adjacent district in *Kham*, situated in the low-lying *Li-chu* valley to the south-west of *Minyak*. It is the birthplace of the Seventh *Dalai Lama*, *Kelsang Gyatso*.

Lobpon སློབ་དཔོན་ slob dpon *ācārya*

See **Acarya** and **Dorje Lobpon**

Lojong (tib.) བློ་སྦྱོང་ blo sbyong

A unique group of practices related to the training of one's **mind** in the generation of *bodhicitta* and living one's life in accord with the principles of a *bodhisattva*. One of the main characteristics of this practice is the skilful transformation of circumstances, which might normally be considered adverse or harmful, into conditions favourable to one's practice. The origin of the texts related to this approach can be traced to the Indian master *Dharmarakshita*, author of *THE WHEEL OF SHARP WEAPONS*. This tradition was continued in Tibet by *Atisha* and his immediate disciples. The most famous Tibetan text on *Lojong* is the celebrated *EIGHT VERSES OF THOUGHT TRANSFORMATION* by *Geshe Langri Thangpa*. See *EIGHT VERSES OF THOUGHT TRANSFORMATION* and **Kadam**.

Loka(s) (skrt.) འཇིག་རྟེན་ 'jig rten *loka*

Literally meaning 'world' or 'world-system', the *Sanskrit loka* refers to each world-system (as defined in **Buddhist cosmology**) contained within the trichiliocosm or billion world universe expounded in *abhidharma* literature. These include the so-called 'world of patient endurance' (*sahalokadhatu*) - our own world-system, which is occupied by six distinct classes of living beings including *devas*, *asuras*, humans, animals, *pretas* and **hell**-beings. In English the expression 'six *lokas*' has sometimes been used mistakenly to refer to these six classes of living beings, rather than the world-system they inhabit. See **Six Realms**.

LONGCHEN NYINGTHIG (tib.) ཀློང་ཆེན་སྙིང་ཐིག་ klong chen snying thig

See **Nyingthig**.

Longchenpa (tib.) ཀློང་ཆེན་པ་ klong chen pa

Longchen Rabjampa or *Drime Ozer* (1308-1363) is undisputedly the greatest scholar of the *Nyingma* tradition. A prolific writer who systematised the philosophical structures and technical terminology of *Mahayoga*, *Anuyoga* and *Atiyoga* in relation to the *sutra* and *shastra* traditions of ancient India, his highly respected compositions include the collection of *SEVEN TREASURIES (MDZOD-BDUN)*, *THE TRILOGY OF MIND AT REST (NGAL-GSO SKOR-GSUM)*, *THE TRILOGY OF NATURALLY LIBERATED INTENTION (RANG-GROL SKOR GSUM)* and *THE TRILOGY OF DISPELLING DARKNESS (MUN-SEL SKOR GSUM)*. He is also renowned as a discoverer and redactor of *Terma* teachings, which are contained in the *FOURFOLD INNERMOST SPIRITUALITY (SNYING-THIG YA-BZHI)*.

Losar (tib.) ལོ་གསར་ lo gsar

The traditional Tibetan new year day which normally falls around the end of February. The Tibetan calendar is based on a complex combined system of solar, lunar and astrological calculations. Therefore, the first day of the new year varies in relation to the Western calendar. The exact date can be determined by consulting the official Tibetan calendar produced by scholars of **astrology** towards the end of each year. *Losar* is accompanied by public ceremonials such as the Great Prayer Festival (*smon-lam chen-mo*), monastic dances and picnicing.

Loseling (tib.) བློ་གསལ་གླིང་ blo gsal gling

One of the two principal philosophical colleges of *Drepung* monastic university, the other being *Tashi Gomang*. Prior to 1959, *Loseling* was probably the largest college of all the monastic institutions in Tibet with over 4000 resident scholars. Although the major philosophical works of both Indian and Tibetan masters were studied in the two main philosophical colleges of *Drepung*, each college had its own special textbooks. The textbooks used at both *Loseling* and the *Shartse* college of *Ganden* monastic uni-

versity are the commentarial works of *Panchen Sonam Drakpa* (sixteenth century). '*Loseling*' literally means 'the abode of scholars or clear intelligence'.

Lotsawa (skrt.) ལོ་ཙཱ་བ།/སྒྲ་སྒྱུར lo tsā ba/sgra sgyur *lokacakṣuḥ/anuvādaka*

Although this term refers to translators in general, it is most commonly reserved for the translators of Buddhist literature. It is the Tibetan transliteration of the *Sanskrit* compound *lokacakshuh*, meaning 'eye of the world'. This term was not translated into Tibetan, perhaps to preserve its honorific form and to express the deep appreciation accorded to translators for their great contribution towards the establishment of Buddhism in Tibet.

Love/Loving Kindness བྱམས་པ།/བརྩེ་བ byams pa/brtse ba *maitrī*

In a Buddhist context, love or loving kindness is defined as a **mental factor** characterised by a sincere wish that others enjoy happiness. According to this definition, **love** is one of the eleven 'wholesome **mental factors**' categorised in the **abhidharma** literature. However, in the case of the **four immeasurables**, the word **love** is used as an abbreviation for 'great **love**' (*mahamaitri* in **Sanskrit** or *byams-pa chen-po* in Tibetan) which refers to an altruistic mental attitude that is unbiased in its **love** towards all beings and is also spontaneous and natural. It is said that such a spontaneous sense of universal or unqualified **love** can only arise as a result of a systematic meditative training.

Madhyamaka (skrt.) དབུ་མ dbu ma *Madhyamaka*

Derived from the **Sanskrit** expression *madhyamapratipad*, meaning the 'Middle Way' between the extremes of **eternalism** and **nihilism**, which was expounded by **Shakyamuni Buddha, Madhyamaka** is the name of the most influential among the four major philosophical schools of **Indian Buddhism**. Within the context of the *Madhyamaka* school, the Middle Way refers to the doctrine of **emptiness**, which is held to be the true nature of all things. According to this view, all phenomena, both mental and physical, cannot be found to possess any independent and **self**-validating natures and their existence and **identity** are regarded as valid only within a relative framework of worldly convention. Further, it is propounded that not only do phenomena exist solely in dependence on causes and conditions, but even their **identities** depend on our conceptions and labelling. Nevertheless this school holds that, unlike mere fantasies, such as unicorns for example, phenomena do exist conventionally and their ontology must be accepted as valid. Such a metaphysical position is the Middle Way in that it is the mid-point between the extremes of total non-existence (**nihilism**) and the positing of an ultimate, independent existence of **reality** (**eternalism**/absolutism). Founded by **Nagarjuna** in the second century AD, the *Madhyamaka* school was later classified into two sub-divisions: **Prasangika** and **Svatantrika**, based on the different interpretations of **Nagarjuna's** views which were made by **Buddhapalita** and **Bhavaviveka** respectively. The Tibetan tradition, while recognising **Bhavaviveka's** contribution to Buddhist logic and philosophy, generally considers the *Prasangika* technique of consequential reasoning and also the use of *reductio ad absurdum* to be the most refined logical method in Buddhism for establishing the view of **emptiness**. See **Emptiness**. For the tradition known as the **Great Madhyamaka**, see **Shentong**.

MADHYAMAKAVATARA (skrt.) དབུ་མ་འཇུག་པ dbu ma 'jug pa *Madhyamakāvatāra*

One of the most celebrated Indian works on the study of **emptiness**, by

Medicine Buddha

Trisong Detsen

Candrakirti. Written in verse, the work consists of ten chapters, each corresponding to the ten levels or **grounds of a bodhisattva**. It was written as a supplement to ***Nagarjuna's*** principal exposition of the doctrine of **emptiness**, the *MULAMADH-YAMAKAKARIKA*, this text being extensively discussed in the sixth chapter of ***Candrakirti's*** book. The *MADHYAMAKAVATARA* is regarded in the Tibetan tradition as one of the most authoritative texts on the **Madhyamaka Prasangika** view, and it is still used today as the primary text for the study of **Madhyamaka** philosophy by most monastic universities in Tibet.

Madhyamika (skrt.) དབུ་མ་པ་ dbu ma pa *Mādhyamika*

An adherent of the **Madhyamaka** school. See **Madhyamaka**.

MADHYANTAVIBHAGA (skrt.) དབུས་མཐའི་རྣམ་འབྱེད་ dbus mtha'i rnam 'byed *Madhyāntavibhāga*

One of the **five works of Maitreya** principally expounding the philosophical views of the **Cittamatra** school of Buddhism, and also considered by some as expounding the tenets of the **Great Madhyamaka** school. See **Five Works of Maitreya** and **Shentong**.

Mahakala (skrt.) ནག་པོ་ཆེན་པོ་ (མགོན་པོ་) nag po chen po/mgon po *Mahākāla/nātha*

A **protector** who is a **wrathful** manifestation of ***Avalokiteshvara***. There are various aspects of **Mahakala**, the meditative practices associated with this **protector** being popular in all four traditions of **Tibetan Buddhism**. The **Gelug** school regards **Mahakala** as the **protector** associated with the training of one's **mind** in the practices of the 'great scope'. See **Three Scopes**. The **protectors** associated with the other two scopes are ***Vaishravana***, associated with the 'middling scope', and *Kalarupa*, associated with the 'initial scope' practices.

Mahamudra (skrt.) ཕྱག་རྒྱ་ཆེན་པོ་ phyag rgya chen po *Mahāmudrā*

Literally meaning 'great seal', the term ***Mahamudra*** is defined according to either the *sutra* or *tantra* classes of teachings. According to the *sutra* explanation, ***Mahamudra*** refers to the comprehension of **emptiness** as the all-encompassing **ultimate** nature of **reality**. **Emptiness** is called the great seal, in this context, for it is posited that nothing extraneous to it exists, and all phenomena, both physical and mental, are in their **ultimate** natures **empty** of **inherent existence**. According to the explanation of the *tantras* in general, ***Mahamudra*** refers to the state of **buddha**hood, the conclusive result or supreme accomplishment. It is called '*mudra*' because the **realisation** of the three **kayas** is sealed in the accomplishment of supreme unchanging bliss. With respect to this attainment, there is neither increase nor decrease and, on account of its atemporal nature, it endures as long as space endures. It is called 'great' because the three greatnesses of

the *Mahayana* - **renunciation**, **realisation** and mental cultivation - are fully ripened. In *Mahayoga*, *Mahamudra* refers to the great seal of **buddha-body** which secures the **consciousness** of the ground-of-all (*alayavijnana*) as the mirror-like **pristine cognition**. *Mahamudra* practice may also be considered in terms of ground, path and result. As a path, it comprises a sequence of systematic advanced **meditations** on **emptiness** and pure appearance. See *Dharmakaya*. This meditative approach applies both **calm abiding** and **penetrative insight** whilst focusing on the nature of the **meditator's** own **mind**. This type of **meditation** is popular in both the *Kagyu* and *Gelug* schools of **Tibetan Buddhism**.

Mahapandita (skrt.) པཎྜི་ཏ་ཆེན་པོ pan di ta chen po *mahāpaṇḍita*

A great scholar, a very learned person. '*Maha*' literally means 'great' and '*Pandita*', the one who is well-versed in the five sciences. The five sciences are the five subjects of traditional scholarship in Buddhist India, namely: art, medicine, grammar, logic and **epistemology**, and inner science/Buddhist philosophy.

Mahasiddha (skrt.) གྲུབ་ཐོབ་ཆེན་པོ grub thob chen po *mahāsiddha*

A *yogin* or *yogini* with *siddhi* or great spiritual accomplishments. '*Maha*' means great and '*siddha*', one who has attained spiritual accomplishments. The term is usually reserved for those *tantric yogins* or *yoginis* who have attained very high levels of spiritual **realisation**. *Tantric* literature mentions eighty-four such *Mahasiddhas* of ancient India. These include such *yogins* as *Saraha*, *Tilopa*, *Virupa* and many others. See **Siddhi**.

Mahasukha (skrt.) བདེ་བ་ཆེན་པོ bde ba chen po *mahāsukha*

Literally meaning '**great bliss**' or 'joy', this *Sanskrit* word is often used in Tibetan *tantric* ritual literature as an exclamation of the great joy and ecstasy which the **meditator** experiences during deity *yoga* **meditation** and other specific *tantric* practices. In the context of *Anuttarayogatantra*, **great bliss** refers to the blissful states experienced when the **meditator** enters into union with a partner (either in visualisation at the beginner's level or in actuality at an advanced stage). In both cases, the experiences, to be valid, have to arise as a result of the dissolution of gross mental conceptuality and the subtle energy **winds** which propel it. Such a blissful state of **mind**, when generated within a direct experience of **emptiness** becomes what is known as, the union of bliss and **emptiness**.

Mahayana (skrt.) ཐེག་པ་ཆེན་པོ theg pa chen po *Mahāyāna*

One of the two main systems or vehicles of Buddhism, the other being *Hinayana*. Philosophically, *Mahayana* is the systemisation of the Buddhist teachings conducive to complete **liberation** from the various **delusions** and misconceptions concerning phenomenal existence, whilst the *Hinayana* systemisation is not conducive to a full appreciation of **emptiness**. In terms of motivation, the practitioner of *Mahayana* emphasises altruism and has the **liberation** of all others as the principal objective, whilst the practitioner of *Hinayana* emphasises the individual's own freedom from **cyclic existence** as the primary motivation and goal. The *Mahayana* system comprises both *sutra* and *tantra* aspects. The *sutra* aspect is also known as the *Bodhisattvayana* or the '*bodhisattva's* vehicle', and *Paramitayana* or the 'perfection vehicle'. As the word *Mahayana* ('greater vehicle') suggests, the *bodhisattva* path is analogous to a large carriage which can transport a vast number of people to **liberation**, as compared to a

smaller vehicle for the individual practitioner. *Maitreya*, in the
MAHAYANASUTRALAMKARA, defines **Mahayana** as '*Maha*' or
'great' in seven ways, in that it possesses the following features of
greatness: 1) great objective *(dmigs-pa chen-po)*, 2) great attainment *(sgrub-pa chen-po)*, 3) great **pristine cognition** *(ye-shes
chen-po)*, 4) great perseverance *(brtson-'grus 'dzom-pa chen-po)*,
5)great **skilful means** *(thabs-mkhas chen-po)*, 6) great genuine
accomplishment *(yang-dag 'grub-pa chen-po)*, and 7) great enlightened activities *(phrin-las chen-po)*. Other sources define the greatness of the *Mahayana* in terms of its **renunciation, realisation**
and mental cultivation. The principal philosophical schools of the
Mahayana are *Cittamatra* and *Madhyamaka*.

Mahayana Ordination ཐེག་ཆེན་གསོ་སྦྱོང་ theg chen gso sbyong
Mahāyānaposadha

A twenty-four hour long **vow** to maintain eight **precepts**, which
Mahayana practitioners take on important religious occasions.
The eight **precepts** are: abstinence from killing, sexual misconduct, stealing, lying, drinking alcohol, frivolous activities, sitting
and lying on elevated beds or seats etc, and eating after lunch.
These **precepts** are taken within the context of an altruistic motivation of *bodhicitta*, the aspiration to attain full **enlightenment**
for the benefit of others.

MAHAYANASUTRALAMKARA (skrt.) ཐེག་པ་ཆེན་པོ་མདོ་སྡེ་རྒྱན་ theg pa
chen po mdo sde rgyan *Mahāyānasūtrālaṃkāra*

One of the **five works of Maitreya** known for its detailed treatment of important *Mahayana* topics such as *buddha*-**nature**,
refuge in the **Three Precious Jewels**, the *Mahayana* paths, and
also a presentation of the doctrine of **emptiness**. The work consists of twenty-one chapters and, like many of the classic Indian
texts of its time, it is written in verse. It is identified as one of the
main sources for the interpretation of **emptiness** by both the *Cittamatra* and *Shentong* schools of Buddhist thought.

Mahayoga (skrt.) རྣལ་འབྱོར་ཆེན་པོ་ rnal 'byor chen po *Mahāyoga*

The first of the three inner classes of *tantras* according to the
classification of the *Nyingma* school. *Mahayoga* emphasises the
generation/creation **stage** of **meditation**, and the gradual visualisation of elaborate *mandalas* of **deities**. It comprises eighteen
basic *tantras*, such as the *GUHYAGARBHA*, *GUHYASAMAJA* and
BUDDHASAMAYOGA, as well as a vast number of *tantra*-texts associated with the so-called eight classes of means for attainment
(*sadhana*), which focus on the **deities** *Yamantaka*,
Hayagriva, *Shriheruka*, *Vajramrita*, *Vajrakila*, *Matarah*, *Lokas-
totrapuja* (*'jig-rten mchod-bstod*), and *Vajramantrabhiru* (*rmod-pa
drags-sngags*). These texts are all contained in the *COLLECTED
TANTRAS OF THE NYINGMAPA* (*RNYING-MA'I RGYUD-'BUM*) and
important examples of each are also contained in the *Kangyur*.
See **Nine Yanas**.

Maitreya (skrt.) རྒྱམས་པ་ byams pa *Maitreya*

Maitreya is an embodiment of the 'great **love/loving kindness**' (*mahamaitri*) of all the *buddhas* (the fully enlightened **mind**) as visualised in the form of a **meditational deity**. *Maitreya* therefore represents the perfected state of the faculty of **love/loving kindness** inherent within each individual's mental continuum. In addition, there is also an eminent historical figure known by the name of *Maitreya*, a *bodhisattva* who is included among the eight principal *bodhisattva* disciples of the *Buddha Shakyamuni*. It is to him that the FIVE WORKS OF *MAITREYA* are attributed. According to the classical *sutra* literature it is the *Bodhisattva Maitreya* who is the coming *buddha*, fifth in the line of the thousand *buddhas* (*Buddha Shakyamuni* being the fourth) who will descend to this world during the aeon of illumination and good auspices. Currently he is said to be residing in the *deva* realm of *Tushita*.

Major and Minor Marks མཚན་དཔེ་ mtshan dpe *lakṣanavyañjana*

The thirty-two major and eighty minor marks of a *Buddha's* body have been interpreted from different standpoints - outer, inner, secret and most secret - which derive respectively from the *Buddha's* expressive power, the purity of his energy **channels**, the purified seed of his **enlightened mind**, and the single savour of his supreme bliss. In general, as explained in texts such as the *ORNAMENT OF CLEAR REALISATION* and the *ORNAMENT OF THE SUTRAS OF THE GREATER VEHICLE*, the *Buddha's* body is said to have thirty-two important marks, each of which reflects his pre-eminence, noble personality, or extensive accumulations of **merit**. These include the wheel-like markings on his palms and soles, the protrusion on the crown of his head, the golden complexion and delicate skin, the *Brahma*-like voice, the hair-ringlet between the eyebrows, and so forth. By contrast the eighty minor marks refer to various secondary complementary features.

Manasarovar (skrt.) མཚོ་མ་ཕམ་ mtsho ma pham *Manasarovara*

A sacred lake near Mount *Kailash* in Western Tibet. Like Mount *Kailash*, the lake is associated with the Buddhist *tantric* **deity** *Cakrasamvara*. *Hindus* consider it a sacred site of Lord *Shiva* and his consort *Parvati*.

Mandala (skrt.) དཀྱིལ་འཁོར་ dkyil 'khor *maṇḍala*

The basic definition of the *Sanskrit* word *mandala* is circle, wheel, circumference, and also a totality, assembly or literary corpus. In the context of *Anuyoga* and *Atiyoga*, the expression 'three *mandala*' refers to the scope of *buddhabody*, *buddha*-**speech** and *buddha*-**mind** respectively. In its general usage, this term, which is rendered in Tibetan as *dkyil-'khor* (pronounced '*kyil-khor*'), indicates the central (*dkyil*) and peripheral ('*khor*) **deities** described in the *tantra*-texts. These **deities** reside within a celestial palace, known as the *vimana*, which has a perfectly symmetrical design - with four gateways and four main walls composed of five layers of different colours, each of these features corresponding to a specific aspect of the principal **deity's**, and thereby the meditator's, **enlightened mind**. Therefore, the *mandala* represents a perfected state of being and perception encompassing all phenomena. The celestial palace itself and the **deities** within it symbolise the perfected states of the **meditator's** own five **aggregates**, five elemental properties, etc. When such *mandala* are represented symbolically, they may take the form of a two-dimensional image on painted cloth or may be made of coloured sand, or are constructed as a three-dimensional structure, carved from wood or other materials. The visualisation of ***mandala*** (in their three-dimensional form) plays a crucial role in ***tantric*** meditations during the **generation**/creation **stage**. Here, these 'abodes of the **deity**' are never perceived of as independently existing universes but as manifestations of the **enlightened mind** of the principal **meditational deity** being meditated upon. The ***tantric mandalas*** are therefore never visualised without the presence of their related **deities**. See **Meditational Deity**.

Mandala Offering མཎྜལ་ mandal *maṇḍala*

A specific ritual of **offering** which involves visualisation of the entire universe and mentally **offering** this to an object of **refuge** such as one's ***guru***, a **meditational deity** or the **Three [Precious] Jewels**.

Manibhadra (skrt.) ནོར་བུ་བཟང་པོ་ nor bu bzang po *Maṇibhadra*

One of the retinue of the wealth **deity** *Vaishravana*. There is also a **meditational deity** of the same name who is an aspect of *Avalokiteshvara*.

Manjushri (skrt.) འཇམ་དཔལ་(དབྱངས་) 'jam dpal (dbyangs) *Mañjuśrī(ghoṣa)*

Manjushri is an embodiment of the **discriminative awareness** (***prajna***) of all the ***Buddhas*** (the fully enlightened **mind**) as visualised in the form of a **meditational deity**. ***Manjushri*** therefore represents the perfected state of the faculty of intelligence inherent within each individual's mental continuum. He is normally depicted holding a sword in his right hand (representing **discriminative awareness** which realises **emptiness**) and a scripture in his left hand (indicating his mastery of all **knowledge**). In Buddhist iconography one finds various aspects of ***Manjushri***, some with multiple faces and arms. ***Manjushri*** is also the name of an eminent historical figure who was one of the eight principal ***bodhisattva*** disciples of the ***Buddha***.

Mantra (skrt.) སྔགས་ (lit. ཡིད་སྐྱོབ་) sngags *mantra*

Mantra is composed of two syllables, *mana* and *tara*, respectively suggesting '**mind**' and '**protection**'. Hence '***mantra***' literally means 'protection of the **mind**'. The essential indication here is the protection of the **mind** from the overwhelming influence of ordinary perceptions and conceptions. Such ordinary perceptions and conceptions give rise to **deluded** states of existence, thus inhibiting the full expression of the ***buddha***-nature. The overcoming of ordinary perceptions and conceptions in ***tantra*** is achieved through the cultivation of the perceptions and **identity** of oneself as a **deity**, a practice known as **deity** ***yoga***. In a Buddhist context, ***mantra*** is a synonym of ***tantra*** and it refers to a specific practice of spiritual training involving the above features. More specifically, ***mantra*** refers to the pure sound which is the perfected speech of an **enlightened** being. The **seed-syllables**

and names of the various deities are recited and visualised within a set **Sanskritic** formula, in order to effect the transformation of mundane sound into **buddha-speech**. See **Generation Stage**.

Mara (skrt.) དུད་ bdud *māra*

Buddhist literature mentions four kinds of **mara** (evil influences) which are the obstacles that impede one's spiritual transformation. These are the evil influence of: 1) one's own impure **aggregates**; 2) **dissonant emotions**; 3) *'deva's* son'; and 4) the bringer of death. The first **mara** refers to the psycho-physical **aggregates** which are the products of one's own **dissonant emotions** and negative **karmic** forces. The second refers to **dissonant states** such as attraction or **desire**, hatred/anger, pride and jealousy, which commonly dominate our **minds** and bring harm. The third refers specifically to sensual **desires** and temptations, whereas the fourth refers to ordinary death, which comes about without choice as a consequence of our own past actions.

Marpa (tib.) མར་པ་ mar pa

(1012-1097) One of the greatest Tibetan *lotsawa* (translators) and the founder of the **Kagyu** school of **Tibetan Buddhism**. Trained at the feet of such pre-eminent Indian masters as **Naropa** and *Maitripa*, **Marpa** translated into Tibetan many **tantric** texts, including, in particular, authoritative works on the **GUHYASAMAJA** and **CAKRASAMVARA tantras**. **Marpa** was also the main teacher of the renowned Tibetan poet-saint **Milarepa**.

MEDICAL TANTRAS གསོ་རིག་གི་རྒྱུད་རྣམས་ gso rig gi rgyud rnams *cikitsatantra*

The four principal works on Tibetan medicine, redacted from or composed on the basis of Indian medical sources by Tibet's foremost medical authority *Yutok Yonten Gompo* during the ninth century and rediscovered by *Trapa Ngonshe* during the eleventh century. The four works are: 1) *ROOT TANTRA (rtsa-rgyud)*, 2) *EXEGETICAL TANTRA (bshad-rgyud)*, 3) *INSTRUCTIONAL TANTRA (man-ngag-gi rgyud)*, and 4) *SUBSEQUENT TANTRA (phyi-ma rgyud)*.

Medicine Buddha སངས་རྒྱས་སྨན་ལྷ་ sangs rgyas sman lha *Bhaiṣajyaguru*

The '**Buddha** of Medicine', the principal figure in the Buddhist **medical tantras**. According to certain sources, the **Buddha Shakyamuni** is believed to have assumed a specific form when teaching the **medical tantras** and that aspect of the **Buddha** is called *Vaidurya*, the 'Beryl **Buddha** of **Medicine**'. He is normally depicted in paintings as being blue in colour and holding in his left palm an alms bowl filled with the fruits of a medicinal plant, chebulic myrobalan. According to the **lineage** of the **medical tantras**, there are eight different aspects of the **Medicine Buddha**.

Meditation སྒོམ་ sgom *bhāvanā*

Meditation is defined as a disciplined mental process through which a person cultivates familiarity with a chosen object, be it an external object like an image, or even a trivial object such as a pebble, etc., or an internal object such as one's own **mind** or personal **identity**. There are two main types of **meditation**, one emphasising the faculty of stability and single-pointedness of **mind** and the other emphasising analysis and discrimination. The first type of **meditation** is absorptive, and produces a quality of mental placement and tranquillity (see **calm abiding**), and the latter is penetrating, and generates a higher insight into the profound natures of the chosen object (see **penetrative insight**). Buddhism perceives **meditation** on its own as a mere technique by which one can develop a disciplined state of **mind**, which can then be utilised towards higher spiritual training.

Meditational Deity ཡི་དམ་ yi dam *devatā*

Forms or resonances of the fully enlightened **mind** whose characteristics are defined or revealed by the specific *tantric* practices on the basis of which they are visualised/cultivated. A **meditator** on the *tantric* path takes such a **deity** as a particular object of **meditation**, seeking to cultivate experientially union with the qualities of *buddha*-**body, speech** and **mind**. Such a **meditational deity** should not be perceived as an externally existing or independent being, but rather as a manifestation of *buddha*-**mind** itself. This non-dual approach is one of the most essential elements of **deity yoga** meditation. See **Generation Stage** and *Mantra*. When contrasted with the *guru* and the *dakini*, union with the meditational **deity** is said to effect supreme *siddhi*, whereas **meditation** on the *guru* results in the conferral of **blessing** (*byin-rlabs*) and the **meditation** on the *dakini* results in the actualisation of enlightened activities.

Meditative Concentration བསམ་གཏན་ bsam gtan *dhyāna*

The fifth of the **six perfections**, defined as the one-pointed abiding in the unwavering state of **mind** which is free from the taint of the **dissonant emotions**. It is called *bsam-gtan* in Tibetan because this one-pointed abiding is definitive or established, and on its basis all the aspects of discernment and logic common to the *Hinayana* and *Mahayana* paths can be accomplished. See **Concentration** and **Four Concentrations**.

Mental Factors སེམས་བྱུང་ sems byung *caitasika*

In contrast to the primary **mind**, mental events or factors are the modalities of **mind** which relate in specific ways to the perceived object. There are two principal categorisations of **mental factors** in Buddhist *abhidharma* literature. *Asanga's* ABHIDHARMASAMUCCAYA lists fifty-one **mental factors** whereas *Vasubandhu's* ABHIDHARMAKOSHA enumerates forty-six. See **Mind**.

Mental Pliancy སེམས་ཤིན་སྦྱངས་ sems shin sbyangs *cittaprasrabdhi*

Suppleness of **mind** attained when the **mind** is temporarily free of mental lethargy and heaviness, achieved as a result of successful single-pointed **meditation**. True **mental pliancy** allows the **mind** to focus on any chosen object of **meditation** for a prolonged period of time. 'Pliancy' also refers to the **mental factor** of pliancy which serves as the causal basis which, through proper training, can mature into full **mental pliancy**. This is one of the eleven wholesome **mental factors** mentioned in *abhidharma* literature. See **Mental Factors**.

Merit བསོད་ནམས་ bsod nams *puṇya*

The wholesome tendencies imprinted in the **mind** as a result of positive and skilful thoughts, words and actions that ripen in the experience of happiness and well-being. According to the *Mahayana* schools, it is important to dedicate the **merit** of one's wholesome actions for the benefit of all **sentient being**s, ensuring that others also experience their good karmic results.

MIGTSEMA (tib.) དམིགས་བརྩེ་མ་ dmigs brtse ma

A very popular prayer of praise to *Tsong Khapa* originally composed by the great *Sakya* scholar *Rendawa Zhonu Lodro*, one of the principal teachers of *Tsong Khapa*. The prayer pays homage to *Lama Tsong Khapa* as an embodiment of *Avalokiteshvara*, *Manjushri* and *Vajrapani*, thus perceiving him as the human manifestation of the **compassion, discriminative awareness** (*prajna*) and energy of all the *buddhas*. There are several variants of this eulogy and from these there has developed an extensive collection of practices focusing on *Lama Tsong Khapa* within the *Gelug* tradition.

Milarepa (tib.) མི་ལ་རས་པ་ mi la ras pa

(1040-1123) The great twelfth century poet-saint of Tibet. He is known for his magnificent perseverance and determination in his quest for spiritual accomplishment and learning, even at the cost of tremendous hardships encountered under *Marpa's* tutorship. His reputation for **meditation** and practice is such that all the four main traditions of **Tibetan Buddhism** accept that *Milarepa* attained full **enlightenment** within a single lifetime. He is particularly remembered for his collection of inspiring poems and songs, relating his experiences on the spiritual path. Principal among his disciples were *Gampopa*, the founder of *Dagpo Kagyu* school, and *Rechungpa*.

Mind སེམས་/ ཡིད་ sems/yid *citta*

In Buddhism, **mind** is defined as a dynamic process which is simply the awareness of an object or event. In its technical usage '**mind**' is contrasted with '**mental events or factors**'. In the context of this differentiation the primary function of '**mind**' is to be aware of the referent object as a whole, whereas the modalities which relate to the specific aspects of the object are defined as '**mental factors**'. In *tantra* various levels of **mind** corresponding to subtleties of the vital energies (**winds**) are also discussed. It is important to understand, however, that **mind** in Buddhism should not be conceived of as a static thing or as something composed of a spiritual substance. Although some Buddhist philosophical schools of thought do identify **mind** as the essence of being or personal **identity**, the notion of **self** or person is not an essential component of the Buddhist concept of **mind**. See **Consciousness**.

Mind Training བློ་སྦྱོང་ blo sbyong

An alternative translation of the Tibetan word *Lojong*, often also translated as **Thought Transformation**. See **Lojong**.

Mindfulness དྲན་པ་/ དྲན་པ་ཉེར་བཞག་ dran pa/dran pa nyer bzhag *smṛti/smṛtyupasthāna*

One of the five **mental factors** of ascertainment. **Mindfulness** is the faculty of our **mind** which enables the **mind** to maintain its attention on a referent object, thus allowing for the development of familiarity with the object and also the ability to retain its imprint within memory for future recollection. Together with mental alertness, it is one of the most crucial faculties of our **mind**, it being indispensable when developing '**calm abiding**'. **Mindfulness** is the factor that counteracts the arisal of forgetfulness, one of the greatest obstacles to a successful cultivation of mental stability. **Mindfulness** also refers to a specific set of introspective **meditations** known as the four foundations of **mindfulness**, which form the basis of the **thirty-seven** aspects of the path to **enlightenment**. These are: the **mindfulness** of body, feeling, **mind**, and phenomena. See also **Four Mindfulnesses**.

Mindroling (tib.) སྨིན་གྲོལ་གླིང་ smin grol gling

One of the most important monasteries of the **Nyingma** school of **Tibetan Buddhism**. Founded in the seventeenth century by the great treasure finder (**Terton**) *Terdag Lingpa* in the *Lhokha* region of Central Tibet, it served as a great learning centre until 1959, and is now undergoing reconstruction. A branch of the monastery has been established within the exiled Tibetan community at Clement Town, near *Dehra Dun, Uttar Pradesh*, India.

Monlam Chenmo (tib.) སྨོན་ལམ་ཆེན་མོ་ smon lam chen mo

The 'Great Prayer Festival' was initiated by **Tsong Khapa** to commemorate the **Buddha Shakyamuni's** victory over some of his contemporaries who challenged the **Buddha** in a contest of supernatural feats. Celebrated in the *Jokhang*, the central cathedral of **Lhasa**, in the presence of *Jowo* **Rinpoche**, the most sacred image of the **Buddha** in Tibet, the festival soon became a major religious event in the Tibetan calendar. The festival focuses around the chanting of praises to the **Buddha** and other great masters, sung by large congregations of monks and nuns gathered from all over Tibet. It is during the 'Great Prayer Festival' that the **Geshe Lharam** candidates of that year sit for their final **Geshe** examinations. See **Geshe**.

Mudra (skrt.) ཕྱག་རྒྱ་ phyag rgya *mudrā*

Literally meaning 'hand seal', the term *mudra* has three basic senses. Firstly, it refers to the various hand gestures which are performed in specific **tantric** ritual practices, and by extension to the symbolic hand implements (*phyag-mtshan*) such as the **vajra** and the bell. Secondly, *mudra* may refer to the appropriate sexual partners known as *Karmamudra* (a live consort) and *Jnanamudra* (a visualised consort) that a practitioner at high levels of **tantric completion/**perfection **stage** practice unites with, in order to arouse **great bliss** (*mahasukha*). Thirdly, in the context of **Mahayoga**, where the four seals are secured, these comprise the seal of commitment (*samayamudra*), which secures **buddha-mind**, the seal of doctrine (*dharmamudra*) which secures **buddha**-speech, the seal of action (*karmamudra*) which secures **buddha**-activities, and the great seal (*mahamudra*) which secures **buddha-body**. **Mahamudra** is also the name for an

important meditative tradition. See **Mahamudra**.

Nadi (skrt.) རྩ་ rtsa *nāḍī*
See **Energy Channels**.

Naga ཀླུ་ klu *nāga*
A powerful water-spirit which may take the form of a serpent or a semi-human form similar to a mermaid/man. Some *naga* are regarded as custodians of doctrinal treasure and are depicted as arising out of the sea. Others have a malign influence, the treatments for which are expounded in the texts of Tibetan medicine. *Naga* are classified as one of the eight classes of **demons** or spirits (*sde-brgyad*), the foremost representatives of which are the *naga* kings such as *Ananta* and *Taksaka*.

Nagarjuna (skrt.) ཀླུ་སྒྲུབ་ klu sgrub *Nāgārjuna*
A second century Indian scholar and the founder of the **Madhyamaka** philosophical school of Buddhist thought. Undisputedly one of the greatest **Mahayana** thinkers of ancient India, his philosophy of **emptiness** soon became the dominant Buddhist philosophical system within India, attracting such outstanding followers as *Buddhapalita*, **Bhavaviveka**, **Shantarakshita**, **Candrakirti** and **Shantideva**. The Tibetan tradition considers **Nagarjuna** one of the two most important personalities in Indian **Mahayana** Buddhism (the other being **Asanga**), and among the multitude of classical Indian scholars his authority outshines all others. **Nagarjuna's** works include six treatises which form the corpus of reason (*yuktikaya*), including his famous *MULAMADHYAMAKA-KARIKA*, and various treatises forming the corpus of eulogies (*stavakaya*). There is a tradition, the **Great Madhyamaka**, which interprets the doctrines of *tathagatagarbha* and *buddha*-nature on the basis of the latter corpus. Traditional literature also attributes to him several pre-eminent works on *tantra*, especially on *Guhyasamaja*, *Hayagriva* and *Mahakala*.

Nalanda (skrt.) ན་ལན་ད་ na lan da *Nālandā*
The most important seat of Buddhist learning in ancient India. Located in Bihar, near *Rajgir* where the **Mahayana sutras** were first delivered by **Shakyamuni Buddha**, and on the site where the **Buddha**'s foremost disciple *Shariputra* had passed away. *Nalanda* is considered to have been the greatest Buddhist university of its time (fifth to tenth century), producing outstanding scholars such as **Bhavavikeka**, *Buddhapalita*, **Candrakirti**, *Dignaga*, *Dharmakirti* and **Shantideva**.

Naljorma (tib.) རྣལ་འབྱོར་མ་ rnal 'byor ma *yoginī*
See **Yogini** and **Vajrayogini**.

Naropa (skrt.) ནཱ་རོ་པ་ nā ro pa *Nāropāda*
An eleventh century Indian master. *Naropa* was an accomplished scholar from *Nalanda* university who became a **yogin** meditating under the tutorship of the **Mahasiddha Tilopa**. He was the teacher of **Marpa Lotsawa**, the famous Tibetan translator and principal teacher of **Milarepa**. *Naropa* is particularly known for his presentation of a specific set of *tantric* practices known as the SIX YOGAS OF NAROPA. See SIX YOGAS OF NAROPA.

Nechung (tib.) གནས་ཆུང་ gnas chung

One of the main **protector deities** of Tibet and of the *Dalai Lama*. The **deity's** medium is the state **oracle** of Tibet who is consulted on many important matters of state. The propitiation of the **deity** and the rituals connected with the invocation of the **deity** are undertaken by *Nechung* Monastery, a monastery named after the **protector deity**. In Tibet, the monastery is located adjacent to *Drepung* monastic university, and in India, the abode of the state **oracle** is in *Dharamsala*, the seat of the exiled Tibetan government in the Himalayan foothills of *Himachal Pradesh*.

Ngagpa (tib.) སྔགས་པ་ sngags pa *mantrin*

A *mantra*-adept or master of *tantra*. The word is popularly used to denote those practitioners of *tantra* who choose to maintain a family life in contrast to the celibate life of a monk or a nun.

Ngondro (tib.) སྔོན་འགྲོ་ sngon 'gro

Preliminary practices which are normally undertaken by a **meditator** prior to engaging in *tantric* practice. There are both outer **preliminaries**, in the form of analytic **meditation**s which turn the **mind** of the practitioner away from worldly distractions and towards spiritual practice, and inner **preliminaries**, designed to purify the basic **dissonant emotions**. Outer **preliminaries** concern **meditation** on: the advantages of human birth, **impermanence**, the workings of *karma* and the **suffering** of living beings within cyclical existence. Inner **preliminaries** are the taking of **refuge** in conjunction with the performance of one hundred thousand prostrations (which purifies pride), cultivation of *bodhicitta* (which purifies jealousy or mundane ambition), the recitation of *Vajrasattva's* hundred-syllable *mantra* (which purifies hatred/aversion), the *mandala* **offering** (which purifies **attachment**), and *guruyoga* (which purifies **delusion**).

Ngor (tib.) ངོར་ ngor

Originally the name of an important *Sakya* monastery in Western Tibet, it soon evolved into a term referring to a sub-school within the *Sakya* tradition following the **lineage** of such great *Sakya* masters as *Ngorchen Kunga Sangpo, Konchok Gyaltsen* and *Konchok Lhundrup*.

Ngorpa (tib.) ངོར་པ་ ngor pa

The followers of the *Ngor* sub-school of the *Sakya* tradition.

Niguma (skrt.) ནི་གུ་མ་ ni gu ma *Nigumā*

The sister of the famous Indian *Pandita* and **yogin** *Naropa*. *Niguma* was herself a great *tantric yogini* and from her evolved an entire system of *tantric* practices known as the SIX *YOGAS* OF *NIGUMA*. See *SIX YOGAS OF NIGUMA*.

Nihilism ཆད་ལྟ་ chad lta *ucchedāśraya*

One of the two extreme views which must, according to Buddhist thought, be transcended in order for any philosophical position to be considered well-founded. **Nihilism** in general refers to the view that denies the existence of objects, particularly those which can be directly perceived through our empirical **knowledge** of the world. Also denied are the laws of **cause and effect** and the principle of **dependent origination**. However, based on one's metaphysical position with regard to the nature of **reality**, the criteria of what constitutes a denial of the existence of phenomena or the law of **cause and effect** etc., may differ.

Nine Modes of Practice ཐེག་པ་རིམ་པ་དགུ་ theg pa rim pa dgu *navayāna*

See **Nine Yanas**.

Nine Stages of Calm Abiding སེམས་གནས་དགུ་ sems gnas dgu

The **nine stages** of **meditation** which lead to the eventual attainment of **calm abiding** as explained in **Maitreya's MAHAYANASUTRALAMKARA**. The **nine stages** are: 1) placing the **mind**; 2) continual placement; 3) replacement; 4) close placement; 5) controlling; 6) pacifying; 7) completely pacifying; 8) single-point-edness; and 9) placement in equipoise. The above refer to progressive levels of mental development, each characterised by specific features marking progress, such as the ability to prolong one's mental focus and to refocus easily when the attention is lost. See **Calm Abiding**.

Nine Yanas ཐེག་པ་རིམ་པ་དགུ་ theg pa rim pa dgu *navayāna*

According to the **Nyingma** tradition, the entire Buddhist path is divided into what are known as the **nine yanas**, or the nine vehicles on the path to **buddha-hood**. The **nine yanas** are: 1) **Shravaka**; 2) **Pratyekabuddha**; 3) **Bod-hisattva**, which are the three causal vehicles based on the **sutras**; 4) **Kriyatantra**; 5) Ubhayayatantra (or **Caryatantra**); 6) **Yogatantra**, which are the outer **tantras** advocating austere conduct as well as **meditation**; 7) **Mahayoga**; 8) Anuyoga; and 9) Atiyoga, which are the three inner **tantras**, focusing respectively on the **generation**/creation **stage**, the perfection/**comple-tion stage**, and the Great Perfection (*rdzogs-pa chen-po*).

Nirmanakaya (skrt.) སྤྲུལ་སྐུ་ sprul sku *nirmāṇakāya*

Among the aspects of the **buddha**-body, on which see **Kaya(s)**, **Nirmanakaya** is the emanational body, the visible and usually physical manifestation of fully enlightened beings which arises spontaneously from the expanse of **Dhar-makaya**, thus serving the diverse dispositions of **sentient beings**. Classical liter-ature lists three principal types of **Nirmanakaya**: 1) supreme emanations (*mchog-gi sprul-sku*) such as **Shakyamuni Buddha** and the other **buddhas** of this aeon who initiate a new doctrine; 2) diversified emanations (*sna-tshogs sprul-sku*), including oases, food, medicine and other such material manifestations which are of benefit to living beings, as well as emanations of artistry (*bzo-bo sprul-sku*); and 3) those of birth (*skye-ba sprul-sku*) such as those **Shakyamuni** assumed in previous lives, e.g., Prince *Shatshvetaketu* in the **deva** realm of **Tushita**.

Nirvana (skrt.) སྱུང་འདས་ myang 'das *nirvāṇa*

The Tibetan term *myang-'das* (pronounced *'nyangde'*) literally means the 'state beyond sorrow'. As such, *nirvana* refers to the permanent cessation of all **suffering** and the **dissonant emotions** which cause and perpetuate **suffering**. It is defined as the total extinction of all our misconceptions, afflictive emotions and negative tendencies within the **ultimate** sphere of **emptiness**. Since it is through the misapprehension of the nature of **reality** that our conscious states of **delusion** arise, a total elimination of these **delusions** can only be effected by generating a genuine insight into the true nature of **reality**. Such an insight must be a **direct perception** of **emptiness**, which is in perfect union with **calm abiding**. Classical Buddhist literature mentions three types of *nirvana*: 1) *nirvana* with residue (the initial state of *nirvana* when the person is still dependent upon his or her old psychophysical **aggregates**); 2) *nirvana* without residue (an advanced state of *nirvana* when the old **aggregates** have also been consumed within **emptiness**); and 3) non-abiding *nirvana* (***Buddha's nirvana*** which is a state that has transcended both the extremes of conditioned **cyclic existence** and also the isolated peace of *nirvana*).

Non-Virtue མི་དགེ་བ་ mi dge ba *akuśala*

In the Buddhist ethical context, **virtue** and **non-virtue** are defined in terms of both motivation and the consequences of the action. In order for an action to be defined as either virtuous or non-virtuous there are certain pre-requisite features which must be present. These are: 1) motivation; 2) the actual execution of the act; and 3) the conclusion. An act is non-virtuous if it is: a) motivated by negative intentions; b) committed by the agent in a sane **mind** and with full knowledge; and c) the person derives a sense of satisfaction from having accomplished the act. Such actions can be physical, verbal or mental. Broadly speaking, **non-virtuous** actions are categorized into the following ten types: 1) killing; 2) stealing; 3) sexual misconduct, (which are the three bodily actions); 4) lying; 5) divisive speech; 6) harsh speech; 7) meaningless gossip, (which are the four verbal actions); 8) covetousness; 9) harmful intent; and 10) distorted views (which are the three mental actions).

Norbulingka (tib.) ནོར་བུ་གླིང་ཁ་ nor bu gling kha

The summer palace of the ***Dalai Lama***s in ***Lhasa***, constructed from the eighteenth century onwards.

Nyarong (tib.) ཉག་རོང་ nyag rong

A forested district in the *Yalung* river valley south of *Kanze*, in the province of ***Kham***, the South-eastern region of Tibet.

Nyingma (tib.) རྙིང་མ་ rnying ma

The oldest school of **Tibetan Buddhism**, based on the teaching

traditions and texts introduced to Tibet during the earliest phase of Buddhist propagation, which coincided with the reigns of the Buddhist kings of the *Yarlung* dynasty in the eighth to ninth centuries. These traditions were introduced from India by **Padmasambhava**, **Vimalamitra** and others, and maintained in Tibet by the twenty-five disciples of **Padmasambhava**. The distinction between the old and new schools of **Tibetan Buddhism** is made on the basis of the interregnum which followed the persecution of Buddhism during the ninth century and preceded the second or later phase of Buddhist propagation when a different corpus of Buddhist literature was introduced from India by **Marpa**, *Drokmi Lotsawa*, **Atisha**, *Rinchen Zangpo* and others during the eleventh century. **Lineages** derived from the earlier phase and works translated before the interregnum are known as **Nyingma**, or the 'Ancient Translation School' *(snga-'gyur rnying-ma)*, in contrast to those which emerged thereafter and are known as **Sarma**, or the new schools. The original *tantric* literature of the **Nyingma** corpus includes eighteen **Mahayoga tantras**, such as *GUHYAGARBHA* and *GUHYASAMAJA*, and eight cycles of *Mahayoga* means for attainment (**sadhana**), as well as the particular *tantra* texts of *Anuyoga* and *Atiyoga*. See **Dzogchen** and **Nine Yanas**.

Nyingthig (tib.) སྙིང་ཐིག་ snying thig *cittatilaka*

The 'Innermost Spirituality' or 'Heart Essence' *(snying-thig)* is the most important and essential class of teachings within the esoteric instructional class *(upadeshavarga)* of **Atiyoga**. Two distinct **lineages** of these teachings were introduced from India by **Padmasambhava** and **Vimalamitra**, and then transmitted with great secrecy in Tibet until the time of *Longchen Rabjampa* (fourteenth century) who integrated them in his *FOUR-PART INNERMOST SPIRITUALITY (SNYING-THIG YA-BZHI)*. Diverse teachings on **Nyingthig** are practised within the **Terma** *(gter-ma)* traditions of the **Nyingma** school, perhaps the most influential being the *INNERMOST SPIRITUALITY OF **LONGCHENPA** (KLONG-CHEN SNYING-THIG)*, which was revealed during the eighteenth century by *Rigzin Jigme Lingpa* on the basis of his inspirational visions of *Longchen Rabjampa*, and which has since become the most popular recension of **Nyingthig** teachings throughout Tibet. See *VIMA NYINGTHIG*.

Nyung Ne (tib.) བསྙུང་གནས་ bsnyung gnas *upavāsa*

A fasting ritual which is very popular among the Tibetan laity. It is normally performed with the **meditational deity Chenrezig** as its basis, the practice being commonly undertaken during the first two weeks of *Vaishakha*, the fourth month of the lunar calendar, during which are commemorated the anniversary of the birth, **buddha**hood and **parinirvana** of the **Buddha**. The ritual is usually led by a monk or a nun.

Obscurations སྒྲིབ་པ་ sgrib pa *āvaraṇa*

There are two main categories of **obscurations** *(sgrib-pa)*, namely, the **dissonant emotions** which are the **obscurations** to **liberation** *(nyon-sgrib)*, and the **ignorance** which is the **obscuration** to **knowledge** *(shes-sgrib)*. As the terms themselves indicate, the first category of **obscurations** obstruct the individual from gaining total freedom from the **karmically** conditioned **cycle of existence**, and the latter, from attaining a direct and non-deceptive **knowledge** of all aspects of **reality**. The **obscurations** to **liberation** include not only the conscious states of our **deluded mind**, such as **desire**, **hatred**, jealousy, harmful intent, etc., but also the psychological tendencies which are imprinted by these states, which serve

Yeshe Tsogyal

Padmasambhava

as seeds for their continuity and recurrence. The second category of **obscurations** refers to the 'propensities for deceptive **dualistic** appearance' (*gnyis-snang khrul-pa'i bag-chag*s), the subtle dispositions and latent tendencies which are deeply ingrained within an individual's psyche and which are the origins of our **dualistic** perceptions of the phenomenal world and of our own **consciousness**. A total overcoming of both **obscurations** marks the attainment of **Buddha**hood.

Obstructions བགེགས་/ བར་ཆད་ bgegs/bar chad *vighna/anantara*

Obstructions are those interfering forces, both external and internal, which hinder one in the accomplishment of a task. The task may be a highly spiritual endeavour such as embarking on a path to **enlightenment,** or a mundane work such as building a house.

Oddiyana ཨོ་རྒྱན་ O rgyan *Oḍḍiyāna*

Oddiyana, or **Orgyen** in Tibetan, is the name of an ancient kingdom, probably in the remote north-west of the Indian subcontinent, where a large corpus of **tantric** literature is said to have been propagated in the human world for the first time. The land of **Oddiyana** is associated with the great **tantric** master **Padmasambhava** in particular. It is described in **tantric** literature as a land of many **siddhas, meditators** with high **tantric realisation**. On the basis of traditional pilgrimage accounts, such as that written by *Orgyenpa Rinchenpel,* modern writers identify *Oddiyana* as having been in the region of the *Swat* valley in Pakistan. The Tibetan form of *Oddiyana,* **Orgyen,** is also by extension a name for **Padmasambhava** himself.

Odiyan (skrt.) ཨོ་རྒྱན་ O rgyan *Oḍḍiyāna*

See **Oddiyana.**

Offering སྦྱིན་པ་ sbyin pa *dāna*

See **Puja.**

Om (skrt.) ཨོཾ་ Om *OṂ*

A **Sanskrit** letter which symbolizes the **vajra** body of all the **Buddhas** and which is also the seed syllable of the **Buddha Vairocana,** representing the perfected state of our **aggregate** of form. **OM** is a combination of three sounds, *A, U,* and *M,* which respectively represent **buddha**-**body, speech** and **mind**. Their combination into a single composite **Om** signifies that **buddha**-**body, speech** and **mind** are essentially indivisible. The syllable is used as the prefix of many **mantras,** e.g., **Om** *Mani Padme Hum.*

Omniscience རྣམ་མཁྱེན་/ ཐམས་ཅད་མཁྱེན་པ་ rnam mkhyen/thams cad mkhyen pa *sarvajñā*

In a Buddhist context the word is reserved only for the all-knowing **pristine cognition** *(sarvajnana)* of the **buddhas**. Although the original **Sanskrit** and Tibetan terms, like their English equivalent, do carry with them the literal connotation of all-knowingness, the principal meaning of the Tibetan word should be understood in terms of a direct and simultaneous perception of the dual aspects of **reality**, i.e., of the phenomenal aspects (valid only within the relative framework of our ordinary perceptions) and their **ultimate** nature, **emptiness**. In other words the term refers primarily to a non-conceptual simultaneous perception of the **two truths** within a single mental act.

One Day Precepts བསྙེན་གནས་ཀྱི་སྡོམ་པ་ bsnyen gnas kyi sdom pa *upavāsasaṃvara*

One of the eight divisions of the ***Pratimoksha* vows**. This is a lay person's vow of abstinence from eight actions, taken only for twenty-four hours. The **precepts** are the abstinence from killing, sexual misconduct, stealing, lying, drinking alcohol, frivolous activities, sitting and lying on high seats and beds, and eating after lunch. The difference between '***Mahayana* Ordination**' and '**One day precepts**' is that the former requires the motivation of ***bodhicitta*** whereas the latter does not. Another distinguishing feature between these two is that although '***Mahayana* Ordination**' is open to all practitioners, '**One day precepts**' in the context of the ***Pratimoksha* vows** cannot be taken by fully ordained monks or nuns since that would constitute a degrading of their commitments from a lifelong vow to a twenty-four hour vow. In terms of the actual **precepts** of abstinence from these eight actions, however, there is no difference between the two. See **Mahayana Ordination.**

Oracle སྐུ་བསྟེན་ sku bsten

A person who acts as a medium for a **protector deity** such as ***Nechung***. An authentic **oracle** must be initiated through the ceremony of 'channel opening' (*rtsa-sgo 'byed-pa*) into the role of such a medium by a high ***lama*** who has a special relationship with the **protector deity**. This is to ensure that not only a smooth possession of the **protector deity** takes place within the medium's body but also that the medium is not misused by other unwanted forces during the trance. Although not essentially a Buddhist practice, the tradition of **oracles** has remained an important part of **Tibetan Buddhism**, and, like **divination**, it is used as an element of **skilful means** in promoting the well-being of **sentient beings**.

Orgyen (tib.) ཨོ་རྒྱན་ O rgyan *Oḍḍiyāna*

See **Oddiyana**.

ORNAMENT OF CLEAR REALISATION མངོན་རྟོགས་རྒྱན་ mngon rtogs rgyan *Abhisamayālaṃkāra*

The English title of the ***ABHISAMAYALAMKARA***. See ***ABHISAMAYALAMKARA*** and **Maitreya**.

Padma (skrt.) པད་མ་ pad ma *padma*

A lotus, particularly the variety which grows in water. In poetry and the visual arts it is often used as a symbol of purity. The lotus grows from an unclean mire, yet it is clean and unpolluted by the mire surrounding it. One finds the lotus depicted as the cushion or seat of many **meditational deities** in Buddhist *tantric* iconography. Among the five enlightened families, the ***Padma*** or Lotus family (*pad-*

ma'i rigs) is that of the **Buddha Amitabha**, indicating the analytical qualities of discernment/perception.

Padmakara (skrt.) པདྨ་འབྱུང་གནས་ padma 'byung gnas
Padmākara

The principal form of **Guru Rinpoche**, from whom the so-called eight manifestations of the **Guru** (*gu-ru mtshan-brgyad*) derive. **Padmakara** literally means 'Lotus Born'. See **Guru Rinpoche**.

Padmasambhava (skrt.) པད་མ་སམ་བྷ་ཝ་ pad ma sam bha va
Padmasambhava

One of the eight or twelve manifestations of **Padmakara** or **Guru Rinpoche**. See **Guru Rinpoche**.

Palyul (tib.) དཔལ་ཡུལ་ dpal yul

Palyul *Namgyal Changchub Ling* is the name of a large **Nyingma** monastery, located on the *Nguchu* tributary of the *Yangtze*, south of *Derge* in the province of **Kham**. It was founded in the seventeenth century by *Rigzin Kunzang Sherab*.

PANCAKRAMA (skrt.) རིམ་པ་ལྔ་ rim pa lnga *Pañcakrama*

An important **tantric** text on the **completion**/perfection **stage** of the **GUHYASAMAJA TANTRA** written by **Nagarjuna**. As the title **PANCAKRAMA** (*FIVE STAGES*) indicates, the text analyses the **completion stage** in five stages, namely: 1) Isolation of Body (*lus-dben);* 2) isolation of **Mind** (*sems-dben); 3*) **illusory body** (*sgyu-lus);* 4) **clear light/inner radiance** ('od-gsal); 5) coalescence/union (*zung-'jug).*

Panchen Lama (tib.) པཎ་ཆེན་བླ་མ་ paṇ chen bla ma

A title, meaning '**Guru** who is a great scholar', which was given to *Panchen Choki Gyaltsen*, the Fourth **Panchen Lama**, by his student the Fifth **Dalai Lama** during the seventeenth century, and which was also given retrospectively to his previous emanations. The **Panchen Lama** is revered as an emanation of the **Buddha Amitabha**, and after the **Dalai Lama**, is regarded as the second most influential potentate within the spiritual and political hierarchy of Tibet. The **Panchen Lama** is the head of **Tashilhunpo** monastery and as with the successive **reincarnations** of the **Dalai Lama**, is also brought up in a rigorous monastic academic environment and assigned important spiritual duties. Although, unlike the **Dalai Lama**, the **Panchen Lama** is never given prime position as temporal head of the government, the influence of the successive **Panchen Lamas** in the political area has still been considerable. The late Tenth **Panchen Lama** who passed away in 1989 directed his power and influence towards the restoration of Buddhism in Tibet before his untimely death. Past **Panchen Lamas** have also been referred to as the '*Tashi Lama*' by some non-Tibetan modern writers.

Pandita (skrt.) པཎྜི་ཏ་ paṇ ḍi ta *paṇḍita*

A scholar, a very learned person. See **Mahapandita**.

Paramitas (skrt.) ཕར་ཕྱིན་ phar phyin *pāramitā*

In the *sutra* system of the path to *buddha*hood the entire *bodhisattva's* way of life or conduct is founded upon the practice of the *paramita(s)* or perfections, which number either six or ten. The **six perfections** are those of: 1) generosity; 2) ethical discipline; 3) patience; 4) perseverance or joyous effort, 5) **meditative concentration**; and 6) **discriminative awareness** or **wisdom** (*prajna*). These six are known as perfections when, for example, the practice of generosity is: 1) motivated by the altruistic aspiration to attain full **enlightenment** for the sake of all beings; 2) undertaken within a sixfold combination of all the perfections; and 3) performed with an awareness of the **emptiness** of the agent, the act, and the object in question. The enumeration of ten perfections includes, in addition to the above six, the perfections of **skilful means**, power, aspiration, and **pristine cognition**. In the aspirational sense the word *paramita* or 'perfection' is used to denote a means to perfection. When describing the corresponding perfected result at the attainment of *buddha*hood, the term means 'transcendent perfection', in accord with its literal meaning, 'gone beyond'.

Parinirvana (skrt.) ཡོངས་སུ་མྱ་ངན་ལས་འདས་ yongs su mya ngan las 'das *parinirvāṇa*

'Final *nirvana*' or *parinirvana*, like the non-residual or non-abiding *nirvana* described above, is the state of total cessation of all **sufferings, dissonant emotions** and also the psychological tendencies and imprints which cause our **dualistic** perceptions and lead **sentient beings** to a state of confusion within a conditioned existence. Specifically it refers to the passing away of *buddhas* and others who have attained that state, e.g., to the last among the twelve principal deeds of the *Buddha Shakyamuni* - his death at *Kushinagara*. There is also a *sutra* in the *Kangyur,* the **Tibetan Buddhist** canon, by the above name.

Path and its Fruit ལམ་འབྲས་ lam 'bras *mārgaphala*

In its technical usage this phrase refers to a specific set of practices in the *Sakya* tradition known as *Lamdre,* the **path and its fruit**. See **Lamdre**.

Peaceful and Wrathful Deities ཞི་ཁྲོའི་ལྷ་ཚོགས་ zhi khro'i lha tshogs *śāntakrodhadevatā*

In general, this term refers to the **peaceful and wrathful meditational deities** who form the *mandala* of the indestructible expanse *(vajradhatumandala)*, i.e. the purity in the expanse of the **aggregates**, sensory bases, elemental properties, etc. See *mandala*. The **peaceful deities**, who from the point of view of the practitioner of *Vajrayana* are associated with the purification of attachment, symbolise the quiescent aspects of *buddha*-nature and the **wrathful** *herukas*, who are associated with the purification of hatred/aversion, symbolise the dynamic aspect of the **peaceful deities** in their role of transforming deeply-seated **dissonant emotions** into **buddha**-nature. There are diverse *tantra* and *sadhana* cycles which present the meditative sequences associated with the diverse **peaceful and wrathful deities**. Perhaps the most fundamental, in which the forty-two **peaceful** and fifty-eight **wrathful deities** are fully integrated, is the *GUHYAGARBHA TANTRA* from which the ZHI-KHRO (pronounced 'ZHITRO') literature of the

Nyingma school, including the *TIBETAN BOOK OF THE DEAD,* is derived. See *GUHYAGARBHA* and **Wrath.**

Pema (tib.) པད་མ་ pad ma *padma*

The Tibetan way of pronouncing **Padma.** See **Padma.**

Penetrative Insight ལྷག་མཐོང་ lhag mthong *vipaśyanā*
See **Lhagthong.**

Phabongkha (tib.) ཕ་བོང་ཁ་ pha bong kha

A **lineage** of **reincarnate *lamas*** of the **Gelug** tradition named after a place of **retreat** north-east of **Lhasa** and close to **Sera** Monastery, which has ancient associations with the king **Song-tsen Gampo** and the first seven monks of Tibet. Early **Phabongkha** hierarchs include *Khonton Paljor Lhundrup,* an important holder of the **Nyingma lineage tradition.** During the nineteenth century, the celebrated *lama Phabongkha Dechen Nyingpo* was one of the most prolific writers and respected teachers. One of his special gifts was his ability to present even the most complex topics in everyday simple language. Principal among his disciples were the two late tutors of the Fourteenth **Dalai Lama,** **Kyabje Ling Rinpoche** and **Kyabje Trijang Rinpoche.** *Je Phabongkha,* as he is often referred to, is particularly known for his lucid guide to **Lamrim** practice entitled *LIBERATION IN THE PALM OF YOUR HAND (LAM-RIM RNAM-GROL LAG-'CHANG).*

Phowa (tib.) འཕོ་བ་ 'pho ba *saṃkrānti*

A unique *tantric* practice undertaken to transfer the **consciousness** of a dying person to a realm of existence with a favourable migration, preferably to the unconditioned state of the **realisation** of *dharmakaya,* or to the **pure realm** of a **meditational deity** or *dakini.* The practice of *phowa* is commonly associated with the **six *yogas* of *Naropa*,** but may be undertaken on the basis of many diverse texts, **lineages,** and **deities,** the most popular being *Amitabha.* The **meditator** must train thoroughly in advance before actually performing *phowa* at the time of death, whether on one's own behalf or on behalf of another. A sign of a successful transference of the dying person's **consciousness** is a minute hole which will appear at the crown aperture of the dead person's body. The manuals on transference *yoga* emphasise the critical significance of determining the appropriate timing of its application. Numerous signs indicating a possible death within a certain period of time are said to appear at various stages prior to death and attempts must be made to reverse these signs as far as possible. However, when the signs recur constantly and definite indications of the moment of death arise, only then must the transference *yoga* be resorted to. *Phowa* literally means 'transference' or 'transformation'. It is in the latter sense that the term 'great transformation' *('pho-ba chen-po)* refers to the actual attainment of the **Rupakaya,** as a rainbow-like body, during the practices of *Atiyoga.*

Phurba ཕུར་པ་ phur pa *kīla*

A ritual dagger which symbolises the **meditational deity** *Vajrakila*, an embodiment of *buddha*-activities. The ritual implement is generally made of iron or acacia wood, with the motif of a **deity's** head surmounting an eight-faceted shaft, a sea-monster's head *(makara)* at the base of the shaft and below this a triangular blade, the latter symbolising the transformation of ignorance (as to the true nature of reality), attachment and hatred/aversion. The meditative cycles associated with the *VAJRAKILA TANTRAS* are of particular importance within the *Nyingma* and *Sakya* schools. The word *phurba*, in its everyday usage, refers to a tent peg or tethering stake.

Physical Pliancy ལུས་ཤིན་སྦྱངས་ lus shin sbyangs *praśrabdhi*

Suppleness of the body attained as a result of having focused one's mental **concentration** on a chosen object of **meditation** during the practice of **calm abiding**. When this practice is successfully applied, not only the **mind** but also the physical body of the **meditator** is said to become free from lethargy and heaviness (which normally cause our bodily discomforts and tensions) and thereby the body becomes serviceable to any prolonged period of sitting in **meditation**. See **Mental Pliancy** and **Concentration**.

Pious Attendant ཉན་ཐོས་ nyan thos *śrāvaka*

See **Shravaka**.

Potala (skrt.) པོ་ཏ་ལ་ po ta la *Potala*

The winter palace of the *Dalai Lama*, the spiritual and temporal leader of Tibet. Although the original construction of a palace at the site of the *Potala* was undertaken by the great Tibetan monarch *Songtsen Gampo* in the seventh century, the *Potala* as it stands now was built by the Fifth *Dalai Lama*, Ngawang Lobsang Gyatso and his **regent** Desi Sangye Gyatso during the latter half of the seventeenth century. Undisputedly the most famous architectural structure in Tibet, the *Potala* is a vast complex, with an imposing presence, built on a hill known as *Marpori*, which overlooks the town of *Lhasa*. Before 1959, it not only served as the winter palace of the *Dalai Lama* but also housed, in addition to various officials, the monks of *Namgyal* Monastery.

Prajna (skrt.) ཤེས་རབ་ shes rab *prajñā*

This term translates most lucidly into English as discriminative awareness, although many translators have often used the word '**wisdom**' instead, probably in consideration of the remarkable achievements of Edward Conze who translated over the years a voluminous series of texts devoted to *Prajnaparamita*. *Prajna* is generally defined as 'the discriminative awareness of the essence, distinctions, particular and general characteristics, and advantages and disadvantages of any object within one's own perceptual range, at the conclusion of which doubts are removed'. In other words, this is the faculty of intelligence or discriminating awareness inherent within the mental continuum of all living beings, which enables them to examine the characteristics of things and events, thus making it possible to make judgements and deliberations. In *abhidharma*, *prajna* is one of the five **mental factors** of ascertainment which arise during all mental events of a veridical nature. In *Mahayana*, the perfection of this faculty of discriminative awareness (*prajnaparamita*) leads a *bodhisattva* to a total overcoming of all types of scepticism and **ignorance** and to the **realisation** of the **emptiness** of all things. In conjunction with **skilful means** or method (*upaya*), the term *prajnopaya* refers to the integration of the two principal aspects of the path to **enlightenment**. In this context, the sixth perfection, *prajna*, or true insight into **emptiness**, which is the ultimate nature of phenomena, is united in perfect union with the **skilful means** and great **compassion** present in the previous five perfections, constituting the essence of the *Mahayana* path to full **enlightenment**. In *tantric* traditions, the union of *prajnopaya* is often depicted iconographically in the union of the male and female **deities**, and in the symbolic hand implements such as the *vajra* and the bell. In terms of the fully enlightened perception of a *buddha*, the aspect of *buddha*-**mind** known as the **pristine cognition** of discernment (*pratyavekshana-jnana*) indicates the full maturation of *prajna*.

Prajnaparamita (skrt.) ཤེས་རབ་ཀྱི་ཕར་ཕྱིན་ shes rab kyi phar phyin *Prajñāpāramitā*

One of the **six** *Paramitas* or **perfections**. The term *Prajnaparamita* has three different applications: 1) *Prajnaparamita* as the resultant perfected **discriminative awareness** of a *buddha ('bras-bu sher-phyin)*; 2) as the *bodhisattva* paths leading to such a perfection of **discriminative awareness** (*lam sher-phyin*); and 3) as the literature which outlines the essential aspects of such paths and their goals (*gzhung sher-phyin*). The resultant *Prajnaparamita* refers to a *buddha's* **discriminative awareness** (*prajna*) which is totally non-dual, free of all **obscurations**, and perceives spontaneously in a single mental act the dual aspects of all phenomena. (See **Two Truths**). *Prajnaparamita* as a path refers to the *bodhisattva's* path which blends at the most profound level the **discriminative awareness of emptiness** and the **skilful means** of great **compassion**. *Prajnaparamita* as a series of texts refers to the category of *Mahayana* **sutras** known collectively as *Prajnaparamita* **sutras**. See also **Paramitas**. *Prajnaparamita* is depicted iconographically in the form of a female **meditational deity** and the *Sanskrit Prajnaparamita sutra* texts themselves are invariably entitled BHAGAVATIPRAJNAPARAMITA, THE TRANSCENDENTAL LADY WHO IS THE PERFECTION OF DISCRIMINATIVE AWARENESS.

Pramana (skrt.) ཚད་མ་ tshad ma *pramāṇa*

A complex philosophical term used commonly by both Buddhist and non-Buddhist Indian philosophical schools of thought. Etymologically, *Pra* means 'first', 'fresh', 'full', 'primary', and *Mana*, 'to know', 'to apprehend', and 'to cognise'. Together the word literally means 'prime cognition' or 'first hand **knowledge**'. However, in its actual philosophical usage the word has acquired both logical and epistemological dimensions, and is often translated into English as 'valid cognition'. *Pramana* in its epistemological sense refers to both our empirical **direct perceptions** of the world and also our conceptual, inferential, cognitive thought processes as well. In other words *Pramana* includes both our empirical

knowledge and inferential **knowledge**. Although some philosophical schools of thought may insist on a strict definition of valid cognition (*Pramana*) which demands that absolute **truth** and certainty be essential elements, the original *Sanskrit* term itself admits the possibility of inference, but it does presuppose the **truth** and validity of the cognition within a consistent frame of reference. *Pramana* in its logical sense refers to a valid proof capable of generating inference based on the validity of certain premises. Here valid cognition or reasoning is defined as a form of argument which is based on valid premises and established logical principles. In classical Indian and Tibetan logic there are two main types of **valid reasoning**: 1) **consequential** reasoning; and 2) **syllogistic** reasoning. The first category is a unique form of reasoning which is primarily aimed at showing internal inconsistencies within an opponent's position. The second category is a more established and conventional mode of reasoning commonly used in presenting philosophical perspectives or arguments. A valid 'syllogistic reasoning' (technically known in traditional logic as a 'correct sign') is characterised by the 'three logical marks' of a valid proof. These are: 1) the proof should be a property of the subject *(phyogs-kyi chos)*; 2) the proof must entail the predicate *(rjes-khyab)*; and 3) the negation of the predicate must entail the negation of the proof *(ldog-khyab)*. In Buddhist logic the validity of an argument is determined not merely on the basis of its structure but also on the basis of whether or not it leads to a correct inference. The most authoritative classical source for the study of Buddhist logic is *Dharmakirti's* **PRAMANAVARTTIKA**.

PRAMANAVARTTIKA (skrt.) ཚད་མ་རྣམ་འགྲེལ་ tshad ma rnam 'grel *Pramāṇavārttika*

One of the most important works on Buddhist logic and **epistemology** written by the great Indian logician *Dharmakirti*. It is an extensive **commentary** on *Dignaga's* PRAMANASAMUCCAYA; it is divided into four chapters dealing respectively with the topics of inference, validation, **direct perception**, and forms of argument such as **syllogism**, **consequential reasoning**, etc. Like many works of its time, it is written in metered verse. It is now used as the primary text by most major monastic universities of **Tibetan Buddhism** in their study of logic and **epistemology**.

Prana (skrt.) སྲོག་འཛིན་ (གྱི་རླུང་) srog 'dzin (gyi rlung) *prāṇa(vāyu)*

The 'life-bearing wind' *(srog-'dzin)* which is one of the ten kinds of wind or vital energy permeating the body. See **Winds.**

Prasangika (skrt.) ཐལ་འགྱུར་བ་ thal 'gyur ba *prasaṅgika*

One of the two sub-schools of *Madhyamaka* philosophy. The division of the *Madhyamaka* school into two sub-schools resulted from a classic philosophical dispute between *Bhavaviveka* and *Candrakirti*. The dispute focused on *Buddhapalita's* interpretation of *Nagarjuna's* thought, defended by *Candrakirti*. The essence of *Bhavaviveka's* criticism was his allegation that *Buddhapalita's* system lacked any systematic process of reasoning leading to a successful proof of a positive thesis. Although the difference in methodology appears to be the explicit issue under dispute, the differences between the *Madhyamaka* schools are considered to be more profound. The distinctive feature of the *Prasangika* school is its total denial of any ontology implying **inherent existence** of either external objects or subjective **consciousness**. *Prasangika* literally means 'consequentialist', a term deriving from the school's emphasis on consequentialist reasoning. See **Consequence, Svatantrika** and **Madhyamaka.**

Pratimoksha (skrt.) སོ་སོར་ཐར་པ་ so sor thar pa *prātimokṣa*

An individual's practice of ethical discipline which acts as a firm foundation for the aspirant's spiritual endeavour whilst on the path towards the attainment of **liberation** from **cyclic existence**. There are eight types of *Pratimoksha* **vows**: 1) one-day **lay precepts** *(bsnyan-gnas);* 2) lay man's **vows** *(dge-bsnyan pha);* 3) lay woman's **vows** *(dge-bsnyan ma);* 4) novice monk's **vows** *(dge-tshul pha);* 5) novice nun's **vows** *(dge-tshul ma);* 6) probationary nun's **vows** *(dge-slob ma);* 7) fully ordained monk's **vows** *(dge-slong pha);* and 8) fully ordained nun's **vows** *(dge-slong ma).* *Pratimoksha* literally means 'individual **liberation**', or the initial stage of release from the impulsive force of **non-virtuous** habits. *Prati* means 'individually' or 'first', and *moksha,* 'release', 'freedom', or '**liberation**'.

Pratityasamutpada (skrt.) རྟེན་ཅིང་འབྲེལ་བར་འབྱུང་བ་ rten cing 'brel bar byung ba *pratītyasamutpāda*

See **Dependent Origination**.

Pratyekabuddha (skrt.) རང་སངས་རྒྱས་/ རང་རྒྱལ་ rang sangs rgyas/rang rgyal *pratyekabuddha*

The term, sometimes translated in English as '**solitary realiser**' or 'self-centred *buddha*', indicates one who attains the state of **liberation** without relying on a teacher, following a natural predisposition. The *Pratyekabuddha* is superior to the *Shravaka* in two (or three) principal ways: 1) unlike the *shravaka* he accumulates merit over a hundred aeons and obtains a similitude of a *buddha's* **major and minor marks**; 2) just as his own **liberation** is attained without relying on verbal transmission, he communicates with others mainly non-verbally; and 3) according to some sources, he realises the **emptiness** of the external phenomena composed of atomic particles, in addition to the **emptiness** of the individual personality, as realised by the *shravaka*. However, according to these same sources, he fails to realise the **emptiness** of the inner mental phenomena composed of temporal moments, for which reason he is said to be realised in 'one and a half parts of **selflessness**'. The realisation of a *pratyekabuddha* depends not only on the **renunciation** or monastic discipline (which is undertaken by *Shravakas*) but also on their comprehension and reversal of the **twelve links** of **dependent origination**.

Precepts ཁྲིམས་/ སྡོམ་པ་ khrims/sdom pa *nigraha/saṃvara*

Sets of specific ethical codes which a practitioner voluntarily makes a deliberate pledge to adopt, as a means of establishing a firm foundation for spiritual endeavour. The **precepts** can be adopted for a short period, as in the case of **One Day Precepts**, or they can be a life-long commitment, as in the case of other *Pratimoksha* **vows**, such as the **precepts** of a fully ordained monk or a nun. *Bodhisattva* **precepts** and also *tantric* **vows** are taken on the basis that they are to be maintained, if possible, even

through the successive lives of a practitioner, until the ultimate aim of bringing about the welfare of others is fulfilled.

PRECIOUS GARLAND རིན་ཆེན་ཕྲེང་བ་ rin chen phreng ba *Ratnāvalī*

An important *Mahayana* work written by *Nagarjuna* as a letter of advice to a king. Although explicitly dealing with state matters and how best the king may serve his countrymen, whilst remaining faithful to the humanitarian principles of Buddhism, the work also addresses other subjects of profound significance to the *bodhisattva* path. These include: the practice of the **six perfections**, cultivation of **compassion** and *bodhicitta*, the progressive levels of the *bodhisattva* path, the unique **qualities of a *buddha***, and the process through which the **wisdom** (*prajna*) realising **emptiness** should be conjoined with the **skilful means** of great **compassion**. Some Tibetan scholars list this work as one of the six treatises that form *Nagarjuna's* 'corpus of reason' (*yuktikaya*).

Preliminaries སྔོན་འགྲོ་ sngon 'gro

See **Four Preliminaries** and **Ngondro**.

Preta (skrt.) ཡི་དྭགས་ yi dvags *preta*

See **Hungry Ghost**.

Pristine Cognition ཡེ་ཤེས་ ye shes *jñāna*

See **Jnana**.

Protector སྲུང་མ་/ཆོས་སྐྱོང་ srung ma/chos skyong *dharmapāla*

Literally translated as 'doctrinal **protectors**' or '**protectors** of the *dharma*', the *Dharmapala* are beings assigned with the important task of protecting the Buddhist teachings and its sincere practitioners. There are two main categories of **protectors**: 1) supramundane **protectors** who are the **wrathful** manifestations of **enlightened** beings; and 2) worldly **protectors** (many of whom were originally malevolent forces) who were subdued by advanced *tantric* mystics and then assigned to protect the teachings. Such **protectors** can have male or female forms.

Puja (skrt.) མཆོད་པ་ mchod pa *pūjā*

A sacramental **offering**, which is a means of venerating and producing delight in the *guru* or an appropriate object of veneration, such as a **meditational deity**. In general, there are **offerings** associated with body, speech and **mind**. Thus, an **offering** can be of material substance such as flowers, scented water and food, or a verbal **offering**, such as the recitation of songs of praise, or a mental offering, such as the **offering** of the positive potentials which one may have accumulated as a result of having engaged in wholesome deeds beneficial to others. More specifically, the *tantras* identify four kinds of **offering** which are to be made; they are: outer, inner, secret and definitive **offerings**. The outer **offerings** of enjoyment (*phyi nyer-spyod-kyi mchod-pa*) are the eight associated with the eight **offering** goddesses, namely: water for the mouth and water for the feet, flowers, incense, light, perfume, food, and sound, as well as song, dance, and **meditation**. Inner **offerings** of commitment (*nang gi mchod-pa*) refer to the pure physical essences such as semen, blood and flesh. Secret **offerings** are those of sexual union (*gsang-ba'i mchod-pa*) and definitive **offerings** are those of great sameness (*de-kho-na-nyid mchod-pa*); namely the union of bliss and emptiness. It is worth noting that the word *puja* has also acquired a corrupt English usage as a mistranslation of the **Sanskrit** *vidhi* (tib. *cho-ga*) meaning a ritual practice in general, whether **offerings** are made or not. See also **Tsog**.

Pure Realm དག་ཞིང་ dag zhing (*śuddha*)*kṣetra*

Realms of existence which spontaneously arise as an imprint of the altruistic aspirations of a *buddha*. Such realms are environments which are totally free from **suffering**, both physical and mental. Beings who take **rebirth** in a **pure realm** are those who have established strong *karmic* links with the particular *buddha* associated with the **pure realm**. **Pure realms** commonly mentioned in Buddhist *tantric* literature are the **pure realms** of *Amitabha*, *Avalokiteshvara*, *Maitreya* and *Vajrayogini*. It is said that **sentient beings** who have not yet attained the state of an *arhat*, i.e., a permanent release from the bondage of **cyclic existence**, when born in such **pure realms**, do become temporarily free from not only the manifest **sufferings** of the body and **mind** but also the pervasive **sufferings** of *karmic* conditioning as well.

Purification སྒྲིབ་སྦྱོང་ sgrib sbyong *pariśodhana*

The verb 'to purify' has two distinct meanings in a Buddhist context. Firstly, **purification** can refer simply to the **purification** of non-virtuous habits, **dissonant emotions**, etc. in which the objects of **purification** are, without qualification, totally eradicated from one's mental continuum. In the second meaning, which arises more in the context of *tantra*, the term **purification** has rather different implications. Here, the significance of the word is understood in terms of transmutation from an impure, polluted state into an unstained, purified state. *Tantric* literature explains such a process in terms of what is called the transmutation of death, **intermediate state**, and **rebirth** into the path as the three *kayas* (*sku-gsum lam-mkhyer*). Ordinary death, **intermediate state**, and **rebirth** as experienced choicelessly, as a result of karmic forces, are the bases of **purification**. The *trikaya* **meditations** of *tantra* are the purifying paths and a *buddha*'s three *kayas* are the purified results.

Qualities of the Buddha སངས་རྒྱས་ཀྱི་ཡོན་ཏན་ sangs rgyas kyi yon tan *buddhaguṇa*

See **Enlightened Attributes**.

Rangtong (tib.) རང་སྟོང་ rang stong

Literally meaning 'intrinsic **emptiness**', *Rangtong*, in contrast to the view held by advocates of extraneous **emptiness** (*gzhan-stong*), refers to the dialectical method through which *Madhyamaka* philosophy comprehends **emptiness** as the absence of **inherent existence** in all phenomena. See also **Emptiness** and **Shentong**.

Ratnasambhava རིན་ཆེན་འབྱུང་གནས་ rin chen 'byung gnas *Ratnasambhava*

The *Buddha* of one of five **enlightened-families** corresponding to the perfected states of an individual's five **aggregates**. *Ratnasambhava* is the perfected state of our faculty of feeling and is the manifestation of the *buddha's* **pristine cognition** of sameness. *Ratnasambhava* is usually depicted as yellow in colour. *Ratnasambhava* literally means 'the Source of the Precious'. See **Enlightened-Families.**

Realisation རྟོགས་པ་ rtogs pa *adhigama*

The most basic division of the *dharma* is that which distinguishes **realisation** (*adhigama*) from scriptural **transmission** (*agama*). The former refers to the spiritual experiences that a practitioner gains through insight into and transformation of the mental continuum whilst on the path to **enlightenment,** and to the resultant attainment of **liberation** or *buddhahood*. The latter, by contrast, refers to the texts and oral teachings which communicate that **realisation** to others. Therefore, it is important to note that the *Sanskrit* term *adhigama*, and its Tibetan equivalent *rtogs-pa*, imply both the dynamic unfolding or uncovering of **realisation** achieved by those who follow a specific path to **enlightenment,** and the passive **realisation** of the *buddhas* which is effected atemporally. The process of dynamic unfolding is also known as 'emergent/clear **realisation**' (Skrt. *abhisamaya*, Tib. *mngon-rtogs*).

Reality ཆོས་ཉིད་ chos nyid *dharmatā*

In the context of the glossary, the term **reality** or actual **reality** is mostly used as a synonym for the **emptiness** or lack of **inherent existence** in all phenomena. See **Dharmata** and **Emptiness.** The apparent or apparitional aspect of **reality** (*dharmin, chos-can*) embraces the entire expanse of existence both material and mental. See **Two Truths.**

Rebirth སྲིད་པ་/སྐྱེ་བ་ཕྱི་མ་ srid pa/skye ba phyi ma *bhava/punarbhava*

An individual's migration into a subsequent life after death. Like many ancient Indian philosophical schools of thought, Buddhism also asserts the continuity of being after the physical death of the person. The principal premises upon which the Buddhist doctrine of **rebirth** is based are: 1)the principles of causality; 2) the doctrine of *karma*; and 3) the acceptance of a beginingless continuum of **consciousness. Mind** and body, though inseparable at the subtlest energy level, are distinct and thus possess separate continua during the successive individual lives of a being. Although they mutually influence each other, they can never become one another, as a corn seed cannot produce a rice sprout. It is the *karmic* forces which remain as subtle potentials within the mental continuum of the person which, when activated, cause the bringing together of **mind** and body thus constituting a particular state of existence in the **cycle of existence.** When the potentials of that particular *karmic* force are exhausted, then the separation of the mental continuum from a particular bodily existence takes place, which is called death. It must be stressed that Buddhism does not accept any notion of unchanging eternal souls which transmigrate from one life to another. Detailed arguments supporting the doctrine of **rebirth** can be found in *Bhavaviveka's* TARKAJVALA and the second chapter of *Dharmakirti's* PRAMANAVARTTIKA. See **Cause and Effect** and **Karma.**

Refuge སྐྱབས་འགྲོ་ skyabs 'gro *śaraṇagamana*

This term in Buddhist usage indicates the act of entrusting one's spiritual growth and well-being to the **Three Precious Jewels**. The **Three Precious Jewels** are the objects of **refuge**, and the nature of the **refuge** sought from each of the three differs. In the *Buddha*, the fully **enlightened** teacher, perfect expression of the qualities of **enlightenment** is sought; in the *dharma*, the true path, **realisation** of the path is sought; and in the *sangha*, the spiritual community, perfect companionship on the path to *buddhahood* is sought. The successful taking of **refuge** in the **Three Precious Jewels** requires the following two conditions: 1) a genuine anxiety in the face of the potential for future **suffering** in **cyclic existence**; and 2) a genuine confidence in the capacity of the **Three Precious Jewels** to offer protection from these potential **sufferings**. Motivated by these two considerations the spiritual well-being of the practitioner is then entrusted to the **Three Precious Jewels**. The deeper meaning of taking **refuge** in the **Three Precious Jewels** emerges when the objects of **refuge** are the perfected states of one's own inner potentials. In this context the *buddha* is the resultant state of one's own *buddha*hood; the *dharma* refers to the resultant states of one's own experiences on the path, and the *sangha* refers to one's own advanced states as an *arhat*, *bodhisattva* and so forth. This interpretation of **refuge** accords with the fundamental Buddhist approach of placing greater emphasis on **self**-reliance. The Tibetan tradition considers the seeking of **refuge** in the **Three Precious Jewels** as the mark of becoming a practising Buddhist. In the context of *tantric* preliminary practices, **refuge** is also taken in the so-called 'three roots' (*rtsa-ba gsum*) - the *guru*, **meditational deity** and *dakini*, along with the doctrinal **protectors**. See **Meditational Deity**.

Regent རྒྱལ་ཚབ་ rgyal tshab *yuvarāja*

The representative of an incarnate hierarch who presides over a monastic community during the infancy or minority of the actual hierarch. **Regents** often have a political role and are responsible for the administration of monastic estates. The most prominent example of this occurs during the period between the death of a *Dalai Lama* and his formal re-adoption of office, when a senior **reincarnate** *lama* of the highest rank becomes the **regent**, or acting head of the government in Tibet. The **regent's** main responsibilities, in addition to his functions as head of state, are to ensure a successful recognition of the new *Dalai Lama* and to administer a smooth transition of power to the *Dalai Lama* at his majority.

Reincarnation ཡང་སྲིད་ yang srid

The Tibetan term *yang-srid* indicates a holy being, or the sacred incarnation of a great *lama* from the past. See **Nirmanakaya**.

Renunciation ངེས་འབྱུང་/སྤང་བ་ nges 'byung/spang ba *naiśkramya/prahāṇa*

The English term **renunciation** translates both the Tibetan terms

nges-'byung (Skrt. *naiskramya*) and *spang-ba* (Skrt. *prahana*). In the former sense, **renunciation** refers to ***Shakyamuni Buddha's* renunciation** of the household life and thus it is considered to be one of the **three principal aspects of the path**. **Renunciation** is defined as a mental attitude free from impulsive clinging to all forms of worldly qualities such as wealth, fame, position and the thought of a favourable **rebirth** in a future life. It is only on the basis of such an attitude that the practitioner can spontaneously generate within him or herself a genuine wish to be free from the **cycle of existence**. Hence the real meaning of **renunciation** lies not just in mere physical separation from objects of **desire**, but more importantly in a quality of mental **liberation** which is free from even the slightest degree of craving for mundane values. The Tibetan word *Nejung* literally means a 'definite emergence', indicating a definite emergence from the bonds of our normally narrow-minded **attachment** to worldly pleasures. See **Three Principal Aspects of the Path**. In the latter sense, the **renunciation** cultivated on the paths followed by adherents of the *sutra*-based vehicles has two aspects, corresponding to the two aspects of **realisation** described above. **Renunciation** can refer either to the active removal of the **obscurations** covering the enlightened **mind**, or equally to the *fait accompli* or resultant state consequent on their removal.

Reting (tib.) རྭ་སྒྲེང་ rva sgreng

Name of a ***Kadampa*** monastery in Central Tibet, located in the Upper *Kyichu* valley, which was founded by ***Atisha's*** student *Dromtonpa* in the eleventh century. The last ***Reting Rinpoche*** served as the **regent** of Tibet (1933-47) following the death of the Thirteenth ***Dalai Lama*** and headed the search for his **reincarnation**, leading to the successful recognition of the present Fourteenth ***Dalai Lama***.

Retreat མཚམས་/ བསྙེན་པ་ mtshams/bsnyen pa *sīmā/āsevita*

In technical usage, these terms refer to intensive silent periods of **meditation** undertaken in regular sessions for a stipulated period of time. A **retreat** can either be short term, and is often specifically dedicated to the practice of a particular **meditational deity**, or long term, which would normally mean a period of three years or more. The short term **retreats**, *las-rung (pronounced 'lerung')* as they are known in Tibetan, usually involve intensive practice of a **deity's *sadhana***, after completion of which the yogin is authorised to engage in certain advanced **meditations** related to the **deity** such as **self-empowerment** into the ***mandala***. The general Tibetan words for **retreat** are *bsnyen-pa* (pronounced 'nyen pa') and *mtshams* (pronounced 'tsam'). The former emphasises the 'service' *(asevita)* that the practitioner cultivates in **retreat** through realising a deeper relationship with the **meditational deity**, and the latter meaning 'interval' or 'boundary' *(sima)*, suggests that during periods of **retreat** the limits of social intercourse are well defined.

Rigpa (tib.) རིག་པ་ rig pa *vidyā*

As a verb, ***rig-pa*** means 'to know', and 'to be aware'. When used as a noun it has several distinct though not unrelated meanings: 1) as a general term encompassing all experiences of **consciousness** and mental events; 2) intelligence or mental aptitude; 3) as a science of **knowledge**; 4) as a pure awareness. The last of these meanings is found in ***Dzogchen*** terminology, where *rang-rig* refers to an intrinsic or natural awareness which is the fundamental innate **mind** in its natural non-

Naropa

Atisha

dual state of spontaneity and purity, beyond the alternating states of tranquillity and motion. As such, *rig-pa* gives the meditator access to *buddha*-**mind** itself.

Rime (tib.) རིས་མེད་ ris med

A non-sectarian or eclectic movement which crystalised during the nineteenth century in Eastern Tibet where the study and integration of all schools of **Tibetan Buddhism** were encouraged by the leading figures of that period, namely: *Jamyang Khyentse Wangpo*, *Jamgon Kongtrul Lodro Thaye*, *Chogyur Dechen Lingpa*, and *Ju Mipham Gyatso*. A principal feature of the *Rime* movement was the emergence of a new literature. This consisted primarily of compendiums of major works of all the major and minor schools of **Tibetan Buddhism** on convergent topics of thought and practice.

Rinpoche (tib.) རིན་པོ་ཆེ་ rin po che

This term literally means 'high in value or esteem', and in ordinary language indicates a precious gemstone. By extension, in **Tibetan Buddhism,** the term came to refer to an incarnate master who is 'high in value' or 'most precious'. Accordingly, the title '*Rinpoche*' is widely used by Tibetans to refer to any incarnate *lama*.

Ritroma (tib.) རི་ཁྲོད་མ་ ri khrod ma *Śabarī*

A female **meditational deity** associated with practices related to the healing of certain illnesses. She is usually depicted with a semi-**wrathful** expression and wearing a skirt of leaves, indicating that she is a forest dweller. *Ritroma* literally means 'the lady of the mountain ranges'.

Rupakaya གཟུགས་སྐུ་ gzugs sku *rūpakāya*

See **Form Body**.

SACRED WORD OF MANJUSHRI འཇམ་དཔལ་ཞལ་ལུང་ 'jam dpal zhal lung

Written by the Fifth *Dalai Lama* the *SACRED WORDS OF MANJUSHRI* is an important commentarial work on *Lamrim* meditative practice.

Sadhana (skrt.) སྒྲུབ་ཐབས་ sgrub thabs *sādhana*

Sadhana literally translates as 'means for attainment'. *Tantric* literature is classified into *tantra*-texts and *sadhana*-texts. The former are general expositions concerning the ground, path and result associated with a particular *mandala* of **deities**, while the latter are specific blueprints derived from and inspired by the former as the detailed means for attainment or meditative **realisation** of a specific *mandala* of **deities**. Such practices have four phases, which are often known as the 'four branches of ritual service and attainment'. These are: ritual service (*seva*), further ritual service (*upaseva*), means for attainment (*sadhana*) and great

means for attainment (*mahasadhana*), which respectively entail: 1) ***mantra*** recitation and one-pointed visualisation of the **deity**; 2) prayers that the **blessing** of the **deity** will descend to transform mundane body, speech and **mind** into ***buddha*-body, speech** and **mind**; 3) the absorption of accomplishments from the actual **deity** into the visualised **deity** and thence into oneself; and 4) the **realisation** of primordial purity experienced when body, speech and **mind** are identical to those of the **deity**. All of these steps are incorporated into the *sadhana* practices themselves. In short, *sadhana* mainly embodies the essential practices relating to the **generation stage**. See **Generation Stage**.

Sakya (tib.) ས་སྐྱ་ sa skya

One of the four principal schools of **Tibetan Buddhism**, named after a monastery of the same name which was founded by *Khon Konchok Gyalpo* in the eleventh century in Western Tibet, at a site which has a slightly whitish rock surface. *Sakya* literally means 'pale earth'. The widespread influence of the early *Sakya* masters soon evolved into a whole new school of **Tibetan Buddhism**, the school reaching its full maturity during the time of the *Sachen Gongma Nga*, the five great founders of *Sakya*, and in particular through the influence of perhaps the greatest of these, *Sakya Pandita Kunga Gyaltsen*. The essence of the *Sakya* school's thought and practice is enshrined in the sets of instructions called 'the **path and its fruit**' (*lam-'bras*).

Samadhi (skrt.) ཏིང་ངེ་འཛིན་ ting nge 'dzin *samādhi*

The *Sanskrit* term *samadhi* literally means 'union' or 'combination', and its Tibetan equivalent *ting-nge-'dzin* suggests an 'adhering to that which is profound and definitive'. *Samadhi* is a profound meditative state, sometimes rendered in English as contemplation or contemplative stabilisation, in which the **mind** is totally focused into a rapt, single-pointed absorption on the object of **meditation**. The word is used in a variety of contexts: in ***abhidharma*** literature, *samadhi* is listed along with discriminative awareness (***prajna***) among the five **mental factors** of ascertainment. The *Mahayana sutras* enumerate a large number of *samadhis*, contemplative stabilisations, in which *Shakyamuni Buddha* is said to abide, e.g., profound illumination (*zab-mo snang-ba*). In the *tantras*, *samadhi* refers to the profound **meditations** of the **generation/** creation and **completion**/perfection **stages** of **meditation**. The term is to be contrasted with the following different but related terms: ***dhyana***, which comprises four kinds of meditative **concentration** cultivated either to achieve higher **rebirth** in cyclical existence or the fifth of the **six perfections** on the ***bodhisattva*** path; *bhavana*, which is the path of **meditation**, among the five paths to **enlightenment** followed by followers of the *sutra* vehicles; and the technique of ***shamatha*** (**calm abiding**/tranquillity), which is cultivated through **nine stages** of mental development. See **Calm Abiding, Nine Stages of Calm Abiding and Meditation**.

Samantabhadra (skrt.) ཀུན་ཏུ་བཟང་པོ་ kun tu bzang po *Samantabhadra*

Literally meaning 'all-good', 'all-positive', and 'ever perfect', *Samantabhadra* has many meanings depending upon the context. It may be: 1) the name of a particular ***bodhisattva*** who is one of the eight principal ***bodhisattva*** disciples of the *Buddha Shakyamuni*; 2) a synonym for ***buddha*-nature** in general; and 3) a synonym for ***dharmakaya***, in the form of the primordial *Buddha Samantabhadra*, from whom, according to the *Nyingma tantras*, the diverse

buddha*-bodies** emanate and from whom the higher ***tantric* lineages** arise. As such, ***Samantabhadra is also the result attained through the ***Dzogchen*** practice of Cutting through Resistance (*khregs-chod*). This resultant ***Samantabhadra*** has three aspects, namely, the male aspect, ***Samantabhadra***, who represents the luminosity or apparitional aspect of the ***dharmakaya***; the female aspect, *Samantabhadri*, who represents its **emptiness** or apparitionless nature; and the non-dual aspect *kun-bzang yab-yum*, who represents the coalescence of pure appearances and **emptiness**. See **Dharmakaya**.

Samaya (skrt.) དམ་ཚིག་ dam tshig *samaya*

A sacred commitment or pledge taken by a practitioner which is a prerequisite for the **meditational** practice of a particular ***tantric* deity**. The Tibetan equivalent '*dam-tshig*' literally means 'binding word', indicating that the person becomes bound by a solemn oath. Each class of ***tantra*** has its own category of ***samaya*** commitments, just as there are diverse **vows** taken by adherents of the ***sutra*** based or causal vehicles. ***Samaya*** may therefore entail the observation of general **precepts**, which are common to a whole class of ***tantra***, or individual **precepts**, such as never deriding women, which must be observed in relation to specific **meditational deities** such as ***Vajrayogini***. When such commitments are broken they must be restored through appropriate ***tantric*** ritual practices, for their degeneration may cause serious hindrances to progress on the path.

Sambhogakaya (skrt.) ལོངས་སྐུ་ longs sku *sambhogakāya*

See **Enjoyment Body** and **Rupakaya**.

Samsara (skrt.) འཁོར་བ་ 'khor ba *saṃsāra*

See **Cyclic Existence**.

Samye (tib.) བསམ་ཡས་ bsam yas

Recognised as the first Buddhist monastery to have been constructed in Tibet. It was built by the Tibetan king ***Trisong Detsen***, with the assistance of ***Shantarakshita*** and ***Padmasambhava*** during the latter half of the eighth century, and is said to be modelled on the famous *Otantapuri* temple in *Bihar*. ***Samye*** is renowned as the centre where the early translations of ***sutra*** and ***tantra*** texts were made from ***Sanskrit*** originals under the supervision of ***Padmasambhava***, ***Vimalamitra*** and other great ***panditas***. Nowadays, the monastery combines three traditions together - ***Nyingma***, ***Sakya***, and ***Gelug***, reflecting three distinct phases of political influence in this region over the centuries.

Sangha (skrt.) དགེ་འདུན་ dge 'dun *saṅgha*

In its classical Buddhist usage, the term refers mainly to the spiritual communities of ordained practitioners, both monks and nuns. The actual ***sangha***, when viewed as an object of **refuge** in the

context of the **Three Precious Jewels**, is a sublime, highly realised assembly of those who have gained a direct insight into the true nature of **reality, emptiness,** i.e., those who have attained the path of insight. The monastic community conventionally represents such spiritually accomplished beings. See **Arya** and **Refuge**.

Sanskrit (skrt.) ལེགས་སྦྱར་ legs sbyar *saṃskṛta*

The refined ancient Indian language used by many classical Indian scholars for literary composition, in contrast to the Prakrits, the common languages of that period. *Sanskrit* is noted for its complex grammar and rich vocabulary, ideal for philosophical precision and poetic expression.

Saraha (skrt.) ས་ར་ཧ་ sa ra ha *Saraha*

One of the eighty-four *Mahasiddhas* of ancient India. *Saraha* is especially remembered for his collection of mystical songs known as *Doha*. See **Mahasiddha** and also **Doha**.

Sarma (tib.) གསར་མ་ gsar ma

The *tantras* translated from Indian sources from the period of the great *Lotsawa Rinchen Sangpo* (the late tenth century) onwards are called the *tantras* of the new translation schools *(gsang-sngags gsar-ma)*. Principal among this category of literature are such prominent *tantras* as: *GUHYASAMAJA, CAKRASAMVARA, KALACAKRA, VAJRABHAIRAVA, VAJRAYOGINI* and *HEVAJRA*. Consequently, the practices of these *tantras* constitute the core of the *tantric* practices for the *Kagyu*, *Sakya* and *Gelug*, the three Tibetan traditions which are known as the new translation schools. One should note, however, that the *Nyingma* or ancient translation school also possesses recensions of the *GUHYASAMAJA* and certain other *tantras* which were retranslated in the later period. For a historical perspective, see **Nyingma**.

Sarnath (hindi) དྲང་སྲོང་ལྷུང་བ་ drang srong lhung ba *Ṛṣipatana*

A place of great historical importance in northern India, now in the state of *Uttar Pradesh*. It was the site of the first public discourse given by the *Buddha Shakyamuni* following his attainment of *buddhahood* attained whilst meditating under the shade of the Bodhi Tree in *Bodhgaya*. The nearest town to *Sarnath* is *Varanasi*, also called *Benares*. *Varanasi* was for a long time the intellectual and cultural heart of India, serving as the seat of numerous philosophical movements. See **Benares**.

Sarvastivada (skrt.) ཐམས་ཅད་ཡོད་པར་སྨྲ་བ་ thams cad yod par smra ba *Sarvāstivāda*

One of the primary *Vinaya* orders and an important division of the *Vaibashika* school in ancient India. The school developed from the teachings of *Buddha Shakyamuni's* son *Rahula* and its main tenet is the acceptance of the substantial existence of all five categories of phenomena, technically known as the five bases: 1) matter; 2) **mind**; 3) **mental factors**; 4) unassociated or disjunct compositional factors; and 5) non-products or uncompounded entities. The school is also known as the *Mulasarvastivada*. See **Vaibashika**.

Satipatthana (pali) དྲན་པ་ཉེར་བཞག་ dran pa nyer bzhag *smṛtyupasthāna*

See **Four Mindfulnesses**.

Sautrantika (skrt.) མདོ་སྡེ་པ་ mdo sde pa *Sautrāntika*

One of the four main schools of Buddhist philosophical thought in classical India, the other three being *Vaibhashika*, *Cittamatra* and *Madhyamaka*. The main tenets of this school are the acceptance of an objective external **reality** (*vayartha*) and an intrinsic **self**-cognising faculty of **consciousness** (*svasamvedana*). This **self**-cognising faculty is regarded as validating all our cognitive mental events and also as validating itself - this implying an **inherent existence** of **consciousness**. **Consciousness** is also said to perceive sensa directly, as an intermediary, rather than actual objects. Unlike the *Vaibhashika* school, the *Sautrantika* reject the notion of imperceptible forms which sustain a behavioural pattern throughout the past, present and future (*prapti*), instead holding a nominalistic position regarding the ontology of universals. The school is especially noted for its extremely comprehensive and systematic philosophies of logic and **epistemology** and offers the main rival alternative theories to the Buddhist metaphysics of the *Mahayana* schools. The main classical sources for the study of this school in the Tibetan canon are the first two chapters of *Dharmakirti's* PRAMANAVARTTIKA and *Bhavaviveka's* TARKA-JVALA. It is ironic that in spite of the *Sautrantika* school's great importance in the early development of Buddhist philosophy hardly any substantial original works exist in Tibetan literature attributed to a philosopher of this school.

Seed Syllable ཡིག་འབྲུ་ yig 'bru *bīja*

Each of the **peaceful and wrathful meditational deities** is said to emerge in the course of **meditation** from a specific **seed-syllable**, which in turn emerges from **emptiness**. For example, in the case of the **meditation** on *Avalokiteshvara*, the meditator visualises a *Sanskrit* syllable *HRIH* from which arises the entire meditative image of the **deity**. With respect to the central **deities** of the **five enlightened-families**, according to the *GUHYAGARBHA TANTRA* and the *GUHYASAMAJA TANTRA*, *OM* is the seed-syllable of *Vairocana*, *HUM* is that of *Akshobhya*, *SVA* is that of *Ratnasambhava*, *AH* is that of *Amitabha*, and *HA* is that of *Amoghasiddhi*. The seed-syllables *OM AH* and *HUM* are also identified respectively with the emanational basis of *buddha*-**body**, *buddha*-**speech** and *buddha*-**mind**, while the syllables *A SU NRI TRI PRE DU* are respectively associated with the emanational basis of the **six realms** of existence, which may be assumed by **sentient beings**, namely those of: **gods**, **antigods**, humans, animals, **hungry ghosts**, and denizens of **hell**.

Self བདག/ང་ bdag/nga *ātmā*

The *Sanskrit atma* and its Tibetan equivalent *bdag*, which are translated in English as 'self', have diverse connotations in Buddhist philosophy. 'Self' can mean simply the conventional notion of a person's **identity**, as in the concept of 'self and others'. Such a conventional **self** functions as the subject for predicating various properties, both in language and thought. The mode of being of

this conventional idea of **self** is, however, recognised by all Buddhist schools to be not independently distinct from the psycho-physical **aggregates** that constitute the person. Not only is the existence of **self** dependent on these **aggregates**, but our perception of its **identity** is also dependent on the nature of these **aggregates**. The concept of **self** is therefore intimately linked to the notion of personal **identity**, and there are various views of personal **identity** based on the diverse metaphysical standpoints of the various Buddhist philosophical systems. It must be pointed out, however, that none of the Buddhist schools accept a **self** in the sense of an eternal, unchanging soul which can inhabit the body independently. Indeed, the *Sautrantika* and all the *Mahayana* philosophical schools extend their notions of **self** to external phenomena also and speak of their **selflessness**, i.e., their lack of **self**-substantive **identities**. But again what is meant by lack of **self-identity** differs significantly from one school to another.

Self-Identity བདག་ཉིད་/ རང་གི་ངོ་བོ་ bdag nyid/rang gi ngo bo *ātman/svabhāva*

The expression '**self-identity**' may be used to translate either the *Sanskrit* term *atman* (Tib. *bdag-nyid*) or in certain contexts *svabhava* (Tib. *rang-bzhin*). The former is the independent or substantial **self** known to the eternalistic philosophies of Hinduism and Jainism. The latter refers to the **inherent existence** which such schools project onto phenomena. Contrary to the view of **emptiness** or actual **reality** (*dharmata*), phenomena are in this case perceived to possess some kind of **self**-evident nature, something which is capable of maintaining its own **identity**, independently. For example, when we perceive a car our pre-analytic notion of the car is a car which has a concrete and substantial **identity**. But upon reflection we will find that apart from the parts which compose the car there is no such thing as a concrete car independent of its parts and our perception of it, as we pre-supposed. **Self-identity** is negated by the Buddhist concept of **selflessness**. However, the notion of **selflessness** differs among the various Buddhist philosophical schools of thought. See **Self** and **Selflessness**.

Selflessness བདག་མེད་ bdag med *nairātmya*

Selflessness in Buddhist philosophy is understood to imply the lack of **inherent existence** both in terms of personal or **self-identity** and in terms of physical and mental phenomena. The *Hinayana* schools such as *Vaibhashika* and *Sautrantika* expound the doctrine of **selflessness** only in terms of personal **identity**. They propound that **selflessness** refers to the absence of an independently existing '**self**' or 'I', emphasising that the **self** is not substantial or **self**-sufficient. Nowhere among the **aggregates** of the person, either individually, collectively, or even in their continuity, can one find a substantial or solid being. Material objects are nothing but a series of indivisible atomic particles, and **consciousness** is nothing but a series of indivisible time moments. Such a view is called *nairatmya* (the 'no-**self**' doctrine). However, the *Cittamatra* and *Madhyamaka* schools extend this notion of **selflessness** to embrace all physical and mental phenomena. All such phenomena are equated with **emptiness** (*shunyata*), and these *Mahayana* philosophical schools therefore speak of both the **selflessness** of person (*pudgalanairatmya*) and the **selflessness** of phenomena (*dharmanairatmya*). Nevertheless, substantial philosophical differences exist between the two *Mahayana* schools in their views on what it is that is being negated by the doctrine of **emptiness**.

Semdzin (tib.) སེམས་འཛིན་ sems 'dzin

An abbreviation for *sems-nyid-la ngo-'dzin*, which refers to the recognition or introduction to **mind**-as-such. Among the esoteric instructions (*upadesa*) which expound the Esoteric Instructional Class of **Atiyoga**, the Great Perfection, there are texts on Cutting through Resistance (*khregs-chod*) and All-Surpassing **Realisation** (*thod-rgal*). Practical manuals such as *khrid-yig ye-shes bla-ma* indicate the special **preliminaries** (*sngo-'gro*) which have to be performed before the *yogin* can engage in such advanced practices. The **preliminaries** include: 1) training in the *yoga* of the four **elements**; 2) practices which distinguish between **samsara** and **nirvana** (*khor-'das ru-gshan*), i.e., between mundane body, speech and **mind** and **buddha**-body, **speech** and **mind**; 3) introduction to the nature of **mind**-as-such, which includes various techniques, such as **Vajra** Posture (*rdo-rje sdug-stangs*), and Recitation, which refine mundane body, speech and **mind** respectively into **buddha**-body, **speech** and **mind**. This last category is also known as *sems-'dzin*. More specifically, a series of twenty-one *sems-'dzin* is enumerated in the *tantras* of the Esoteric Instructional Class, such as the COALESCENCE OF SUN AND MOON (*NYI-ZLA KHA'-'BYOR*).

Sentient Being སེམས་ཅན་ sems can *bhūta/sattva*

In a Buddhist context the expression '**sentient being**' has a technical usage which contrasts with the concept of a **buddha**. The term refers to beings in **cyclic existence** and also those who have attained **liberation** from it but who have not attained full **buddhahood**. The **Sanskrit** gati (Tib. *'gro-ba*) literally means 'goer' and *sattva*, a 'living being'. The Tibetan equivalent of the latter, *sems-can*, literally means 'sentient' or 'a being with **mind**', as it does in English.

Sera (tib.) སེ་ར་ se rā

One of the three great **Gelug** monastic universities around **Lhasa**. Founded by *Jamchen Choje Shakya* **Yeshe** in 1419, the monastery gradually grew into one of the largest monastic learning centres of Tibet with over six thousand resident scholars before 1959. **Sera** has three colleges - *Ngakpa* for the study of **tantra**, and two philosophical colleges, **Sera Je** and **Sera Me**, both of which have also been re-established amongst the exiled Tibetan community in *Karnataka* state, south India.

Seven Limbed Practice ཡན་ལག་བདུན་པ་ yan lag bdun pa *saptāṅga*

A preliminary practice which is normally undertaken as a preparation for **tantric** ritual and **meditation** practices, including **sadhana**s of specific **deities**, and also for the systematic **meditation**s of **Lamrim**. The seven limbs together constitute a comprehensive practice for purifying negative potentials and accumulating **merit**, thus laying a stable basis for a successful **meditational** session. The seven limbs are, in their proper sequence: 1) prostrations; 2) making **offerings**; 3) purifying **non-virtuous** habits; 4) rejoicing in the wholesome actions of others and oneself;

5) requesting the **Buddhas** to teach; 6) appealing to the **Buddhas** not to enter into **Parinirvana**; and 7) dedicating **merit**.

SEVEN POINT THOUGHT TRANSFORMATION རྦློ་སྦྱོང་དོན་བདུན་མ་ blo sbyong don bdun ma

The title of one of the most celebrated manuals on the practice of **Lojong**. Written by the **Kadampa** master **Chekhawa**, the text expounds, within the framework of seven points, the essential practices for training the **mind** in the generation of **bodhicitta** and integrating the **bodhisattva** ideals into daily life. The seven points are: 1) the preliminary practices of **Lojong**; 2) the main practice - training the **mind** in the practice of the two kinds of **bodhicitta;** 3) transforming adverse circumstances into favourable conditions on the path to **enlightenment**; 4) methods for integrating this practice into daily life; 5) the measure of determining the success of one's mental training; 6) the commitments associated with **Lojong** practices; and 7) the **precepts** to be followed by a **Lojong** practitioner.

Sevenfold Reasoning རྣམ་བདུན་གྱི་རིགས་པ་ rnam bdun gyi rigs pa

A specific form of **Madhyamaka** reasoning applied to prove the **emptiness** of the **inherent existence** of person or **self** by drawing an analogy with the characteristics of a chariot. This is an elaboration of a form of reasoning which **Nagarjuna** employed extensively in his *MULAMADHYAMAKAKARIKA* and which came to be known as the fivefold reasoning. The **sevenfold reasoning** was first employed by **Candrakirti** in his *MADHAYAMAKAVATARA,* the supplement to **Nagarjuna's** root text. The seven elements of the reasoning are these: The 'self' or the 'person' does not exist inherently because: 1) the **self** or person is not identical to the **aggregates**; 2) nor is it a distinct entity independent from the **aggregates**; 3) nor is it the basis of the **aggregates**; 4) nor is it inherently based on the **aggregates**; 5) nor does it inherently possess the **aggregates**; 6) nor is it the collection of **aggregates**; and 7) it is also not the form of the **aggregates**. In the analogy with the chariot, the **self** is the chariot and the **aggregates** the parts of the chariot. See **Self** and **Selflessness**.

Seventy Topics མངོན་རྟོགས་རྒྱན་གྱི་དོན་བདུན་བཅུ་ mngon rtogs rgyan gyi don bdun bcu

According to the *ORNAMENT OF CLEAR REALISATION*, the **bodhisattva's** path to **enlightenment** and eventual **buddha**hood, as expounded in the **Prajnaparamita** literature, has eight fundamental aspects which sequentially concern the theoretical understandings of the ground, the realisation of the **path to enlightenment**, and the resulting attainment of the **Dharmakaya**. These eight aspects are then elaborated in a series of seventy topics, thirty of which concern the theoretical understanding, thirty-six the actual realisation of the path, and four the resultant **Dharmakaya**.

Seven Spiritual Wealths འཕགས་ནོར་བདུན་ 'phags nor bdun *saptadhana*

More accurately translated as the 'seven riches of the sublime ones' or 'superiors', this expression refers to seven mental qualities which sustain the enrichment of a person's life. Unlike material wealths, acquisition of the spiritual riches gives rise to a sense of lasting fulfilment based on an ethically sound conduct. The seven riches are: 1) self-confidence; 2) ethical discipline; 3) learning; 4) generosity; 5) propriety; 6) sound conscience; and 7) **discriminative awareness**.

Shakyamuni (skrt.) ཤཱ་ཀྱ་ཐུབ་པ་ shā kya thub pa *Śākyamuni*

The historical **buddha** who was born as the prince *Siddhartha* and became the fully **enlightened buddha** whilst meditating under the shade of the *Bodhi* Tree in **Bodhgaya**. The name **Shakyamuni** (Sage of the *Shakyas*) indicates that the historical **buddha** was born into the *Shakya* clan. Classical Buddhist literature lists **Shakyamuni** as the fourth among the thousand **buddhas** who are predicted to come to the earth during this 'auspicious aeon' (*bhadrakalpa*). The **Buddha Shakyamuni** is said to have lived in the sixth century BC and is credited as the progenitor of nearly all the contemporary Buddhist lineages. His life-stories include the famous *BUDDHACARITA* by **Ashvagosha**. See **Buddha**, **Sutra** and **Tantra**.

Shamatha (skrt.) ཞི་གནས་ zhi gnas *śamatha*

See **Calm Abiding**.

Shambhala (skrt.) ཤམ་བྷ་ལ་ sham bha la *Śambhala*

A mysterious land, associated with the **tantric meditational deity Kalacakra**, which is said to exist in the northern direction of the world or universe, and is often identified with Central Asia. The salvific myth of **Shambhala** is very strong among the Tibetan laity where it is commonly believed that in the future, when human greed and **hatred** manifest in their full destructive form, the world will be enmeshed in a ceaseless cycle of war and conflict and eventually ruled by an evil empire. At that point the kingdom of **Shambhala** will subdue the evil ruler and save the people of this earth from tyranny. There is a popular folk belief that those who are able to participate in a **Kalacakra empowerment** will subsequently be reborn in **Shambhala**. See **Kalacakra**.

Shangpa (tib.) ཤངས་པ་ shangs pa

One of the main sub-schools of the **Kagyu** school of **Tibetan Buddhism**. This particular division of the **Kagyu** school originated from the great Tibetan **tantric** master *Khyungpo Naljor*. He visited India and Nepal three times and sought instructions and **transmissions** to numerous **tantric** practices from over one hundred Indian teachers including *Maitripa*. The name of the school **Shangpa** derives from the name of a valley in the **Tsang** province of Tibet called *Shang*, where *Khyungpo Naljor* established his first monastery. See **Kagyu**.

Shantarakshita ཞི་བའི་འཚོ་ zhi ba'i 'tsho *Śāntarakṣita*

An **abbot**, or more precisely a monastic preceptor, and exponent of **Madhyamaka** philosophy from *Zahor* who officiated at **Nalanda** before his arrival in Tibet at the invitation of King *Trisong Detsen*, during the eighth century. In Tibet, he was responsible for the construction of **Samye** Monastery, which he modelled after the design of the *Odantapuri Vihara* in *Magadha*. At

Samye, he introduced the monastic ordination of the *Sarvastivada* school, which subsequently became known as the Lower Tibetan *Vinaya* lineage. Together with *Padmasambhava* and *Trisong Detsen*, he came to form the trio known as the abbot/preceptor, the master and the spiritual king *(mkhan-slob-chos gsum)* who were jointly responsible for establishing Buddhism as the state religion of Tibet.

Shantideva (skrt.) ཞི་བ་ལྷ་ zhi ba lha *Śāntideva*

A great *bodhisattva* of classical India and a strong proponent of the *Madhya-maka Prasangika* school who lived between the end of the seventh and the middle of the eighth century. *Shantideva* is most noted for his two works: the *BODHISATTVACARYAVATARA* and the *SIKSASAMUCCAYA*, both of which are practice oriented and outline the essential qualities of a *bodhisattva's* conduct. Among *Mahayana* practitioners, the *BODHISATTVACARYAVATARA* is one of the most popular works ever written. The text, in ten chapters, is composed in a very lucid poetic style yet at the same time never compromises its detailed presentation of complex philosophical and ethical subjects. Many say that it is still by far the best book for introducing to a new reader the rich spiritual and philosophical traditions of *Mahayana* Buddhism. See **Bodhisattvacaryavatara**.

Shastra (skrt.) བསྟན་བཅོས་ bstan bcos *śāstra*

The authentic **transmissions** of the *Buddha Shakyamuni's* teachings *(agama)* are divided into the transmitted **precepts** actually delivered by the *buddha* *(pravacana)* and the authentic commentaries or treatises elucidating their meaning *(shastra)*. The *Sanskrit* term '*shastra*', meaning **commentary** or treatise, is interpreted to have two senses, because an authentic treatise: 1) diminishes and purifies the **obscurations** of the reader; and 2) protects the reader from **igno-rance** as to the actual meaning and from the **suffering** of conditioned existences. The term therefore implies the bringing about of a transformation in the reader's **mind** and the protection from the potential dangers of **cyclic existence**. Trea-tises are traditionally classified in six ways, according to: 1) the standard of their composition; 2) the purpose of their composition; 3) their individual composers; 4) the manner of their composition; 5) the transmitted **precepts** of *buddha*-word which they explain; and 6) the meaning which they express.

Shedra བ་ཤད་གྲྭ་ bshad grva

A college for the theoretical study of Buddhist texts in contrast to the **meditation** hermitages known as *drupdra (sgrub-grva)*. A number of important monasteries in Tibet have been known for their illustrious colleges, such as the *Shri Simha She-dra* at *Dzogchen* in *Kham*.

Shentong (skrt.) གཞན་སྟོང་ gzhan stong

An interpretation of the doctrine of **emptiness**, based on N**agarjuna**'s '*CORPUS OF EULOGIES*' *(Stavakaya)*, which contrasts with the views established in *Nagar-juna's* six treatises of the '*CORPUS OF REASON*' *(Yuktikaya)*. The **view** of extrane-ous **emptiness** *(gzhan-stong)* was elaborated in Tibet by the *Jonang* school, which was founded and developed by *Yungmo Mikyod Dorje*, the *Kalacakra* master *Dolpo Sherab Gyaltsen*, and *Kunpang Thukje Tsondu*. The essence of the doctrine of extraneous **emptiness** is that **emptiness**, or **ultimate truth**, should be understood in terms of a non-dual pristine awareness which is empty of the con-ventional natures of dependence and mental constructs, and that the alternative to this coalescence of pure appearances and **emptiness** is **nihilism**. The school maintains that such an understanding of **emptiness** is superior to the *Prasangika's* **view** of intrinsic **emptiness**. They also contend that this **emptiness** is only perceptible by direct experience and hence it is not an object of conceptual thought. Such a non-dual awareness is regarded as absolute and beyond conventionality. This **view** has been the focus of extensive debate over the centuries. It has been criticised by many great scholars of various traditions at various times, most notably by *Buton Rinchen Drup* and *Tsong Khapa*, and it has been upheld or elucidated by other great scholars such as *Karmapa Rangjung Dorje* and *Longchen Rabjampa*. In the *Rime* movement which developed in Eastern Tibet during the nineteenth century, philosophers such as *Ju Mipham Gyatso* came to uphold a 'non-dual **emptiness**' (*gnyis-med stong*) which integrates both the **views** of intrinsic **emptiness** (*rang-stong*) and that of extraneous **emptiness** (*gzhan-stong*), showing that they are in fact without contradiction. The former **view** is clarified analytically through the application of consequentialist logic, leading to the understanding of **emptiness** as an absence of all conceptual elaboration and inherent existence. Then, the latter **view**, cultivated in meditative experience, reveals how all *buddha*-attributes are a coalescence of pure appearance and **emptiness**, extraneously empty of all the impure phenomena associated with **cyclic existence**. The term '**Great *Madhyamaka***' is used to describe this **view** when contrasted with or complemented by the **view** established through *Madhyamaka* dialectic, which in this context is referred to as outer *Madhyamaka*. See **Rangtong** and **Tathagatagarbha**.

Shravaka (skrt.) ཉན་ཐོས་ nyan thos *śrāvaka*

In the *sutra*-based texts of Buddhist literature, three types of spiritual trainees with distinct natural inclinations are mentioned, namely: 1) **pious attendants/hearers** (*shravaka*); 2) self-centred *buddhas*/**solitary realisers** (*pratyekabuddha*); and 3) spiritual heroes of **enlightenment** (*bodhisattva*). Among these the first two types follow the *Hinayana* tradition while the third follows the *Mahayana*. Both the *shravaka* and the *pratyekabuddha* are naturally inclined to seek merely their own individual **liberation** from **cyclic existence,** but there are two primary differences between them. The first is made on the basis of their degree of accumulation of **merits** and the manner in which they attain the final **liberation** or *nirvana*: the *shravaka* accumulates only a limited amount of **merit** and places greater emphasis on destroying the mistaken belief in personal **identity** (*pudgala*) by overcoming the primary and secondary **dissonant emotions**, while the *pratyekabuddha*, in addition to eliminating these dissonant states, comes to realise the **emptiness** of all external phenomena composed of atomic particles, accumulates **merit** over a hundred aeons and obtains a similitude of the *buddhas* **major and minor marks**. Second, the *shravaka* depends heavily on verbal instruction both for the attainment of *nirvana* and also when giving guidance to others on the path; whereas the *pratyekabuddha*

does not depend on verbal communication. Unlike both these types of trainee, the **bodhisattva** is one whose entry onto the path is principally motivated by an altruistic concern for the welfare of others. The original **Sanskrit** word '*shravaka*' suggests someone who hears or attends the **buddha**-word in a pious manner and narrates that which has been heard to others. It is therefore translated into English on occasions as '**pious attendant**' or '**hearer**'.

Shunyata (skrt.) སྟོང་པ་ཉིད་ stong pa nyid *śūnyatā*

See **Emptiness**.

Siddha (skrt.) གྲུབ་ཐོབ་ grub thob *siddha*

See **Mahasiddha**.

Siddhi དངོས་གྲུབ་ dngos grub *siddhi*

Spiritual accomplishments which may be supramundane or common. The former (*mchog-gi dngos-grub*) refers to the accomplishment of **buddha**hood, transcending **cyclic existence**. The latter (*thun-mong-gi dngos-grub*) are a series of mystical powers gained through meditative practices which are based on **mantra** recitation in the context of specific rituals. **Tantric** literature mentions eight such types of common accomplishment: 1) the power of creating pills that can sustain life without conventional food for a long period (*ril-bu'i dngos-grub*); 2) the power of creating an eye lotion which can extend one's vision (*mig-sman-gyi dngos-grub*); 3) the power to walk underground without obstruction (*sa-'og-gi dngos-grub*); 4) the power to ride on a flying sword (*ral-gri'i dngos-grub*); 5) the power to fly (*phur-ba'i dngos-grub*); 6) the power to become invisible (*mi-snang-ba'i dngos-grub*); 7) the power to prolong one's life (*'chi-ba med-pa'i dngos-grub*); and 8) the power to heal diseases (*nad 'joms-pa'i dngos-grub*). The above accomplishments are mundane in that the purposes they fulfil are ordinary and such feats can be acquired without any experience of **emptiness** or **bodhicitta**.

Sidpa Bardo (tib.) སྲིད་པའི་བར་དོ་ srid pa'i bar do

One of the four (or six) **intermediate states**, as expounded briefly in some of the early **Mahayana sutras** and in greater detail in the texts of the **Nyingma** school concerning the transitional periods in the course of a **sentient being's** progression through **cyclic existence**. See **Bardo**. In the **intermediate state** of the process of **rebirth** (*srid-pa'i bar-do*), an ordinary person will experience a form of life-review, a process of **self**-judgement and premonitions of the type of future existence that might be entered into. The deceased undergoes these experiences, not with a corporeal body composed of atomic matter, but a subtle mental body (*yid-lus*) which has all its sensory capacities intact, which arrives at each place as it is thought of and which can pass through matter without obstruction. Accordingly, there are instructions conducive to **liberation** or advantageous **rebirth** based on: recognition of the nature of this mental body, the identification of the illusory nature of the **self**-judgement process, the transformation of **attachment** and hatred/aversion, and the recognition of various lights and images associated with the six classes of living beings, enabling the deceased to avoid **rebirth** in unfavourable forms. According to **abhidharma** literature *sidpa bardo* is a synonym for **bardo**, i.e., the intermediate state between death and birth. See also **Chikai Bardo** and **Chonyi Bardo**.

Simhanada (skrt.) སེང་གེ་སྒྲ་སྒྲོགས་ seng ge sgra sgrogs *Siṃhanāda*

One of the eight manifestations of ***Guru Rinpoche***. See **Guru Rinpoche**.

Six Perfections ཕར་ཕྱིན་དྲུག་ phar phyin drug *ṣatpāramitā*

The perfections of: 1) generosity; 2) ethical discipline; 3) patience; 4) perseverance or joyous effort; 5) meditative **concentration**; and 6) **discriminative awareness *(prajna)***. See **Paramitas**.

Six Realms རིགས་དྲུག་གི་སྐྱེ་གནས་ rigs drug gi skye gnas

A birth in **cyclic existence** is characterised as occurring in one of **six realms** depending on the nature and maturity of the individual's karmic propensities. The **six realms** are divided into three of favourable birth and three of unfavourable birth. The former are: 1) ***deva*** (mundane celestial beings whose primary mental state is one of exaltation); 2) ***asura*** (anti-**gods** or demi-**gods** who are predominantly hostile and jealous); and 3) human beings (who are influenced by all five **dissonant emotions**). The latter are: 4) animals (who are under the sway of **delusion**); and 5) tormented spirits or **hungry ghosts** (who are under the sway of **attachment** and unsatisfied craving), and denizens of **hell** (who are overwhelmed by **hatred**, anger and fear). Since all five **dissonant emotions** have influence on human beings, it is not inappropriate to look upon all of these conditions also as extrapolations of human psychological states. See **Cyclic Existence**.

Six Session (Guru) Yoga ཐུན་དྲུག་བླ་མའི་རྣལ་འབྱོར་ thun drug bla ma'i rnal 'byor

A specific sequence of ***tantric*** **meditations** systematised for their ease of daily practice by the Fourth ***Panchen Lama***, *Lobsang Chogyen*. The **meditations** include such basic ***Mahayana*** Buddhist practices as taking **refuge** in the **Three Precious Jewels**, reinforcing the ***bodhicitta*** motivation and developing **love** and **compassion** towards all beings. The main aim of the practice is to enable the average practitioner who cannot spend the majority of each day in **meditation** to observe successfully the **vows** and commitments taken during a ***tantric*** **empowerment**. The commitments consist mainly of the pledge to reinforce six times during each twenty-four hour period, the altruistic motivation to help others, to review all the ***bodhisattva*** and ***tantric*** **vows**, and to reaffirm the commitment to seek full **enlightenment** for the benefit of all. In '***Six session yoga***' all the above practices are undertaken on the basis of a strong ***guruyoga*** **meditation**, thus providing the average practitioner with a comprehensive daily practice containing most of the essential elements of the ***Mahayana*** path.

Six yogas (or doctrines) of Naropa ནཱ་རོ་ཆོས་དྲུག་ nā ro chos drug

A unique system of advanced ***tantric*** **meditation** originating

from the great Indian master **Naropa**. The SIX *YOGAS* OF *NAROPA* constitute the heart of **completion stage** practice in the **Kagyu** school and later became popular amongst **Gelug** practitioners as well. The **six yogas** are: 1) the **yoga** of inner heat *(gtum-mo)* ; 2) the **yoga** of **inner radiance/clear light** *('od-gsal)*; 3) the **yoga** of the **illusory body** *(sgyu-lus)*; 4) the **yoga** of the **intermediate state** *(bar-do)*; 5) the **yoga** of **consciousness transference** *('pho-ba)*; 6) the **yoga** of resurrection *(grong-'jug)*. Alternative systems of enumerating the **six yogas** substitute **bar-do** with the **yoga** of coalescence/union *(zung-'jug)* or *grong-'jug* with **dream yoga** *(rmi-lam)*.

SIX YOGAS (OR DOCTRINES) OF NIGUMA ནི་གུའི་ཆོས་དྲུག ni gu'i chos drug

A **lineage** of *tantric* practice similar to **Naropa's six yogas** which originated from the **yogini Niguma**. The **six yogas** are the **yogas** of: 1) the **inner heat** *(gtum-mo)* ; ; 2) the **illusory body** *(sgyu-lus)*; 3) **dream yoga** *(rmi-lam)*; 4) the **inner radiance/clear light** *('od-gsal)*; 5) **transference of consciousness** *('pho-ba)*; and 6) the **intermediate state** *(bar-do)*.

Sixteen Emptinesses སྟོང་ཉིད་བཅུ་དྲུག stong nyid bcu drug *ṣoḍaśaśūnyatā*

In the **Mahayana** **sutras** the doctrine of **emptiness** is presented as embracing the entire expanse of **reality**. It is stated that a genuine insight into the profound nature of **emptiness** will dispel the **ignorance** and misconceptions which lie at the root of our **suffering** within **cyclic existence**. Such expositions are put forward on the basis of explaining the notion of **emptiness** in relation to various categories of phenomena. Based on the varied categorisations of phenomena one finds different enumerations of **emptiness** in the *sutras*. Popular among them is the list of **sixteen emptinesses**. These are: 1) **emptiness** of the internal *(nang stong-pa-nyid)*; 2) **emptiness** of the external *(phyi stong-pa-nyid)*; 3) **emptiness** of both internal and external *(phyi-nang gnyis-ka stong-pa-nyid)*; 4) the **emptiness** of **emptiness** *(stong-pa-nyid stong-pa-nyid)*; 5) **emptiness** of the vast *(chen-po stong-pa-nyid)*; 6) **emptiness** of the ultimate *(don-dam-pa stong-pa-nyid)*; 7) **emptiness** of the produced *('du-byas stong-pa-nyid)*; 8) **emptiness** of the unproduced *('du-ma-byas stong-pa-nyid)*; 9) **emptiness** of the extremes *(mtha'-las 'das-pa'i stong-pa-nyid)*; 10) **emptiness** of that which is without beginning or end *(thog-ma-dang mtha'-ma med-pa stong-pa-nyid)*; 11) **emptiness** of that which is not to be abandoned *(dor-ba med-pa stong-pa-nyid)*; 12) **emptiness** of **self-identity** *(rang-bzhin stong-pa-nyid)*; 13) the **emptiness** of all things *(chos thams-cad stong-pa-nyid)*; 14) the **emptiness** of **self**-defining characteristics *(rang mtshan-nyid stong-pa-nyid)*; 15) **emptiness** of the non-referential *(mi-dmigs-pa stong-pa-nyid)*; and 16) **emptiness** of the absence of substantiality *(dngos-po med-pa'i stong-pa-nyid)*. The principal sources for the study of the **sixteen emptinesses** are the **Prajnaparamita sutras** and the literature of **Madhyamaka** philosophy, particularly **Candrakirti's MADHYAMAKAVATARA** and its related commentaries.

Skandhas (skrt.) ཕུང་པོ phung po *skandha*

See **Aggregates**.

Skilful Means ཐབས thabs *upāya*

The **Sanskrit** term **upaya** (tib. *thabs*) translates into English as **skilful means**. In **Mahayana** Buddhism, learning in **skilful means** *(upayakausalya/thabs-la mkhas-pa)* refers to the first five **paramitas**, generosity and so forth, when inte-

Marpa

Milarepa

grated with **discriminative awareness** (*prajna*), the sixth *paramita*, to form a union of **discriminative awareness** and means. The perfection of **skilful means** is also separately enumerated among the ten *paramitas*, where it indicates the inestimable result acquired by dedicating the **merit** of one's virtuous deeds, however small, for the benefit of all **sentient beings** in general and for the sake of great unsurpassed **enlightenment** in particular. In *tantric* literature, the path of **skilful means** (*thabs-lam*) refers to the sexual practices (*sbyor-ba*) in which the internal *yogas* of the energy **channels**, **winds** and seminal fluids are activated. Also, according to the *Nyingma* school, the three inner classes of *tantra* are sometimes referred to as the 'vehicles of overpowering means' (*thabs dbang-'bsgyur-ba'i theg-pa-rnams*), in the sense that they carry on the path all the **dissonant emotions** which are renounced in lower paths.

Smrityupasthana (skrt.) དྲན་པ་ཉེར་བཞག་ dran pa nyer bzhag *smṛtyupasthāna*

See **Four Mindfulnesses**.

Sojong གསོ་སྦྱོང་ gso sbyong *poṣadha*

A fortnightly confessional ceremony which is an essential element of monastic discipline held alternately on the full moon and new moon days. During the ritual, monks and nuns declare various transgressions of their **vows** which may have occurred over the past two weeks, thereby reinforcing their resolve to abide according to the rules prescribed by the monastic order.

Solitary Realiser རང་རྒྱལ་ rang rgyal *pratyekabuddha*

See **Pratyekabuddha**.

Songtsen Gampo (tib.) སྲོང་བཙན་སྒམ་པོ་ srong btsan sgam po

The great seventh century Tibetan monarch who first actively encouraged the introduction of Buddhism into Tibet. *Songtsen Gampo* is also the king who dispatched to India his learned minister *Thonmi Sambhota* in order that a script could be devised for the Tibetan language, capable of rendering Buddhist terminology and at the same time consistent with the monosyllabic nature of the Tibetan language. Politically, *Songtsen Gampo* unified the whole of Tibet for the first time, and established *Lhasa* as his capital. He entered into marriage alliances with the neighbouring king of Nepal and emperor of China. Tibetans consider him to be a human emanation of Tibet's patron **deity** *Avalokiteshvara*, the *bodhisattva* of **compassion**. Together with *Trisong Detsen* and *Tri Ralpachen*, he is revered as one of the 'three ancestral rulers who were spiritual kings'.

Stupa (skrt.) མཆོད་རྟེན་ mchod rten *stūpa*

Originally a symbol of *Dharmakaya*, constructed in a dome-shape to hold the remains of *Shakyamuni Buddha*, the *stupa* has become the most well-known sacred monument in the Bud-

dhist world. *Stupas* are constructed to a specific architectural design, usually in the shape of a dome, raised on a square base of several layers, from which rises a multilayered column. The veneration of *stupas* is closely connected with the earliest phase of *Mahayana* Buddhism; the original *stupa*-design developing during this period into the *Caitya*, or monastic *vihara* (large temple) of ancient India. There are many types of *stupa*, and, in Tibet, a series of eight well-known *stupa* forms is frequently constructed, symbolising different events in the life of *Shakyamuni Buddha*. Others are extraordinarily large, like those of *Bodhnath* and *Svayambhu* in Nepal, or *Sanchi* in India and *Borabodur* in Indonesia, and some enclose within them entire *mandalas* of deities, such as the *Pelkhor Chode stupa* at *Gyantse* in *Tsang* province, Tibet. The symbolism of the *stupa* is complex - representing the progression to **buddhahood** or **enlightenment**, the **five elements** and so forth. Smaller *stupas* are built normally as a funerary memorial for a high *lama*, often enshrining sacred ashes or embalmed remains.

SUBLIME CONTINUUM རྒྱུད་བླ་མ་ rgyud bla ma *Uttaratantra*

See **UTTARATANTRA**.

Subtle Body ཕྲ་བའི་ལུས་/ ཡིད་ལུས་ phra ba'i lus/yid lus

In contrast to our gross physical body, which is composed of flesh, bones and blood, the **subtle body** refers to the type of form which arises as a natural expression of the interaction of the subtle **mind** and the **subtle winds** or energies on which it depends. Though all **sentient beings** possess such a composite of awareness and energy, (which is in fact the essence of their existence and the factor that carries the mental continuum through successive **rebirths**), its true nature lies unapparent within an ordinary person when alive. During our normal conscious states our **mind** remains active on a conceptual or sensory level thus inhibiting the essential subtle **mind** from manifesting its nature. A similitude of such a **subtle body** can be experienced by some during the dream state when the level of **consciousness** is relatively subtle and deep, due to the temporary cessation of active sensory processes. The mental body (*yid-lus*) experienced during the **intermediate state** of **rebirth** is also a form of **subtle body**. However, the most advanced level of **subtle body**, known in *tantra* as the **illusory body** (*sgyu-lus*), is experienced only when an indivisible unity of *buddha*-**body, speech** and **mind** has been actualised.

Subtle Wind(s) ཕྲ་བའི་རླུང་ phra ba'i rlung

In correspondence to the various levels of **consciousness**, the **subtle winds** are the **winds** of vital or subtle energy that propel these **consciousnesses**, and accompany their subtle experiences. Such experiences become possible only when gross sensory experiences and conceptions have dissolved. See **Winds**.

Suffering སྡུག་བསྔལ་ sdug bsngal *duḥkha*

In a Buddhist context, the term 'suffering' is used in a broad sense and includes not only physical sensations but also mental experiences. In fact the concept of **suffering** or *dukha* includes all the essentially unsatisfactory experiences of life in **cyclic existence**. The various forms of **suffering** can be categorised into three groups: 1) the **suffering** of **suffering** (*sdug-bsngal-gyi sdug-bsngal*); 2) the **suffering** of change (*'gyur-ba'i sdug-bsngal*); and 3) the **suffering** of pervasive conditioning (*khyab-pa 'du-byed-kyi sdug-bsngal*). The first category refers to all our physical sensations and also to the mental experiences which are **self**-evident to us as **suffering** and toward which we have spontaneous feelings of aversion. The second category includes all our experiences which are normally recognised as pleasant and desirable. Nonetheless they are *dukha* in that persistent indulgence in these always results in the changed attitude of dissatisfaction and boredom. It is only through reflection that the unsatisfactory nature of such experiences can be realised. The third category of **suffering** refers to the basic **suffering** which pervades life in **cyclic existence**. This **suffering** serves as the cause of our experiences of the two other classes of **suffering**. It is called pervasive because it extends to all forms of life in this cycle of existence, irrespective of whether or not life-forms within it are endowed with bodily existence.

Sugata བདེ་བར་གཤེགས་པ་ bde bar gshegs pa *sugata*

An epithet of the **Buddha**, which literally translates as 'One who has gone to bliss'. See **Buddha**.

Suhrllekha (skrt.) བཤེས་སྤྲིངས་ bshes springs *Suhṛllekha*

See ***Letter to a Friend***.

Sukhavati (skrt.) བདེ་བ་ཅན་ bde ba can *Sukhāvatī*

The **pure realm** of *Amitabha*. See **Pure Realm**.

Suryarashmi (skrt.) ཉི་མ་འོད་ཟེར་ nyi ma 'od zer *Sūryaraśmī*

One of the eight manifestations of *Guru Rinpoche*. See **Guru Rinpoche**.

Sutra (skrt.) མདོ་ mdo *sūtra*

The original discourses which *Buddha Shakyamuni* taught publicly to his disciples whilst teaching, as a fully ordained *Bhikshu*, consequent to his attainment of *buddha*hood. In the context of the three successive turnings of the doctrinal wheel, the *Buddha* expounded respectively: 1) the *shravaka* discourses on the doctrine of the **four noble truths**; 2) the *Prajnaparamita*, *Ratnakuta* and related *sutras* which emphasise signlessness, aspirationlessness and **emptiness**; and 3) the *Tathagatagarbha sutras* which emphasise *buddha*-nature and the thorough analysis of *buddha*-attributes. Among these the first category is the corpus of *Hinayana sutras*, and the last two are the *Mahayana sutras*. Each of the major divisions of *Hinayana* Buddhism had or has its own recension of 'first turning **sutras**'. Among these, the *Sthaviravada* (or *Theravada*) collection is fully extant in *Pali*. The *Mahasanghika* and *Sammitiya sutras* are no longer extant (although their *vinaya* and *abhidharma* literature do partially survive in Chinese and *Sanskrit*). The *Sarvastivada* collection largely survives in Chinese translation, but only a small representative number of their 'first turning *sutras*' were actually translated into Tibetan. As far as the *Mahayana sutras* are concerned, a few do survive in the original *Sanskrit*. However, the vast majority of the 740 extant *sutras* in the earliest version of the Chinese *Tripitaka* are *Mahayana sutras*, and of the 351 extant *sutras*

in the Tibetan canon, almost all represent the **Mahayana**, in either its second or third turning aspects. The original teachings of the **Buddha Shakyamuni**, which are described in the **tantric** literature as having been given by the **Buddha** whilst assuming the esoteric appearance of various **meditational deities**, are known as **tantras**. Although **tantra**-texts are represented in the Chinese **Tripitaka**, the most extensive collection of all **four classes of tantra** is contained in the **Kangyur**, the fourteenth century anthology of **sutras** and **tantras** extant in Tibetan translation. Older **tantra**-texts are contained in the *Collected **Tantras** of the **Nyingma**pa (rnying-ma'i rgyud-'bum).* See **Kangyur**.

Sutrayana (skrt.) མདོའི་ཐེག་པ་/ ཕར་ཕྱིན་ཐེག་པ་ mdo'i theg pa/phar phyin theg pa *sūtrayāna/pāramitāyāna*

According to **Mahayana** Buddhism the entire path towards the attainment of **buddhahood** is presented within the framework of two main systems or vehicles (**yana**), the **sutrayana** and **tantrayana**. **Sutrayana** includes those systems of the path based on the 'causal method' of the **sutras**, while **tantrayana** includes those based on the 'resultant method' of the **tantra** texts. In **sutrayana** there is a causal progression from **ignorance** to **enlightenment** which takes place over an immeasurable period of time (calculated at three times ten to the power of fifty-seven years). The practice entails a rational, intellectual and systematic approach to **mind training**, based on a stable foundation of ethical discipline and a fully developed single-pointedness developed through **calm abiding**. The practitioner of the **sutrayana** pursues five successive paths: the path of provision or accumulation, on which **pristine cognition** is cultivated and **merit** is gathered, the path of connection or preparation on which meditative experiences of warmth and satisfaction are refined, the path of insight on which the true nature of **reality** free from **obscurations** is experienced over sixteen successive moments of insight, the path of **meditation** on which familiarity with that insight is cultivated and **enlightened attributes** are refined, and the path of no-more-learning on which the result is attained. There are three divisions within **sutrayana**, namely: the *shravakayana* followed by **shravakas**, the *pratyekabuddhayana*, followed by **pratyekabuddhas**, and the **bodhisattvayana**, followed by **bodhisattvas**. The first two lead to the result of **arhat**hood, while the last leads to the attainment of perfect **buddhahood** through the cultivation of **bodhicitta**, integrating the **six perfections** and a spontaneous motivation to seek full **enlightenment** for the benefit of all others. The **bodhisattva** experiences the first seven **bodhisattva** levels or **grounds** during the **path** of insight and the initial stage of the **path** of **meditation**; and the last three during the latter stage of the **path** of **meditation**. See **Grounds and Paths** and **Grounds of a Bodhisattva**.

Svabhavikakaya (skrt.) ངོ་བོ་ཉིད་སྐུ་ ngo bo nyid sku *svabhāvikakāya*

See **Kayas**.

Svatantrika (skrt.) རང་རྒྱུད་པ་ rang rgyud pa *svātantrika*

One of the two divisions of the **Madhyamaka** philosophical school of thought. This school emerged as a separate system of thought following **Bhavaviveka's** extensive criticism of *Buddhapalita's* interpretation of **Nagarjuna's** thought and the subsequent counter-attack on **Bhavaviveka** by **Candrakirti**. As the name *svatantrika* (autonomous) implies, the main tenet of this school is the exposition of **Nagarjuna's** doctrine of **emptiness** within the framework of autonomous logical **syllogisms**. According to later opponents such as **Candrakirti**, the **svatantrika** position entails the acceptance of ontological standards, implying that they admit to a certain degree of **inherent existence**. *Svatantrika* itself was to evolve into two subdivisions: *Svatantrika Sautrantika* and *Svatantrika Yogacara*. *Bhavaviveka* is associated with the former trend, and *Shantarakshita* and *Kamalashila* with the latter. See **Prasangika** and **Bhavaviveka**.

Syllogism སྒྲུབ་ངག་/ རྟགས་སྦྱོར་ sgrub ngag/ rtags sbyor *hetuprayoga*

A specific form of argument, similar to Aristotelian **syllogism**, which employs such logical principles as: entailment, the law of the excluded middle and the law of non-contradiction. A typical example of a **syllogism** would run as follows, in positing a rose as changeable: 1) entailment - 'anything which is a product is changeable'; 2) example - 'like the dying flame of a candle'; 3) proof - 'The rose is also a product.' Unlike Aristotelian logic this type of **syllogism** does not state the conclusion of the argument explicitly other than by demonstrating the parallels between the example and the subject in question. The standard **syllogism** must be structured in the above three-faceted form and, in addition, in order for the **syllogism** to lead to a correct inference with respect to the conclusion, the stated proof in the argument must be valid. The most highly regarded source for the study of Buddhist logic is *Dharmakirti's* classic work on logic and **epistemology** the *PRAMANAVARTTIKA*. See **Pramana** and **Valid Reasoning**.

Taglung (tib.) སྟག་ལུང་ stag lung

In Central Tibet there are two monasteries by this name. North *Taglung*, north of *Penyul* in the upper *Kyichu* region, is the name of a monastery and sub-school of the *Phakmodrupa* **Kagyu**, founded by *Taglung Tashi Pal* in 1180. South *Taglung* is located by the shores of Lake *Yamdrok* in the administrative region of *Nakartse Dzong*. It is a branch monastery of *Dorje Drak*, one of the two most celebrated *Nyingma* monasteries in Central Tibet.

Tantra (skrt.) རྒྱུད་ rgyud *tantra*

The *Sanskrit* word *tantra* and its Tibetan equivalent *rgyud* literally mean a 'continuum' or 'unbroken stream' flowing from **ignorance** to **enlightenment**. *Tantra* has two basic meanings in Buddhism - it refers to the continua of ground, path and result, and to the literature or *tantra*-texts which expound these continua in the context of the **four classes of** *tantra*. The former is the actual meaning of *tantra*. Through the continuum of the path (*lam-gyi rgyud*) the atemporally present continuum of the ground (*gzhi'i rgyud*) is realised or fully manifested as the continuum of the result (*'bras-bu'i rgyud*). Because *tantra* includes sophisticated techniques which, unlike the *sutra* path, enable dissonant emotions, such as **desire**/attraction and hatred/aversion, to be transmuted into blissful states of **realisation**, without **renunciation** or rejection, the practitioner can cultivate an uninterrupted

continuum between the practitioner's ordinary initial **mind**, the advanced **mind** on the path, and the resultant fully **enlightened mind** of a *buddha*. It is said that on the basis of the fulfilment of the **generation** and **completion stages** of *Anuttarayogatantra*, full **buddhahood** can be attained in a single life-time. The **four classes of** *tantra*-texts namely: *Kriyatantra, Caryatantra, Yogatantra* and *Anuttarayogatantra*, are all said to have been taught by the *Buddha Shakyamuni* whilst taking the form of diverse **meditational deities**. See **Four Classes of Tantra**.

Tantrayana (skrt.) རྒྱུད་ཀྱི་ཐེག་པ་ / སྔགས་ཀྱི་ཐེག་པ་ rgyud kyi theg pa/sngags kyi theg pa *tantrayāna/mantrayāna*

Tantrayana and *sutrayana* are the two basic subdivisions of the vehicle or systematisation of the path to **buddhahood**. The former is based on the *tantra*-texts and their underlying **three continua** of ground, path and result. *Tantrayana* is said to be superior to *sutrayana* on account of its 'four complete purities'. These are the complete purity of: 1) the environment; 2) the body; 3) resources; and 4) deeds. By naturally dissolving into **emptiness** all perceptions and conceptions of ordinariness, in relation to the environment, body, resources and deeds, the **meditator** assimilates the experiences of the resultant **buddhahood** whilst on the path. *Tantrayana* is also called *Vajrayana* because this path is characterised by the **realisation** of the indestructible **reality** of *buddha*-**body, speech** and **mind** at the subtlest energy level. It is also known as *Mantrayana* because engaging in this path ensures the protection of the **mind** from dualistic perceptions and conceptions. See **Tantra** and **Sutrayana**.

Tara (skrt.) སྒྲོལ་མ་ sgrol ma *Tārā*

A female **meditational deity** who is regarded as the embodiment of all the *buddhas*' (the fully enlightened **mind's**) enlightened activity. Naturally, therefore, she is strongly associated with both **pristine cognition** and **compassion** and is often spoken of as the 'mother' of all the *buddhas*. As an object of propitiation, she is said to protect from the eight 'great fears', including fear of the **elements**, worldly tragedies and so forth. There are many different aspects of *Tara*, and an enumeration of twenty-one aspects in the *tantric* Buddhist pantheon is well documented in prayers, liturgies, sculpture and painting. The most popular of these are Green *Tara* (mainly associated with protection) and White *Tara* (often associated with healing and longevity practices). Practices associated with *Tara* are widespread among all the four main traditions of **Tibetan Buddhism**, and amongst the laity the more common of *Tara's* verse praises are known by heart. *Tara* literally means 'saviouress' or 'she who liberates'. See **Cintamani Tara**.

Tarig (tib.) ཏྟགས་རིགས་ rtags rigs *liṅgayukti*

The study of signs *(linga)* and reasoning *(yukti)*, or *rtags-rigs* (pronounced 'tarig'), is usually undertaken in the Tibetan monastic universities as a preliminary to higher studies of logic and **epistemology**. *Tarig* covers such topics as: establishing the validity of an argument, types of **valid reasoning**, and the fundamental logical principles that govern the nature of proofs. The curriculum of *tarig* was essentially designed as an introduction to logical terminology and the complex concepts associated with this terminology. All students in a Tibetan monastic university are trained in *tarig* from an early age, before they begin their actual study of philosophy. The study of *tarig* follows on from the study of *dura* (**Collected Topics**). As with the study of *dura*, the emphasis is on assisting students to develop a sharp, enquiring, analytical and logical **mind**. See **Collected Topics**.

Tashilhunpo (tib.) བཀྲ་ཤིས་ལྷུན་པོ་ bkra shis lhun po

The seat of the **Panchen Lama** in *Shigatse*, capital city of the **Tsang** province of Tibet. Founded by the First **Dalai Lama**, *Gedun Drup* in 1447, **Tashilhunpo** became the largest monastery in **Tsang** and an important philosophical learning centre. Its reputation as a seat of learning grew to the extent that it is often classed alongside **Sera**, **Drepung** and **Ganden** as one of the four great **Gelug** monastic universities of **Utsang**.

Tathagata (skrt.) དེ་བཞིན་གཤེགས་པ་ de bzhin gshegs pa *tathāgata*

A synonym for '**Buddha**,' used frequently in the **sutras**. *Tatha* literally means 'thus' and *gata*, 'gone' or 'departed'. The word is interpreted in different ways, corresponding to the different classes of **Mahayana sutras** and **tantras**, but in general it is defined as 'one who has departed in the wake of the conquerors of the past', or as 'one who has manifested the great **enlightenment** dependent on the **reality** that does not abide in the two extremes of existence and quiescence'. See **Buddha**.

Tathagatagarbha (skrt.) བདེ་གཤེགས་སྙིང་པོ་ bde gshegs snying po *tathāgatagarbha*

The 'nucleus of the **tathagata**' (*tathagatagarbha*) refers to the seed of **Buddhahood** or **buddha**-**nature**, present but uncultivated in the mental continuum of all **sentient beings**, and without which the attainment of **enlightenment** or **buddhahood** would be impossible. This seed of **buddhahood** is said to be partially purified by **arhats** and **pratyekabuddhas**, and to be fully manifested by **bodhisattvas** of the highest level or by perfect **buddhas**. **Tathagatagarbha** is also the title of a famous **Mahayana sutra**, which discusses the subject of **buddha-nature** in detail, drawing analogies with illustrative examples. Many, though not all, schools consider the class of **tathagatagarbha sutras**, represented by this and related texts, to belong to the **sutras** of the 'third **turning of the** doctrinal **wheel**', and so to expound the thorough analysis of **enlightened attributes**. The **tathagatagarbha sutras** are the primary sourcesfor **Maitreya's** MAHAYANOTTARA-TANTRASHASTRA, and the **view** of extraneous **emptiness**, **shentong** (*gzhan-stong*). In Tibet, during the fourteenth century, this **view** was developed in particular by the *Jonang* school, under the influence of the **Kalacakra** master *Dolpo Sherab Gyaltsen* and *Kunpang Thukje Tsondru*. See **Buddha-Nature** and **Shentong**.

Ten Aspects of Knowledge རིག་གནས་བཅུ་ rig gnas bcu *daśavidyā*

A classical Indian division of **knowledge** into ten disciplines of academic scholarship. The ten fields of **knowledge** broadly fall into two separate but inter-related groups known as: a) the five

major sciences and b) the five minor sciences. The five major sciences are: 1) medicine; 2) visual arts and craftsmanship; 3) logic and **epistemology**; 4) grammar; and 5) Buddhist philosophy/inner science. The five minor ones are: 1) poetry; 2) synonymics; 3) composition; 4) drama; and 5) **astrology**. The *Sanskrit* word for a scholar, *pandita*, implies that one is learned in the five major sciences or **knowledge**s. See **Knowledge**.

Ten Non-Virtues མི་དགེ་བ་བཅུ་ mi dge ba bcu *daśakuśalāni*

See **Non-Virtue**.

TENGYUR (tib.) བསྟན་འགྱུར་ bstan 'gyur

The Tibetan Buddhist Canon comprises both the *Kangyur*, which contains the translated transmitted **precepts** of the *Buddha Shakyamuni (pravacana)*, and the ***TENGYUR***, which contains authoritative commentarial works by classical Indian scholars related to these texts. ***TENGYUR*** literally means the 'translated commentarial works'. Like the ***KANGYUR***, this collection of classical Indian materials was compiled by the great Tibetan encyclopaedist and scholar *Buton Rinchen Drup*. See ***KANGYUR***.

Terma (tib.) གཏེར་མ་ gter ma *nidhi*

The texts and oral teachings of Buddhism have been handed down in two distinct ways: through a 'distant oral **lineage**', i.e., handed down from one generation to the next (*ring-brgyud bka'-ma*) and through a 'close **lineage** of revealed teachings', which are believed to have a more immediate impact, i.e., to be more relevant to a particular time (*nye-brgyud gter-ma*). The *Sanskrit nidhi* (Tib. *gter-ma*), translated in English as 'treasure' or 'revealed teaching' (*gter-chos*), refers to those texts and sacred objects which were concealed in the past in order that they might be protected and revealed in the future for the benefit of posterity. The tradition of concealing texts as treasure is extremely ancient in India and China. Within **Indian Buddhism**, it is well known that the *Prajnaparamita sutras* are said to have been revealed when *Nagarjuna* received them in the form of treasure from the *nagas*. A recension of the *sadhana* class of *Mahayoga tantras* is also said to have been revealed to eight great masters, including *Nagarjuna*, in the *Sitavana* charnel ground near *Bodhgaya*. In Tibet, the tradition of the treasures was introduced by *Padmasambhava* and his students, who concealed texts and sacred objects at geomantic power points on the landscape, entrusting them to their respective custodians or treasure-lords (*gter-bdag*) or **dakinis** for safe-keeping, with the prediction that these would be discovered at some future time by a prophesied treasure-finder (*gter-ston*). Accordingly, it is believed that the students of *Padmasambhava* have continued to emanate in the forms of treasure-finders in successive centuries in order to reveal these treasure-doctrines. Other kinds of treasure-doctrine revealed directly from the enlightened intention of *buddha-mind* in a telepathic manner (*dgongs-gter*), or in a pure visionary experience (*dag-snang*) are also recognised. There are many such **lineages** extant at the present day, and these are maintained mostly, but by no means exclusively, by the *Nyingma* school.

Terton (tib.) གཏེར་སྟོན་ gter ston

The *tantric* master who successfully reveals a hidden treasure-text or sacred object, in full accordance with the prophesies made by the original master who hid the scripture. *Terton* literally means 'treasure-finder'. See **Terma**.

Thangka (tib.) ཐང་ཀ་ thang ka

A traditional Tibetan painting which may include *buddhas*, *bodhisattvas*, **meditational deities**, great teachers, *mandalas* and so forth. A *thangka* is usually framed in a rich colourful silk brocade and has a thin silk veil covering the front surface.

Tharpa (tib.) ཐར་པ་ thar pa *mokṣa*

See **Liberation**.

Theravada (pali) གནས་བརྟན་པའི་སྡེ་ gnas brtan pa' sde *Sthavīravāda*

Theravada is the *Pali* equivalent of the **Sanskrit** term *Sthaviravāda*, or 'way expounded by the elders', which is one of the four primary *Vinaya* orders of the ancient Indian *Hinayana*. The *Theravada* tradition is maintained principally in Thailand, Burma, Cambodia and Sri Lanka, and its canon is fully extant in Pali. See **Hinayana, Mahayana, Sutra** and **Vinaya**.

Theravadin (pali) གནས་བརྟན་པའི་སྡེ་པ་ gnas brtan pa' sde pa *Sthaviravādin*

A follower of the *Theravada* school

THIRTEEN GOLDEN DHARMAS གསེར་ཆོས་བཅུ་གསུམ་ gser chos bcu gsum

The teachings of the *Tsharpa* tradition of the **Sakya** school of **Tibetan Buddhism**, which are closely associated with the monastery at *Chakpori*. The **THIRTEEN GOLDEN DHARMAS** are a collection of *sadhana* cycles comprising: the *TRILOGY OF KHECARI* (*mkha'-spyod skor gsum*), the *TRILOGY OF THE GREAT RED ONE* (*dmar-chen skor gsum*), the *TRILOGY OF THE SMALL RED ONE* (*dmar-chung skor gsum*), the *CHIME DORJE LHAMO*, *RED JAMBHALA*, *SIMHAVAKTRA*, and *BLACK MANJUSHRI*.

Thirty Five Buddhas of Confession ལྟུང་བཤགས་ཀྱི་ལྷ་སོ་ལྔ་ ltung bshags kyi lha so lnga

Thirty-five *buddhas* associated with a specific practice of purifying **non-virtuous** habits. This practice of confession involves recitation of the names of each of the *buddhas* and paying homage to them (usually enacted in conjunction with physical prostrations). The practice is based on a *Mahayana sutra* called the '*SUTRA OF THE THREE AGGREGATES*' (*TRISKANDHAKA*).

Thirty Seven Factors of Buddhahood བྱང་ཕྱོགས་སོ་བདུན་ byang phyogs so bdun *saptatriṃśabodhipakṣadharma*

More usually rendered as the '**thirty-seven** aspects of the path to **enlightenment**' (*bodhipakshadharma*), these are the sequential aspects of the path experienced in the course of attaining **enlightenment**. Although associated with both *Hinayana* and *Mahayana* Buddhism, this division of the path into **thirty-seven**

factors or aspects is more common in the *Hinayana* literature. The **thirty-seven factors** are grouped under seven main headings which in turn correspond to specific stages of the five paths to *buddha*hood. See **Grounds and Paths**. The seven sequential groups are: 1) the **four mindfulnesses**; 2) the four correct **renunciation**s; 3) the four supports for miraculous ability; 4) the five faculties; 5) the five powers; 6) the seven branches of **enlightenment**; and 7) the noble eightfold path.

THIRTY SEVEN PRACTICES OF A BODHISATTVA རྒྱལ་སྲས་ལག་ལེན་སོ་བདུན་མ་ rgyal sras lag len so bdun ma

A set of practices which embraces all the essential aspects of the *bodhisattva's* conduct and path to full **enlightenment**. This set of **thirty-seven practices** is based on a text written by the great Tibetan *bodhisattva Ngulchu Thogme Zangpo* entitled *THE THIRTY-SEVEN PRACTICES OF A BODHISATTVA (RGYAL-SRAS LAG-LEN SO-BDUN-MA)*. Commentaries based on this text are popular among all four schools of **Tibetan Buddhism** and teaching, based on this text, is often given as a preliminary to advanced *tantric* discourse.

Thought Transformation བློ་སྦྱོང་ blo sbyong

See **Lojong**.

Three Baskets སྡེ་སྣོད་གསུམ་ sde snod gsum *tripiṭaka*

See under **Three Higher Trainings**.

Three Continua རྒྱུད་གསུམ་ rgyud gsum

The **three continua** of ground, path and result, through which the mental continuum progresses to the full **realisation** of *buddha*hood, as expounded in the *tantra*-texts. See **Tantra**. There is also a specific teaching with this title in the **'Path and its Fruit'** *(lam-'bras)* literature of the *Sakya* school.

THREE ESSENTIAL MOMENTS སྙིང་པོའི་སྐབས་གསུམ་ snying po'i skabs gsum

A unique meditative practice related to the **transference of consciousness** to the **pure realm** of *Sukhavati*. The manual on this practice was composed by the First *Dalai Lama*, *Gedun Drup*, and it deals in a systematic order with the appropriate practices related to the transformation of three stages of our existence in *samsara*, namely: death, the **intermediate state** and **rebirth**. These three periods in our existence are called the '**three essential moments**', and a successful utilisation of these three phases can greatly enhance progress on the spiritual path. The three associated practices to be undertaken at these '**three essential moments**' are: 1) the **transference of consciousness** at the time of death; 2) the blending of all appearances with emptiness during the **intermediate state**; and 3) meditating on **deity *yoga*** when alive.

Three Higher Trainings ལྷག་པའི་བསླབ་པ་གསུམ་ lhag pa'i bslab pa gsum *triśikṣā*

A system of classification common to both *Hinayana* and *Mahayana* Buddhism, the **three higher trainings** provide a framework which encompasses the entire range of spiritual practice in the Buddhist tradition. The three trainings are: 1) higher training in **ethics**; 2) higher training in **meditation**; and 3) higher training in **discriminative awareness** (*prajna*). This classification of the Buddhist path into three trainings is related to the threefold scriptural division of the

Buddha Shakyamuni's discourses technically known as the *Tripitaka* or the 'three baskets'. The scriptural category which is primarily concerned with the higher training in **ethics** is the *Vinaya* pitaka; the one related to **meditation**, the *Sutra* pitaka; and the category dealing principally with discriminative awareness, the *Abhidharma* pitaka.

Three Humours ཉེས་པ་གསུམ་ nyes pa gsum *tridoṣa*

See **Humours**.

Three (Precious) Jewels དཀོན་མཆོག་གསུམ་ dkon mchog gsum *triratna*

The *buddha*, or expression of the **ultimate** nature; *dharma*, the true path and the consequent states of freedom it leads to; and *sangha*, the ideal spiritual community. These three are regarded as the perfect objects in which **refuge** can be sought from the unsatisfactory nature of life in **cyclic existence** in general, and particularly from the potential **suffering** of unfavourable future existences. The three objects are called 'precious jewels' because, like **wish-fulfilling jewels,** in their metaphorical sense, they possess the capacity to provide protection from the perils of life within **cyclic existence**. See **Refuge**.

Three Natures མཚན་ཉིད་གསུམ་/ ངོ་བོ་ཉིད་གསུམ་ mtshan nyid gsum/ngo bo nyid gsum *trilakṣaṇa/trisvabhāva*

A philosophical concept developed by both the *Cittamatra* and *Tathagatagarbha* schools. The concept of the **three natures,** which is discussed in *sutras* representative of the third **turning of the** doctrinal **wheel**, embraces the entire expanse of *samsara* and *nirvana*, and provides a metaphysical framework for the detailed analysis of all phenomena and **enlightened attributes**. According to the *Cittamatra* school all things can be analysed according to these **three natures** or categories, namely: 1) the imaginary (*parikalpita*), which includes the nominal (names and symbols) and the delimited (mistaken view of **self** with respect to the individual and phenomena); 2) the dependent (*paratantra*), which includes impure dependence i.e., **aggregates** *(skandha)*, **elements** *(dhatu)*, sensory activity fields *(ayatana)*, etc. and pure dependence, i.e., *buddha*-attributes; and 3) the absolute or thoroughly established phenomena (*parinispanna*), which includes **emptiness** (*dharmadhatu*) and the irreversible states of cessation. According to the *Tathagatagarbha* school, the imaginary nature and impure dependent nature are exactly the same, but the pure dependent nature is intrinsic **emptiness** or *rangtong* (the lack of **inherent existence** in imaginary phenomena) rather than *buddha*-attributes, and the absolute nature is the *buddha*-attributes themselves which are extraneously empty (*shentong*) of the dependent nature. Scholars sometimes refer to the former (*Cittamatra*) view as the 'pivotal model' of the **three natures** because the transformation of the imaginary into the absolute is effected by a pivotal movement from the impure dependence of

aggregates etc. to the pure dependence of *buddha*-attributes, while the latter (*Tathagatagarbha*) view is called the 'pyramidal model' because, in succession, the pure dependent nature is experienced as the intrinsic **emptiness** of the imaginary and the absolute nature as the extraneous **emptiness** of the dependent, i.e., intrinsic **emptiness** and its scope. In other words, the *Cittamatrin* views *buddha*-attributes as dependent while the adherent of the *Tathagatagarbha* school views them as absolute.

Three Poisons ད᠋ུག་གསུམ་ dug gsum

A term used to describe the three primary **dissonant emotions**: **attachment**, **hatred**/aversion and **delusion** (as to the true nature of **reality**). Amongst the **dissonant emotions** these three are considered the most fundamental and deeply rooted in the **minds** of all ordinary **sentient beings**. Together with pride, mundane ambition or envy, and wrong views they constitute the category of **mental factors** known as 'the six root **dissonant emotions**'.

THREE PRINCIPAL ASPECTS OF THE PATH ལམ་གྱི་གཙོ་བོ་རྣམ་གསུམ་ lam gyi gtso bo rnam gsum

Renunciation, *bodhicitta* and the correct **view** of **emptiness**. The practice of these three essential aspects of the path embraces the entire process of mental training and development towards fulfilling the ultimate aim of a *bodhisattva*, i.e., to attain *buddha*hood for the sake of all beings. The tradition of categorising all the aspects of the path within these three principal topics of meditative practice was first initiated by the founder of the *Gelug* school, *Tsong Khapa*. This succinct approach and also the term 'the three principal aspects of the path' developed from a letter written in verse by *Tsong Khapa* to one of his disciples outlining the essential methods for training the **mind**. The letter was entitled '*THE THREE PRINCIPAL ASPECTS OF THE PATH*' (*LAM-GYI GTSO-BO RNAM-PA GSUM*).

Three Scopes སྐྱེས་བུ་གསུམ་ skyes bu gsum

A classification of spiritual trainees according to three distinct classes of natural inclination and mental capacity. It was the great Indian master *Atisha* who first coined the term *skyes-bu gsum*, the '**three scopes**' or the 'trainees of three capacities' in the context of *Lamrim*. The **three scopes** refer to the initial, middling and great capacities of **mind**. A trainee is defined as being of initial scope or capacity if the primary motivation in spiritual practice is to obtain a favourable existence in the next life; as middling if the primary aim is to attain an individual **liberation** from **cyclic existence**; and great if the principal motivation is to attain complete *buddha*hood for the benefit of all beings. The tradition of outlining the essential practices of the path within the framework of these **three scopes** developed first from *Atisha's* celebrated work the *THE LAMP FOR THE PATH TO ENLIGHTENMENT* (*BODHIPATHAPRADIPA*). The distinction between superior, mediocre and inferior capacities (*dbang-po mtho-'bring-mtha' gsum*) is also generally made in other commentarial works where the scopes are related to diverse capacities.

Three Vehicles ཐེག་པ་གསུམ་ theg pa gsum *triyāna*

In a three-fold division of the vehicles (*yana*), the *Hinayana* is subdivided into the vehicle of *shravakas* and the vehicle of *pratyekabuddhas*, while the third vehicle is the *Mahayana*. See **Yanas**, **Shravaka**, and **Pratyekabuddha**.

Three Visions སྣང་བ་གསུམ་ snang ba gsum

The foundational practices based on the *sutras*, a prerequisite to the practice of *tantra*, according to the unique **Path and Fruit** (*lam-'bras*) instructions of the **Sakya** tradition. The **three 'visions'** or 'perspectives' are: 1) an impure perspective (*ma-dag-pa'i snang-ba*); 2) the perspective of an experienced *yogin* or *yogini* (*rnal-'byor nyams-kyi snang-ba*); and 3) the pure perspective (*dag-pa'i snang-ba*). The first phase of the path includes such **preliminary practices** (*sngon-'gro*) as **meditation** on the unsatisfactory nature of life in **cyclic existence**, developing conviction as to the validity of the laws of ***karma***, etc. The second phase of the path includes training in the cultivation of **love**, **compassion** and ***bodhicitta***; and the third stage includes reflection on the exalted qualities of the fully **enlightened *buddhas***.

Throneholder ཁྲི་འཛིན་ khri 'dzin

See **Tripa**.

TIBETAN BOOK OF THE DEAD བར་དོ་ཐོས་གྲོལ་ bar do thos grol

More accurately rendered in English as the '*GREAT LIBERATION BY HEARING IN THE INTERMEDIATE STATE*', the ***TIBETAN BOOK OF THE DEAD*** is a well-known guidebook, the recitation of which is said to assist the dying to take advantage of the experiences of death, actual **reality** (**inner radiance/clear light** and the appearance of the **peaceful and wrathful deities**), and the processes preceding **rebirth**, as they arise in succession. It is a section of the *NATURAL LIBERATION OF THE ENLIGHTENED INTENTION OF THE PEACEFUL AND WRATHFUL DEITIES* (*ZHI-KHRO DGONGS-PA RANG-GROL*), a text concerning the practices pertaining to the hundred **Peaceful and Wrathful Deities**, which are desrcibed in the fundamental ***GUHYAGARBHA TANTRA***. This text is said to have been concealed by ***Padmasambhava*** as *gter-ma* during the eighth century, and to have been discovered subsequently in the fourteenth century by *Karma Lingpa*. See **Bardo, Chikai Bardo, Chonyi Bardo, Sidpa Bardo**, and **Terma**.

Tibetan Buddhism བོད་ཀྱི་ནང་པའི་གྲུབ་མཐའ་ bod kyi nang pa'i grub mtha'

The form of Buddhism which evolved in Tibet following the gradual introduction of Buddhist teachings into that country from the seventh century onwards. **Tibetan Buddhism** is characterised by its successful integration of all three primary facets of Buddhist thought and practice. That is to say that the basic *shravaka* practices as taught in the ***Hinayana sutras***, the extensive ***bodhisattva*** principles of the ***Mahayana sutras***, and the profound and sophisticated paths of the ***Mahayana tantras*** are all integrated into graduated practice systems. Based on the early and later dissemination of Buddhism in Tibet, **Tibetan Buddhism** developed into four main schools: ***Nyingma, Kagyu, Sakya*** and ***Gelug***.

Tilbupa (tib.) དྲིལ་བུ་པ་ dril bu pa *Gaṇṭhapāda*

The Tibetan equivalent of *Ganthapada*, a great **lineage** master of classical India and one of the human progenitors of the **CAKRASAMVARA TANTRAS**. The *Ganthapada* tradition of **Cakrasamvara** evolved from his unique interpretation of this cycle, based on his own mystical meditative experiences.

Tilopa (skrt.) ཏི་ལོ་པ་ ti lo pa *Tilopāda*

One of the eighty-four *mahasiddhas* of ancient India and the *guru* of the great scholar and **meditator Naropa**. *Tilopa* is regarded as the first human holder of the *Dagpo Kagyu* **lineage**, having received this **lineage** of esoteric instructions directly from the primordial *buddha*, *Vajradhara*.

Tonglen (tib.)

See **Giving and Taking**.

Torma (tib.) གཏོར་མ་ gtor ma *bali*

A ritual cake usually made from dough and often decorated with colourful butter sculptures. *Tormas* can be of various shapes and sizes and they have different symbolic functions. Sometimes they are embodiments of the **meditational deities** associated with particular ritual practices, or they may be food **offerings** made to various **deities** or **protectors** visualised in the context of **meditation**. Yet again, *tormas* may act as physical symbols into which diverse aspects of negativity are absorbed, transformed, and ejected through ritual practices.

Transference of Consciousness (རྣམ་ཤེས་གོང་དུ་) འཕོ་བ་ (rnam shes gong du) 'pho ba *(vijñāna) saṃkrānti*

See **Phowa**.

Transmission ལུང་/ བརྒྱུད་པ་ lung/brgyud pa *āgama/paraṃparā*

In Buddhism, the *dharma* is considered in terms of either its **realisation** (*adhigama*) or authoritative **transmission** (*agama*). The latter comprises the oral teachings and scriptures delivered by the *buddhas*, as well as the related commentaries, which have been transmitted in an uninterrupted **lineage** or succession from ancient times. In **Tibetan Buddhism**, it is regarded as essential that a **transmission** of both the text and its oral **commentary** is formally received from an authoritative **lineage**-holder, if any significant spiritual experience is to be cultivated, since a mere theoretical understanding of these topics is not regarded as sufficient.

TREASURY OF KNOWLEDGE ཤེས་བྱ་མཛོད་ shes bya mdzod

A three-volume encyclopaedia of **Tibetan Buddhism** written by *Jamgon Kongtrul Yonten Gyatso* in 1864. The encyclopaedia is divided into ten main sections dealing with the following ten topics: 1) cosmological systems; 2) appearance of specific *buddhas* within these cosmological systems; 3) the philosophical structures of Buddhism; 4) history of the propagation of the *sutras, tantras* and five sciences; 5) analysis of the three kinds of **vows** associated with higher **ethics**; 6) study of the sciences, vehicles and so forth; 7) development of higher discriminative awareness (*prajna*) based on reflection; 8) attainment of higher contemplation (*samadhi*) based on **meditation**; 9) traversal of the *bodhisattva* levels

Khon Konchok Gyalpo (founder of Sakya monastery, Tibet, in 1073)

The First Karmapa, *Dusum Khyenpa*

and paths based on spiritual **realisation** and experiential cultivation; and 10) the result which is conclusive **liberation** or *buddha*hood.

Tripa (tib.) ཁྲི་པ་ khri pa

A general term used in conjunction with the title of high spiritual offices, which denotes that the so-titled person is the acting incumbent. For example, to emphasise that someone is the acting **abbot** of a monastery he will be called *Khenpo tripa*. *Tripa* literally means the 'present throne holder' or the 'incumbent who occupies the chair'.

Tripitaka (skrt.) སྡེ་སྣོད་གསུམ་ sde snod gsum *tripiṭaka*

See **Three Higher Trainings**.

Trishiksa (skrt.) བསླབ་པ་གསུམ་ bslab pa gsum *triśikṣā*

See **Three Higher Trainings**.

Trisong Detsen (tib.) ཁྲི་སྲོང་ལྡེ་བཙན་ khri srong lde btsan

The thirty-eighth king of Tibet, and son of King *Tride Tsukten* and the Chinese princess *Jingcheng*. Despite his accession to the throne at a tender age and the opposition of ministers such as *Mazhang* and *Nanam* who were **Bon** sympathisers, he established Buddhism as the state religion of Tibet. In the early years of his reign he also engaged in military campaigns against *Tazik*, *Zahor* and the *Tang* dynasty of China, but following the peace treaty of *Qing Shui Xian* in 783 he devoted his energies to the propagation of Buddhism. He invited both **Shantarakshita** and **Padmasambhava** to construct Tibet's first monastery at **Samye** and to transmit the diverse Indian lineages of the *vinaya*, *sutras* and *tantras*. He became a realised practitioner of the *tantras* in his own right, under the guidance of **Padmasambhava**, and actively sponsored the education and projects of his highly organised translation teams.

Triyana (skrt.) ཐེག་པ་གསུམ་ theg pa gsum *triyāna*

See **Three Vehicles**.

Trizin (tib.) ཁྲི་འཛིན་ khri 'dzin

A synonym of *tripa*. See **Tripa**.

Truth བདེན་པ་ bden pa *satya*

A term in Buddhism which may denote either the **four noble truths** as expounded in *sutras* of the first turning, or the **two truths** (relative/conventional and **ultimate**/absolute) which are the subject of discussion in *Mahayana* texts. See **Two Truths**.

Truth Body ཆོས་སྐུ་ chos sku *dharmakāya*

See **Dharmakaya**.

Tsalung (tib.) རྩ་རླུང་ rtsa rlung *nāḍī/vāyu*

The yogic practices of the perfection/**completion stage**, through which the energy **channels** are refined and control of the **winds** and seminal points within the body is matured. See **Bindu, Cakra, Channels,** and **Winds**.

Tsang (tib.) གཙང་ gtsang

The province to the west of Central Tibet, which has *Shigatse* as its capital, and occupies the regions north and south of the *Brahmaputra* to the west of its confluence with the *Kyichu*, including the fertile *Nyangchu* river valley. The capital of *Tsang* is *Shigatse*, a former capital of Tibet and the location of *Tashilhunpo*, the seat of the *Panchen Lamas*. *Gyangtse* is the second city of the province.

Tsharpa (tib.) ཚར་པ་ tshar pa

One of the sub-schools of the *Sakya* tradition. See **Thirteen Golden Dharmas**.

Tsenshab (tib.) མཚན་ཞབས་ mtshan zhabs

A spiritual and philosophical assistant to a high *lama*, such as the *Dalai Lama*. *Tsenshab* are highly qualified scholars who serve as spiritual colleagues to high *lamas* and assist in their study of philosophy, literature, poetry and other related topics. In the case of the *Dalai Lama, Tsenshab* have official rank in the Tibetan government and, in some cases, are later elevated to the esteemed position of a tutor.

Tsepon (tib.) ཙིས་དཔོན་ rtsis dpon

A government official who is the 'chancellor of the exchequer'.

Tsog (tib.) ཚོགས་ tshogs *sambhāra/gaṇa*

The Tibetan word '*tshogs*' translates either the *Sanskrit* *sambhara* or *gana*. In the former case it indicates 'provisions' or 'accumulations', and in the latter case it is an abbreviation for *ganacakra (tshogs-kyi 'khor-lo)*, meaning 'feast-**offering**'. In the sense of *sambhara*, the term refers to the '**two accumulations** or provisions of **merit** (*punya*) and **pristine cognition** (*jnana*), which are gathered on the path to **liberation**. According to the *sutras*, these are gathered sequentially over an inestimable period of time (three times ten to the power of fifty-seven years). The fulfilment of the '**two accumulations**' constitutes the fruition of the entire *Mahayana* path to **enlightenment**, resulting in the attainment of the *rupakaya* and the *dharmakaya* respectively. In the latter sense of the term (*ganacakra*), in the context of *tantric* practice, the rituals and *mandala* of feast-**offerings** are regarded as an indispensable means for conferring accomplishment and pacifying obstacles. There are three aspects to the feast-**offering**: 1) the gathering of fortunate *yogins* and *yoginis* who participate in the feast; 2) the outer, inner and secret sacraments of the ritual which are offered and consumed during the feast; and 3) the *mandalas* of *buddha*-**body** and *buddha*-**mind**, whether actual or visualised, who receive the **offerings** and bring the ritual to its successful conclusion. The overall purpose is to distribute **merit** (*punya*) and **pristine cognition** (*jnana*) in the context of a specific *tantric* ritual.

Tsong Khapa (tib.) ཙོང་ཁ་པ་ tsong kha pa

(1357-1419) One of the greatest philosophers of Tibet and the founder of the

Gelug school and *Ganden* monastic university. Born in the *Tsongchu* valley in north-eastern *Amdo*, he travelled to Central Tibet at an early age and studied extensively under the greatest living masters of all the traditions, especially those of the *Kadam* and *Sakya* schools, including *Remdawa*. *Tsong Khapa* is renowned as an emanation of *Manjushri*, and is said to have actually appeared as *Manjushri* in five different visionary forms. His main contribution lies in his successful marriage of profound meditative spirituality and meticulous logic. He clarified a number of spiritual and philosophical misconceptions concerning *Nagarjuna's* doctrine of **emptiness** and the fundamental principles of *tantra*-texts such as *GUHYASAMAJA* and *CAKRASAMVARA*. In addition he emphasised the indispensability of a pure ethical discipline as the foundation for a successful spiritual training and re-instituted a comprehensive tradition of *Vinaya* practice amongst his followers. His works run into eighteen volumes, covering the full array of Buddhist thought and practice, and include his most celebrated two works, *THE GREAT EXPOSITION OF THE STAGES OF THE PATH TO* **ENLIGHTENMENT** *(LAM-RIM CHEN-MO)* and *THE GREAT EXPOSITION OF* **TANTRA** *(SNGAGS-RIM CHEN-MO)*.

Tsurphu (tib.) མཚུར་ཕུ་ mtshur phu

An important monastery of the *Kagyu* tradition situated in a side-valley of the *Tholung* river, north-east of *Lhasa*. Founded by the first *Karmapa Dusum Khyenpa* in 1189, *Tsurphu* is the seat of both the *Karmapa* and his **regent** *Gyaltsab Rinpoche*. It is one of the two principal monasteries of the *Karma Kagyu* sub-division of the *Kagyu* school, the other being *Karma Gon* in southern *Nangchen*, Eastern Tibet.

Tulku (tib.) སྤྲུལ་སྐུ་ sprul sku *nirmāṇakāya*

Literally meaning the 'emanational body' of a *buddha*, the term is used in two related but distinct senses. In its philosophical and classical usage it refers to *Nirmanakaya*, the emanation body of a *buddha*. See **Nirmanakaya**. However, based on this concept of emanation, a different usage developed in Tibet following the inception of a tradition to recognise formally the incarnations of high *lamas* after their death. The first such *tulku* to be given formal recognition was *Karma Pakshi*, the Second *Karmapa*. There exist numerous methods for determining the authenticity of such **reincarnations**; principal among these being observations based on the mystical experiences of high *lamas*, consultation with **oracles**, various forms of **divination**, and testing of the infant candidate in a process whereby the articles belonging to the past incarnation are presented, mixed with others, for successful identification. Depending upon the position of the departed *lama* within the spiritual hierarchy the complexity of the examination procedures may vary. The *Dalai Lama* is a classic example of such a **reincarnate** *lama*.

Tummo (tib.) གཏུམ་མོ་ gtum mo *caṇḍāli*

Literally meaning 'the Fierce One' it is the name of an energy

channel connected with the *cakra* of the heart-centre inside the body. In terms of practice, *gtum-mo* (pronounced *'tummo')* is generally associated with and translated as 'inner heat', a reference to the perfection stage practice which utilises the energy **channels**, currents and seminal points to generate the sensation of heat within the body. The successful practice of *tummo* is said to ignite the bliss which burns away all delusive cognitive states and allows the co-emergent **pristine cognition** of bliss and **emptiness** to manifest. See *SIX YOGAS OF NAROPA* and *SIX YOGAS OF NIGUMA*.

Turning of the Wheel ཆོས་འཁོར་བསྐོར་བ་ chos 'khor bskor ba
dharmacakrapravartaṇa

See **Dharmacakra**.

Tushita (skrt.) དགའ་ལྡན་ dga' ldan *Tuṣita*

The **pure realm** of the *Buddha Maitreya*. *Tushita* is also the name given to one of the *deva* realms in the **desire realm**. In the second usage, *Tushita* refers to a celestial realm which is part of the **karmically** conditioned **cycle of existence**. See **Pure Realm**.

Twelve Deeds of the Buddha མཛད་པ་བཅུ་གཉིས་ mdzad pa bcu gnyis
dvādaśākārya

The classical literature on the life of the *Buddha Shakyamuni* speaks of the twelve principal deeds of the *Buddha*. These are: 1) descending from the celestial realm of *Tushita*; 2) entering the mother's womb; 3) taking birth; 4) displaying mastery in worldly arts and skills; 5) enjoying the women of the harem; 6) renouncing the worldly way of life; 7) undergoing severe physical penances; 8) meditating under the *Bodhi* Tree; 9) overcoming the forces of evil (*mara*); 10) attaining *buddha*hood; 11) **turning the wheel** of *dharma*; and 12) entering the peaceful state of final *nirvana*.

Twelve Links (རྟེན་འབྲེལ་གྱི་) ཡན་ལག་བཅུ་གཉིས་ (rten 'bral gyi) yan lag bcu gnyis
dvādaśāṅga(pratītyasamutpāda)

As expounded in a number of *sutras* including the *PRATITYASAMUTPADAVI-BHANGANIRDESA* which is contained in the *Kangyur*, the doctrine of **dependent origination** (*pratityasamutpada*) explains the **twelve links** in a chain which constitute the process through which the external world and the **sentient beings** within it revolve in a **cycle of existence** propelled by **karmic** propensities and their interaction with **dissonant emotions** and conditions. The **twelve links** are: 1) **fundamental ignorance**; 2) habit-forming propensities (*samskara*); 3) **consciousness**; 4) name and form; 5) sensory fields; 6) contact; 7) sensations; 8) **attachment**; 9) grasping; 10) maturation toward **rebirth**; 11) birth; and 12) aging and death. Although, in the ultimate sense there is no beginning to the continuum of **mind**, a relative beginning can be spoken of on the basis of a single instance of **rebirth** in *samsara*. Every instance of birth in *samsara* must have a cause and such causes are ultimately rooted in our **fundamental ignorance**, which misapprehends the true nature of **reality**. **Ignorance** gives rise to habit-forming propensities, which in turn give rise to the chain reaction of the other links. For an ordinary **sentient being** all the **twelve links** are interconnected and each component of the chain contributes to the perpetuation of the cycle. It is only through a deliberate reversal of the **fundamental ignorance** (*avidya*) that one can succeed in bringing the whole cycle to an end. Habit-forming propensities (*samskara*) are stored in the **consciousness** (*vijnana*); name and form (*namarupa*) refer to the psycho-physical **aggregates** which are products of that dualising **consciousness**, and which manifest during the post-conception period; sensory fields (*ayatana*) provide the subjective and objective framework for sensory activity in its initial stages of development; contact (*sparsha*) refers to the maturation of sensory perception which occurs as an unborn child develops a sensitivity to its environment inside the womb; sensation (*vedana*), **attachment** (*trishna*), grasping (*adana*), maturation toward **rebirth** (*bhava*) - these three together indicate the process through which birth (*jati*) actually occurs, and these in turn lead to old age and death (*jaramarana*). The reversal of the **twelve links** is a feature of the meditative path followed by ***pratyekabuddhas***, particularly in the awesome setting of a charnel ground. See **Dependent Origination**.

Twenty One Categories of Uncontaminated Wisdom

ཟག་མེད་ཡེ་ཤེས་སྡེ་ཚན་ཉེར་གཅིག   zag med ye shes sde tshan nyer gcig *ekaviṃśatikāṇḍānāsravajñāna*

The uncorrupted **pristine cognition** (*anasravajnana*, tib. *zag-med ye-shes*), translated here as uncontaminated **wisdom**, is the sixty-eighth topic discussed in the ***ORNAMENT OF CLEAR/EMERGENT REALISATION (ABHISAMAYALAMKARA)***. In the discussion on ***dharmakaya***, which forms the final chapter of that text, *svabhava* and ***jnana*** are differentiated as objective and subjective aspects of ***dharmakaya***, respectively the ***dharmadhatu*** expanse and the ***buddha*-mind**. The latter (*jnanadharmakaya*) comprises twenty-one uncorrupted aspects of **pristine cognition**, namely: 1) the **thirty-seven factors** of **enlightenment** (*bodhipaksha*); 2) the **four immeasurables** (*aprameya*); 3) the eight kinds of **liberation** (*vimoksha*); 4) the **nine stages** of mental development in **calm abiding** (*samapatti*); 5) the ten consummations of the **elements** (*kshaya*); 6) the eight kinds of charismatic overpowering (*abhibhuya*); 7) undeluded contemplation (***samadhi***); 8) **knowledge** based on aspiration; 9) the six supernormal cognitive powers (*abhijna*); 10) the four kinds of individual intrinsic awareness (*pratisamvid*); 11) the four purities (*shuddha*); 12) the ten powers (*vasita*); 13) the ten abilities (*bala*); 14) the four fearlessnesses (*vaisaradya*); 15) the three things not to be guarded (*arakshya*); 16) the three foundations of **mindfulness** (*smrityupasthana*); 17) actual **reality** (*dharmata*); 18) destruction of propensities (*vasananirodha*); 19) great **compassion** (*mahakaruna*); 20) the eighteen distinct properties/characteristics of the ***buddhas*** (*ashtadashavenikabuddhadharma*); and 21) **omniscience** (*sarvajna*).

Two Accumulations ཚོགས་གཉིས་ tshogs gnyis *dvisambhāra*

See **Tsog**.

Two Fruits འབྲས་བུ་གཉིས་ 'bras bu gnyis *dviphala*

The **two fruits** refer to the ***Rupakaya*** and ***Dharmakaya*** of a ***buddha***, which are actualised as the result of accomplishing the **two accumulations** on the path to **enlightenment**. See **Kayas** and **Tsog**.

Two Truths བདེན་པ་གཉིས་ bden pa gnyis *dvisatya*

All Buddhist philosophical schools of thought formulate their metaphysics within the framework of the two truths: the conventional or relative truth *(samvrtisatya)* and the ultimate truth *(paramarthasatya)*. However, their definition of the two truths differs according to their different epistemological interpretations. In addition, the notion of two truths is also used in the resultant teachings of the **Vajrayana** where there are also a number of different standpoints. See **conventional truth** and **ultimate truth**.

Udrayana (skrt.) ཨོ་རྒྱན་ O rgyan *Oḍḍiyāna*

A different way of spelling *Oddiyana*. See **Odiyan**.

Ultimate Truth དོན་དམ་བདེན་པ་/མཐར་ཐུག་བདེན་པ་ don dam bden pa/mthar thug bden pa *paramārthasatya*

Cittamatra and *Madhyamaka*, the two **Mahayana** schools of thought which emphasise the doctrine of the **two truths**, define it as a synonym of **emptiness**, the **ultimate** nature of phenomena. However, in *Anuttarayogatantra* **ultimate truth** refers not to the objective **emptiness**, as above, but to the **inner radiance/clear light** *(prabhasvara)* which is the coalescence of pure appearance and **emptiness**, and the final or **ultimate** nature of **mind**. See **Two Truths** and **Conventional Truth**.

Upaya (tib.) ཐབས་ thabs *upāya*

See **Skilful Means**.

Urgyen (tib.) ཨོ་རྒྱན་ O rgyan *Oḍḍiyāna*

See **Odiyan**.

Urinalysis གཅིན་བརྟག་པ་ gcin brtag pa

A method of diagnosis used in the Tibetan medical system often in combination with the examination of the pulse. The analysis is performed using fresh urine and the colour, density, odour, and nature of the foam that emerges upon stirring are especially noted.

Utsang (tib.) དབུས་གཙང་ dbus gtsang

The provinces of Central Tibet *(dbus)*, pronounced '*u*', which comprises the *Kyichu* valley and the *Lhokha* region to its south, and **Tsang** *(gtsang)* which comprises the areas north and south of the *Brahmaputra*, and west of the *Kyichu*. In ancient and medieval times, the far west of Tibet (from the highland region of *Lato* to the *Indus* and *Sutlej* watersheds) formed a separate administrative region known as *Ngari Korsum*, but this largely unpopulated area was later incorporated within **Utsang**. Currently *Ngari* forms a distinct region within the so-called Tibetan Autonomous Region.

UTTARATANTRA (skrt.) རྒྱུད་བླ་མ་ rgyud bla ma *Uttaratantra*

More accurately known as the *MAHAYANOTTARATANTRASHASTRA*, this text is one of the five treatises of *Maitreya*. The text has four major themes: the **Three Precious Jewels**, the seed of *buddha*-**nature** inherent in all **sentient beings**, the buddha-attributes and the **buddha**-activities. It is particularly famous for its extensive treatment of the subject of **buddha-nature**. The text deals with the doctrine of **emptiness** and the role which development of insight into the nature of **emptiness** plays in the **purification** of the **dissonant emotions** which stain the essentially pure **mind**. It takes as its source the *Mahayana sutras* of the *tathagatagarbha* class, and particularly the *sutra* known as *TATHAGATAGARBHA*.

Vaibhashika (skrt.) ᠍ᢩ᠌ᢅᢅ᠍᠍᠍᠍ᢅ᠍ᢅᢅᢅ bye brag smra ba *Vaibhāṣika*

One of the four major Buddhist philosophical schools of ancient India, the other three being: *Sautrantika*, *Cittamatra* and *Madhyamaka*. The dominant tenet of this school is the acceptance of *dharmas* which are the distinct and independently existing atomic factors that compose the material world and the moments of time that compose **consciousness**. This metaphysic extends to a notion of time in which the past and future are accepted as being equally as real as the present. One of the distinctive postulates of this school is the existence of an imperceptible behavioural pattern (*prapti*), which is said to connect the independent and particular instances of the various *dharmas*, thus constructing a perceptible macroscopic world. One of the principal works of this school is *Vasubandhu's ABHIDHARMAKOSHA*. The school has four main divisions which in turn evolved into eighteen sub-divisions.

Vairocana (tib.) ᢳᢅᢅᢅᢅᢅᢅᢅᢅ rnam par snang mdzad *Vairocana*

The *Buddha* of one of five **enlightened-families** corresponding to the perfected states of an individual's five **aggregates**. *Vairocana* is the perfected state of our **aggregate** of form or **consciousness**, and is the manifestation of the *buddha's* mirror-like **pristine cognition** or the **pristine cognition** of **reality's** expanse, visualised in the aspect of an embodied **deity**. *Vairocana* is usually depicted as white in colour. *Vairocana* literally means the 'Illuminator'. See **Enlightened-Families**.

Vaishravana (skrt.) ᢳᢅᢅᢅᢅ rnam sras *Vaiśrāvaṇa*

There are various aspects of *Vaishravana*: according to *Lamrim*, *Vaishravana* is a **protector deity** associated with the essential practices for spiritual trainees of middling scope. See **Three Scopes**. In the context of the '**four guardians**', *Vaishravana* is the guardian king of the northern direction. Hence images of *Vaishravana* appear in murals outside most Tibetan temples. See **Four Guardians**. *Vaishravana* is also one of the principal wealth **deities**.

Vajra (skrt.) ᢲᢅᢲ rdo rje *vajra*
See **Dorje**.

Vajrabhairava (skrt.) རྡོ་རྗེ་འཇིགས་བྱེད་ rdo rje 'jigs byed *Vajrabhairava*

An important **meditational deity** of *Anuttarayogatantra* belonging to the class of deities known as *Yamantaka*. This **deity** is depicted with a buffalo's face and multiple arms and legs. *Yamantaka* is a wrathful manifestation of *Manjushri* and has various aspects. Based on the different texts within the *YAMANTAKA* corpus and also on different translations of the root *tantras*, there developed several different systems of *Yamantaka* practice in Tibet. In fact, all major schools of **Tibetan Buddhism** have systems of practice based on this deity. The *Nyingma* system is derived from *Nupchen Sangye* Yeshe, who introduced *YAMANTAKA TANTRAS* from Nepal in the ninth century. The *Kadam* system associated with the translator *Rwa Lotsawa* later became the most dominant and widespread. Then the study and practice of the *Yamantaka* **deities** became particularly important in the *Gelug* school, following *Tsong Khapa's* fourteenth century exposition of the *Vajrabhairavatantra*.

Vajradhara (skrt.) རྡོ་རྗེ་འཆང་ rdo rje 'chang *Vajradhara*

Vajradhara is an expression of the *Dharmakaya*, spontaneously arising from the pure, pristine expanse of **inner radiance/clear light**, in a form complete with all the perfect resources of the *Sambhogakaya*. *Vajradhara* is thus regarded as the root of all the **enlightened-families**, the pristine source from which emerge the **five enlightened-families** who represent the five psychophysical **aggregates** in their purified or transmuted state. Consequently, he is also known as the sixth **enlightened-family**. Many *tantra*-texts and **lineages** attribute their origin directly to the *Dharmakaya* - either represented in the form of *Samantabhadra* or in the form of *Vajradhara*. Other *tantra*-texts and **lineages** claim that *Vajradhara* is a form assumed by the *Buddha Shakyamuni* when giving esoteric teachings on *tantra*. In Tibet, the *Kagyu* **lineage** in particular is one regarded as ultimately derived from *Vajradhara*, directly. *Vajradhara* is said to become manifest when one has totally overcome all dualistic conceptions and actualised *buddha*hood. He is usually depicted as seated and holding a *vajra* and bell in his crossed palms. *Vajradhara* literally means the 'holder of the *vajra*'. See **Dharmakaya** and **Samantabhadra**.

Vajrakrodhakala (skrt.) རྡོ་རྗེ་ཁྲོ་བོ་ནག་པོ་ rdo rje khro bo nag po *Vajrakrodhakāla*

A **wrathful** male **deity** associated with the practice of *Chod* in the *Nyingma* tradition.

Vajrakrodhikali (skrt.) རྡོ་རྗེ་ཁྲོ་མོ་ནག་མོ་ rdo rje khro mo nag mo *Vajrakrodhīkālī*

A **wrathful** female **deity** associated with the practice of *Chod* in the *Nyingma* tradition.

Vajrakila (skrt.) རྡོ་རྗེ་ཕུར་པུ་ rdo rje phur pu *Vajrakīla*

A **meditational deity**, literally meaning 'Dagger of Indestructible **Reality**', who belongs to the **enlightened-family** of enlightened-activity (*karma* family). The *tantras* of *Vajrakila* are contained in the *sadhana* class of *Mahayoga*, and preserved in the *COLLECTED TANTRAS OF THE NYINGMAPA (rnying-ma'i rgyud-'bum)*. Only one small fragment, translated by *Sakya Pandita*, is to be found in the *KANGYUR,* although longer *VAJRAKILA TANTRAS* are also found in Chinese translations from the *Sanskrit*. The practices associated with the **deity** comprise both higher rites *(stod-las)* conducive to the supreme accomplishments of **libera-**

tion and **buddhahood,** and lower rites *(smad-las)* which through the **fourfold activities** of pacification, enrichment, influence/subjugation and wrathful force, bring about protection and removal of obstacles. The **deity** is sometimes depicted with the lower part of the body in the form of a dagger *(phur-bu)*, the three facets of the pyramidal blade representing the transformation of **ignorance** (as to the true nature of **reality**), attachment (**desire**) and aversion (**hatred** or fear).

Vajra Mind ཐུགས་རྡོ་རྗེ་ thugs rdo rje *citta vajra*

The expression *thugs rdo-rje* translates into English as '*vajra-mind*' or 'indestructible **reality**' of *buddha*-mind. The fully **enlightened mind,** i.e., that of a *buddha*, is called *vajra*, meaning indestructible and indivisible, for it is invulnerable to all degrees of mental defilement and is naturally and perfectly indivisible from the subtle energies which constitute the exalted body of a *buddha*. Similarly, a *buddha's* body and speech are also called *vajra* body and *vajra* speech. This term emphasises the indestructible qualities of a *buddha's* body, speech and **mind.**

Vajrapani (skrt.) ཕྱག་ན་རྡོ་རྗེ་ phyag na rdo rje *Vajrapāṇi*

The embodiment of the power *(bala)* and **skilful means** of all the *buddhas* (the fully enlightened **mind**) as visualised in the form of a **meditational deity.** *Vajrapani* is depicted as being **wrathful** in aspect, holding a *vajra* in his right upraised hand and a skull-cup in his left. There are various aspects of *Vajrapani* and associated with these there are related **meditational** practices.

Vajrasattva (skrt.) རྡོ་རྗེ་སེམས་དཔའ་ rdo rje sems dpa' *Vajrasattva*

Literally rendered in English as 'Spiritual Hero of Indestructible **Reality**', *Vajrasattva* is an aspect of *Akshobhya*, the **deity** associated with the *vajra* family, who may appear in a blue form *(mi-bskyod-pa/mi-khrugs-pa)* or a white form *(rdo-rje sems-dpa')*. The most well-known primary *tantra*-text associated with *Vajrasattva* in the *Nyingma* tradition is the *GUHYAGARBHA TANTRA*, in which, according to most commentaries, he appears at the centre of the *mandala* of the peaceful **deities.** There are also a great many *sadhanas* dedicated to *Vajrasattva*, and their practice is popular among all four schools of **Tibetan Buddhism.** In the context of the preliminary practices, in particular, the recitation of *Vajrasattva's* hundred-syllable *mantra* is said to bring about the **purification** of anger and **hatred** specifically. As a **lineage**-holder, *Vajrasattva* is credited with the **transmission** of *Atiyoga* into the human world, appearing in the form of the *deva* Adhicitta *(lhag-sems-can)* before Prahevajra *(dga'-rab rdo-rje)* in a vision. He is depicted as seated, holding a *vajra* in his right palm close to the heart and a bell in his left hand close to the left side of his hip.

Vajravarahi རྡོ་རྗེ་ཕག་མོ་ rdo rje phag mo *Vajravārāhī*

A female **meditational deity,** the 'Indestructible Sow', who may

appear as the central figure of the *mandala* in her own right or as the consort of the **meditational deity** *Cakrasamvara*, also known as *Paramasukha*. She is red in colour and carries the emblem of a sow's head above her own. When she appears without the sow's head, she does so in a form known as *Vajrayogini*.

Vajrayana (skrt.) རྡོ་རྗེ་ཐེག་པ་ rdo rje theg pa *Vajrayāna*

See **Tantrayana**.

Vajrayogini (skrt.) རྡོ་རྗེ་རྣལ་འབྱོར་མ་ rdo rje rnal 'byor ma *Vajrayoginī*

A female **meditational deity** belonging to the *Anuttarayogatantra*. The meditative practice of this **deity** is popular in the *Kagyu*, *Sakya* and *Gelug* schools and the most well known aspect of the **deity** is the one known as *Kecari* according to **Naropa's** system *(na-ro mkha'-spyod)*. *Vajrayogini* is usually depicted as red in colour with a semi-**wrathful** facial expression.

Valid Reasoning རིགས་པ་ཡང་དག་ rigs pa yang dag *yukti*

On **valid** cognition or **reasoning**, see **Pramana**.

Vasubandhu (skrt.) དབྱིག་གཉེན་ dbyig gnyen *Vasubandhu*

The younger brother of *Asanga* and a great Indian Buddhist scholar in his own right. Born during the fourth century, *Vasubandhu* first established himself as a great scholar within the *Vaibhashika* school of *Hinayana* Buddhism. As a *Kashmiri Vaibashika* he wrote the highly admired treatise on *abhidharma* entitled *ABHIDHARMAKOSHA* and its auto-**commentary**. Both of these texts are, to this day, still considered two of the most authoritative treatises on *abhidharma*. Later in life *Vasubhandu* turned to *Mahayana* Buddhism, under the influence of his brother *Asanga*, and he became one of the primary commentators on the mentalist traditions, influencing developments within the *Cittamatra* school, the *Yogacara-Svatantrika Madhyamaka* school, and also the *Tathagatagarbha* school.

Vibhaga (skrt.) རྣམ་འབྱེད་ rnam 'byed *vibhāga*

In the collection known as the FIVE WORKS OF *MAITREYA* there are two texts, known as the 'two analyses' or 'two distinctions' *(vibhaga)*, namely: the *ANALYSIS OF PHENOMENA AND ACTUAL REALITY (DHARMADHARMATAVIBHAGA)* and the *ANALYSIS OF THE MIDDLE WAY AND EXTREMES (MADHYANTAVIBHAGA)*.

Vidyadhara རིག་འཛིན་ rig 'dzin *vidyādhara*

'Holder of awareness' *(vidyadhara)* is an expression referring to accomplished practitioners of the *tantras* who have realised through profound **skilful means** the awareness of *buddha*-body, speech and **mind**, embodied respectively in the divine *mandalas*, the *mantras* and the **pristine cognition** that is supreme bliss. The resultant vehicles of the *tantras* are sometimes referred to as the vehicle of the awareness-holders, and the canonical *tantra*-texts as the *pitaka* (collection) of the awareness-holders. In general, as explained in the *BUDDHASAMAYOGA*, awareness-holders are said to have seven distinctions of **enlightened** attributes, namely: they abide in contemplation *(samadhi)*, they possess the five supernormal cognitive powers, they act on behalf of living beings in various fields, they lack envy or attachment, they enjoy limitless desires as supreme bliss, they transcend the span of human life, and abide in a mental body. Four kinds of aware-

Tsong Khapa

The Fifth Dalai Lama, *Ngawang Lobsang Gyatso*

ness-holder are particularly identified, and their realisations are said to parallel those of the **bodhisattva** and **buddha** levels, namely: the awareness-holder of maturation *(rnam-smin rig-'dzin)*, the awareness-holder with power over the life-span *(tshe-dbang rig-'dzin)*, the awareness-holder of the great seal *(phyag-chen rig-'dzin)*, and the awareness-holder of spontaneous presence *(lhun-grub rig-'dzin)*.

View, Meditation and Action ལྟ་སྒོམ་སྤྱོད་གསུམ་ lta sgom spyod gsum

A broad way of referring to the entire scope of a spiritual trainee's path to **enlightenment**. The cultivation of a correct philosophical perspective is regarded as an essential foundation from which a successful practice of **meditation** can emerge. The correct **view** and its contemplation in **meditation** consequently gives rise to sound ethical action. Although such a consequential development is considered vital at the initial stage, as the practitioner advances in **realisation**, a co-ordinated simultaneous application of all three factors is equally emphasised.

VIMA NYINGTIG (tib.) བི་མའི་སྙིང་ཐིག་ bi-ma'i snying thig

The *INNERMOST SPIRITUALITY* or *HEART ESSENCE of **VIMALAMITRA** (BI-MA'I SNYING-THIG)* is a collection of esoteric instructions belonging to the Esoteric Instructional Class of **Atiyoga**. This particular collection was introduced to Tibet by the master **Vimalamitra** during the early ninth century, and then secretly transmitted by *Nyangben Tingzin Zangpo* and his successors in Central Tibet until the lifetime of **Longchen Rabjampa** in the fourteenth century. **Longchenpa** redacted the collection as part of his own *FOUR PART INNERMOST SPIRITUALITY (SNYING-THIG YA-BZHI)*, and the original texts are contained in Vols. 7-9 of his later anthology. See **Nyingthig**.

Vimalamitra (skrt.) དྲི་མེད་བཤེས་གཉེན་ dri med bshes gnyen *Vimalamitra*

A Kashmiri **pandita** who visited Tibet during the reign of king **Trisong Detsen**, in the early ninth century, and was responsible for the translation of many texts belonging to the **sutras** (e.g., the *HEART **SUTRA***) and the **tantras** (e.g. his works on the **Mahayoga** cycle of **GUHYAGARBHA**, and his **Atiyoga transmission** of the *INNERMOST SPIRITUALITY OF **VIMALAMITRA***). **Vimalamitra** himself is said to reside continuously on the five-peaked mountain range of *Wu Ta'i shan* in China, in the form of the *Mahasamkrantikaya* (the rainbow-light body). See **Vima Nyingthig**.

Vinaya (skrt.) འདུལ་བ་ 'dul ba *vinaya*

Literally meaning 'discipline', the term generally refers to monastic discipline and especially to the observance of the ethical codes which regulate the life of an ordained monk or nun. The collection of **Buddha Shakyamuni's** discourses which elucidate and define the principles of monastic **vows** and discipline (including the

administrative guidelines for running a monastery) is known as the *Vinayapitaka*, which is one of the three primary collections of discourses which comprise the Buddhist canon or *Tripitaka*. Based on different interpretations relating to the subtler points of the *Buddha's* discourses on *Vinaya* there emerged, in India, several distinct *Vinaya* schools. These include the *Sthaviravada*, *Sarvastivada* *Mahasanghika*, and *Sammitiya*. The *Vinaya* tradition which became predominant in Tibet is that of the *Sarvastivada* system.

VINAYASUTRA (skrt.) འདུལ་བ་མདོ་(ཚ་) 'dul ba mdo(rtsa) *Vinaya(mūla)sūtra*

The most important Indian **commentary** on the study and practice of *Vinaya* within the *Sarvastivada* tradition. Written by the *Vinaya* master **Gunaprabha**, the text outlines in detail all the essential points of monastic discipline: the nature and specifications of the ethical codes, a definition of what constitutes their transgression, methods of restoration, the procedures for conducting an ordination ceremony and guidelines for monastic administration. The *Vinayasutra* is used as the primary text for the study of *Vinaya* in most Tibetan monastic universities.

Vipashyana (skrt.) ལྷག་མཐོང་ lhag mthong *vipaśyanā*

See **Lhagthong**.

Vipassana (pali) ལྷག་མཐོང་ lhag mthong *vipaśyanā*

The Pali spelling of *Vipashyana*. See **Lhagthong**.

Virtue དགེ་བ་ dge ba *kuśala*

Virtue can be defined either passively or actively. The former refers to the practice of abandoning and refraining from the ten kinds of non-virtuous actions which are enumerated in Buddhist texts. The latter is the positive engagement in virtuous actions with an altruistic motivation. See **Non-Virtue**.

Virupa (skrt.) བི་རཱུ་པ་ bi rū pa *Virūpa*

One of the eighty-four *Mahasiddhas* of ancient India who was the progenitor of the profound instructions set down in the *Lamdre* of the *Sakya* school. See **Lamdre**.

Voidness སྟོང་པ་ཉིད་ stong pa nyid *śūnyatā*

See **Emptiness**.

Vows སྡོམ་པ་ dom pa *saṃvara*

Sets of **precepts** or injunctions voluntarily adopted in the course of Buddhist practice, which enable practitioners to transform their entire way of life into a spiritual pursuit. The integration of the **vows** associated with the *Hinayana*, *Bodhisattvayana* and *Tantrayana* is a particular feature of spiritual practice within all four schools of the Tibetan tradition. *Tantrayana* **vows** are also known as commitments (*samaya*). See **Samaya**.

Vultures' Peak བྱ་རྒོད་ཕུང་པོའི་རི་ bya rgod phung po'i ri *Gṛdhrakūṭa*

A hill near the town of *Rajgir*, north of *Bodhgaya* in *Bihar* state, where the *Buddha Shakyamuni* is said to have taught, in particular, the *sutras* of the 'second turning', principally the ***Prajnaparamita sutras***.

Wheel of Life སྲིད་པའི་འཁོར་ལོ་ srid pa'i 'khor lo *bhavacakra*

An illustrative metaphor which depicts the process of an individual's passage through **cyclic existence** and the relationship between the **twelve links of dependent origination**. In the innermost circle of the wheel are images of a pig, a bird and a snake each holding the tail of the other and rotating in a circle. These three respectively represent: **delusion**, **attachment** and **hatred**/aversion. The intermediate circle is divided into six parts each representing the **six realms** of existence in *samsara*; and the perimeter is divided into twelve sections each containing images which illustrate one of the **twelve links**. The whole wheel is depicted as being ensnared by the jaws of *Yama*, the lord of death, this symbolising the **truth** of our being at the mercy of dissatisfaction, frustration and **suffering** for as long as we remain within a **karmically** conditioned existence.

Wheel of Sharp Weapons མཚོན་ཆ་འཁོར་ལོ་ mtshon cha 'khor lo

A text on the practice of *Lojong* written by the Indian master ***Dharmarakshita***. The text is written in verse and outlines the essential practices of a ***bodhisattva***, emphasising various practical methods for transforming adverse circumstances into favourable conditions on the path.

Winds རླུང་ rlung *vāyu*

The ***Sanskrit*** term *vayu* (tib. *rlung*) is rendered into English as 'vital energy' or 'wind'. This term has a broad range of meanings. In traditional medicine, it refers to the humour of wind, one of the **three humours** which must be in balance if sound health is to be maintained. Within the physical body and its subtle counterpart, which is refined through the meditative practices of the perfection/**completion stage**, there are said to be ten different kinds of vital energy - five inner vital energies *(nang-gi rlung lnga)* which influence the body's inner motility, and five outer vital energies *(phyi'i rlung lnga)* which have specific effects on the outward motility of the body. The former are the vital energies associated with the **five elements** (earth, water, fire, air, space) and their respective colour-tones (yellow, white, red, green, blue). The latter comprise life-breath *(prana/srog-'dzin)*, muscular movement *(vyapin)*, digestion *(samana)*, semiotic/vocal movement *(udana)*, and reproduction/waste disposal *(apana)*. In the context of the perfection/**completion stage**, the **subtle winds** or vital energies of *karma (las-kyi rlung)* on which the various aspects of **consciousness** depend are refined, along with their respective **consciousnesses**, and absorbed with them, into the central channel *(avadhuti)* of the body, where they are transformed into the vital energy of **pristine cognition** *(ye-shes-kyi rlung)*.

Wisdom

Translators have frequently employed the English word **'wisdom'**

to translate indiscriminately the **Sanskrit** terms *prajna (shes-rab)* and *jnana (ye-shes)*, when, in fact, the word is inadequate in both cases. Each of these original terms implies perceptual activity rather than a store of **knowledge**. *Prajna* is the discriminative awareness or intelligence developed by **bodhisattvas** on the path to **enlightenment**, enabling them to assess and understand all phenomena in terms of **emptiness** and so forth. *Jnana* is the **pristine cognition** or natural awareness of the **buddha-mind** in its diverse facets of perception. In many instances, it is not always easy to determine which sense the translator intends without access to the original source. See **Jnana**, **Prajna** and **Knowledge**.

Wish–Fulfilling Jewel ཡིད་བཞིན་གྱི་ནོར་བུ་ yid bzhin gyi nor bu *cintāmaṇi*

A unique jewel said to exist in the **deva** and **naga** realms which has the capacity to fulfil the mundane wishes of its owner; such as providing shelter or creating wealth and fortune. However, both Buddhist and non-Buddhist classical Indian literature often allude to this ancient myth using the term metaphorically, and in a supramundane sense, when referring to the spiritually 'wish-fulfilling' properties of a particular notion or object.

Wrath དྲག་(པོ་མངོན་སྤྱོད་) drag (po mngon spyod) *abhicāra*

The concept of **wrath** in the context of Buddhist *tantra* should not be understood in terms of even the subtlest egocentric violence or fierceness. **Wrath** here refers to the enlightening process of transformation from a delusive state to an enlightened state. **Wrath** is the purified form of **hatred**/aversion which actively transforms delusive states. The face, posture, ornaments etc. of a **wrathful meditational deity** are therefore fierce and awesome, but this face is the display of the enlightened awareness which transforms delusion. See **Fourfold Activities**. One of the principal primitive emotional states is anger or **hatred** and a successful transmutation of this state is essential to spiritual practice. It is in the context of this objective that one visualises one's own pristine fundamental awareness (i.e., realisation of **emptiness**) in a wrathful manifestation (i.e., in the form of a **wrathful meditational deity**) and based on this meditative state a unique sense of **identity** is cultivated in one's practice, in which one's own delusive states are energetically transformed. The *mandala* of wrathful deities is explained to represent the expressive power or energy of the *mandala* of peaceful deities, arising in the face of the most enduring and subtle aspects of egoism, and without which such **obscurations** could not be transformed into **enlightened attributes**. In the meditative practices of the **completion**/perfection stage and the **Great Perfection**, it is said that the peaceful deities naturally abide in the heart of the meditator, while the wrathful deities naturally abide in the skull. According to **Nyingma** teachings on the *bardo*, the **consciousness** of the deceased, in the **intermediate state** of actual **reality** *(chos-nyid bar-do)*, comes to perceive the hundred **peaceful and wrathful deities** in succession. In order that the deceased might recognise their true nature without fear or confusion, it is regarded as extremely important, in the course of one's life, to cultivate experientially the meditative practices associated with such deities and develop familiarity with them. See **Bardo** and **Peaceful and Wrathful Deities**.

Yama གཤིན་རྗེ་ gshin rje *Yama*

YAMANTAKA (skrt.) གཤིན་རྗེ་གཤེད་ gshin rje gshed *Yamāntaka*

A class of important **meditational deities** belonging to *Anuttarayogatantra*. There are various aspects of *Yamantaka* including: Red *Yamantaka*, Black

Yamantaka, and *Vajrabhairava*. These all function as the meditative opponents of the aspects of *Yama*, the forces of death, which are the embodiments of **impermanence** and the laws of **cause and effect**. See **Vajrabhairava**.

Yana ཐེག་པ་ theg pa *yāna*

See **Three Vehicles** and **Nine Yanas**.

Yantra (skrt.) འཁྲུལ་འཁོར་ 'khrul 'khor *yantra*

In Buddhism, the **Sanskrit** term **yantra** (tib. 'khrul-'khor) refers to a series of vigorous yogic exercises which enable the meditator to develop the physical flexibility necessary for the subtle meditative practices of the perfection/**completion stage**, when the energy **channels** are refined and control of the **winds** and seminal points within the body is matured. Such yogic exercises are associated with the practice of different **meditational deities**, and are well known in all traditions.

Yeshe (tib.) ཡེ་ཤེས་ ye shes *jñāna*

See **Jnana**.

Yeshe Tsogyal ཡེ་ཤེས་མཚོ་རྒྱལ་ ye shes mtsho rgyal

According to the *INJUNCTIONS OF PADMA (PADMA'I BKA'-THANG)*, **Yeshe Tsogyal** was the daughter of *Namka Yeshe* and *Nubmo Gewabum*, born at *Drongmoche* in *Dra* into the *Kharchen* clan, for which reason she became known as the 'princess of *Khar*'. She married the Tibetan king **Trisong Detsen** who subsequently offered her to **Padmasambhava**. Consequently, she became **Padmasambhava's** innermost consort and was empowered and became accomplished in the **mandala** of **Vajrakila**. She compiled **Padmasambhava's** oral teachings and concealed them throughout Tibet in the form of treasures (**terma**) to be discovered by later generations. Her most extensive biography appears to be that revealed by *Taksham Nuden Dorje*, which has been published in translation under the titles: *SKYDANCER* and *MOTHER OF KNOWLEDGE*.

Yidam (tib.) ཡི་དམ་/ལྷག་པའི་ལྷ་ yi dam/lhag pa'i lha *(iṣṭa)devatā*

See **Meditational Deity**.

Yoga (skrt.) རྣལ་འབྱོར་ rnal 'byor *yoga*

The **Sanskrit yoga**, literally meaning 'union', is rendered in Tibetan as *rnal-'byor*, meaning 'union with the fundamental nature of **reality**'. In Buddhism therefore, **yoga** refers to the diverse meditative techniques through which the meditator unites with the qualities of the **meditational deity** in the context of the **generation stage**, and the nature of fundamental **reality** on the perfection/**completion stage** of the spiritual path. In terms of the latter it includes mental and physical practices which refine the energy **channels**, and mature control of the currents and seminal points

within the body; these practices cultivate **discriminative awareness** (*prajna*), and the coalescence of bliss with **emptiness**, radiance with **emptiness**, or non-discursiveness with **emptiness**, and so forth.

Yogacarin (skrt.) རྣལ་འབྱོར་སྤྱོད་པ་བ་ rnal 'byor spyod pa ba *Yogācārin*

A follower of the *Yogacara* school, a term which originally seems to have indicated those following in *Asanga's* tradition of yogic practice, in contrast to *Nagarjuna's* tradition which emphasises profound **emptiness** and its **view**. Some authors have used this term as a synonym for *Cittamatrin* or *Vijnanavadin*. See **Cittamatra**.

Yogatantra (skrt.) རྣལ་འབྱོར་གྱི་རྒྱུད་ rnal 'byor gyi rgyud *Yogatantra*

See **Four Classes of Tantra**.

Yogin (skrt.) རྣལ་འབྱོར་པ་ rnal 'byor pa *yogin*

A male practitioner engaged in intensive meditative practices. See **Yoga**.

Yogini (skrt.) རྣལ་འབྱོར་མ་ rnal 'byor ma *yoginī*

A female practitioner engaged in intensive meditative practices. See **Yoga**.

Yongdzin (tib.) ཡོངས་འཛིན་ yongs 'dzin

A tutor on spiritual and philosophical subjects to a high *lama* such as the *Dalai Lama*.

Zhangzhung (tib.) ཞང་ཞུང་ zhang zhung

A place mentioned in *Bon* literature cited as being the place where the *Bon* tradition took root in Tibet and the birthplace of its original Tibetan exponent *Shenrab Miwoche*. The renowned scholar and translator *Goe Lotsawa Zhonu Pal*, in his *BLUE ANNALS*, identifies *Zhangzhung* as being in the region of *Guge* in the western part of Tibet, and this is now generally recognised. It has been speculated, however, that the true origins of *Bon* are to be found outside Tibet, either in Iran or North-west India, indicating Zoroastrian or Kashmiri influence. See **Bon**.

APPENDICES

INDEX OF RESOURCES

INDEX OF BIOGRAPHIES

INDEX OF ILLUSTRATIONS

ILLUSTRATION CREDITS

Front cover image of Buddha Shakyamuni © Bhikshuni Ngawang Chodron

All line drawings are copyright © Robert Beer